October 3–5, 2011
Pisa, Italy

**Association for
Computing Machinery**

Advancing Computing as a Science & Profession

SIGDOC'11

Proceedings of the 29th ACM International Conference on

Design of Communication

Sponsored by:
ACM SIGDOC

Supported by:
Serious Games Institute, CNR, and ISCTE

**Association for
Computing Machinery**

Advancing Computing as a Science & Profession

The Association for Computing Machinery
2 Penn Plaza, Suite 701
New York, New York 10121-0701

Notice to Past Authors of ACM-Published Articles
ACM intends to create a complete electronic archive of all articles and/or other material previously published by ACM. If you have written a work that has been previously published by ACM in any journal or conference proceedings prior to 1978, or any SIG Newsletter at any time, and you do NOT want this work to appear in the ACM Digital Library, please inform permissions@acm.org, stating the title of the work, the author(s), and where and when published.

ISBN: 978-1-4503-0936-3 (Digital)

ISBN: 978-1-4503-1357-5 (Print)

Additional copies may be ordered prepaid from:

ACM Order Department
PO Box 30777
New York, NY 10087-0777, USA

Phone: 1-800-342-6626 (USA and Canada)
+1-212-626-0500 (Global)
Fax: +1-212-944-1318
E-mail: acmhelp@acm.org
Hours of Operation: 8:30 am – 4:30 pm ET

ACM Order Number: 613110

Printed in the USA

Foreword

It is our great pleasure to welcome you to ACM SIGDOC 2011, the *29th ACM International Conference on Design of Communication*. This year's conference continues its tradition of being the premier forum for presentation of research work and experience reports on communication and information, information science, design studies, cognitive and computer science, etc. Furthermore, ACM SIGDOC aims to continue expanding its creative interactions and energies in Europe, hosting this year's conference in Pisa, Italy, at the Grand Hotel Continental.

The mission of the conference is to share novel ideas, theories, model and application environments in the areas of Information Design and Information Architecture, Technical Documentation, Open Source, Collaborative Writing Processes, Usability, Human-Computer Interaction (HCI/CHI), Computer-Mediated Communication, Learning Systems/Environments, Legal and Ethical Dimensions of Communication, Serious Games and Virtual Worlds, etc. and identify new directions for future research and development. ACM SIGDOC '11 gives researchers and practitioners a unique opportunity to share their perspectives with others interested in the various aspects of communication design and technology.

The call for papers attracted 75 submissions from Asia, Europe, and the Americas. The program committee accepted 36 as full papers and 9 as short papers, and 5 posters. In addition, the program includes a Workshop on *Augmenting the learning experience with virtual simulation systems* and two prestigious keynote speakers. We hope that these proceedings will serve as a valuable reference for all the participants.

Putting together *SIGDOC'11* was a team effort. We first thank the authors for providing the content of the program. We are grateful to the program committee who worked very hard in reviewing papers and providing feedback for authors. Finally, we thank the hosting institution ISTI-CNR, and our sponsor, ACM SIGDOC.

We hope that you will find this program interesting and thought-provoking and that the conference will provide you with a valuable opportunity to share ideas with other researchers and practitioners from institutions around the world.

Aristidis Protopsaltis
SIGDOC'11 General Chair
Serious Games Institute, CU, UK

Nicolas Spyratos
SIGDOC'11 General Co-Chair
University of Paris-South, France

Carlos J. Costa
SIGDOC'11 Program Co-Chair
ISCTE-IUL, Portugal

Carlo Meghini
SIGDOC'11 Program Co-Chair
ISTI-CNR, Italy

Table of Contents

Session 8: New Frontiers in Documentation II
Session Chair: Kathy Haramundanis *(Hewlett-Packard Company)*

Session 9: Social Media II
Session Chair: David Novick *(The University of Texas at El Paso)*

Keynote Address 2
Session Chair: Carlo Meghini *(CNR)*

Session 10: Social Media and Learning
Session Chair: Michael Albers *(East Carolina University)*

Session 11: Poster Session

SIGDOC 2011 Conference Organization

General Co-Chairs: Aristidis Protopsaltis *(Serious Games Institute, Coventry University, UK)*
Nicolas Spyratos *(University of Paris-South, France)*

Program Co-Chairs: Carlos J. Costa *(ISCTE-IUL, Adetti-IUL, Portugal)*
Carlo Meghini *(ISTI-CNR, Italy)*

Local Arrangements Chair: Francesca Borri *(STI-CNR, Italy)*

SIGDOC Chair: Brad Mehlenbach *(North Carolina State University, USA)*

SIGDOC Co-Chair: Robert Pierce *(IBM, USA)*

SIGDOC Treasurer: Liza Potts *(Michigan State University, USA)*

Program Committee: Adam Qureshi *(Plymouth University, UK)*
Antonio Cerone *(United Nations University, USA)*
Aristidis Protopsaltis *(Serious Games Institute, Coventry University, UK)*
Ashley Williams *(Bridgeline Software, USA)*
Brad Mehlenbach *(North Carolina State University, USA)*
Brian Butler *(University of Pittsburgh, USA)*
Carlos J. Costa *(ISCTE – IUL, Portugal)*
Cesar Teixeira *(UFSCar, Brazil)*
Chara Balasubramaniam *(Saint Georges, University of London, UK)*
Charalampos Bratsas *(Aristotle University of Thessaloniki, AUTH, Greece)*
Clay Spinuzzi *(University of Texas at Austin, USA)*
Daniel Lucrédio *(UFSCar, Universidade Federal de São Carlos, Brazil)*
Dave Clark *(University of Wisconsin-Milwaukee, USA)*
David Farkas *(University of Washington, USA)*
David Novick *(The University of Texas, USA)*
David Panzoli *(University of Lille, France)*
Daniela Giordano *(University of Catania, UNICT, Italy)*
Dimitra Papa *(NCSR Demokritos, Greece)*
Douglas Eyman *(George Mason University, USA)*
Eduardo Fernandez *(Florida Atlantic University, USA)*
Eleni Kaldoudi *(Demokritous University of Thrace, DUTH, Greece)*
Eli Blevis *(Indiana University, USA)*
Fotis Liarokapis *(Coventry University, UK)*
George Tsaramirsis *(Kings College, UK)*
Hans Liesenberg *(UNICAMP, Brazil)*
Hélio Guardia *(Universidade Federal de São Carlos, Brazil)*
Henry Lieberman *(Massachusetts Institute of Technology, USA)*
Ian Dunwell *(Serious Games Institute, UK)*
Ivan Ricarte *(FEEC, UNICAMP, Brazil)*
Jarkko Mylläri *(University of Helsinki, Finland)*
Jason Swarts *(North Carolina State University, USA)*

ACM SIGDOC 2011 Sponsor & Supporters

Sponsor: **SIGDOC** Special Interest Group on Design of Communication

Supporters:

SGI
Serious Games **Institute**

Consiglio Nazionale delle Ricerche

ISCTE
Instituto Superior de Ciências
do Trabalho e da Empresa

The Communicative Functions of Animation in User Interfaces

David Novick
The University of Texas at El Paso
El Paso, TX 79968-0518

novick@utep.edu

Joseph Rhodes
Georgia Institute of Technology
Atlanta, Georgia 30332

jrhodes@gatech.edu

Wervyn Wert
Georgia Institute of Technology
Atlanta, Georgia 30332

wervyn@gmail.com

ABSTRACT

To develop a model that relates the purpose of the communication to the nature of the animation, we surveyed existing user interfaces that use animation, analyzed these uses with respect to type of animation and communicative function, and considered ambiguous or otherwise difficult cases. From this analysis, we constructed a matrix with appropriateness/inappropriateness values for all combinations of communicative functions and animation types covered by our survey. To illustrate how the model could be applied to graphical user interfaces and to assess the model's plausibility, we used the model to develop two versions of a user interface for an MP3 player.

Categories and Subject Descriptors

H.5.2 [**Information Interfaces and Presentation**]: User Interfaces – *graphical user interfaces (GUI), style guides, Theory and methods.*

General Terms

Design, Human Factors, Standardization

Keywords

Animation, design patterns

1. INTRODUCTION

> *Most people equate animated content with useless content.*
> —Jakob Nielsen [17]

Nielsen aimed his maxim at designers of user interfaces who use Flash with, as he put it, no purpose beyond annoying people. But designers who seek to use animation in a more integrated way, as an inherent part of the user interface rather than as something merely to catch the eye, find scant support in the interface-design literature. Developers can rely on resources that provide design patterns that, incidentally, use animation, but they are largely on their own if they seek more generally applicable, model-based advice. What do different kinds of animation communicate to the user? When should a designer consider introducing animation into an interface, or changing the nature of an existing animation in an interface? Answers to these sorts of questions, which touch on fundamental but relatively unexplored issues in the design of communication, require a more comprehensive and systematic connection between the form of different animations and what they communicate. In this paper we claim that the key communicative functions of animation in user interfaces can be characterized by a model that relates the purpose of the communication to the nature of the animation. Such a model could support designers who seek to use animation to expand the effectiveness and usability of user interfaces.

In this paper, then, we review the state of art with respect to models of animation in user interfaces, survey the uses of animation in existing and proposed user interfaces, present an initial model that describes the appropriateness of different animation types for different communicative functions, and illustrates how the model could be applied to graphical user interfaces by presenting two versions of a user interface for an MP3 player. We conclude with a discussion of the strengths and limitations of the model.

2. REVIEW OF RELATED RESEARCH

Definitions of animation in user interfaces have ranged from specific to general. Vodislav [25] distinguished three categories of animation: (1) demonstration of program behavior, such as algorithm animation and data visualization, (2) feedback for users' actions to provide more realistic interaction, and (3) predefined animation, unaffected by either the user or the program. The latter category, the most conservative view, defines animation such as videos presented in help systems [e.g., 10, 21]. And to the three categories could be added a newer and often more annoying one: animation as a visual attractor [8], such as the elements of on-line advertisements that try to grab the viewer's attention—the very function that was the target of Nielsen's comment.

In this paper, we define animation broadly, with a view toward building as general a model as possible. As expressed by Thomas and Calder [22 (p. 199)], the "goal is to apply animation to the interface itself—to enhance or augment the effectiveness of human interaction with applications that present a graphical interface." Animation as an inherent part of the user interface, as opposed to a predefined animation, can reduce the user's cognitive load by enabling the user to follow and understand changes in the interface's appearance; that is, the interface uses animation to replace sudden changes with smooth transitions [5, 6]. These transitions can be spatial or qualitative. For example, developers of toolkits for interfaces with this sort of animation have provided motion, scaling, and change of color [13], and change of position and change of shape [9].

Providing the means for building animation into user interfaces leaves developers with a need for design guidance for the use of animation. Thomas and Calder [22] articulated a set of principles (attachment, reluctance, smoothness, and anticipation) that served as animation counterparts to Norman's familiar principles [18] for direct-manipulation interfaces. For example, the principle of attachment [22 (p. 203)] is that

> the objects being manipulated should at all times remain attached to the pointer, which maintains the impression that the user is always in control of the action.

Similarly, Chang and Ungar [5] articulated three main principles of animation: solidity, exaggeration, and reinforcement. For example, the appearance of solidity can be enhanced by motion blur and through proper treatment of arrivals and departures.

While these sorts of principles offer help in the implementation of animation, they fall short as help in the choice of the kind of animation. As Chatty [6] asked, what information should be coded by animation, and how? Should a change in information or in state be represented by a change in place? In shape? In color? In scale? In fact, there are few design rules for animation in user interfaces, and what design knowledge there is becomes more sparse and vague as animations take on communicative and metaphoric functions [6].

2.1 Design Patterns

One approach to answering these questions could rely on first principles, starting with the science of visual perception, eventually linking to semiotics. This approach was problematic for this initial research effort, in part because the scope of work would have been beyond that of an exploratory inquiry, and in part because the semiotics of change and movement do not appear to be well developed. As an alternative approach we chose to codify emerging practices, with a view toward understanding what implemented designs suggest about the implicit principles that underlay the developers' design choices. In many aspects of human-computer interaction, these design choices would be expressed as design patterns; as we discuss, however, for animation these resources remain limited with respect to communicative functions.

Developers of user interfaces can consult sources for design patterns for many kinds or components of graphical user interfaces. However, review of these sources suggests that they provide neither strong support for developers who use animation nor a generally applicable model of the functions of animation in human-computer interaction.

Reference materials that include design patterns for user interfaces (e.g., [20], [23]) provide patterns that help developers implement elements of the traditional canon of interaction elements, such as dashboards, navigation, and progress indicators. This probably should be expected, as design patterns represent known solutions to known problems. They do, in part, address animation, but this tends to be either as part of a traditional design pattern (e.g., scrolling) or as a specific technique (e.g., transitions). Review of these resources did not disclose animation patterns of general applicability, nor a higher-level model of when animation in its various forms would be useful or appropriate.

Several on-line sources, including Patternry [19] and UI Patterns [24], provide additional advice, in the form of design patterns, for developers of graphical user interfaces. While the patterns these sites provide may incidentally include animation as part of the interaction, the patterns are not patterns for animation. Rather, both Patternry and UI Patterns provide interaction- or task-specific patterns that solve specific interaction problems in ways that may or may not include animation. For example, Patternry's "Tag an object" pattern solves the problem of a user wanting to attach his or her own keyword or set of keywords to an object for organization and later retrieval and does not appear to include animation. Patternry's "Endless scrolling" pattern solves the problem of the user needing to view large data sets where loading all the data at once would cause a notable delay in page load; because it involves scrolling, this design pattern necessarily includes animation, but the pattern's focuses on the interaction problem and its solution rather than providing a more abstract view of movement of text. UI Patterns offers design patterns that cover much the same ground—and in some cases almost exactly the same ground (e.g., the "Continuous scrolling" pattern solves the problem of user needing to view a subset of data that are not easily displayed on a single page).

2.2 Design Guidelines

Even if design of animation in user interfaces with respect to communicative function has not yet been codified through design patterns, developers can nevertheless consult the prescriptive advice of design guidelines.

Microsoft provides clear and helpful advice [16] for using animation in user interfaces, including some points about relating the animation to the task. Overall this documentation contains a mix of high-level concepts, several specific design patterns, and several implementation considerations. The design patterns are at the level of "Hover feedback: To show where the interaction point is" and "Attractor: To show that something needs the user's attention." Each design pattern describes Windows's animation vocabulary for the particular task. For example, the design pattern for hover feedback suggests displaying the hover effect (bounding rectangle, highlight, enlargement) with a fade in/fade out effect for smoothness, and the design pattern for attractor suggests flashing, moving, pulsing, glowing, and gleam. As noted, the advice is largely sound, and the patterns are useful and detailed. But even though they, implicitly, reflect broader ideas of the uses of animation, the advice and the patterns represent a set of design decisions specific to Windows; they do not represent themselves as or constitute a general model of use of animation in user interfaces.

Likewise, Apple's Human Interface Guidelines [3] provide correspondingly Apple-specific advice for developers of user interfaces. The advice is useful and clear, although it covers animation only implicitly, as when describing the use of drag and drop. The guidelines offer general design advice for graphical user interfaces (e.g., "Reflect the user's mental model"), along with ways to avoid particular design pitfalls (e.g., "Don't assign new behaviors to existing objects"). For developers who use animation, Apple does offer a guide, the Core Animation Programming Guide [2], but it focuses exclusively on implementation rather than use. That is, the animation guide and its related linked documents describe basic concepts involving the timing and animation classes. The animation guide assumes that the developers already have an animation design and now seek to implement it.

The Android Developer's Guide [1] does not address design patterns or guidelines for animation. Indeed, it covers animation only implicitly, as, for example, when it describes the API for dragging and dropping. Design advice is limited to accessibility, performance, responsiveness, and seamlessness, with, in the latter case for example, explanations of how to avoid dropping data and avoiding overloading a single activity screen. Again, developers are free to use their design imaginations in creating user interfaces, but the developer's guide does not provide much support on how to use that freedom when using animation as part of the interaction.

2.3 Need for a Model

From this survey of design patterns and guidelines for the user of animation in user interfaces, it appears that developers have solid support for implementing standard interface elements that might incorporate animation but that they lack support for designing innovative interfaces that use animation in novel ways to improve the effectiveness of communication with users. What is missing is a model that could include the insights about animation inherent in the design patterns and in animation as it is actually used in interfaces and that would enable generalization of and extension from these specific cases. In short, the goal is to build a comprehensive model of the communicative functions of animation by generalizing from existing and proposed uses of animation in user interfaces.

3. AN INTIAL MODEL

To develop a model that relates the purpose of the communication to the nature of the animation, we surveyed existing and proposed user interfaces that use animation, analyzed these uses with respect to type of animation and communicative function, and considered ambiguous or otherwise difficult cases. From this analysis, we constructed a matrix with appropriateness or inappropriateness values for all combinations of communicative functions and animation types covered by our survey.

In this section, then, we review uses of animation in user interfaces, and then relate the types of animation to the communicative functions they embody, producing an initial model. In Section 4, we apply the model to illustrate its use in developing useful and usable interfaces.

3.1 Uses of Animation

In this exploratory study, we surveyed uses of animation in user interfaces across a wide range of interfaces and applications. We looked at GUIs for operating systems, office automation applications, video games, commercial Web sites, proposed future interfaces, and other specialized interfaces.

The GUIs for operating systems included Apple OS X, the Apple iPhone, Microsoft Windows, and Microsoft Surface.

Commercial Web sites surveyed included Fred Stuart (http://fred-stuart.com/FS.html), which uses animation to make digital objects appear and act like their real world counterparts, SectionSeven Inc. (http://www.sectionseven.com/), which uses animation to convey a book metaphor to navigate their client list and show off their portfolio, NOFRKS Design (http://www.nofrks.com/), which uses spatial animation to move smoothly from one page of the site to another, thus letting users feel like they are looking at one large page, and AgencyNet Interactive (http://www.agencynet.com/), which enables navigation by clicking on actual office rooms to discover different aspects of the company, with the animation flying into the room of choice so that users feel they are actually visiting and talking with the workers.

Our survey of proposed future interfaces included Microsoft Future Vision: Healthcare [15], Microsoft Future Vision 2019 [9], the 'Stand Up' Mac dock mockup [11], the Smart Inspector dynamic palette mockup [12], and Bumptop [4]. Other interfaces

we studied included Compiz Fusion [7] and dynamic weather maps. Video games we studied included "Left 4 Dead 2" and "Mass Effect 2."

Such a survey is inherently non-comprehensive. The number of actual user interfaces employing animation is large, and even our team of three researchers working for months could not hope to cover more than a tiny fraction of these interfaces. We strove, then, to look at a range of different types of interfaces that would help us catalogue (a) broad types of animations and (b) kinds of communicative functions embodied in these animations, and then populate the entries in the animation-function matrix. Our resulting model thus reflects the selection of interfaces that we analyzed and should be considered as a starting point rather than as a model with universal truth. Indeed, as we note below in the discussion, we can already identify additional types of animation that could be employed in user interfaces.

From the interfaces that we studied, we catalogued instances of animation types according their communicative functions. For example, here is an excerpt of our survey dealing with change of shape and expression of context:

iPhone: The map page curls to reveal new controls but keeping the same context.
Interface Builder: The interface uses drag-and-drop morphing.

Similarly, here is an excerpt of the survey dealing with change of color and expression of salience:

iPhone: An email message's alpha value is faded to zero when trashed
Microsoft healthcare vision: The ring around the prescription bottle pulses green when it is time to take the given medication. After it is taken, the ring turns to red.
Microsoft healthcare vision: The nerve of the eye the doctor is examining turns to green to indicate that it is important while the others are gray.

From this catalogue, we summarized across animation types and communicate functions to produce high-level taxonomies. This exploratory process sought to minimize the number of categories in the taxonomies while preserving useful distinctions. We identified seven types of animation used in the interfaces we studied, as shown in Table 1. Likewise, we identified seven basic communicative functions served by the animations, as shown in Table 2.

The types of animation were relatively easy to distinguish. The categories did not overlap, except perhaps for gesture, and rather plainly covered all of the examples we had catalogued.

The communicative functions, in contrast, underwent repeated iterations as we distinguished, combined, and refined them. For example, some iterations combined status, importance and urgency as a single function, and some iterations included speech acts as a category. In our view, the problems of this process reflected uncertainty, ambiguity, and conflict among various models of communicative function. We faced a tension between over-generalization and over-specificity; the number of categories thus reflects both (a) the limits of generalizing from the roughly 60 observations that comprised our data and (b) our goal of producing practical guidance. The categories listed in Table 2 provided the greatest clarity in our analysis, but the categories' dynamic quality suggests that further refinement should be expected as this research continues, even as they provide current practical assistance for developers of user interfaces based on animation.

Table 1. Types of Animation.

Change of place
Change of size
Change of color
Change of shape
Gesture
Rotation
Blur

Table 2. Communicative Functions.

Signal different context
Signal different value
Signal different status
Signal importance, or urgency
Signal different function
Signal referent (pointing)
Signal salience

3.2 Relation of Types and Functions

The seven animation types and the seven communicative functions provided the axes for a matrix that described the appropriateness of using a particular animation for a particular function. We judged appropriateness based on (a) the prevalence of the animation-function relationship in the user interfaces we studied and (b) the theoretical plausibility of the relationship given generally accepted models of affordances in user interfaces (e.g., [18]). We used the more theoretical approach particularly in assessing the appropriateness of animation-function combinations where instances of these combinations were sparse or non-existent in our survey of animation in user interfaces. We did not, however, necessarily assign low-appropriateness values for combinations with few instances in the survey. The survey's coverage stressed breadth rather than representativity, so the raw number of instances of a combination might not carry real significance. So where the number of instances of a combination was low, we assessed appropriateness using the affordance models.

The result of this analysis, our model of the relationship between animation types and communicative functions, is presented in Figure 1. Each of the cells in the matrix represents the use of an animation style for a communicative function, and the value of the cell represents our estimate of the appropriateness of the animation-function combination for effective user interfaces. A value of 2 means that the combination is highly appropriate, a value of 1 means that the combination is moderately appropriate, a value of -1 means that the combination is moderately inappropriate, and a value of -2 means that the combination is highly inappropriate. A value of 0 is neutral. In Figure 1 the shadings of the cells reflect their values; in this representation, brighter is better.

Before turning to an extended example of application of the model, presented below in Section 4, we first note a few of the model's broader implications. The model suggests that:

- No single animation style is appropriate for expression of all communicative functions.

- Some animation styles (e.g., change of color and change of place) have a greater number of appropriate uses than others (e.g., blur and gesture).
- Some communicative functions (e.g., function and referent) provide greater opportunity for inappropriate animation.
- Some communicative functions (e.g., status) have a clearly most-appropriate way of being expressed through animation.

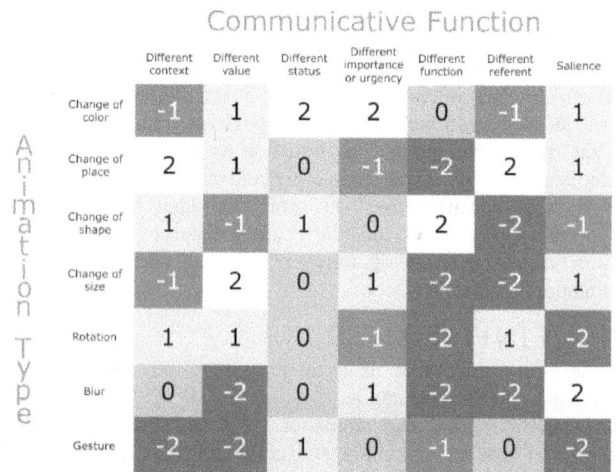

Communicative Function

Animation Type	Different context	Different value	Different status	Different importance or urgency	Different function	Different referent	Salience
Change of color	-1	1	2	2	0	-1	1
Change of place	2	1	0	-1	-2	2	1
Change of shape	1	-1	1	0	2	-2	-1
Change of size	-1	2	0	1	-2	-2	1
Rotation	1	1	0	-1	-2	1	-2
Blur	0	-2	0	1	-2	-2	2
Gesture	-2	-2	1	0	-1	0	-2

Figure 1. Model of communication of animation.

Some of the model's results seem to reflect common sense and common practice. For example, the model suggests that the most appropriate way of expressing value is through size. But the model also surprised us. For example, the model suggests that the most appropriate way of expressing salience is through blur, which few user interfaces use.

4. APPLICATION OF THE MODEL

To illustrate how the model could be applied to graphical user interfaces and to assess the model's plausibility, we used the model to develop two versions of a user interface for an MP3 player.

The first version, shown in Figure 2, uses [animation type, communicative function] pairs that, according to the model, have high appropriateness. For example, the model posits that the best way to signal a change of function is to change the shape of the relevant interface element; this pairing is plausibly appropriate because the different shapes can carry clear meanings. In the animation-appropriate MP3 player, the player's function (i.e., *play* or *stop*) is signaled by change of shape between an arrow and a square. Figure 2 thus depicts a user interface that should be among the most usable animation-based interfaces.

The second version, shown in Figure 3, uses [animation type, communicative function] pairs that, according to the model, have low appropriateness. For example, the model posits that one of the poorest ways to signal a change of function is to change size of the relevant interface element; this pairing is plausibly inappropriate because change in size does not clearly carry with it a new meaning related to function. In the animation-inappropriate MP3 player, the player's function (i.e., *play* or *stop*) is signaled by the same rectangle, just larger or smaller. Figure 3 thus depicts a user interface that should be among the least usable animation-based interfaces.

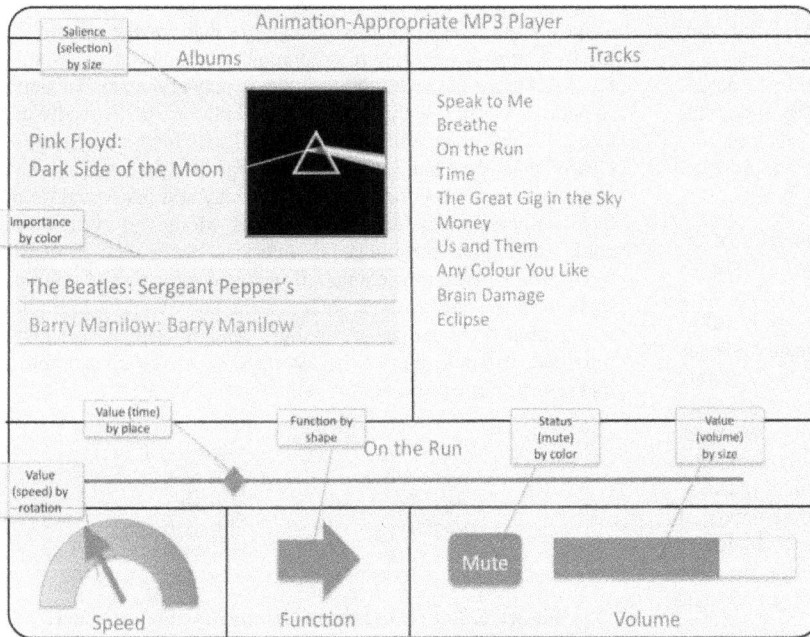

Figure 2. Animation- appropriate user interface

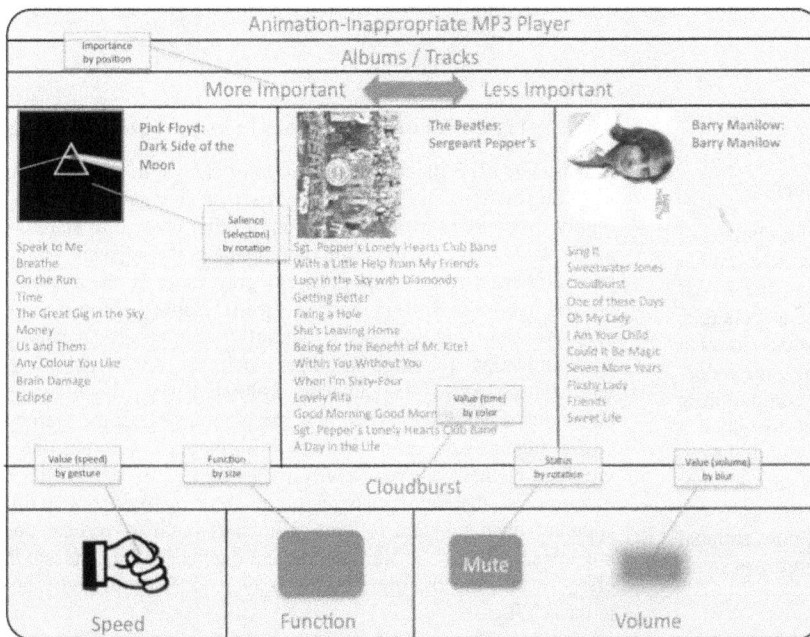

Figure 3. Animation-inappropriate user interface

Working mock-ups of the user interfaces of animation-appropriate and animation-inappropriate MP3 players can be found at *http://www.cs.utep.edu/novick/mp3examples/*. In the mock-ups, which were implemented in PowerPoint, users can see the animations in action. In the authors' admittedly subjective opinions, the animation-appropriate interface feels intuitive and natural, and the animation-inappropriate interface feels awkward to the point of hilarity.

We now turn to a comparison of the specific animation features in the two mock-up interfaces, explaining how the design choices came from values in the model.

Salience. The MP3 player's major use of salience involved displaying which album was selected. The model suggests that change of size would be a moderately appropriate animation to communicate change of salience, so in the animation-appropriate user interface (henceforth "AAUI"), selection is indicated by expansion of the album's information block. The selected album has a larger bounding rectangle and shows the album cover; the unselected albums have been minimized. The model suggests that blur is a highly appropriate means of communicating salience, but in this case blur would have indicated selection of an album at the cost of making it more difficult for the user to select another album. Selection is not the only instance of salience, so blur would be useful in other cases.

The model suggests, conversely, that rotation is a highly inappropriate animation for salience, so in the animation-inappropriate user interface ("AIUI"), selection is indicated by a 90-degree rotation of the album cover. Comparison of the selection animations in the two interfaces confirms that change of size is more effective than rotation: it's immediately clear in the AAUI that the Pink Floyd album has been selected, while in the AIUI it's relatively difficult (a) to discern which album has been selected and (b) the identity of the unselected albums.

Importance. The model suggests that importance is most appropriately signaled by change of color. Accordingly, the AAUI uses color to distinguish "important" albums from "unimportant" albums, and a change in importance would be reflected in a change in color. In this example, the titles of the Pink Floyd and Beatles albums are presented in red, and the title of the Barry Manilow album is presented in blue. Conversely, the AIUI communicates importance through change of place, which the model suggests is moderately inappropriate. Indeed, the use of location as a signal of importance was so weak that we felt we had to include informational arrows in the AIUI explaining what the positions meant. Comparison of the two animation styles is easier in the full color of the PowerPoint mock-ups than in the monochrome of Figures 2 and 3, but to the extent that the color red is understood as communicating urgency, the color change should be more effective than a change in position.

Value (time). The MP3 player includes a widget that indicates a value, namely the time elapsed as the track plays. The model suggests that change of place would be a moderately appropriate animation for communicating change of value, so the AAUI uses a moving slider to indicate elapsed time. The model suggests, too, that change of size is a highly appropriate animation for communicating change of value; our mock-up could also have used an expanding bar to represent elapsed time. Conversely, the model suggests that change of color is a moderately inappropriate means of communicating change of value, so the AIUI uses change of color, through shades of green, yellow, orange and red, to indicate elapsed time. It might have been possible to include color reference values (i.e., a sample of green to mean the beginning and a sample of red to mean the end), but the very awkwardness of doing so serves to underline how inappropriate change of color is for indicating change of value.

Value (speed). The MP3 player also includes an indicator of the speed of playback; that is, the track might be playing faster or slower than normal. The model suggests that rotation is a moderately appropriate means of communicating change in value, so the AAUI has a dial with a rotating pointer to indicate playback speed. The model also suggests that gesture would be a highly inappropriate way of communicating value, so the AIUI uses gesture to indicate playback speed. In the PowerPoint mock-up, the fist icon extends its index figure one or more times, depending on the speed, alternating between the images in Figure 4. Comparison of the two animations suggests the clear advantage of the rotation over the gesture: the rotation shows the change in speed right away while the gesture takes time (and the problem gets worse as the track speeds up!), and the value indicated by the rotated pointer appears to be immediately interpretable while the meaning of the gesture may depend on the user's ability or willingness to count the number of times the finger points.

Figure 4. Speed gesture in inappropriate interface.

Value (volume). The MP3 player's last function is change of volume. The model suggests that change of size is a highly appropriate way to communicate change of value, so the AAUI indicates greater volume by increasing the length of a rectangle. Moreover, the rectangle is in a box, which provides users a reference value for the maximum volume. Conversely, the model suggests that blur is a highly inappropriate way to communicate value, so the AIUI indicates volume by the extent to which a rectangle is blurred. Figure 5 shows three values of volume, from low to high, indicated by blur. Aside from the fact that it's not clear whether greater blur means greater volume, the growing-shrinking rectangle in the AAUI provides a conventional representation of value that users will likely find easier to interpret.

Figure 5. Value buttons in inappropriate interface.

Function. Like other interfaces for playing audio, our mock-up MP3 players include a widget for controlling whether a track plays or pauses. The nature of the function—play or pause—is indicated by the representation of the button; as the button's function changes, its representation changes. The model suggests that change of shape is a highly appropriate way of communicating change of function, so the button in the AAUI presents an arrow or a pair of parallel lines, depending on whether

the button's function is play or pause. Figure 6 shows these shapes. Conversely, the model suggests that change of size is a highly inappropriate way to communicate change of function, so the AIUI has a larger button to indicate play and a smaller button to indicate pause. Figure 7 shows these buttons. As the reader may easily see, the change in shape communicates function much more clearly than the change of size, in large part because we have canonical shapes for functions such as play and pause and do not have canonical sizes for these functions. Moreover, even if sizes could have such meanings, an interface using change of size would still be hard to use unless it included some sort of reference scale to judge size: without such a scale, how would a user know if a button were larger or smaller? And if such a scale were provided, it would clutter the interface in a way comparable to that of the reference colors for value.

Figure 6. Function buttons in appropriate interface.

Figure 7. Function buttons in inappropriate interface.

Status. The MP3 illustrates animation of change in status through its mute button. The model suggests that change in color is a highly appropriate means of communicating change in status, so in the AAUI clicking the mute button causes the adjacent volume bar to change color from green to gray (and, if the button is clicked again, back from gray to green). Conversely, the model suggests that rotation is a neutrally appropriate means of communicating a change in status, so in the AIUI clicking the mute button causes the adjacent volume bar to rotate from a horizontal orientation to a vertical orientation (and, if the button is clicked again, back from vertical to horizontal). Graying out an interface element conventionally indicates loss of availability or function, so the color change in the AAUI provides a readily apparent meaning. But rotation from horizontal to vertical does not appear to have a similar conventional meaning, and so the effect of clicking the mute button is more difficult to understand in the AIUI.

5. CONCLUSION

Our review of resources for designers of user interfaces indicated that although designers have access to design patterns for specific tasks and for proprietary design schemes, they lack access to a broader and more comprehensive model of the use of animation in user interfaces. From a survey of a range of user interfaces employing animation, we identified seven basic types of animation and seven basic communicative functions that they embodied. Using the information from the survey, we developed a model of the appropriateness of the various combinations of animation types and communicative functions. We then applied the model in developing two example user interfaces for an MP3 player, one using appropriate animation-function relations and the other using inappropriate animation-function relations. We explicated the use of the model in developing the example interfaces.

Our research suggests that the key communicative functions of animation in user interfaces can be characterized by a model that relates the purpose of the communication to the nature of the animation. Such a model would have three principal benefits: First, designers could apply the model to static user interfaces that could benefit from the use of animation. Second, designers could apply the model to critique existing use of animation in user interfaces. And third, designers could use the model to develop novel animation-based user interfaces. As our inappropriate-animation example suggests, not all innovation is necessarily useful. But through exploration of the design space, guided by the model, designers may be able to find new and useful animation-based user interfaces.

Aspects of our methodology, some less avoidable than others, limit the results of our research.

A first limitation involves the number and kind of the interfaces we surveyed in developing the model. Clearly it would be impossible to examine all interfaces past, current and proposed. But how many should be enough? We chose to look at different kinds of interfaces and different uses of animation, favoring unique examples over cumulative examples, so that we could attempt to have at least one example in as many of model's matrix cells as possible. We rapidly figured out that we would be unlikely to find examples for all the cells. After all, many of the cells represent poorly appropriate use of animation, so to the extent that designers of animation-based user interfaces developed reasonably appropriate interfaces, we should expect to have many cells unfilled. However, with the large but still limited number of examples we surveyed, we cannot be sure if a cell is empty because it represents a poor combination of animation type and communicative function, or if we just did not run across an existing example of a good combination.

A second limitation involves the categories of animation types and communicative functions. As we discussed in Section 3, we refined and modified these categories as our research progressed and the model matured. This suggests that, although useful for present purposes, the categories might be further refined or extended. Indeed, we are presently considering whether to add *transparency* and *entrance/exit* as animation types.

A third limitation arises from our methodology for constructing the model. We used a qualitative approach because our survey sought breadth of examples rather than quantity of examples. It might conceivably be possible, given much more time and human resources, to conduct a sort of random sample of interfaces, and then to produce quantitative results, where the number of examples in each cell of the model's matrix would indicate the appropriateness of the [animation, communication] pair. However, the problems with this sort of quantitative approach look insurmountable. How would we determine the population of interfaces to sample? Should we weight this by use? Should we look at every animation in the sampled interfaces? If so, this might (a) give too much weight to more extensive interfaces and (b) produce misleading indicators of appropriateness where a particular combination is used repeatedly but ineffectually. With the methodology we used, we tried to avoid the problem of examples of inappropriate combinations indicating apparent value, largely by applying our own judgment, based on traditional Norman-like cognitive models of human-computer interaction, to

the examples we surveyed. But this approach necessarily involves the subjectivity of the researchers' judgments.

If additional resources were available, clearly would have been better to be able to survey many more interfaces. But from the examples we examined, we were able to construct the model, so we feel it is fair to say that it is possible to build a model that relates the key communicative functions of animation in user interfaces to the nature of the animation. The model is likely valid at least for the functions, features, and relationships disclosed in our survey.

Given these limitations, we suggest that future work on this topic should focus on enlarging the fund of examples in the survey, fostering discussion in the research and practice communities on the categories of animation type and communicative functions, and leveraging this discussion to extend the qualitative analysis from which the values in the model were determined. In particular, we look forward to reports from practitioners on the model's usefulness and validity.

6. ACKNOWLEDGMENTS

Our thanks to Georgia Tech-Lorraine for hosting this project and to the members of UTEP's Interactive Systems Group for their help in refining our ideas. We also thank the reviewers for their comments, from which we were able to strengthen this paper significantly.

7. REFERENCES

[1] Android (2011). Developer's guide. Available at http://developer.android.com/guide/index.html.

[2] Apple Inc. (2010). Core animation programming guide. Available at http://developer.apple.com/library/mac/#documentation/Coc oa/Conceptual/CoreAnimation_guide/Introduction/Introducti on.html#//apple_ref/doc/uid/TP40004627-SW1.

[3] Apple Inc. (2010). Apple human interface guidelines. Available at http://developer.apple.com/library/mac/#documentation/User Experience/Conceptual/AppleHIGuidelines/XHIGIntro/XHI GIntro.html.

[4] Bumptop.com (undated). BumpTop 3D Desktop Prototype, available at http://www.youtube.com/watch?v=M0ODskdEPnQ.

[5] Chang, B.-W., and Ungar, D. (1995). Animation: From cartoons to the user interface, *Proceedings of the 6th annual ACM symposium on User Interface Software and Technology (UIST '93)*, 45-55.

[6] Chatty, S. (1992). Defining the behaviour of animated interfaces. *Proceedings of the IFIP conference on Engineering Human-Computer Interfaces (EHCI '92)*, 95-11.

[7] Compiz (undated). Compiz Fusion. Available at http://www.compiz.org/.

[8] Hong, W., Thong, J.Y.L., and Cheung, Y.M. (1997), The impact of animation characteristics and task conditions on online user behavior, *Proceedings. of the First China Summer Workshop on Information Management*, 7-11.

[9] Hudson, S.E., and Stasko, J.T. (1993). Animation support in a user interface toolkit: flexible, robust, and reusable abstractions, *Proceedings of the 6th annual ACM symposium on User interface software and technology (UIST '93)*, 57-67.

[10] Kang H., Plaisant C., and Shneiderman B. (2003). New approaches to help users get started with visual interfaces: Multi-layered interfaces and integrated initial guidance, *Proceedings of the Digital Government Research Conference*, 141–146.

[11] Lang, K. (undated). 'Stand Up' Mac Dock Mockup, available at http://vimeo.com/6695160.

[12] Lang, K. (undated). Smart Inspector — a mockup of a dynamic Inspector Palette, available at http://vimeo.com/8109356.

[13] Maloney, J.H., and Smith, R. (1995). Directness and liveness in the morphic user interface construction environment, *Proceedings of the 8th annual ACM symposium on User Interface Software and Technology (UIST '95)*, 21-28.

[14] Microsoft (undated). Microsoft Future Vision : Healthcare, available at http://www.youtube.com/watch?v=V35Kv6-ZNGA.

[15] Microsoft (undated). Microsoft's Future Vision 2019. Available at http://www.youtube.com/watch?v=g9JBSEBu2q8.

[16] Microsoft (updated). Animations and Transitions. Available at http://msdn.microsoft.com/en-us/library/aa511285.aspx#patterns.

[17] Nielsen, J. (2005). Top ten Web design mistakes of 2005. Available at http://www.useit.com/alertbox/designmistakes.html.

[18] Norman, D.A. (1998). *The design of everyday things*, MIT Press.

[19] Pattern Factory Oy (Ltd.) (2011). Patternry.com. Available at http://patternry.com.

[20] Pawan, V. (2009). *Web application design patterns*, Morgan Kaufmann.

[21] Plaisant, C., and Shneiderman, B. (2005). Show me! Guidelines for producing recorded demonstrations, *Proceedings of the 2005 IEEE Symposium on Visual Languages and Human-Centric Computing* (VL/HCC'05), 171-178.

[22] Thomas, B.H., and Calder, P. (2001). Applying cartoon animation techniques to graphical user interfaces, *ACM Transactions on Computer-Human Interaction*, 8: 198–222.

[23] Tidwell, J. (2011). *Designing interfaces* (2nd edition), O'Reilly Media.

[24] Toxboe, A. (2011). User interface design patterns. Available at http://ui-patterns.com.

[25] Vodislav, D. (1997). A visual programming model for user interface animation, *IEEE Symposium on Visual Languages*, 344-351.

Usability Evaluation of Acoustic Interfaces for the Blind

Mexhid Ferati
Indiana University
School of Informatics

535 West Michigan Street
Indianapolis, Indiana 46202

mferati@iupui.edu

Steve Mannheimer
Indiana University
School of Informatics

535 West Michigan Street
Indianapolis, Indiana 46202

smannhei@iupui.edu

Davide Bolchini
Indiana University
School of Informatics

535 West Michigan Street
Indianapolis, Indiana 46202

dbolchin@iupui.edu

ABSTRACT

With the rapid advent of touchscreen devices, opportunities are increasing to develop innovative interfaces, including applications that combine touch input with auditory feedback to serve the blind and visually impaired (BVI) community. Targeted to blind high-school children, our innovative design, AEDIN (Acoustic EDutainment INterface), uses non-speech sounds simultaneously as navigational prompts and content icons/signifiers for recorded text-to-speech educational essays, which are the main content of this application. A study of two versions of AEDIN was conducted with 20 participants from a K-12 school for the BVI to evaluate its usability and identify ways to improve it. Through the collection of quantitative and qualitative data, we discovered key design improvements that made AEDIN a highly usable and enjoyable interface for these users. The paper highlights good design practices for acoustic interfaces.

Categories and Subject Descriptors

H.5.2 [User Interfaces] Auditory (non-speech) feedback.

General Terms

Human factors, design.

Keywords

Audeme, sound, auditory communication, auditory design, acoustic, touchscreen, interface, blind and visually impaired, children, usability evaluation.

1. INTRODUCTION

Of the approximately 1.5-2 million Americans (and approx. 160 million worldwide) with blindness or severe visual impairment, too few progress through the educational levels required to pursue professional careers. Most blind and visually impaired (BVI) students are overwhelmed by the logistical and emotional obstacles that confront them in standard, vision-centric educational curricula, textbooks and support materials. This has been particularly true in STEM (science, technology, engineering and math) education, which is heavily dependent on visual pedagogy. Ironically, in recent years there has also been increased international concern for improving access to and engagement

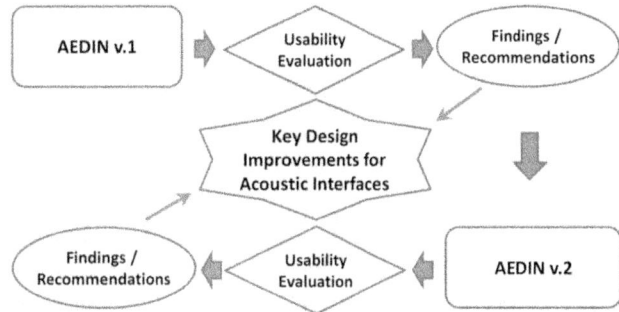

Figure 1. AEDIN evaluation and re-design flow.

with STEM education especially in K-12 grades. A government study in Australia cited "considerable evidence that interventions and resources aimed at encouraging student engagement in STEM thus need to capture the imagination of students in the upper primary and early secondary school years" [19].

To address the particular needs of the BVI community and support their learning, we here at the IUPUI School of Informatics have developed an acoustic touchscreen interface called AEDIN (Acoustic EDutainment INterface). AEDIN facilitates interactions with large collections of educational essays through the use of "audemes," an original type of non-speech sound symbol similar to auditory icons [15, 16]. Audemes are collages or concatenations of two or more sounds (snippets of music and/or sound effects) typically 3-7 seconds long. Audemes generate meaning depending on the identity or meaning of the sounds concatenated. For instance, an audeme collaged from a sound of keys *jangling* (signifying "keys") plus the sound of a car ignition *cranking-revving* (signifying "car") conveys the meaning of "starting the car" and strongly implies "begin a drive." Adding a third sound of surf *crashing* generates the concatenated meaning of "a drive to the beach." Depending on the context, and the presence of other audemes, this concatenated "drive/beach" audeme can be metaphorically extended to signify "vacation."

Our past research [16] has demonstrated that audemes function as powerful mnemonic prompts, and can also emotionally engage BVI students in the competitive challenge of decoding them. To leverage this power, AEDIN was designed to deliver educational content through game-like interactions [6] with audemes used as aural mnemonic prompts and/or as riddles to decode to signify the theme or content of recorded essays. In this paper we review our more recent usability testing of AEDIN, evaluate the integration of audemes into the interface, and provide an overall assessment of AEDIN's logic and user experience.

The first series of usability tests was conducted with AEDIN v.1. The results of these tests suggested possible improvements which were implemented in AEDIN v.2, followed by more usability testing (see Figure 1). Findings from the first and second rounds of usability testing are discussed in the results section. We also provide a synopsis of key design improvements based on those findings.

2. RELATED WORK

AEDIN builds on three main areas of research: auditory feedback, accessible design for the BVI, and touchscreen input.

2.1 Auditory Feedback

The use of non-speech auditory feedback in interfaces has been studied for over 30 years [5, 13]. Critical advances came with the invention of earcons [1] and auditory icons [8]. Earcons are abstract tones with varying pitch, timbre, number and duration, and have been shown to successfully signal functions or help users identify objects in a graphical user interface [3]. Auditory icons replicate common mechanical or natural sounds, and are used as aural analogies to also signal objects and actions in a user interface. They have been successfully evaluated in two auditory interfaces, SonicFinder [9] and ARKola [10]. More recently, a new type of sound cue called a spearcon has been developed by speeding up a text-to-speech word naming a target object/action. Spearcons are played so fast that they essentially become abstract sounds (although with compressed aural similarities to the word heard at normal speeds), and were evaluated as successful prompts in a menu-only interface [20].

In our basic design concept for audemes, we draw upon these other types of aural signifiers, but attain a higher level of semantic complexity through our strategy of combining sounds. This gives audemes a nearly linguistic level of meaning beyond a simple sign or signal, and enables them to convey complex content by acting as a compound icon (e.g. "drive/beach"); or as a metaphor ("drive/beach" = "vacation"); or as an implied micro-narrative ("We got our keys, started the car and drove to the beach."). Although we have yet to investigate which of these explanations is most accurate, we have demonstrated that audemes facilitate memory of multiple facts and ideas associated with their signified themes. [15, 16].

2.2 Accessible Design

The use of auditory feedback has been an important element in designing accessible interfaces for BVI users, or in applications for sighted users in "eyes free" contexts such as driving. One study [4], which tested drivers with auditory and visual interfaces, demonstrated better lane performance with auditory interfaces. Another successful use of auditory feedback is found in BlindSight, a mobile application in which users engage a cell phone keypad and receive auditory feedback, all without looking at the screen [14].

2.3 Touchscreen Input

In the recent past, with the widespread use of touchscreen devices, researchers and developers have successfully demonstrated the power of auditory feedback. In the Slide Rule [11] interface, blind users read names of screen objects and actions on hand-held touchscreens by employing finger gestures. Similarly, No-Look Notes is an eyes-free text-entry application that leverages the iPhone's multi-touch capabilities to increase its accessibility for the blind [2].

Our aim with AEDIN is to demonstrate another successful integration of touchscreen input and auditory output in an interface suitable for BVI users. In our previous paper [6] we described the design of AEDIN and introduced its features and functionalities. This current paper is a follow-up to that work, presenting results of the usability evaluations conducted on AEDIN (v.1 and v.2), and explaining key design improvements made to AEDIN.

3. AEDIN: AURAL/TOUCH INTERFACE

AEDIN (Acoustic EDutainment INterface) is an auditory and touchscreen interface built to support education for BVI students. AEDIN was developed at the School of Informatics, IUPUI, and tested at the Indiana School for the Blind and Visually Impaired (ISBVI). It functions as a knowledge base of aural educational content (comprising recorded essays and quiz questions about these essays) that is navigated through touch input with audio output or feedback (comprising audemes, as well as navigational feedback sounds).

The overall interactive structure of AEDIN offers a game-like learning experience. Users progress through the game by selecting a succession of audemes, all of which are optional selections, and listening to the essays associated with these audemes. At unpredictable times AEDIN challenges users to answer simple yes/no quiz questions based on the essays they have already heard. Users accumulate points by correctly answering those questions [6]. The goal of the initial game is to accumulate as many points as possible. AEDIN offers users 49 audemes, each associated with and serving as a trigger for an individual essay. These audemes are arranged in a virtual, 7-by-7 grid of 49 squares (called the bookshelf), each square containing one audeme. All 49 squares of the bookshelf are not displayed on the screen at once. Instead, the bookshelf is accessed through a screen of nine squares (called the window). The window can be virtually moved throughout the bookshelf (Figure 3) to access any of the 49 squares. Thus, AEDIN avoids confronting users with a screen of 49 relatively small, difficult-to-navigate squares, and instead offers users individual squares with reasonable touch affordance (approx. 2x3 inches on a medium-sized laptop or desktop screen). Theoretically, AEDIN could easily be expanded to a bookshelf of 64, 81, 100 squares or more.

AEDIN features three modes of operation. The primary or initial mode, called the Home Screen, features all audemes in a set arrangement in the bookshelf. In the Shuffle Mode users employ a semi-circular left-to-right finger swipe on any square to trigger a "reshuffling" of the eight audemes displayed in the window. The reshuffled window screen displays the eight audemes that are most semantically relevant to the swiped audeme, which automatically relocates to the upper left corner of the window. (Once the Shuffle Mode is engaged, the bookshelf is disabled, i.e. the user cannot virtually move the window. To restore this movement function, users must return to the Home Screen, effectively re-initializing AEDIN.) The final mode is the Quiz Screen, which is triggered at random after the user has listened to at least two essays. An internal random number generator in the AEDIN program determines when to launch the Quiz Screen.

3.1. AEDIN Sound Categories

The sounds displayed by AEDIN are categorized as either content sounds or feedback sounds.

3.1.1 Content Sounds

The great majority of sounds in AEDIN convey content to users through *audemes*, recorded text-to-speech *essays* and *quizzes*.

Figure 2. Interacting with AEDIN on a touch-screen.

Audemes in AEDIN are used to signify the content or theme of the associated verbal essay by offering users an iconic, metaphoric or micro-narrative representation of that verbal content. Although experienced audeme listeners can often anticipate the content associated with new audemes by decoding them deductively, audemes generally make greater sense (and thus more powerfully prompt memory) after users hear the associated essay content and can best understand and imprint the semantic connection [16].

Essays are text-to-speech (TTS) recordings lasting 1-2 minutes at 160 words per minute. Although any academic subject, notably the STEM disciplines, could provide the material for these essays, in the current version of AEDIN all essay themes were drawn from US history lessons appropriate for the early high school level. Each essay contains a mixture of important figures, facts and analyses consolidated from reliable websites and standard textbooks.

Quizzes, presented as TTS, challenge users with true or false statements to test their knowledge of essays they have already heard during that game session. AEDIN contains 147 quiz statements, three each from the 49 essays. Users hear these statements then must answer the question: Is this true? Yes or No.

3.1.2 Feedback Sounds
AEDIN uses feedback sounds to inform users about the position of objects on the interface or the running state of the interface. These feedback related sounds could be *positional* or *background* sounds.

Positional feedback sounds have the role of communicating to the user the object under their fingertip as they tap the screen. As such, audemes can function as positional sounds to inform users of their location within the bookshelf. When users tap on any affordance on the screen, they will hear a sound revealing the underlying object/function. If the user taps on a functional command button, they will hear its aural label (in TTS), e.g. "Up" or "Left" to indicate the intended movement of the window through the bookshelf (see Figure 3).

Background sounds inform users as to which screen mode the interface is running at that moment. Each screen features a different continuous background sound playing at lower volume whenever the user is not engaging anything on the screen. Once the user taps on an audeme or any command/function button, the background sound stops, but resumes once the audeme or command sound ends.

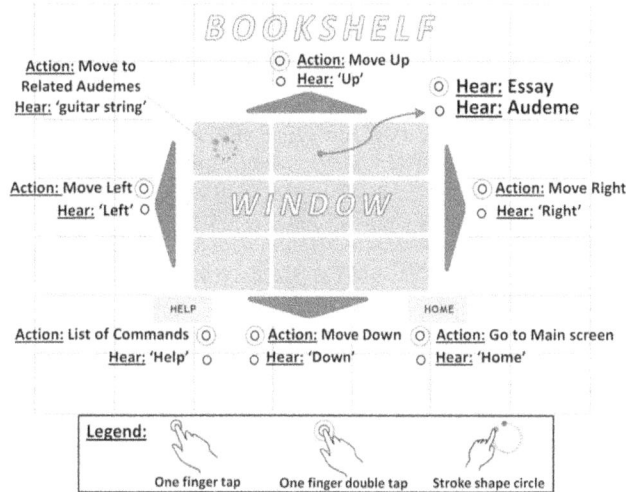

Figure 3. AEDIN: touch-based browsing through audemes.

Continuous background sounds can become annoying; to avoid this we designed background sounds to be soothing and/or pleasant. For example, the Home Screen plays a *soft wind* sound; the Shuffle Screen has a sound of slow *dripping water*. The Quiz Screen plays the audeme related to the question being presented at that moment. As demonstrated in our previous study [16], playing the relevant audeme improves recall of facts from its associated essay. Thus we anticipated that using the specific relevant audeme as a background sound would similarly improve performance for AEDIN's quiz takers.

4. AEDIN v.2
Our analysis of training and usability testing sessions with the first user group, along with comments from the users, generated numerous ideas to improve AEDIN.

4.1 Increased Speed of Essays
For our initial AEDIN implementation, TTS essays were recorded at a speed of 160 words per minute, a rate roughly equivalent to a lively conversation. Our ISBVI student subjects, however, considered this too slow, and requested an increase in speed to make listening less tedious. We increased the TTS essays to around 250 words per minute based on previous research demonstrating that 275 words per minute is a rate that does not significantly affect comprehension or retention [7].

4.2 Designing for Overlapping Affordances
One of our significant observations in our study arose from the participants who were totally blind, and did not always apply to the visually impaired. Blind participants using AEDIN often tapped on the non-functional "empty space" surrounding the four arrow-shaped buttons used to move the window up, down, left and right. These arrows were positioned along the physical screen edges corresponding to the direction of movement. In the design of AEDIN v.1, the arrow-shaped screen graphics exactly overlapped the touchscreen haptic affordances.

For AEDIN v.2 we maintained the same size and shape of the visual affordance but increased the area of touch/haptic affordance to a rectangle in which the arrow fit. This rectangular area was invisible on screen, but accessible through touch. This design decision resulted in decreased empty space on screen, and greater ease-of-use for blind users. This was extensively explained in our previous paper [6].

4.3 Improved Feedback Sounds

Results of our first round of usability testing also suggested changes to AEDIN's feedback sounds. Initially AEDIN's TTS voice automatically announced the cumulative quiz score each time the participant answered a question. However sensible and straightforward this feedback strategy originally seemed to researchers, participants experienced it as needlessly annoying. In AEDIN v.2 we re-configured the TTS announcement "Your Score is [number]" as an on-demand feature accessible through a new on-screen "Score" button, or by pressing the keyboard space bar.

Initially most of the aural labels for command buttons featured a robotic-sounding synthesized voice announcing the function of each (e.g. Home, Up, Left, etc.). Researchers chose this voice in an attempt to create a humorous or distinctive atmosphere for the entire interface. After participants expressed a general dislike of this voice quality, we re-recorded all aural labels with more humanlike voices.

In the initial design, we unintentionally created an ambiguous aural label for the button that triggered replay of the question, labeling it simply "Replay." Our participants suggested we change this aural label to "Replay Question," a phrase which more clearly identified its function.

5. EXPERIMENTAL DESIGN

5.1 Purpose and Overview

AEDIN was carefully designed following guidelines from existing acoustic interfaces aimed for BVI users, e.g [17]. For the evaluation of AEDIN we conducted two usability tests at the Indiana School for the Blind and Visually Impaired (ISBVI). AEDIN was installed in ten touchscreen computers in an ISBVI lab. These were used for all testing. For the first usability test we used AEDIN v.1. After analyzing data from the first usability test, we designed and implemented improvements to produce AEDIN v.2, which we used to conduct the second usability test. In both usability tests, participants were given a 60-minute training session to familiarize them with the current version of AEDIN. Two days later, with no interim opportunity to practice, each participant was tested for 30 minutes for their ability to smoothly operate all aspects of AEDIN. In that test, participants performed eight tasks, then answer five open-ended satisfaction questions, and then answer 19 Likert scale satisfaction questions. Additionally, researchers made direct observation of participant behavior to generate additional usability data.

The purpose of the evaluation was to substantiate our design decisions and help identify key design principles for effective design of acoustic interfaces. To this end, we will compare two versions of AEDIN and discuss the relations between the two.

5.2 Participants

A total of 20 participants (10 male, 10 female, seven blind and 13 visually impaired/partially sighted) took part in this study. For the usability test of AEDIN v.1, we had nine participants (four males, five females, two blind and seven visually impaired/partially sighted). For the second usability test using AEDIN v.2, we had 11 participants (six males, five females, five blind and six visually impaired/partially sighted).

Through the ISBVI administration, a call for volunteers was sent to all middle-school and high-school students. Students who volunteered for the research were randomly assigned to one of the two test groups. Initially both groups comprised 10 students, but

since a student assigned to participate in the first usability test missed the training session, this student participated in the second usability test. All participants were paid.

5.3 Design

This research was a mixed methods design using quantitative and qualitative methods. Quantitative methods were the user satisfaction ratings. Qualitative methods included user comments recorded while they performed the tasks, open-ended questionnaires and observation notes made by researchers. This type of design was used for both usability tests.

5.4 Procedure

We met with participants of the first usability test in the ISBVI computer lab. The first session was a training and familiarization with AEDIN v.1. All nine participants took the hour-long training session at the same time. Two days later the same participants underwent individual usability testing, four with one researcher in one room, and the other five with another researcher in a different room. Each participant spent approximately 30 minutes performing eight tasks and completing questionnaires verbally, while researchers recorded the answers.

Based on our direct observation of the training session and participants' comments while using AEDIN v.1, we defined and implemented improvements in the interface design to create AEDIN v.2. This version was used the following week for the second usability test with the remaining 11 participants. The session tasks and questionnaire were the same as those used in the first usability test.

5.5 Data Collection

The following four types of data were collected in both usability tests performed with a total of 20 participants:

5.5.1 Participant Comments

Researchers took extensive notes about participants' comments during a training session with AEDIN v.1. Changes implemented for AEDIN v.2 mainly derived from these comments.

5.5.2 Satisfaction Questionnaire

In both usability tests, for AEDIN v.1 and v.2, participants performed the specified tasks then completed a satisfaction questionnaire based on their experience in using that version of AEDIN. The questionnaire contained 19 questions to be answered in a five-point Likert scale (Strongly Disagree, Disagree, Neutral, Agree and Strongly Agree). In order to make the process smoother and avoid participant fatigue, the questions were read by researchers to each participant in individual interview sessions. Participants answered verbally with the appropriate value. For example, a researcher read the question "*Using the interface is enjoyable,*" and asked the participant to rate this from 1 to 5, with 1 indicating Strongly Disagree and 5 indicating Strongly Agree.

5.5.3 Open-Ended Questionnaire

After the task performance sessions and satisfaction questionnaires, we also administered a set of five open-ended questions for each usability test. The goal was to gather broader insight into participant experience and uncover issues that we did not anticipate in earlier, more specific questions.

5.5.4 Observation

Researchers took notes on the participants' behavior during the training sessions and during their actual performance of the tasks.

Important usability issues were uncovered through these observations.

6. ANALYSIS AND FINDINGS

6.1 Factor Analysis

Initially, to detect relationships between questions presented in both usability tests, we examined the factorability of the 19 satisfaction rating questions. Ten out of nineteen questions correlated with each other, suggesting reasonable factorability (Table 1). The Keiser-Meyer-Olkin test of sampling adequacy was .51, and Bartlett's test of sphericity was significant, $\chi^2 (45) = 99.12, p < .001$. The Cronbach's Alpha is .731.

Table 1. Extracted factors from satisfaction post-hoc questions

Factor	Questions
Factor 1. *Enjoyability of AEDIN*	**Q16.** The interface is fun to use. **Q15.** Using the interface is enjoyable. **Q17.** I would use this interface again.
Factor 2. *Meaningfulness of AEDIN*	**Q8.** Audemes were meaningful. **Q5.** The bookshelf metaphor makes sense. **Q4.** Our explanation was sensible after you experienced the interface.
Factor 3. *Easiness of using the touchscreen*	**Q19.** Using the touchscreen was comfortable. **Q18.** Using the touchscreen was easy.
Factor 4. *Appropriateness of feedback sounds*	**Q11.** Feedback sounds were meaningful. **Q13.** Feedback sounds were short enough.

Table 2. Question loadings for each factor

Rotated Component Matrix[a]			
Component / Factor			
1	2	3	4
Q16 .932			
Q15 .855			
Q17 .811			
Q8	.915		
Q5	.850		
Q4	.815		
Q19		.951	
Q18		.950	
Q11			.866
Q13			.855

Extraction Method: Principal Component Analysis.
Rotation Method: Varimax with Kaiser Normalization.
a. Rotation converged in 5 iterations.

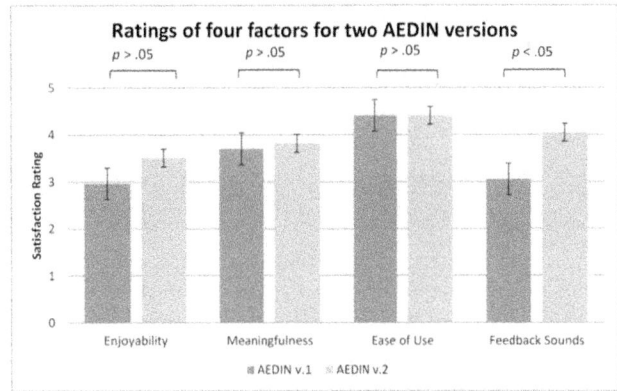

Figure 4. Satisfaction ratings for all four factors in both versions of AEDIN.

Four factors were extracted (see Table 2 for the questions loading on each factor). The first factor is the *enjoyability of AEDIN*, which explained 30.83% of the total variation. The second factor is the *meaningfulness of AEDIN*, which explained 22.68% of total variation. The third factor measured the *easiness of using AEDIN as a touchscreen interface*, which explained 16.89% of total variation. Finally, the fourth factor, measuring the *appropriateness of the feedback sounds*, explained 13.86% of total variation. Table 1 lists the four factors and the questions loading on each factor.

6.2 Consistent Improvement

We have compared the satisfaction rating for both versions of AEDIN and discovered a trend that AEDIN v.2 was rated higher than AEDIN v.1, especially on factor 4 (*F4: Appropriateness of feedback sounds*), which demonstrated a significant difference ($p < .05$). For this factor, participants using AEDIN v.1 ($M = 3.06, SD = 1.24$) gave lower ratings compared to participants using AEDIN v.2 ($M = 4.05, SD = 0.88$), $t(18) = 2.09, p < .05, d = .92$. Satisfaction rating for each factor is shown in Figure 4.

An interesting finding is the high rating given to both versions of AEDIN for factor 3 (*F3: Easiness of using touchscreen*) which leads us to believe that our designed division of space for screen objects was successful. We think this success results from the physical size and placement of the designed buttons and affordances, and the ability of users to easily orient the position of their hands by touching the physical edges of the monitors with their fingers, and by doing so quickly developing an easily remembered "feel" for the centered and symmetrical arrangement of the on-screen affordances. This self-orienting physical easiness was matched by the easily-learned processes of AEDIN's functionality.

The lowest rating, although still above average, was given for factor 1 (*F1: Enjoyability of AEDIN interface*). The reason for this low rating can be found in the post-hoc open-ended questions where users commented that the interface provided too few quiz questions, and that these few were generally perceived as *too* easy to answer. Similarly, participants commented that AEDIN offered too few audemes and essays; and that in general the game logic of AEDIN did not offer participants a sufficient challenge to become truly fun or enjoyable. Based on these findings, we believe that our initial concept for AEDIN was balanced too evenly between its function as an educational knowledge base vs. a game designed

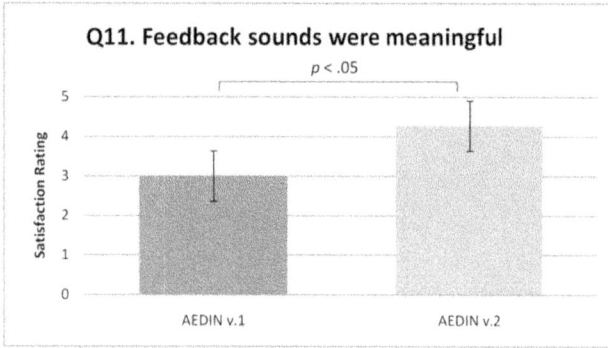

Figure 5. Feedback sounds in AEDIN v.2 were rated significantly higher than AEDIN v.1.

to be played for its own sake rather than for its educational value. In this balance we conflated ease of use with easiness of content. Future developments of AEDIN will strive for a greater degree of mental challenge (see section 7.3 Underdeveloped Game Logic).

In order to better understand the underlying reasons for the significant difference found in factor 4, we further analyzed its two constituent questions: *Q11. Feedback sounds were meaningful*, and *Q13. Feedback sounds were short enough*. In our analysis of Q11, we found that participants who were tested with AEDIN v.2 ($M = 4.27$, $SD = 1.01$) rated the feedback sounds significantly higher than participants using AEDIN v.1 ($M = 3.00$, $SD = 1.50$), $t(18) = 2.26$, $p < .05$, $d = .99$. This result validates our decision to make significant changes to the feedback sounds from AEDIN v.1 to AEDIN v.2 (see section 4.3 Improved Feedback Sounds). Satisfaction rating for Q11 comparing the two versions of AEDIN are shown in Figure 5.

Although we had available only one week to make improvements in AEDIN, our changes resulted in significant increase of enjoyability of the interface. Our analysis of Q13, although showing some gender effect (discussed in section 6.3 Gender Effect) did not suggest the need to reconsider the duration of feedback sounds. Figure 6 shows that for *Question 15: Using the interface is enjoyable*, there was significant difference between the participants using AEDIN v.1 ($M = 2.78$, $SD = 0.83$) compared to participants using AEDIN v.2 ($M = 3.64$, $SD = 0.92$), $t(18) = 2.16$, $p < .05$, $d = .98$. This shows that AEDIN is still an interface that needs improvement, but also that we can achieve significant improvements with relatively minor changes.

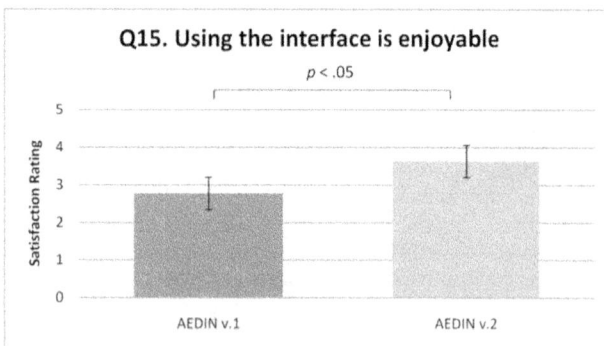

Figure 6. AEDIN v.2 was rated significantly more enjoyable than AEDIN v.1.

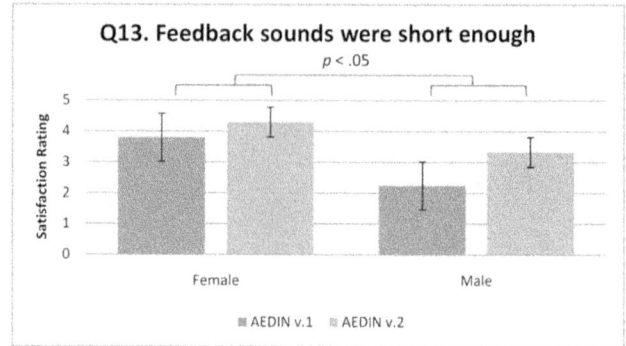

Figure 7. Female participants rated the length of AEDIN feedback sounds significantly higher than male participants.

6.3 Gender Effect

The results show that female participants ($M = 4.10$, $SD = 0.88$) rated the appropriate duration of feedback sounds higher than male participants ($M = 3.64$, $SD = 0.92$), $t(18) = 2.16$, $p < .05$, $d = .98$. It appears that females like feedback sounds to be short and succinct rather than long. Satisfaction rating for Q13 comparing the two versions of AEDIN for females and males are shown in Figure 7.

6.4 Impairment Effect

In both usability tests our participants were blind or visually impaired/partially sighted. For *Question 15: Using the interface is enjoyable*, we noticed a significant difference in the perception of AEDIN as enjoyable. Overall, blind participants ($M = 4.00$, $SD = 1.00$) rated the enjoyability of AEDIN significantly higher than partially sighted ($M = 2.85$, $SD = 0.69$), $t(18) = 3.05$, $p < .05$, $d = 1.34$. Figure 8 shows that there was a big jump in the enjoyability factor from AEDIN v.1 to v.2 for blind participants, while for partially sighted users v.2 offered no significant improvement in enjoyablity. This result is in line with the changes we implemented in overlapping affordances, where our goal was to increase the usability for the blind but not negatively impacting it for the partially sighted (see section 4.2 Designing for Overlapping Affordances).

One of the limitations of the study is the relative small sample size (20). This size, however, is consistent with most published user studies with the blind and visually impaired. To provide a more comprehensive picture of the results, we report here that the power test shows that the impairment effect (partially sighted vs. blind) has a satisfactory statistical power (above 80%). The other effects were above 60%.

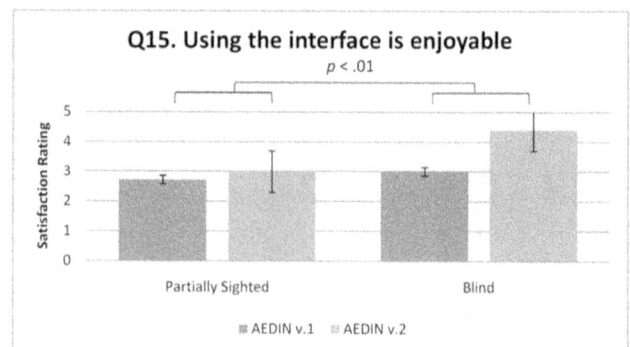

Figure 8. Blind participants rated the enjoyability of AEDIN significantly higher than partially sighted participants.

7. DISCUSSION AND KEY DESIGN IMPROVEMENTS

7.1 Simple Design Changes Yield Significant Improvements

Our usability tests indicate a consistent improvement from AEDIN v.1 to AEDIN v.2, with the greatest improvement shown in the use of feedback sounds. This validates our analysis of the first round of usability tests, and the decision to implement relatively simple changes to these elements of the AEDIN design.

7.2 Touchscreens Highly Usable for the Blind and Visually Impaired Users

Contrary to what may be a "commonsense" belief that touchscreens represent an interaction modality inaccessible and unsuitable to blind users, our results reveal the highest satisfaction rating for touchscreen interactions. Although glass touchscreens inherently lack the tactile dimension of a haptic "technology" such as Braille, they can offer a high degree of proprioception (self-awareness of body/physical positions), particularly for hand/finger positioning within a comfortable field of interaction, as is found with most computer screens. This proprioception can be strengthened by audio feedback. This same positional/audio combination is experienced in playing the piano of the guitar, where all objects/surfaces are essentially indistinguishable except by virtue of their physical location relative to the user's body, and by virtue of the distinct sounds produced when different objects are engaged. A similar study [12] highlights the importance of using the physical edges and corners of a touch screen as useful landmarks for blind users. With its carefully designed feedback sounds and simple, logical layout, our design for AEDIN leverages both the audio and positional dimensions.

7.3 Underdeveloped Game Logic

Compared to the overall satisfaction rating, the enjoyability of AEDIN showed the lowest score, although still above the average. We believe this can be attributed to the underdeveloped design of its game rules and logic, which do not provide enough mental challenge or ludic experience for this group of users. Participants commented that quiz questions were too easy. Besides adding more questions and making them more complex, a few students suggested penalizing players by subtracting points for incorrect answers.

Further, based on several participant comments that the bookshelf design and content were too-easily learned, we believe that participants may be capable of recognizing and remembering more complex bookshelf designs or maps; and that AEDIN could be improved by increasing the number of audemes and essays, achieved by expanding the bookshelf either two-dimensionally or even three-dimensionally in layers. This is to suggest that there may be a natural "field of comprehension" or content map that users can easily hold in their minds for sets of ideas. Conceptual territories smaller than this field may be perceived as too simple and thus boring. Territories larger than this field provide greater opportunities for a serendipitous experience of knowledge discovery or rediscovery.

Further study of these possibilities could be correlated to research into mental maps as well as domains such as urban design (We note that the blind and visually impaired are long accustomed to navigating large urban spaces based on aural cues.) We also speculate that there is an inverse reciprocal relationship between the complexity of the "playing field" and its game logic: That if one is perceived as too simple, the other must assume greater complexity or variability in order to sustain user enjoyment.

7.4 Females Rate Feedback Sounds Higher

An interesting finding is the gender difference in the perception of AEDIN feedback sounds. Compared to males, female participants rated the length of the feedback sounds more positively or as more appropriate. We are unsure what this finding may demonstrate, and neither our observations nor qualitative data indicate an explanation for this result. Although some research has produced relevant findings that females prefer audio experiences more strongly than males in navigational contexts [18], how this correlates to a preference for shorter aural cues remains an open question. Further study should be dedicated to this matter.

7.5 Designed for an Aural Rather than Visual Experience

Our goal was to make AEDIN usable for the blind and visually impaired/partially sighted, although we did not fully anticipate the differences between these groups in terms of their expectations for screen-based interactions. The initial design (AEDIN v.1) was rated as average in terms of being enjoyable to use. Partially sighted users, who could discern the overall graphic design of the interface, commented that the interface was dull and not enjoyable to look at it. This is not surprising since our main goal was to design AEDIN as a highly aural user experience, and we deliberately used simplistic visual strategies and elements. The graphic quality of AEDIN will be addressed in future versions. We believe that simple enhancements to the colors or patterns of screen objects could yield significant improvements to the enjoyment experienced by partially sighted users. As suggested above (see section 7.3 Underdeveloped Game Logic), making the game logic or content infrastructure more complex or variable may compensate for the perceived simplistic quality of the visual design.

The completely blind participants reported different dissatisfactions, which were substantiated by researchers' observations. The areas of haptic affordance in AEDIN v.1 were not always easily accessible for these users. In AEDIN v.2 we designed haptic affordances that overlapped but went beyond the visual affordances designed, particularly for movement command/function buttons (see section 4.2 Designing for Overlapping Affordances). This increased the enjoyability of the interface for the blind, while having no negative effect for the partially sighted.

7.6 Further AEDIN Improvements

The usability findings give us clear indications on several ways in which the AEDIN interface can be improved. First, the game logic should be further developed to provide challenging experiences. For example, levels of difficulty (either in content, quizzes or by challenging users to remember specific content locations) could be introduced to accommodate both novice and expert users and provide appropriate complexity. Second, to address the needs of partially sighted users, we should provide a more interesting visual interface with colors, other graphic elements or images. One participant suggested providing an image to go along with each audeme/square. We recognize the appeal of such a multimodal (audio/visual) approach, but also appreciate the difficulty of introducing effective visual signifiers that would reinforce but not cognitively distort the complex metaphoric impact of audemes. Third, we could expand the virtual dimensions of the bookshelf to offer users more variety, complex discovery and retrieval challenges, and serendipity. Fourth and finally, we could apply the AEDIN infrastructure to knowledge/content domains other than education, and thus offer experiences that appeal to different aspects of young lives, such as popular culture, music or social networking. For example, AEDIN could be adapted as a music archive with snippets of songs to identify content categories, or as a "phonebook" with snippets of friends' voices used as identifying sound symbols.

8. CONCLUSIONS

In this paper we presented usability results of AEDIN, an acoustic interface that enables exploration of a complex knowledge base using touchscreen input and auditory output.

We highlighted three main points. First, we presented the design and implementation of a system that enables access to a knowledge base for blind and visually impaired users. Second, we conducted user studies of two versions of AEDIN designs. Third, we presented results from the user study comparing the two designs that demonstrated significant usability improvements with only minor quick improvements.

In the future we will apply our findings to further improve AEDIN. Our goal is to design innovative aural interfaces for the BVI, offering enjoyable user experiences that are also efficient and effective in facilitating interaction with target content. This content may be large knowledge bases of educational material or other categories of useful information. In designing these interfaces, our challenge will be striking the most appropriate balance between the ease and/or difficulty of these interactions. This balance may vary for different types of content, overall purpose (education, entertainment or communication), specific user groups and chosen platform (desktop, laptop, tablet or smaller handheld).

9. ACKNOWLEDGMENTS

This work was supported by a grant from the Nina Mason Pulliam Charitable Trust. The researchers were also partially supported by the National Science Foundation under Grant #1018054. We thank the students and the staff of ISBVI as well as Microsoft's Imagine Cup 2011 judges for providing suggestion on improving AEDIN and delivering an honorable mention certificate. The study has been approved by the IUPUI (Indiana University-Purdue University Indianapolis) IRB #IRB-01-0704-74B.

10. REFERENCES

[1]   Blattner, M., Sumikawa, D. and Greenberg, R. Earcons and icons: Their structure and common design principles. Human-Computer Interaction, 4 (1). 11-44.

[2]   Bonner, M., Brudvik, J., Abowd, G. and Edwards, W. No-Look Notes: Accessible eyes-free multi-touch text entry. Pervasive Computing. 409-426.

[3]   Brewster, S., Wright, P. and Edwards, A. An evaluation of earcons for use in auditory human-computer interfaces. Proceedings of the INTERACT '93 and CHI '93 conference on Human factors in computing systems. 222-227.

[4]   Brumby, D., Davies, S., Janssen, C. and Grace, J. Fast or safe? How performance objectives determine modality output choices while interacting on the move.

[5]   Deatherage, B.H. Auditory and other sensory forms of information presentation. Human engineering guide to equipment design. 123-160.

[6]   Ferati, M., Mannheimer, S. and Bolchini, D. Acoustic interaction design through audemes: experiences with the blind. Proc. of the 27th ACM International Conference on Design of Communication (SIGDOC), Bloomington, IN. 23-28.

[7]   Foulke, E., Amster, C.H., Nolan, C.Y. and Bixler, R.H. The comprehension of rapid speech by the blind. Exceptional Children.

[8]   Gaver, W. Auditory icons: Using sound in computer interfaces. Human-Computer Interaction, 2 (2). 167-177.

[9]   Gaver, W. The SonicFinder: An interface that uses auditory icons. Human-Computer Interaction, 4 (1). 67-94.

[10]   Gaver, W., Smith, R. and O'Shea, T. Effective sounds in complex systems: The ARKola simulation. Proceedings of the SIGCHI conference on Human factors in computing systems: Reaching through technology. New Orleans, Louisiana, United States. 85-90.

[11]   Kane, S.K., Bigham, J.P. and Wobbrock, J.O., Slide rule: making mobile touch screens accessible to blind people using multi-touch interaction techniques. in, (2008), ACM, 73-80.

[12]   Kane, S.K., Wobbrock, J.O. and Ladner, R.E. Usable Gestures for Blind People: Understanding Preference and Performance.

[13]   Kantowitz, B.H. and Sorkin, R.D. Human factors: Understanding people-system relationships. Wiley, 1983.

[14]   Li, K.A., Baudisch, P. and Hinckley, K., Blindsight: eyes-free access to mobile phones. in CHI 2008, (2008), ACM, 1389-1398.

[15]   Mannheimer, S., Ferati, M., Bolchini, D. and Palakal, M. Educational Sound Symbols for the Visually Impaired. Universal Access in HCI, Part I, HCII 2009 Proceedings, Springer-Verlag LNCS 5614, San Diego, CA. 106-115.

[16]   Mannheimer, S., Ferati, M., Huckleberry, D. and Palakal, M. Using Audemes as a Learning Medium for the Visually Impaired. Proceedings of HEALTHINF'09, Porto, Portugal. 175-180.

[17]   McGookin, D., Brewster, S. and Jiang, W.W., Investigating touchscreen accessibility for people with visual impairments. in, (2008), ACM, 298-307.

[18]   Siochos, V. and Eisenhauer, M. A user evaluation study of a multi-modal mobile navigation aid for pedestrians with respect to gender differences.

[19]   Tytler, R., Osborne, J., Williams, G., Tytler, K. and Clark, J.C. Opening up pathways: Engagement in STEM across the Primary-Secondary school transition.

[20]   Walker, B., Nance, A. and Lindsay, J. Spearcons: Speech-based earcons improve navigation performance in auditory menus. Proceedings of ICAD'06. 63-68.

AccessibilityUtil: A Tool for Sharing Experiences About Accessibility of Web Artifacts

Thiago Jabur Bittar
UFG - Catalão - GO, Brazil
USP - ICMC
São Carlos, SP, Brazil

jabur@icmc.usp.br

Leandro Agostini do Amaral
USP - ICMC
Caixa Postal 668
São Carlos, SP, Brazil

ordnael@icmc.usp.br

Renata Pontin de Mattos Fortes
USP - ICMC
Caixa Postal 668
São Carlos, SP, Brazil

renata@icmc.usp.br

ABSTRACT

Existing guidelines on how to develop web applications with accessibility are currently not applied in many organizations. The lack of "closeness" of these guidelines to the developers is one of the most significant reasons for this scenario, as developers often do not know them or find it difficult to apply them. As a proposed solution to increase the use of guidelines in development practices, we present a proposal of a collaborative tool for sharing and disseminating experiences. The proposal is based on capturing and disseminating Design Rationale (DR) related to experiences with developing web artifacts, following the Web Content Accessibility Guidelines (WCAG) 2.0.

Categories and Subject Descriptors

D.2.2 [**Design Tools and Techniques**]: User Interfaces;
H.5.4 [**Hypertext/Hypermedia**]: User issues;

General Terms

Design, Human Factors.

Keywords

Accessibility, WCAG 2.0, Collaboration, Design Rationale

1. INTRODUCTION

Millions of people have limited access to content and functionality available on the web due to interaction artifacts are not in accordance with accessibility guidelines. The challenge in this area is to design elements of the web sites that enable any user to perceive, understand and interact with its content [13][20][24].

Considering the various technologies such as desktop computers, notebooks, tablets and cell phones, accessibility can become more complex to developers; this can make it be partially or completely ignored by developers [7][15][1].

The aim of web accessibility is to provide equal opportunities for all, to have access to the extensive content available on the online environments for education, business, government, commerce and entertainment.

The motivation for this research is directly related to the issue of how to solve or mitigate the problem of non-use of web

development best practices, especially regarding the W3C accessibility guidelines, by developers. Currently, in fact, many barriers are found [15][1][7][24].

One problem is the lack of efficient mechanisms to assist the developers, informing and supporting them to make effective use of successful experiences during the process of web applications [20][24]. Whereas a development team often has a lack of standardization in the way of implementation, not being consulted prior experience and with little documentation of the well-succeeded cases, which would be very useful for facilitating the development concerning the accessibility guidelines.

According to Freire, Russo and Fortes (2008), despite the efforts at developing the accessibility guidelines, the developers often do not know them, the organizations have not been involved in applying them and the authoring tools do not provide adequate support to their employment. The research describes a study that involved 605 people engaged in web development projects. They were asked for answering a survey; 48% of respondents did not use any method to incorporate or evaluate accessibility in their projects [7].

Based on the problematic context of the developers not being aware of the accessibility guidelines, we propose a collaborative tool for helping an organized exchange of experiences on development of web interaction artifacts concerning the accessibility guidelines. We have used a Design Rationale (DR) method, as part of the development process that requires the documentation of decisions, discussions, argumentation and comments on the final product.

In the DR proposal the design decisions and their impacts are registered as good or bad. This is because such decisions could lead to success or failure of a project. Documentation is important to build a knowledge base for future projects by avoiding rework and enabling better decisions [16].

Another point to consider is that this type of approach to design and its dissemination is common to human experience. Most people often observe others' comments as builders of knowledge, in this case features of using guidelines in projects to improve accessibility.

The purpose of this paper is to present concepts and results of the study, planning and development of our tool, highlighting the discussion about how DR and collaboration can be useful in the field of development using best practices. Thus and because the limited size of this paper, we do not we focus on the further implementation details, but on the design and rationale of the proposed development.

The proposed tool for promote discussion and experience sharing about accessibility, called AccessibilityUtil, is available online in

Portuguese and English, to expand the contribution of aggregation and knowledge of experts from around the world. The overall aim is to allow the dissemination of information and make resources available to other developers, providing mechanisms to assist development with good accessibility.

In Figure 1 we present the conceptual first attempt for the picture of the proposed tool.

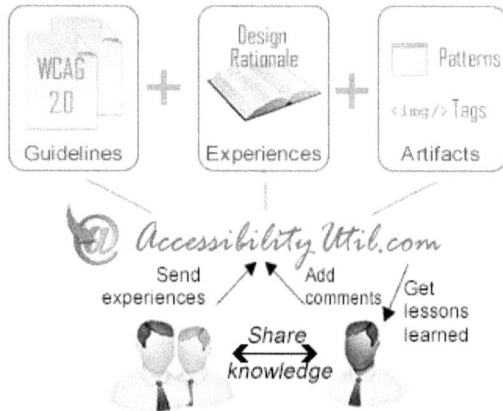

Figure 1 – AccessibilityUtil concept and collaboration model

To clarify the usage scenarios resulting from the tool use and its contributions, we show the following 3 main examples of possible use:

1. A developer wants to insert and share a technique related to a particular pattern or tag;
2. A developer who used a technique and has positive or negative comments about it;
3. A developer wants to use a certain pattern and will consult the tool to ponder over existing techniques and what other developers and experts argue about them before using.

With the collaboration model proposed, we intend to achieve a number of relevant assessments and contributions for each artifact registered with the purpose to enable developers and other interested persons to consult a database aiming to support the creation of websites more accessible using official guidelines. The tool is available at the URL *"http://www.accessibilityutil.com/"* and can be used from the creation of a user account to full access to view and contribute with artifacts and assessments.

This paper is organized as follows: Section 2 presents the concept of web accessibility, with the problems involved and a summary of accessibility guidelines. In Section 3 we present the concepts of DR and then show the methodology for the research we conducted in Section 4. Section 5 presents a summary of the development of the supporting tool to our proposal. Finally, in Sections 6, 7 and 8, we discuss the results, related work and conclusions, respectively.

2. WEB ACCESSIBILITY
Accessibility can be broadly interpreted as the possibility of using some resource universally, without barriers or with alternative ways to access and use. In web context, the contents of the pages are this resource. So this concept is related to every user, using every agent, can understand and interact with the offered content [19][21].

In general, there are three fundamental reasons why organizations must make their sites accessible:

Social reasons: organizations must be motivated to be socially responsible and work to eliminate discrimination and promote the human rights [10].

Commercial reasons: there is no economical justification for organizations to alienate about 10% of potential users who may have some disability [10]. Companies having an inaccessible website may result in the migration of disabled users to competing sites.

Legal justification: in 1993, the United Nations released the *Standard Rules on the Equalization of Opportunities of Persons with Disabilities*. This document is only a guideline and includes the recommendation that nations must "develop strategies to make information services and documentation for different groups of people with disabilities" [2]. In Brazil there is the 5296's Law Decree from December 2nd, 2004 which regulates, in its article 47, the obligation of accessible governmental websites within one year. After approximately seven years what we can see is that we are still far away from what was regulated.

2.1 Issues overview
There is a significant gap of knowledge from developers and experts in accessibility. Most programmers have no necessary knowledge or experience to ensure that their code attends the accessibility requirements. It is a common practice to consider accessibility in a project developing advanced stages or when applications are already coded. At this point, making applications accessible is a real challenge of redesign and reprogramming.

Martín, Cechich and Rossi (2011) ponder about the importance of modeling accessibility requirements in the development early stages and not only in evaluations after the product performed [13]. An essential feature for them is that the application of accessibility concepts requires a special treatment during web developing. There's an idea that must predominate accessibility global features that are independent of device and implementation types. Thus, they propose an independent aspect-oriented approach for inclusion of accessibility good practices in web development.

These authors also comment that the use of past experiences reports are very important for the accessibility successful solutions reuse, saving time and investment from developers. Thus, it is indicated the use of patterns and templates. The design support must be performed with a universal design for an efficient inclusion in the project [1].

According to Bigham, Brudvik and Zhang (2010) very few developers have been trained explicitly for accessible pages creation. Evaluate pages using assistive technology may reveal problems, but these software take time to install and can be complex for this use.

To facilitate the developers learning, these authors propose an accessibility approach by demonstration. The idea is that one person using an assistive technology may find problems and report it to the website developers.

Creating accessible content can be subjective and a difficult task for developers, who are mostly not trained in accessibility. Guidelines and standards serve as an entry point, but may not capture many factors that influence the accessibility and usability of a page [3].

2.2 Web Content Accessibility Guidelines (WCAG)

Aiming to explain more about how to produce accessible content for the Web, W3C, through its *Web Accessibility Initiative* (WAI), released a collection of accessibility guidelines, called *Web Content Accessibility Guidelines* (WCAG). These guidelines represent recommendations to produce accessible web content (texts, images, forms, sounds) to persons with disabilities, including blindness and low vision, deafness and poor hearing, learning difficulties, dyslexia, cognitive limitations, limitations of movement, inability to speak, photosensitivity and combinations thereof.

These guidelines are in its 2.0 version since December 2008. The goal is that they serve to supporting developers and subject to testing by automated tools and humans.

Its composition is hierarchical, being on top of its structure are four principles underlying 12 guidelines and 61 success criteria. A summary of these principles and guidelines is shown below [21]:

Principle 1: Perceivable - information and user interface components must be presentable to users in ways they can perceive. Its guidelines are:

Guideline 1.1 - Text Alternatives: provide text alternatives for any non-text content so that it can be changed into other forms people need.

Guideline 1.2 - Time-based Media: provide alternatives for time-based media.

Guideline 1.3 - Adaptable: create content that can be presented in different ways without losing information or structure.

Guideline 1.4 - Distinguishable: make it easier for users to see and hear content including separating foreground from background.

Principle 2: Operable - user interface components and navigation must be operable. Its guidelines are:

Guideline 2.1 - Keyboard Accessible: make all functionality available from a keyboard.

Guideline 2.2 - Enough Time: provide users enough time to read and use content.

Guideline 2.3 - Seizures: do not design content in a way that is known to cause seizures.

Guideline 2.4 - Navigable: provide ways to help users navigate, find content, and determine where they are.

Principle 3: Understandable - information and the operation of user interface must be understandable. Its guidelines:

Guideline 3.1 - Readable: make text content readable and understandable.

Guideline 3.2 - Predictable: make web pages appear and operate in predictable ways.

Guideline 3.3 - Input Assistance: help users avoid and correct mistakes.

Principle 4: Robust – the content must be robust enough that it can be interpreted reliably by a wide variety of user agents, including assistive technologies. It guideline is:

Guideline 4.1 - Compatible: maximize compatibility with current and future user agents, including assistive technologies.

For each one of the 12 guidelines, there are several success criteria to be tested. The W3C documents all criteria in WCAG and outlines solutions to comply them in different applications [21], though they remain far from practical reality of most web application developers, without a direct connection with the various existing artifacts.

Besides this problem, those who know of the existence of these guidelines often do not follow them, by its demand a greater effort in developing applications, considering a relatively small audience. The challenge thus is to bring closer the guidelines from the developer environment in a facility, practical and clear guidance for applying them.

3. DESIGN RATIONALE

Gruber and Russell (1991) and Moran & Carroll (1996) define Design Rationale (DR) as a reference to the reasoning that justifies a project and to descriptions that justify choices structures on other alternatives. MacLean (1989) and Lee (1997) consider that the DR not only includes a description of potential artifact, but also the reasons for decisions, experiences, alternatives and arguments that led to the decision.

Wang and Burge (2010) show that the DR can be used to capture and management architectural knowledge, which is extremely important in software projects including information from the environment and reasons for the design and negotiation process defining the outcome a final product.

However, storing DR can take significant time and be expensive. What can you do to try to resolve this issue is to automate the capture process and associate it most with the work object, i.e. the development itself.

The use of the DR helps the learning of a project as a whole and may represent a solution to help designers to identify issues that might otherwise go unnoticed [9], also contributing to inappropriate identification of premises and decrease the tendency of designers in not perceive possible alternatives on important decisions.

The knowledge has demonstrated a decisive factor in today's world, being the focus of the institutions that need to use it, making decisions constantly. Likewise, the DR is recovered to capture and record decisions made on projects and their impacts, good or bad. This is because such decisions can lead to success or failure of a project. Documenting experiences is important to build a knowledge base for future projects by avoiding rework and enabling better decisions.

The explicitness of the DR allows us to offer a common vocabulary, to produce artifacts most complete in less time with less effort and enabling a better maintenance and development, ensuring design quality. But there are limitations that difficult its use in practice, as presented Regla *et al.* (2000) and Conklin and Burgess-Yakemovic (1996): the developers' difficulties to retrieve information captured, the difference between information that developers wish to record and that the system allows, the generally of the tools and the not contributing to the natural progression project activities.

Other useful employment of this methodology, according to Dutoit *et al.* (2006), is to promote collaboration and knowledge among team members, facilitate maintenance and reuse, improve the quality of the artifacts and base new design decisions.

4. METHODOLOGY

To achieve the objectives of presenting concepts, results of the study, planning and deployment of the proposed tool, we adopt initially exploratory and collaborative research to obtain information from reality, filter them and compose a knowledge base to help developers.

Thus, for planning and development tool we selected the Requirements Engineering (RE) to assist in planning and recording of the necessary functionality. Then, stages were made for analysis (to understand and make inferences about the data) and design (which is the description and implementation of steps to reach the final product or process) [18].

Thus, the first step was to determine what the goals and requirements for application, and then we developed a document with the planning and requirements.

The team assigned in this work was composed of undergraduate computer science students, masters and doctorate researchers with work area related to accessibility. With prior knowledge of the team in the area we were able to reduce development time.

Team discussed necessary to approximate the data collected and development decisions with findings of previous studies and the consolidated rules, optimizing and enabling a relationship of knowledge. So we choose the relationship with WCAG 2.0 because it is a set of official guidelines from W3C.

Thus, the tool concepts were was defined: it is not enough we only collect information and design decisions about accessibility, there is a need to organize them in accordance with the guidelines established.

User profiles have been defined including the information that each profile will be allowed access into the tool. This is an important point seen in the planning: the collaboration needs some mediation, to preventing duplication of information and invalid data are not kept in tool.

An issue of the methodology was verified as having high importance: the tool must be accessible, and then it has permeated all programming with implementation of verifications and periodic adjustments in its accessibility. Thus, we used successfully the tool AChecker[1] and manual inspections. How some pages require user authentication, we did manual access in AccessibilityUtil and copy its HTML code for subsequent tool checking.

As the first version of our tool become available, we did the planning of how to make the dissemination, which is important for project success. Thus, developers, students and web interested persons were invited by e-mail and using social networks to participate in the project, just as experiences viewers or as content collaborators.

5. TOOL DEVELOPMENT

The tool was developed in PHP language as code for application on the server side, using the JQuery framework for handling events in the interface and using MySQL as the Database Management System (DBMS). This development has required effort for about four months and we are making improvements and refinements to include new features.

AccessibilityUtil allows the users registration to be able to create artifacts, to visualize the ones who have already done assessments, inserting their experiences and project's decisions, contributing with use's report and techniques to have the complete criterions of accessibility for each artifact, from a collaboration methodology between the accessibility specialists.

---

[1] http://achecker.ca

The database model allowed the inclusion of all principles, guidelines and success criteria with their descriptions and codes, as documented in WCAG 2.0. Thus the creation of the database was defined with the creation of 11 tables with associations (relationships) between them, as can be seen in Figure 2.

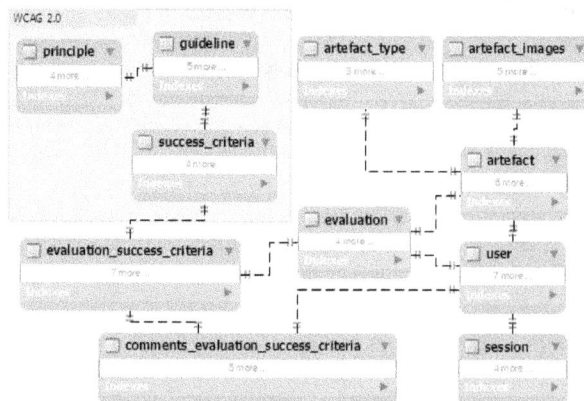

Figure 2 – AccessibilityUtil data model

Besides the content guidelines, this database also includes the registration of users with their personal data, level of expertise and profile if they have administrator or participant permissions.

We choose register the web artifacts, turning the system more flexible, instead of supporting just patterns, for example. In this context, we consider as artifacts any element present in the web construction, which have some accessibility's consideration.

The administrator can manage the system accepted artifacts types, visualize utilization's report, list the users and make a mediation of the sent contents.

The participants can create artifacts related to the administrator inserted types, visualize all the system previous registered artifacts and evaluate them.

The artifacts types' creation helps its better organization, ranking them. As initial categories we have inserted: "patterns", "tags" and "others".

The objective of the generic category "others" is to permit flexibility in the initial categorization, in cases of having lots of artifacts in this category, administrators will be able to verify and a new category can be created to arrange them.

The tool was created to support two languages, Portuguese and English, aiming to be international and also to explore the knowledge of researchers from abroad. Its home screen in the English interface can be seen in Figure 3, below.

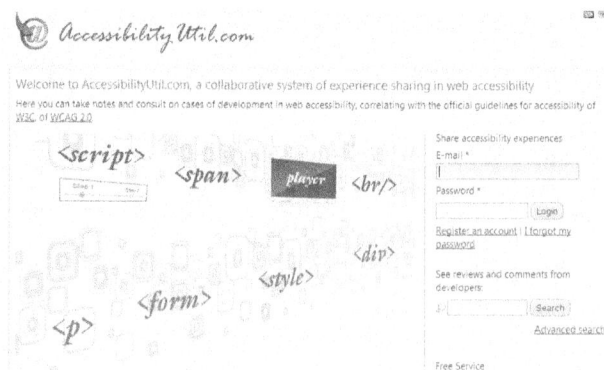

Figure 3 – Home screen in the English interface

The Figure 4 shows the main page presented to the participant, in which the user has: the registered artifacts number information from each artifact type contained in the tool, access to the artifact registration page, access to all registered artifacts. Additionally, with the objective of contributing with information retrieve, keyword artifacts search is available too.

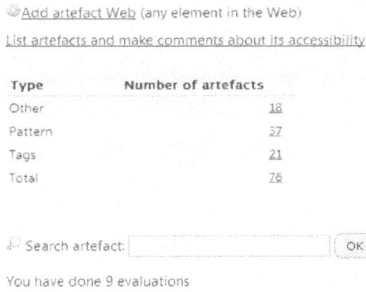

Figure 4 – Participant home

The artifact registration form can be visualized in the Figure 5, in which are requested information as the administrator previously registered artifact type, the name, its description, the associated images and the literary references. Besides the Portuguese version, it's possible to attribute the translations to the English language in the fields.

In addition to inserting artifacts, the participant can perform evaluations about the use of accessibility techniques according to a guideline and adding comments in evaluations of an artifact.

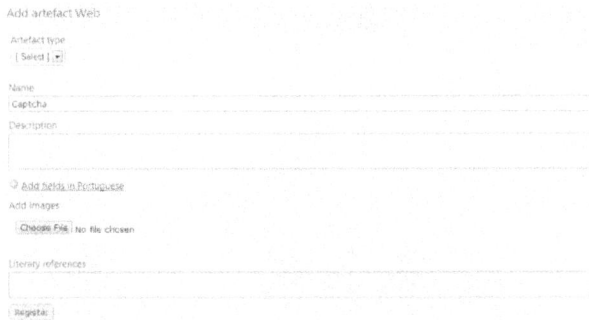

Figure 5 – Adding a web artifact

The Figure 6 presents an artifact visualization associated with an image and the evaluation form.

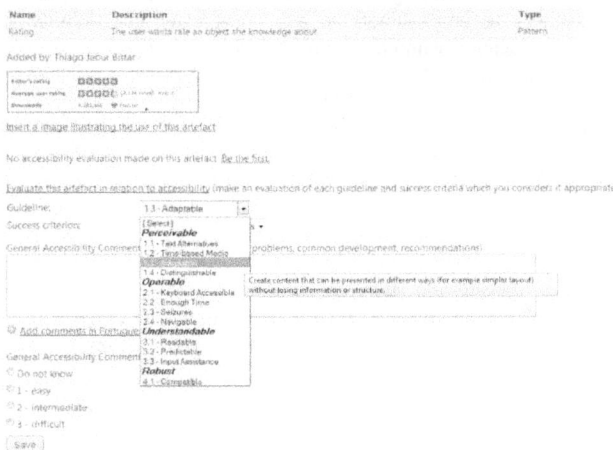

Figure 6 – Viewing artifact details and performing an evaluation

As showed in the previous figure, the evaluation can be made by the selection of the accessibility guideline and after choosing the success criterion qualified by guideline selection. The two other fields to be filled out are the accessibility general comments and the accessibility develops difficulty rating.

It's important to detach that the interface was planned to support the ones who don't have depth knowledge about WCAG 2.0, showing the related text when the user stays some seconds with the focus or the mouse pointer in each option, by "title" attribute. In case it was a requirement knowing the Guidelines to do the evaluation, it would be an obstacle to the developers, and then, with the AccessibilityUtil offered form helps its dissemination.

From the administrator's main page, showed in Figure 7, the registered artifacts types appears, it's possible the generation of user's accesses and registration, beyond artifacts types creation.

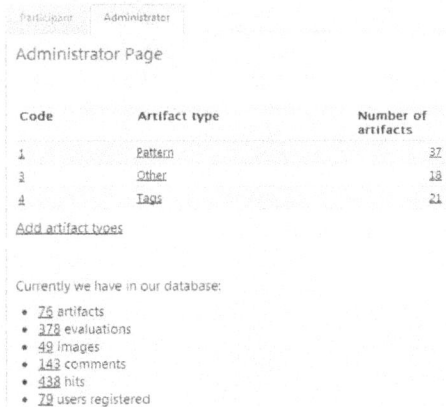

Figure 7 – Administrator's main page profile

So, the AccessibilityUtil tool was developed respecting the initial objectives, inserting all guidelines and principles documented by W3C (WCAG 2.0), from which the participants' experiences are assigned with artifacts present in the database.

6. RESULTS

In addition to tool developing, as presented in the previous section, which consumed significant time and effort, allowing the validation of the involved idea in the accessibility DR's capture, we have as results the its initial application.

Thus, since its recent release in early May, 2011, 206 accesses were computed in AccessibilityUtil tool. In its database were registered 79 users and 76 artifacts distributed in three types according to Table 1, as following.

Table 1 - Initial distribution of artifacts

Artifact types	Quantity
Patterns	37
Tags	21
Others	18
Total	76

The selected patterns in this initial registration were selected from Welie (2011) [25] and the *Yahoo! Design Pattern Library* collection (2011) [26].

The artifacts registration is made in a way to make duplications difficult. When a participant enters with the artifact name, the tool performs a search to show potential candidates in tool database which describe the same artifact desired by the user. If the artifact name already exists in the system, the participant may make evaluation without having to register it again.

In each artifact can be inserted images to illustrate it and collaborate with its description. For accessibility reasons, each image, to be sent, requires its textual description.

About the evaluations made until late June 3, we have the results shown in Table 2.

Table 2 - Collaborations in the tool

Collaboration types added	Quantity
Experiences	378
Images	49
Comments	143
Total	570

This successfully initial use of the tool, with positive users' feedback, brings confidence to the proposed database model. We verified that this model completed its function capturing and transmitting DR in web accessibility field, which requires everyone's efforts to improve the inadequacy situation of many artifacts in relation to established guidelines.

Another positive point was some definitions made that don't involve the data's model, as the choice of name and domain in the application: for the wider coverage of the project, including international was chosen their access through the domain ".com". This important feature allows the project don't being associated with an institution's domain, because it involves different institutions and others may join as partners.

Whereas the project is open for the user to insert images into the artifacts database, and for protection, the sent was limited to the maximum of 7 images per artifact. Thus, we do not have the risk of a user tries, by the use of any tool, overloading the server.

Another interesting result feature is in relation to different reports that can be generated from the AccessibilityUtil tool database. Such reports involve different views, for example, knowing which success criterion was most commented by the contributors and which artifacts it applies. This report can be seen in Figure 8, indicating the evaluations number per success criterion.

Name	Evaluations
Principle: 1 - Perceivable	
1.1 - Text Alternatives	
1.1.1 - Non-text Content	14
1.2 - Time-based Media	
1.2.1 - Audio-only and Video-only (Prerecorded)	0
1.2.2 - Captions (Prerecorded)	0
1.2.3 - Audio Description or Media Alternative (Prerecorded)	0
1.2.4 - Captions (Live)	0
1.2.5 - Audio Description (Prerecorded)	0
1.2.6 - Sign Language (Prerecorded)	0
1.2.7 - Extended Audio Description (Prerecorded)	0
1.2.8 - Media Alternative (Prerecorded)	0
1.2.9 - Audio-only (Live)	1
1.3 - Adaptable	
1.3.1 - Info and Relationships	26
1.3.2 - Meaningful Sequence	7
1.3.3 - Sensory Characteristics	13
1.4 - Distinguishable	
1.4.1 - Use of Color	7

Figure 8 – A part of the list of evaluations per success criterion

Analyzing the tool's data, as the ones seen in Figure 8, we can make relationships and investigations with the evaluations results and comments inserted. For example, we can know the reasons for users don't send artifacts development experiences in a particular guideline.

We can make good measurements on the sharing of experiences in the tool through a qualitative analysis. Some rich examples are given below:

- **Success criterion:** 3.1.1 - Language of Page

- **Artifact:** <p> (tag)

- **Experience reported:** "The paragraph attracts the user attention. It makes him look at the text, starts reading and then want to read the whole text. A text without paragraph is boring; it's neither organized nor interesting".

- **Success criterion:** 2.1.1 - Keyboard

- **Artifact:** <select> (tag)

- **Experience reported:** "The combo-box make the navigation easier. It helps not just people with difficulty, but it helps everybody sparing us to type something that is already defined. Instead of typing it you can just click in the word and it's ready".

- **Success criterion:** 1.3.1 - Info and Relationships

- **Artifact:** Accordion menu (pattern)

- **Experience reported:** "Accordions are a good way to organize a web site. It's just necessary to be read by the program-reader. The accordions make faster the localization of subjects in the site, because everything is divided in topics, so the navigation becomes easier".

Therefore, the main contributions of this work can be summarized as following: **i)** connect participants with accessibility guidelines to allow visualizations from different points of view for the same evaluation; **ii)** participants cooperation to the completeness of experiences and views about accessibility guidelines for a particular artifact, **iii)** creation, development and dissemination of a practical experiences about development with usability relating it with artifacts and official guidelines and **iv)** enable consulting about already evaluated artifacts presenting important data to novice developers, providing good practices learning and identification of inadequate premises.

We note that these contributions are valued within a valorized context at these days, the collaboration by different researchers and others society's actors to achieve greater accessibility in relation to scientific and technological advances.

7. RELATED WORK

When searching about tools for this field, it was verified that the majority seeks to deal with the accessibility in already developed elements, making its evaluation according to guidelines. Differently of these, the AccessibilityUtil tool aims to be used during the analysis and development processes. So, it's expected to arrive in the assessment time with the less number of errors as possible, considering also the cost of modifications after an effectuated development is much higher than if the correction, or good development, had been practiced in previous stages.

Bailey and Pearson (2011) describe a web tool's development of accessibility knowledge administration, called Accessibility Evaluation Assistant (AEA), focalized in help the accessibility evaluation process for novice appraisers.

These authors reported that evaluation tools aren't easily understood for these users yet. One of the causes is the hard correct understanding of WCAG for beginners. The AEA tool was successfully tested for a 38 under-graduating students group.

An idea presented by these authors that deserve to be pointed out is the organization of special necessities users in 10 groups: dyslexics, learning disabilities, low vision, physical disabilities, English as a foreign language, elderly, visual impairments in color perception, hearing impairments and seizure disorders.

This organization's motive, according to the authors, is to help the evaluators to recognize real users and encourage them to find commons accessibility principles that aid in the accessibility verification process. It can be incorporated in the explained tool of this paper over time, but the own guideline is already discoursed about which disability they're applied.

AccessibilityTips.com already has offered a collection of tips, guidelines and practical suggestions for accessible web development. Its format differs from the developed work in AccessibilityUtil proposed here, because that is structured as blog form, it is not possible the collaboration between users (inclusively the commentaries option is disabled). In such case, all the posts are from a unique author. Another characteristic that differ them is that in this site there is no relation between the suggestions presented and the official guidelines from W3C. One point that must be jutting out is that the last post of this site is reported on 2009, indicating a possible downgrade and discontinuity.

In relation of the DR use, involving the description of experiences related to accessibility, it was not found significant published researches. The performance line realized in this work comes to turn the hypothesis about the benefice with the alliance between the two areas valid. We verified it's a way to get a proven methodology for the storage and recover of experiences with reasons that motivated a determined development.

Wald *et al.* (2011) in turn, presents the web2Acess[2] that allows the users to evaluation a site according to WCAG 2.0 and others Guidelines. The difference with the AccessibilityUtil is the idea of assessment of a web site and not a generic artifact. The important information to be considered in web sites evaluation is the time factor, because a site can be frequently changed and, with it, the accessibility characteristics can also change, and the tool's posted data becomes outdated.

In Almeida and Baranauskas work (2010) it's made an interesting relation between universal design principles, the WCAG and the ISO's norm, that deal with the ergonomics of the physical environment. These relations can be included in the tool presented here, with user's comments about how the environment's ergonomics affects the accessibility, for example.

With regard to the pattern's use documentation can be pointed out the work of Wang and Burge (2010) that objectify the association between DR and patterns. The showed concept is from an architecture to help software's architects choosing one solution among the candidates patters. For this, they developed an extension for the application called Software Engineering Using RATionale (SEURAT) [23].

The differentiation to the AccessibilityUtil is that the SEURAT is not web, being a plug-in for the IDE Eclipse's[3] tool, and there's

not the specification to deal with accessibility in accessibility patters.

We have verified that the undertaken work for the proposed AccessibilityUtil tool presents innovations in order to relate developer's discussions and comments with the officials Guidelines, allowing an incentive for the collaboration between developers about good practices dissemination as guaranty of accessibility.

8. CONCLUSION

In this work, the purpose was to show the project's decisions, planning, development and results of a collaboration tool for evaluation with the use of DR of pre-registered artifacts and for artifacts registered by the own participants.

The idea behind the work is to associate artifacts present on web with the W3C accessibility guidelines; for it we picked up and fed the tool with the WCAG 2.0's guidelines. We hope that it can contribute to approximate experiences of development real cases (in artifacts form) to the guidelines and allow the collaboration with comments between developers and stakeholders.

Through the system access and assessment's comments, we'll have conditions to evaluate what issue is considered by the tool development's staff as its strong point: use DR to help developers choosing which techniques to use.

The tool has been divulged in the community among the different expertise for assessment of numberless artifacts created by them. From the generation of artifacts suitable with the accessibilities Guidelines documented by WCAG 2.0, it's intended in a near future, associate the artifacts with models, based on the objects oriented development methodology.

As another future work, another guideline's sets will be able to be added to the system, with the purpose of advance in the accessibilities requisites and turn the artifacts more and more accessible. Another possibility is to integrate the comments about the artifacts in development's environments as models, making easier the developer's use, who will be able to visualize recommendations and practical experiences in development's mode, for example, by dragging and dropping an element and then appears advice's texts and guidelines helping him.

9. ACKNOWLEDGMENTS
Our acknowledgments to the Institute of Mathematics and Computer Sciences - University of São Paulo (USP) and also to the FAPESP, project number 2010/05626-7.

10. REFERENCES
[1] Almeida, L. and Baranauskas, C. Universal Design Principles Combined with Web Accessibility Guidelines: A Case Study. In *Proceedings of IX Brazilian Symposium on Human Factors in Computing IHC 2011, 2010. v. 1. p. 169-178*. IX IHC - 2010. Belo Horizonte-MG, October, 5 to 8, 2010.

[2] Bailey C. and Pearson E. 2011. An educational tool to support the accessibility evaluation process. In *Proceedings of the 2010 International Cross Disciplinary Conference on web Accessibility* (W4A '10). ACM, New York, NY, USA, Article 12, 4 pages.

[3] Bigham J. P., Brudvik J. T. and Zhang B. 2010. Accessibility by demonstration: enabling end users to guide developers to web accessibility solutions. In *Proceedings of the 12th ACM SIGACCESS Conference on Computers and accessibility* (ASSETS '10). ACM, New York, NY, USA, 35-42.

---

[2] http://www.web2access.org.uk/

[3] http://www.eclipse.org

[4] Caslon Analytics. (2002). *Caslon Analytics Online Accessibility Guide.* Available at: http://www.caslon.com.au/accessibilityguide2.htm. Accessed November, 2010.

[5] Conklin, E. J. and Burgess-Yakemovic, K. C. (1996). *A process-oriented approach to design rationale.* In Moran, T. P. and Carroll, J. M. (Eds.), Design rationale: Concepts, techniques, and use, 393-427. Mahwah, NJ: Lawrence Erlbaum Associates.

[6] Dutoit, A. H., McCall, R., Mistrík, I. and Paech, B. *Rationale Management in Software Engineering: Concepts and Techniques.* Mistrík I. and Paech B. (eds.), Rationale Management in Software Engineering, Springer, p. 1-48, 2006.

[7] Freire, A. P.; Russo, C. M. and Fortes, R. P. M. A survey on the accessibility awareness of people involved in web development projects in Brazil. In: *International cross-disciplinary conference on Web accessibility (W4A), 2008, Beijing, China.* Proceedings of the 2008 international cross-disciplinary conference on Web accessibility (W4A). New York, NY, USA: ACM Press, 2008. v. 1. p. 87-96.

[8] Grubber, T. R. and Russel, D. M. *Design Knowledge and Design Rationale: A Framework for Representation, Capture, and Use.* Technical Report KSL 90-45, Knowledge Systems Laboratory, Standford, California, 40p. 1991.

[9] Horner, J. and Atwood, M.E. *Effective Design Rationale: Understanding the Barriers.* Dutoit, A.H.; McCall, R.; Mistrík, I. et al., Rationale Management in Software Engineering, Springer Berlin Heidelberg, pp. 73-90, 2006.

[10] HREOC, (2002). *World Wide Web Access: Disability Discrimination Act Advisory Notes 3.2.* Available at: http://www.hreoc.gov.au/disability_rights/standards/www_3/www_3.html. Accessed February 10, 2011.

[11] Lee, J. *Design Rationale Systems: Understanding the Issues.* IEE expert/Intelligent Systems and Their Applications, v. 12, n. 3, p. 78-85, 1997.

[12] Maclean, A.; Young, RM. and Moran, T. (1989), *Design rationale: the argument behind the artifact,* SIGCHI Bull. 20, pp. 247-252.

[13] Martin, A.; Cechich, A. and Rossi, G. Accessibility at early stages: insights from the designer perspective. *Proceedings of the International Cross-Disciplinary Conference on Web Accessibility, W4A 2011,* Hyderabad, Andhra Pradesh, India, March 28-29, 2011.

[14] Moran, T. P. and Carroll, J. M. *Design Rationale: Concepts, Techniques, and Use Computers, Cognition, and Work.* New Jersey: Lawrence Erlbaum Associates, 659p, 1996.

[15] Power, C. and Petrie, H. Accessibility in non-professional web authoring tools: a missed web 2.0 opportunity?

Proceedings of the 2007 international cross-disciplinary conference on Web accessibility (W4A). New York, NY, USA : ACM Press. 2007. p. 116-119.

[16] Regli, W. C., Hu, X., Atwood, M. and Sun, W. A Survey of Design Rationale Systems: Approaches, Representation, Capture and Retrieval. Engineering with Computers: An *International Journal for Simulation-Based Engineering, special issue on Computer Aided Engineering in Honor of Professor Steven J. Fenves,* v. 16, p. 209-235, 2000.

[17] Sloan, D. 2006. *The Effectiveness of the web Accessibility Audit as a Motivational and Educational Tool in Inclusive web Design.* Ph.D. Thesis, University of Dundee, Scotland. June, 2006.

[18] Sommerville, I. and Sawyer, P. *Requirements Engineering – a good practice guide.* New York: John Wiley & Sons Ltd, 1997, 391p.

[19] Thatcher, J.; Cynthia, W.; Henry, S.; Swierenga, S.; Urban, M.; Burks, M.; Bohman, P. *Constructing Accessible Web Sites.* 1a. ed. [S.l.]: Glasshaus, 2002. 415 p.

[20] Trewin, S.; Cragun, B., Swart, C.; Jonathan, B and Richards, J. 2010. Accessibility challenges and tool features: an IBM Web developer perspective. In *Proceedings of the 2010 International Cross Disciplinary Conference on Web Accessibility (W4A) (W4A '10).* ACM, New York, NY, USA, Article 32, 10 pages.

[21] W3C. *Web Content Accessibility Guidelines (WCAG) 2.0,* 11 dez. 2008. Available at http://www.w3.org/TR/WCAG20/. Accessed may, 2011.

[22] Wald, M.; Draffan, E. A.; Skuse, S.; Newman, R. and Phethean, C. 2011. Southampton accessibility tools. In *Proceedings of the International Cross-Disciplinary Conference on web Accessibility* (W4A '11). ACM, New York, NY, USA, Article 23, 2 pages.

[23] Wang, W. and J. E. Burge. 2010. Using rationale to support pattern-based architectural design. In *Proceedings of the 2010 ICSE Workshop on Sharing and Reusing Architectural Knowledge* (SHARK '10). ACM, New York, NY, USA, 1-8.

[24] Watanabe, W. M; Neto, D. F.; Bittar, T. J. and Fortes, Renata R. P. M. 2010. WCAG conformance approach based on model-driven development and WebML. In *Proceedings of the 28th ACM International Conference on Design of Communication (SIGDOC '10).* ACM, New York, NY, USA, 167-174.

[25] Welie, M. van. *A Pattern Library for Interaction Design.* Available at: http://welie.com/. Accessed April, 2011.

[26] Yahoo. *Yahoo! Design Pattern Library.* Available at: http://developer.yahoo.com/ypatterns/. Accessed April, 2011.

Tapping as a Measure of Cognitive Load and Website Usability

Michael Albers
East Carolina University
Department of English
Greenville NC 27858
252-328-6374

malbers@acm.org

ABSTRACT

This article examines how cognitive load theory applies to website design and then considers using a tapping test as a practical method of measuring cognitive load. By identifying the design elements causing cognitive overload, the designer can potentially redesign the website to reduce it. The results of a pilot tapping test study are discussed which respect to its ability to determine if it can identify points of cognitive overload in a design. The results showed that the tapping test was an acceptable method, which could be easily integrated into current usability testing procedures.

Categories and Subject Descriptors

H.0 Information Systems: General

General Terms

Measurement, Documentation, Design, Economics, Human Factors.

Keywords

Empirical findings, usability method, usability data analysis

1. INTRODUCTION

As web design continues to evolve, websites are becoming more complex with deeper and more interrelated structures containing a wealth of information. But this poses a design problem. "Data analysis and recursive decision-making are cognitively very burdensome; people have little cognitive workload available for dealing with unusable interfaces [or poor information presentation] regardless of format of presentation" [21, p. 103].

Although design teams strive to create a website which is as user-friendly as possible, poor usability still challenges users with unclear information structures and impedes finding information [16]. Usability testing works to identify problem spots, but many of the testing methods do not pinpoint the exact spots on the page causing the problems. As web page information increases in complexity, the need for methods of identifying the problem points increase so the designer can focus on improving those specific points and for follow-on tests to verify that any changes did improve the usability.

The goal of this article is to consider if cognitive load measurement methods are a viable addition to the usability testing toolbox and if it can be practically implemented. If designers and testers can measure how users' cognitive load fluctuates as they interact with a design, then specific points causing cognitive overload can be identified, and the design reworked to reduce the cognitive load in the problem areas. Cognitive load measurement methods can be small scale and lend themselves to inexpensive and discount usability testing methods. On the other hand, like all usability measurement tools, cognitive load has limitations. Cognitive load measurements can identify specific trouble spots, but cannot measure overall usability. It also requires a relatively high-fidelity prototype which provides real-time interaction responses. Unfortunately, they are difficult to apply to early or paper prototypes, where changes can be fast/cheap.

One major element which interferes with effective interaction with any complex information system is the amount of cognitive resources needed can exceed the amount available. "An ever expanding array of complex systems is being found in both industry and the military. This increase in complexity is placing a larger burden on operators because interactions with these systems require higher-level cognitive processes such as problem-solving and decision-making" [7, p. 185]. Working to identify and minimize individual problem points can greatly improve overall system usability by removing bottlenecks. When used in conjunction with other forms of usability testing, it can help the design team gain a full understanding of the HCI.

The paper first discusses cognitive load, cognitive resources and cognitive overload and considers their importance to comprehending information. Next, it examines different methods of measuring cognitive load. Finally, it reports the results of an exploratory study, which examined a tapping method to determine if it would provide a reliable method of measuring cognitive load during a usability test.

2. COGNITIVE LOAD

Cognitive load refers to the total amount of mental activity that a person has to maintain in memory at any one time. Measurement of cognitive load can help to pinpoint design problems. Psychology and human factors researchers have a long history of using cognitive load measures to determine specific points of high cognitive load. For example, design of control panels in both aviation and industrial plants, especially nuclear control rooms, normally includes studies of operator cognitive load while interacting with the systems. High cognitive load results in increased errors as well as lower comprehension and performance; identifying these places within a web design should improve the overall usability, increase information comprehension, and decrease errors.

2.1 Cognitive Resources

People possess a pool of cognitive resources which they devote to the various tasks they are performing (Figure 1) that, unfortunately, is a small fixed-size pool. Cognitive load is the amount of cognitive resources which are actually being used at any specific time. Depending on the researcher and how their specific theory is constructed, the amount of cognitive resources and how they are allocated to tasks can vary, but across all models, the actual amount of cognitive resources is very low [e.g.,1, 4, 29]. Miller's [13] well-known work on 7 +/- 2 information chunks was early research into memory and can be interpreted as a reflection of limited cognitive resources.

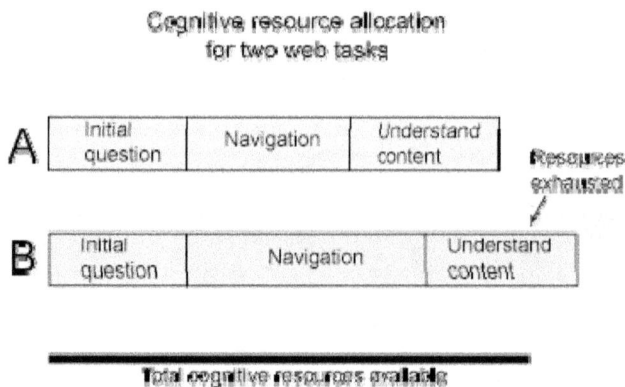

Figure 1. Cognitive resource allocated across various tasks. When working with a website, people typically have allocated resources for answering the initial questions which brought them to the site, site navigation, and to read and analyze the content. Part A shows the cognitive load imposed by well designed site, which does not exceed available resources. Part B shows an overload problem caused by poorly designed navigation which requires more resources.

. Methods of measuring cognitive load are based on the psychological research of the cognitive resources people possess and how they allocate them to tasks [24]. It is the highly limited nature of cognitive resources and how people handle them which can be used as an explanation for issues such as difficulties in multitasking and forgetting previously read information

The more complex the task and the lower the experience level, the higher the task load [15]. With increasing experience, the level of cognitive processing drops. Experts handle larger amounts of information as single chunks, thus handle more information before cognitive overload occurs. Consequently, adjusting for cognitive overload within the design process is complicated as cognitive load levels and users experience levels are interrelated and constantly changing.

Besides design factors, which design teams can control, many external factors influence the amount of cognitive resources a user has available. The amount of cognitive resources is not fixed for each person, but can increase or decrease over time (although it can be considered a fixed size for any specific interaction). Stress, time pressure, and lack of sleep are but a few factors, which can decrease the available cognitive resource pool [28].

Mead, Spaulding, Sit, Meyer, and Walker [12] concluded that a majority of the difficulties older users experience are linked to memory limitations, which tie directly to reduced cognitive resources as people get older. Thus, some of the differences between typical usability testing and real-world software use can be attributed to the different cognitive resources available. During the usability test the person may be stressed because they are in an unfamiliar environment or they may feel less stress than their job normally entails since they are in a low-distraction test environment. In either case, the usability research results become skewed because of different underlying cognitive resource demands of the test situation and reality.

2.2 Cognitive overload

Since cognitive resources are allocated from a small fixed-size pool, once the resources are exhausted, the user suffers from cognitive overload. The cognitive overload problems occur because people do not function in a state of cognitive overload; they cannot use mental resources they do not possess. Instead, they reduce the load, typically without considering the implications of the reductions, by adopting simplifying strategies or heuristics [6] or shedding tasks. Because cognitive resources are very limited, cognitive overload can occur easily when manipulating poorly designed websites because the extra manipulations required to interact with the design exhausts the available resources. When cognitive overload occurs, several things happen to a person's performance:

- Error rates dramatically increase. The failures that occur when playing the higher levels of Tetris occur because of cognitive overload from having to rapidly calculate and perform the required rotations.

- Tasks are shed. Rather than trying to mentally juggle multiple tasks, the user sheds (stops doing) one or more tasks.

- Frustration increases. People may quit performing the task or simply pick any answer to avoid further interactions (essentially, they address the frustration by task shedding). Frustration also leads to negative views of overall system usability and usefulness.

- Information may be accepted without evaluating its quality. As the information increases in quantity and complexity, contrary to intuition, people do not increase the complexity of their analysis strategy [6, 26]. People avoid cognitive overload by simplifying the analysis and just accept information at face value.

- Information is disregarded and the person goes with stereotypical responses. Instead of working to incorporate new or updated information into their current mental model, information is ignored.

Interestingly, until a person reaches cognitive overload, the level of cognitive load has minimal effect on task performance (Figure 2). After reaching the point of cognitive overload, performance decreases abruptly and dramatically. For example, the sudden onset of errors a person experiences on reaching a new level of Tetris or other related games results from the game requiring more cognitive resources than are available. In other research, Wickens and Carswell [27] point out that graphs reduce cognitive load by shifting the load to visual perception. Lohse [9] claims that the effects of reducing cognitive load will only be noticeable in complex task which are normally constrained by cognitive resources since it frees up resources for use elsewhere. In terms of figure 2, the effect is only seen when the cognitive load point is exceeded.

The minimal decline in performance until cognitive overload occurs complicates trying to measure cognitive load. Most measurements of cognitive load focus on finding the points where overload occurs and performance degrades. However, if subjects are operating just below overload then they will show minimal performance degradation, but only slightly higher cognitive demands will cause much lower performance. Tests for cognitive load must try to determine the design factors causing the overload point.

Decline in Performance from Cognitive Overload

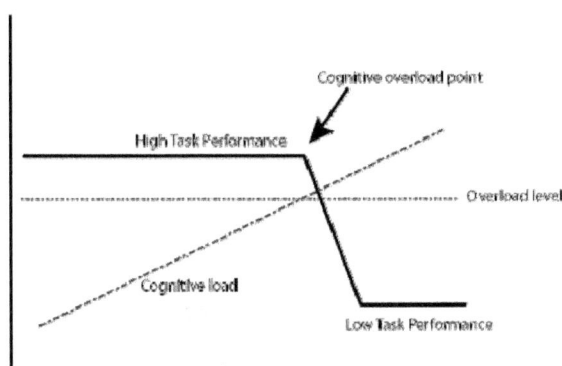

Figure 2.When the cognitive load level (increasing line) crosses the overload threshold (dotted line); the performance (heavy line) drops abruptly.

2.3 Web Usability Problems

This section takes the previous generic discussion of cognitive resources and considers how it can be applied to web usability.

For maximum usability, "successful user interfaces must respect the limits of human cognitive processing, since the goal of the user is to locate the highest quality of sources in the shortest amount of time" [2]. However, poor website usability is a roadblock for anyone using or maintaining websites. It is easy to generate a long list of web design mantras, such as: "if the user can't find it, it doesn't exist" or "people have no second thoughts about leaving a webpage." Discussions of the effect of violations of various design principles consistently list cases where people quit looking for a feature or product, or fail to see it even when they navigate to the proper page; one possible explanation may be that cognitive overload interfered with mentally processing the information. High cognitive load is not the cause of unusable webpages, but, rather, is a symptom which can be tested for.

Users rely on design teams to provide them with current, reliable sources and the functionality to locate those sources. While this statement sounds obvious, many website architectures present the users with major obstacles to overcome. The overwhelmed/confused reactions that users often experience may be due to the abundant options that increase cognitive load [3] and tax a user's memory [2]. Including measurements of cognitive load as an element of usability testing should help lead to designs which reduce feelings of confusion or being overwhelmed. More

importantly, it can also provide input into the specific points of the design which are causing the problem.

Each mental task consumes resources, especially when the tasks must be done in parallel, such as navigating a web site and interpreting the site's content. All website interactions have at least two distinct components: site navigation and content integration. The issue from a design viewpoint is that that at least some of the user's cognitive effort is devoted to performing the interface action, as distinct comprehending the content's meaning. The navigation forms the *extraneous cognitive load*: effort required to accomplish the task but not a direct element in comprehending the information. Interpreting the content forms the *intrinsic cognitive load*: the effort directly applied toward comprehending the information. Together, they make up the total cognitive load for a task. When the navigational design causes increased cognitive demands on a user, there are fewer available cognitive resources to be devoted to content integration which results in lower comprehension [20]. Thus, designing for easy manipulation and assimilation of information requires minimizing cognitive effort of activities not directly tied to the information [26]. All of the extraneous cognitive resources devoted to the interface are not available to be used as part of the intrinsic cognitive load and mentally processing the information contained in that interface. And, thus, the need to make the interface and navigation as transparent as possible.

The more complex the interaction, the harder time a person has comprehending the information since they are devoting too many resources to the interface and not enough to the content. Seufert, Jänen, and Brünken [23] looked at the use of hyperlinks and comprehension, finding that although they reduced extrinsic cognitive load and improved comprehension for high knowledge people, they did little for improving comprehension of complex information for low knowledge people. The complexity level required to comprehend the information contributes substantially to the cognitive load and, as this study points out, what works for one situation or audience may not be adequate for another. For a recent review on cognitive load and how it effects reading hypertext documents, see [5].

A highly usable site minimizes the amount of cognitive resources required for navigation, freeing more cognitive resources to concentrate on the details of the "to-be-used" information. But extraneous demands on cognitive load, such as poor information architecture or non-intuitive navigation, caused by inefficient design often impede this process. For example, consider how poor navigation can force the user to figure out cryptic categories or link names. These draw cognitive resources away from the user's primary task of finding and comprehending the website's information. Rather than being able to devote a majority of the cognitive resources to understanding the problem, the user is forced to allocate a substantial amount of resources toward simply working with and understanding the interface.

The following list shows some examples of common web usability and design problems which can cause high cognitive load. Obviously, other factors also come into play, but cognitive resource load helps to explain a significant part of the difficulties people encounter.

- People can handle vertical scrolling without a problem, but dislike having to scroll horizontally. The basic problem is they have to remember the current text while scrolling, which imposes an additional cognitive load since they have to deal with remembering text and navigating while reading.

- Vague link names force a user to try and figure out what the link leads to. The mental analysis of the link meaning, coupled with the person's engagement in their task, can cause overload. Typically, rather than exert a high level cognitive effort, people avoid cognitive overload by just trying each link, which takes extra time and then requires resources to evaluate the relevance of the new page.

- Direct manipulation interfaces benefit from the commitment of fewer cognitive resources in order to complete a given task. Overall cognitive effort and total cognitive load is minimized if the system interface maps directly into a user's view or mental model of a specific task. Also, rather than having to devote resources to remembering part of the task, it is shifted to the external display.

- Improper chunking of information forces the person to mentally work with and integrate the individual chunks. Properly chunked information lets the person mentally handle it as a single unit. Manipulating multiple chunks of information requires more cognitive resources.

3. MEASURING COGNITIVE LOAD

This article argues that once a website has a working prototype, one aspect of usability testing is measuring the cognitive load that the site imposes on a user. There are many different methods of measuring cognitive load, ranging from direct measurement of neuro-physiological response to post-event questions. While techniques measuring physical responses such as EEG and pulse rates are accurate, they are also expensive and require special equipment and training. Although physiology studies such as these can be vital for safety-critical systems, their expense, expertise requirements, and test time prohibit their application to most software or web-based interactions.

This section examines two simple methods of measuring cognitive load. It then looks at tapping in more detail as a method which can be easily used during a usability test.

3.1 NASA TLX

The NASA TLX test was developed to measure the overall work load of equipment operation "in various human-machine environments such as aircraft cockpits; command, control, and communication (C3) workstations; supervisory and process control environments; simulations and laboratory tests." [10]. The concept of the NASA TLX is to allow the user time to assess the workload situation once an action is complete. For example, the person would complete a NASA-TLX form after each major step, such as after removing a panel cover and then after disconnecting a piece of equipment.

To assess the workload experienced while completing multiple tasks, the person rates their effort on six scales: mental demand, physical demand, temporal demand, performance, effort, and frustration (JTAP). The user rates each of these on a Likert scale and then answers 15 questions that pairs two scales and asks the user to select the one that is the most important contributor to the workload of the task.

Although recognizing the NASA TLX as a method of measuring cognitive load (and some may argue it is the gold standard), it is a post-event measure and cannot identify the specific areas on a web page causing difficulty. Unfortunately for usability testing, NASA TLX does not test the user while they are in the process of completing the task; workload is measured post hoc. The user is forced to rely on what they remember and provide an opinion based on memory. It can capture the cognitive load of the entire task, but not specific actions or elements. Also, NASA TLX is designed for workloads with high physical components (such as complex equipment operation or maintenance) rather than web navigation and computer mouse operations.

3.2 Tapping Task

The tapping task is a simple method of imposing a secondary load on a user, with a long history of use in psychology and human factors.

During the test, users are asked to tap with either one finger or multiple fingers. If both hands are required, such as for data entry work, toe tapping can also be used. Tapping is as simple as it sounds; it is no more than rhythmically (1 beat per second) tapping the fingers on a desktop or recorder key. The main requirement is to tap at a steady rate and hard enough to allow the tapping to be heard or recorded. While a seemingly trivial task, it does require cognitive resources to continue to rhythmically tap. (As a simple demonstration, try tapping while multiplying 384 x 3902, or any pair of large numbers.)

Here's an example of tapping and usability testing. A person using a website encounters a list of poorly written links. They are too vague and don't really communicate what is behind them. As the person reads over the list, she has to interpret the meanings to decide which one to click. Performing that mental effort of interpreting a list of links imposes a high cognitive load, as a result she slows or stops tapping until she makes a decision. Once the decision on which link to click has been made, then cognitive load drops and she resumes tapping. During the post-test interview, the person can be specifically asked about what caused the slowdown. The design team gets focused feedback that link wording needs to be improved.

Tapping works to directly measure cognitive load by imposing a secondary task on the user [18]. The primary task may not have a high enough load level to exhaust a person's cognitive resources and thus the person does not show any measurable performance decrease which could identify points of overload. However, the primary and secondary tasks both draw from the person's cognitive resources, which make an overload situation more likely (figure 3). Until the person reaches cognitive overload, the taps will remain constant. Once cognitive overload occurs, since they cannot work in cognitive overload, people drop tasks. Figure 2 showed the abrupt performance degradation when cognitive resources are exhausted.

Most people respond to an overload situation by sloughing the secondary task to concentrate resources on the primary task. The tapping serves as a secondary task, which helps push the user into cognitive overload. If the user's concentration is focused at processing information other than tapping, it is hard for participants to apply the concentration needed to execute the tapping task [14]. As usability issues increase, the user's cognitive load increases and the cognitive resources required for the primary task increases. To maintain focus on the primary task, the secondary task loses cognitive resources and, consequently, the tapping task is dropped. The point of cognitive overload is found by monitoring the performance of the secondary task and recording when performance degrades.

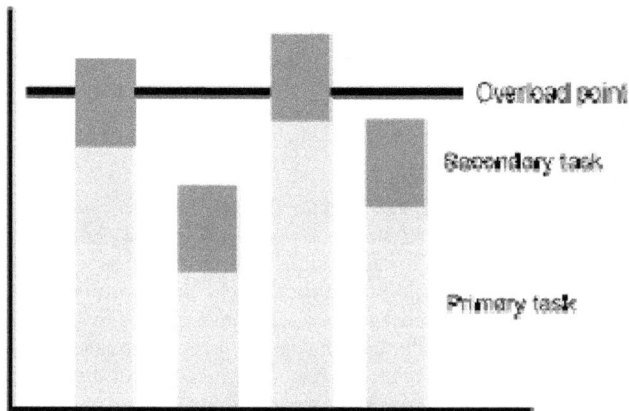

Figure 3. While performing the primary task, a secondary task is introduced. A secondary task will push the user to the cognitive overload load level, resulting in a decrease in performance and the dropping of the secondary task. Without the secondary task, none of these four actions would result in cognitive overload and performance decrease, but with the secondary task, the two which exceed the overload line will show overload effects. The designer can then focus on improving those particular areas of the design.

4. TAPPING TASK EXPERIMENT

This section provides a summary of a exploratory tapping study reported elsewhere [25]. The goal of the experiment is to determine if a tapping task could be used as measures of cognitive load for usability purposes. Approval was gained through The University of Memphis Institutional Review Board prior to beginning. The test was performed in the offices of a local Memphis business.

4.1 Participants

To recruit participants, an email was sent to employees asking for participation in the study. The company employees a wide range of people, anyone from very skilled programmers to the novice computer user. The company's purpose is to sell airline and marine parts through an in-house maintained website. Therefore, all of the employees were required to use an intranet and the Internet on a daily basis. An overview of the project, participant requirements, and a time allocation, were included in the email. A convenience sample consisting of 10 male and 8 female participants, with a mean age of 35 was the end result. The study included participants that merely used in-house software and email to computer programmers with extensive computer backgrounds and computer knowledge. The participants were given a schedule with a choice of three days divided in to 30 minutes time slots. They were asked to sign up for a 30-minute time slot on the day that was most convenient for them.

4.2 Design and Procedure

A pilot test was conducted several weeks prior to the actual experiment. The pilot test revealed some issues with the length and difficulty of the questions, which were revised and retested before the actual test session.

Three testing sessions were carried out using two conferences rooms. Before beginning the experiment, participants were asked to read and sign a disclaimer, and listen to a set of instructions explaining how the experiment was conducted and its purpose.

Two websites, *How Stuff Works* and *National Institutes of Health* were used to perform the tapping task. They were selected because they were not used on a daily basis, and not of a personal nature. Both sites have been extensively redesigned since this study.

The participants started with the NIH site and then used the How Stuff Works site.

For each website, participants were asked a series of five questions with 2 ½ minutes for each question. Participants were given a card the questions so they could refer to at any time during the experiment, and were told they would be stopped at 2 ½ minutes. The questions were presented in identical order for each website and participants were instructed to return to the homepage at the end of each question. Because the tapping task required use of a hand, we did not want participants typing information to locate answers to the questions. Therefore, participants were told o use the mouse as their only navigation tool and not to use the search feature.

4.3 Tapping Task

Each participant was asked to sit facing the computer with one hand on a table or book, and the other hand positioned on the mouse. As participants navigated the given website with the mouse they were asked to rhythmically tap at about one tap per second. Participants were informed of the importance of tapping as naturally as possible, i.e. try not to think about the tapping task and let it come naturally. Participants were also instructed to the tap as steady and rhythmically as possible, and to not stop tapping at any point if possible.

Participants were then instructed to navigate the given website while answering the questions. A recorder (Morea) was used to record both the tapping sound and the area of the website the participant was navigating.

4.4 Results and Discussion of the Tapping Task Experiment

The tapping task is a clear indicator of a high cognitive load situation. The participants displayed a range of tapping fluctuations. As their cognitive load increased the tapping become slower, quieter, and/or less rhythmical. This fluctuation tended to match other user responses, which indicate problem areas. Post-analysis with Morea found trends between navigational elements and tapping fluctuations.

Table 1 compares the differences of tapping fluctuations found in three different problem areas. In all cases the non-technical user more than doubled the technical user results. Of course, it would be expected that expert level users would demonstrate lower levels of cognitive load for the same task. In the analysis, by technical we mean those participants who spend a majority of work and/or free time using a personal computer. Non-technical are those participants that use a personal computer for a necessary-based task only. With the rather simple web navigation our tests entailed, the technical computer users (in this case, web programmers) showed very little slowdown.

Human factors research traditionally has used tapping across all skill levels. Many of the users in that research involved groups of highly skilled individuals, such as pilots or plant operators. On the other hand, our tapping results showed that usability test designers must consider participant experiences when analyzing the results. Although the findings provide some insight, additional research must be conducted on the "technical" versus the "non-technical" participant and how it affects the results.

Table 1. Tapping variations based on user type. The table shows the number of users who encountered noticeable tapping variation, not the number of instances.

	Link	Reading	Scrolling
Technical	5	6	4
Non-Technical	12	12	19
Total Instances	17	18	23

The participants for our study ranged in age of approximately 25-60. The participants 40 and older seemed to experience more difficulty multi-tasking the questions and tapping than did the 40 and younger participants. Our findings, while requiring further research, are preliminarily consistent with other findings related to age. A study by Mead, Spaulding, Sit, Meyer, and Walker [12] concluded that a majority of the difficulties older users experience are linked to memory limitations, which tie directly to cognitive resource demands. We noted that the 40 and older users had twice as many instances of navigation issues than did our 40 and younger group. On the other hand, the younger users were also the majority of the technical group, which confounds the analysis.

5. USABILITY TEST USING TAPPING

This section presents a basic description of using tapping during a usability test and applying the lessons learned during the tapping experiment.

5.1 Designing the questions

Create a series of questions the participants will answer. However, testing the usability of a complex system must be regarded as fundamentally different from simple systems [21]. Rather than a lack of information, the failure to anticipate people's needs forms the basis of most information problems and poor decision making. As such, the questions need to reflect the real-world scenarios in which the information will be used and simple information look-ups (such as "what is the phone number for xxx").

Because the tapping task requires use of a hand, the questions typically need to be designed so they require the mouse as their primary interaction tool, rather than typing.

5.2 Performing the test

Tell the participant to tap as naturally as possible (i.e. try not to think about the tapping task and let it come naturally) with a rhythmically rate of about one tap per second. They should try to tap at a steady rate and not stop. Depending on the tapping surface, it may be easier to use a pen for tapping purposes; some people may tap with the fleshy part of their finger which is very quiet. It also works to have them tap on top of a three ring binder, which functions as a small echo chamber.

The taps need to be recorded along with a screen image so the points of slowing down can be analyzed. We used Morea in the study we reported, but any screen recorder with audio will work.

We observed some "oops, sorry" statements from test participants who had stopped tapping. It is important to tell the participants upfront and reassure them that you expect them to stop or slow down on their tapping during the test and that the irregularities are what you are looking for. Otherwise, they might get very frustrated or feel they are failing to perform adequately if they constantly vary their tapping rate.

5.3 Analyzing the test

Review the recording and flag the points where the rhythmical tapping either slows or stops. Determine what the person was doing at this point. If it was a mouse movement such as scrolling, it might just be muscle interference, but if they were hovering over an area of the webpage, then it becomes an area to examine closer. A post-test walk through with the participants can be very revealing since it serves to highlight the areas worth discussing and you can ask what caused the stoppage.

In our study, we found participant's external reactions, which are normally noted in a usability test (sighing, mumbling, gestures) when they become frustrated, lost and/or confused, matched with fluctuations in tapping. Interestingly, and highly useful for identifying design problem points, the change in tapping rhythm often preceded the external reactions. In other cases, there were tapping changes without external reactions. In these cases, it would have been hard for an observer to note a problem point. The observed frustration was often caused by problems induced from an earlier cognitive overload situation. The tapping slowdown indicated the actual point of trouble, whereas going simply by external reactions; the analysis may have resulted in misdiagnosing the problem as being caused by later/next part of the interface interaction.

The variation in tapping also makes it easier to spot usability issues across pages, such as when navigational elements that appear on multiple pages are problematical. After the first or second interaction, a person may adjust to how the navigational element works and, consequently, would not show the typical interaction problems noted by a test observer. But the high cognitive load could still be measured on the initial interactions. Or, the navigational elements might only provide a slight stumble (minor irregular tapping) which would not be of concerned if it occurred a single time, but if the irregular tapping persists across the same design elements on many pages, then the design should be reexamined.

5.4 Motor interference with tapping tests

Post-test analysis revealed multiple participants encountering issues during scrolling, which is consistent with previous research on paging versus scrolling [19]. We found instances where participants completely stopped tapping while scrolling. Although there was some potential increase in cognitive load while scrolling, since a person tends to be skimming the new information as it appears, there is also a possible interaction with motor interference.

It is difficult to tap and scroll simultaneously since one index finger is tapping and the other index finger is rolling the scroll wheel [22]. Motor interference explains why it is difficult to do something different with both index fingers at the same time; the mental commands get mixed up [11]. The old pat your head rub your stomach adage comes to mind. Human muscles naturally want to act together and when the action prevents them from doing so, there is a performance penalty.

On the other hand, while motor interference can be a confounding factor with tapping, some of its effects can be mitigated when the tapping is combined with the observer notes or screen captures. In the tapping experiment, we found participants with the highest frustration levels or those obviously experiencing difficulties also were more prone to stopping tapping during scrolling. Also, motor interference should only occur when the mouse hand has to perform fine finger motions, such as operate the scroll wheel, versus the basic point and click movement, which for most user has become essentially an automatic reaction.

6. CONCLUSION

Observations of usability tests often reveal the participants dropping tasks, failing to follow through with an action, disregarding information, or not seeing information on a page. Although many factors can lead to these symptoms, all of these problems are also indications of cognitive overload. Performing an effective redesign requires knowing the underlying cause. Norman [17] addressed the need for considering user needs in terms of psychological goals and user thought processes, rather than just observing explicit user behavior. Current usability testing often uses think-aloud protocols but, while effective, can be time-consuming to analyze and can interfere with the action itself.

The tapping task is a simple method of imposing a secondary load on a user, with a long history of use in psychology and human factors. Granted, tapping also interferes with a task, but less so than a think-aloud and the user is less self-conscious of performing it. Use of tapping helps to pinpoint the page elements that cause the user's cognitive overload and, as a result, provide a focused starting point for redesigns to fix the problems.

To perform a tapping task during a usability study, users are asked to tap with either one finger or multiple fingers. If both hands are required, such as for data entry work, toe tapping also works. Tapping is the rhythmical tapping of the fingers on a desktop or recorder key. The main requirement is to tap at a steady rate and allow the tapping to be heard or recorded.

While a seemingly trivial task, tapping requires cognitive resources to continue to rhythmically tap. The tapping serves as a secondary task, which helps push the user into cognitive overload. If the user's concentration is focused at processing information other than tapping, it is hard for participants to apply the concentration needed to execute the tapping task. As usability issues increase, the user's cognitive load increases and the cognitive resources required for the primary task increases. To maintain focus on the primary task, the secondary task loses cognitive resources and; consequently, the tapping task is dropped. The less mental effort a user exerts on web navigation and content interaction, the more the tapping will remain constant.

As websites becomes more information rich and complex, the person's interaction is essentially driven by their thought process. The usability toolbox needs to be expanded to contain multiple ways of monitoring and measuring those thought processes. Tapping provides a tool that measures cognitive load, adding to the usability toolbox another method of getting at the user's thought processes and measuring the cognitive obstacles imposed by a design. Although a simple test, tapping can show where a person is experiencing excessive cognitive load issues. It requires virtually no expense or time and can be recorded as part of the tests general task recording.

7. REFERENCES

[1] Baddeley A. 2001 Is working memory still working? American Psychologist, 56.11, 851–64.

[2] Balogh, J., Cohen, M. and Giangola, J., 2004. "Voice User Interface Design: Minimizing Cognitive Load." *InformIT*. May 13, 2004. Accessed: September 3, 2007. <http://www.informit.com/articles/article.aspx?p=170792&rl=1>.

[3] *Celt: Centre for Enhancing Learning and Teaching*. "Evaluating multimedia packages." 8 Aug. 2004. <http:www.csu.edu.au/division/celt/edtech/multimedia/Mmeval.htm>.

[4] Chandler, P. and Sweller, J. 1996. Cognitive load while learning to use a computer program." *Applied Cognitive Psychology 10*. 151–170.

[5] DeStefano, D. and LeFevre, J. 2007. Cognitive load in hypertext reading: A review. *Computers in Human Behavior, 23,* 1616–1641.

[6] Fennema, M., and Kleinmuntz, D. 1995. Anticipation of effort and accuracy in multi-attribute choice. *Organizational Behavior and Human Decision Processes, 63.1*, 21–32.

[7] Fiore, S., Cuevas, H., and Oser, R. 2003. A picture is worth a thousand connections: The facilitative effects of diagrams on mental model development and task performance. *Computers in Human Behavior 19.2.* 185–199.

[8] Gregor, S. and Benbasat, I. 1999. Explanations from intelligent systems: a review of theoretical foundations and empirical work. *MIS Quarterly, 23*, 497–530.

[9] Lohse, G. 1997. The role of working memory on graphical information processing. *Behaviour & Information Technology, 16.6*, 297–308.

[10] Manning. 1998 "NASA-TLX (Task Load Index)." *Human Engineering"*. 12 Dec. 2005 <http://www.manningaffordability.com/S&tweb/HEResource/Tool/Shrtdesc/Sh_NASATLX.htm>.

[11] Marteniuk RG, and Mackenzie C. 1980. A preliminary theory of two handed coordinated control. In G.E. Stelmach and J.Requin (Eds.), Amsterdam: North-Holland.

[12] Mead, S., Spaulding, R., Sit, B., and Walker, N. 1997. Effects of age and training on World Wide Web navigation strategies. *Proceedings of the Human Factors and Ergonomics Society*, 152-156.

[13] Miller, G. 1956. The magical number seven, plus or minus two: Some limits on our capacity for processing information. *The Psychological Review, 63*, 81-97.

[14] Miyake, Y., Onishi, Y., and Poppel, E. 2004. Two types of anticipation in synchronization tapping. *Acta Neurobiol 64.* 415–426.

[15] Neerincx, M. and Griffioen, E. 1996. Cognitive task analysis: Harmonizing tasks to human capacities. *Ergonomics, 39.4*, 543-561.

[16] Nielsen, J. 1999. *Designing Web Usability: The Practice of Simplicity*. Indianapolis: New Riders Publishing.

[17] Norman, D. 1986. Cognitive engineering. In D. Norman and S. Draper (Eds.), *User Centered System Design: New Perspectives on Human-computer Interaction.* (pp. 33-62). Mahwah, NJ: Erlbaum.

[18] Olive, T. 2004. "Working memory in writing: Empirical Evidence from the dual-task technique." *European Psychologist 9.1.* 32–44.

[19] Piolat, A., Roussey, J.Y., and Thunin, O., 1998. Effects of screen presentation on text reading and revising, *International Journal of Human Computer Studies 47,* 565–589.

[20] Pitts, C., Ginns, P., and and Errey, C. 2006. Cognitive load theory and user interface design: Making software easy to learn and use. 26 April 2006. <http://www.ptg-global.com/papers/psychology/cognitive-load-theory.cfm>

[21] Redish, J. 2007. Expanding usability testing to evaluate complex systems. *Journal of Usability Studies 2.3* 102–111.

[22] Riek S, Carson RG and Byblow WD. 1992. Spatial and muscular dependencies in bimanual coordination. *Journal of Human Movement Studies. 23.* 251–265.

[23] Seufert, T., Jänen, I., and Brünken, R. 2007. The impact of intrinsic cognitive load on the effectiveness of graphical help for coherence formation. *Computers in Human Behavior, 23,* 1055–1071.

[24] Sweller, J. 1988. Cognitive load during problem solving: Effects on learning. *Cognitive Science, 12,* 257–285.

[25] Tracy, J. and Albers, M. 2006. Measuring cognitive load to test the usability of web sites. *Society for Technical Communication 53rd Annual Conference.* Las Vegas, NV. May 7-10, 2006.

[26] Thuring, M., Hannemann, J., and Haake, J. 1995. Hypermedia and cognition: Designing for comprehension. *Communications of the ACM, 38,* 57-66.

[27] Wickens, C. D., and Carswell, C. M. 1995. The proximity compatibility principle: Its psychological function and relevance to display design. *Human Factors, 37,* 473–494.

[28] Wickens, C. and Hollands, J. 2000. *Engineering Psychology and Human Performance.* Upper Saddle River, New Jersey: Prentice Hall.

[29] Wickens, C. 2002. "Multiple resources and performance prediction", *Theoretical Issues in Ergonomics Science,* 3.2: 150–177.

Context Sensitive Accessibility Aid to Middle-Aged Adults and Elderly Users in Web Systems

Silvana M. Affonso de Lara
Institute of Mathematics and
Computer Sciences,
University of São Paulo, São Carlos,
Brazil
silvana@icmc.usp.br

Denis Oliveira
Federal Institute for Education,
Science and Technology of São Paulo
Campus São Carlos
Brazil
denis.olvr@gmail.com

Renata P.M. Fortes
Institute of Mathematics and
Computer Sciences,
University of São Paulo, São Carlos,
Brazil
renata@icmc.usp.br

ABSTRACT

This paper describes an interaction mechanism aimed at enhancing the accessibility of Web pages to middle-aged adults and seniors. The proposed approach builds on previous research on problems commonly encountered by these users. The presented solution encompasses the customization of Web page layouts and the use of automatically-generated voice prompts to users. One of the main contributions of this work is the use of contextualized aids according to the genre of Web pages and the types of features they contain. An automatic page categorization scheme has been developed, alongside with a tool to collect knowledge from users about the nature of pages. The preliminary results from a usability inspection of the tool are discussed, and proposals for future investigations on the impact of this technology on the accessibility of websites for middle-aged adults and senior users are also outlined.

Categories and Subject Descriptors

H.2.2 [Design Tools and Techniques]: User Interfaces; H.5.4 [Hypertext/Hypermedia]: User issues

General Terms

Accessibility, Human Factors.

Keywords

Web accessibility, middle-aged adults, elderly, adaptation

1. INTRODUCTION

Demographic and epidemiological changes have brought a significant increase in the population of middle-aged adults and seniors in Brazil. It is estimated that the period 2000 to 2050 will encompass the largest increase in the proportion of elderly, from 5.1% to 14.2% and in 2025, the population over 60 will reach 34 million people [1].

One way to quantify the quality of life of an individual is by means of the degree of autonomy with which he/she performs the day-to-day tasks and his/her ability to carry on tasks such as looking after personal hygiene, cooking, organizing their finances, ability to make purchases, among others [1].

The Web can be regarded as an essential facilitator to obtain information and services, especially when one begins to show functional decline associated with aging, which prevents him/her from performing their daily tasks. Therefore it is of fundamental importance that an individual can perform their interactions with the Web in a satisfactory manner, despite possible difficulties.

Most Web sites, in order to offer increasingly sophisticated pages, use technical resources that can become barriers to access for certain groups of user. This includes middle-aged adults with limited experience using computers, the elderly and the people with special needs.

The demand for productivity and the development speed of sites often leads the developers not paying attention to the human aspects. The time pressure makes them worry primarily about creating technologically efficient environments, but leaving aside specific needs of certain groups of users.

To facilitate the experience of people in interactions with the Web, it is essential to take into account the needs of different user profiles. However, currently solutions have failed to address problems such as lack of skill in the use of web applications and learning difficulties of such applications by middle-aged adults and the elderly.

This paper presents a support mechanism for Web interaction developed as an add-on, which aims to enhance browser functionality, allowing people with differing needs to access the services originated from interaction with the Web in a more natural way and as much independently as possible, providing improvements in quality of life, and promoting their social integration and also their inclusion.

This paper is organized as follows: in Section 2 are shown the main problems associated with aging that influence the interaction of middle-aged adults and elderly with Web pages, in Section 3 is presented the proposed mechanism, called Tuki, which was developed to support interaction with the Web and in Section 4 are presented the conclusions and future work.

2. OLDER ADULTS AND THE WEB

The definition of middle-aged adults, for the purposes of this study, was considered as adults who are older than 40 years and below 60 years of age, and seniors as those aged over 60 years. According to the literature [2], there is no physical or biological marker to determine accurately the point in time when the end of the maturity or the onset of old age. This process is influenced by several factors such as gender, socioeconomic status, physical and mental health conditions, habits and lifestyle, and others [2].

According to the N/N Group [3], the main reasons why older adults are using the Web, aside from work demands, are: catching up with news, finding out about diseases and medications, reading about hobbies, travelling, finding recipes, religion-related activities, among others, and especially to communicate with family and friends. Part of these users also uses the Web to shop online and to carry out banking activities.

By means of field observations, we could really see that Web use by middle-aged adults and elderly people currently has more to do with entertainment than with the actual need of carrying out day-to-day tasks. It was also noted that many users have no awareness of the benefits of Web use and blame themselves for the difficulty in learning, using as an excuse their lack of experience with technology resources and their cognitive difficulties of memorization of procedures [4].

Several studies have been found in the literature addressing the effects of aging on cognition. Most of them have focused on major cognitive functions such as memory, reasoning, problem solving, and language, among others. The skills that present declines during the aging process are especially those that require an efficient working memory [5] [6] and fast processing [7], which means that the cognitive activities that rely more heavily on fluid intelligence, such as cognition and spatial reasoning, dealing with the maintenance and manipulation of visual images tend to be negatively affected by aging [8]. Studies have reported that early spatial deficits appear around 40 years of age and may become more pronounced after 50 years of age [9].

Working memory or the ability to keep information active declines with age and often appears as a limiting factor in performance in speech understanding, handling quantitative representations, and others [10]. In some situations, these limitations of working memory can be reduced by the exercise of constant practice of certain tasks (memory tasks) or by means of formation of planning strategies, or support to the work environment, with the objective of reducing memory demands.

Compared with younger adults, older adults are slower and less successful in acquiring new procedures, once they process information more slowly. The differences between ages increase with task complexity, particularly with respect to activities that require coordination of multiple tasks simultaneously [10]. With regard to attention, both visual selective attention (scanning in a visual display) and the dynamic visual attention (redirecting the focus of attention) show declines during aging [10].

Therefore, according to Fisk et al. [10], older adults are benefiting by receiving guidance and suggestions to get your attention in design elements. Following this approach a support mechanism was created to enhance the interaction of middle-aged adults and seniors with Web pages that will be described in the following section.

3. THE TUKI MECHANISM

Aiming to reduce demands on working memory, the Tuki mechanism was prepared in order to facilitate and encourage Web interaction by middle-aged adults, seniors and people with special needs.

The Tuki mechanism was designed with the aim of being a lightweight program, to add functions to enhance usability and accessibility for user interaction with the Web page, providing greater integration between them. Its main function is to provide aids and support during the interaction of middle-aged and older adults with the Web.

To create a mechanism capable of providing appropriate aids to the interaction of middle-aged adults and elderly with the Web it was necessary to make a categorization of Web pages accessed by the most common target audience and also those who would bring them more benefits if used in old age.

The categorization was the automatic identification of the main elements of interaction present in information-intensive Web (online newspapers, government pages, wikis, etc.), shopping sites, banks and services, form pages, and others. From the assignment of a page into a given context-category, it is possible to elaborate set of messages and tips that would be appropriate use for the user.

To perform the automatic categorization of a Web page, the engine extracts information items of the source code of the page, which encompass an analysis of their own page URL, metadata, titles, and the quantification of links, paragraphs, images and objects in flash, among others, a weight is assigned to each item, in order to help categorize it. The total values used for the classification are: minimum relevance (2), low relevance (5), relevant item (10) and maximum relevance (50).

The relevance of an item is described by its weight confirmation, or how this item can confirm that the page belongs to a particular category. The higher the weight of the item of relevance is the best match for the category. For example, the greater weight (50) is attributed to the presence of significant URLs of pages for a particular category or due to the presence of metadata, such as %tube% in URL for video category. The main categories observed and used as the basis for the construction of the behavioral actions of the support mechanism are: informational pages, online newspapers, government pages, collaborative pages, business pages (that place products on sale online), pages of banks (little relevant information can be extracted from this type of page because of the fact that they are secure pages) and pages containing forms.

It is noteworthy that the choice of items was performed by observing the source code and programming patterns present in most HTML pages accessed, where we selected the tags that are repeated more or uniquely identifying the category of Web page.

In addition to the automatic processing performed by the Tuki mechanism, another plug-in for Mozilla Firefox was developed, which allows the deployment of the classification according to the perception that users had the page. It was decided to make this collection due to the fact that the access to a free Web-based tool is a viable technology for the creation of a large corpus of classified Web pages according to the user's perspective.

After installing the classifier mechanism, in each new Web page that is accessed by the user, a form of classification appears, in which the user must report his/her age, choose the most appropriate category to that page and send to server application, which registers the number of ratings per URL/category. The user can stop running the plug-in at anytime. In this first period made available an initial simple set of categories, such as information, banking, sales/purchases, videos and collaborate pages. The target audience used for this index was primarily undergraduate and postgraduate students in areas related to computing, because it is a public that has greater experience in using Web resources.

The Tuki mechanism, when activated, performs an automatic classification for the current Web page and the browser checks for a benchmark classification outside (free sort collected via Web user participation) for that page. After completion of the classification of context-category of Web page, behavioral actions are performed by the engine (Figure 1).

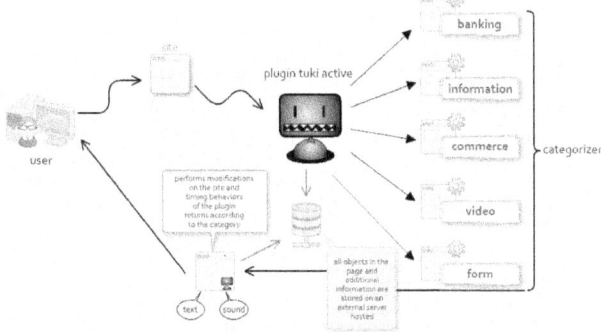

Figure 1: scheme of operating the facility TUKI

The first step is to make changes in page layout, eliminating pop-ups, banners and other elements that have been shown to affect this audience interaction with Web pages. The definition of the Tuki mechanism behavior depends directly on the elements present in the Web page itself concerned. Suppose, for example, that the current Web page is a Wikipedia page. In the first step it will be categorized as a Wiki page. From there, it will extract the present options on their menu, so the engine can instruct the user as to how he can use the page and what options he can access, as shown in Figures 2 and 3.

The mechanism of support for wiki pages highlights the main elements by including a border around the option while it reproduces an explanatory text via voice. For the option of creating accounts (Figure 2) the user hears: "If you want to create a user account or enter an existing account click the mouse in this region". By highlighting the left side menu (Figure 3) is reproduced the following statement: "To the left of the screen are the navigation menu, click the mouse on an item to access it".

If the Web page in question contains a form, the Tuki mechanism identifies the elements present and puts an outline around the input fields to give greater prominence to them at the same time it instructs the user via voice message to click the mouse on the highlighted field and start typing using the keypad, and the explanation of alternative means of access, such as shortcut keys, among others (Figure 4). Immediately after completing the field by the user, the Tuki mechanism sends a text message on the interface "field filled!" and performs the highlight of the next field.

The implementation of the mechanism, was performed using a development tool for add-ons from Mozilla Labs called Jetpack Prototype [11] and its APIs [12]. This tool enables the

development of scripts that can change the interface pages that are displayed by the browser Mozilla Firefox.

Figure 2: highlighting the option of creating accounts

Figure 3: focus on the options menu

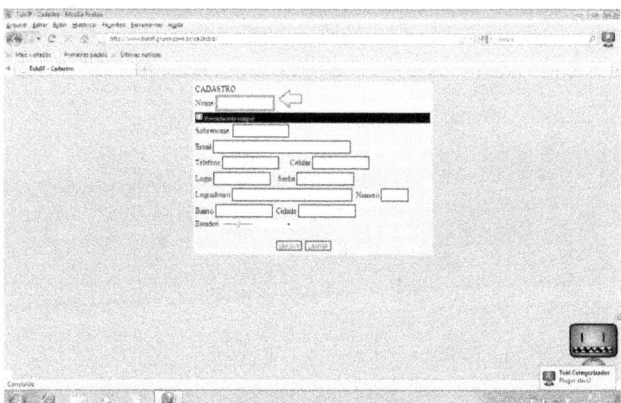

Figure 4: emphasis on the field to be filled

The platform on which the Jetpack Prototype plug-in was developed acts in the superficial layer of the browser, using HTML elements that have already been interpreted to make any such modifications. Considering that the development platform is based on JavaScript (with support for jQuery), CSS and HTML, this language associated with the DOM, it enabled the plug-in to do the identification, addition or removal of elements, such as pop-up windows and banners, by keywords (located on the page source) that tend to be standardized by the developers of the sites.

For playback of voice messages via software was used TextAloud [13], which converts text documents like txt, html, pdf, doc, rtf in natural language, including Portuguese language.

It is worth noting that with the Tuki mechanism it is possible to extract any information that is present in the tags of the source code of the webpage, and that the higher the level of information contained in these tags, the better its performance in helping to interact with the pages.

The main objective of this mechanism of usability and accessibility is to encourage middle-aged adults and seniors to use the Web in their day to day in order to reap the benefits that this interaction can give them, especially when they reach old age.

4. CONCLUSIONS AND FUTURE WORK

The growth in Internet usage has occurred in parallel with its own evolution, since it is no longer just a repository of static pages that provided information to its users and now offers support in various segments of their lives. Currently, in addition to providing applications for communication, entertainment and services online, it must be also offered support for the realization of the interaction between users and resources available on the Web.

Initially a usability inspection was performed on Tuki mechanism, according to the Nielsen heuristics for evaluation of prototypes and initial designs [14], where the main suggestions made by experts were: inclusion of the indication that the mechanism is active or not (on/off); addition of the symbol [x] to close it, aiming to avoid potential clicks on the image of Tuki; although the image used by the engine was very striking to the user, it is not explicit in its appearance that it is a mechanism to support accessibility; possible adjustments in calculations of time spacing between one another for help and action on registration pages, based on the average time of filling in fields for real users and also the capture of task completion by the user; inclusion of documentation and assistance to the user in the interface of the mechanism. This absent of documentation occurred because the Tuki mechanism was designed to be a plug-in for Mozilla Firefox browser, and because of its nature, must be very light on his activity, so that the documentation concerning its operation will be included in their respective page of installation.

The evaluation of Tuki mechanism by middle-aged and elderly is currently underway, and the results of the analysis should provide more insight into the impact of the use of such a mechanism on the interaction of these users with Web sites.

The next step in the development of this mechanism is to capture user interactions, and from that interaction be able to provide appropriate aids to the desired interaction, such as what users can do from where they are. Other features include splitting a complex task into smaller steps, recovering previous navigations as a way to remember a forgotten procedure, and others.

The next stages of this work should consider the extent of modeling behavioral actions of the Tuki mechanism, to work in pages of e-commerce, collaborative editing, among others, and

also the storage of data about the interaction, allowing the user to remember their steps and achievements, showing when prompted, everything has been done in terms of navigation, how and which transactions were conducted, among others, to reduce the demands on working memory and prior knowledge.

5. ACKNOWLEDGMENTS

FAPESP Project # 2010/05626-7.

6. REFERENCES

[1] Cavalcanti A., Galvão C. 2007. Fundamentação & Prática. ISBN: 9788527712859, editora Guanabara Koogan, 566 pgs, (2007).

[2] Neri, A. L. 2005. Palavras Chave Em Gerontologia. Editora Alinea, Campinas, SP.

[3] Coyne, K. P., and Nielsen, J. 2002. Web Usability for Senior Citizens: 46 Design Guidelines Based on Usability Studies with People Age 65 and Older, Nielsen Norman Group Report.

[4] Lara, S. M. A; Fortes, R. P. M. 2009. Usabilidade universal para adultos de meia-idade em interações com a Web. In: XXXV Latin American Informatics Conference, Pelotas. Proceedings of CLEI, 2009. v. 1. p.1-10.

[5] Salthouse, T. A. 1990. Working memory as a processing resource in cognitive aging. Developmental Review, 10, 101-124.

[6] Van der Linden, M., & Hupet, M. 1994. Le vieillissement cognitif [Cognitive aging]. Paris: PUF.

[7] Salthouse, T. A. 1985. Speed of behavior and its implications for cognition. In J. E. Birren & K. W. Schaie (Eds.), Handbook of the psychology of aging (pp. 400-426). New York: Van Nostrand Reinhold Company Inc.

[8] Rozencwajg P., Cherfi M., Ferrandez A. M., Lautrey J., Lemoine C., Loarer E. 2005. Age Related Differences in the strategies used by middle aged adults to solve a block design task, The International Journal of Aging and Human Development. Volume60, Number2.

[9] Kirasic, K. C., & Allen, G. L. 1985. Aging, spatial performance and spatial competence. In N. Charness (Ed.), Aging and human performance (pp. 191-223). New York: John Wiley & Sons, Ltd.

[10] Fisk, A. D., Rogers, W. A., Charness, N., Czaja, S. J. and Sharit, J. 2004. Designing for Older Adults: Principles and Creative Human Factors Approaches (Boca Raton: CRC Press).

[11] Mozilla Labs Jetpack Prototype. 2011. Disponível em https://jetpack.mozillalabs.com/.

[12] API Jetpack. 2011. Disponível em https://wiki.mozilla.org/Labs/Jetpack/JEPs.

[13] Text Aloud. 2011. Conversor de texto para voz natural. Disponível em http://www.nextup.com/.

[14] Nielsen, J. 1993. Usability Engineering. Academic Press.

Scenario-based Serious Games Repurposing

Aristidis Protopsaltis
Serious Games Institute
Coventry University Tech Park
Cheetah Road, Coventry, CV1 2TL, UK
aprotopsaltis@gmail.com

Laurent Auneau
Succubus Interactive
17 rue Paul Bellamy
44000 Nantes, France
laurent.auneau@succubus.fr

Ian Dunwell, Sara de Freitas, Panagiotis Petridis,
Sylvester Arnab, Simon Scarle, Maurice Hendrix
Serious Games Institute
Coventry University Tech Park
Cheetah Road, Coventry, CV1 2TL, UK
{IDunwell, SFreitas, PPetridis, SArnab, SScarle, MHendrix}@cad.coventry.ac.uk

ABSTRACT

Serious games are very content-rich forms of educational media, often combining high fidelity visual and audio content with diverse pedagogic approaches. This paper introduces scenario-based serious games repurposing and demonstrates repurposing a serious game into new learning objects. The process uses the scenario editor called "mEditor". Two case studies based on the Happy Night Club serious game are presented. The article describes exploratory work which continues the work that started within the mEducator project regarding repurposing serious games in order to enable their use and reuse in the same or different educational contexts.

Categories and Subject Descriptors

J.m Computer Applications: Miscellanesous

General Terms

Experimentation

Keywords

Information systems education, Computer-assisted instruction (CAI), Computer science education, Collaborative learning, Serious Games; Interactive learning environments; Virtual reality; Simulations; Media in Education

1. INTRODUCTION

Serious games usage within the current educational context has been growing steadily over the last decade. Serious games are very suitable for learning and they are a very good environment for improving the learning experience, by increasing motivation and diversify the content delivery media. Considering however the time, effort, resources, cost and complexity of developing serious games it is imperative that such a game can be repurposed effectively adaptively into educational practices and curricula. This includes updating, changing, enriching serious games to reflect new functionalities, amending to different pedagogies, technologies, representations, cultures, contexts and learners. Such repurposing therefore, is a desirable activity, reducing organisational resource consumption and opening up new opportunities for learning, maximising the capabilities of existing learning objects. Therefore, being able to repurpose game content reduces the need to continually rebuild content, and offers potential to efficiently adapt serious games and game elements to meet the needs of wider audiences and application areas.

The term repurposing refers to the changing of a learning resource or object initially created for a specific educational context, to a new educational context (or contexts) [1], and should be distinguished from reuse, which refers to the use of the same learning resources or objects without any changes [2].

Work in the field of repurposing learning objects has been focused greatly on automatic learning object repurposing. For example, Zaka et al. [3] work on creating new PowerPoint presentations from a repository of existing presentations. Furthermore, the ALOCOM project created an ontology and a framework that was used to disassembles PowerPoint presentations and then reassembles them in a more meaningful way [4-6]. Further, the TRIAL-SOLUTION project defines an ontology for learning objects which aims to produce and deliver adaptive teaching materials from existing documents on mathematics at undergraduate level [7]. While Singh's [8] work had focused on repurposing text.

On a slightly different direction other researchers focused on web-based technologies. For example, the DART project focused on the subject of anthropology has investigated how web-based technologies and digital resources can be used and reused to enhance student learning [9]. One important conclusion from this project was that repurposing aids the successful reuse of learning objects, and that involving the teacher in the design process is an essential part of repurposing since he is the one to use the new object to fulfil his learning objectives.

Multimedia repurposing has also been an area which received considerable attention by researchers. Steiger et al. [10] have worked on an MPEG-based personalized multimedia content delivery system while Hjelsvold, et al. [11] have showed a web-based interactive video repurposing framework. Hossain et al. [12, 13] have introduced a multimedia content repurposing framework using Web Services.

Contrary to the area of multimedia repurposing the area of games repurposing is still in its infancy and there are no exhaustive works addressing the issue. In one study, Burgos et al. [14] describe the use and the repurposing of what they called "generic" games, referring to commercial games. The focus of their work was mainly on the different pedagogic approaches in game repurposing. They described two different approaches where in one a game is fully integrated in the learning flow while in the other a game is used as an autonomous learning object disconnected from the learning flow.

In previous work [15] some of the authors started identifying the key issues faced when repurposing serious games. They proposed a theoretical framework for the repurposing of serious games in medical education and three case studies based on the Climate Health Impact serious game were developed. These case studies demonstrated the ability to repurpose a serious game into new learning objects, covering three different paradigms of content repurposing, language, content and pedagogy. The different paradigms for content repurposing have been developed by the mEducator consortium [16, 17]. This work has shown that the need for programming skills by the educators in order to be able to repurpose serious games is a limiting factor for widespread repurposing of game content. As a result, the authors formulated recommendations that readily assist serious games repurposing. Having the content separated is really important in order to facilitate the efficient repurposing of a game. A general recommendation would consider eliminating the need for programming skills by separating the content from the game engine changing the balance between what an educator cannot manipulate (i.e. due to a lack of programming skills or access to the source files) and what they can (i.e. eXtended Markup Language (XML) files) towards the latter. Content can be stored in separate files and educators would only have to access and modify those files and nothing else. Such tasks do not require advanced programming skills and therefore educators would be able to complete them with relative ease. Another suggestion that could simplify serious games repurposing and even games repurposing that came from this work [15] refers to scenario-based games repurposing. Scenario-based games are branching scenarios, where users' decisions lead to effects, both immediate and simulation wide, altering the events, characters and situations encountered. Players are usually faced with multiple scenarios and they can change the situations and challenges they are involved in, in the game. The scenario can be modified to fit individual needs and situations and feedback is provided seamlessly as a natural progression throughout the experience. Usually, the scenario in serious games is scripted inside the game dynamics and therefore quite often inaccessible for repurposing after being compiled. However, sometimes the script files are accessible after the game is being compiled, as they are actually only interpreted during runtime and therefore one will still need programming skills to understand them. A solution therefore could be to present the scenario loaded inside a bespoke editor. Therefore, the scenario can be edited and manipulated without programming knowledge and then directly integrated into the game. However, this bespoke editor would be entirely dedicated to the game engine in use, and thus scenario data could not be reused in another technology.

Examples of authoring applications that use environment editing are UnrealEd, the level editor of the Unreal 3 engine; and e-Adventure [18, 19]. UnrealEd was developed by and for professional game developers, and is as such very powerful, but also very complex. Another approach was adopted by van Est et al. [20], which allows instructors to define and edit scenarios, using high-level actions and events and some basic logic. However, these authoring applications are focusing more on providing alternative scenarios rather than repurposing serious games and learning objects.

Bar the work from Burgos and colleagues [14] and our own within mEducator (www.meducator.net) [15], our research uncovered no other current studies regarding repurposing of serious games content. Our current mEducator study therefore aims to provide the mechanisms with which to discuss and analyse the repurposing of game-based content using case studies as a research method. This work is an extension of our previous work [15] on serious games repurposing and focuses on scenario-based repurposing.

2. GAMES DESIGN AND SERIOUS GAME DESIGN

Regarding game design in general we can identify two main aspects, one technical which contains the game engine while the other one contains game rules, scenario, behaviours, background etc. and is the game mechanics.

In this way modern entertainment game development very much follows a data-driven software engineering paradigm. In that the underlying software, the Game Engine, is intended with minimal alteration to be useable on multiple game projects. The game's playable content, scenario and mechanics are codified as so-called runtime objects and these are then the data which is acted upon by the engine. This is an important part of the modern entertainment game industry business model, in that it allows for maximum re-use of software and more rapid development of game content. An ancillary component of the software for the Game Engine is its "Asset Pipeline", this will be a suite of software applications which take various forms of input from the artist and designers (e.g. 3-D objects, 2-D images, sound, description of AI and possible interactions) and converts them into templates for the required runtime objects. The tools which constitute this pipeline are increasingly becoming more generically useable, but are still primarily aimed at being used by professional games designers and artists.

Serious games design approaches derive from these general game design approaches. Work undertaken by one of the authors outlines how serious games design principles can be mapped against traditional game design processes and principles. From their review of game-based learning, de Freitas and Jarvis [21] derive five game-based learning development principles: foster positive attitudes, appropriate selection of games, learning and usability design criteria, adopt a participatory design approach, use formative evaluation methodologies. This is mapped against games principles and supported by specific tools and techniques based upon the four dimensional framework [22]. Pre-prototyping, human factors analysis, scenario creation tools and learning needs analysis approaches are adopted. Tate et al., [23] also outline design principles including defining fun as a main criterion for serious game design.

3. REPURPOSING AND PEDAGOGY

Pedagogy is a very important aspect of serious games repurposing. When repurposing to different pedagogical approaches one needs to consider that learning objects usually are created with specific teaching method in mind. However, repurposing can change the teaching approach, or the learning objectives or the assessment method and so on. Pedagogical repurposing might or might not require adaptation of the learning object itself.

The approach of the instruction methodology for example can be changed from a simulation based to a combination of a problem-based and exploratory learning. Learners are active during the learning process by constructing their own knowledge through exploration and action and serious games seem to aid such exploration.

From a pedagogy perspective well designed games have different learning theories integrated in the design and take advantage of their characteristics. These pedagogic approaches include Problem-Based Learning (PBL), as well as contextual and experiential learning models [24]. However, recent pedagogic trends have seen situative and experiential approaches move to the forefront [25]. In such approaches an emphasis is placed on indirect learning which occurs through exposure to situations that mirror real-world problems and environments.

Therefore the challenge of serious games repurposing does not only relates to the technical aspects of a serious games but also involves the pedagogic and instructional methods used to deliver the material. However, it is outside the scope of this paper to cover this aspect since the work presented here focuses on the technical challenges of serious games repurposing.

4. THE REPURPOSING CONTEXTS

Educational content repurposing is a very popular activity between educators and it can broadly be distinguished into ten different categories as proposed by the mEducator consortium [1, 15, 17]. The categories include: 1) Actual content, 2) Languages, 3) Cultures, 4) Pedagogical approaches, 5) Educational levels, 6) Disciplines or professions, 7) Delivery content types, 8) Technology, 9) Educational context, 10) Different abilities.

As shown in Figure 1 using these 10 definitions of repurposing types, we begin to deconstruct the various elements common to serious games and illustrate the strongest links between repurposing types and game elements. This provides a preliminary guide outlining which elements of a game are likely to be needed to effectively perform a given type of repurposing. For example, language repurposing may require a simple translation if the content are kept into separate files while cultural repurposing may require animations, sounds and game dynamics to be changed to reflect differences in gameplay and gestures between cultures, which demands for a lot more effort and specialized knowledge.

5. THE mEducator APPROACH

The scenario in a game can be split into two types: narrative and behavioural. The narrative scenario refers to dialogs and texts and how they will be displayed successively to the player. This part is easy to repurpose as only few things needs to be touched, and most of them could be available in separate non binary files. The behavioural part of a scenario describes how the game will react to user input (i.e. if I click on a blue door and I have the blue key in my inventory, then the blue door should open) and is very hard to repurpose because it is described as source code, not as a model, and thus needs specific skills (programming skills) to be understood. Some solutions exist, even if they are quite limited:

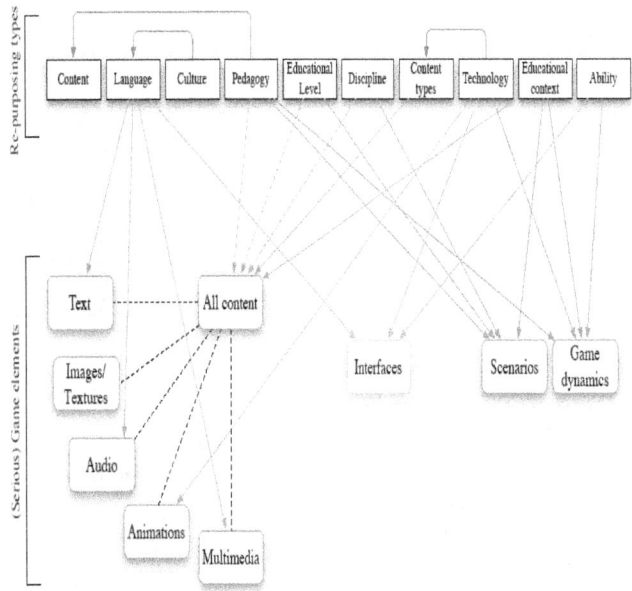

Figure 1. Hypothesised relationships between repurposing types and common game elements

- The first one consists in using a dedicated graphical editor that presents the model to the game designer, and hides the implementation. The limitation comes from the fact that this authoring tool is tightly bound to the game engine, and thus scenario files can't be used in a separate project using a different technology.

- The second approach lets developers use script files instead of compiled source code. The scenario is thus available, but still very hard to understand when you're not a computer scientist.

- The last solution consists in opening an API so that users can "mod" the game. It is the most open solution, letting other developer entirely modify and reuse the original creation, but is also the most difficult one, as it is mandatory to perfectly understand everything from the original work.

To handle all problems related to scenario repurposing, the mEducator approach aims to consider scenario as content, and not as plain text and source code. And so on, this content should be available in separate non binary files, should be described as a logical and understandable model, and a graphical editor should be provided to edit and author the model. More importantly, the model itself should be technology agnostic, meaning it doesn't need to be aware of the game engine that will run it.

6. THE MEDITOR

In order to have a generic tool that could allow game designers to directly integrate their designed scenario content into a game, the model needs to be extremely generic and technology agnostic. A mix between visual programming and workflow management was created, letting designers model how the game should react to user input. The model itself is represented as a directed acyclic graph, and is stored in simple XML files.

The agnosticity is achieved by declaring to the editor the features of the game engine, allowing the effective cross compatibility between game engine if they both share the same features. The XML files store references to game engine features as well as to branching generic features (such as "IfThenElse"). These files are read by the game engine that will "run" the scenario, calling at the right moment its own dedicated functions that were declared to the scenario editor.

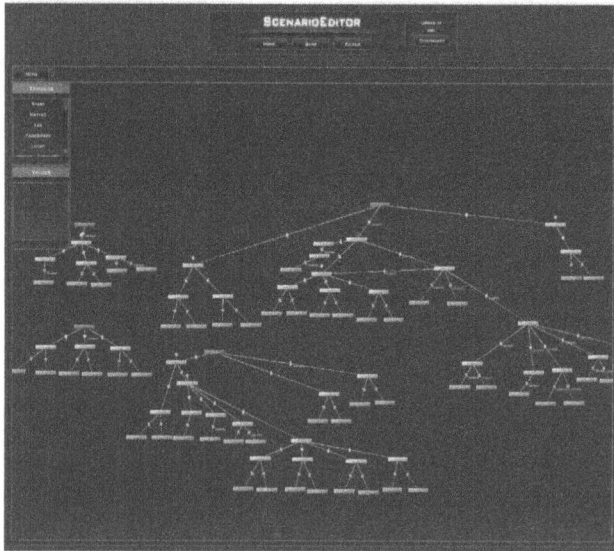

Figure 2. SUCCUBUS meditor for scenario-based repurposing

The model is split into six elements:

- Triggers (red nodes) are the entry points to the graph. They represent events fired by the game engine, themselves commonly created upon user input (i.e. "Player clicked on the door", or "Player gained a level")

- Branching nodes (yellow nodes) are used to choose between several paths in the scenario (ie. "IF player has the blue key THEN open the door, ELSE display a hint message") or to go into multiple paths at once (do all of these following actions at once, or sequentially)

- Engine node (orange nodes) are references to engine features such as "Walk to a specific place", "Display a message", "Trigger a door open / close", etc. These nodes needs to be declared at first so that the game designer has a set of features he or she can use to create some actual scenario

- Functions and operators (green nodes) are quite the same as orange nodes the main difference being that they return a value upon execution. They can be specific engine features ("HasItem" returns a boolean value indicating if the player has a given item in his inventory) or more generic ("+" adds two integer values together and returns the result)

- Values (blue nodes) are used to store text, number and boolean values that can be constant or change over time.

- Groups (purple nodes) contain a collection of other nodes and provide a simple way of using multiple times the same behaviour.

7. METHOD
The research method used in the current research is case study.

7.1 Material: the game
The case studies are based on the Happy Night Club game[1] developed by SUCCUBUS Interactive, a partner in the mEducator project. Happy Night Club is a serious game that explains to teenagers the dangers associated to binge drinking. It is a part of a bigger communication campaign (print, web, TV, radio) that was launched in the city of Nantes, France. Furthermore, the Happy Night Club scenario itself works as a test bed for the scenario editing and repurposing tools accessible on www.succubus.fr/meditor.

Figure 3. Happy Night Club game

All the files that can be found in the Happy Night Club game directory can be sorted into three different categories: content files, interface elements and game dynamics.

7.1.1 Content files
Content files contain every data used by the game, from parameters defining the rules of the game to text or images to be displayed on the screen. Objects other than text like images, clips or sounds are often referred to as assets in the context of a game project. Content is represented as XML files in this format allow for the structuring of heterogeneous types of content. Contents in the game are represented as a single record, and structured into many fields that can be text elements or numbers. Assets cannot be included directly in such files and are therefore referred to by their URL.

7.1.2 Interface elements
Interface elements consist of panels, graphic widgets, buttons and containers ready to display the content. As Happy Night Club is a web-based game, the interfaces are written in Adobe Flash. Adobe Flash is a programming environment for developing animations and graphics. A flash player is then required to play the files. In Happy Night Club, the entire game screen is a Flash panel that recursively contains other Flash panels. All these panels have been designed by web-designers.

The interfaces integrate and present the content from the XML files (texts, images, etc). They may also include labels for titles,

---

[1] The game is available online at http://www.succubus.fr/ and http://www.meducator.net/

tabs, buttons, etc. which are usually not represented as separated content but hard coded inside the Flash files.

7.1.3 Game dynamics

Finally, the game dynamics bring the interfaces and the content together to create the game. Game dynamics are written using scripts and algorithms in a specific programming language (e.g. C++, Java, C#, Flex etc.). The Happy Night Club game has been programmed in the Flash environment, from Adobe, which allows the production of rich internet applications (RIAs) which includes collections of predefined components and the ActionScript scripting language. Game dynamics have three roles; first, they are responsible for loading the content and the interfaces and building the main game screen, second, they load the content into the interfaces, and third, will listen to the interfaces for user events (button clicked, text input, etc.) and trigger specific behaviours accordingly (change a panel, update a text in the interface, etc.).

The game elements and the workflow presented in this section are commonly found in games and they are a benefit when designing a game. However, they can also be an essential step towards repurposing the content.

8. PROCEDURE

The process of repurposing was completed in five steps. First step included extraction, from the source code of the game, of all "string" variables. Second step included filtering the strings, to keep only those that needed to be translated. Next, the translation and the adaptation of the text file took place. After translation the reintegration took place: the translated text strings were placed back into the source code, at the appropriate position. Finally, testing and debugging made sure that all errors that might have been introduced during the reintegration were fixed.

The work started by translating the text in the XML files. The work was conducted using Adobe Flex.

9. THE CASE STUDIES

9.1 Happy Night Club: Language Repurposing

The first case study considers repurposing the game to a different language, which basically involves the translation of every text displayed in the game. The content-related parts were fairly easy to process as XML files can be edited by any text processor and translated without requiring any programming skills. Once translated, the content was seamlessly integrated into the game by the interfaces provided the right fonts have been embedded in the Flash panels.

The labels and tags on the Flash based interfaces are different. Not only does editing a Flash file require some programming skills but these files also come compiled as Small Web Files (SWF), whereas the FLA (Flash file in the Macromedia Flash authoring program) source files are needed to perform any modification. Although some software allow users to de-compile a SWF file into a Flash source file, it may not work properly and re-compiling the source file into a new SWF file that can be integrated back into the game can be problematic. The main suggestion consists of replacing the hard-coded labels by variables that can be separated in XML files just as any type of content. Figure 4 shows the French repurposed version of the Happy Night Club game. The text has been translated by editing all the XML content files using the mEditor.

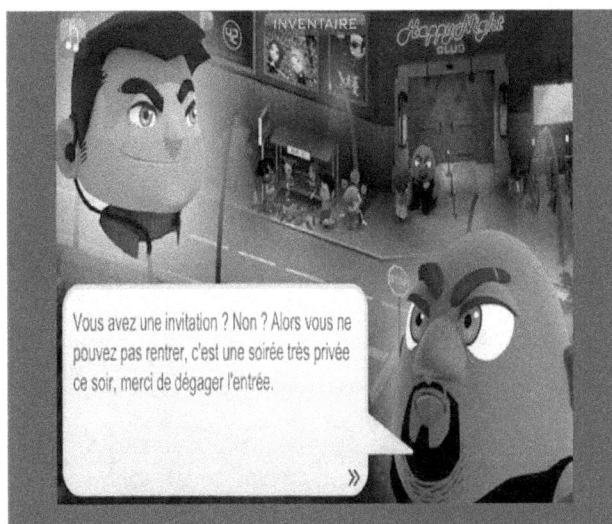

Figure 4.   Happy Night Club game in French

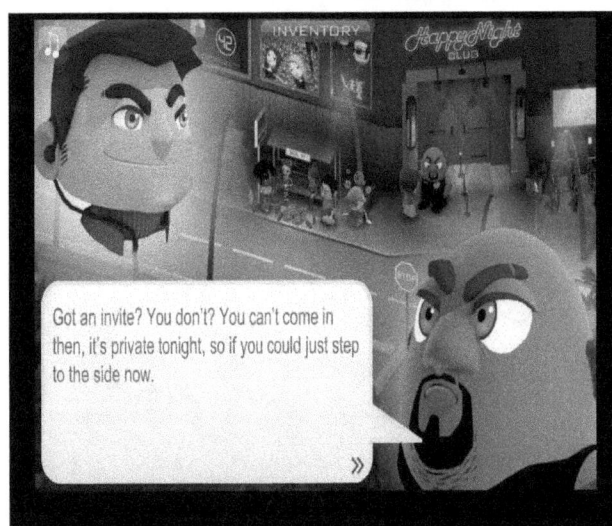

Figure 5.   Happy Night Club game in English

9.2 Happy Night Club: Scenario repurposing

The second case study consisted of repurposing the scenario of the game. Using the scenario editor we created a totally new scenario using existing characters and manipulating their actions. We made Jacques, the main character, to talk to Lucas the security at the club's door and we placed the entrance point at Lucas. In its properties we selected "Mouth"; an arrow appears and then we defined the actions that will follow the choice "act with mouth" on Lucas. Several actions will be performed sequentially; first move to be in front of Lucas and then a text bubble will pop up. Blue arrows indicate actions' parameters; *MoveNpc* needs the name of the characters to move to its destination, while *Info* requires the name of the character on whom the bubble will show up with the text content.

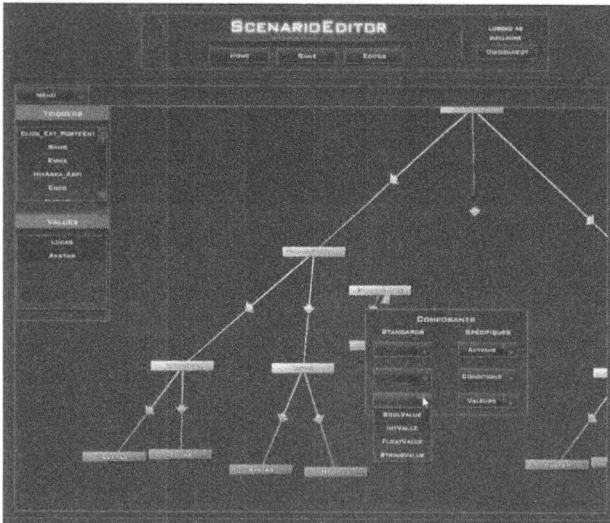

Figure 6. Happy Night Club new game using the Scenario Editor

Figure 8. Happy Night Club new game with text

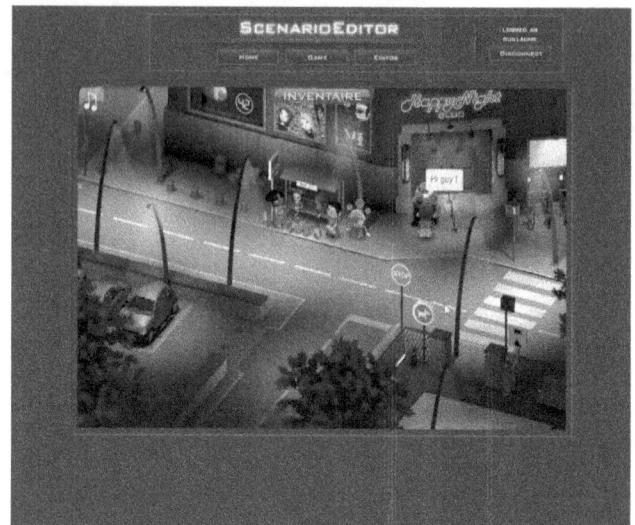

Figure 7. Happy Night Club new game

When playing the game, we act on Lucas by selecting the mouth icon available to us, as it can be seen in figure 7. Jacques then moves to Lucas' and when he arrives, the text shows (see Figure 8).

We create three values: the character's name, which will be used twice, so we select "module" in its properties, this value now shows up in the left hand side menu. We call that value "Avatar", its value is Jacques: the name recognized by the renderer. The name won't be reused so it's a temporary variable. For the text in the bubble when the character talks: the text constant used once (temporary). For the destination of our character, here we tell to the renderer to use the Lucas' position on the scene. We then save and test our scenario.

We can always go back to the editor, to improve or complete our scenario in order to introduce more dialogue or actions for the characters. We can copy the actions of our previous scenario so we do not have to start from the beginning and use them again.

Now we can insert a condition with the *IfThenElse* action. This action leads to different actions following a conditional statement, if that statement is true, we will then have to introduce a *Then* statement to the left hand side action sequence, *Else* it will execute the right hand side sequence. To check that we have talked once to Lucas we can add a *ChangeState* action to the first sequence that will change the state of a Boolean value. We will put "true" from a temporary constant to a temporary variable which default state is false.

The conditional block is composed of an *IsTrue* operator that evaluate the variable's state and a *Not* operator, so that while the variable is false, the condition is true and we execute the left hand side sequence. Finally we change the text of the right hand side block.

To test the game we need to save and load the game again. We then can talk to Lucas however because it is the first time to do so Jacques says "hi", using the previously created action, the variable takes the "true" state and then we can talk to Lucas again, since the system knows that we have already talked to him once and therefore shows a different text.

In the same way we can carry on introducing more dialogues and actions to create the scenario that fits our aims. All the processes in the scenario editor are automated either in menu or drop down lists.

10. DISCUSSION

Due to the technical nature of game content, a limited knowledge amongst educators regarding how games are designed and programmed is still a limiting factor for widespread repurposing of game content. Consequently, game developers should realise the needs of educators who using serious games content as a relevant source of educational material and provide the tools and interfaces required to realise its potential. Therefore the aim of this work is to provide an alternative method of game repurposing based on the serious games scenario editor created within the mEducator project. To supply game developers and game companies with standards and recommendations that will help them to create serious games that can be easily repurposed and reused by educators either within the same context or not. The role of researchers is to provide game developers with recommendations and frameworks that would enable this repurposing at the lowest cost. To that end, future research should focus on developing technical solutions that can bridge the gap between technical skills required for the repurposing an external module, serious game, simulation or virtual world and an e-learning system.

These two case studies have been realised in the specific context of the mEducator project but they have led us to formulate different recommendations that readily apply beyond this context. Having the content separated is really important in order to facilitate the efficient repurposing of a game. A general recommendation would consider pushing the limit between what an educator cannot manipulate –due to a lack of programming skills or access to the source files– and what they can towards the latter. For example, regarding the interfaces, it is possible to have Flash considering a text field as a variable (a Dynamic Text Field in Flash terminology) by assigning it an identification name. Consequently, the same way content is loaded into the interfaces at runtime, the interfaces labels, buttons or titles can be separated into a file, preferably XML, and loaded by the game dynamics.

The same recommendation applies, albeit to a lesser extent, to the game dynamics. In some cases, they can be considered as content and stored in separate files, provided appropriate ways of representing them are found. Scenario-based games provide a perfect illustration. Usually, the scenario of such a game is scripted inside the game dynamics and therefore inaccessible for repurposing after being compiled. In the context of the mEducator project, research has been initiated to find ways of representing scenarios as content in order to ease their repurposing. A solution is to present a scenario loaded inside a bespoke editor such us mEditor. Therefore, the scenario can be edited and manipulated without programming knowledge by manipulating the menu and the actions via the drop down lists provided in the editor and then directly integrated into the game. Additionally, these elements can be reused to form a basis for the game without having to start from scratch. Educators' actions and decisions lead to effects, both immediate and simulation wide, altering the events, characters and situations encountered.

Another, great advantage of the editor is that it was designed so that it can be used with any game engine. However, "bindings" of the game engine must be provided to the editor, and that is made possible using xml files. Inside the game engine, some code must be able to read and interpret the xml files coming out of the scenario editor, but this is fairly easy to be developed, and runtimes for Flash, JavaScript, PHP and C++ can be provided.

Finally, the work on repurposing will assist towards reducing the development costs of serious games and expand the target market by supporting the process of localisation and by creating reusable games and game tools which in turn appeals both, to game developers as to the organizations that implement them.

11. CONCLUSION

This paper has presented a framework for serious game-based learning design, and interrogated how game content can be repurposed. Additionally, we presented the scenario based editor called mEditor created to assist in serious games repurposing. The case studies demonstrate that two new serious game learning objects were created by repurposing the Happy Night Club serious game. The conclusion makes clear that a separation between the content and the behaviour of the game is a great facilitator to such repurposing and the serious game editor offers the flexibility and the ability to the educators to create bespoke serious games to serve their learning objectives. With the scenario based editor, educators and users' decisions lead to effects, both immediate and simulation wide, altering the events, characters and situations encountered.

12. ACKNOWLEDGMENT
This paper has been fully supported by the mEducator project which is funded by the eContent*plus* programme by the European Commission.

REFERENCES
[1] Dovrolis, N., et al., "Depicting Educational Content Re-purposing Context and Inheritance", in *International Conference on Information Technology and Applications in Biomedicine (ITAB)*: Larnaca, Cyprus, 2009.

[2] Meyer, M., et al., "Requirements and an Architecture for a Multimedia Content Re-purposing Framework", in *Innovative Approaches for Learning and Knowledge Sharing*, W. Nejdl and K. Tochtermann, Editors, Springer-Verlag: Berlin / Heidelberg. p. 550-556, 2006.

[3] Zaka, B., et al., "Topic-Centered Aggregation of Presentations for Learning Object Repurposing" in *World Conference on E-Learning in Corporate, Government, Healthcare, & Higher Education (E-Learn)*, Las Vegas, USA, 2008.

[4] Verbert, K. and E. Duval, "ALOCOM: a generic content model for learning objects", International Journal on Digital Libraries, 9 (1): p. 41, 2008.

[5] Jovanović, J., et al., "Ontology of learning object content structure" in *12th International Conference on Artificial Intelligence in Education*, Amsterdam, The Netherlands, 2005, 322–329.

[6] Verbert, K., et al., "Ontology-Based Learning Content Repurposing: The ALOCoM Framework", International Journal on E-Learning, 5 (1): p. 67-74, 2006.

[7] Lenski, W. and E. Wette-Roch, "The TRIAL-SOLUTION Approach to Document Re-use Principles and Realization", in *Workshop on Electronic Media in Mathematics*: Coimbra, Portugal, 2001.

[8] Singh, G., "Content repurposing", IEEE Multimedia, 11 (1): p. 20-21, 2004.

[9] Bond, T.S., C. Ingram, and S. Ryan, "Reuse, repurposing and learning design – Lessons from the DART project", Computers & Education, 50 (2008): p. 601–612, 2008.

[10] Steiger, O., T. Ebrahimi, and M.D. Sanjuan, "MPEGBased Personalized Content Delivery", in *IEEE International Conference on Image Processing (ICIP)*: Barcelona, Spain, 2001.

[11] Hjelsvold, R., S. Vdaygiri, and Y. Ldautd, "Webbased personalization and management of interactive video" in *10th International Conference on World Wide Web*, Hong Kong, 2001, 129-139.

[12] El Saddik, A. and S. Hossain, "Content repurposing: Multimedia", in *Encyclopedia of Wireless and Mobile Communications*, B. Furht, Editor, Taylor & Francis, 2008.

[13] Hossain, S.M., A.M. Rahman, and A. El Saddik, "A Framework for Repurposing Multimedia Content" in *CCECE 2004/CCGEI 2004*, Niagara Falls, 2004.

[14] Burgos, D., C. Tattersall, and D. Koper, "Re-purposing existing generic games and simulations for e-learning", Computers in Human Behavior, 23 (6): p. 2656-2667, 2007.

[15] Protopsaltis, A., et al., "Repurposing Serious Games in Health Care Education" in *XII Mediterranean Conference on Medical and Biological Engineering and Computing (MEDICON 2010)*, Chalkidiki, Greece: Heidelberg, Springer, 2010, 963-966.

[16] Dovrolis, N., et al., "Depicting Educational Content Re-purposing Context and Inheritance" in *International Conference on Information Technology and Applications in Biomedicine (ITAB)*, Larnaca, Cyprus, 2009.

[17] Kaldoudi, E., C. Balasubramaniam, and D.P. Bamidis, "mEducator D.3.1 Content Repurposing: Definition of Repurposing Reasons & Procedures", 2010.

[18] Moreno-Ger, P., et al., "Rapid Development of Game-like Interactive Simulations for Learning Clinical Procedures" in *Fifth International Game Design and Technology Workshop and Conference (GDTW2007)*, Liverpool, UK, 2007, 17-25.

[19] Moreno-Ger, P., I. Martínez-Ortiz, and B. Fernández-Manjón, "The <e-Game> Project: Facilitating the development of educational adventure games" in *Cognition and Exploratory Learning in the Digital age (CELDA 2005)*, Porto, Portugal: IADIS, 2005, 353–358.

[20] van Est, C., R. Poelman, and R. Bidarra, "High-Level Scenario Editing for Serious Games", in *International Joint Conference on Computer Vision, Imaging and Computer Graphics Theory and Applications*, Springer: Vilamoura, Algarve, Portugal, 2011.

[21] de Freitas, S. and S. Jarvis, "Towards a development approach to serious games", in *Games-Based Learning Advancements for Multi-Sensory Human Computer Interfaces: Techniques and Effective Practices*, M. Stansfield, T. Connolly, and L. Boyle, Editors, IGI Global: London. p. 215-231, 2009.

[22] de Freitas, S. and M. Oliver, "How can exploratory learning with games and simulations within the curriculum be most effectively evaluated? Special Issue", Computers and Education, 46 (3): p. 249-264, 2006.

[23] Tate, R., J. Haritatos, and S. Cole, "HopeLab's Approach to Re-Mission", International journal of Learning and Media, 1 (1): p. 29-35, 2009.

[24] Pappa, D., et al., "Game-based learning for knowledge sharing and transfer: the e-VITA approach for intergenerational learning", in *Handbook of Research on Improving Learning and Motivation through Educational Games: Multidisciplinary Approaches*, P. Felicia, Editor, IGI Global, 2011.

[25] Hulme, K., et al., "Experiential Learning in Vehicle Dynamics Education via Motion Simulation and Interactive Gaming", International Journal of Computer Games Technology, (2009): p., 2009.

On the Design and Player Satisfaction Evaluation of an Immersive Gestural Game: The Case of Tortellino X-Perience at the Shanghai World Expo

Marco Roccetti
Computer Science Department
University of Bologna
Mura A. Zamboni 7
40127, Bologna, Italy

roccetti@cs.unibo.it

Angelo Semeraro
Computer Science Department
University of Bologna
Mura A. Zamboni 7
40127, Bologna, Italy

semeraro@cs.unibo.it

Gustavo Marfia
Computer Science Department
University of Bologna
Mura A. Zamboni 7
40127., Bologna, Italy

marfia@cs.unibo.it

ABSTRACT

The role of human-computer interaction technologies has become a prominent factor that most can determine the successful introduction of new computer games. Players, in fact, wish to experience playful exchanges with the objects and characters that compose games. To reach this aim, new technologies have come into the play that comprise the use of video cameras and gesture recognition software. The great news is that such types of technologies could be exploited not only while playing at home on a console, but also in public spaces, thus broadening the use of games to new segments of customers. Nonetheless, to the best of our knowledge, neither relevant exemplars of such specific type of games (that can be played in public spaces) have yet emerged, nor extensive measurement studies exist regarding how players enjoy games in public immersive environments (e.g., fairs, museums and exhibits), the motivation being that those technologies that support completely hands-free gaming have been commercialized only very recently. Hence, our contribution with this article is twofold: on one side we want to illustrate the main design principles we have devised to design a gestural game to be played in a public space, based on novel hand following and gesture recognition techniques. On the other side we wish to report on real measurements we took when over one hundred players enjoyed our gestural game at the Shanghai 2010 World Expo.

Categories and Subject Descriptors

H.1.2 [**Models and Principles**]: User Machine Systems – *human factors, human information processing.*

General Terms

Design.

Keywords

Hands free gaming, player experience, immersive environments, gestural gaming, Shanghai World Expo.

1. INTRODUCTION

Major producers of game consoles are engaged in a technological race that aims at providing their respective customers with the most exciting and natural human-computer interfaces. Recent trends show that the more realistically a game can be played, the higher will be its chances of beating its competitors in the market share arena. This means that customers are no longer happy of holding joysticks, pressing keyboard buttons or sliding mice, but want to be able to play games where they perform the same natural body movements that would be performed in reality.

The first innuendos that have raised the expectations of computer players have been caused by the experience of playing with the Nintendo Wii, where realistic human body movements are supported by the combination of infrared and accelerometer technologies. The Wii has succeeded in letting players move as they were playing on a real field, especially in the case of games that required them swinging an arm, such as tennis or bowling. A further step forward has been moved with the launch of Kinect, an advanced video camera and software system that supports human body recognition on the Microsoft Xbox console. In Kinect-supported games, players can move and control their avatar, which mimics their movements, just as dreamt by many generations of youngsters.

This comes at a cost: the use of non-cheap, advanced video cameras, namely *depth sensing* cameras, which, combined with infrared sensors, are capable of estimating the distance from the real objects that are captured in real-time, thus adding 3D information to 2D images.

Besides playing at home on a console, a new alternative trend is emerging where a crowd of players joins a specific open area (we refer to it as the *gaming arena*), while waiting for their turn to have fun with a game. When a player enters the gaming arena, he/she faces a wall screen (or any other immersive display technology) where a virtual gaming world is presented. Then, a video camera is placed above the arena to record his/her movements, with particular attention to the location where arms and hands are waved. It is worth noticing that such type of settings is attracting an increasing consideration as it can be deployed within public spaces, where ludic exhibitions take place (think of museums, fairs and theatres, for example).

However, although *hands-free* gaming has been successfully introduced at home, neither relevant examples exist of using such technologies in public spaces, or open areas, probably due to the novelty of such approach, nor player results have been yet publicly made available gathered from extensive sets of measurements taken within immersive gaming environments.

Within this framework, the contribution of this work is then twofold. First, we want to describe and discuss the process that led us to develop some novel hand following and gesture recognition techniques that can be easily applied to develop games to be played in public spaces. This latter aspect, in some sense, extends the scope of our work and brings an important contribution to the DOC (Design Of Communication) field, as our techniques could be more generally exploited to provide a technological support to all those performing events thant can be enjoyed publicly, where a predefined set of gestures need to be automatically recognized to permit a natural experience to customers/players. More technically speaking, we specifically developed a set of new recognition algorithms that have revealed the good property to be robust and easy to implement. For this reason, these algorithms are particularly suited for public gaming scenarios where settings can often change or adapted to new requirements or needs. [2], [3].

Second, with this paper we wish also to illustrate how over one hundred players enjoyed at the 2010 Shanghai World Expo our game *Tortellino X-Perience*, a *hands-free* game (implemented based on our algorithms) which teaches how to prepare the famous Tortellini Pasta. In particular, we provide both survey results summarizing how a large set of people, of all ages, enjoyed playing the game, and also experimental results from technical tests performed on our software. Although we neither provide nor discuss here a new methodology for measuring player's behavior in these new challenging contexts of immersive gaming environments, nonetheless we have supplied a contribution in terms of a thorough analysis of such games, through the exemplar of *Tortellino X-Perience*. Moreover, as this game was deployed in a very realistic, as well as environmentally complex, setting, we feel confident that the data we got may be of use for future studies and the development of principled theories on this subject.

The rest of this article is organized as follows. In the second Section, we provide a succinct overview of some alternative methods. In the third Section we describe the gaming scenarios we are interested in along with the algorithms we implemented in our system. In the fourth Section, we report on the use of our system at the 2010 Shanghai World Expo [1]. The fifth Section concludes this article.

2. BACKGROUND ON GESTURE RECOGNITION

In the past decade, a wealth of research has been devoted to finding new and more natural means of interaction between humans and computers. Here we simply provide a succinct overview on those technologies that have seen a widespread adoption in popular gaming consoles, while omitting other intriguing proposals that do not have any commercial counterpart [2].

A famous controller capable of supporting the tracking of a player's movements is the Nintendo Wiimote [3]. The Wiimote is equipped with an infrared camera sensor, which provides high speed tracking of up to four infrared light sources.

This infrared camera computes the distance of the Wiimote from two light emitting sources placed within the sensor bar (typically positioned above or below the TV set). The Wiimote transmits such information to the console via a Bluetooth interface and also

carries an accelerometer. Seen from a different perspective, a Wiimote acts as an intermediary between the gestures a player performs and its console.

Recently, after a long marketing process that has started from the presentation of the Natal Project and finally ended with the commercialization of the Kinect sensor, computer game players have been able to enjoy body free gaming with Microsoft Xbox. Kinect is a horizontal bar that is placed either above or below the TV set. However, it comprises a specialized depth sensor in addition to the RGB camera, which is capable of recording the distance of all objects that lie in front of it [4]. This information is then processed by a software engine, which extracts human body features of players, thus enabling the interaction between physical and virtual worlds.

Sony, before Microsoft, offered to its customers mixed reality experiences with the Playstation Eye. This product is based on a digital camera that feeds the captured video stream to software algorithms, designed to infer game input commands, which implement edge detection and color tracking techniques to detect movements that should be performed only in correspondence of specific given areas. Although millions of the described consoles have been sold around the world, little or no knowledge is known concerning the opinions of gamers on *hands-free* gaming experiences.

3. ON THE DESIGN OF A GESTURE RECOGNITION SYSTEM FOR GAMES IN PUBLIC SPACES

Our hand gesture recognition system was devised to work within an immersive gaming scenario, where a game is played within an open space (termed *gaming arena*), with each new player who can join every few minutes. We have in mind not a typical console but a situation where a queue of players is waiting on his/her turn to play within that public space, like during a visit to a museum, or to a fair or to any other exhibit event.

Playing essentially amounts to waving hands within the arena, while watching a wall screen that displays the game graphical environment. A video camera is placed above and hands are detected as those motion patterns that reach farthest away from the player's body. This may be achieved, for instance, also having a player leaning over a desk, which may further represent a restriction of the gaming arena.

The goal is that of recognizing gestures performed by hands that move freely above a given surface (e.g., a tabletop or simply the floor), and below a video camera that captures frames. We here discuss and report on the process that has led us to devise a system able to recognize players gesture within this context.

In particular, in the next Subsections we will provide details about the series of three different algorithms on which our system is based. As a preliminary comment (confirmed by the experimental results we reported at the end of this paper), we wish the reader notice that all the devised algorithm are robust enough and easy to implement. This makes them particularly suited for public gaming scenarios where settings can often change or adapted to new requirements. Each of them was implemented in Java.

To anticipate how all this work, it is worth considering that the first of these algorithms computes the luminance differences between the static scene before the hands come into play and the scene after that the player has begun to move his/her hands. Such process leads to the identification of those specific areas that the player traverses while waving his/her forearms and hands.

Once individuated, the second algorithm filters out those areas to identify the farthest positions reached by a player's hands (termed *extreme points*). This has been done considering that the games of our interest require a player to stretch out his/her hands in front of him/her, and hence a hand can be significantly identified with the point that reaches farthest away from the player's body.

A third and final algorithm recognizes gestures while tracking those extreme points, based on the consideration that each movement a player performs involves a starting zone from which a hand commences its movement, a trajectory to be followed, and finally an ending zone where the hand completes its gesture. We describe each algorithm in detail. A comprehensive representation of the three algorithms is provided in Figure 1.

3.1 Algorithm 1: Detecting Hands

This algorithm computes the luminance difference between the initial state of the surface below and the current frame as captured by the camera above the hands.

At the very initial stage, before anyone plays, but not with each new player, a very fast calibration phase is performed. Such phase involves dividing the underlying surface rectangle into an N x M grid of blocks, and storing the maximum and minimum RGB luminance values for a subset of K pre-defined pixels within each block.

N and M are chosen large enough to provide the granularity sufficient to detect a typical hand with its arm, whose width is about 5 centimeters. K, instead, represents a trade-off between the increasing computation effort required utilizing larger values and the decreasing detection accuracy deriving from the use of smaller ones (from our experiments, the values of $N = M = 9$ and $K = 4$ has given optimal results in terms of both accuracy and speed).

Then, for every chosen pixel p in a given block, the minimum and maximum luminance values (min_p, max_p) are taken, after an observation lasting for a sufficient, but short, amount of time. This eliminates any problem due to small luminance variations that are possible, even in settings subject to constant illumination.

After that, with each new frame, the algorithm checks for the presence of a hand above any of the K pixels of each block. First, a low-pass Gaussian filter is applied to smooth out any color peak due to small object movements and/or random brightness variations, providing as a result a filtered video frame.

Second, for each block, a check is done to verify if the luminance value of each of the K pixels p lies within the *[min_p, max_p]* interval of reference. If that luminance value is greater than max_p, or smaller than min_p, the pixel is considered as changed. With this comparison, the number of pixels that changed is counted for each block. If this number exceeds a given threshold (e.g., 0.75 times K), then the entire block is considered as changed.

However, to be sure that the area comprised of changed blocks contains a recognizable hand, all those changed blocks must be adjacent (two blocks are pair-wise adjacent if they share an edge, or even a vertex).

To this aim, the final part of this algorithm checks whether all the changed blocks represent an area, termed *active area*, comprised of all adjacent blocks, without any form of interruption between blocks. Only in such case, and at the end of this process, we can conclude that that active area represents a player's hand. The top part of Figure 1 delivers a pictorial representation of all the process we have described.

3.2 Algorithm 2: Following Hands

Once the active areas with the two hands have been identified, the problem is to find an efficient mechanism to follow those hands.

Achieving such result means determining one relevant point to follow for each of them. Some authors, in similar cases, choose the center of mass; we, instead, as relevant point to follow for each hand, have chosen the already mentioned *extreme point*.

The motivation for this is that the extreme points are those that reach the farthest positions of a player's hands, while waving them freely in the air. A large class of games, in fact, entails that a player extends his/her hands in front of him/her, and hence a relevant information for following, and then for recognizing, gestures is concerned with that precise point that reaches farthest away from the player's body. Finding both the extreme points (right and left hands) can be performed utilizing the following algorithm.

We start by mapping the underlying rectangular surface, above which hands are waved, into a Cartesian coordinate system. In this coordinate system a unit of length is taken as the linear dimension of a block. The y and x axes have their origin at the bottom leftmost corner of the surface, where y points externally away from the player's body, while x points towards the right side of the surface, as shown in the bottom leftmost part of Figure 1.

In the first step of this algorithm, each active area is transformed into a bar chart. More precisely, for any given block correspondent to a point along the x axis, a bar is inserted into the chart, whose height y equals the distance of that point from the player's body (for a given x, bars of lower height are replaced by bars of higher heights). Simply said, as shown in the leftmost chart of the bottom leftmost part of Figure 1, each bar represents the highest y value (for each x body's position), where a hand, or a part of it, was detected.

The second step of the algorithm (that is, determining the coordinates of the extreme point of the first hand) is a simple task, as that point is simply given by that bar with the maximum y value among all the represented bars in the chart.

For instance, in the aforementioned leftmost chart, the extreme point of the first hand is detected at position $x = 12$, with value $y = 7$.

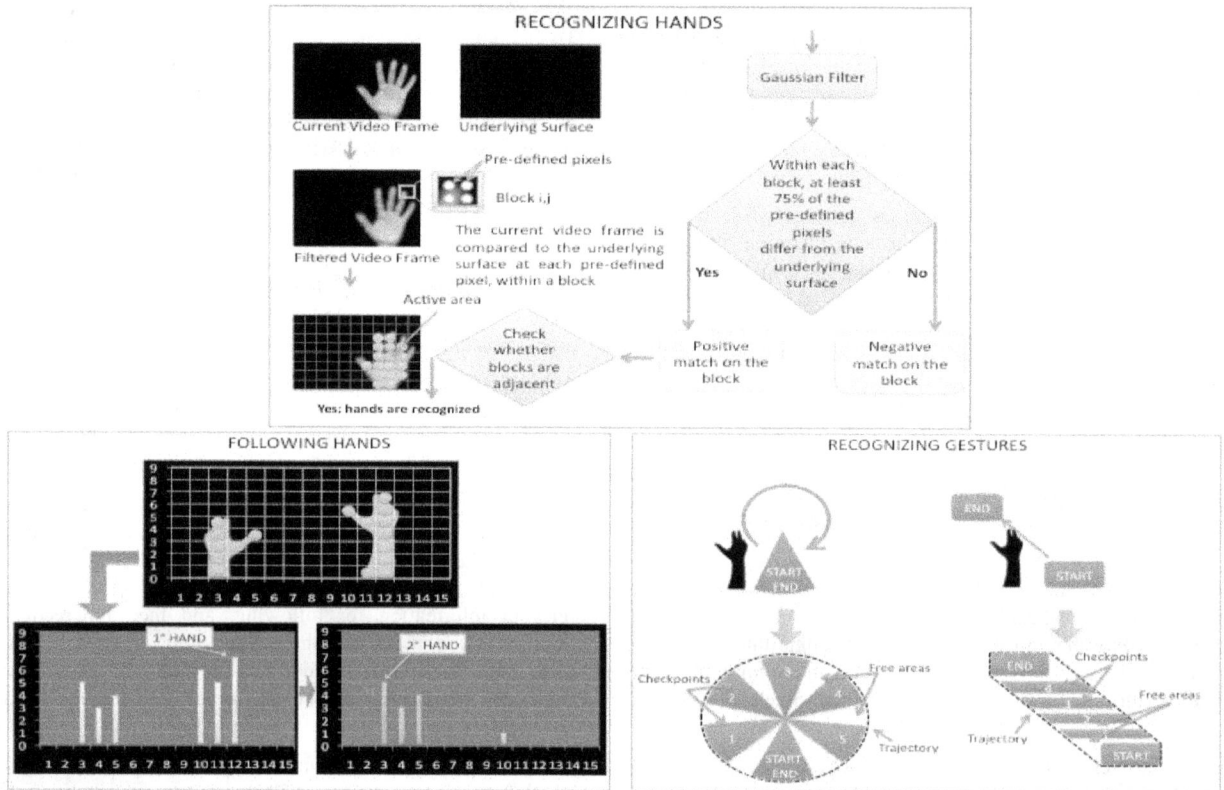

Figure 1. Algorithms for detecting hands, following hands, recognizing actions (anticlockwise from top).

Trickier is the problem of finding the extreme point of the second hand, as it cannot simply be individuated in correspondence with the position where the second (or third) highest y value is found in the chart. These, in fact, could correspond to local maximum values that are representations of lower points of still the first hand. In essence, we are seeking for another maximum y value, while excluding all those bars that still pertain to the first recognized hand.

Thus, with the aim of filtering out all these possible *fake* maximum values, our algorithm constructs a new bar chart, based on the first one, where each new bar is created as follows. The height (y) of each bar of the old chart is contrasted with a so-called *minimum* (whose value is progressively updated).

We start with the next bar at the left (or at the right) of that for which the global maximum was found. If the difference between the height of this current bar and the *minimum* is positive, then a new bar is inserted in the new chart, whose height equals the value of this difference.

If the difference is negative, instead, the bar is not imported in the new chart. Obviously, the *minimum* represents the y value of the lowest bar encountered so far, and is updated as long as the search proceeds, with each new bar under consideration.

This methodology applied to the leftmost chart of Figure 1 yields the correspondent rightmost chart of the same Figure.

In fact, if we move along the direction of decreasing x values, we obtain a new chart where at position $x = 11$, we have $y(11) =$ $max(5 - 7, 0) = 0$, as the minimum y value encountered so far corresponds to the value of the global maximum, that is 7. After that, the new minimum y value is updated to 5, and hence for the position $x = 10$, we obtain a new bar in the new chart, whose y value is equal to $max(6 - 5, 0) = 1$. Again, at the position $x = 5$, the minimum value computed until that point is 0 and hence $y(5)$ $= max(4 - 0, 0) = 4$. If we iterate this until the entire old chart is completely scanned, a new chart is produced with $y(4) = 3$, $y(3)$ $= 5$, respectively. On the new chart, a new global maximum can be searched. That new maximum y value corresponds to the extreme point of the second hand. In our example, it is identified at the position $x = 3$. With the extreme point of each hand, we can now follow hands and their movements.

3.3 Algorithm 3: Recognizing Actions

To recognize actions, we exploit the fact that each gesture requires the player move his/her hand between an origin and a destination, along a given trajectory connecting the two areas.

Moreover, the action of following a given trajectory must be done within a given time period, after which that movement has been performed too slowly to be considered correct.

This is true for all the movements that a player is required to perform within a very large gamut of games where hands can be moved freely.

Hence, the idea behind our algorithm is that of tracking the extreme point of each hand, while verifying that this point starts its movement from the origin, completes it in correspondence with the destination, and traverses a set of checkpoints set along the chosen trajectory (see the bottom rightmost part of Figure 1).

Therefore, each trajectory followed by an extreme point is recognized as correct if it flows within a stripe of a given size (in essence, a certain degree of tolerance is allowed).

This mechanism was devised to make our algorithm able to consider as correct a wider set of movements with slightly different trajectories that differentiate only for a few geometric differences. This scheme can be applied to trajectories of either linear or circular shape.

4. PLAYING WITH TORTELLINO X-PERIENCE IN SHANGHAI: GAME RULES AND USER SATISFACTION

We developed an educational cooking game where the player is instructed on how to cook a typical Italian recipe: the Tortellini Pasta. The cooking steps the player has to imitate using hands are as follows:

- Initially, we have an empty cooking board, with flour and eggs at its right hand side. The player is required to bring the ingredients at the center of the board;
- The yolks and the albumen of the opened eggs float squeezed within the flour. The action required is to use hands to knead the ingredients, adding some water, ending up with a smooth ball of dough;
- The ball of dough needs to be rolled out with a rolling pin;
- A thin foil of dough is lying on the cooking board. It needs to be cut into squares, using a cutting wheel;
- Each square of dough has to be stuffed with meat and cheese;
- The pasta has to be closed to obtain a Tortellino. This is done by joining different pairs of opposite angles of the pasta;
- The Tortellino is ready to be cooked.

Figure 2, 3 and 4 below illustrate the real case of use of our game during the Shanghai World Expo [7], following some of the rules we have just described. We now supply an analysis of such game, which, thanks to the environmentally complex setting where it was deployed, provided us the opportunity of collecting user experience information from heterogeneous groups of players. To this aim, we here present the most prominent result coming from our Chinese experience. We supply two types of data: the first type is concerned with the quantitative behavior of our system when stressed under the pressure of a continuous queue of customers wishing to play.

Table I. Tortellino X-Perience speed results.

Average Delay	Number of Experiments
< 20 ms	103
> 20 ms	4

The second type of results, more traditionally take qualitative measurements of the degree of satisfaction of players during their gaming sessions. With reference to the first type, we first checked the speed and robustness of our system. A first set of experiments assessed the speed of the cascade of our algorithms, measuring the time they took to return a result on a given action performed by a player. These results are shown in Table I, where we can appreciate that on over 100 events detected by our algorithm, less than 4% required more than a 20 milliseconds processing time, never, however, exceeding a 30 milliseconds delay.

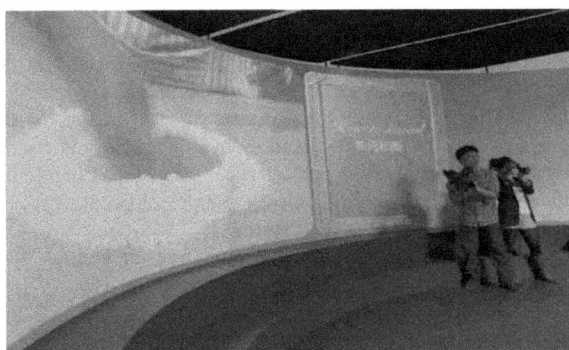

Figure 2. Explaining the actions.

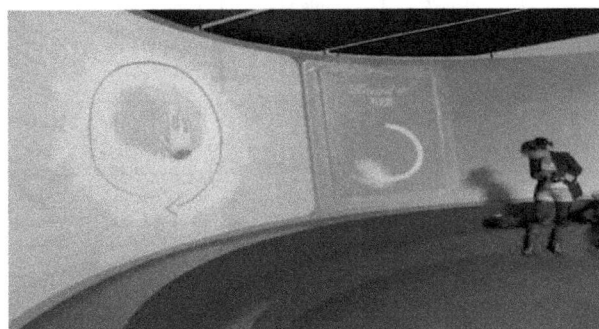

Figure 3. Virtual cooking board.

A second set of experiments was employed to assess the robustness of our algorithms in positively identifying a player's hands, and to contrast it with a gesture recognition system that employs color-tracking techniques implemented with the OpenCV libraries.

Figure 4. Playing the game in Shanghai.

Table II reports the results obtained from using both recognition systems over 50 trials and with 4 different players.

Table II. Tortellino X-Perience robustness results.

Gesture Recognition System	Positive Matches
Custom	88%
OpenCV-based	81%

Analyzing the results, we have concluded that OpenCV-based is slightly outperformed by our gesture recognition system for the following reason. Most misses while using OpenCV, over 70%, have been observed while the third player was engaged in the game. The same problems have not been observed with the same player when a recalibration phase has been performed before the beginning of a game. For this reason we are confident in saying that the calibration phase required by the color tracking algorithm used in OpenCV, in this case, was the source of its underperforming.

Table III. Tortellino X-Perience survey results.

Age Range	Did you enjoy the game?	Was it easy and intuitive to play?	Prefer a remote control?	# of answers
< 18	3.8	4.8	30 NO 3 YES	33
18-50	4.3	4.5	64 NO 9 YES	73
50-70	4.5	4.7	17 NO 0 YES	17
> 70	4.8	4.3	4 NO 0 YES	7

Finally, taking into consideration qualitative aspects, we performed a survey among a large sample of players that played a game. We asked the following set of simple to understand questions:

1. Did you enjoy the game?
2. Was it easy and intuitive to play?
3. Would have you preferred playing it with a remote control (or something similar to control the game)?

Players were asked to give a score, between 1 and 5, to answer the first two questions, while they were asked to simply give a positive or negative answer to the last one. The outcome of this survey is reported in Table III (answers are clustered by the age ranges of participants). The second column, which reports the average score of answers to the first question, clearly shows there has been a high appreciation for the game, which has especially been enjoyed by older people, we believe because of its theme. The third column, instead, shows that, when answering the second question, there has been no significant difference between people of different ages: the innovative human-computer interface has been appreciated, on average, by all. This fact has also been confirmed by the answers we received to the third question, summarized in the fourth column,

where most players clearly affirmed that they preferred our *hands-free* interaction scheme to the use of a controller, as a remote control. Interestingly, we obtained a few preferences for the use of a remote control among players whose age ranged between the late thirties to the late forties; therefore all people belonging to the generation that most has used such type of hardware interface (with the exception of 3 over-70 who were not able to respond to this question).

5. CONCLUSIONS

We have discussed on the design process and on the user experience of a *hands-free* gaming system deployed in an immersive and public environment. We have specifically reported on a real case study of a food game (termed the Tortellino X-Perience) we developed, which has been publicly enjoyed by over one hundred players at the Shanghai 2010 World Expo [1, 6, 8]. We feel that our work brings an important contribution to the DOC (Design Of Communication) field, as our techniques can be generally expoited to provide a support to all those performing events to be enjoyed publicly, where a predefined set of gestures need to be automatically recognized.

6. ACKNOWLEDGMENTS

Our thanks to the Italian Projects DAMASCO (FIRB) and ALTER-NET (PRIN).

7. REFERENCES

1. M. Roccetti, G. Marfia, M. Zanichelli, "The Art and Craft of Making the Tortellino: Playing with a Digital Gesture Recognizer for Preparing Pasta Culinary Recipes," *ACM Computers in Entertainment*, ACM, 8(4), December 2010.

2. S. Mitra, T. Acharaya, "Gesture Recognition: A Survey," *IEEE Trans. On Sys., Man and Cyb.*, 37(3): 311-324, May 2007.

3. J. C. Lee, "Hacking the Nintendo Wii Remote," *Pervasive Computing,* IEEE, (7)3:39-45, July-Sept. 2008.

4. A. D. Wilson, "Depth-Sensing Video Cameras for 3D Tangible Tabletop Interaction," *Proc. of the Second Annual IEEE International Workshop on Horizontal Interactive Human-Computer Systems,* Newport (RI), 2007, 201-204.

5. R. Y. Wang, J. Popovic, "Real-time hand-tracking with a color glove," *ACM Trans. Graph.*, 28(3):1-8, August 2009.

6. J. Giles, "One per Cent: Video Games Teaches You To Make the Perfect Tortellini, *New Scientist*, Jan. 2011, accessed online January 26th, 2011: http://www.newscientist.com/blogs/onepercent/2011/01/computer-game-that-teaches-you.html

7. H. H. Aviles-Arriaga, L.E. Sucar, C.E. Mendoza, "Visual Recognition of Similar Gestures," *Proc. of the 18th International Conference on Pattern Recognition,* Hong Kong, 2006, 1100-1103.

8. M. Roccetti, G Marfia, "Recognizing Intuitive Pre-defined Gestures for Cultural Specific Interactions: An Image-based Approach", *Proc. 3rd IEEE International Workshop on Digital Entertainment, Networked Virtual Environments, and Creative Technology*, Las Vegas (NV), 2011, 1-5.

Player Agents for Langrid Gaming

Akihiro Yamaguchi, Keisuke Tsunoda[*], Reiko Hishiyama
Graduate School of Creative Science and Engineering
Waseda University
{ weathering_13@ruri., 93489410@toki., reiko@}waseda.jp

ABSTRACT

Gathering players is unavoidably costly when we run large-scale "Langrid Gaming", which is a Language Grid-linked multilingual and multinational gaming simulation. If people can be replaced in the gaming simulations, the cost decreases. Thus, a player agent has been introduced. First, game experiments were conducted in natural language, and parallel texts and player agents were developed by analyzing the experiments. Second, experiments were conducted in Japanese (Experiment 1) and in Japanese and Chinese (Experiment 2). Negotiation protocols were analyzed, and new parallel texts were developed from Experiments 1 and 2. Third, experiments were conducted in Japanese (Experiment 3) once again, and Experiments 1, 2, and 3 were compared and analyzed. The following results were obtained. (1) Using parallel texts enables a player agent to be introduced. (2) Various negotiation protocols can be extracted by repeating an experiment with a greater variety of participants. (3) Valid parallel texts can be extracted by analyzing negotiation protocols and functions of utterances. (4) Adding new parallel texts reduces fruitless utterances and changes the negotiations protocol.

Categories and Subject Descriptors

H.5.3 [**Group and Organization Interfaces**]: Computer-supported cooperative work. Synchronous interaction.

General Terms

Design, Experimentation, Human Factors

Keywords

Intercultural collaboration, participatory approach, gaming simulation, language-grid, negotiation protocol

---

[*]He now works at Nippon Telegraph and Telephone Corporation (NTT).

1. INTRODUCTION

"Langrid Gaming", which is a Language Grid [1]-linked multilingual and multinational gaming simulations, has been suggested as a solution to complex and multinational problems [2, 3]. However, doing a large-scale gaming simulation across several different languages and countries currently involves substantial costs in terms of time, effort, and money. In addition, the larger the simulation, the more difficult it is to observe the all players at the same time. Thus, by using parallel texts, we designed player agents to cut the costs of gathering players and understand the human players more easily and deeply. Moreover, we extracted new parallel texts gradationally by analyzing negotiation protocols from experimental results.

2. RELATED WORK

2.1 Gaming Simulation

Duke [4] describes gaming simulations with "future language" and definite gaming simulations as a language that can make a better future for a lot of participating stakeholders. Whereas a conventional simulation is accompanied by the mathematics model construction that has a numerical formula as its base and is minute, the gaming simulation is intuitive, heuristic, and applicable to complex problems that include a lot of stakeholders, like environmental or city planning problems. In addition, we can expect an educational effect because players can acquire knowledge directly by participating in a game. In this way, gaming simulations are a communication tool that can be used to educate and solve complicated problems.

2.2 Participatory Approach

Participatory simulation is a simulation in which people participate. By using participatory simulation, we can not only analyze participants' actions but also adopt a variety of viewpoints when we design an institution. Many researchers have used the participatory approach for solving complex problems [5, 6]. Torii et al. [7] proposed a modeling process using a participatory approach. They used their method in a real case study of agricultural economics in the northeast of Thailand. They proposed the following four steps as a construction process for the negotiation model in these studies: (1) Investigation of the object domain. (2) Role playing game. (3) Interaction design. (4) Participatory simulation

2.3 Multilingual Collaboration

In the field of multilingual collaboration, Tsunoda et al. [2, 3] researched gaming simulations in a multilingual environment. In this study, they thought of gaming simulations as a tool that provides a controlled environment, and they used gaming simulations to try to overcome the poor quality of mechanical translations. Furthermore, they suggested an agent that could support a conversation. However, in this study, all participants were human beings. Therefore, assembling participants required a lot of time, effort, and money.

In addition, parallel texts is another method for overcoming the poor quality of mechanical translations. Although making parallel texts requires much time, effort, and money, unlike mechanical translation, mistranslations do not occur. Therefore, parallel texts are often used when highly accurate translation is necessary, such as in medical fields [8].

3. PROPOSAL

In this paper, by using parallel texts, we designed player agents to cut the costs of gathering players and understand the players more easily and deeply. Moreover, we extracted new parallel texts gradationally by analyzing negotiation protocols and tried to diversify communications and secure general versatility of examples. Figure 1 shows the research process.

The process of this study is as follows.

1. Preliminary experiment in natural language

2. Analysis of the conversation in the preliminary experiment

3. Making parallel texts

4. Analysis of the players' behavior in the preliminary experiment

5. Design of the player agent

6. Experiment in the same language (Experiment 1)

7. Experiment in multiple languages (Experiment 2)

8. Analysis and consideration of Experiment 1 and 2

9. Analysis of negotiation protocols

10. Making new parallel texts

11. Experiment with new parallel texts (Experiment 3)

12. Analysis and consideration of Experiment 3

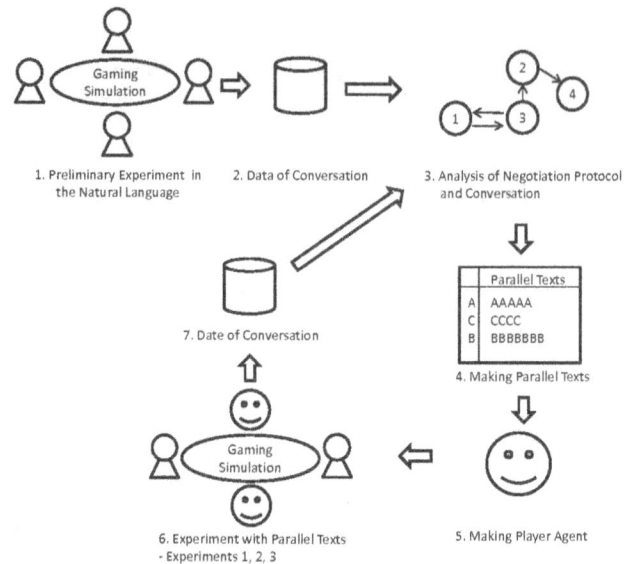

Figure 1: Research process

4. SYSTEM FOR EXPERIMENT

4.1 Language Grid

Language Grid is an Internet-based language service infrastructure created by the National Institute of Information and Communications Technology (NICT), Kyoto University, and Nippon Telegraph and Telephone Corporation (NTT). This base is intended to support multilingual communication. In this study, we utilized the parallel text service of Language Grid and designed a multilingual participatory gaming simulation.

4.2 Renewable Energy Game

The game used in this study involved negotiations over a problem with introducing renewable energy [9]. The players form a virtual city consisting of four citizens and share one renewable energy institution. The players are given names: Player A, Player B, Player C, and Player D. Each player aims at maximizing their "economic clout" and "contribution degree", and the maximum degrees are different for each player. Economic clout can gained by money. Players can get money depending on economic clout per round. The contribution degree can increased by doing something good for the group such as improving a jointly owned energy institution and dealing with trouble. The collective aim is to prevent environmental degradation. Over the course of the game, the environment degrades and bigger troubles occur. Players can prevent the environment from degrading by improving renewable energy institution. We designed it so that the players had to negotiate to decide their course of action in response to various events.

Figure 2 shows the game flow. One round contains three phases.

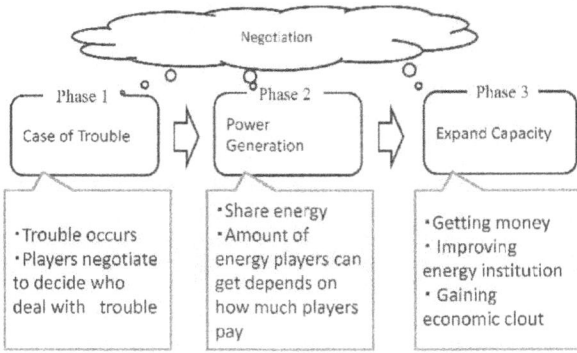

Figure 2: Game flow

In phase 1, trouble occurs. Players decide who will deal with this trouble. More than one player can be chosen. Whoever deals with the trouble must pay money. In phase 2, a renewable energy institution generates energy, which players share. Energy allocation is prioritized on the basis of how much money each player pays. Energy is necessary for operating economic clout. In phase 3, players can intensify economic clout and improve renewable energy institution. If a player meets the victory conditions at the end of phase 3, that player is the winner. If no players meet the victory conditions, a new round begins from phase 1 again. Players choose their utterances from a list connected to the Language Grid parallel text service during the game. This is because the player agent cannot make natural utterances and quality of mechanical translation is poor. Figure 3 outlines the proposed system.

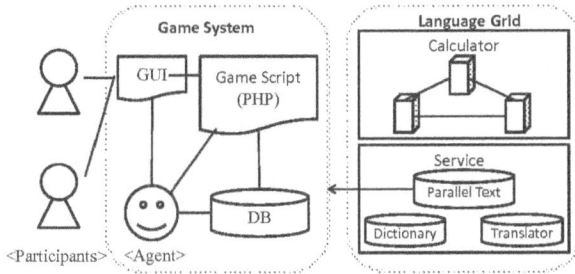

Figure 3: Outline of proposed system

4.3 Player Agent

The player agents were designed on the basis of the following process.

Step 1 Experiment in natural language (preliminary experiment)

Step 2 Parallel texts making and extraction of strategy by analyzing conversation

Step 3 Design of the player agent

We twice carried out game experiments and extracted an action protocol, the strategy of players, and utterance patterns for agent-making information. In addition, we validated the game through this preliminary experiment and adjusted various parameters.

4.3.1 Step 1: Experiment in Natural Language (preliminary experiment)

We conducted game experiments twice in natural language as a preliminary experiment. Participants were eight in all. All participants were Japanese and chatted throughout the game. We had each participant read a manual before the game started, and clarified the rules. We answered all questions from participants during the game.

After the preliminary experiment, we tried to extract the action protocol, strategy, and utterance patterns of each player through an interview and analysis of their utterance log and action log.

Table 1 shows the total number of utterances in the preliminary experiment.

Table 1: Total number of utterances in preliminary experiment

	1st	2nd
Number of utterances	127	117

4.3.2 Step 2: Parallel Text Making and Extraction of Strategy by Analyzing Conversation

We made parallel texts and extracted strategies from results of the preliminary experiment. Table 2 lists the actions of each player in both experiment games. "Dealing with troubles", "Improving energy institution", "Financial assistance" detail the amounts of money that players used in each action. "Gaining economic clout" details the number of times that players increased their economic clout.

Table 2: Action pattern in preliminary experiment

	A	B	C	D
Dealing with troubles	11	10	2	4
Improving energy institution	66	107	11	25
Financial assistance	4	3	4	1
Gaining economic clout	6	9	8	2

As for strategy, players tended to almost always dislike dealing with troubles. In fact, players expanded their "contribution degree" by "Improving energy institution" and "Financial assistance". They tended not to expand their "contribution degree" by "Dealing with troubles". However, players with much money tended to contribute money for dealing with troubles when they were requested to several times.

There were many conversations conforming with the rules of the game. That is to say, "Request financial assistance", "Request dealing with troubles", "Request improving energy institution", "Accept", and "Reject" were the main types of utterances. We made parallel texts of these five types of utterances and used them in the rest of the experiments. Tables 3 and 4 show specific conversations. In Table 3, Player A deals with troubles as requested by Players D and B.

Table 3: Example of conversation log in preliminary experiment

Speaker	Words
Player D	Please pay, A
Player B	According to the rules, the person with the most money should pay.
Player A	I paid

On the other hand, in Table 4, Player B receives requests from Players A and D to deal with troubles, but refuses because Player B prioritized winning ahead of helping the group. When a player was asked to perform an action that did not meet the victory conditions, the player tended to reject such requests. When a player requested other players to do things, they tended to ask the player who had much money.

Table 4: Example of conversation log in preliminary experiment

Speaker	Words
Player B	Please pay
Player A	You have the most money, so please pay, B
Player B	I don't pay. My victory conditions don't include doing so.
Player B	Please pay quickly
Player D	Please pay, B

4.3.3 Step 3: Design of the Player Agent

On the basis of results of the preliminary experiment, we designed the player agent. Utterance patterns are the same as those in the parallel texts we made: "Request financial assistance", "Request dealing with troubles", "Request improving renewable energy institution", "Accept", and "Reject". The main strategy for a player agent is to prioritize winning. However, if it has much money or is responding to a request from other players is that meet the victory conditions, it tends to accept requests. Figure 4 shows the agent's action protocol we designed.

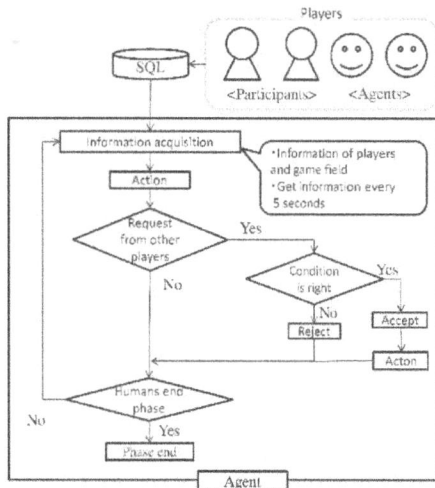

Figure 4: Agent protocol

5. EXPERIMENT 1: EXPERIMENT IN THE SAME LANGUAGE

5.1 Settings

We conducted Experiment 1 with this game system in the same language (Japanese). The participants were two human beings and two player agents. Human beings were four Japanese native speakers. We performed three experiment games. Although participants were told that two players were agents, they did not know which.

5.2 Results

In this study, we paid attention to and analyzed human behavior to inspect the effect of introducing a player agent. Table 5 shows the number of average utterances per round (total number of utterances/(total number of rounds × total number of players)) from human beings to player agents and from a human being to a human being in Experiment 1. "Accept" means acceptance, "Reject" means rejection, and "Request" means the sum of the three request utterance. "Total" means the sum of the five utterance patterns.

Table 5: Average number of utterances in Experiment 1

	Human⇒Human	Human⇒Agent
Accept	0.19	0.19
Reject	0.40	0.35
Request	1.33	3.21
Total	1.91	3.75

The number of utterances from a human being to a player agent is almost twice that from a human being to a human being. This is because the human beings tried to understand the structure of the player agent. Here, "structure" means the conditions in which a player agent accepts a request from others.

All human players distinguished the player agents from the other human being at an early stage in Experiment 1, and through utterances to the agents, players tended to try to understand in what kind of condition a player agent accepted requests. As a result, the number of utterances from humans to agents became larger.

Table 6 shows a specific conversation in which a player tried to understand the structure of a player agent.

Table 6: Example of conversation log in which player tried to understand agent structure in Experiment 1

Speaker	Word	Conversation partner
Player C (Japanese)	Give me $1	Player B (Agent)
Player B (Agent)	No	Player C (Japanese)
Player C (Japanese)	Give me $1	Player B (Agent)
Player B (Agent)	No	Player C (Japanese)
	(Repeat)	

In this conversation, Player C (the person) repeated the same request to Player B (the agent). Player C thought that

Table 7: Example of conversation log in which player requested other players perform actions in Experiment 1

Speaker	Words	Conversation partner
Player C (Japanese)	Decrease 2 Trouble Matter	Player A (Japanese)
Player A (Japanese)	No	Player C (Japanese)
Player C (Japanese)	Decrease 2 Trouble Matter	Player B (Agent)
Player C (Japanese)	Decrease 2 Trouble Matter	Player D (Agent)

a player agent would accept a request at random, so Player C repeated the same request to the player agent. Player C later confirmed this in the interview. As a result, Player C, who was not able to make Player B accept the request, concluded that Player B did not accept or refuse at random, so Player C stopped repeating the same request beyond necessity. On the other hand, when a human was rejected by the other human, he tended to give up the request, make a compromise request, or make the same request after performing action for other players. Consequently, the number of utterance from human to human was smaller than that from human to agent.

Table 7 shows another specific conversation. "Decrease 2 Trouble Matter" means that the speaker requests the conversation partner to pay $2 towards dealing with trouble. As shown in Table 7, Player C asked Player A (both humans) to deal with this trouble. However, because Player C's request was rejected, Player C requested other players to deal with trouble, unlike when Player C requested a player agent to do so. The results of Experiment 1 showed that when we conduct gaming simulations with player agents and human players who can distinguish a player agent from a human being, human players tended to try to understand the structure of the player agent. Players tended to repeat requests of the same sort until they succeed in understanding the structure of a player agent or give up. From these results, we extracted a negotiation protocol that players implement in the gaming simulations in which player agents are introduced. Figure 5 shows this protocol.

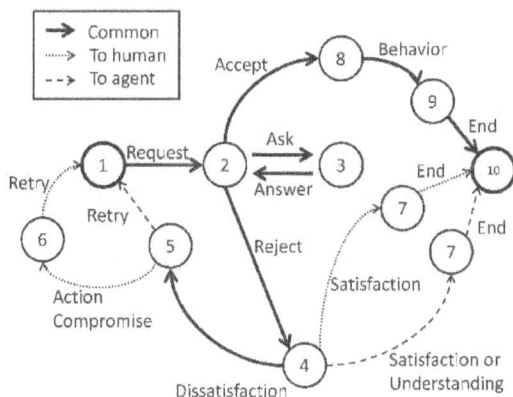

Figure 5: Negotiation protocol in Experiment 1

In Figure 5, "Satisfaction" means that players are satisfied with the response from the conversation partner, and "Understanding" means that players succeed in understanding the structure of a player agent.

When players make a request to a player agent and are dis-

satisfied with the response, negotiation protocol shifts to State 5 and the player repeats the same request. In addition, when players' requests are rejected by a player agent, if the players succeed in understanding the structure of the player agent (Understanding) or players are satisfied with the response (Satisfaction), negotiation protocol shifts to State 7 and players end the negotiation. When players make requests to human beings that are rejected and are dissatisfied with the rejection, negotiations may go into a loop. In this case, after having performed either behavior pattern, players repeat the same request. These two behavior patterns are "performing action for other players (Action)" and "making a compromise request (Compromise)". However, even if a negotiation goes into this loop, players end the negotiations with human beings earlier than those with a player agent.

6. EXPERIMENT 2: EXPERIMENT IN THE MULTIPLE LANGUAGES

6.1 Settings

We conducted Experiment 2 in multiple languages. The participants were two human beings and two player agents. Human beings were two Japanese and two Chinese, and they used their mother tongues. A pair of human beings was Japanese and Chinese. We performed four rounds of experiment games. Just as in Experiment 1, although participants were told that two players were agents, they did not know which.

6.2 Results

Table 8 shows the number of average utterances per one round from a human being to a player agent and from a human being to a human being in Experiment 2. "Accept" means acceptance, "Reject" means rejection, and "Request" means the sum of the three request utterance. "Total" means the sum of the five utterance patterns.

Table 8: Average number of utterances in Experiment 2

	Human⇒Human	Human⇒Agent
Accept	0.26	0.46
Reject	0.39	0.31
Request	1.26	1.71
Total	1.91	2.49

Unlike in Experiment 1, there is almost no difference between the number of utterances from human to human and from human to agent. This is because few players distinguished a player agent from human beings in Experiment 2, whereas almost all players did so in Experiment 1. Some

Table 9: Conversation log in which player makes request to other players in Experiment 2

Speaker	Word	Conversation partner
Player C (Chinese)	Decrease 1 Trouble Matter	Player A (Japanese)
Player A (Japanese)	No	Player C (Chinese)
Player C (Chinese)	Decrease 1 Trouble Matter	Player B (Agent)
Player B (Agent)	No	Player C (Chinese)
Player C (Chinese)	Decrease 1 Trouble Matter	Player D (Agent)
Player D (Agent)	No	Player C (Chinese)

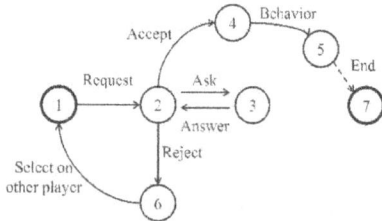

Figure 6: Negotiation protocol in Experiment 2

players remarked that they could not distinguish a player agent from a human being. One of these player's negotiation protocol was to make a request to one player, and wait for a response, and make a request to other players by matter of response. Table 9 shows a specific conversation this player had. In Table 9, the Chinese player requested without distinguishing a player agent from the other human being (Japanese player). Figure 6 shows the negotiation protocol from this result. If a players' request is rejected, negotiation protocol shifts to State 4 and the player choose another player and requests once again.once again. Moreover, one player distinguished a player agent from a human being but did not try to understand the structure of a player agent and made a request to another player who had much money, another player failed to understand the structure and made unnatural requests such as repeating same request to one agent that scarcely accepted, and another player made the same request to all players at one time unconcerned about which players were agents.

7. ANALYSIS AND DISCUSSION

7.1 Intercultural Collaboration

The numbers of utterances from human to human in Experiments 1 and 2 do not differ much. Thus, conversations in multiple languages neither increased nor decreased the number of utterances. In addition, players remarked in interviews that they had no communication problems when speaking to players who had a different mother tongue. We succeeded in overcoming the communication barrier between different languages.

7.2 Design of the Player Agent

Since the player agent serves as a substitute for a human, the player agent has to be indistinguishable from human beings. Thus, we asked players who could distinguish a player agent from a human why they were able to. The main reason was "difference in the response time". When a human being makes responses, his/her response times usually differ

because his/her thinking time differs. This difference in response time was different between humans and agents, and helped players to distinguish a player agent from a human. Since the current player agents make responses by consistently getting information every given number of seconds, agents' response times tended to be the same. Therefore, we can make a player agent that is indistinguishable from a human being by making its response time more like that of a human, or by making a player agent disregard a request from other players.

Another reason is "difference in strategy". Human beings use a bold strategy of borrowing large amounts of money and taking advantage of rules of the game. Difference in strategies between human beings and player agents helped some players to distinguish player agents from humans. Therefore, we can make a player agent that is indistinguishable from human beings by letting a player agent use various strategies.

7.3 Negotiation Protocol

We extracted one negotiation protocol from Experiment 1 in which players distinguished a player agent, understood its structure, and made most of their requests to the player agent. Additionally, we extracted new negotiation protocols from Experiment 2, which was conducted in multiple languages. In these new negotiation protocols, players could not distinguish a player agent from a human and players made requests unconcerned about which players were agents. We cannot allege that the difference between Experiments 1 and 2 was caused by the difference between monolingual communication and multilingual communication, but we thought that having a wider variety of participants created a significant effect on extracting a variety of negotiation protocols. Figure 7 shows all negotiation protocol patterns we extracted from Experiments 1 and 2.

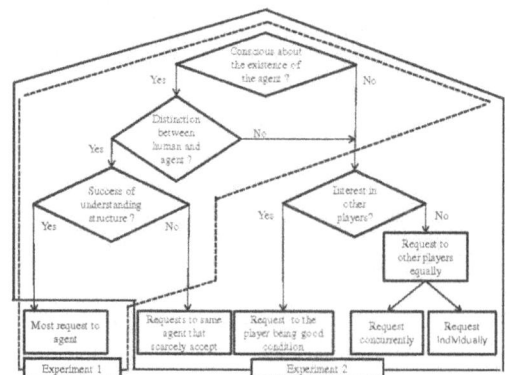

Figure 7: Negotiation protocol pattern

From the results of Experiments 1 and 2, we obtained various negotiation protocols that could be extracted by repeating an experiment with a variety of participants. Although we extracted only one negotiation protocol from Experiment 1, we extracted four new negotiation protocols from Experiment 2, making five negotiation protocols in total. Using these five negotiation protocols, we made five new player agents with different patterns. Introducing these new player agents into a gaming simulation, we conducted experiments in a situation in which a greater variety of players participated.

8. MAKING NEW PARALLEL TEXTS

8.1 Analysis

Figure 5 shows that negotiations may go into a loop when players' requests to human beings are rejected and they are dissatisfied with this rejection. In this case, after having performed either two behavior patterns, players repeat the same request. These two behavior patterns are "performing actions for other players (Action)" and "making a compromise request (Compromise)" This loop enlarged the number of fruitless utterances and could block negotiations. Therefore, we needed to make new parallel texts that could prevent negotiations from going into this loop.

8.2 Making New Parallel Texts

We believed that one action players took when negotiations went into the loop was to say "I will do α, so please do β". Therefore, a new parallel text we should make is "I will do α, so please do β(Negotiation)", which plays the role of "offer + request". As for making a compromise request, we try to prevent negotiations from going into this loop by utterance from conversation partner. In this case, we made a new parallel text saying "I will do γ", which plays the role of "offer". This parallel text was expected to prevent players from making a compromise request by showing limit that they can pay.

9. EXPERIMENT 3: EXPERIMENT WITH NEW PARALLEL TEXTS

9.1 Settings

We conducted Experiment 3 with the five parallel texts used in Experiments 1 and 2 and two new parallel texts. The participants were human beings (all Japanese) and two player agents. We performed three rounds of experiment games. Just as in Experiments 1 and 2, although participants were told that two players were agents, they did not know which.

9.2 Results

Table 10 shows the number of average utterances per round from a human being to a player agent and from a human being to a human being in Experiment 3. "Accept" means acceptance, "Reject" means rejection, and "Request" means the sum of the three request utterance. "Negotiation" means "I will do α, so please do β", and "Proposal" means "I will do γ".

Table 10: Average number of utterances in Experiment 3

	Human⇒Human	Human⇒Agent
Accept	0.20	0.17
Reject	0.22	0.30
Request	0.59	0.80
Negotiation	0.24	0.64
Proposal	0.00	0.02
Total	1.13	1.94

Figure 8 shows the average number of utterances without distinguishing between humans and agents in Experiment 1, 2, and 3 in graphs.

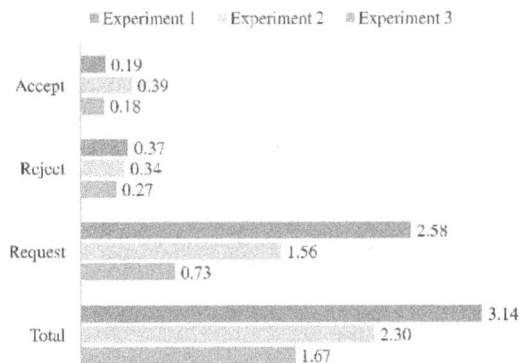

Figure 8: Average number of utterances

10. DISCUSSION

10.1 New Parallel Texts

10.1.1 Effect

The number of average utterances in Experiment 3 was smaller than those in Experiments 1 and 2. The number of Requests especially decreased. This was because negotiations were prevented from going into the loop in Experiments 1 and 2. Figure 5 shows that the negotiation loop increased the number of utterances. New parallel texts prevented negotiations from going into the loop, so the number of Requests decreased in Experiment 3. Although negotiations went into the loop sometimes in Experiment 3, they escaped the loop more quickly in Experiment 3 than in Experiments 1 and 2 because players acquired Satisfaction early. As a consequence, the number of Requests decreased.

10.1.2 Usability

Next, we discuss the usability of new parallel texts. Although the number of Negotiations was as large as that of Requests, the number of Proposals was very small. This was because Proposals were used when players were requested to perform actions. As pointed out above, players could receive satisfaction early by using the new parallel texts. Since negotiations were finished before Proposals were used, the number of Proposals was very small. Even if players tried to use a Proposal actively, the number of Proposals, which plays the role of "offer", sometimes decreased because Negotiation, which plays the role of "offer + request", had a superior function. There was even a case where players felt a Proposal was an obstacle. Therefore, although we can make new parallel texts that have broad utility from analyzing negotiation protocols, parallel texts that have the same function must be removed.

10.2 Negotiation Protocol

Adding new parallel texts created a new negotiation protocol. If players had the experience of having their request refused (Reject), they tended to accept a request from other players (Accept request from other players).

Figure 9 shows the new negotiation protocol from Experiment 3.

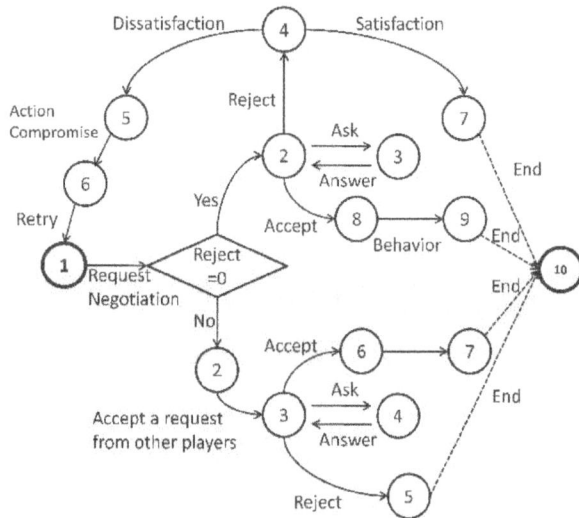

Figure 9: Negotiation protocol in Experiment 3

In the new negotiation protocol, players who were going to use "Request" or "Negotiation" branched condition if the number of rejections was 0 (Reject = 0) or not. If they had not had requests rejected, they tended to adopt the negotiation protocol shown in Figure 5. However, if they had the experience of having requests rejected, they tended to accept a request from other players, and after that they made a request. As a result, if they were rejected, negotiations tended not to go into the loop.

We considered that the reason such negotiations protocol came into being was players' desire to boost relations with other players. In Experiments 1 and 2, players performed actions aimed at helping them win and helping players win with a view to boosting relations with other players. However, players did not accept requests from other players to boost relations with other players in Experiments 1 and 2. We considered that this difference between Experiments 1 and 2 and Experiment 3 resulted from psychological guidance given by new parallel texts. Although parallel texts only played the role of request in Experiments 1 and 2, new parallel texts played the role of "offer + request" in Experiment 3. A form of "give & take" to make other players accept requests was set up from the beginning in the experiment. We thought that players were more likely to give thought to accepting a request from other players if they saw the form of "give & take" from the beginning in the experiment.

11. CONCLUSION

In this study, we designed player agents to cut the costs of gathering players and understand the human players more easily and deeply by using parallel texts. As a result, we found that various negotiation protocols could be extracted by repeating an experiment with a variety of participants. Moreover, we found that we could extract valid parallel texts by analyzing negotiation protocols and functions of utterances and that adding the new parallel texts reduced fruitless utterance and changed the negotiations protocol.
We need to create more agents that have more negotiation protocol patterns and strategies with a view to controlling experiment environments.

12. REFERENCES

[1] T. Ishida: Language Grid: An Infrastructure for Intercultural Collaboration. *IEEE/IPSJ Symposium on Applications and the Internet (SAINT-06)*, pp. 96-100, 2006

[2] Keisuke Tsunoda and Reiko Hishiyama: Design of Multilingual Participatory Gaming Simulations with a Communication Support Agent, *28th ACM International Conference on Design of Communication (SIGDOC 2010)*,pp19-27,2010

[3] Keisuke Tsunoda and Reiko Hishiyama: Langrid-Gaming: A multilingual participatory gaming approach for global solution and innovation, *The 2nd International Service Innovation Design Conference(ISIDC 2010)*, 2010.

[4] R. D. Duke: Gaming:THE FUTURE'S LANGUAGE, New York:Sage Publications,U.S, 1974.

[5] N.Gilbert, S.Maltby, and T.Asakawa :Participatory simulations for developing scenarios in environmental resource management,*In Proceedings of Third Workshop on Agent-Based Simulation*,pp. 67-72, 2002

[6] M. E. Camargo, P. R, Jacobi and R. Ducrot, Role-playing games for capacity building in water and land management: Some Brazilian experiences, *Jounal of Simulation and Gaming*, Vol. 38, No. 4, pp472-493, 2007.

[7] Daisuke Torii, Toru Ishida, Francois Bousquet: Modeling agents and interactions in agricultural economics,*5th International Joint Conference on Autonomous Agents and Multiagent Systems (AAMAS2006)*,pp.81-88,2006

[8] Mai Miyabe, Kunikazu Fujii, Tomohiro Shigenobu, and Takashi Yoshino: Parallel-text Based Support System for Intercultural Communication at Medical Receptions, *The First International Workshop on Intercultural Collaboration (IWIC2007)*, pp.182-192, 2007.

[9] Painuly JP: Barriers to renewable energy penetration a framework for analysis, *Renewable Energy 24*, pp.73-89, 2000.

3D Environments with Games Characteristics for Teaching History: The VRLerna Case Study

Barbatsis Kostas
Informatics Teacher
Regional Directorate of
Primary and Secondary
Education of Central
Macedonia
Greece
+302310320801
barbatsis@gmail.com

Economou Daphne
School of Electronics and
Computer Science
University of Westminster
W1W 6UW, United
Kingdom
+44 (0)20 7911 5000 ext
64506
D.Economou@wmin.ac.uk

Papamagkana Ioanna
Department of History and
Archaeology Aristotle
University of Thessaloniki

Greece
+302106095492
ioapapa@hotmail.com

Loukas Dimos
Department of
Accounting
School of Management
and Economics
A.TEI of Thessaloniki
Greece
+302310853679
dloukas@uom.gr

ABSTRACT

The latest rapid advancement of technology of informatics and communication brought new prospective to education. However, the potential of those technologies could have been exploited further in order to transform students from passive data receivers, to active actors in the learning process. The scope of this paper is the presentation of a theoretical educational framework for the use of interactive three dimensional virtual environments with game characteristics that aims at the initiation of motivation and enhancement of learning. To evaluate the effectiveness of the theoretical framework a prototype educational application called "VRLerna" has been implemented and evaluated with real users. VRLerna is an interactive reconstruction of the central building of a prehistoric population at Lerna of Argolis which is used to teach history at Key stage 5. The paper describes the methodology used to evaluate the prototype and via this the theoretical educational framework and presents the evaluation results that portray the success of the prototype to attract the students interest and keep them engaged and motivated.

Categories and Subject Descriptors

K.3.2 [**Computers and Education**]: Computer and Information Science Education – *Computer science education*

General Terms

Theory

Keywords

History education, virtual environments, video games, constructivism, motivation.

1. INTRODUCTION

The most wide spread theories of learning psychology suggest that the learner's activation and engagement in an energetic learning process are prerequisites for achieving certain learning goals. According to Rogers active learning is linked with motivation [55].

At the same time, modern history teaching considers the ability of being critical on all historical narratives [38] and encounters the understanding of time, change or continuity [35] as very important educational goals. It is therefore broadly acknowledged that teaching facts through textbooks is no longer enough in order to appreciate the past. As a result, archaeological evidence seems to become more valuable under the new circumstances [27] [59] [3] [45]. Hamilakis (2004) suggests that archaeology in education can help students develop critical, as well as synthetic, analytical and hypothetical abilities as they come to understand the dialectic relation between the past and present through the study of material culture. In order to address those goals motivating, challenging and interactive means that avoid one-dimensional narrative [62] and can support the students to gain a non-fragmented view of the past are required. Those are pursued in modern technology which provides the tools for reconstructing what time has destroyed and offers the environments in which the learner can engage a rich empirical experience [16].

As a result, it is considered necessary to enhance the existing learning process by adding elements that aid into motivating and engaging the students. Learning technology can play an important role in achieving this. More specifically, technologies such as Virtual Reality (VR) and video games could be used as learning tools in order to create the context into which the students could remain active through entertainment, commitment and motivation.

VR is a technological discovery which allowed to overcome the classical way of interaction with personal computers through static means of interface such as the mouse and the keyboard and step through the computer screen into a three dimensional (3D) artificial world. It is a multi-sensory experience, based on: real-time 3D computer graphics; stereoscopic rendering; head/eye/body tracking; and binaural vision [22]. In a virtual environment (VE) the users with the help of suitable devices has the sense of immersion in an artificial world in which they have the sense of moving and interacting with its content in a intuitive and natural way [10], while the reproduced environment changes reflecting the user's movements.

VR offers the potential to create pioneering educational environments [43] [44] and the ability to explore and interact with objects and the environment [42]. It uses metaphors borrowed from the games and the theater, promoting sentimental elements in the interface [37]. Many scholars and teachers believe that VR offers many advantages which can support the learning process [49]. For some, these advantages focus on its ability to facilitate the use of constructivist learning activities [68]. For others, it is the fact that it offers alternative ways of learning which can help different types of students, as for example optical ones. Until today there has been many examples of the use of VR for educational purposes and subjects [48], including those of history [57] [46], as it has all those characteristics which allow the "revival" of the past (archaeological finds and sites) and the study of historical issues.

Nevertheless, a common problem experienced in VEs is the lack of structured activities and processes [19] [31]. This is because the initiative of exploration in the VE moves to the users themselves. Another problem focuses on the lack of 3D VEs to offer the necessary dynamics in order to provide a rich and focused interaction, which can trigger the student's interest and motivate them to fulfill certain learning goals.

At the same time, video games technology is a rapidly evolving technological field. It is considered a technology which penetrates more and more in modern societies and is becoming one of the main, most lucrative and effective forms of entertainment, maybe the most popular among young people [2] [33]. Many scholars support the use of video games as a means that aids learning. This opinion is based on the enormous influence of games upon young people as well as on the fact that they seem to motivate students with a more constructive way than the one used by conventional learning methods [36] [54] [20] [34]. Boyle (1997) considers that games are able to give an attractive and pleasant form to learning, by offering a strong "pattern" on which we can design effective learning environments. Papert (1993) also supports that video games give a vivid and interesting pace to teaching, in regards to conventional means used in most schools, which turn teaching into a slow and unattractive process [65]. Modern students are familiar with video games technology and are most likely to enjoy a learning experience incorporated in a video game [5] [54].

An educational video game should accomplish two goals: entertainment and learning. Both goals should be accomplished in a rather satisfying level in order to achieve an effective educational environment.

Entertainment is very important and strongly connected with student motivation [25] [60] [2]. Successful entertaining educational video games are considered the ones that offer intriguing challenges, have a clear goal and specific outcome, as well as precise, constructive and encouraging feedback and offer elements such as those of curiosity and imagination [40]. Prensky [53] suggests that educational games which lack entertainment disorientate and offer nothing more than conventional teaching software. In addition, learning is achieved only in an environment which offers the necessary "teaching support", meaning adopting such pedagogical and teaching principles (learning theories, educational methods, and learning tools) which are consistent with the video games' character and can lead to achieving educational goals [54].

Nevertheless, through literature review of prior attempts to develop educational video games, it is being realized that the achievement of a balance between entertainment and learning is complicated. This is the reason why there are few successful educational games [12]. Indicative of the problem is Brody's [9] opinion, who mentions that the attempts to combine educational content and entertaining elements have produced some unsuccessful educational video games and some ineffective entertaining learning experiences. As a result, there is a need to design and develop educational games which will combine stimulating elements with clear learning goals and a satisfying educational content.

The main purpose of this paper is to present a theoretical framework for designing and developing educational 3D VEs that reflect the main characteristics of video games (see Section 2). In order to evaluate the effectiveness or this theoretical framework a pilot educational application is implemented, the "VRLerna" (see Section 3). Section 4, presents the methodology that has been used to evaluate the educational outcome, while section 5 presents and discusses the evaluation results. Finally, the paper closes with conclusions and future recommendations (see Section 6).

2. EDUCATIONAL FRAMEWORK

The basic goal of the theoretical framework discussed in this paper is the reinforcement of learning results by initiating motivation. However, in order to accomplish this goal it is essential to understand the main factors that motivate learner and what is the desirable learning outcome. The desirable outcome includes the focus of learners' attention, the degree of their excitement and involvement in the learning process and insisting on achieving the learning goals [13] [51]. Moreover, motivated learners should feel enthusiastic, focused and engaged by their goal. Their interest for learning should be evident and the learning process should be pleasing.

The discussed theoretical framework consists of two sections: the educational framework to be satisfied and the educational tools to be used to achieve this (see Figure 1). The educational framework consists of the pedagogical background which is being adopted. The later includes learning theories and educational methods which help keeping the learners engaged and motivated and addresses the characteristics of the chosen educational tools. More specifically, it includes the constructive learning theory, which focuses on the learner, who is called to act in order to obtain knowledge [58] [56] [18] [17] [28]. The educational methods that have been adopted as part of the educational framework are those of experiential and discovering learning. Those address the basic goals of the theoretical framework, which is to motivate the learner, as well as the basic principles of constructive learning theory, as they give an impulse to learning through experience and personal knowledge discovery.

The educational tools that have been adopted are based on 3D VEs and video games, that can enhance the learning process, as stated earlier (see Section 1), if the educational dynamic of certain characteristics is triggered, like those of: fantasy; curiosity; rules/goals; control; and as partial but equally important those of interaction (piloting, choosing objects etc); realism (graphics, sound); and the video game's environment. The activation of such educational characteristics can be realized through integrating those video games' factures in a certain educational framework [21]. As a result, the elements that have been chosen are consistent with basic principles of the constructive learning theory, the educational methods of experiential and discovering learning and those which have the ability to engage and motivate the learner. In addition, the elements that have been chosen can be addressed in a 3D VE.

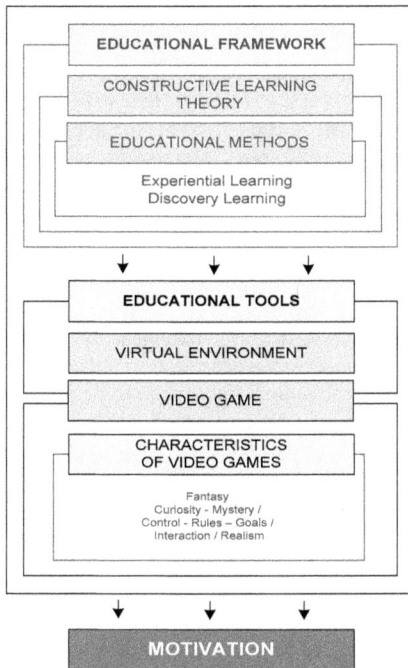

Figure 1 The structure of the theoretical framework for the reinforcement of learning by initiating motivation.

3. VRLerna case study

The basic elements of the theoretical framework stated earlier (see Section 2) have been applied in the "VRLerna" pilot application. The VRLerna pilot is an interactive 3D VE with educational goals and the basic characteristics of a video game.

This project is based on the reconstruction of the "House of Tiles" in Lerna, an archaeological site with a particularly long history, reflected in the Greek mythological tradition. The edifice is dated in the Early Helladic Period (3000- 2000 b.C.) [11]. One of the reasons for choosing this site for reconstruction is the presence of thorough archaeological publication related to it, which provides the required data for its reconstruction. Another reason for choosing to work around this site is that it can help to cover the great economic and social changes which led to the development of the hierarchic society in the Early Helladic Period, a subject of great importance which however, it is not covered by the Greek history curriculum. Last but not least, the building itself is of immense importance due to its impressive dimensions, its elaborate construction and its rare architectural type [23] (what is most important is its function, as it has been considered by many scholars as the house of certain members of the local elite, a community center, a center for exchanging commodities, or a site for the redistribution of community wealth) [65].

The main educational goal of the current project is to teach certain aspects of the ancient Greek history in the secondary education using methods that reinforce structure and facilitate learning. More specifically, the current project aims at presenting elements that are not covered in the ordinary teaching process. Moreover, it is believed to assist the students to have a first acquaintance with the Early Helladic Period in the Greek mainland in order to acquire basic skills in making interpretations about the period and associating it with latter social developments.

The structure of VRLerna consists of three different levels: the operational level; the multimedia level and the VR level. During the execution of basic functions using VRLearna those three levels either interact with each other, or they function separately. The operational level is the "brain" of the system, defining how and when the two other levels will function. The most important element of the operational level is a data base. This data base manages user actions (a table where the actions of the user and his answers to the knowledge questions are being stored), objects (a table where the objects – archaeological finds that are chosen and observed by the user are being stored) and VE (where the route followed by the user is being stored). The multimedia level consists of the application graphics, as well as applications that store instructions for the game, explanations about the game's goals, information about the historical background of the "House of Tiles", and user feedback according to their actions are presented. The VR level consists of all the VEs and 3D objects of VRLerna.

The implementation of VRLerna consists of the 3D reconstruction of the "House of Tiles", the application interface and finally the unification of all the structural elements in a common interactional environment. The 3D reconstruction was a rather difficult and time consuming process, as a thorough study of the bibliography (the publication, articles, previous reconstructions and photos of the archaeological site and its artifacts) was required. For building the three dimensional models a 3D modeling software has been used (3D Studio MAX of Autodesk). For programming the basic interactions of the VE (navigation in the VE, basic interaction in the VE and objects in it) Virtual Reality Modelling Language (VRML) has been used. Adobe Photoshop and Flash software were used for creation two dimensional graphics and presenting the informative material respectively. Finally, for bringing all the elements together in a unified interactive environment HTML, PHP and mysql programming languages have been used.

Figure 2. 3D recreation of the "House of Tiles" in Lerna, Argolis dated in the Early Helladic Period (3000- 2000 b.C.)

VRLerna has been designed and implemented addressing the principles of the constructive learning theory. The learners take active part in the educational process as they explore the rooms of the House of Tiles, discovering archaeological findings and obtaining new knowledge. The learners interact almost naturally with the environment in a way which simulates everyday activities. As a result, knowledge for the life in this specific historical period is obtained through their own experiences and not through narratives and descriptions [67].

The experience of interaction with the VRLerna application incorporates elements which trigger the imagination and the curiosity, enhance the mystery atmosphere and have the potential to keep the learners focused and interested. The realistic VE is rather satisfying as it offers the ability to get oriented in the space and adjust to it. The interaction (navigation, choosing and manipulating objects) was designed on well known forms/ frames so that the user would not be disorientated.

The 3D recreation of the space offers new potential of visualisation and interaction with the educational material by using basic pedagogical principles [8].

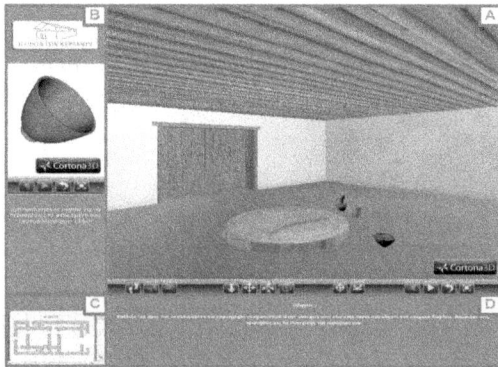

Figure 3. Snapshot of the basic interface of VRLerna. The interface consists of the four following areas: (a) depicts the 3D reconstruction of the environment; (b) is a window that allows the user to view a selected object closer ; (c) is a top view of the reconstruction that shows the current position of the user; and (d) is a dialog box were basic directions to the user are provided.

Realism (geometrical models, textures and lighting) is rather satisfying as it offers the ability to get oriented in the VE and get adjusted to it.

Navigation in the VE has been designed to assist the users not to get disoriented and remain focused on the important activities taking place in the VE [14] [19]. It adopts the natural movement of walking, one of the most efficient movements in VE, as it simulates a user's everyday life experience [61]. The user viewpoint follows the self-centred frame, according to which the user observes the space in a way similar to the one they do in real world. The navigation as well as the interaction with objects in the VE takes place by using the mouse and the direction arrows of the keyboard. It is an interaction which is based on the users' previous knowledge and so it facilitates their orientation in the VE [47].

The navigation in the application triggers the learners' imagination. The learners come in touch with the past which is not part of their conventional everyday life and cannot be approached otherwise. Previous researches claim that the incorporation of imagination elements in the educational environment can cause greater interest and advanced learning outcome [13] [51].

When entering the VE a dialogue box appears which informs the learners about the game's basic goal which is tracing archaeological finds and the ways to achieve this. Next, a short presentation enriched with text, diagrams and photos provides information about the historical period the settlement and the building. The information is clear, simple and without lengthy details. The clear presentation of the goals and the rules before

engaging with the game's activities contributes in motivating the learner. Related research has shown that sparing information [40], surprise, unexpected outcomes [6] and the inability to predict future developments [30], enhance the sense of mystery. As mystery elements can be considered the incorporation of activities in a context that enforces imagination [4], the quest for archaeological finds and the exploring of unfamiliar spaces of the building. Also, Malone and Lepper [40] consider that mystery triggers curiosity which is one of the main factors that lead to learning.

The learners have to explore and access all the levels of the game (one in the house yard, six in the basement and one on the floor). In each one of them they can see various artefacts which are three dimensional reconstructions of archaeological finds from the Lerna excavations. The learners are called to trace those (using the game instructions). By selecting an artifact in the VE, a 3D reconstruction of it appears in a separate window at the left side of the screen, where it can be rotated and observed closer (see figure 3). This feature is very important, as according to the constructivist learning theory, the ability to observe an object under many and different sights contribute to making an issue simpler and easier to understand [29].

In order to move to the next level the learners have to complete a quiz assessing their knowledge gained by playing the game (see Figure 4). The quiz questions concern the relevant level of the game. The quiz questions are of increasing difficulty in order to enhance motivation and learner's performance [39]. Malone and Lepper [40] claim that players are challenged by quizzes of medium difficulty. In those cases where the difficulty level is either too low or too high according to the learners' abilities, the player/learner's interest is getting lost soon enough and any effort is being abandoned respectively [52]. After the learners have gone through the knowledge assessment quiz they receive feedback about their achievement. If the users answer a question correctly they continue to the next level. If they fail answering correctly they have the chance to try again. User feedback during the game motivates and prompts them to readjust their behavior according to their performance [32]. During the exploration process the system assists the learners by providing short instructions regarding the directions they have to follow and the action they have to take every time.

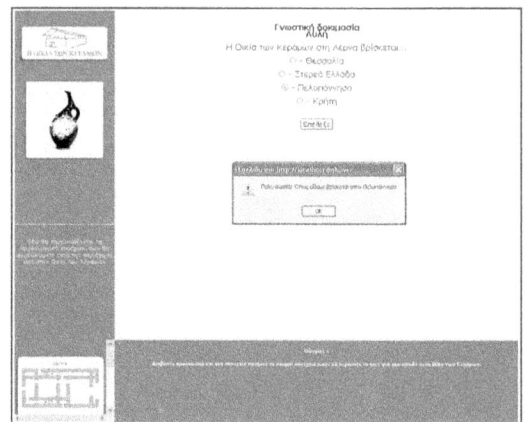

Figure 4. A snapshot of the quiz the learners have to complete after they have navigated through a level of the VRLerna game and they have gone through the objects contained in it.

In order for the application to function a PC is required with a minimum 2GHz processor, a 1GB RAM memory, and a 1024x768 screen analysis. As to the required software a network explorer must be available (Mozilla Firefox 2.0 or latter, Internet Explorer 5.5 or later, Netscape Navigator 6.0 or later) which can support the HTML 4.0 and CSS models. It is also considered necessary to have installed programs that allow the projection of VRML (wrl) and Adobe Flash (swf) files.

4. EVALUATION

The VRLerna pilot application was evaluated in order to:

- assess its efficiency as a learning tool

- examine its dynamics to motivate the learner

- study the effectiveness of the theoretical framework.

The evaluation took place among students of the 3rd high school grade class (Key Stage 5 students, 16–18 years old) in a small town in central Greece. The particular class has been chosen based on the fact that in the past they have been involved in activities related to Early Helladic Period. Seventeen students aged 14-15 years old, eight of which were girls and nine boys took place at the study. The sample size was determined by the number of the students in the 3rd grade class.

During the preliminary stage of the evaluation the principle and all the involved teachers and students were contacted and informed about the aims and the goals of the research in order to obtain their active participation and provide assurance of the confidentiality of the personal data.

The method chosen for the evaluation of the educational efficiency of the interventionist method (interaction with the pilot application) is that of the pre and post-test. According to this the data collected assessing the students' knowledge before and after their interaction with the educational application is compared.

The evaluation study took place in two phases. The first one took place inside the ordinary school class where a twenty five minutes lecture was given covering themes related to the historical topic dealt with at the VRLerna pilot, followed by a discussion. Next, the students had to complete a questionnaire or the pre-test, which apart from specifying the sex it comprised of ten "closed" statistical questions. Seven of those were related to the educational content of the application and aimed to explore the students' previous knowledge. The other three concerned the learners' attitude towards personal computers, their experience with using them as educational aids and their familiarisation with video games. It should be noted that in order to ensure anonymity and be able to compare results in pre-test and post-test, no names were used, instead a unique number – code for each questionnaire was used.

In the second phase of the study the students interacted with VRLerna in the school's computer lab. The students shared one PC in pairs. At the beginning the students were asked to use an experimental 3D VE, which gave them the ability to get familiar with navigating in a VE. Before entering the VRLerna the students had the chance to interact with an educational multimedia application that covered the theory they have been taught during the first phase of the study. Next, the students were left alone to interact with VRLerna for a typical teaching hour (forty-five minutes). The main activities to take place were given to the

students by the system. The researchers supervised the process and interfered to resolve problems, mostly technical ones.

After the end of the interaction with VRLerna the students were asked to complete a post-test questionnaire, that was also anonymous and the relation with the pre-test questionnaire was ensured with the aforementioned unique code. The post-test questionnaire consisted of two parts. The first part similarly with the pre-test questionnaire consisted of seven multiple choice questions assessing the learning outcome. The second part consisted of 19 questions (16 "closed ones" and 3 "open") that targeted at ascertaining directly and in-directly if the application managed to keep the students motivated throughout the interaction with it. More specifically, the questions chosen aimed in finding out if the specifications laid by the structural elements of the theoretical framework caused the expected learning results (motivation, learning reinforcement).

The main keystones of the study revolve around the pedagogical framework and the educational tools. As a result, the questionnaire comprises questions aimed at extracting knowledge related to the application features to support imagination, the sense of mystery and curiosity, the way that the game's goals and rules are presented to the learner, the efficiency of interaction between the learner and the system and elements that enhance realism in the VE. Also, there were questions assessing the constructive approach the application adopted for presenting educational material, as well as those application features to motivate the students and how this affected the learning outcome. The questionnaire includes also some open questions allowing the students to express their likes and dislikes and what they would like to see being added to the application.

5. RESULTS

This section presents the evaluation results of the study described above (see Section 4) are presented. Figure 5 below presents the results that derived from the pre-test and post-test comparison, in relation to the learning potential of the interventionist method that have been used. The results indicate that there has been an impressive change in the number of students that answered correctly after using the pilot application. More specifically, the mean of the correct answers given by the students rose from 7,57 during the pre-test to 13,43 after the post-test. In order to compare the learning performance before and after the interaction with the pilot application the Wilcoxon criterion has been used, which is considered suitable when the sample is small and there are serious doubts about the regularity of the population [66] [68] [69]. The results showed that the raise in the learning efficiency was statistically important (Z=--2,226, p=0,026).

One of the basic aims of the present study is to motivate the learners. Motivation helps retaining the learners' attention and focus until the expected learning goals have been fulfilled [1]. The results that derived from the post-test study showed that the application's environment triggered in a certain degree characteristics such as, the imagination and mystery, which indirectly affected the learner's motivation (Figure 6). More specifically, it appears that when the learning content is characterized by elements of imagination it attracts more the learners, it causes greater interest and it contributes to advanced learning results [13] [51] [1] [52]. Many students that interacted with the application (35%) consider that the environment contributed much or very much in triggering their imagination.

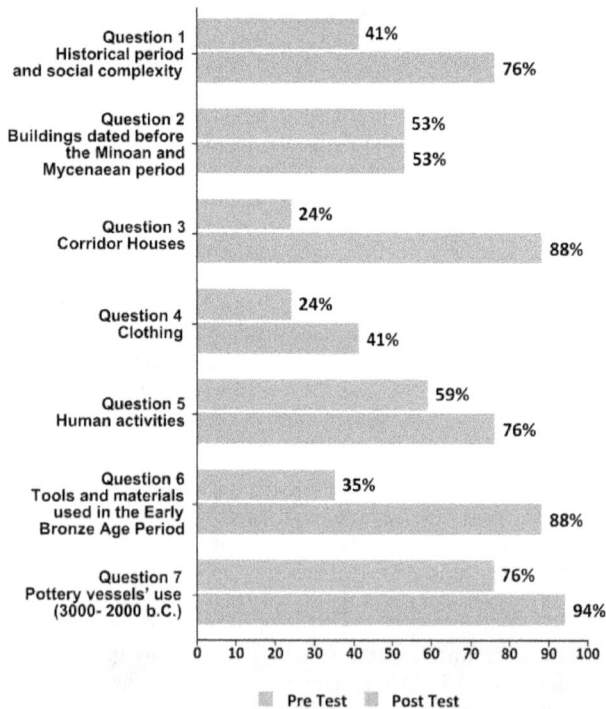

Figure 5. A comparison of the percentage of students' correct answers on topics that have been covered during pre and post-test

However, taking in mind the percentage of those who answered little (48%) and not at all (18%), it is considered that further activities that trigger the learners' imagination should be included. As to the elements of mystery and curiosity, Malone and Lepper [40], suggest that they can become important factors in assisting learning, if they are included in the learning process. The answers of the students during the evaluation prove that the above characteristic exists in VRLerna in some degree, as the 47% of the sample mentioned that the game's action created a mysterious atmosphere that generates curiosity. At this point, it should be mentioned that the due to their subjective nature imagination and mystery are difficult to be measured and lead to objective conclusions.

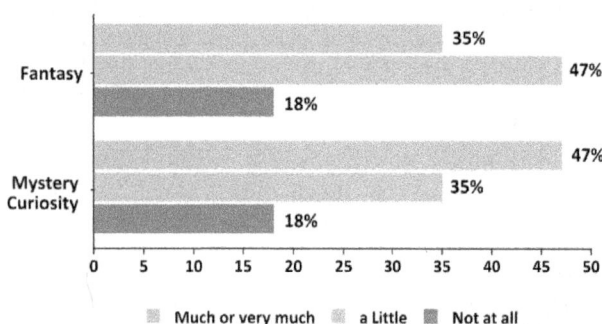

Figure 6. The graph depicts the students' response assessing how much the VRLerna environments stimulated their fantasy – mystery/curiosity.

Significant are the results regarding stimulating motivation, like attracting the learners' interest and entertainment (see Figure 7). The evaluation results showed that 64% of the students found the experience of interacting with the pilot application as very, or extremely interesting. This result is very important since related bibliography mentions that interest, motivation and learning are directly connected [15] [50] [4] [63].

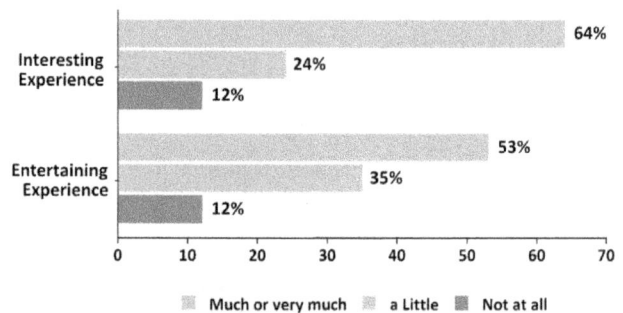

Figure 7. The graph depicts the students' response assessing if they found the VRLerna game interesting and entertaining.

Also, the entertaining factor of video games is of major importance since its existence or absence is directly linked with learners' engagement and consequently their motivation [25] [60] [13] [2] [54]. Malone [41] consents with this opinion and suggests that successful educational games are entertaining and as a result motivating. The results showed that 53% of the students considered that their experience interacting with the educational VE was very, or extremely entertaining.

Finally, the results regarding the reinforcement of the learning outcome (see Figure 8) showed that 59% of the students using VRLerna considered it contributed much or very much in understanding the educational content and more specifically the prehistoric period in Greece. Results showed that the ability to present an artifact in a different window and providing the opportunity to rotate and manipulate it was very helpful. This way of presentation and interaction with objects follows one of the basic principles of the constructivist theory, according to which an object observation via different viewpoints contributes to simplification and easiest appreciation of it [28]. The above opinion is being confirmed by the research results according to which the 64% of the students considered that this ability contributed much, or very much to the careful observation of the archaeological finds.

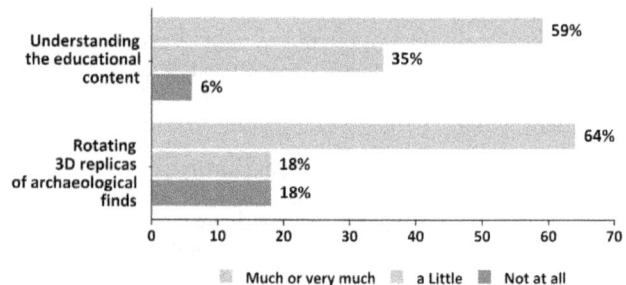

Figure 8. The graph depicts of the students' response assessing if the use of VRLerna environment contributed to their understanding of the educational content and how helpful they found the feature of having a closer look and rotation an object.

6. CONCLUSIONS

The previous sections presented the design, the realisation and the evaluation of the pilot application VRLerna. It is an interactive 3D VE which holds the main characteristics of a video game. Its educational content aims to facilitate the teaching of historical/ archaeological issues and it addresses to Secondary Education students (high school). The application's realisation follows a series of specifications which are part of a theoretical framework which aims at stimulating motivation and improving the learning efficiency. The analysis of the data which were gathered during the evaluation of the application with real users showed that the pilot application contributed in a significant degree in improving the learning efficiency of the students. It was also established that the theoretical framework on which the application is based can trigger the interest, entertain and motivate satisfactorily the learners. Nevertheless, there is a need for further improvements as failings and weaknesses have been noted. More specifically, as it has been realised by answering the questionnaires used at this study, realism should be improved (graphics, textures, sound and lighting) so that the application will approach environments similar to those of popular commercial video games. Finally, secondary factors that contribute to enhance the learners' motivation should be isolated and studied separately, like mystery, and imagination.

7. ACKNOWLEDGMENTS

We would also like to thank the school's principal, the teachers and the students for their excellent cooperation.

8. REFERENCES

[1] Ahdell, R. & Andresen, G. 2001. Games and simulations in workplace elearning: How to align eLearning content with learner needs. Master of Science Thesis, Norwegian University of Science and Technology.

[2] Amory, A., Naicker, K., Vincent, J., and Claudia, A. 1998. Computer Games as a Learning Resource. In Proceedings of ED-MEDIA, ED-TELECOM 98, World Conference on Education Multimedia and Educational Telecommunications. Vol. 1, 50-55.

[3] Aschersonn N. 2000. Editorial, Public Archaeology, 1(1). 2.

[4] Asgari, M., and Kaufman., D. 2004. "Relationships among computer games, fantasy, and learning." 2nd International Conference on Imagination in Education. (Vancouver, Canada, 2004). Retrieved November 30, 2009, from http://www.ierg.net/confs/2004/Proceedings/Asgari_Kaufman.pdf.

[5] BECTA. 2002. British Educational Communications and Technology Agency: http://www.becta.org.uk/research/research.cfm?section=1&id=519

[6] Berlyne, D. E. 1960. Conflict, arousal, and curiosity. New York: McGraw-Hill.

[7] Boyle, T. 1997. Design for Multimedia learning. London, Prentice Hall.

[8] Bricken, M., and Byrne, C. 1993. Summer Students in Virtual Reality: A Pilot Study on Educational Applications of Virtual Reality Technology. In A. Wexelblat (Ed.), Virtual Reality: Applications and Explorations. CA: Academic Press, San Diego, 199-217.

[9] Brody, H. 1993. Video Games that Teach?. Technology Review, 96(8), 51-57.

[10] Brown, D.J., Cobb, S.V. & Eastgate, RM. 1995. Learning in Virtual Environments (LIVE). Virtual Reality Applications, R.A. Earnshaw, J.A. Vince & H. Jones (eds), Academic Press pp. 245-252.

[11] Caskey, J.L. 1968. Lerna in the Early Bronze Age. American Journal of Archaeology.72, 313–316.

[12] Ciavarro, C. 2006. The Design, Development and assessment of an educational sports-acrion video game: implicity changing player behavior. Master Thesis, Simon Fraser University,.

[13] Cordova D. I., and Lepper M. R. 1996. Intrinsic motivation and the process of learning: Beneficial effects of contextualization, personalization, and choice. Journal of Educational Psychology, 88, 715-730.

[14] Darken, R.P., and Sibert J.L. 1996. Wayfinding strategies and behaviours in large virtual worlds. In Proceedings of the CHI '96 conference on Human Factors in Computing Systems (Vancouver, Canada, 1996). New York: Association for Computing Machinery.

[15] Deci, E., and Ryan, M. 1985. Intrinsic motivation and self-determination in human behavior. Plenum, New York.

[16] Dimaraki, E. 2007. Ψηφιακή διαμεσολάβηση της μάθησης για το παρελθόν: σχεδιασμός εφαρμογών για την ενορχήστρωση μαθησιακής δραστηριότητας. In Νικονάνου Ν, Κασβίκης Κ., Εκπαιδευτικά ταξίδια στο χρόνο, Εμπειρίες και ερμηνείες του παρελθόντος, Πατάκης, Αθήνα.

[17] Driscoll, M. P. 1994. Psychology of learning for instruction, Needham Heights, MA: Allyn and Bacon.

[18] Duffy, T.M., and Jonassen D.H. 1992. Constructivism and the technology of instruction. Lawrence Erlbaum Associates Publishers: New Jersey.

[19] Economou, D. 2001. The role of Virtual Actors in Collaborative Virtual Environments for Learning, Ph.D. thesis. Department of Computing and Mathematics, Manchester Metropolitan University, Manchester.

[20] Facer, K. 2003. Computer games and learning. Retrieved 15 December 2009 from Future Lab, innovation in education: http://www2.futurelab.org.uk/resources/documents/discussion_papers/Computer_Games_and_Learning_discpaper.pdf

[21] Garris,R., Ahlers,R., and Driskell,.J.E. 2002. Games, motivation and learning, Simulation and gaming, An Interdisciplinary. Journal of Theory, Practice and Research. 33(4), 441-467.

[22] Gigante, M.A. 1993. Virtual Reality: definitions, history and applications. Virtual Reality Systems, R.A. Earnshaw, M.A. Gigante & H. Jones (eds.), London: Academic Press, ISBN 0-12-22-77-48-1, pp. 3-14.

[23] Hagg, R., and Konsola, D. 1986. Early Helladic architecture and urbanization. In Proceedings of a seminar held the Swedish Institute (Athens, June 8, 1985). SIMA, 76. Goteborg.

[24] Hamilakis, Y. 2004. Archaeology and the politics of pedagogy, World Archaeology, 36(2), 287–309.

[25] Inkpen, K., Upitis, R., Klawe, M., Hsu, D., Leroux, S., Lawry, J., Anderson, A., Ndunda, M., and Sedighian, K. 1994. We Have Never Forgetful Flowers in Our Garden: Girls' Responses to Electronic Games. Journal of Computers in Mathematics and Science Teaching, 13(4), 383-403.

[26] Inkpen, K., Upitis, R., Klawe, M., Hsu, D., Leroux, S., Lawry, J., Anderson, A., Ndunda, M., and Sedighian, K. 1994. We Have Never Forgetful Flowers in Our Garden: Girls' Responses to Electronic Games. Journal of Computers in Mathematics and Science Teaching, 13(4), 383-403.

[27] Jameson, J. 2004. Public Archaeology in the United States. In N. Merriman, Public Archaeology, Routledge, New York, 21- 58.

[28] Jonassen, D. 1994. Thinking technology: Toward a constructivist design model. Journal of Educational Technology, 34 (2), 34-37.

[29] Jonassen, D.H., Campbell, J.P., and Davidson, M.E. 1994. Learning with media: Restructuring the debate. Journal of Educational Technology Research and Development, 39(3), 5-14.

[30] Kagan, J. 1972. Motives and development. Journal of Personality and Social Psychology. 22, 51-66.

[31] Kaur, K. 1998. Designing virtual environments for usability. PhD thesis. Centre for HCI Design, City University London.

[32] Kernan, M. C., and Lord, R. G. 1990. Effects of valence, expectancies, and goal-performance discrepancies in single and multiple goal environments. Journal of Applied Psychology, 75, 194-203.

[33] Kirriemuir, J. 2002. Video gaming, education and digital learning technologies. D-Lib Magazine, 8(2).

[34] Kirriemuir, J., and McFarlane, A. 2004. Literature review in games and learning: A report for NESTA Futurelab, Retrieved 30 November 2009 from Future Lab, innovation in education: http://www.futurelab.org.uk/resources/documents/lit_reviews/Games _Review.pdf

[35] Kissock, J. 1987. Archaeology and its place in the primary school curriculum. Archaeological Review from Cambridge, 6(1987), 119 – 28.

[36] Klawe, M. 1999. Computer games, education and interfaces: The E-GEMS project. In Proceedings of the Graphics Interface 1999 Conference. Ontario, Canada, 36-39.

[37] Laurel, B. 1993. Computers as Theatre, Addison-Wesley.

[38] Liakos, A. 2007. Πως το παρελθόν γίνεται ιστορία;. Πόλις, Αθήνα.

[39] Locke, E. A., and Latham, G. P. 1990. A theory of goal setting and task performance, Englewood Cliffs, NJ: Prentice Hall.

[40] Malone, T. W., and Lepper, M. R. 1987. Making Learning Fun: A Taxonomy of Intrinsic Motivations for Learning. In R. E. Snow and M. J. Farr (Eds.), Aptitute, Learning and Instruction: III. Conative and affective process analyses. Hilsdale, NJ: Erlbaum.

[41] Malone, T.W. 1980. What makes things fun to learn? A study of intrinsically motivating computer games. Palo Alto Research Center, Xerox.

[42] Mantovani, G. 1996. New Communication Environments From Everyday to Virtual, Taylor & Francis.

[43] McLellan, H. 1996. Virtual realities. In D. H. Jonassen (Ed.), Handbook of research for educational communications and technology, Macmillan Library Reference, New York, USA, 457–487.

[44] McLellan, H. 2003. Virtual realities. In D. H. Jonassen and P. Harris (Eds.), Handbook of research for educational communications and technology (2nd ed), Lawrence Erlbaum Associates, New York, USA, 461–498.

[45] McManamon, F. 2000. Public education. A part of archaeological professionalism. In Smardz and Sh. J. Smith (eds.), The archaeology education handbook. Sharing the past with kids, Altamira Press and Society for American archaeology: Walnut Creek, 17-24.

[46] Mitchell, W.L. and Economou, D. 1999. Understanding Context and Medium in the development of Educational Virtual Environments. In Proceedings of the Workshop on User Centered Design and Implementation of Virtual Environments, University of York, 109-115.

[47] Neale, D. C., and Carroll, J. M. 1997. The role of metaphors in user interface design. In Helander, M. G., Landauer, T. K., and Prabhu, P., editors, Handbook of Human-Computer Interaction, 2nd edition. Elsevier Science.

[48] Pantelidis, V. S. 1991–2007. Virtual reality and education: Information sources; a bibliography. Retrieved November 10, 2007, from Virtual Reality and Education Laboratory, Department of Library Science
College of Education, East Carolina University, Greenville, NC USA: http://vr.coe.ecu.edu/vpbib.Html

[49] Pantelidis, V. S. 1995. Reasons to use virtual reality in education. VR in the Schools, 1(1), 9. Retrieved September 29, 2007, from Virtual Reality and Education Laboratory, Department of Library Science
College of Education, East Carolina University, Greenville, NC USA: http://vr.coe.ecu.edu/reas.html

[50] Papert, S. 1993. The Children's Machine: Rethinking School in the Age of the Computers. Basic Books, New York.

[51] Parker, L. E., and Lepper, M. R. 1992. Effects of fantasy context on children's learning and motivation: Making learning more fun. Journal of Personality and Social Psychology, 62, 625-633.

[52] Pivec, M., Dziabenko, O., and Schinnerl, I. 2003. Aspects of game-based learning. In Proceedings of International Conference on Knowledge Management (Austria, Gratz, July 2-4, 2003). I-KNOW '03. 216-225.

[53] Prensky, M. 2000. Digital Game-Based Learning. New York, McGraw Hill.

[54] Prensky, M. 2002. The motivation of gameplay. On the Horizon, 10(1).

[55] Rogers, A. 1999. Η εκπαίδευση ενηλίκων. Μεταίχμιο, Αθήνα.

[56] Salomon, G., Perkins, D., and Globerson, T. 1991. Partners in cognition: Extending human intelligence with intelligent technologies. Educational Researcher.

[57] Sanders, D.H. 2000. Archaeological publication using virtual reality: case studies and cavets. Virtual Reality in Archaeology, J.A. Barcelo, M. Forte and D. Sanders (eds.), ArchaeoPress, Oxford, 2000, (British Archaeological Reports International Series S843 2000), ISBN: 1 84171 047 4, pp. 37-46.

[58] Scardamalia, M., Bereiter, C., McLean. R.S., Swallow, J., and Woodruff, E. 1989. Computer-supported intentional learning environments. Journal of Educational Computing Research, 5(1), 51-68.

[59] Schadla-Hall, T. 1999. Editorial: Public Archaeology. European Journal of Archaeology., 2(2), 47-158.

[60] Sedighian, K. 1997. Challenge-Driven Learning: A Model for Children's Multimedia Mathematics Learning Environments. Conference of Educational Multimedia and Hypermedia and Educational Telecommunications, 1997, Calgary, Canada.

[61] Slater, M., and Wilbur, S. 1995. Through the looking glass world of presence: FIVE: a Framework for Immersive Virtual Environments. In Proceedings of FIVE '95: Framework for Immersive Virtual Environments. (London, 1995). University of London.

[62] Smith, K.C. 1991. At Last a Meeting of the Minds. Archaeology, 50(1), 36-46, 80.

[63] Virvou, M., Katsionis, G., and Manos, K. 2005. Combining Software Games with Education: Evaluation of its Educational Effectiveness. Educational Technology and Society. Journal of International Forum of Educational Technology and Society and IEEE Learning Technology Task Force, 8(2).

[64] Virvou, M., Manos, K., Katsionis, G., and Tourtoglou, K. 2002. Incorporating the Culture of Virtual Reality Games into Educational Software via an Authoring Tool. In Proceedings of the IEEE International Conference on Systems, Man and Cybernetics (SMC 2002), Tunisia, 422-428.

[65] Weiberg, E. 2007. Thinking the Bronze Age, Life and Death in Early Helladic Greece, Uppsala Univertitet.

[66] Wilcoxon, F. 1945. Individual Comparisons by ranking methods. Journal of Biometrics Bulletin, 1(6), 80-83.

[67] Winn, W., 1993. A conceptual basis for educational applications of virtual reality. Retrieved 10 February 2010 from Human Interface Technology Laboratory: http://www.hitl.washington.edu/publications/r-93-9/.

[68] Youngblut, C. 1998. Educational uses of virtual reality technology. Alexandria, A: Institute for Defense Analyses.

[69] Γιαλαμάς, Β. 2005. Στατιστικές τεχνικές και εφαρμογές στις επιστήμες της αγωγής. Εκδόσεις Πατάκη, Αθήνα.

[70] Ρούσσας, Γ. 1994. Στατιστική συμπερασματολογία: Έλεγχος υποθέσεων. Εκδόσεις Ζήτη, Θεσσαλονίκη.

Game Description Language and Frameworks for Langrid Gaming

Itaru Suziki, Keisuke Tsunoda *, Reiko Hishiyama
Graduate School of Creative Science and Engineering, Waseda University
3-4-1 Okubo, Shinjuku-Ku, Tokyo, Japan.
{ itaru-suzuki@asagi., 93489410@toki., reiko@ }waseda.jp

ABSTRACT

Langrid Gaming, which provides multilingual communication for gaming simulations using translation services provided on the Language Grid, is a useful educational tool and can contribute to the resolution of international social conflicts. This tool has been enhanced on the basis of the experience and know-how obtained from the participants' comments and suggestions.

However, the object and the model object of the gaming tool are usually defined as Java or PHP objects, which makes it difficult for non-programmers to develop a new game. In this study, we propose a framework to implement various types of Langrid Gaming easily. In particular, we designed a new domain specific language (DSL) called 'Karina' to describe targeted games, and implemented a translator to convert Karina script into CGI programs. This script development environment makes game building easy and simplifies the development procedures, regardless of whether the gaming developer is a programmer or not.

Categories and Subject Descriptors

H.5.3 [**Group and Organization Interface**]: Computer-supported cooperative work. Synchronous interaction

General Terms

Design, Experimentation, Human Factors, Languages

Keywords

Intercultural Collaboration, Language Grid, Gaming Simulation

1. BACKGROUND AND MOTIVATION

Nowadays, gaming simulations are widely used for educational purposes in place of lecture-style approaches as a

---

*He now works at Nippon Telegraph and Telephone Corporation (NTT).

formal teaching style in classrooms. Compared to the traditional lecture or tutorial method for teaching students, the benefit of using the gaming simulation is that the participants in gaming simulations can learn through observing the simulated environment and have a vivid sense of reality by making their decisions and monitoring results of their decisions as the game progresses. Gaming simulations are especially powerful tools when we want to think through intercultural or international issues because the game is a universal activity.

Among them, Langrid Gaming, which provides multilingual communication for gaming simulations using translation services provided on the Language Grid, is useful for intercultural communication because it can help users communicate effectively by using their mother tongues (MT) or the languages they know best to successfully support their collaboration by overcoming the mistranslations of machine translation.

On the other hand, gaming users expect game designers to provide various types of games for their intercultural education using Langrid Gaming not only in schools but also in social educational institutions such as community centers or recreation centers. If we can provide tools to make game building as simple as possible, users will be able to design and provide their own games in accordance with their own needs and circumstances. Therefore, we aim to design and develop easy-to-use game design tools for Langrid Gaming users who want to develop original games by themselves.

Previous works include lots of frameworks on the Web with which programmers can easily make Langrid Gamings. However, since most frameworks are designed for programmers, they are not easy for non-programmers to use. Furthermore, the people who are Langrid Gaming users, for example, teachers and researchers interested in intercultural problems, are not expected to be good at programming. Developing educational materials using Langrid Gaming is difficult for them because almost none of them can write programs to run on a computer. In this study, we propose a framework that makes it easy for non-programmers to implement a game using Langrid Gaming. We made a new description language to describe a Langrid Gaming scenario that is easy to understand even for non-programmer and made a translator that translates the scenario into an "implementation", which is a program running on a computer as game using Langrid Gaming.

2. RELATED WORKS

Gaming is a "Future Language," a new form of communication emerging suddenly and with great impact across many countries and in many problem situations [6]. Gaming approaches have been successfully used in education, business, training, and intercultural collaboration.

For multilingual communication, Ishida [8] proposed a base network named 'Language Grid' to align language services on the Internet. Language Grid is an online multilingual service platform that enables easy registration and sharing of language services such as online dictionaries, bilingual corpora, and machine translations. This service platform is providing 106 language services as of Feb, 2011 and makes multilingual web services easy to construct.

Tsunoda and Hishiyama [4] implemented an international food problems game on the Language Grid and showed it achieves intercultural collaboration and communication. In this study, participants could overcome mistranslations of machine translator because they shared the rules of the game. They could fathom thoughts of other participants on the basis on these rules. It has become obvious that gaming simulations can be used as backgrounds to understand each other in intercultural communications.

Simplifying the overwhelming complexity of human interaction to enable human minds to begin to understand it is, in fact, the whole challenge of social sciences, and computerized simulation is a highly useful tool with which to take on this challenge [2].

Greenblat [1] proposed a framework to design games for education. She says that designers should extract elements essential for education from complex simulations and assign felicitous symbols to elements in order to give participants the intended experience.

To design the computer games and simulations, some frameworks has been designed and developed. Spot Oriented Agent Role Simulator (SOARS), which is a spot oriented agent role simulator proposed by Tanuma et al. [3], is a new agent-based simulation language that requires no language programming skills. This simulation language is designed for everyone who does not have any specialist skills in computer science. This platform also supports making web-based gaming simulations. To make the simulation on the SOARS platform, game designers must write action rules for agents. Humans can switch positions with agents. Designers can make an interface to prompt humans to input their decisions. However, games made using this framework are not expected to run alone or be extended by external programs.

Ishida [7] proposes scenario description language 'Q', which is a language for designing interaction scenarios among agents and human communities. These scenarios focus on the protocols between agents and humans for their social interactions. The languages proposed for describing agents have been based on agents' internal mechanisms. On the other hand, Q is a language between agents and humans based on agents' external roles. However, in the process of designing, three kinds of designers (application designer, interaction designer, and agent designer) are required interact to conduct the simulation. Among them, only agent designer is expected to be a computing professional. The application designers can write the agents' interaction rules without specialist computer science knowledge because it is easy to write the rules using the scenario description language 'Q'. However, they cannot implement their game directly without the aid of agent designers.

3. APPROACH

Our challenge is to ensure that a person without specialist skills in computer programming can design and implement the gaming simulation easily. To this end, we developed a new domain specific language (DSL) called 'Karina' to describe targeted games and implemented a translator, which converts Karina script description files into CGI execution programs. The translator automatically generates applications that the user can play as a gaming simulation. This enables non-programmers to develop gaming tools on Langrid Gamings by themselves and provides the capability to improve/modify the games if needed. In the current gaming tool development process in Langrid Gaming, we need specific frameworks or software. To realize the proposed frameworks, we designed versatile functions and forms for games to be designed on Langrid Gaming. This framework, Karina, and its gaming code, and user interface (UI) generator, can perform as an automatic coding system, freeing both programmers and non-programmers from many time-consuming tasks.

The Framework has three main steps. In the first step, we developed the common architecture of the Langrid Gamings that explains the Langrid Gamings by a board game analogy. It is believed that our proposed architecture is easy for non-programmers to understand because the platform is independent of the gaming implementation and that game designers are likely to be familiar with board games.

In the second step, we designed and produced the language on the basis of this architecture. We designed so that the programming language is as simple and easy to understand as the architecture. A function in Langrid Gamings is a declarative description of a component in the common architecture. Here, we call a description about a game in that language a 'Scenario'.

In the final step, we made a translator to translate scenarios into web applications automatically. It enables non-programmers to implement Langrid Gaming without specialist knowledge about computers, networks, or programming languages.

4. COMMON ARCHITECTURE

4.1 The overall architecture

Different kinds of gaming simulations do not share one style. Therefore, in this study, we focus on versatile games that fulfill the below requirements:

- Games that simulate the real world numerically.

- Only participants' actions can change the environment. Their possible actions are defined in the rules of game.

- Educational effect of games on participants is independent of implementation. In other words, the people who play the games, whether the game is implemented as a table game or a computer game, can obtain the full educational benefit.

The user analyzes the target game and extracts information on functional components from it. Then the user divides these components into the following three categories:

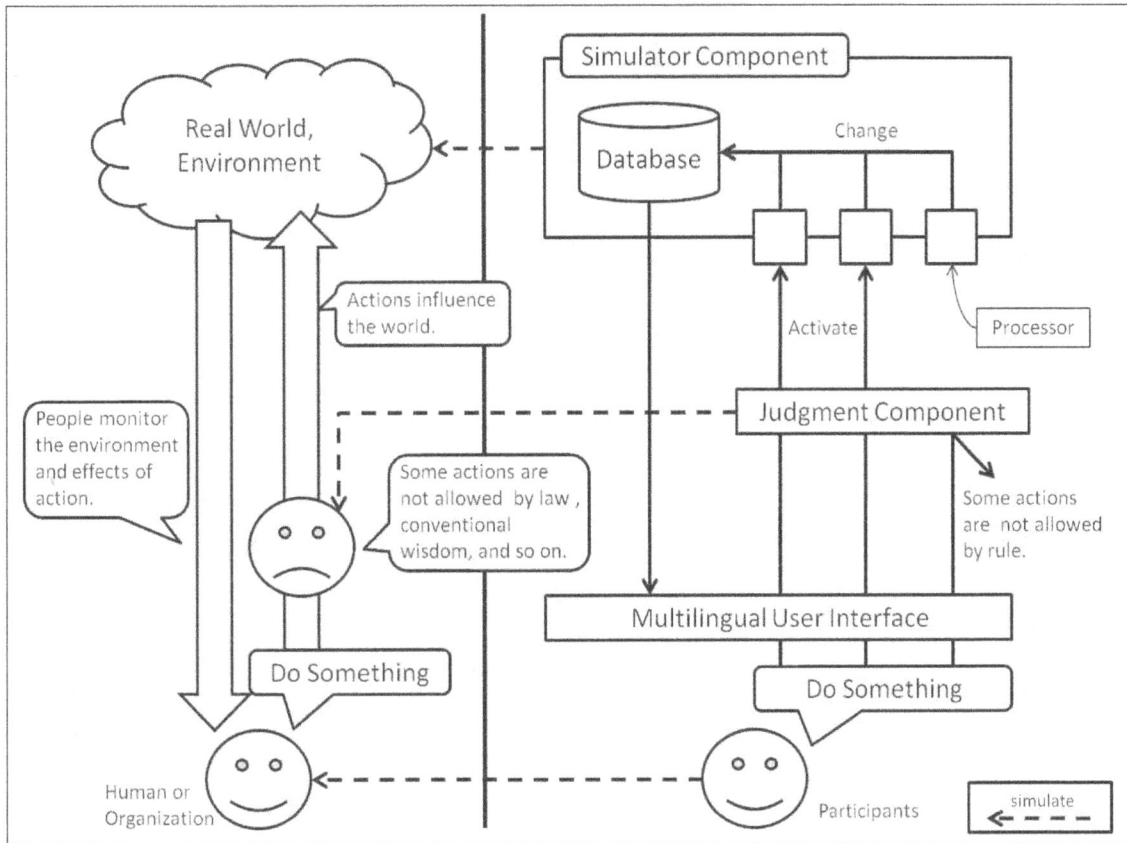

Figure 1: The common architecture

simulator components that simulate the real environment, multilingual interface components that show circumstances of the game to participants, and judgment components that tell participants what actions are possible. A simulator component is subdivided into two sub-components: a database that stores the game data about the environment and an interface that updates it. Figure 1 shows our proposed architecture for target games, which is the processing flow of gaming interaction.

4.2 The operator: judgment function

The Operator takes the judgment role in the game using his judgment function. He tells participants what action the user will be able to take in the user's situation. Then he continues to wait until someone (one of the users) makes the decision. If that decision follows the rules, he starts up the Processors. We explain the function of the Processor below.

4.3 Cards

All possible actions are represented using cards in this architecture. A card contains the name and the caption of the action and some blanks. A participant fills in blanks and plays to declare his/her decision or action. Figure 2 shows an example of a card.

The operator tells participants possible actions and deals cards corresponding to them and then collects cards corresponding to impossible actions from participants.

4.4 Processors

Processors provide an interface to update the database,

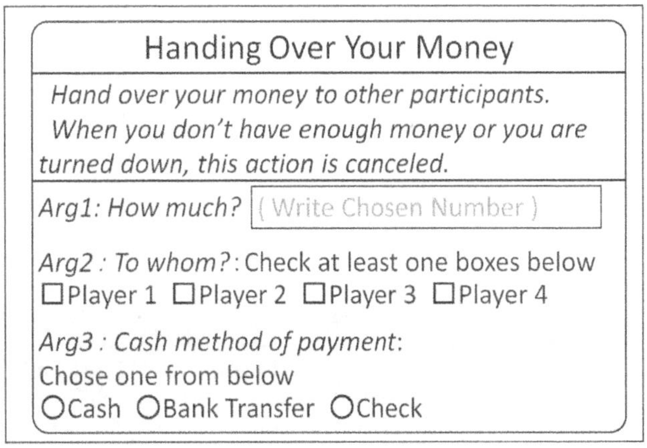

Figure 2: Card Example

but participants cannot access interfaces directly. Only the operator can access them. Thus, they pass cards to ask the operator to activate processors.

After the operator receives a card, he starts up the corresponding processors in accordance with the rules. The operator knows who plays that card. Sometimes he use that information. For example, 'Player A' plays a card shown in Figure 2, with the space next to 'how much' filled in with '$10' and the "Player B" box under 'to whom' ticked and the "Cash" circle under 'Method of payment' marked, then the operator starts up 'Add' processor with arguments: 'Player

B money', '10' and 'Sub' processor with arguments: 'Player A money', '10'.

In this study, we prepared the following three processors: 'Add', 'Sub', and 'Set'. Obviously any other processors can be added as a predicate argument.

4.5 The multilingual user interface

The multilingual user interface shows the participants the gaming parameter and its values in their native language and translates other participants' remarks during the progress of the gaming. This provides users the ability to communicate with others by chatting in their mother tongue within the real-time, dynamic online communication environment. In this study, therefore, we suppose that the participants communicate through multilingual chatting.

4.6 Steps of the Game

Using this common architecture, which we have previously outlined, the gaming has the following seven steps. That is, by following these seven steps, we can conduct the gaming.

1. The Operator initializes the database

2. The interface shows participants circumstances of the game

3. The Operator deals cards to participants

4. A participant plays a card

5. The Operator start up corresponding processors

6. Processors updates the database

7. Game returns to Step 2 unless it is over

5. SCENARIO DESCRIPTION LANGUAGE 'KARINA'

To describe a game that is based on the common architecture, we propose a new scenario description language codenamed 'Karina'. Karina is a small procedural language similar to the programming language Pascal. It provides a control structure with value parameters to define the gaming functions. The gaming procedure (here called a 'scenario') written in Karina is divided into three parts: (1) a default part written about the database initialization, (2) a card part written about all possible actions and cards for participants, and (3) a scene part written about the rule defining when and which actions become possible. A structure of the scenario is illustrated in figure 3.

We will explain how to write scenarios with an example scenario "The Tragedy of the Commons". In this game, participants play managers of a factories. They must decide which they will install a purification unit on their factory or not. Without that unit, participants' factories pollute the nearby river. All participants must pay the cost to purify that river.

Purification cost is smaller than installation cost until all factories start to pollute the river. Participants can cut the installation cost if other participants install units. But if all participants think the same way, they must pay highest cost.

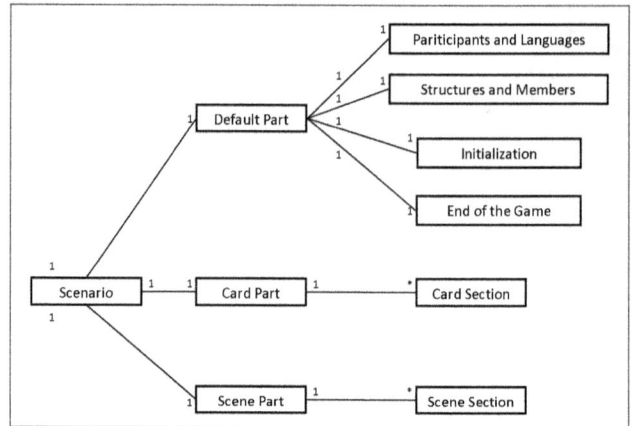

Figure 3: Structure of Scenario

5.1 Multilingual description

All captions and messages in a senario must be written in English. They are translated by machine translation services on the Language Grid when the scenario is translated to executable format.

Oh the other hand, conversations among players on the Web chat are are translated in real time. Participants can use their chosen languages.

5.2 Default part

The default part is subdivided into the following four sections: Participants and Languages, Structures and Members, Initialization, and End of the Game.

An example in Figure 4 shows syntax of the default part. And Figure 5 show how that script initializes the database.

"Participants and Languages" is a section to write list of names of participants and languages they use. Messages in the game are translated to languages written here.

In the "Structures and Members" section, designers define structures. It is similar to structures in C language or records in Pascal. A structure is a collection of variables under a single name. Variables of a structure are called 'members of a structure'. Designers describe names of structures, members, and their default values.

In the "Initialization" section, parameters and their default values are defined. Parameter values of the game should be a numerical number, a string, a list of them, or a structure. When a structure is set in a parameter, it is possible to give new values to its members. If not, its members are initialized by default values.

In the "End of the Game" section, some conditions are described that refer to the parameters of the gaming environment. Once any of the conditions are met, the game is over.

5.3 Card part

The card part is a set of card sections. A card section contains the name of the card, its caption, some blank definitions, and a script describing how to call processors.

A blank definition contains a name next to the blank and says how to fill in the blank. There are three methods to fill in the blanks: input, check, and radio. Blanks next to the input-method are filled in with a chosen number. Blanks next to the check-method are filled in with a list of num-

```
// this is a comment
Participants-and-Languages
  FactoryManagerA  ja;
  FactoryManagerB  en;
  FactoryManagerC  zh;
  FactoryManagerD  fr;
end


Structures-and-Members
  Player
    strategy = "Not yet";
    cost = 0;
  end
end


Initialization
  Turn = 1;
  RiverPollutation = 0;

  FactoryManagerA = new Player;
  FactoryManagerB = new Player;
  FactoryManagerC = new Player;
  FactoryManagerD = new Player;
end

Game-Over
  When(Turn > 10);
end
```

Figure 4: An Example of Default Section

Parameter		Value
Turn		1
RiverPollutation		0
FactoryManagerA	strategy	"Not yet"
	cost	0
FactoryManagerB	strategy	"Not yet"
	cost	0
FactoryManagerC	strategy	"Not yet"
	cost	0
FactoryManagerD	strategy	"Not yet"
	cost	0

Figure 5: Initialized Database

```
defcard MakeStrategicDecision
  Caption:
    "You must make a strategic decision."
    "Will you install a clarify unit?"

  strategy = radio([ "Install the Unit"
                   , "Pollute the River"]);

  player.strategy = decision;
  if decision == "Pollute the River" then
    P.add(RiverPollution, 1);
  end
end
```

Figure 6: An Example of Card Part

```
defscene CostPaymentPhase
  Caption:
    "All participants made decision.""
    "Now you must pay cost"
    "for installation and clearification."

  for pl in [ FactoryManagerA, FactoryManagerB
            , FactoryManagerC, FactoryManagerD ]:
    if num_of_played(PayCost, pl) < 1 then
      deal(pl, PayCost);
    end
  end

  next_scene_if num_of_played(PayCost) >= 4
  then
    next_scene_is(MakeDecisionPhase);
  else
    next_scene_is(CostPaymentPhase);
  end
end
```

Figure 7: An Example of Scene Part

bers or strings. Participants select one or more numbers or strings from alternatives. Blanks next to the radio-method are filled in with a number or string. Participants select one number or string from alternatives.

The script of a card contains processer-calling statements and control statements representing conditional branching and iteration. The operator calls processors on the basis of that script.

The example in Figure 6 shows syntax of a card part. Participants play this card to show their strategy. When they play this card, they must fill the blank named "strategy" by choosing one strategy from two alternatives: "Install the Unit" or "Pollute the River". Operator write player's strategy on the database. And if "Pollute the River" is selected, Operator raises the pollution level

5.4 Scene part

'Scene' provides the games' states. Rules about dealing cards and scene transition are bound to a scene. When a participant plays a card, the scene transfers to another scene after the database is updated. The scene also has a

name and a caption, which are displayed properly in the user interface and show participants circumstances of the game with parameters.

For example, in a game simulating factory management, participants may be dealt 'write purchase order' and 'post all orders' cards in the 'Procurement' scene. Then, when all participants post their orders, the scene moves to 'Fabrication' and participants receive new cards like 'open production lines', 'modify fabrication planning slightly', and so on.

The scene part is a set of scene sections. A scene section contains the name of the scene and rules about card dealing and transition.

The card contains a list of captions written in each language defined in the language declaration.

Rules about card dealing define possible actions in that scene. The operator deals cards depending on that rule. Possible actions may change depending on the condition.

The rule about transition defines the next scene of that scene. Each time a card is played, this rule is checked and the scene transfers.

The example in Figure 7 shows syntax of a scene part. In this scene, participants are dealt "PayCost" cards. After all participants play that card, scene transits to "MakeDecision".

6. TRANSLATOR

The translator parses a scenario written in Karina and generates a Web application.

Generation flow is illustrated in Figure 8. Solid lines mean generation and dotted lines mean reference. The translator generates three files: initialization program, structures information file, and CGI program file. To start a game, the initialization program needs to be started up. It initializes the database referring to the structures information file.

Corresponding relationship between the architecture and the implementation is shown in Table 1.

7. VALIDATION

To evaluate the availability and utilization of the language Karina and the translator, we describe a game called "The world food crisis", which was made by Tsunoda and Hishiyama [5].

7.1 Overview of the game

This game simulates a world food crisis. Each participant plays the role of a country in a role-playing game. Participants make decisions about food production in their own country to feed their citizens. If citizens go hungry, the security situation deteriorates. However, not all countries can produce enough food by themselves. Some countries have a shortage of land to produce the foods. In some countries, some crops do not grow. Therefore participants need to help each other. This game provides an opportunity for participants to think about social dilemmas, or in other words, an opportunity to face typical international dilemmas. This game simulates food production and consumption numerically, and only participants' decisions change the environment. This game can be written in Karina.

7.2 Results and Consideration

We verified that this game can be written using our proposed description language Karina and that the scenario of this game can be translated into a Web application that can be accessed in either Japanese or Chinese. Figures 9 shows the interfaces in Japanese and Chinese.

Table 2 compares the number of steps taken by the original code written in HTML, PHP, and MySQL and by the script code written in Karina.

It shows that the effort needed to learn programming languages and to describe games is reduced by using Karina. Because of this, the proposed framework can be said to enable non-programmers to make games easily.

8. CONCLUSION

In this paper, we proposed a new framework to make the games on Langrid Gamings. By using Karina, which is a language based on the common architecture of Langrid Gamings, and its translator, ximplementing various types of the games on Langrid Gamings is made easier not only for programmers but also non-programmers.

As a future work, we will try to expand the translator to translate captions automatically. Additionally, we will expand the generated game to log the game for reflection.

9. REFERENCES

[1] Cathy Stein Greenblat. Designing Games and Simulations: An illustrated handbook. Sage Publications, Inc, 1988.

[2] David Garson. Computerized Simulation in Social Science: A Personal Retrospective. *Simulation Gaming*, Vol. 25, No. 4, pp.477-487, 2002.

[3] H. Deguchi, H. Tanuma, T. Shimizu. Soars: Spot oriented agent role simulator: Design andimplementation. *Post-Proceeding of the AESCS International Workshop 2004*, pp.49-56, 2004.

[4] K. Tsunoda, R. Hishiyama. Design of multilingual participatory gaming simulations with a communication support agent. *28th ACM International Conference on Design of Communication(SIGDOC 2010)*, pp.17-25, 2010.

[5] Reiko Hishiyama, Keisuke Tsunoda. Langrid-gaming: A multilingual participatory approach for solutions and innovation. *2nd International Service Innovation Design Conference(ISIDC2010)*,pp.451-458, 2010.

[6] R. D. Duke: Gaming:THE FUTURE'S LANGUAGE,New York:Sage Publications,U.S, 1974.

[7] T. Ishida. *Q*: A scenario description language for interactive agents. *IEEE Computer*, Vol. 35, No. 11, pp.42-47, 2002.

[8] T. Ishida. Language grid: An infrastructure for intercultural collaboration. *IEEE/IPSJ Symposium on Applications and the Internet*, pp.96-100, 2006.

Table 1: Corresponding Relationship

In architecture	In implementation
Operator	CGI Program on the Server
Cards	HTML Form to access CGI Program
Processors	External Programs
Database	Database on Server

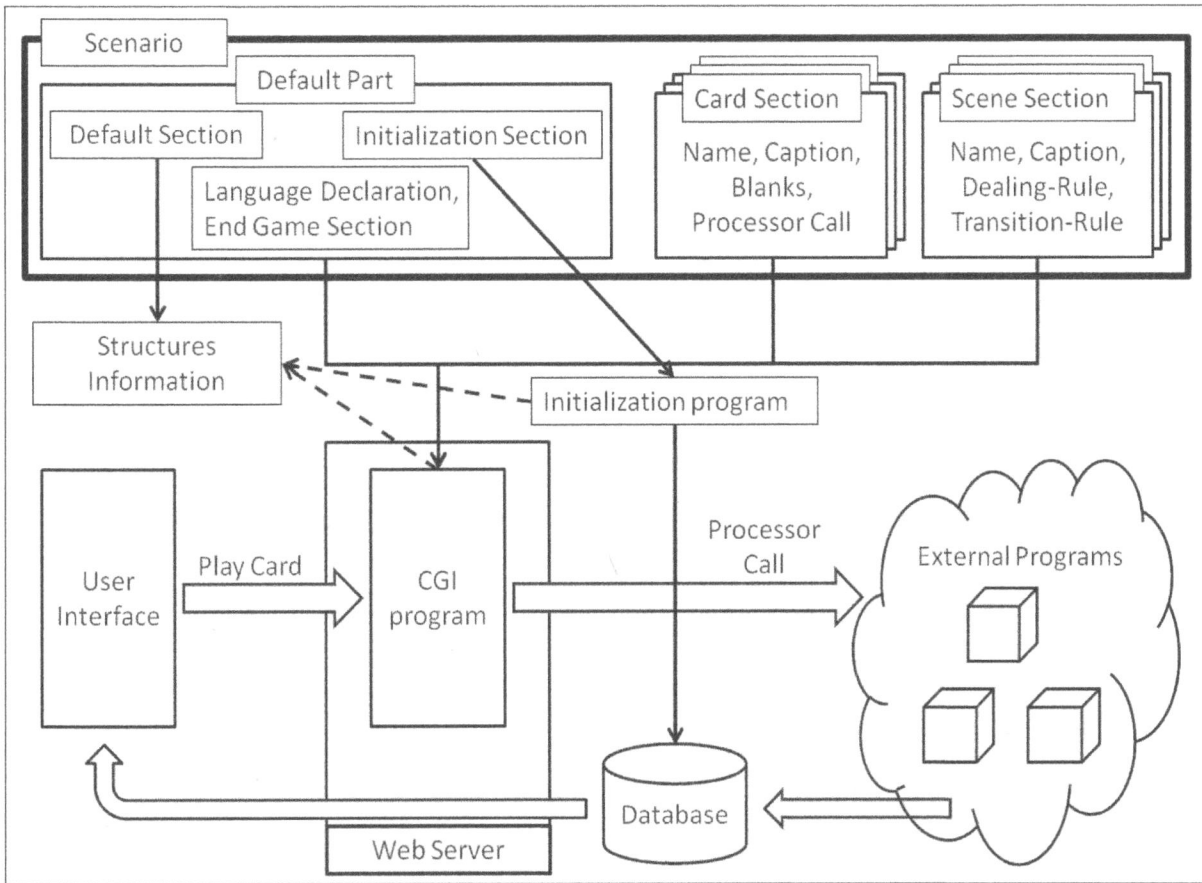

Figure 8: Generation Flow

Table 2: Comparing Results

Items to compare	Implementation by Tsunoda et al.	Proposed Framework
Used prog. languages	HTML, PHP, MySQL	Karina
Number of lines	1772	469
Number of files	21	1

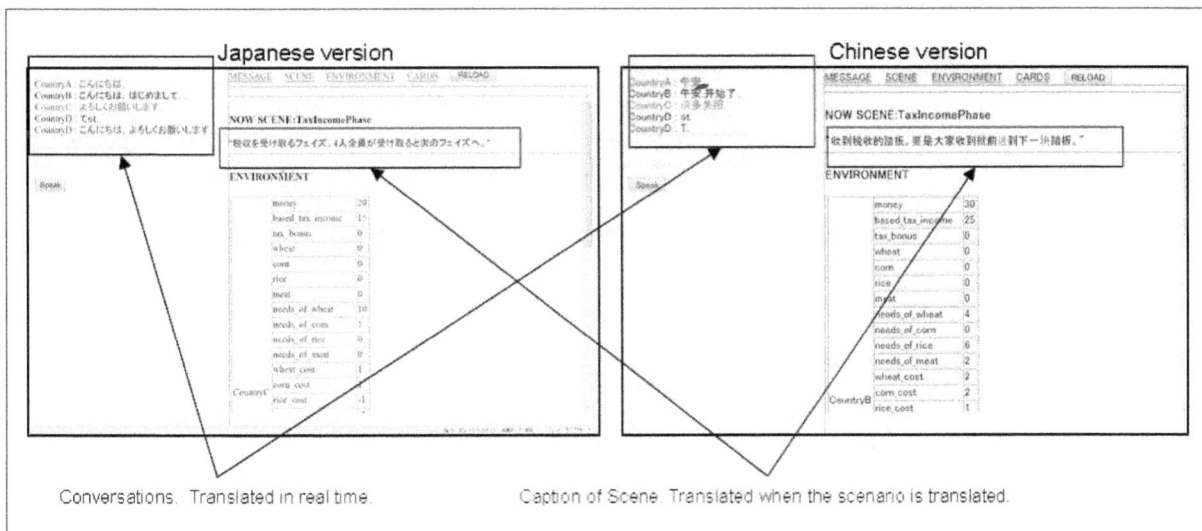

Figure 9: Generation Flow

Conceptual Model for Web Games with Application in Local Promotion

Carlos J. Costa
Adetti- IUL/ISCTE – University Institute of Lisbon
Lisboa, Portugal
carlos.costa@iscte.pt

Pedro Costa
UNIDCOM – IADE
Lisboa, Portugal
pedro.costa@iade.pt

ABSTRACT

In this paper, we propose guidelines to a conceptual model for Web game design in the context of local promotion. First, supported in the literature review, we discuss the importance of the artistic point of view in game design. Then, an empirical study was performed to identify the main dimensions of a game. The importance of games dimension on the global evaluation of the game was also analyzed.

Categories and Subject Descriptors

H.5.2 **[Information interfaces and presentation]**: User Interfaces - *Evaluation/methodology, Theory and methods*

General Terms

Design, Experimentation, Theory.

Keywords

Web game, promotion game, conceptual framework, user interface, TAM.

1. INTRODUCTION

In the actual development of Internet and mobile devices, people have increased the amount of time they spend on-line to work and having fun. Playing on-line is an increasing activity and can be taken the opportunity to use on-line games for local promotion. This is one more chance to become visible to local stakeholders, like tourism entities, cultural institutions and local authorities to reach more people and get to know their culture, history, tourism products and places to visit.

This conceptual model corresponds to a set of guiding principles to designing games on the Web. Those games have as aim promoting a particular local, city or region, by promoting cultural, artistic and historical aspects of that place [24].

Digital games now occupy an important position in the leisure industry, constituting itself as the cultural product with higher economic growth in recent years. It is estimated that in 2012 the digital game industry move 68.40 billion dollars. [1]

In Portugal this is an industry in upheaval, having been produced in this country about 12 games for the international market, only in first 4 months of 2011. In the year 2010 was produced almost a quarter of all games produced so far in Portugal, as described in the report of the Portuguese Society of Videogames Science [2].

The publication "2011 essential facts about the computer and video game industry" [3] gives a set of data about gender and age of gamers on population of the United States. The most purchased games in age rate are the "E" (Everyone) with 44% of the sales, while adult Games rated with "M" (Mature) represent 24% of sales. [3] [4]

By this study we targeted our conceptual game model to a large audience, mostly over 18 years old, with "E" rated content and with the ability to be played on mobile devices.

The game concept, as a work with aesthetic value, is connected with the cultural and artistic values that are intended to transmit to users. In the aspect of playability, as long the game pretends to be a casual game, for different people, with different ages and cultural background, the main focus of communication should be in the visual field. Concerning playability and clarity of the message, is desirable to have a good balance between the two, first to keep people in the activity by giving enjoyable tasks that gives a feeling of fun and second to be accessible to most of the people as possible.

In this context, we discuss the importance of the artistic point of view in game design. We also perform an empirical study to identify main dimensions of a game.

In the following section, we present the literature review, where we analyze the importance of art in game design. Then, we identify promotion games in the context of serious games.

2. REVIEW OF THE LITERATURE
2.1 Game as art

The discussion about the inclusion of art in videogames and about looking at games as artistic works comes its genesis. In 1984 Chris Crawford [5] stated that game was a potential art form, although, at the time of the *Space Invaiders* and *Pac Man* games, he considered that they were still undeveloped. At the time games were considered too simple, trivial and frivolous to be considered as art. The debate was opened across the new media and contemporary art, which puts on the table two opposing visions of culture: entertainment and artistic expression.

In the case of digital games, the artistic object is very dependent of the technological field. Game development involves a multidisciplinary team that can include: artists, designers, programmers, producers, songwriters and a set of increasing technical staff as the narrative complexity and visual effects increases.

Crawford defends digital games as an art form because it presents its audience with fantasy, exhorting with this experience, emotion. However this reasoned justification is not a line of thought. Immanuel Kant [6] distinguished artistic expression of aesthetic pleasure, putting in his *critique of pure reason*, aesthetics and logic in different fields. This conceptual dualism separated the areas of science and aesthetics. However we can find ways of rapprochement in several authors, as Heidegger [7] who claims the essence of art is Poetry and the essence of Poetry is the instauration of the truth.

The thought of Hegel [8] reinforces the concept of physical presence and function of religious contemplation. For this philosopher, an art work assumes a "here and now" (*hic et nunc*) who awarded the authenticity and value his reverential authority. This attribute Walter Benjamin [9] called "aura", denouncing their systematic disappearance as reproduction techniques were being developed, such as the press, photography and cinema.

From the text of Walter Benjamin "The work of art in the age of mechanical reproduction" [10], Gérard Lebrun [11] argues that what for Hegel would be the "death of art", is actually the semantic change of its definition. Reproduction transposes to other level the meaning of truth and a new dialectic between material and immaterial objects.

Game is gaining their own place in the art panorama, like cinema did in the past. About the purpose of the cinema as an artistic expression, Walter Murch [12] uses the parallelism between cinema and the work of Wagner to describe their multiple expressive nature.

Current developments on digital media, new communication and information technologies has brought to New Media more people, creating a greater acceptance in viewing New Media as a cultural object.

Lev Manovich [13] in his research proposes new forms of art using New Media, stating that Web sites, CD-ROM and games are natural evolutions of cinema, both in technical terms and in the configuration of a new aesthetic language.

First, cinema appeared as a technological object, and the first movies were a simple record of everyday tasks; however it is now celebrated as an art form, no longer present in museums, as the other art forms of the past, but among the audience, as underline Panofsky [14].

The complexity of current digital games, with complex devices and narratives, controlled by increasingly sophisticated interfaces requires by the creators a higher level of expertise and a big coordination of team work. This is why Barragán [15] and Santaella and Arantes [16] states that is required a more intense dialogue between the fields of art and technology.

In Videogames Conference 2010, Falcão et al. [17] raises the question of artistic nature of the work of art, making parallel with other New Media and with the cinema and reminding that this issue is still not fully resolved and more research work is needed to the stabilization of concepts and the development of a language all its own.

2.2 Research in Local Promotion Games

Serious Games are currently applied in several fields, for example, military, education, training and simulation, urban planning, rehabilitation, social awareness, and others.[22] Among them, we may identify local promotion games [24].

Learning Games are one of the fields studied and that usually underlies Serious Games once the computer has as strong support information. [18].

To test the effectiveness of several promotional Web games it was made a survey in the game section of www.visiteurope.com a European Travel Commission (ETC) Website. ETC is an association of National Tourism Organizations (NTOs) to promote Europe as a destination to long-haul tourism markets. In this Website users are invited to play a game and "get some pre-flight educational entertainment" [20].

Among the dimensions of the games, we may identify interface characteristics [21][25].

To study game dimensions Rosemary Garris and colleagues [19] identified different game dimensions along several authors.

TAM is an approach proposed to evaluate the main dimensions involved in the acceptance of technology [23]. Yusoff [26] used TAM (Technology Acceptance Model) for studying serious games. In this model, the influence of different variables is mediated by two main individual beliefs: perceived ease of use and perceived usefulness. These two dimensions affect the attitude and intention of the user in using a technology.

3. EMPIRICAL STUDY

An empirical study was performed to identify main dimensions related to local promotion game. This study was composed of two approaches: a quantitative and a qualitative.

In the first approach, we identified dimensions resulting from the aggregation of variables of a survey. This was obtained through factorial analysis. The survey was supported in the variables from Technology Acceptance Model. To this survey each user played all 8 games and should choose 2 games, one of the most appreciated and the least favorite. Each user responded to questionnaires (one per each game chosen). In the questionnaires was used a scale of 7 points. Data analysis was performed using statistical software. In order to treat data analysis was done factorial core components.

We also used other approach to identify game dimensions. It was performed a qualitative approach supported in a study from Rosemary Garris and colleagues [19]. These dimensions are described briefly as: FANTASY is the imaginary or fantasy context, themes, or characters; RULES/GOALS are the setting of clear rules, goals, and feedback on progress towards goals; SENSORY STIMULI is the dramatic or novel visual and auditory stimuli; CHALLENGE is the optimal level of difficulty and uncertain goal attainment; MYSTERY is the optimal level of informational complexity; CONTROL refers to the ability to control an activity.

4. RESULTS

As we mentioned previously, a survey was used in order to identify main game promotion dimensions.

Table 1- Factorial analysis with Varimax rotation.

Qn	Question	F 1	F 2	F 3	F 4	F 5
A22	After playing this game, it will be easier for me to plan a trip in the future.	0,888				
A24	The game will be useful to inform people of the various places to visit.	0,858				
A23	This game will help me to use best available services in places.	0,835				
A9	I feel that I can plan a new journey, after playing the game.	0,821				
A21	The game can help people achieve the same pathways in a real situation.	0,790				
A10	I feel that I can use the skills to identify new paths.	0,707				
A12	I feel that I have acquired knowledge and skills in the course of the game.	0,638				0,560
A8	This game helps me learn, for allowing me to find answers out of the game.	0,610				0,643
A7	This game allows me to find answers to my own speed.	0,593				
A11	After playing, I feel that I have learned and gained new abilities.	0,510				0,612
A13	I felt rewarded when the game displays messages of congratulations to my answer.				0,690	
A2	The graphics of the game helped to better understand the region shown.			0,750		
A14	I am encouraged to learn more when the game displays congratulating messages.				0,708	
A6	I can apply previous knowledge to accomplish tasks in the game.					0,623
A15	The game increases my confidence and motivates me to continue playing when congratulatory messages are displayed.				0,794	
A16	I feel that the congratulatory messages are important to my learning.				0,753	
A4	The game's visual references (colors, photos and other useful elements) facilitate the understanding of the site.			0,727		
A19	I think it is easy to use game, because I'm familiar with the functioning of the buttons and mouse.		0,558			
A3	I am motivated, if a game is similar to what I want to learn.			0,816		
A20	I think it is easy to learn, if the game is simple and direct.		0,625			
A18	I think the game is easy to use.		0,857			
A1	I can learn better if I can relate the experiences within a game to my experience in real life.			0,741		
A17	Learn how to play this game was easy.		0,823			
A5	I have a full control of the game, while I play.				0,636	

In the surveys, 52 students from undergraduate and graduate classes, aged between 18 and 36 years answered a questionnaire. The Factorial analysis of main components allowed to extract 5 factors or dimensions (see table 1). In order to facilitate their interpretation was made the Varimax rotation. Total variance explained is 76,112.

These factors have been assigned the following names: Factor 1. Usefulness of Learning; Factor 2. Ease of use; Factor 3. Connection Game-Reality; Factor 4. Reward and control and Factor 5. Use and acquisition of knowledge.

In the table 2, we identify the extent to which these factors explain the overall assessment of the game and the will to use the game. Thus, linear regressions were performed two multiple dependent variables were respectively the variable A29 (global assessment of the game). It shows the quality of regression and allows identifying the weight of each of the factors in the explanation of the dependent variable. The factor 4 (reward and control) is what provides greater weight in the overall assessment of the game.

Table 2 - Regression Analysis

SOURCE	DF	SS	MS	F	Prob.> F
Regression	5	155.838	31.168	21.205	0.000
Residual	82	120.526	1.470		
Total	87	276.364			
Dependent Variable: "A29"					

R	R2	F	Prob.>F	DF1	DF2
0.751	0.564	21.205	0.000	5	82
Adjusted R Squared = 0.537					
Std. Error of Estimate = 1.212					

Variable TOL	Beta	B	Std.Error VIF	t	Prob.>t
Factor 4	0.440	0.785	0.130	6.037	0.000
Factor 1	0.399	0.711	0.130	5.470	0.000
Factor 3	0.384	0.684	0.130	5.264	0.000
Factor 5	0.187	0.333	0.130	2.558	0.012
Factor 2	0.169	0.302	0.130	2.322	0.023
Constant = 4.636					

To collect more information about each game it was made an open question about what they liked the most and the least in each chosen game. To analyze the open questioner of these 8 games we used the methodologies pointed by Garris et al., which supported content analysis.

In this study it was found game characteristics that can be designated in terms of six general dimensions or categories: fantasy, rules/goals, sensory stimuli, challenge, mystery, and control.

In this analysis it was identified the answers in the different variables and picked up the frequency each variable is referred by users.

Analyzing the frequency that different dimensions appeared in the answers it raises three most reported: *Sensory stimuli* with 39, *Declarative* with 30 and *Rules/goals* with 25. This can be read in two different points of views, both useful to the current study: these are the dimensions people valorize the most, or these are the dimensions these games have more highlighted.

Table 3 – Frequency of answers by different dimensions

Dimension	freq	Dimension	freq
FANTASY	6	SKILL	21
RULES/GOALS	25	CONFIDENCE	8
SENSORY STIMULI	39	TASK INVOLVEMENT	16
CHALLENGE	17	DECLARATIVE	30
MYSTERY	13	PROCEDURAL	10
CONTROL	9	STRATEGIC	4
INTEREST	9	AFFECTIVE	8
ENJOYMENT	8		

As the *sensory stimuli*, is the dimension connect to the narrative, visual stimuli and sound, areas where it's important the artistic touch, we can infer that the artistic dimension is important for the users of the studied games.

The *declarative* dimension includes the knowledge of facts and data required for task performance and is a learning outcome. This shows the importance to have some learning objective in the game.

Clear rules and goals with feedback on progress towards goals is a natural response that players demands and it's connected with the concept of most games.

One aspect that users very often mentioned is the *playability*, which is a very diffuse concept that can be the joining of different dimensions depending on the type of game, and can be object of a separate study.

5. CONCLUSIONS

Designing a conceptual model to a Web game is a challenging task that needs several approaches. In this paper it was highlighted the dimensions of game design. It was studied the dimensions that explain the overall assessment of the game and the increasing will to use it.

We concluded that reward and control is one of the factors that provide greater acceptance in the use of these games, but the sensory stimuli is a very important issue to users in their game experience.

6. ACKNOWLEDGMENTS

The present research was partially financed by FCT – Fundação para a Ciência e Tecnologia, Portugal.

7. REFERENCES

[1] PricewaterhouseCoopers. 2008. *Global Entertainment and Media Outlook; 2008-2012*. PricewaterhouseCoopers.

[2] Sociedade Portuguesa de Ciências dos Videojogos: http://www.spcvideojogos.org/

[3] 2011 Essential Facts About the Computer and Video Game Industry, Entertainment Software Association

[4] 2008 Essential Facts About the Computer and Video Game Industry, Entertainment Software Association

[5] Crawford, C. 1984. *The Art of Computer Game Design*. McGraw Hill/Osborne Media, Berkeley.

[6] Kant, I. 1855. *Critique of pure reason*. Henry G. Bohn, London.

[7] Heidegger, M. 1977. *Der Ursprung des Kunstwerks*. Vittorio Klostermann. Frankfurt-Am-Main.

[8] Hegel, G. W. Friedrich, 1993. *Estética*. trad. Álvaro Ribeiro e Orlando Vitorino, Guimarães Editores, Lisboa.

[9] Benjamin, W. 1996. *Obras escolhidas*. Volume 1, Brasiliense, São Paulo.

[10] Benjamin,W. *1936. A Obra de Arte na Era de sua Reprodutibilidade Técnica*. Segunda versão do texto, iniciada por Walter Benjamin em 1936 e publicada em 1955.

[11] Lebrun, G. 2006. *A filosofia e sua história*. Cosac & Naify, São Paulo.

[12] Murch, W. 1999. *A digital cinema of the mind? Could be*. In: The New York Times, New York, May 2.

[13] Manovich, L. 2000. *The Language of New Media*. MIT Press, Cambridge.

[14] Panofsky, E. 1969. *Estilo e meio no filme*. In: LIMA, Luiz Costa (org.), *Teoria da cultura de massa*, Saga, Rio de Janeiro.

[15] Barragán, H. 2008. *Software: ¿Arte?* In: LA FERLA, Jorge (org.). Artes y Medios, Buenos Aires

[16] SANTAELLA, L & A. 2008. *Estéticas Tecnológicas: novos modos de sentir*, Priscilla (orgs.) Educ, São Paulo.

[17] Falcão, L., Neves, A., Ramalho, G., Campos, F., Oliveira, B. Game as Art: A Matter of Design. In *Proceedings of the Videojogos 2010* (16- 17, 2010) Porto Salvo, Portugal.

[18] Van Eck, R. 2007. *Building artificially intelligent learning games*. In D. Gibson, C. Aldrich, & M. Prensky (Eds.), *Games and simulations in online learning* (pp. 271– 307). Hershey, PA: Information Science.

[19] Garris, R., Anlers, R., Driskell, J. 2002. Games, Motivation, and Learning: A Research and Practice Model. In *Simulation and Gaming* 33, p. 441-467

[20] http://www.visiteeurope.com/Share/Fun/Content/Games

[21] Costa, C.J. & Costa, P., 2010. Wemoga. In *ACM SIGDOC European Chapter/ Eurosigdoc Workshop on Open Source and Design of Communication - OSDOC '10*. ACM SIGDOC European Chapter/ Eurosigdoc Workshop. Lisbon, Portugal, p. 61

[22] Costa, J.P. & Costa, C.J., 2010. Market game. In *ACM SIGDOC European Chapter/ Eurosigdoc Workshop on Open Source and Design of Communication - OSDOC '10*. ACM SIGDOC European Chapter/ Eurosigdoc Workshop. Lisbon, Portugal, p. 59-60

[23] Davis, F. D. 1989. *Perceived usefulness, perceived ease of use and user acceptance of Information Technology*. MIS Quarterly, 13(3), 318-339.

[24] Costa, P., 2010. Map gaming for local promotion. In *ACM SIGDOC European Chapter/ Eurosigdoc Workshop on Open Source and Design of Communication - OSDOC '10*. ACM SIGDOC European Chapter/ Eurosigdoc Workshop. Lisbon, Portugal, p. 45-48

[25] Pena, J. & Costa, C.J., 2010. Open source isometric browser games framework. In *ACM SIGDOC European Chapter/ Eurosigdoc Workshop on Open Source and Design of Communication - OSDOC '10*. ACM SIGDOC European Chapter/ Eurosigdoc Workshop. Lisbon, Portugal, p. 51-54

[26] Yusoff, A. 2010. *A Conceptual Framework for Serious Games and its Validation*. Thesis for the degree of Doctor of Philosophy, University of Southampton

Simulation Game for Training New Teachers in Class Management

Vassiliki Bouki
School of Electronics and
Computer Science
University of Westminster,
New Cavendish Street
W1W 6UW,London, UK
+44 (0)20 7911 5000
boukiv@westminster.ac.uk

Markos Mentzelopoulos
School of Electronics and
Computer Science
University of Westminster,
New Cavendish Street
W1W 6UW,London, UK
+44 (0)20 7911 5000
mentzem@westminster.ac.uk

Aristidis Protopsaltis
Serious Games Institute
Coventry University Tech Park
Cheetah Road, Coventry
CV1 2TL, UK
+44 2476 158252
aprotopsaltis@gmail.com

ABSTRACT

Games are used in education at all levels for quite long time. Most educational games intend to introduce trainees to a new subject and present them with new knowledge when others allow then to acquire and improve certain skills. This paper presents the "Teaching Game", an implementation that explores the possibility to create a simulation of a classroom event in the format of a game. It is offered as a training tool for new teachers who want to get prepared for the class. The educational aim of the game is to put players in the place of a teacher who comes across some unforeseen circumstances and to allow them to test and improve their skills in class management.

The 'teaching game' has been implemented in Game Maker 7 and it is a tool developed for the needs of the "Virtual Training Environment (VTE) for Teachers" at the University of Westminster.

Categories and Subject Descriptors

D.2.2 [**Design Tools and Techniques**]: User Interfaces; I.2.1 [**Applications and Expert Systems**]: Games

General Terms

Algorithms, Documentation, Performance, Design, Experimentation.

1. INTRODUCTION

How should teachers respond when they come across unforeseen situations in the classroom? Any person involved with education could tell that there are no recipes or ready-made solutions that a teacher could follow in order to handle a new or difficult situation in a classroom. There are so many unpredictable factors such as teacher's and students' goals, reactions, specific cognitive and emotional conditions

as well as conditions related to a particular, most of the times unique, event that it is not possible to provide useful instructions to a new teacher.

It is only after many years of experience when teachers start to realise the best ways to handle unforeseen situations and they start becoming proactive in order to prevent an unpleasant situation or incite a specific reaction from students. By facing and asking to handle several different, new, unexpected and mostly difficult situations, new teachers could improve their skills to understand students' reactions, manage the classroom better and avoid disturbing factors.

A training environment that will help new teachers to get prepare for the class, should offer trainees the chance to face real life situations and allow then to experiment with them. Both are essential features of any training environment [6] The "Teaching Game" is an implementation that explores the possibility to create a simulation of a classroom event in the format of a game. The educational aim of this game is to put players in the place of a teacher who comes across some unforeseen circumstances and to allow them to test and improve their skills in class management. It is a tool developed for the needs of the "Virtual Training Environment (VTE) for Teachers" - a platform created at the School of Electronics and Computer Science (ECS), University of Westminster, London.

2. OBJECTIVES OF TEACHING GAME

The main objective for the 'teaching game' was to introduce players to 'real-life' situations. It was absolutely essential to use genuine situations instead of 'made scenarios.' There are some good reasons for that. On one hand 'made scenarios' have been criticized for being disconnected from their real-world context [2]. As a result, knowledge conveyed through 'made scenarios' tends to be situated in the context of the theoretical framework within these scenarios have been constructed rather than the context in which actual events took place. On the other hand learning situated in real-world contexts has been shown to have positive impacts on learning and learner motivation (Duffy Cunningham, 1996) [1].

In order to collect authentic data, we interviewed lecturers at the School of Electronics and Computer Science (ECS), University of Westminster. The "teaching game" we present in this paper reproduces, in game format, an event that took place during an exam at ECS. The event was described to

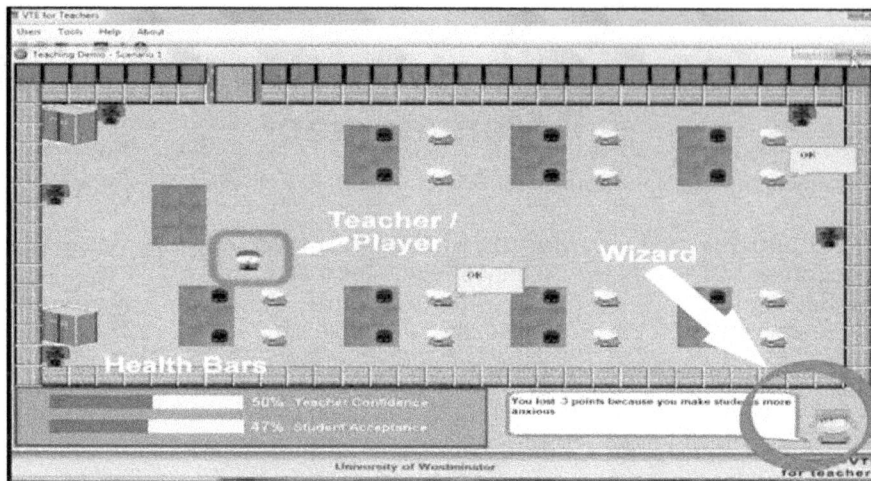

Figure 1: The Teaching Game: Health bars -Instructions and Help -Main game Characters.

us by the lecturer who took part in it and had to handle this specific situation.

3. THEORETICAL BACKGROUND

There are two main questions we had to answer before we started the design of the game. The first one is 'what exactly we try to simulate in this game'. Apparently, the initial approach to this question is that it is the 'teaching environment' and the 'teaching process' that we have to simulate. The 'teaching environment' is a self-explanatory concept and it consists of all those persons, machines (e.g. computers) or other tools (e.g. projector, boards or software) that are present or used in the classroom.

The 'teaching process' is not such straightforward to define term. 'Teaching' has been described in many different ways: as "the art of explaining", "a profession", "the result of experience", a "skill", a "charisma" etc. All these definitions try to capture different aspects of 'teaching'. For this particular application we started with the main remark that whatever teaching is, it is mainly achieved through linguistic communication between the teacher and the students. Apparently there are more ways for a teacher to pass a message to students (e.g. body language, intonation) but language is the most common and ultimate tool, teachers use.

As it is common in any discourse students try to decode the message given by the teacher and then they code their own linguistic messages. After that, it is the teacher who has to decode students' messages in order to continue the communication. All the other non-verbal actions and signals are used in order to underline and clarify the linguistic message. The linguistics messages that teachers and students exchange do not convey only information or knowledge related to a specific subject. They also pass information about understanding, emotions and intentions. The linguistic choices teachers make indicate intentions and trigger reactions from students. For example a lecturer who tells student during the very first day of a class "my module is very difficult with a very difficult exam" and a lecturer who tells them "only half of you will manage to pass my module" try to pass the same message (that students have to work hard to pass the module) but the choices they make cause different impressions, feeling and reactions from students.

The second question we had to answer was what kind of actions will be available to players. Having defined teaching as (mainly) a linguistic communication the actions we provide players with are linguistic actions. For the needs of the game we created alternative ways for the teacher to react to specific problems by generating different linguistic actions. Such alternatives were constructed after discussions with teachers and students. These actions are presented to players as different sentences. The player has to choose the "correct" sentence that corresponds to a certain attitude towards the students and a certain way to communicate with them. Apparently, no answer could be considered as a 100 % "correct" or assumed that it will work will all students. From experience we could say that a certain attitude might lead to a "quicker" solution and definitely - because this is a real life story- we could say which one worked in the given situation. There is no assurance that the same choices will work with a different class.

It goes without saying that the view that 'teaching is a linguistic action' is a relative narrow approach and it limits the number of actions players are allowed to take in order to play the game. The development of this principle along with the "characters" of the students must be considered in the future, in order to create a more sophisticated game that will be much closer to the "real environment".

4. SOFTWARE CHOICES

Two pieces of software currently used for computer games graphics and implementation were studied, namely "Game Maker" and "True Space 7".

"Game Maker" (download from the address: http://www yoyogames.com/make) is an easy-to-learn Windows and Mac IDE originally developed by Mark Overmars[3] as a teaching aid for his students. It is gaining recognition as a useful teaching tool in primary and secondary schools because of its easy entry and sophisticated scripting language.

"True Space 7" offered by Caligari Corporation (http:// www.caligari.com/products/ trueSpace/ts75/Brochure/ intro.asp) is a fully-featured 3D authoring package. It is a more sophisticated package with more advanced graphics but it requires more learning time. True Story is used for

modeling, apply texture and light, animate and rendering 3D content.

Both packages produce executables. We decided to use 'Game Maker' taking into consideration its full functionality and the less learning time it requires.

4.1 Design

4.1.1 Instructions and Help

Students get the following instructions at the beginning of the game: "You are the lecturer of the first year computer science module 'Programming 1' and you organise a lab exam. Students are already in the lab waiting for your instructions - they have no previous experience of University lab exams and they might be a bit anxious... They expect to work in an undisturbed and 'peaceful' environment." The user plays the role of the teacher.

During the game players can get help from a "wizard" who appears at the right bottom corner of the screen. The wizard provides feedback to players after each action and explains why they gain or lose points.

4.1.2 Aim, Actions and Health Bars

The aim of the game, as it is set in the instructions, is for the teacher to make sure that the exam goes smoothly whatever unexpected problems occur. Time plays a crucial role. The teacher has to resolve any problem that comes up as soon as possible and - in an ideal world - to foresee and avoid it.

The user has to select among three sentences and decide which action and which phrasing will lead to a quick solution. At the bottom of the screen there are also two health bars: "students' acceptance" and "teacher's confidence". At the beginning of the game both health bars are in the middle (50). Every action that helps to resolve problems which arise add to "students' acceptance" and "teacher's confidence" when wrong decisions that cause further unnecessary delay reduce the score.

Figure 2 shows the screen of the "Teaching Game". According to the real event we simulate a late student enters the room and a serious of disturbing events start. Each time the player clicks on the teacher he is provided with three linguistic actions to choose from as it is shown in the following figure (Fig 3). In order to create the options offered to players, several studies on how to be more productive in classroom and how to deal with difficult students were used [5, 4].

5. IMPLEMENTATION

The case study was built using GameMaker (GM) 7 engine. We selected to represent avatars from interactive representation of a human figure in a games-based two-dimensional interactive graphical environment. The term was made popular by Neal Stephenson in his novel 'Snow Crash'. For example a person in a virtual meeting or the tutor in a distance learning context may be represented by their avatar dealing with students. Usually an avatar will have human characteristics, including speech and facial expressions.

For this game there are three main avatars. The lecturer, the students initial in the class (all with the same avatar representation) and the student that appear delayed after a certain time (fig 3). The game has been designed to use the common WASD keyboard entry with the help of the mouse

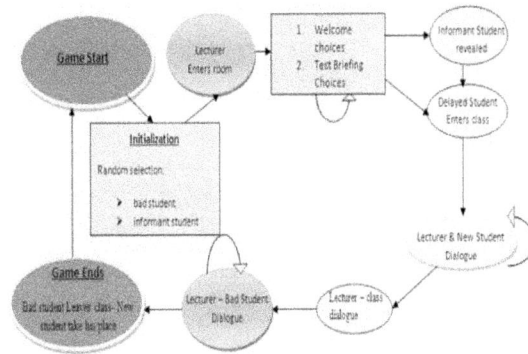

Figure 3: General FSM design for the Teaching Game. The curved arrows show that depending from the selection options of the dialogues from the user, there might be delays in the propagation from the current state to the next one.

to select options over dialogues, or to initiate time events using the left click. The game general FSM (Finite State Machine) can be seen in Figure 3.

6. PILOT TESTING

The "Teaching Game" has been pilot tested several times over the course of two days by one expert. It has been very well delivered and it is easy to use. The dialogues are very informative, easy to read and easy to select. Only very few minor problems were identified, which are presented below in two sections along with some suggestions.

6.1 Apparatus

Computers were used to display the hypertext. Pentium IV 2.0 GHz custom computer with 1024MB memory were used. The monitor was a Dell Professional 1909W 19 inches colour monitors. The monitors' resolution was 1360 x 768 / 60 Hz.

6.2 Usability aspects

Since the game is educational a welcome message would be more appropriate at the start of the game instead of the three choices of how to proceed with the game. Then, only the "Start" option should be displayed in the middle of the game. It was suggested that for reasons of consistency with the rest of the game's screens (the health bars appear at the bottom), the other two (Help and Save and Exit) option should be moved to the bottom space. It is unlikely that the user will use these choices again and again, and therefore could easily be moved at the bottom of the screen. In addition, these two functions should be available to the user throughout the game, in order to give to the user the opportunity to again read the guidelines, if needed, or to leave the game at any time he/she wishes to do so. Furthermore, the opportunity to go back to the main/start screen should be given to the user without having to quit the game altogether.

In the "Help" file, where the functions of the different keys are explained, an explanation about the "Esc" key is needed, since it is a key used in the game and an explanation is not provided. Also, it need to be said that the Esc key has a

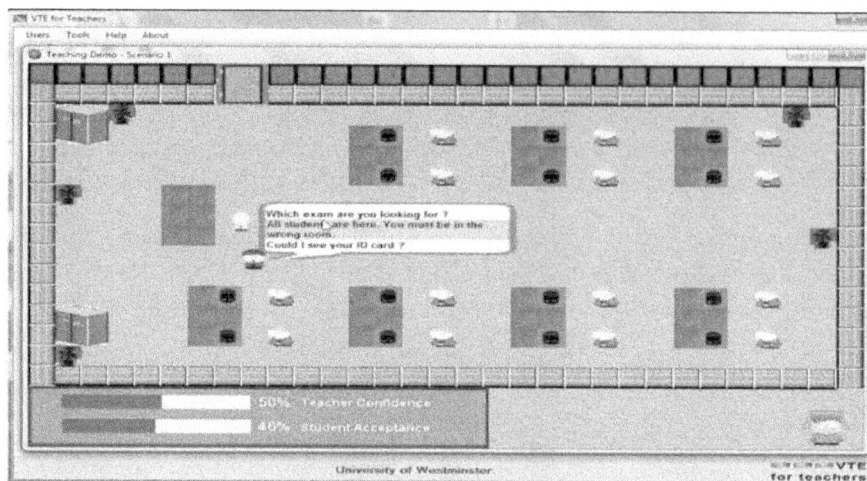

Figure 2: The Teaching Game: Potential simulation problem that arises when a student is entering the class for his practical examination and all seats are taken. Option Menu selection for the lecturer with three possible choices. All different choices are evaluating to different case scenarios.

double function, as a return key from the help and as a quit key in the game.

Also, it needs to be made clear that the Esc key has a double function, as a return key from the help and as a quit key in the game.

Besides, when the user clicks on the Help (F1) button and moves to the help screen it is not clear how he/she can get back to the main screen, therefore, a message like "press esc to return to the main screen" needs to be displayed in the screen, and it needs to be clearly visible. This is only happening at the beginning of the game and it might take a while until the user will realise that he/she needs to click again on the lecturer in order to continue. A message like "click on the lecturer to continue" from the wizard could be very useful and it could improve the pace of the game. The user might not remember what he/she needs to do to proceed, and an instruction will help him/her to proceed with the rest of the game.

Finally, in some of the responds/explanations from the wizard, when the respond is less informative and the user looses points, it is not clear, if those points refer to the confidence levels or not, since the health bars display percentages. However, if it is, this is inconsistent with the health bars and a change it should be made, so both use the same metric scheme and therefore the relationship between the two is transparent.

6.3 Technical aspects

A technical problem was identified when the teacher is moved at the end of the classroom, after the second row of desks. When the teacher stands there and the new student enters the room, he/she turns back immediately and moves around, outside the class/wall, presumably trying to find another entrance. After he/she finishes moving around the classroom, enters the room, goes towards the lecturer, the interaction starts and the game continues.

7. FUTURE WORK

The "Teaching Game" (as a tool offered through the "Virtual Training Environment (VTE) for teachers") is an ongo-

ing project. We continue to expand and develop it. We also work on more complicated real-life scenarios that could be re-created in the form of a game. Further developments will include additional student avatars with different AI for each one. That could lead to import additional features for each student such as psychological profiles and confidence, which the teacher should take into account with time constraints. Also, all the usability and technical issues revealed by the pilot testing will be resolved. Expand the GUI of the game to include face avatars and information selection for all students within the class. Create a database to keep reference of user's actions in order the game AI to update itself to increasing level of difficulty.

8. REFERENCES

[1] T. Duffy and D. Cunningham. *Constructivism: Implications for the Design and Delivery of Instruction.* In D. Jonassen (Ed.), Handbook of research on educational communications and technology. New York: Simon Schuster, 1996.

[2] L. M. Lunce. Simulations: Bringing the benefits of situated learning to the traditional classroom. *Journal of Applied Educational Technology*, 3(1), Summer 2006.

[3] M. Overmars. *The Game Maker's Apprentice: Game Development for Beginners.* 2006.

[4] F. Report. Improving learning in mathematics at key stages 1 2: a research and development project in conjunction with enfield education authority's primary mathematics network. *G023 Middlesex University*, 2007.

[5] A. Rumpus. Giving effective lectures: Transforming information into learning. *Educational Initiative Centre, University of Westminster*, 2004.

[6] A. M. Schmidt and J. K. Ford. Learning within a learner control training environment: The interactive effects of goal orientation and metacognitive instruction on learning outcomes. *Personnel Psychology*, 56(2):405–429, Summer 2003.

Model-Based Customizable Adaptation of Web Applications for Vocal Browsing

Fabio Paternò, Christian Sisti

CNR-ISTI, HIIS Laboratory
Via Moruzzi 1, 56124, Pisa, Italy

{fabio.paterno, christian.sisti}@isti.cnr.it

ABSTRACT

In this paper we describe a solution to make Web pages more suitable for vocal browsing by analyzing and modifying their logical structure. The solution exploits intermediate logical descriptions that are automatically created by reverse engineering techniques. The adaptation engine aims to identify the main logical structure of the Web page components and remove the aspects specific to the graphical modality. Then, a vocal implementation is generated to support browsing, which begins by the user's selecting from the main components. It is possible to customize some parameters of the adaptation transformation in order to better control its results.

Categories and Subject Descriptors

H.5.2 **[Information Interfaces and Presentation]**: User Interfaces – D.2.2 **[Software Engineering]**: Design Tools and Techniques – User interfaces.

General Terms

Design, Human Factors.

Keywords

Adaptation, Vocal Interfaces, Web Applications.

1. INTRODUCTION

Emerging ubiquitous environments call for supporting access through a variety of interactive devices. Vocal technologies and related applications are steadily improving and this makes possible services such as vocal searches and map navigation by Google or others.

Web applications are widely used and a number of approaches and techniques have been proposed to support their adaptation to mobile devices (e.g. [3], [4]). Little attention, however, has been paid so far on how to adapt Web applications for vocal access. This seems useful and important, given the recent improvements in vocal technologies, which can allow users to access their applications when the visual channel is busy (e.g. when driving) or when they are visually-impaired. While solutions exist for supporting blind people in specific domains [5], the general assistive technology for blind people (mainly screen readers) have a number of usability limitations because they usually access the page implementation and require keyboard selection of the elements of interest, with little ability to filter content; only type filtering is currently available (e.g. listing links, headers, or other

types). Thus, often users have to listen to a lot of useless content before reaching the point of interest or are provided with information that is difficult to interpret because they do not know the surrounding context in the Web page [10]. In this paper we present an original solution for transforming graphical Web pages in order to make their content browsable through vocal interaction. Our target is to generate VoiceXML vocal applications, that are semantically equivalent to the originals but accessible through menu-based vocal interaction. The solution exploits intermediate model-based logical descriptions in the MARIA framework [11], which provides one abstract (platform-independent) user interface language, and a number of concrete (platform-dependent) user interface languages. The implementation is based on a pipeline of XSL Transformations. In order to improve the flexibility of our adaptation tool, we also provide designers and developers with the possibility of customizing the adaptation rules, by specifying the values of some parameters that allow them to change the results accordingly. In the paper, after discussion of related work, we introduce our approach and provide an example application with an existing (widely known) Web site to better illustrate the possible results. The next section provides a more detailed description of how the adaptation transformations have been designed and implemented, along with the description of the customization tool. Lastly, some conclusions along with indication of future work are drawn.

2. RELATED WORK

Recognition of natural language input is improving [7] and this opens up the possibility of obtaining vocal user interfaces able to recognize any user input.

A number of authoring environments for multimodal user interfaces has recently been proposed. The main goal of the MultiModal Web Approach's authoring environment [15] is enhancing the dissemination of knowledge used by proven solutions to recurring problems in the multimodal context. XFormsMM [8] is an attempt to extend XForms in order to derive both graphical and vocal interfaces. In this case the basic idea is to specify the abstract controls with XForms elements and then use aural and visual CSS for vocal and graphical rendering, respectively. The problem in this case is that aural CSS have limited possibilities in terms of vocal interaction and the solution proposed requires a specific ad hoc environment in order to work. We propose a more general solution able to derive implementations in the W3C standard Voice XML. An approach to providing a portal engine with the capability to communicate and receive inputs using voice is presented in [1]. This solution indicates guidelines for developing multimodal Web sites exploiting combination of graphical and vocal modality but does not provide any specific tool to support automatic conversion from graphical to vocal or multimodal. In contrast to [16], which aims to understand how cognitive models can be useful to predict usability issues for screen reader users, we exploit models of user interfaces to build the logical descriptions and then adapt them for vocal browsing. A work that has similar goals is DANTE [9], which provides semantic transcoding for visually-impaired users. For this purpose it uses ontology-based annotations that are manually created and included in the Web page. Such annotations are then used for automatically transforming the original pages into pages more easily accessible for the visually-impaired. In our case we aim to obtain a tool that is able to automatically analyze the content of a Web page and transform it into a vocal application that is sufficiently usable, with the possibility to customize some adaptation parameters. For this purpose we consider intermediate model-based representations [6], which aim to represent the logical structure of the user interface and enable relevant reasoning to derive a more suitable structure for the vocal channel. While previous work (e.g. [14]) has considered the use of model-based techniques in the authoring of vocal or multimodal applications, we exploit them in the automatic adaptation from graphical-to-vocal content.

3. THE PROPOSED MODEL-BASED APPROACH TO VOCAL ADAPTATION

As mentioned, we exploit a model-based language [11] for performing a transformation that preserves the semantics of the interaction. The framework provides abstract (independent of the interaction modality) and concrete (dependent on the interaction modality but independent of the implementation) languages. Such languages share the same structure with different levels of refinements. An AUI (Abstract User Interface) is composed of a number of *presentations,* a *data model* and a set of *external functions.* Moreover, each presentation contains a number of user interface elements, called *interactors*, and a number of *interactor composition* operators. Examples of interactor composition operators are *grouping* and *relations* to group/relate different interactors. The interactors are first classified in abstract terms of *editing, selection, output* and *control* and may have a number of associated *event handlers*. While in graphical interfaces the concept of presentation can be easily defined as a set of user interface elements perceivable at a given time (e.g. a page in the Web context), in the case of a vocal interface we consider a presentation as a set of communications between the vocal application and the user that can be considered as a logical unit, e.g. a dialogue supporting the collection of information regarding a user. Examples of interactors are *navigators* (allow moving from one presentation to another) and *description* (allow TTS functionality). A grouping can contain both interactors and other composition interactors (such as groupings itself). Another composition concept used to structure the presentation is the relation operator, which defines a kind of relation between two groups of elements, typical example is a form with one group for editing input values and one for controlling them (clearing, sending to the server, …).

Our solution is based on an *adaptation server*, which provides a number of functionalities (see Figure 1):

- **Reverser**, parses the content of the Web page and the associated style sheets, and builds up a corresponding Desktop Concrete Logical Description;
- **Graphical-to-Vocal Adapter**, transforms the Desktop Concrete Logical Description into a Vocal Concrete Logical Description, which is optimized for vocal browsing;

- **VoiceXML Generator**, a VoiceXML implementation is generated from the vocal concrete description so that the final result can be loaded onto a vocal browser for execution.

The work described in this paper focuses principally on the Graphical-to-Vocal Adapter. In the next sections we first describe an adaptation example obtained with our approach, and then we describe our solution for the Graphical-to-Vocal Adaptation process.

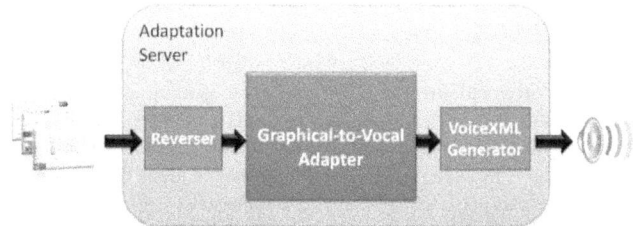

Figure 1: The global adaptation architecture.

4. AN EXAMPLE

In order to illustrate how our approach works, we consider an example of widely known Web site (BBC[2] , see Figure 2).

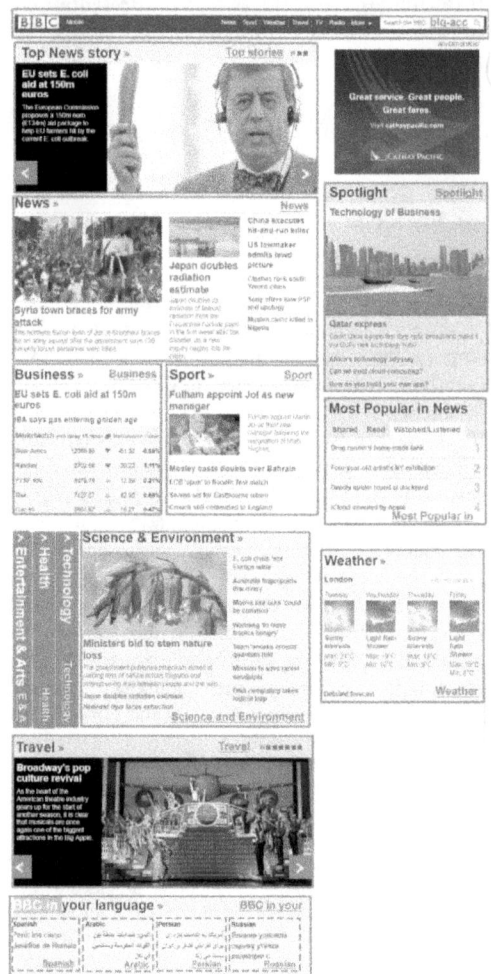

Figure 2: BBC User Interface Logical Structure.

We can thus see how we address one of the most complicated issue in the adaptation: recognizing the different logical parts that a graphical page may be subdivided into, information which is then used to structure the vocal navigation (as explained in Section 5.2). Figure 2 shows the components identified, which are structured into two hierarchical levels.

The screen dump has been annotated with solid lines representing the higher-level sections while the dotted lines represent the nested sub-sections. In addition, we have added the text labels of the corresponding items in the generated vocal menus.

Figure 3 shows an example of the vocal menu structure, in which intermediate nodes are menus while leafs represent content, for the Web page in Figure 2. Adjusting the adaptation process parameters (see next sections) permits increasing or reducing the level of splitting and, consequently, the fragmentation of the result. Another crucial point in the process is the identification of meaningful word/sentences that best describe the content of a logical part. In the next sections we describe the algorithm developed for determining the menu items and explain what the possible sources of information are.

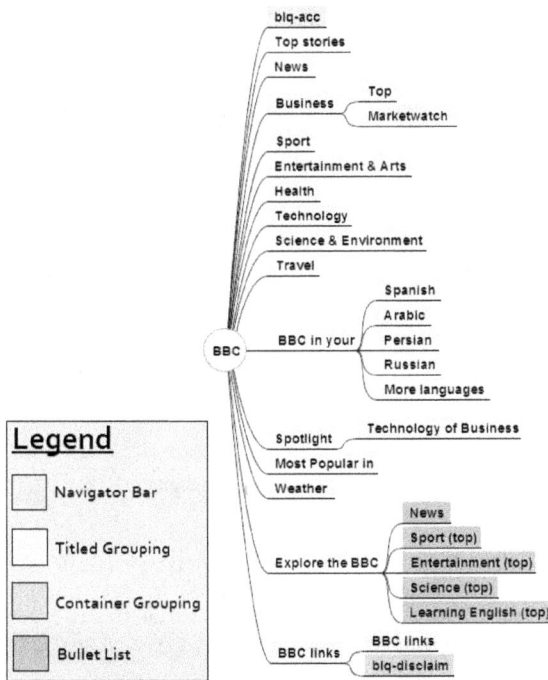

Figure 3: BBC Vocal Menu Structure.

The table below shows an example of a possible resulting dialogue.

	Input / Output	Description
System:	Welcome to BBC Main Menu. Choose one of the following sections: ..., Business, Sport, ...	*Introduction of a menu section*
User:	Sport	*Menu Activation*
System:	You are in Sport. Fulham appoint Jol as new Manager ...	
User:	Repeat	*Speak again the current dialogue*
System:	Sport. Fulham appoint Jol as new Manager ...	
User:	Next	*Skip to the next part*

System:	Moving to part "Mosley casts doubts". Mosley casts doubts over Bahrain ...	
User:	Previous	*Go back to the previous menu.*
System:	Moving back to the main menu. Welcome to BBC Main Menu. Choose one of the following sections: ..., Business, Sport, ...	
User:	Exit	*Close the interface.*
System:	Goodbye!	

Table 1: The Vocal Dialogue in the Example.

5. THE GRAPHICAL TO VOCAL ADAPTATION

Adapting a graphical Web page into a menu-based vocal one poses a number of specific problems. We summarize them into three categories:

- **Content:** some contents of a graphical page translates poorly into the vocal modality. For example, a Web page could contain text not supported by the target Voice Browsers (e.g. Chinese alphabet symbols).

- **Structure:** although the logical description of a graphical page is a tree (good for menu navigation), the depth and the width are typically too large for vocal browsing. So there is a risk of generating a large number of nested menus with little content on the leaves.

- **Menu Items Naming:** it is crucial to find simple meaningful names for activating the menu items that, in some way, anticipate the corresponding node content.

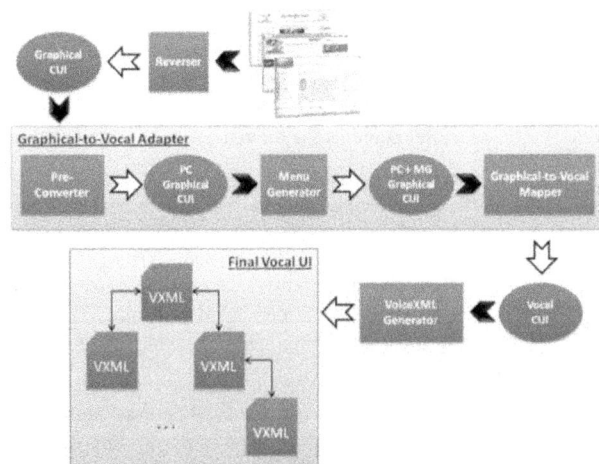

Figure 4: The adaptation process in details.

The adaptation is performed after the reverse engineering phase, in which an analysis of the implementation in terms of all the HTML tags and associated CSS files is performed on the Web page considered in order to build the corresponding logical description. The transformation is carried out through various phases (see Figure 4):

- **Pre-Converter:** 1) performs the *Content Optimization* by removing from the graphical logical description the elements that badly reflect into vocal interfaces (e.g., images without alternative text); 2) performs the

Structure Optimization by recognizing the page components and removing the unnecessary one (e.g., grouping elements used for only formatting purposes); 3) performs the *Calculate Cost* computation (see next sections), whose results are used in the Menu Generator phase.

- **Menu Generator:** a new hierarchical structure is generated in order to allow navigating the interface through menus/submenus.
- **Graphical-to-Vocal Mapper:** the graphical interface elements are mapped onto vocal ones having the same semantic effect.

5.1 Concrete Graphical Description Pre-Conversion

Content Optimization

A logical specification automatically generated by the reverse engineering of graphical desktop Web pages contains elements that might have no sense in a vocal interpretation because they are used for graphical formatting purposes. For this reason, we have developed an algorithm to find and discard elements that are irrelevant. More in detail, this *Pre-Conversion* step performs the following:

- *Remove the interactors not graphically visible*: examples are interactors derived from hidden HTML elements, text with font size equals to zero or image with width, height equals to zero.

- *Remove the images that cannot be rendered vocally:* they are the images without the ALT attribute. In any case the "image links" are preserved and accessed by their destination path.

- *Correct grouping inconsistency:* due to particular graphical page layouts or previous processing, it is possible to have groupings without content or with only one child (so they are no longer definable as groupings). In these cases the groupings are removed and their (possible) contents are moved up in the tree structure.

- *Normalize words:* this feature transforms words containing accents or other diacritics into normalized forms without them (e.g., España is transformed into Espana) to avoid possible encoding errors. This feature can be disabled. More fine-grained normalization techniques will be implemented in future versions. For details about text normalization techniques see [17].

- *Remove unsupported words:* characters not supported by the Voice Browser (e.g., 中文 in English based applications) could cause crashes in the final vocal interface. To avoid this we permit choosing the supported character set. All the words that contain at least one character not in the set are removed. At the moment we provide support for three charsets: 1) Basic Latin 2) Basic Latin + Supplement 3) Arabic. We use regular expressions to recognize the words to delete: for example the following *regular expression* identifies all the words that contain non-Basic Latin characters:

```
\w*\P{IsBasicLatin}+\w*
```

Structure Optimization

The graphical logical description generated by the reverse tool contains hundreds of groupings used only for formatting purposes.

This description, if not appropriately processed, can generate hundreds of vocal menus (and menu items) that will direct to sections with meaningless content. Thus, our solution aims to identify the different kinds of groupings and remove all those useless for vocal navigation.

For this purpose, we defined seven classes of composite interactors: 1) *Root;* 2) *Form:* in MARIA defined as a relation 3) *Bullet List*; 4) *Bullet,*; 5) *Navigator Bars,*; 6) *Titled,* a composition of user interface elements associated with a title by the "titling algorithm"; 7) *Container,* the remaining hybrid composition operators (containing at least one interactor). We then follow this class order to implement a *decision tree* to classify each composite operator in the graphical logical description. Each composition operator that does not belong to any of such classes is removed, and its content is moved up.

Since in HTML there is no strong semantic binding between page components and headings, connecting them is delegated to the user's perception of the actual presentation of the page. The same problem affects the graphical logical description, so the *titling algorithm* aims to perform this binding. After a study of a number of common Web pages we found four patterns. Figure 5 shows the patterns and the algorithm's behaviour.

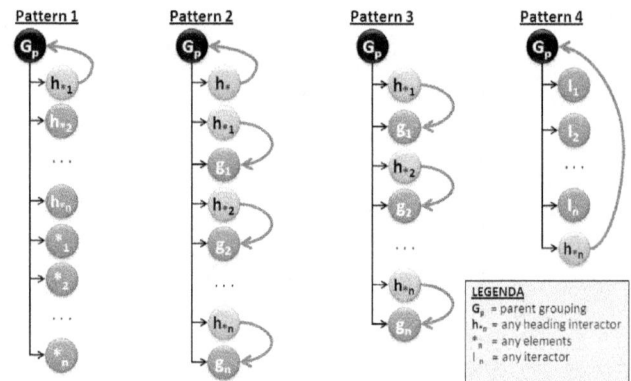

Figure 5: Heading Patterns.

G_p is a grouping containing some children; h_{*n} is a heading interactor (an interactor that has the attribute "role = heading1, heading2, …"); $*_n$ is any possible element and I_n is a generic interactor. The curved arrow indicates the bindings between headings and groupings.

More in detail, *pattern 1* shows a grouping that contains a number of headings as top-child, followed by a series of other elements. In this case the first heading is used as title for the grouping parent. In *pattern 2* we have a heading as first child and then a series of couples [heading-grouping]. Now we use the top child as title for the overall grouping parent and the preceding headings as titles for the relative groupings. *Pattern 3* is similar to the previous one: we have the same couples [heading-grouping] but the top-child to be associated with the grouping parent is missing. Finally, *pattern 4* represents a situation with a number of interactors as top-child and then a heading that is used as title for the grouping parent.

Figure 6 shows the average grouping number and distribution (among the tree levels) before (dotted line) and after (solid line) the structure adaptation process was applied to five well-known Web sites (*w3.org, bbc.com, ebay.com, msn.com* and *yahoo.com*).

On average the number of groupings was reduced from 455.2 to 90.2 and the number of levels from 20 to 9.

Grouping Reduction - Average

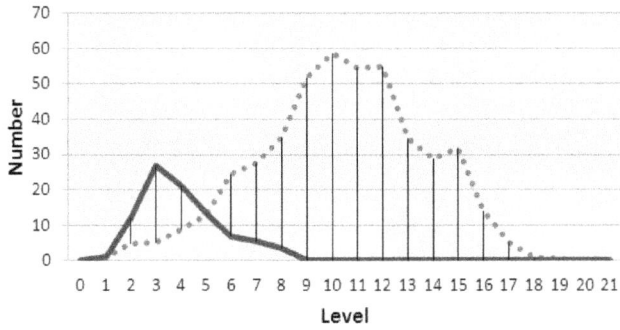

Figure 6: Grouping Reduction Average.

Calculate Cost

The next *Menu Generation* step performs a splitting of the original structure of the graphical logical description into different sections (which will be the new vocal presentations) connected by *menu presentations* (presentations containing the logic for the vocal menu browsing). Our goal is to avoid sections with too much content, so one simple solution would be to split the groupings that contain a large amount of text. This idea seems good but imagine having a grouping that contains two descriptions of ten words each and another grouping with two bullet lists of ten bullets each. Supposing that both groupings have the same overall number of characters, users will most likely find it logical to listen to the first grouping, since it is probably a sequential text that should be accessed as a single logical unit. On the other hand, the second one, which is mainly composed of two different lists of items should be separated. For this reason we introduce a heuristic to calculate the **cost** of each component class giving different **weights** to each of them. To calculate the costs we use the following recursive function:

$$c(n) = \begin{cases} l(n) & \text{if } n \text{ is interactor} \\ w(n) * \sum_{i=0}^{k} c(child(n)_i) & \text{otherwise} \end{cases}$$

Where n is a node , $w(n)$ is a weight associated with the class, $child(n)_i$ is the i-th child of n (with k = number of n children) and $l(x)$ is the function that calculates the amount of synthesizable text in the node x. The stop condition is that the node n is an interactor (not classified).

In other terms, the cost quantifies the size of a well-defined page component depending on its class. The weights define the proportions (in terms of linguistic load) between the different page component classes.

The weights are parameters in the range [1..100]. Increasing the weight of a class means increasing the probability that the elements of that class will be associated with a specific section, and thus will be directly accessible through a separate vocal menu item (see next section for an example). The customization interface (see Section 6) supports the editing of the weights in order to change the structure of the resulting vocal application.

5.2 Menu Generation

The result of the previous phase generates a logical description, which has removed a number of elements deemed useless for the generation of the vocal description. The resulting description is based on the primary groupings, and makes it possible to generate menu sections (with a limited number of choice items) that define a new logical structure of the interface itself. This structure allows the user to better vocally navigate the content. We designed and implemented a recursive algorithm that analyses the presentations in the graphical logical description and recursively splits each of them into multiple presentations until the basic presentations for the vocal interface have been identified. Some of these will contain only one menu and others the actual content, which can be either information to deliver or some interactions to support user-generated input. The purpose of the menu generation phase is to identify when we should create menus that will allow the users to choose among various options. As mentioned each menu will be associated with one single presentation. A presentation is split (and a new menu is generated) if the cost (calculated in the *pre-processing* step) is above a *threshold* (which can be changed through the customization interface).

Figure 7 below shows the general navigation structure generated by the process. Both sections and menus are new presentations. The menus contain the logical description of the mechanism to navigate in the presentation children. The sections instead contain some content retrieved from the original graphical interface. The section itself contains the logical description of the mechanism to navigate through its own different parts.

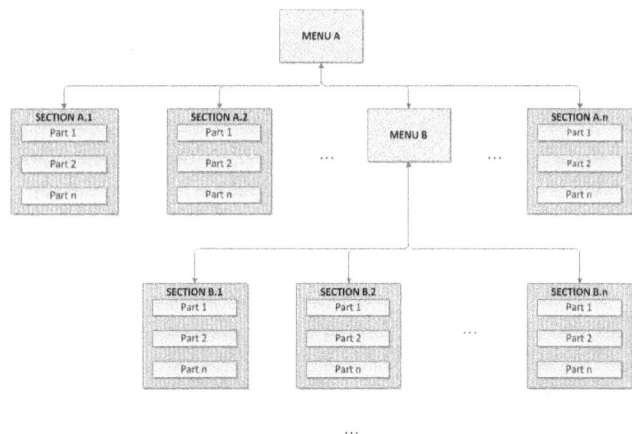

Figure 7: The General Navigation Structure.

The designer can customize the adaptation process choosing the value of the weights. Increasing the values increases the probability that a presentation is split. In the figure below we can see an example of how the weights may influence the splitting.

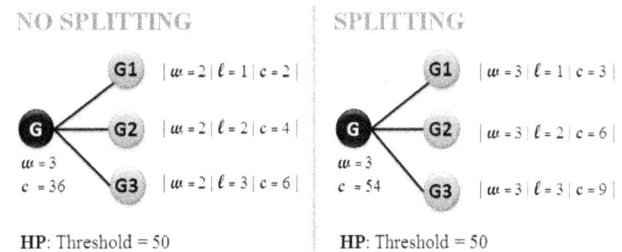

Figure 8: Weight influence in splitting

In the left side we can see that the cost (c) calculated in the node G is below the (predefined) threshold. In this case the child nodes become part of section G and will be evaluated (in the final vocal interface) in the order G1, G2, G3. Increasing the weight (*w*) from 2 to 3, the total cost is above the threshold and the presentation will be split into three new sections (presentations), accessible through a new menu presentation that allow direct access to each one.

One of the main problems in the menu generation is how to find keywords (or short sentences) that summarize the content of the destination. Our algorithm to retrieve the menu items works as described in the following:

1. **If** the node to be referenced has a "title" attribute (obtained in *pre-processing* step) use it.
2. **Else if** the same node has a descendant with a "title" attribute, use the first that is found.
3. **Else if** the node ID has been defined by the original user interface designer then use it.
4. **Otherwise** retrieve the main word from the node.

In order to retrieve the main word, the tool performs an analysis of the content and uses the string of the first description/text with the highest text *role* present in the content considered. The text roles indicated in the graphical concrete description are sorted from the most to the least important in this way: Heading1, Heading2, Heading3, Heading4, Heading5, Heading6, Strong, Emphasis, List_element, Paragraph, Normal. If no text role is specified, then we select the first string that we find in the actual content. In general for each menu items we limit the length at three words.

Testing our algorithm on various Web sites we found that the max number of menu items of the generated menu-based tree can be up to 20. This raises the issue of the user *short term memory effort*. We address this problem by adding a new feature to our Menu Generation process: when there are too many menu items (a limit can be set in the customization interface), the transformation splits the original menu into smaller sub-menus.

5.3 Desktop to Vocal UI Mappings

This is a transformation that takes the elements of the graphical concrete presentations, as modified in the previous stages, and translates them into corresponding elements of the vocal concrete language that have similar effects. It was introduced in [12], each graphical presentation obtained is thus transformed into one vocal presentation.

The presentation *title* is used to build a suitable introduction sentence to use as the *welcome message* for the first time the user accesses the application. A vocal presentation may have a number of associated vocal commands. The transformation enables the following commands: *previous*, to go back to the last menu heard; *main menu*, to go back (at any moment) to the main menu, *next/back*: allows the user to navigate back and forth through different parts of the same section (see Figure 6); *start/stop*, pauses the interface at any time and restarts it at the same dialogue position; *reprompt*, enable repeating the current dialogue; and *exit*, to close the vocal interface.

In the style to emphasis mappings we are constrained by the limited support of the vocal browsers. Regarding the output-only interactors, we provide the following processing. The text elements are directly mapped onto speech elements. If the text element defines a path to the content, we map this information directly onto the speech element. In the case of audio content, if the ALT attribute is set, we use it to give a description of the audio source. The audio element is mapped onto a *prerecorded message* vocal interactor for rendering. In the case of images, if the ALT attribute is specified in the source document, then we

transform the element *image* into a *speech* element that renders the attribute. As in the case of an image, for videos we use the ALT attribute (when present) to vocally render its description, otherwise it is discarded. The *audio* elements are mapped onto the *prerecorded message* interactors; if the ALT attribute is available we use it to provide a general description of the audio resource. Data tables are simply mapped into *vocal tables*. Two table browsing algorithms [13] have been implemented: *linearization*, if the table contains headers, *intelligent browsing*, if no header is present.

Regarding the control interactors we provide for the following processing. The text links are mapped onto the *vocal link* element. The name of the link is used as *activation vocal sentence*. The sentences that users must say to activate a link will be synthesized with higher pitch in order to let the user recognize it. The image link differs because in this case we want to communicate to the user what to say' to activate the link, but we do not have an explicit title for the link. Currently we use the *navigator ID* as the corresponding vocal command, where the ID is that defined by the developers of the original Web pages. Graphical buttons are mapped onto *vocal links*, triggered by pronouncing their labels or, if a button is an image, by pronouncing the corresponding ID. If the button is used to submit the values of a form then it is mapped onto a *vocal submit*. This interactor is automatically enabled when the all the form input fields have been filled.

In the case of graphical interactors supporting selection, they are managed differently depending on whether they support *single* (radio button, list box, drop down list) or *multiple* selections (check box, list box), and consequently associated with the single or the multiple vocal selection interactors. In both single and multiple vocal selection, the labels of the graphical choice elements are used to build either the request or the list of accepted inputs. To explain this kind of interaction to users, the vocal request contains the following sentence: "Single/Multiple Choice. Which would you like to choose: *list of admissible input* ?".

The edit interactors allow users to enter pieces of information of various types. They raise the issue of the generation and use of grammars for vocal interfaces. For *numerical input* (which graphically can be provided by spin boxes, track bars and other similar techniques) we set a grammar able to recognize numbers. In case of *textual input*, we instead introduce two pre-generated grammars: a vocal grammar able to recognize short sentences composed of a well-defined list of words; and a DTMF grammar able to transform the keyboard inputs into words in a way similar to that used to write text messages in mobile phones.

Lastly, once the vocal concrete description has been obtained it can be transformed into a VoiceXML implementation.

6. CUSTOMIZATION TOOL

The adaptation process can be customized by the designers defining a number of parameters. Figure 9 shows the user interface that allows such parameterization: on the left the modifiable parameters, on the right the graphical representation of the structure of the corresponding vocal interface. In particular, the left panel is divided into three sub-panels: *input*, to choose the Web page that will be adapted and to start the process; *FTP Parameters*, to set the parameters of the FTP connection in order to send the generated VoiceXML files to the Voice Browser; *Transformation Parameters*, to set the parameters that influence the adaptation (e.g. the minimum size of an image in order to be considered relevant).

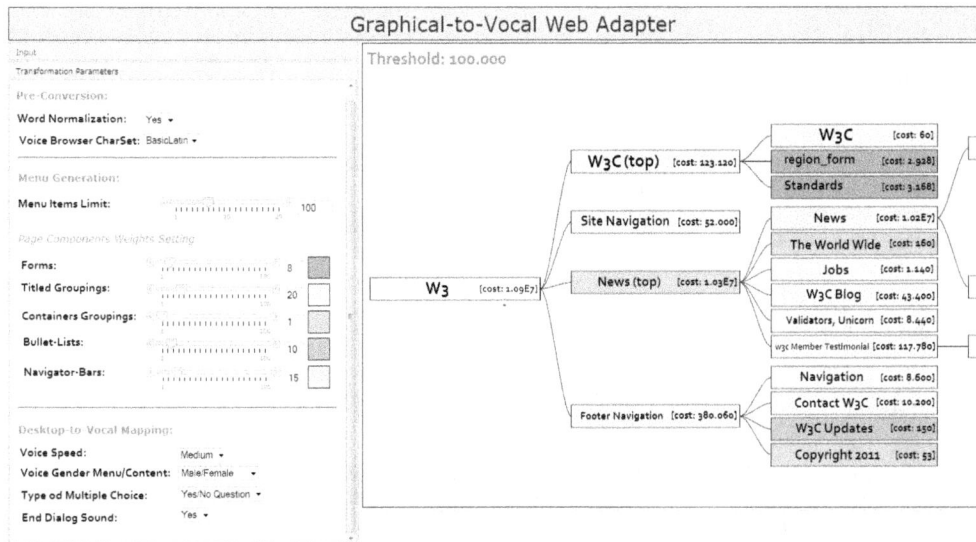

Figure 9: Customization of the Graphical-to-Vocal Web Adapter

The right panel shows the structure and the menu items of the generated vocal page. In this way the designer can decide whether to send the final vocal interface to the Voice Browser or, otherwise, change the transformation parameters in order to obtain a different structure.

7. EVALUATION

7.1 Evaluation Setting

We conducted a user test of our Customization Tool in order to collect feedback about the interface usability and the clarity of the results displayed. To evaluate the tool we recruited ten subjects (eight male and two female). The average user age was ~30.6 with a minimum of 23, a maximum of 42 and a standard deviation of ~6.20. Their education level was: two PhD, five Master Degree, one Bachelor Degree, and two High School.

The users' familiarity with the Web Interfaces was, in a range [1-5], on average ~4.4 with a minimum of 2, a maximum of 5 and a standard deviation of ~1.07. The users' familiarity with the vocal interfaces was, in a range [1-5], on average ~2.7 with a minimum of 1, a maximum of 4 and a standard deviation of ~1.42.

After a short introduction to the adaptation process we asked the users to focus on the first two labels of the *Pre-Conversion* sections (see Figure 9), which we defined as follows: *Word Normalization*, if true, normalize the words that contain accents (e.g. España→Espana); *Voice Browser CharSet*, to delete the words not contained in the selected charset. Then, we pointed out the definitions of the different page components (as described in Section 5.1) in relation to the W3C homepage and explained the weights' role in the menu generation process. At this point we asked the users to perform three adaptations of the W3C homepage with different weights:

- *All the weights at minimum (1);*
- *All the weights at maximum (100);*
- *User setting of free weights.*

As the next task we asked the users to perform two adaptations of the MSN homepage while fixing the *menu items limit* to 100 and 7. The last part of the test focused on the evaluation of the Desktop-to-Vocal customization parameters. We proposed the following definitions: *Voice Speed*, allows changing the speed of the synthesized voice in the final vocal interface; *Voice Gender Menu/Content*, permits selecting the voice gender for the menu and for the contents sections; *Type of Multiple Choice*, enables the user to choose between different kinds of multiple selection (Yes/No Question and Form Grammars); and *End Dialog Sound*, allows adding a sound at the end of each vocal dialog.

At the end of the test, users were asked to complete a questionnaire consisting of both multiple-choice and open questions. The questionnaire principally focused on the evaluation of the three main aspects of the tool: 1) the *pre-conversion*, 2) the *menu generation*, 3) *the desktop-to-vocal mapping*.

We asked for feedback about the clarity of the interface labels and about the usefulness of the associated customization. Moreover, we asked for feedback on the simplicity of the model of the cost-based structure adaptation and its visualization. Furthermore, we investigated the global perception of the proposed solution, asking the users to provide any kind of criticism/suggestion.

7.2 Evaluation Results

On a scale of 1 to 5, the user satisfaction for each of the feature discussed in Section 7.1 was: Pre-Conversion, Average: 4.13, Standard Deviation: 0.84; Menu Generation, Average: 4.26, Standard Deviation: 0.44; Desktop-to-Vocal Mapping, Average: 4.33, Standard Deviation: 0.34. The best result was obtained for *Desktop-to-Vocal Mapping* while *Pre-Conversion* and *Menu Generation*, despite good results, seem to need improvements. This is probably due to the fact that the first two sections of the customization interface are more technical and less intuitive for non-expert users. The overall evaluation of the Customization Tool was ~4.42 (scale [1-5]) with a standard deviation of ~0.54.

We gathered a number of positive user impressions and criticisms that gave us further motivation to investigate the field of adaptation for vocal interfaces. About 80% of the users underlined the lack of a zooming feature for a complete visualization of the tree; 50% asked for some helping mechanism, such as popups or tooltips; 70% found it quite hard to define appropriate weights in a few attempts; and asked for a more immediate feedback from the environment.

For the considered Web sites, the time to perform the adaptation was on average ~40.55 seconds. We expect that this time can be influenced both by the original page dimension as well as by its intrinsic structure. In any case further work will be oriented to reducing processing time both by optimizing the transformations algorithm and adding caching features to the customization tool. Currently, every time that new weights are selected, the tool performs the entire process from the reverse engineering to the VoiceXML generation. The idea is to permit choosing the adaptation part to perform dynamically.

While all the users considered the weights range for the cost calculation suitable, more than half the users asked for a smaller range in the choice of the menu items. Instead of [1..20] they proposed [1..10]. Accessibility was one of the strong points underlined by some users. This approach in fact expands the accessibility horizons, not only for visually-impaired users, but also for people without Internet connection or, moreover, when the visual modality is busy (e.g. checking email when driving a car, follow a recipe while cooking, etc.). Another strong point is the simple navigation, also useful for people who are not used to interacting through vocal interfaces.

Some users criticized the TTS and the Speech Recognizer, but these features are not part of our architecture. Three users considered some of the sentences for menu activation too long, while another one asked for more re-prompting and help hints when the user seems to stop during navigation.

8. CONCLUSIONS AND FUTURE WORK

Our automatic adapting process has been applied to twenty Web sites. The generated VoiceXML vocal interfaces have been tested with the VOXEO Voice Browser and have passed the validation test integrated in it. The applications have been used through VoIP access to the vocal server. A configuration tool was developed in order to change the parameters of the adaptation process and have a preview of the structure of the generated vocal application. This allows the possibility for developers of vocal applications to control the adaptation process and better tailor it to their specific needs.

In general, the results depend on the original content. The solution is not able to manage content such as Flash or Java applets and the results are not as good with Web content that does not follow the standard W3C guidelines for Web applications.

Future work will be dedicated to improving the transformation rules and further performing empirical validation. We are interested in exploiting machine learning techniques in order to investigate the possibility to find the correct weights configuration and in the pattern analysis for the headings identification.

Acknowledgments

We gratefully thank the support from the EU ICT SERENOA Project (http://www.serenoa-fp7.eu/).

REFERENCES

[1] Bergenti F., Lazzari L., et al: Enabling Vocal Interaction in a Web Portal Environment. Lecture Notes in Business Information Processing, Volume 1, Part II, 204-213. Springer, (2007).

[2] British Broadcasting Corporation (BBC), http://www.bbc.co.uk/

[3] Buyukkokten O., Kaljuvee O., Molina H., Paepcke A. and Winograd T.: Efficient Web browsing on handheld devices using page and form summarization. ACM Trans. Inform. Syst. 20, 1, pp. 82-115, (2002).

[4] C. E. Cirilo, A. F. do Prado, W. L. de Souza, L. A. M. Zaina, Model Driven RichUbi - A Model Driven Process for Building Rich Interfaces of Context-Sensitive Ubiquitous Applications, Proceedings SIGDOC 2010, pp.207-214

[5] M. Ferati, S. Mannheimer, D. Bolchini, Acoustic Interaction Design through "Audemes": Experiences with the Blind, Proceedings SIGDOC 2009, pp.32-28

[6] Fonseca J.M.C. (ed.): W3C Model-Based UI XG Final Report, May 2010, available at http://www.w3.org/2005/Incubator/model-based-ui/XGR-mbui-20100504/.

[7] Franz. A., Milch B.: Searching the web by Voice. In proceeding of the 19th international conference on Computational Linguistic - Volume 2, pp. 1-5, Stroudsburg, PA, USA, (2002).

[8] Honkala M., Pohja M.: Multimodal interaction with XForms. Proceedings ICWE, pp. 201-208, (2006).

[9] Yesilada Y., Stevens R., Harper S. and Goble C.: Evaluating DANTE: Semantic transcoding for visually disabled users. ACM Transactions on Human-Computer Interaction 14, 3, Article 14, (2007).

[10] Leporini B., Paternò F.: Increasing usability when interacting through screen readers. Universal Access in the Information Society 3(1): pp. 57-70, (2004).

[11] Paternò F., Santoro C., Spano L.D.: MARIA: A universal, declarative, multiple abstraction-level language for service-oriented applications in ubiquitous environments. ACM Trans. Comput.-Hum. Interact. 16(4): (2009).

[12] Paternò F., Sisti C.: Deriving Vocal Interfaces from Logical Descriptions in Multi-device Authoring Environments. Proceedings ICWE 2010, LNCS 6189, Springer Verlag, pp.204-217, Vienna, July 2010

[13] Spiliotopoulos D., Stavropoulou P., Kouroupetroglou G.: Acoustic Rendering of Data Tables Using Earcons and Prosody for Document Accessibility. HCI (7) pp. 587-596, (2009).

[14] Stanciulescu, A.: A Methodology for Developing Multimodal User Interfaces of Information Systems. Ph.D Thesis, University of Louvain, (2008).

[15] A. Talarico Neto and R. Pontin de Mattos Fortes, Improving multimodal interaction design with the MMWA authoring environment, Proceedings SIGDOC 2010, pp. 151-157

[16] Trewin S., Richards J., Bellamy R., John B. E., Thomas J., Swart C. and Brezin: Towards modeling auditory information seeking strategies on the Web. In Extended Abstracts of SIGCHI Conference on Human Factors in Computing Systems (CHI '10), ACM Press, NY, Extended Abstracts, pp. 3973-3978, (2010).

[17] Uwe D. R., Hartmut. R. P., Text preprocessing for speech synthesis. In Proceedings of the TC-STAR Workshop on Speech-to-Speech Translation, Barcelona, Spain, pp. 207–212, June (2006).

[18] Voxeo Voice Browser, http://www.voxeo.com/.

Comic Computing: Creation and Communication with Comic User Interface

Hiroaki Tobita

Sony Computer Science Laboratories, Inc.

tobita@csl.sony.co.jp

ABSTRACT

We describe a "Comic Computing" method that integrates comics with a user interface for a creation and communication environment. Comics are used to tell stories by combining visual elements and sentences in a way that makes the story visually fun and interesting, and for this reason they are a popular and familiar medium for many people. Our Comic Computing method uses the classical features of comics to create a unique user interface that enhances communication. We first analyzed the comic medium from the viewpoint of a user interface by focusing on information visualization, and then we developed several systems on the basis of the analysis results. Our goal was twofold: comic creation and application, both of which can be used to foster creative and visual communication. In this paper, we describe our method with a focus on the concept itself and its practical applications.

Categories and Subject Descriptors

D.3.3 [**Programming Languages**]: Language Contructs and Features – *abstract data types, polymorphism, control structures*. This is just an example, please use the correct category and subject descriptors for your submission.

Keywords

Comic Computing, Manga Computing, Information Visualization, User Interface, Interactive System, Creation and Communication.

1. INTRODUCTION

Comic books are a graphic art form combining text and images to represent a story. Comics can be read in a wide variety of styles: not only on paper (e.g., magazines and newspapers) but also as electronic content (e-books and the Internet). Without a doubt, comics are one of the most popular and familiar forms of graphic content. People can read comics easily and gain knowledge in the process, so even children can learn about cultures and trends, among other things, through comics.

This is the background against which comic-based computer systems have been developed. These systems, which integrate comics with computers, are mainly divided into two types. One type supports comic creation itself [11, 12, 21]. These systems enable users to create comics interactively by using a computer. The other type uses comics to represent complex information [8, 9,

SIGDOC'11, October 3–5, 2011, Pisa, Italy.

10]. These systems are useful for making content (e.g., chat logs and video content) fun and interesting. However, most previous comic research has focused only on concept and has neglected inquiries into communication design through comics and the relationship between comics and information visualization (IV) [1, 13]. An additional lack is that there is no standard format for combining a comic book with a user interface.

In this study, we used Comic Computing to design comic-based communication through creation. Our goal is to make conventional communication systems more interesting and visual, so we provide several user interfaces based on comics [3, 4, 5, 6, 7]. We first describe the relationship between IV and comic books, because comic-based visualization is quite similar to information visualization: for example, both set information nodes on a timeline. We discuss these shared features in detail. Next, we propose several interfaces (including those that create comic books or utilize comic book jargon) that we developed on the basis of the comic analysis results.

To make a comic, we introduce a simple comic creation method aimed at enhanced communication [3, 4, 7]. Generally, beginners do not have a concrete image of the comic they want to create, so the starting point can be a bit difficult. An effective support for triggering creation is therefore necessary. Our target users are basically beginners and children. Our approach is an interactive system that contains two functions: simple comic creation and unique comic browsing. The creation function requires users to write text to create a comic, after which the system automatically creates a temporary comic by combining the text and predefined images. This is simply a trigger for comic creation as the user then edits and ultimately completes the temporary comic by simple drag and drop manipulations. After creating a comic, users can think about how they want to show it.

To utilize comic jargon, we introduce comic images and video [5, 6]. Our main purpose is to provide an effective thumbnail for image browsing in small devices with characteristic comic deformation. We have developed a technique that supports effective content viewing, and we also utilize movie content to interactively integrate that content with comic books. Conventional systems focus on converting movies into comic books, but our intention is slightly different in that we want to establish a smooth relationship between both movies and comics. Thus, our goal is to provide both a visual summary of a movie and a summarized movie by using comic editing. This enables users to visualize an input movie as a comic book and edit the movie through the visualized comic.

Our proposed comic interfaces use a common format based on XML, so manipulations such as editing or creating a comic book are the same throughout all the interfaces.

2. IV AND COMICS

Comics are quite similar to IV in that both use visual elements to express information and show continuity and relationships within a set of information in a way that users can easily understand. In this section, we describe the similarities and differences between comics and IV.

2.1 Information Nodes and Structure

IV is used to visualize a data set with a simple shape and comics are used to visualize a story with drawing such as characters and speech bubbles. IV depicts information sets as abstracts, so users can interact with them both simply and easily. Simple shapes such as circles, rectangles, spheres, and cubes are used as information units called "information nodes." Defining the information node on the basis of size and position makes the relationship between the feature and the overall information very clear. Needless to say, this is very useful in terms of understanding information visually.

In comics, the information node is a frame unit. The frame unit is usually represented as a rectangle and contains characters and a speech bubble. Comics are a medium that can be defined as set frame units corresponding to a story. The comic structure is hierarchical and contains four elements including story, page, frame, and various frame elements such as characters and speech bubbles (Fig. 1). Characters, the background, and speech bubbles are child nodes of the frame and the frame is a child node of the page. This simple structure makes it easy to treat comics as a data structure. In IV, there are several approaches that use a hierarchical structure to visualize information [14].

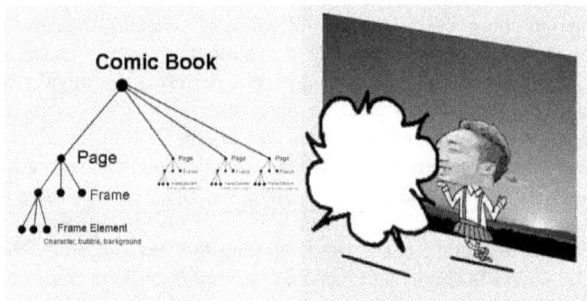

Figure 1. Comic structure.

2.2 Dimension and layout

IV enables users to place information in 2D and 3D space. Using depth information properly makes it possible to combine 2D space with time axis or to set different 2D spaces in 3D space at the same time [17]. In contrast, the comic layout is almost completely fixed in 2D space: there is a 2D timeline, and frame elements are set along it. This timeline starts from the top right in Japanese comics and the top left in Western ones. Although several IV systems visualize information with a bottom-up approach, IV researchers individually design the layout and set rules for how to browse the layout [15]. This system is a bit more flexible than the comic book layout.

Although the comic book layout is basically 2D, each frame has both 2D and 3D elements because comics are treated as 2D content on paper. Although the contents are not animated like in movies and animations, comic creators can express vivid content by using depth information to change an angle or position. Thus, each frame is 2D, but the characters and background objects within the frame are set in a 3D scene.

2.3 Focus and context

Focus and context methods, such as the fisheye view, are some of the more popular IV techniques [16, 18]. They are also effectively used in comics. Focus and context enables users to simultaneously show both an entire information space and a focus area, which is quite useful in terms of understanding the relationship between a part and the whole.

In a comic frame, there are two types of focus and context techniques to create contrast between a feature and a non-feature and to make a story vivid by highlighting character feelings, changing the story tempo, etc. One type is focus and context between a frame and a page. Readers see all frames when they turn a page, and the first thing they focus on is the biggest one. While the size of a page is fixed, the size of each frame depends on the story. A big frame is a focus frame and a small frame is a support frame. The other type is focus and context between feature and non-feature areas in a frame. In each frame, the focus character and character parts are bigger and/or more detailed, and non-focus elements are smaller and/or rougher. By controlling the size and detail, focus character are made clearer and readers can easily understand the most important part of the frame (Fig. 2). A focus line is also used to make the focus clear.

Figure 2. Focus and context.

(a) Attention cuing is defined by angle and length relationship between elements.

(b) Comparisons of attention cuing parameter. Tempo in right figure moves faster than in left because of angle.

Figure 3: Attention cuing.

2.4 Attention cuing

Comic creators can use attention cuing to direct a reader's viewpoint and control a story's tempo. (Note: In this case, tempo does not mean reading speed but rather the flow of the story itself.) As mentioned earlier, characters and text bubbles are primary elements in attention cuing. A reader's viewpoint moves from one element (character or text bubble) to the next. To control the story tempo, the angle and length between the current and next elements (and current and previous elements) are especially important.

The user's viewpoint moves from one element to the next. In Fig. 3 (a), two lines and one angle are shown. The angle at the right of Fig. 3 (b) is steeper than the angle at the left. Therefore, the story tempo of the right figure is faster than that of the left because readers feel a faster tempo when the angle is steep. In the same vein, a wide angle conveys a slow tempo, so the story moves slowly in comparison to a sharp angle. The length between current and previous elements is also important to technically control a reader's viewpoint. Two types of length between the current and next elements are shown in Fig. 3 (a). The length between the second and third elements is longer than that between the first and second elements. Readers feel the story moves at a slower tempo when the length is long, and similarly, a short length conveys a quick tempo, so the story moves faster.

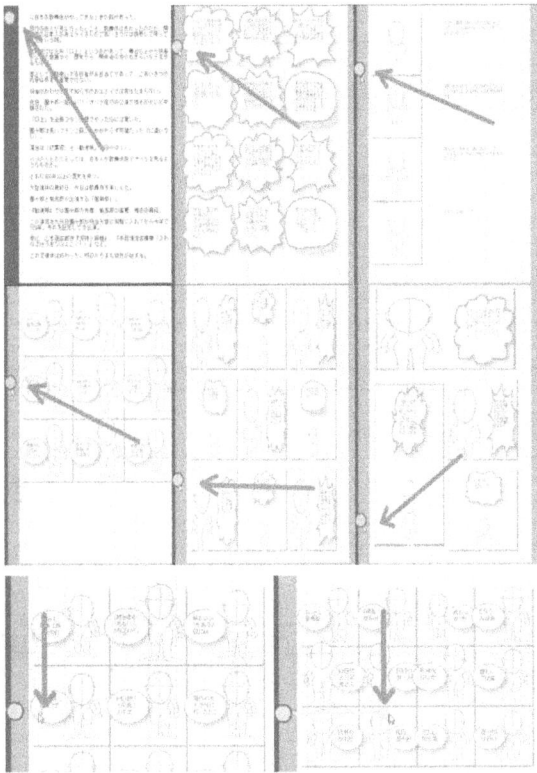

Figure 4: Slider manipulation: Users can select comic style by moving the comic slider. By moving the slider vertically, the system suggests more realistic comic (top). By moving the slider horizontally, the system decreases frame size (bottom).

3. COMIC COMPUTING

Our Comic Computing covers mainly two areas: making a comic and utilizing comic jargon,

3.1 Making a Comic

Our approach of creating comic book is inspired by real comic creation process because it is an effective and established art form. The comic creation process is basically divided into three phases: setting the story plot, roughly drawing a comic, and drawing the comic in detail. In setting the story plot, comic creators write the story outline in four parts: introduction, development, turn, and conclusion. Also, they define their characters' features (e.g., names, sex, age, hobbies, special skills) in this phase. Next, they

roughly draw the comic along with the story plot. In this case, they create frame layouts and roughly draw characters, background, and speech bubbles in each frame. Generally, story plot and rough drawing are important because they are the basic structures of comic books and control whether a comic book is interesting or not. Thus, comic creators spend much time fixing rough drawings and editing story plot and then rough drawing repeatedly to develop the comic. Finally, they draw the comic in detail with pen and ink and screen tones along with additional rough drawing.

3.1.1   Comic Engine
Comic creation with our Comic Engine system [3] is simple. Users input text in the work area and move the comic slider interactively. As the system analyzes the text, a rough comic book is displayed in the work area. By moving the slider vertically, the system suggests a more realistic comic (Fig. 4 (top)) and by moving the slider horizontally, the system increases comic frame size (Fig. 4 (bottom)). Thus, the user manipulates the slider and selects a comic format depending on their design. By using the slider, the three processes of comic creation (writing plot, roughly drawing, and drawing in detail) are naturally integrated.

Figure 5: Comparison between normal and view control comics.

Figure 6: Examples of comic books by Comic Engine.

Generally, the comic style and frame layout are perfectly dependent on the creator's feeling and experience. For example, one creator likes small frames. Another creator uses large frames. Also, one page may contain mainly small frames and another page may have both large and small frames. Thus, the system allows users to select their preferred layout by slider manipulations.

The system provides edit functions, so users can interactively change element information, such as image, position, and scale. Each element, such as face, body, background, and text bubble, is treated as a simple shape mapped to image data. Thus, users can move and resize the elements by considering their design. Our system provides several types of templates, such as for backgrounds, character faces, character bodies, text bubbles, and effects. These templates are especially useful for beginners to create a comic because they do not need to prepare comic elements and can instead focus on creating the comic itself.

Comparisons of a comic created by a conventional system and a comic created by our system are shown in Fig. 5. In the left comic, the comic elements are set simply. The entire page is too simple to be interesting for a reader because the story tempo is always the same. In contrast, the right comic, created by our system, focuses on the Attention Cuing. In the second line, the difference between the current and next frame is clearer, so the story tempo is changed. A character size means the distance between the virtual camera and character positions. Thus, if a character size were increased, the character would become more vivid than the smaller character. The next examples in Fig. 6 show more polished comics created by our system. Each character is designed by professional designers, so users can create more polished comics by simple drag and drop manipulations.

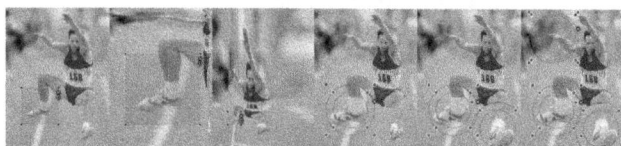

Figure 7: Character deformation.

3.1.2 EnforManga

In EnforManga system [4, 7], the process of comic creation is basically similar to that in conventional systems like ComicLife [5]. A user can manipulate the data by dragging and dropping. After setting a layout for a comic book and setting images by dragging and dropping to create a basic comic book, users deform the basic comic book to make it more interesting. Our system deforms a basic comic book by combining background and character deformations. According to actual comic books, the main character is bigger and more detailed than the other elements, so the background is a kind of extra element. Thus, the background should be rougher than the main character. Moreover, by deforming the main character, a comic becomes more interesting and fun, and the contrast between the character and background is clearer. Our system supports two deformations.

We use non-liner and liner deformation based on the fisheye method for character deformation. Basically, these techniques are common in IV research. The feature area is bigger and clearer and the non-feature area is smaller when using non-linear deformation. We use this deformation technique to make the character bigger and more interesting. By combining non-linear and linear deformations, the inside of a selected area is linearly deformed and the outside of the area is non-linearly deformed. Our system basically uses images to create comic books. Generally, an image contains feature objects, such as humans, animals, and buildings. The system deforms to make such elements clearer.

In an actual comic, a character is one of the most important elements in a comic frame, so we also focus on character deformation. As characters are essential for storytelling, it is important to focus on how to depict them. Generally, by controlling the character's size and position, the readers can easily understand the character's feelings and the comic story. Thus, character deformation is necessary for creating a comic that is similar to an actual comic. Figure 7 shows a simple example of our character deformation process. Our system interactively deforms the user-selected area. A user can deform all or part of the character by focusing on his or her design. For example, a user can deform only the face, hands, arms, or legs of a character. Deforming a part of a character is useful for adding accent or to make a clear contrast between current and previous frames. Also, deformation is useful for making the character more interesting or fun. For example, a character that has a big face and a small body is comical and more interesting.

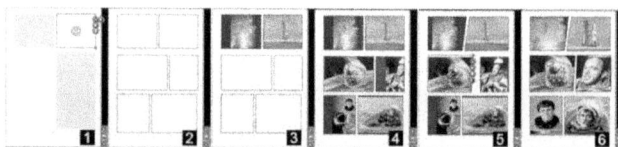

Figure 8: Process of picture comic creation.

Figure 9: Comparison between normal and deformation comics.

Figure 8 shows how to create a comic book using our system. First, a user sets a layout for a basic comic book. As candidates are displayed for user's input, he or she creates a layout by continuously selecting candidates (Fig. 8 (1, 2)). For the layout, the user sets images by dragging and dropping to create the basic comic (Fig. 8 (3, 4)). Next, the user edits the comic book by scaling a frame and moving the image (Fig. 8 (5)). Finally, he or she deforms the characteristic element in each frame. (Fig. 8 (6))

Figure 9 presents a comparison between basic and deformed comic books. The basic comic book is simply created by dragging and dropping images (Fig 9 (left)). This is similar to a comic book created by conventional systems. The deformed comic book is created by focusing on the parts of a character (Fig 11 (right)). In this case, an athlete in each frame becomes more interesting by deforming part of his body.

3.1.3 Comic Browsing

The comic-browsing mode is used to show created comics, in particular to other users. Thus, the main purpose is to share the created comic not only on PCs but also on small display devices, such as cellular phones, PDAs, and portable game devices. These devices have such small displays that showing an entire page is difficult. Our approach is to show a created comic partly through animation, so a static comic becomes a kind of animation. When users read a comic in the real world, their viewpoint moves for the comic. In our approach, a comic moves for the users' fixed viewpoint.

Nodes control virtual camera positions, and the camera moves from one node to the next. The preview window represents a small device display and is used to preview the animation. In the comic area, users set and edit node positions and sizes. The view control function in the system automatically sets the view nodes onto character faces and text bubble positions because the system already contains character and text bubble information. By controlling the scale, users can show a text bubble in detail or enhance a character's attribute. A simple example of setting view nodes is shown in Fig. 10. In this example, a user controls node positions and scale. To achieve browsing animation, the virtual camera moves from one node to the next. The node size controls the camera focus, so the camera zooms in if the node is large and zooms out if the node is small.

Moreover, the system provides several image effects (e.g., color, dissolving, and checker wipe) and some sound effects. This kind of effect is useful for enhancing the representation of the character's feelings. For example, when a character feels shocked, a dissolving effect or a depression sound is more effective than a normal animation.

Figure 10: Comic browsing.

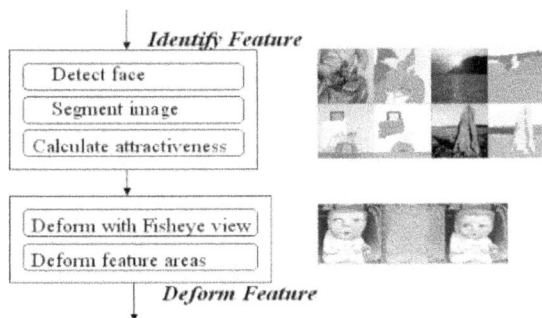

Figure 11: Process of Image Enforme.

3.2 Utilizing Comic Jargon,

We introduce Image Enforme [6] and DigestManga [5] as utilizing comic jargon. Comic deformation is useful for information retrieval, because feature areas in an image become clearer. In movie editing, comic timeline is effective for movie timeline.

3.2.1 Image Enforme

We introduce a deformation technique that enlarges the feature areas in an image while retaining the information in the non-feature areas. Our main purpose is to provide an effective thumbnail that is useful for practical use in small devices (e.g., cellular phone and digital camera). Our approach can quickly deform image features based on a rapid segmentation technique that we have proposed. Moreover, our approach supports multi features as deformation elements. As a result, the feature areas were enlarged and the non-feature areas were reduced at almost a frame rate.

As shown in Fig. 11 (left), there are two processes: extracting the feature areas from an image and deforming the feature areas.

Extracting feature areas: We think that a human face in an image is the most important element, because the image itself would become strange if the system did not recognize a face as a feature. We use the method described by Sabe and Hidai [22]. After the face detection, the system starts an image segmentation process. We have also proposed an image segmentation method [23] that is a practical and readily available method for segmenting images (Fig.11 (right)). Next, the system deletes the background regions using the method proposed by Tanaka [25]. In order to identify highly attractive regions, we used Kansei factors [24]. The factor for each area was based on some parameters (e.g., color, size, and position). Based on the calculated the factor, we can determine which regions of a picture interest for viewers.

Deforming feature areas: We used a multi-fisheye technique to treat multi-features. An image was initially mapped onto a mesh and was then deformed by zooming, using the fisheye method [18]. The system calculates the inside of the rectangles linearly, and calculates the outside of the rectangles non-linearly.

Figure 12 Image thumbnails by Image Enforme.

Two groups of thumbnails are shown in Fig. 12 (top) (121 images, each 256 x 256 pixels). The original images are shown on the left, and the images deformed using the Image Enforme technique are shown on the right. Although the feature areas in the original images were found using image process, the characteristic objects (human faces, buildings, symbols, etc.) were successfully identified and deformed. Since most of the original images contained such objects, the subjects on the right are much clearer. When the feature area was small, the object was deformed more effectively. Two pairs of representative thumbnails are shown in Fig. 12 (bottom); the objects in the feature areas, a building and two people, are clearly almost the same size as in the originals.

3.2.2 DigestManga

Although conventional systems focus on converting movies to comic books, our intention is to establish the smooth relationship between movies and comics (Fig. 13). Thus, our goal is to provide both a visual summary of a movie and a summarized movie by using comic editing, so users can visualize an input movie as a comic book and edit the movie through the visualized comic. In order to visualize an input movie, the system provides both automated and manual approaches. In the automated approach, a comic book is automatically created from an input movie through image processes. In the manual approach, users create a comic by using simple manipulations like drag and drop. Also, the system provides several editing functions such as translating the comic frames and adding extra elements, such as speech bubbles and focus lines.

In addition, our system deforms the movie contents along with the comic visualization. Each comic frame on a page is a kind of impressive or feature scene for the users, because the page is edited by the users and each frame is selected by them. Our deformation technique regards comic frames on a page as feature areas in an input movie. Our deformation is calculated using zooming techniques [6], so the movie contents are deformed without any information loss and naturally connected between the feature and non-feature areas. The contents in the non-feature areas are played more quickly, and the contents in the feature areas are played normally. As a result, users can quickly view the contents and understand the relationships between the entire story and the features.

Figure 13: Movie editing with DigestManga.

$$s' = f(s)$$

$$f(s) = (\frac{dst_s}{src_s}s)$$

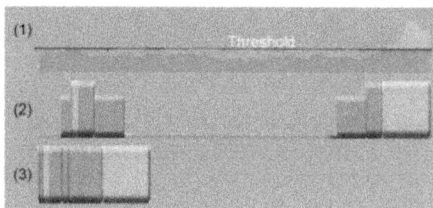

Figure 14: Calculation of play speed.

We use fisheye algorithm to control the play speed of movie, so the feature area is played normally, and the non-feature areas are

played quickly depending on the distance between the frame and the feature frame. The total playing time can be as little as one-fourth that of the original movie. The frame speed calculation is defined by using the following.

In the equations given above, *srcs* is the length of the total playtime of an input image and *dsts* is the distance between the next feature and the current frame (Fig. 14 (top)). In this calculation, each play speed of movie frame depends on the distance between feature and current frames. In our approach, feature area is played normally, and non-feature areas are played quickly depending on the distance between the frame and feature frame. The total playing time can be as little as one-fourth that of the original movie (Fig. 14(bottom)).

4. COMIC FORMAT

Our proposed comic interfaces use the following format based on XML, so manipulations such as editing or creating a comic book are the same throughout all the interfaces.

The comic structure is hierarchical and contains four elements including story, page, frame, and various frame elements such as characters and speech bubbles. Our XML file contains such elements. Figure 15 shows our XML file that contains information such as image, effect, scale, and position.

Figure 15: Example of XML file for comic.

5. DISCUSSION

We have demonstrated our system many times and released our systems as web applications. In particular, a demonstration of our system that was given during a laboratory open house prompted many interesting reactions and comments from visitors.

5.1 Making a Comic

Although comic artists have analyzed comic grammars [2], they have focused on common rules for comic creation. Our concept was to integrate Attention Cuing with comic creation. We demonstrated creating a comic interactively and compared comics created by a conventional system and by our system to explain the Attention Cuing techniques. Although the Attention Cuing was a unique and new approach for comic creation, our design concepts were well received by many visitors. Generally, comics are very familiar to people, most of who often read them, so many of our visitors easily understood our concepts and system features. Moreover, the simple manipulations were also well received. In our system, drawing skills are not necessary, and we observed that many visitors could create a comic by manipulating predefined data. People often have a favorite comic or comic artist. Some visitors created a comic by setting detail angles and layouts in imitation of their favorite comics and authors.

Many images are available because of the development of the digital camera and cellular phones with camera functions. However, there is almost no way to use them for entertainment purposes. Most applications for images are like image albums over a network. Some visitors commented that our system could use these images effectively to create a comic. For real-life comic creation, drawing skills are needed. However, most users generally do not have such skills. They do, however, have access to portable devices. Our system is based on simple manipulations for creating comics, so we think the system would be useful for portable devices. These devices contain a camera, so users can easily obtain image data. The devices also support simple input methods, such as pen input and simple buttons. Thus, our system would work well in such devices, and users could create a comic just as though they were playing a game.

Our target users are basically beginners and children because our system supports simple creation but cannot create a professional comic. However, our system would be useful for professionals if they used our system to create a rough sketch of their comics, called the name process. Generally, professional comic creators draw rough sketches first. In a professional comic creation process, this task is extremely important because it fixes the story and the layout of the comic. In our system, comic elements can be moved and resized freely. Thus, it is also effective for professionals to roughly and quickly create a comic draft.

Our deformed comic books were received good reactions from visitors by showing a comparison between normal and deformed comic books, like in Figure 9. In the deformed comic book, the contrast between the character and background is very clear and the original character becomes more interesting with character deformation, which is similar to actual comics. Users of our system can create a comic by only manipulating predefined image data, so drawing skills are not necessary. Thus, many visitors could start creating a comic after only a simple introduction. Some visitors added accents between the current and previous frames to make a clear contrast between the character and background by deforming the basic comic.

5.2 Utilizing Comic Jargon

The visitors could generally identify the deformed images more clearly than the original images. Most visitors could understand the concept of providing comic like thumbnails. They quickly comprehended the efficiency of doing this by comparing normal and deformed thumbnails and different sizes thumbnails (Fig. 12). The visitors could easily identify the objects in the deformed image even when it was difficult to identify them in the normal image. Also, since the features are produced through a combination of non-linear and linear deformation, most of the deformed images, especially the faces, looked quite funny. Many visitors remarked that the deformed images and thumbnails were interesting. Moreover, since we can adjust the image resolution and mesh flexibly, we can adapt them to the capabilities of the target device. The error rate is related to the size of the feature area and is important because a deformed image is not effective if the original features cannot be retrieved. Since our deformation is

based on fisheye calculation, objects close to deformed features are also deformed. Moreover, the non-feature areas still reside in the deformed image. In contrast, with cropping, unrecognized feature areas are cropped.

Our goal of the DigestManga system was to establish a smooth relationship between movies and comics. Our simple interactions received good reactions from users. We found that many visitors edited comic books from an input movie by using our system after our simple demonstration. They edited a comic book and checked the movie in the preview area over and over again to achieve their design. Through our comic system, an input movie becomes interesting and comical. Also, the playtime of the movie is reduced by our deformation techniques. Thus, users can watch the movie interestingly and quickly.

5.3 Communication with Comic

Many people commented that the system would be useful for Blogging. Blogging is a kind of Internet diary, and most blog sites contain text and image data. These elements are useful for creating a comic with our system, which is effective for translating blog data to a comic format. We believe this type of comic is a good application as a first step in introducing our system. It could become a new type of web content, because most blog content has the same style. In contrast, some visitors requested to add image effects. Our system treats images, so image effects are also important elements. We believe that comic books will become more interesting by adding such effects. We also demonstrated comic creation by using blog data. A blog is a kind of diary on the Internet, and most blog sites contain text content and image data. The text content could be useful for creating a comic, and our system would be effective for converting blog data to a comic. We think this type of comic could become a new type of web content because most blog content has the same style. Several people suggested that our system is useful not only for blogs but also for a wide variety of content, such as documents and manuals. With our system, even boring content could be funny and interesting.

Our approach to comic browsing was also well received, especially with regards to interaction techniques, although it is very simple: setting and following view nodes. In spite of the simple manipulations, users can easily imagine the relationship between a whole page and a focus part of it. We think our browsing method is also useful for presentations. Generally, presenters show slides one by one. After finishing their presentation, they show slide thumbnails for the Q&A session. Our system can set slides as a comic and show a slide or all the slides, so the audience could understand the relationship between the current slide and the entire presentaion.

5.4 Related Work

Comics are a kind of visualization technique and are useful for making complex information fun and interesting. Creation systems for comics have been developed. They integrate comic representations using computers, and there are mainly two types. One system uses comics to convey complex information [8, 9, 10]. These systems are useful for making complex content (e.g., chat logs and video content) more familiar and interesting. The other system supports comic creation itself. These systems enable users to create comics with computers [11, 12].

Comic visualization is useful for complex data. By use of comic features and grammar, such as text bubbles, characters, and frame layouts, complex data such as chat logs becomes interesting and fun. The same can be done for diaries. Some systems translate movie content to comics. These systems are very useful for translating animation data to static images. Through comic grammar, movies are displayed as comics, so users can see the content more quickly and print it out. However, the focus of these systems is to represent a movie in a comic-like format. The representations are simply like image thumbnails and are not a comic. Movie editing systems support the setting of frame data onto a rectangular layout like an image thumbnail. However, these layouts are no longer in a comic format. While a comic is created automatically, the comic is not enough for a user's design and needs. These systems do not provide an edit function. Comics created by the systems are only at a draft level, so editing functions are needed. While some comic creation systems focus on professional use, others provide simple manipulations. For professional comic creation, some systems use a practical comic creation process in the real world. On a computer, these systems can support and manage a user's tasks. However, the GUIs and parameters are very complex, so these elements are problematic for beginners. Users have to learn these complex elements, so this becomes a serious barrier for beginners.

Some systems support simple manipulation for creating comics. They enable users to create a comic by using images and pictures through simple drag and drop manipulations. The drawing process is avoided by using predefined data, such as images and pictures. Thus, users can create a comic only by setting the necessary images, so even beginners can create a comic. However, the created comics are very simple and boring because the images and pictures are used simply.

Thus, the created comics are almost the same tempo, so they just like image thumbnails. We were inspired by the ComicLife system, which provides drag and drop manipulations for comic creation. The system only focuses on background data and bubble images, so our system enhances this concept. A comic consists of many elements, so backgrounds and text bubbles are not enough. Thus, we try to support other types of data (e.g., backgrounds, text bubbles, characters, page layout, and effects) by drag and drop manipulations.

Several systems use 3D CG to represent a comic book [19, 20]. Alves [19] uses 3D CG models to create a comic book. However, 3D CG contains complex elements such as preparing 3D characters and controlling camera perspective. These elements are serious especially for beginners. Moreover, other systems support only some comic elements. For example, systems may focus on how to represent focus lines or may support comic-like drawing. Systems may automatically translate input lines into comic-style drawing. These systems are useful in combination with conventional comic creation systems.

6. CONCLUSION

We described a "Comic Computing" method that integrates comics with a user interface for a creation and communication environment. We first mentioned our concept related with IV researches, and then showed practical applications based on the concept such as Comic Engine, EnforManga, Image Enforme, and DigestManga. We also discussed our systems through users' comments and reactions.

7. REFERENCES

[1] Card, S. K., MacKinlay, J. D. and Shneiderman, B.: Readings in Information Visualization: Using Vision to Think, Morgan Kaufmann, 1999.

[2] S. Mccloud, "Understanding Comics: The Invisible Art", ISBN-10:006097625X, 1994.

[3] H. Tobita, Comic Engine: Interactive Comic Creation System, in Proc of ACM AVI 2010, 2010.

[4] H. Tobita and K. Shibasaki, EnforManga: Interactive Comic Creation System with Drag-and-Drop and Deformation, in Proc of IEEE ISM 2009, 2009.

[5] H. Tobita, DigestManga: Interactive Movie Summarizing through Comic Visualization, in Proc. of ACM CHI 2010 (Extend Abstract), 2010.

[6] H. Tobita and N. Frank, ImageEnforme: Automatic Deformation of Image for Multi-features without Information Loss, Pervasive 2009 (late braking), 2009.

[7] SMOJ http://www.sony.jp/hitokoto/weblabo/comic/

[8] D. Kurlander, T. Skelly, and D. Salesin. "Comic chat", In Proceedings of ACM SIGGRAPH '96, pp. 225-236, 1996.

[9] S. Uchihashi, J. Foote, A. Girgensohn, and J. Boreczky. "Video mange: Generating semantically meaningful video summaries", In proceedings of ACM MultiMedia '99, pp. 383-392, 1999.

[10] Y. Sumi, R. sakamoto, K. Nakao, and K. Mase. "ComiDiary: Representing individual experiences in a comic style", In Proceedings of UBICOMP 2002, pp. 16-32, 2002.

[11] Comic Stadio http://www.celsys.co.jp/

[12] Comic Life http://plasq.com/

[13] Ben Fry: Visualization Data: Exploring and Explaining Data with the Processing Environment.

[14] G. G. Robertson, J. D. Mackinlay and S. K. Card: Cone Trees: Animated 3D visualization of hierarchical information, Proceedings of the ACM Conference on Human Factors in Computing Systems (CHI'91), pp. 189-194, 1991.

[15] M. H. Brown: Algorithm Animation, MIT Press, 1988.

[16] H. Koike, K. Ohno: Snort view: visualization system of snort logs, Proceedings of the 2004 ACM workshop on Visualization and data mining for computer security, 2004.

[17] E. Orimo, H. Koike: Zash: A Browsing System for Multi-Dimensional Data, Proceedings of the IEEE Symposium on Visual Languages (VL' 99), 1999.

[18] G. W. Furnas, Generalized fisheye views. In Proceedings of the ACM Tran. on Computer-Human Interaction 1, 2, pp. 126-160, 1994.

[19] Alves, A. Simoes, R. Figueiredo, M. Vala, A. Paiva, R. Aylett, "So tell me what happed: Turning agent-based interactive drama into comics", *In Processing of the 7th international joint conference on Autonomous agents and multiagent system*, 2008.

[20] W. Eisner, "Comics and Sequential Art: Principles and Practices from the Legendary Cartoonist", ISBN-10: 0393331261, 2008.

[21] A. Salovaara. "Appropriation of a mms-based comic creation: from system functionalities to resources for action, *In proceedings of CHI 2007*, pp. 1117–1126, 2007.

[22] K. Sabe and K. Hidai, Real-time Multi-view Face Detection using Pixel Difference Feature, Recognition, 10th Symposium on Sensing via Image Information (SSII 04), 2004.

[23] R. Nock and F. Nielssen, Statistical Region Merging, Transactions on Pattern Analysis and Machine Intelligence (TPAMI) IEEE CS Press 4, pp. 557–560, 2004.

[24] S. Tanaka, S. Inoue, M. Ishikawa, and S. Inoue, A Method for Extracting and Analyzing "Kansei" Factors from Pictures, In Proceedings of IEEE Workshop on Multimedia Signal Processing 1997, pp. 251–256, 1997.

[25] S. Tanaka, A. Planete, and S. Inoue, A Foreground-Background Segmentation Based on Attractiveness. In Proceedings of CGIM 1998, pp. 191–194, 1998.

Hierarchical Task Instance Mining in Interaction Histories

Benedikt Schmidt,
Johannes Kastl, Todor
Stoitsev
SAP Research Darmstadt
62483 Darmstadt, Germany
firstname.lastname
@sap.com

Max Mühläuser
Telecooperation Group,
Darmstadt University of
Technology
64289 Darmstadt, Germany
max@informatik.tu-
darmstadt.de

ABSTRACT

Knowledge work at computer workplaces involves execution of multiple concurrent tasks with frequent task interruptions. The complexity of the resulting work processes makes task externalization a desired goal towards facilitating analysis and support of knowledge work, e.g. by extracting and disseminating best practices.

In this paper, we present a task mining method that identifies tasks based on interaction histories. The method generates instances of a semantic hierarchical task model which captures an abstraction of the work processes. A specific characteristic of the method is that it mines tasks based on a combination of semantic and temporal features, extracted from enriched interaction histories. The use of semantic similarity results in a high robustness of the system with respect to task interruption and concurrent task execution. An evaluation of our task mining method based on a study with users executing frequently interrupted tasks is presented. One element of the evaluation is the assessment of different algorithms for semantic similarity computing, namely Term Matching (TM), Vector Space Model (VSM) and Latent Dirichlet Allocation (LDA). For an approach using VSM a precision of 0.83, a recall of 0.76 and a F1-measure of 0.79 is reached.

Categories and Subject Descriptors

H.4.1 [**Information Systems Applications**]: Office Automation

General Terms

Human Factors

Keywords

human-computer interaction, task execution support, context, knowledge work support

1. INTRODUCTION

The externalization of knowledge work execution is an efficient foundation for various knowledge work support scenarios such as the mitigation of prospective memory failures [9, 18], the automation of recurring work, improved information access/organization [13], and knowledge dissemination [21]. User interaction histories are frequently used for such externalization [13, 18, 17]. These histories are temporally ordered lists of classified events that stand for user-system interactions, and generally comprise complex mixtures of information about resources a user operated on, using different applications. The complexity of these histories results from the fact that knowledge work in organizations includes frequent disruptions and task-switches [9] that veil the structure of work execution, i.e. it remains unclear which acts serve similar goals and are constrained by situational requirements or individual competencies.

Task mining is the identification of tasks as logical units of work in interaction histories resulting from externalization of work execution. This paper contributes to the research on unsupervised task mining based on interaction histories (c.f. [18, 17, 5]). Our mining method emphasizes robustness of the system with respect to task switches and a process representation of the mined task instances. Task switch robustness is the result of a clustering of interaction history elements based on semantic similarity, not mainly on temporal relations. The process representation follows a Semantic Hierarchical Task Model (SHTM) that presents work execution processes as action and operation hierarchy, following Activity Theory (AT). SHTM enables the mining of abstract process representations of tasks.

The remainder of this paper is organized as follows. First, background on task execution is given. Second, a SHTM to capture task execution processes is presented. Then, a task mining process to generate task model instances is introduced and the task mining is evaluated by a user study. Finally, related work is discussed and the conclusion is given.

2. BACKGROUND

A decent understanding of knowledge work execution at computer workplaces, their formation and externalization opportunities is essential for task mining. Task execution at computer workplaces generally addresses different concurrent goals, resulting in parallel or rapid succession of task executions. Task interruptions occur frequently and stimulate task switches. Studies report 50 task switches over a single week [9]. Thereby, execution processes for similar tasks are not uniform, but emerge in an individual, intentional problem solving process to reach a goal in reaction to situational dependencies [16, 25, 23, 6]. One can distinguish an external and a subjective perspective on the execution process. From an external perspective, a work process manifests as a series of objective observable acts. For a subject, the work process is a dynamic sequence of hierarchically related goal episodes which involve subgoals and the realization by acts [16, 25].

The computer workplace is an environment for work execution, that shapes work execution through its intrinsic design, i.e. supported interactions and available tools. Nevertheless, the mediation by the computer is given implicitly as the computer as tool has no prominent influence on the work. Individuals plan and perceive their interaction with the computer in terms of goals with accompanying tasks rather than in terms of system commands [2]. The technology disappears although it shapes the individual interaction. From this perspective, two characteristics of computer workplaces are striking:

- *Relevance of text:* Computer work boils down to the creation, consumption and transformation of encoded signs that transfer information. The importance of the relationship between text and activity with respect to Vygotsky, Leonitev, Bakhtin and Burke's idea of "Language as Symbolic Action" has been highlighted in [7].

- *Highly structured environment:* Regular computer workplaces include a set of standard software that follows common interaction paradigms. The standardized interaction is familiar to individuals and performed without cognitive efforts i.e. in the form of operations.

The characteristics of the computer workplace shape and structure the work process. Actions and operations of knowledge workers at computer workplaces are not directly observable, as an externalization by an interaction history only includes acts as event representation. Nevertheless, it is beneficial to abstract from observable acts and describe knowledge work processes by means of actions and operations. Such abstraction unfolds the solution processes which structure the work processes of individuals.

3. SEMANTIC HIERARCHICAL TASK MODEL (SHTM)

The SHTM is a task model for work execution at computer workplaces that follows the terminology of activity theory that decomposes activities into actions and operations [14]. This understanding is explained in detail in [20]. SHTM stipulates the transition from objectively observable acts at computer workplaces to the hierarchical structure of operations and actions. The model supports the process of task extraction from interaction histories. SHTM is a semantic model, as it includes information about user-system interaction that enriches information included in interaction histories and enables abstraction from single interaction events to abstract representations of work episodes. For example, for an authoring process with different applications the model does not suggest representing a set of application switches but extraction of the interactions of the different used application and the purpose of the interactions.

SHTM decomposes a task t into knowledge-intensive actions, termed knowledge actions in the following and repre-

sented by the attribute *knowledgeActions* : *Knowledge ActionList* of t. Knowledge actions themselves are decomposed into operations at the computer desktop, termed desktop operations in the following and represented by the attribute *desktopOperations* : *DesktopOperationList* for a knowledge action k. By organizing tasks based on knowledge actions, an abstraction from the actual execution process is realized that describes tasks in terms of aggregated and classified execution process fragments. The connection between the different concepts is visible in figure 1 and is discussed in the following.

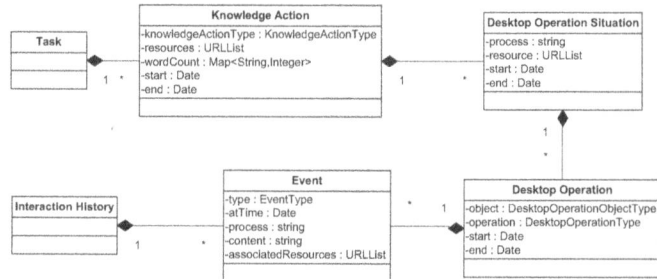

Figure 1: Main elements of SHTM

3.1 Desktop Operations

A desktop operation is a user-system interaction that follows standard interaction-patterns. These paradigms are well trained by individuals and can be applied without much cognitive effort. In terms of AT, a user-system interactions at computer workplaces is situated on the operation level.

A desktop operation d is specified by a tuple of operation and object, represented by the attributes *operation* : *Desktop OperationType* and *object* : *DesktopObjectType*. A desktop operation references events that are the objective indicators of the desktop operation (e.g. a set of events in an interaction history) by the attribute *event* : *EventList*. Additional information is the *start* : *Date* and *end* : *Date* of a desktop operation. The following objects are considered for desktop operations:

- Application: An application is a piece of software that can be run in the computer environment and is used to transform information. An operating system process is a running instance of an application.

- File: A file is a container structure for information. Files have an address and permission structures to organizes access and modification.

- Folder: A folder is a container structure to organize files. Generally, folders have an address, encapsulate an arbitrary number of files and are described by a label.

- Information Object: Information objects are pieces of information presented to the user. This includes, for example, textual information represented by a string of characters. Information objects often have a structure to make them accessible by functionalities of software system. One method to persist information objects are files.

Obj / Opr	App	File	Folder	Information Object	Window
Open	x	x	x		
Close	x	x	x		
Save		x			
Rename		x	x		
Delete		x	x	x	
Cut		x	x	x	
Paste		x	x	x	
Print		x			
Create		x	x	x	
Execute	x				
Focus			x		x

Table 1: Desktop operations: pairs of operation (OPR) and object (OBJ)

Possible associations of desktop operation types and desktop object types are given in table 1.

Desktop operations that are executed in sequence for the same resource using the same application are combined to desktop operation situation. I.e. a desktop operation situation is considered as a continuous work episode with a single application on a specific resource. A desktop operation situation dos has the attributes $process : String$, $resource : URL$, $start : Date$, $end : Date$ and $desktopOperations : DesktopOperationList$.

3.2 Knowledge Actions

Knowledge actions are techniques applied to execute working tasks. These techniques are tangible subgoals that support an individual in structuring a task execution process. An example is the goal of writing a document. An individual structures the respective working process by subgoals that can be directly translated to an interaction with a tool, e.g. using the knowledge action *authoring*. Still, the *authoring* is not straight forward but needs adaptation for the specific task and the specific working situation. Thus, knowledge actions accomplish the transition from planning to actual work execution combined with a process of situative adaptation. At the computer workplace knowledge actions are executed by means of desktop operations. As the adaptation of the technique to an explicit goal requires cognitive efforts, the described techniques are situated on the action level of AT (see also [11]).

For the computer workplace a set of knowledge actions has been identified based on a literature review [11, 24] and discussions. The SHTM includes the following knowledge actions:

- Consuming: A knowledge worker focuses a resource on the computer desktop and focuses his attention to the visual representation of an information.

- Authoring: A knowledge worker creates a representation of information in an existing or new information object through a knowledge transformation process.

- Communicating: A knowledge worker shares information with others.

- Organizing: A knowledge worker organizes existing information resources.

- Browsing: A knowledge worker reviews different information objects in rapid succession.

A knowledge action k is modeled as a classified carrier for desktop operations. k is classified by the attribute $action : KnowledgeActionType$. A knowledge action has the attribute $situations : DesktopOperationSituationList$. To specify knowledge actions, they additionally contain the attributes $resources : URLList$ for all resources required for the execution and $wordCount : Map < String, Integer >$ for an abstract representation of the textual content of the knowledge action (what it is about). The duration is captured by $start : Date$ and $end : Date$.

4. TASK MINING USING A SEMANTIC TASK MODEL

The following section describes task mining as extraction of SHTM instances based on ex post analysis of interaction histories. Basically, the mining process presents itself as connection of the user-interaction events contained in interaction histories with the SHTM in a bottom-up process of data aggregation as depicted in figure 2. Interaction history events are aggregated to desktop operations which themselves are combined to knowledge actions which finally enable the identification of tasks. The task mining method reflects concurrent task executions and task switches, as it ignores temporal information, but focuses completely on semantic similarity of enriched textual content included in the interaction histories.

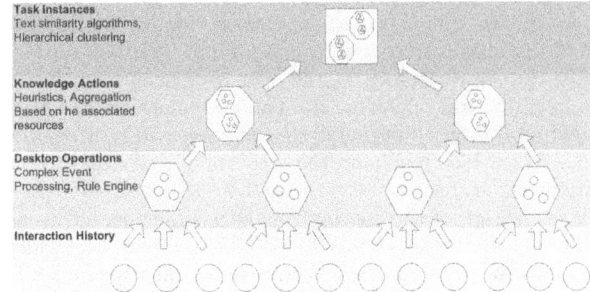

Figure 2: Hierarchy of Behavior Situatedness in Activity Theory

4.1 Interaction History Creation

Interaction histories can be basically considered as logs of user-system interactions. The literature describes different applications to generate this type of data [18, 13]. Interaction history data gives an insight into work as temporally ordered information about user-system interaction. The approach presented in this paper requires interaction histories that extract text displayed to the user and include information about the time frame during which the text was visible. An event e has the attributes $name : String$ to classify an event, $atTime : Date$ to specify the occurrence, $content : String$ for the textual content, $process : String$ for the application generating the event and optionally $associatedResource : URLList$ for resources that are locked by the process

To create interaction histories, a sensor application has been developed for the Windows operating system (see figure 3 for an excerpt from an interaction history). The sensor application has been developed in C# and generates a sensor stream that can be subscribed by other applications via a CORBA interface. The monitor includes a keyboard hub, mouse hub and listeners to different applications (includes: Microsoft Business Office Suite, web browser, Adobe Reader, Process Monitor, Mouse and Keyboard Hub). Additionally, the UI Automation Framework is used to generate rich information about each focused user interface element. Filter methods like black lists and comparison of temporally related events are applied to optimize the quality of the interaction history, as the system events often send events twice or internal methods may fail. The sensor application realizes events as aforementioned. For technical reasons attributes not mentioned here are included additionally in the actual implementation. The sensor application generates an interaction history as a stream of temporal ordered events $e_1...e_n$.

4.2 Desktop Operation Extraction

The SHTM describes desktop operations d as classified by the attributes $d.operation$ and $d.object$. The events delivered by the sensor application are basic events and need to be processed to identify desktop operations. Mapping events to desktop operations is a process of abstraction, as different interaction types are traced back to the basic terminology of desktop operations. This desktop operation identification is identified through complex event processing: rules are modeled to create desktop operations based on sensor events. Extraction of desktop operations requires basic rules RL of the form $antecedent \Rightarrow consequent$. The $antecedent$ relates to the attributes of the events e. The $consequent$ is a new desktop operation d. The aforementioned stream of temporal ordered events $e_1...e_n$ is processed by the rules $RL_1...RL_n$ which results in the creation of new desktop operations $d_0...d_n$.

A realization of the concept has been implemented using Drools Fusion (JBoss Drools, http://jboss.org/drools) which is capable of event processing and temporal reasoning. In total 98 different rules were developed to extract desktop operations. The amount shows the complexity of the abstraction process, as a large set of interaction types needs to be traced back to the respective desktop operations (e.g. rules for 15 different types of file closing were modeled).

4.3 Knowledge Action Extraction

Knowledge actions as work techniques present themselves as disjoint units of continuous work on a single resource, i.e. desktop operations that stand for the same knowledge action are scattered among the interaction history due to disruptions and a mixture of subgoals executed in parallel. Consequently, knowledge action identification turns out as collection and classification of scattered desktop operations belonging to the same knowledge action. The respective method steps are described in the following:

Create situations: Desktop operation situations *dos* are used to organize desktop operations. Two desktop operations d_i and d_j get associated to a situation *dos*, if $d_i.process = d_j.process$ and no d_k exists with $d_k.process \neq d_{i/j}.process$ and $d_i.atTime < d_k.atTime < d_k.atTime$. A list of desktop operation situations $dos_1...dos_n$ is created.

Create unclassified knowledge actions: Sets of desktop operation situations are created. dos_i and dos_j are included in the same set, if $dos_i.process = dos_j.process$ and $dos_i.resource = dos_j.resource$ is valid. This connection to situations as sets of desktop operations based on process and resource is visible in figure 4. Each set of situations represents an unclassified knowledge action k without specification of $k.action$. Knowledge actions, which have a duration of less than six seconds are filtered as irrelevant which is based on detailed review of interaction histories and comparable to [18] where durations below four seconds are filtered.

Classify knowledge actions: For the detected k the type $k.action$ is identified based on heuristics that make use of an application taxonomy. Each unclassified k contains the desktop operations ($k.situations.desktopOperations$) executed at $k.process$. The heuristics decide for a knowledge action based on the types of desktop operations (e.g. consume, focus) and the classification of $k.process$ in the application taxonomy. For example, the usage of Microsoft Word is generalized to the usage of a word processor. Using this information, one can classify the knowledge actions based on the desktop operations they contain. The desktop operation "Creating"-"Information Object", for example, indicates a knowledge action of the type "Authoring". "Renaming"-"Folder" indicates the knowledge action "Organizing".

Content extraction For each classified knowledge action, the map $k.wordCount$ is extracted. Therefore, the $e.content$ attribute of each event contained in $k.situations.desktop$ $Operations.events$ is subject to tokenization, stop-word-detection, part-of-speech tagging, filtering, stemming and term counting to create a bag-of-words. The bag-of-words contains all terms considered relevant (nouns, verbs) and the number of times they occur. The content extraction has been implemented, using a UIMA [10] pipeline of processing resources.

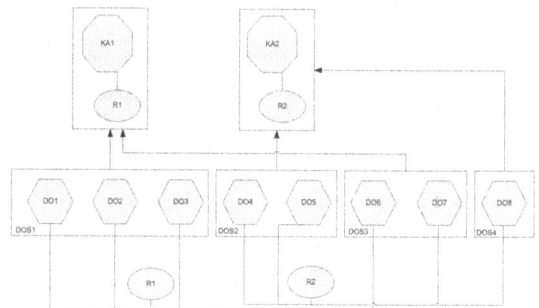

Figure 4: Aggregation of desktop operations to knowledge actions (R=Resource, DO=Desktop Operation, DOS= Desktop Operation Situation, KA=Knowledge Action)

4.4 Task Instance Mining

Task instance mining uses knowledge actions $k_0...k_n$ as generated by the aforementioned method. Each knowledge action stands for a work technique applied at a similar resource with a similar application. Task instances are collections of knowledge actions that serve a similar goal, with other words related knowledge actions.

Here, the term related precisely addresses semantic relatedness. Based on $k.wordCount$ text similarity algorithms

```
<event eventName="FOREGROUND_WINDOW_CHANGED" atTime="01.02.2011 16:19:26.484" eventCategory="Process"><eventattributes>
        <eventattribute name="processname" type="String" value="POWERPNT" />
        <eventattribute name="windowtitle" type="String" value="Microsoft PowerPoint - [Planning-Roundup_v3.pptx]" />
        <eventattribute name="associatedFile" type="String" value="\BaseNamedObjects\MSCTF.Shared.SFM.AFDB" />
        <eventattribute name="associatedFile" type="String" value="C:\Documents and Settings\evaluationuser3\Desktop\work\Planning-
Roundup_v3.pptx" /></eventattributes></event>
<event eventName="FILESYSTEM_OBJECT_DELETED" atTime="01.02.2011 16:19:26.828" eventCategory="Filesystem"><eventattributes>
        <eventattribute name="name" type="String" value="C:\Documents and Settings\evaluationuser3\Desktop\work\Planning-
Roundup_v3.pptx" />
        <eventattribute name="notifyfilter" type="String" value="FileName" /></eventattributes></event>
<event eventName="FILESYSTEM_OBJECT_CREATED" atTime="01.02.2011 16:19:26.828" eventCategory="Filesystem"><eventattributes>
        <eventattribute name="name" type="String" value="C:\Documents and Settings\evaluationuser3\Desktop\work\Planning-
Roundup_v3.pptx" />
        <eventattribute name="notifyfilter" type="String" value="FileName" /></eventattributes></event>
<event eventName="MSPOWERPOINT_EVENT_THROWN" atTime="01.02.2011 16:19:26.968" eventCategory="Application"><eventattributes>
        <eventattribute name="title" type="String" value="Planning-Roundup_v3.pptx" />
        <eventattribute name="content" type="String" value=" Planning Demand and Master Planning Roundup Introduction Author: Andreas
Goeb&#xD;Date: 2011/02/01 Demand Planning Purpose&#xD;improve decisions affecting demand accuracy &#xD;calculation of buffer or
safety stocks &#xD;Results: &#xD;Demand Plan&#xD;Benefit:&#xD;Increased performance of each supply chain entity Master Planning
Purpose&#xD;synchronize the flow of materials along the supply chain&#xD;Range: Mid-term I At least one seasonal
cycle&#xD;Contents:&#xD;Production&#xD;Transport&#xD;supply capacities&#xD;Seasonal stock &#xD;balancing of supply and
```

Figure 3: Excerpt from interaction history

generate input values for a clustering algorithm (used algorithms are given below).

Different methods have been evaluated to calculate semantic relatedness by using a bag-of-words approach. Based on calculations applied to the bag-of-words, the similarity of two bags-of-words is calculated, returning a similarity value between zero and one. An important modification to the bag-of-words was applied here to use the time as relevance factor, i.e. text presented for a longer period of time to a user was considered more important than text presented for a short period of time. Therefore the duration of a knowledge action k was used to weight $k.wordCount$. Three methods to identify semantic relatedness have been applied and compared:

- Term Matching (TM): The number of words that occur in both texts is calculated and scaled by the lengths of both texts (total number of words) [3]. Here, TM is considered as a baseline method.

- Vector Space Model (VSM): The Vector Space Model is an algebraic model to represent text documents [19]. Every text is represented as a term-TF*IDF vector in the N-dimensional space (N representing the number of different terms in both documents). Text similarity is measured by the distance of the vectors within the model.

- Latent Dirichlet Allocation: Latent Dirichlet Allocation is a generative model which regards each text as a mixture of topics and traces each word's creation to one of the text's topics [4]. The model can be applied to realize topic detection and map each text to a probability distribution over the detected topics. The "distance" of two probability distributions can be obtained by utilizing a suitable divergence measure.

The resulting semantic relatedness is weighted based on the temporal closeness of two knowledge actions. The time acts as a gravity for semantic. The technique follows the idea that proximity (spatial or temporal) influences semantic similarity: e.g. homonyms are understood based on a context organized based on spatial and temporal proximity (asking someone for a bank during a finance conversation will most probably not result in a hint for a place to sit down). Therefore the semantic relatedness is weighted by a factor between zero and one that can be calculated by a sigmoid function on all temporal distances between knowledge

actions. The weighted semantic relatedness is input for a hierarchical clustering algorithm [12]. Hierarchical clustering is an unsupervised algorithm which builds a hierarchy of clusters, given a set of input data, an appropriate distance metric, and a linkage criterion. The linkage criterion determines, how the distance between clusters is computed. An average linkage clustering was used, which means that the distance between two clusters is computed by the average distance of all elements within one cluster to all elements within the other cluster. Within the task mining module, an agglomerative variant of hierarchical clustering was implemented, i.e. a "bottom up" approach is used. At the beginning, each knowledge action belongs to its own cluster. Then the algorithm finds the pair of clusters which has the highest similarity. Those clusters are merged into a new cluster and a new level of the hierarchy is created. The algorithm repeats this step until only one cluster remains and the hierarchy is complete. In order to obtain clusters of knowledge actions which are similar to each other and represent a task, a threshold which terminates the algorithm is required.

The last step identifies clusters that belong to one task, even if they are not semantically connected. If a user tended to switch very often between two clusters, i.e. used the applications and resources of both clusters simultaneously or in rapid succession, then the clusters can be merged. For this purpose a matrix that counts all cluster switches is calculated and the clusters are merged, if one of the clusters does not contain more elements than specified by a treshold. As long as clusters are merged, process is repeated.

5. EVALUATION

The following section reports on a study that addresses important aspects of the task mining approach described above. The first aspect is the overall applicability of the approach to task mining in interaction histories. The second aspect is the effect of different methods of semantic similarity calculation (Comparison of TM, VSM and LDA).

The study included eight participants that work for an international software company in the field of IT research. The participants executed a set of predefined, knowledge-intensive tasks (see table 2). Five participants had post-doctoral positions and three participants were PhD students. The tasks were executed in random order and were disrupted during execution. Disruption means that tasks were interrupted randomly to generate task switches as shown in figure

Task 1	Provide information on related work on individual topic
Task 2	Set up meeting to discuss conference paper review
Task 3	Decide on applicant invitation and communicate your decision
Task 4	Plan a trip and inform your colleague with all involved information
Task 5	Present a paper from a foreign language to your colleagues
Task 6	Find Application partners and experts for research project
Task 7	Search for Information on software functionality and save for later use

Table 2: Tasks used for the user study

5. During the execution of the tasks, an interaction history was captured, using the sensor application. The created interaction histories were used as input to the task mining method discussed in the previous section.

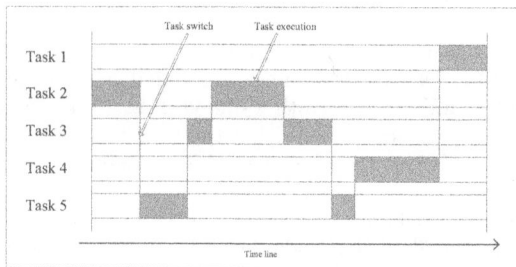

Figure 5: Example for task execution process with task switches

5.1 Evaluation Methodology

The interaction history of each user including the execution process of five frequently switched tasks was input for the task mining method. The mined task instances were assessed against a manually created ground truth. Task instance and ground truth can be considered as clusters of knowledge actions. Input for the creation of a ground truth and task mining were knowledge actions that were extracted from interaction histories based on the aforementioned processes of desktop operation extraction and knowledge action extraction. For these knowledge actions the following process was performed:

- **Ground truth generation:** The study supervisors used interaction logs and notes taken during study execution to validate the quality of knowledge actions and create clusters of knowledge actions that were labeled with the respective task numbers. Thus, the ground truth assigns a task number to each knowledge action extracted from an interaction history.

- **Task mining:** Semantic similarity is the most important aspect of the task mining method. To evaluate the performance of different textual similarity measures, three different cluster distributions (TM, VSM, LDA) were produced and used as input for the hierarchical

clustering algorithm. The algorithm requires a threshold as termination criterion. Tresholds for TM, VSM and LDA were identified in a different study. For the other study, clustering results for input data of interaction histories generated by 90 minutes work executed by 20 users was analyzed to identify optimal treshold values (VSM=0.15, LDA=0.9, TM=0.05).

- **Labeling:** The mined clusters should be similar to the manually labeled clusters of the ground truth, i.e. it should be the same number of clusters, containing the same knowledge actions. In order to compare the knowledge action clusters of the ground truth with the corresponding clusters identified by the system, the following labeling method was applied for each identified cluster: 1) Select a cluster from the task mining as *tolabel* 2) Select the ground truth cluster with the largest percentage of knowledge actions matching the selected cluster as *compareCluster* 3) Label the *tolabel* cluster with the label of *compareCluster* (cf. [5, 17]).

- **Assessment:** A high quality is reached, if a mined task shares many knowledge actions with the corresponding cluster of the ground truth. Three quantitative measures were extracted: 1) Precision: The fraction of knowledge actions in a mined cluster compared to the corresponding manually labeled cluster of the ground truth. The corresponding cluster is the one with the largest matching percentage of items. 2) Recall: The fraction of all knowledge actions in a manually labeled cluster corresponding to a calculated cluster. 3) F1-measure: The weighted harmonic mean of precision and recall. The higher the value of the F1-measure generally the better the result of the algorithm [15].

5.2 Evaluation Results

In total 120 runs of the hierarchical clustering algorithm were analyzed. Table 3 indicates the obtained results. The results for VSM clearly surpass those of both LDA and TM. The low values for TM are expected as it serves as a base line method. The values for the clustering based on LDA are higher than the base line. However, the achieved F1-measure of 0.59 is clearly outperformed by the clustering based on VSM with a F1-measure of 0.79. This result can be partly explained by the amount of input which is used to perform LDA. Only the data, that was collected from an independent run of the task detection system, was used for the similarity calculation step. This is the setup for each similarity algorithm. LDA should produce better results if the complete data of all participants is used to build one single topic model. With an increasing amount of data available, the quality of the inferred topic model will increase [4]. This should be the focus of further investigation regarding the applicability of topic models for task similarity. In the current setup the clustering based on the VSM delivers the best results.

On the total data set average precision of 0.83, a recall of 0.76, and an F1-measure of 0.79 for the Vector Space Model measure was achieved. Figure 6 shows the obtained results for the approach using VSM for the different users. Some differences between the results for the different users are evident. For instance, the system was able to mine tasks with an F1-measure of 0.91 from the task execution of user 2.

	precision	recall	F1-measure
VSM	0.83	0.76	0.79
LDA	0.66	0.57	0.61
TM	0.78	0.41	0.59

Table 3: Average results of the different task similarity measures

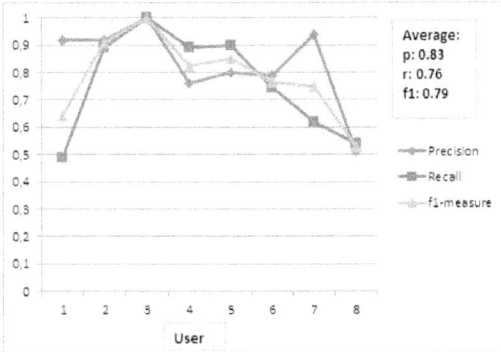

Figure 6: Precision, recall and f1-measure for VSM

For user 8 the system achieved an F1-measure of 0.53. The interaction histories for both task executions were analyzed and show as reason for this difference that user 2 executed the tasks in a fairly straightforward manner. The number of used resources was significantly smaller than what was observed for user 8. This indicates that the more complex the task execution process gets, the harder it is for the task detection system to mine tasks correctly. The combination of semantic and temporal aspects was intended to mitigate this problem, but did not completely resolve it. The task mining method utilizes the full text contents of all associated resources to obtain a notion of task similarity. The assumption underlying the task mining method, that semantic relatedness is key to task clustering when mining interaction histories is central for the discussed approach and brings many advantages but also some disadvantages as discussed in the following:

- **Rejected resources that are semantically not related:** In the study user 8 accessed several web resources that were not relevant for the task. These were for example resources which were accessed and rejected during an information search, because they did not contain the desired information. Such rejected resources were monitored but not assigned to the respective task. Omitting rejected resources brings advantages, as these resources are not relevant for the task.

- **Relevant resources that are semantically not related:** Some resources contain information that can only be assigned to a task with a deeper understanding of semantic relatedness. For example, a web site for currency conversion does contain clearly different textual contents than a web site for flight bookings. A human can link these resources easily if they need to calculate flight ticket prices in a different currency, but as both web sites have different purposes it might be dif-

ficult to relate them semantically in algorithmic fashion. The same applies for resources that use a different vocabulary while describing the same topic. More sophisticated text similarity measures, like LDA, could target this problem, as they do not rely on the exact terms, but built a generative model on how texts are created [4]. Semantic similarities as a measure of task similarity has clear limitations in this respect. The final merge of clusters based on the cluster switches help to mitigate the problem of resources that are not semantically related but belong together.

Overall, the results indicate that the task mining method presented in this paper can sufficiently detect knowledge-intensive tasks. An F1-measure of 0.79 was achieved using the Vector Space Model measure. A precision of 0.83 shows that the identified clusters already sufficiently represent task executions. Overall, the results are promising and indicate that an automatic task detection and task modeling of knowledge-intensive tasks in the computer desktop environment is possible.

6. RELATED WORK

Initial work on interaction histories addressed the analysis of work execution [2]. Interaction histories have proven useful to improve user system interaction, e.g. the UMEA system uses interaction histories to add resources to so called context pools [13]. Many publications involving interaction histories focus on the identification of known task instances generally used to proactively propose resources relevant for the identified task to the user [22, 18]. To provide proactive user support a task repository is required which can be generated manually [1, 8], in a supervised manner through labeled task instances [22] or in an unsupervised manner [5, 17, 18]. Here we focus on unsupervised mining [5, 17, 18] that creates task representations based on interaction histories. Mined tasks are composed of elements of different quality in the different approaches and are evaluated differently. For example Rattenbury et al. [18] evaluate their system by a usefulness study and do not report any values for precision, recall or F1-measure. Oliver et al. [17] and Brdiczka et al. [5] report performance values which are based on different data sets. Thus comparison of the performance is not possible. Nevertheless, in the following different assumptions are given about the evaluations of [17], [5] and the task mining method presented in this paper.

Brdiczka et al. [5] perform task mining based on document usage patterns identified by clustering of events up to a treshold, i.e. the treshold value modifies the number of identified tasks. An F1-measure of 0.32 with a precision of 0.20 is reported for a data set of ten users and 50 tasks, collected over up to three work days. The results are explained by the amount of noise in the input data. By limiting the data set to the six most frequent tasks a f-measure of 0.74 is obtained. Oliver et al. [17] report an F1-measure of 0.58 for a data set of one user and five tasks, collected over about four hours. The results are improved to a recall of 0.76% by using 1 hour chunks of data. Probabilistic latent semantic indexing is used by a mining method that requires a-priori knowledge about the number of tasks in the data set. This previous knowledge about the number of tasks is not required for the method presented in this paper and for [5]. Oliver et al. [17] is related to the approach presented here, as semantic similarity is used. The difference is the amount of text used for the semantic similarity ([17] limits the text to the window titles), knowledge about the task number ([17] requires a-priori knowledge) and the task model ([17] reports about the process but does not provide a task model).

The main difference to existing task mining approach is the obtained task model. While the reviewed systems reduce activities to associated window titles [17], documents [5] or context structures (task relevant information and people) [18], the aforementioned task mining method populates a SHTM to provide an abstraction of the execution process, including details about the execution process. In contrast to existing approaches, mined SHTM instances can be used not only to enable support in the form of resource recommendation, but best practices and next step recommendations. To this point, this quality of support was only possible, if an expert modeled all tasks manually [1, 8].

7. CONCLUSION

Task mining is a relevant research domain to provide a data basis to describe, analyze and support knowledge workers in their daily activities. Mined tasks are foundations for user support systems and contribute to informal learning. This paper contributes a method that mines task instances based on a SHTM. A specific benefit of the SHTM is the hierarchical decomposition of interaction histories into knowledge actions and desktop operations that preserves abstract work execution information. Albeit the expressiveness of the model an automatic identification of model instances in a mining process is possible. We plan to use the mined task instances to propose work execution processes and deliver externalized best practices to knowledge workers.

The method of clustering by semantic similarity has been evaluated, using different approaches, TM, VSM and LDA. The best results were obtained for VSM. The weak results of LDA can be explained as the text corpus of the LDA algorithm was limited to the data of one study participant, each time it was applied. In the future we plan to do a longer study of knowledge workers performing their daily work and believe that LDA will perform better in such a setting with more data. Nevertheless, the results of the task mining method using VSM for semantic relatedness with an F1-measure of 0.79 (precision of 0.83, recall 0.76) are good.

8. REFERENCES

[1] B. Bailey, P. Adamczyk, T. Chang, and N. Chilson. A framework for specifying and monitoring user tasks. *Computers in Human Behavior*, 22(4):709–732, 2006.

[2] L. Bannon, A. Cypher, S. Greenspan, and M. Monty. Evaluation and analysis of users' activity organization, 1983.

[3] J. Bao, C. Lyon, P. Lane, W. Ji, and J. Malcolm. Comparing Different Text Similarity Methods. *UH Computer Science Technical Report 461*, 2007.

[4] D. M. Blei, A. Y. Ng, and M. I. Jordan. Latent Dirichlet Allocation. *Journal of Machine Learning Research*, 3(4-5):993–1022, May 2003.

[5] O. Brdiczka and J. B. Begole. Temporal Task Footprinting : Identifying Routine Tasks by Their Temporal Patterns. *Word Journal Of The International Linguistic Association*, 2010.

[6] K. Byström and P. Hansen. Conceptual framework for tasks in information studies. *Journal of the American Society for Information Science and Technology*, 56(10):1050–1061, 2005.

[7] J. Canny. GaP: a factor model for discrete data. *Proc. of the 27th annual international ACM SIGIR conference on Research and development in information retrieval*, 2004.

[8] B. Cheikes, M. Geier, R. Hyland, F. Linton, and L. Rodi. Embedded training for complex information systems. *Tutoring Systems*, pages 36–45, 1998.

[9] M. Czerwinski, E. Horvitz, and S. Wilhite. A diary study of task switching and interruptions. *Proc. of the SIGCHI*, 2004.

[10] D. Ferrucci and A. Lally. Uima: An architectural approach to unstructured information processing in the corporate research environment. *Natural Language Engineering*, 10:327–348, 2004.

[11] T. Hädrich. Situation-oriented Provision of Knowledge Services. *Dissertation, Martin Luther Universität Halle-Wittenberg*, 2008.

[12] T. Hastie, R. Tibshirani, J. Friedman, and J. Franklin. *The elements of statistical learning: data mining, inference and prediction*. Springer, 2nd edition, 2009.

[13] V. Kaptelinin. UMEA: translating interaction histories into project contexts, 2003.

[14] A. N. Leontiev. *Activity and consciousness*. Progress Publishers, 1977.

[15] C. Manning, P. Raghavan, and H. Schütze. *An Introduction to Information Retrieval*. Number c. Cambridge University Press, 2009.

[16] A. Newell and H. Simon. *Human problem solving*. Prentice-Hall, Englewood Cliffs, NJ, 1972.

[17] N. Oliver, G. Smith, C. Thakkar, and A. Surendran. SWISH: semantic analysis of window titles and switching history, 2006.

[18] T. L. Rattenbury and J. F. Canny. *An Activity Based Approach to Context-Aware Computing*. University of California at Berkeley Berkeley, 2008.

[19] G. Salton, A. Wong, and C. S. Yang. A vector space model for automatic indexing. *Communications of the ACM*, 18(11):613–620, Nov. 1975.

[20] B. Schmidt, H. Paulheim, T. Stoitsev, and M. Mühlhäuser. Towards a Formalization of Individual Work Execution at Computer Workplaces. In *Forthcoming: Lecture Notes in Artificial Intelligence, ICCS*, pages 270–283, 2011.

[21] B. Schmidt, T. Stoitsev, and M. Mühlhäuser. Activity-Centric Support for Weakly-Structured Business Processes, 2010.

[22] J. Shen. Detecting and correcting user activity switches: Algorithms and interfaces, 2009.

[23] T. Trabasso, P. Broek, and S. Suh. Logical necessity and transitivity of causal relations in stories. *Discourse Processes*, 12(1):1–25, 1989.

[24] M. Völkel. *Personal Knowledge Models with Semantic Technologies*. Ph.d. thesis, KIT, 2010.

[25] J. M. Zacks and B. Tversky. Event structure in perception and conception. *Psychological bulletin*, 127(1):3–21, Jan. 2001.

Information Organization on the Internet based on Heterogeneous Social Networks

Eleni Kaldoudi
Democritus University of Thrace
School of Medicine
Alexandroupoli, Greece
Tel. (+30)25510-30329

kaldoudi@med.duth.gr

Nikolas Dovrolis
Democritus University of Thrace
School of Medicine
Alexandroupoli, Greece
Tel. (+30)25510-30322

ndovroli@alex.duth.gr

Stefan Dietze
L3S Research Center
30167 Hannover
Germany
Tel. (+49)551762-17705

dietze@l3s.de

ABSTRACT

The social Web has become an important trend during the last few years with a thriving number of social networking sites that currently address a variety of information needs. Following a first generation of human-centered social networks, the notion of object-centered sociality has been introduced to describe the fact that strong social relationships are built mainly when individuals are grouped together around a shared object. In this paper we attempt to further enhance the notion of the social object and present the concept of heterogeneous social network, where humans and social objects are uniformly treated as equal actors. The paper discusses how this notion can be exploited in different application domains and presents in more detail a particular example from the field of medical education.

Categories and Subject Descriptors

K.0 [**Computing Milieux – General**]. K.3.1 [**Computer Uses in Education**]. J.3.1 [**Life and Medical Sciences**]: Medical Information Systems

General Terms

Design, Experimentation, Theory.

Keywords

Social networking, Semantic technologies, Object-centered sociality, Linked Open Data, Actor network theory.

1. INTRODUCTION

The social Web, or Web 2.0 [1], has become an important trend during the last few years. Among the prominent social web tools, social networking websites focus on creating online communities of individuals who publish their content and activities while exploring others' content and activities, thus creating virtual on-line social groups and associations. This communication paradigm has been taken up by the community of researchers and academics and nowadays there is a thriving number of social networks dedicated to science and professional relations.

At the same time, Semantic Web technologies [2] are specifically designed to address the challenge of data and knowledge management in a world with highly distributed resources. The semantic Web promises an infrastructure that comprises machine understandable content and, therefore, a worldwide Web made of semantically linked data instead of a mere collection of HTML documents.

In this work, these two paradigms of the social Web and the semantic Web are merged for modeling and implementation of heterogeneous social networks of human and nonhuman entities alike that aim to provide alternative ways for rich information organization in different application domains.

More specifically, we propose the use of the actor-network conceptual model [3] to derive working models and subsequently implementations for meaningful and relevant information organization in situations where humans, artifacts (real of digital), organizations and/or concepts interact. Such situations are quite common, and three indicative application areas that we are currently studying include the following: (a) educational content sharing; (b) personalized patient empowerment services; and (c) scientific knowledge management. In all these application domains, the principal idea is to view information organization and management as a heterogeneous social network of humans and various objects, all equal actors as perceived in the actor-network theory. The non-human entities involved are different for each application domain. The basic conceptual principles and the technological approaches for building such networks are presented, and a specific proof-of-concept example is also given.

2. BACKGROUND

As discussed extensively in the literature (see [4] for a thorough overview), in the broader sense 'social' means 'association', as the word derives from the Latin 'socius' meaning a companion or associate. When used in this way, the concept is left open to include anything that can be associated together. However, in the first days of deploying social internet applications, the term 'social' has been used in a way more akin to conventional social theory (e.g. [5],[6],[7]). In this narrower sense, the term is used to refer primarily to human aggregates among themselves. This view is in general indifferent to active nonhuman entities. Things, and for this matter information objects as well, are depicted as tokens and symbols, and they do not have the capacity to act in other ways.

A conventional social network approach concentrates on the network of humans, presumably based on some common social or professional interest – any implied artefacts or concepts are of no interest and are not represented or accounted for in the network

(Figure 1). Here the focus is to establish relationships and connections among humans. These are based on some commonly shared interest, object and/or concept; however this is only implied and not really accounted for in the network. Such an example from the domain of education is the Classroom2.0 social site (http://www.classroom20.com/) which creates a lively forum for discussions on web 2.0 tools and applications in education. Another example (of the many) in the field of healthcare is the CarePages (http://www.carepages.com/) a social network of people collaborating together to share the challenges, hopes and victories of anyone facing a life-altering health event. Finally, LinkedIn (http://www.linkedin.com/), one of the first professional networks connecting people together based on their job profile, is an example of a simple human-only network for scientists (as well as other professionals).

site can be a source of social connectivity, catalysing social networking in virtual spaces. This new approach to sociality has drawn attention, and current state-of-the-art research in the area involves various ways to exploit object-oriented sociality to the benefit of the community. An indicative example from the field of education is Edmodo (http://www.edmodo.com/) a social network for teachers and students who can interact in private virtual classrooms to share educational content and activities. In the healthcare domain, the PatientsLikeMe site (http://www.patientslikeme.com/) connects people based on their health issues and related shared experiences. Finally, an example from the scientific domain is the BioMedExperts (http://www.biomedexperts.com/), where connections between scientists are established based on common authorship of scientific publications.

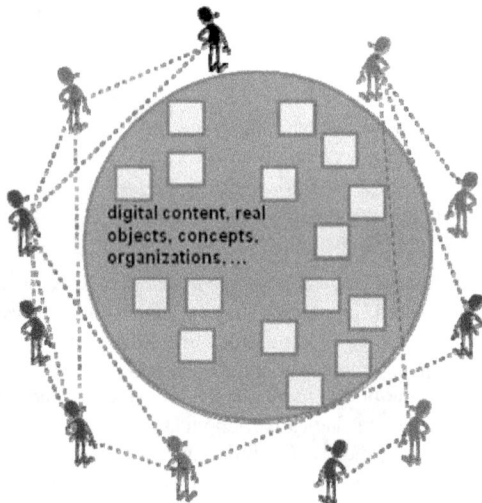

Figure 1. A conventional human-only social network, focusing on human interactions and in essence ignoring objects, concepts, artefacts, etc.

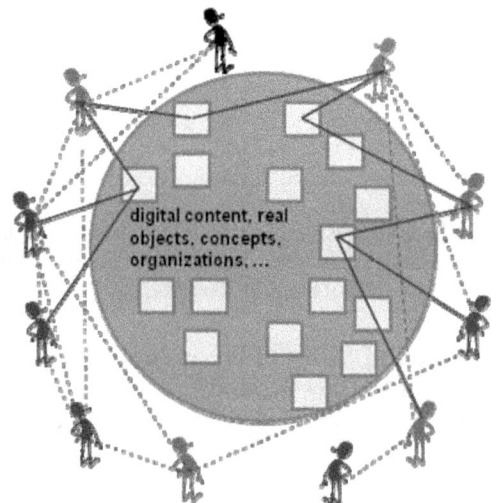

Figure 2. An object-centered network, where the focus is again on the human connections, however as they are formed based on commonly shared objects.

Social networking in this sense is good at realizing and representing links between people, but it doesn't explain what connects those particular people together and what connects those and not others [8]. One way to provide meaning to social networks is to establish relationships and promote self-organization into communities based on shared interests, and even more on specific items of interests. Recently the term 'object-centered sociality' was introduced [9] to describe the fact that strong social relationships are built mainly when individuals are grouped together around a shared object that mediates the ties between them. This can be achieved by organizing the network around the content people create together, comment on, link to, annotate similarly etc. [10]. Digital social objects are at the same time interaction triggers, context providers and communication anchors. Object-centered sociality constitutes today a specific and widespread kind of communication coexisting with others like micro-blogging, mail, forums, etc. An object-centered social network is a social structure formed by people interacting synchronously or asynchronously on a single common social object. In this case emphasis is placed on the connections between the humans and the objects and social interactions is basically established on the basis of commonly shared objects (Figure 2). Therefore, we can assume that each content item on a Web 2.0

In both cases, the focus is not on trying to establish connections based on performative aspects of radically heterogeneous networks, but rather to create associations based on human action, agency and perception. In our work, we attempt to further enhance the notion of the non-human digital object in an on-line social network by relying on the view and concepts of the actor-network theory (ANT). Actor-Network Theory is a sociological theory developed in the 1980's by Bruno Latour, Michel Callon and John Law (for a thorough introduction see [3]). The basis of actor-network theory is the concept of the heterogeneous network, that is, a network containing many dissimilar elements, including both social and technical parts. Moreover, the social and technical are treated as inseparable. This is the so-called principle of generalized symmetry, whereby human and non-human (e.g. artifacts, organization structures) should be integrated into the same conceptual framework and assigned equal amounts of agency. Actor-network theory claims that any actor, whether person, object (including computer software, hardware, and technical standards), or organization, is equally important to a social network. All participating entities can exert agency, i.e. they can have an effect via their interconnections. The outcome is being built unpredictably and collectively only via the interconnections.

3. HETEROGENEOUS SOCIAL NETWORKS

In this paper we present our view for truly heterogeneous social networks where humans and nonhuman entities of various types are integrated into the same conceptual framework and assigned equal amounts of agency. In this way, one gains a detailed description of the concrete mechanisms at work that hold the network together, while allowing an impartial treatment of the all acting entities. Based on the perspective of Actor-Network theory, we followed a 'symmetrical analysis', where the material and non-human elements of a network are not treated as mere social objects but they are rather treated analytically in the same way as the human elements. The focus is on linking and associations among all social entities, human and non-human alike, all represented as actors. This is graphically shown in Figure 3, where the social associations are among humans and among humans and non-human entities, but also among non-human entities themselves.

In implementing such a network, major challenges include a unified treatment and representation of all types of possible actors as well as the development of a social behavior for various nonhuman actors, and subsequently their own associations and networks. Both challenges can be addressed by concepts and technologies of the Semantic Web.

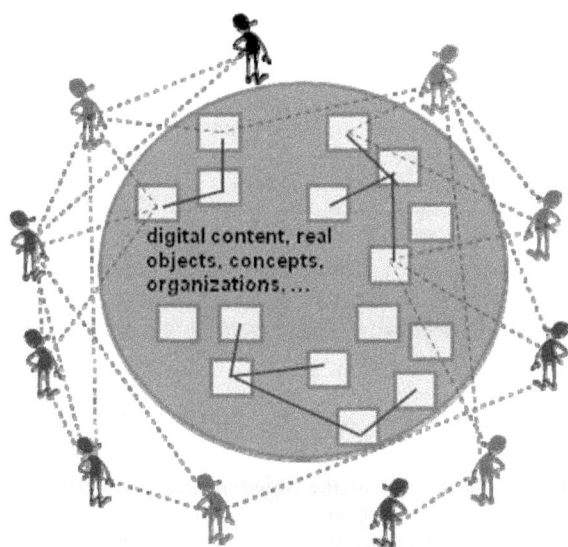

Figure 3. A heterogeneous social network where human and nonhuman entities are treated symmetrically as actors.

In the conventional Web, a resource can be described via an XHTML/XML document, where various tags are used to annotate the document, mainly regarding its presentation, not conveying any semantics about the resource itself. In order to describe a resource the W3C Resource Description Framework (RDF) [11] is commonly used to represent metadata about a resource in the form of triples: subject, predicate, object. Generally, the subject can be the resource itself while the predicate can be any relationship as defined in any XML namespace published on the Web. The object can be an explicit value but also a dereferencable URI. This way, an RDF triple can link the description of a resource with other sources of information on the Web, thus creating a worldwide graph-like linking of resources, what is currently termed Linked Open Data (LOD) cloud [12], [13], a community project of the World Wide Web Consortium's Semantic Web Education and Outreach Group (W3C SWEO).

The building blocks of the Semantic Web are considered to be ontologies, i.e. formal descriptions of parts of the world [14] that guide the specification and generation of the triple generation. There are numerous ontologies that are specific to domain, resource type and objective (also known as application ontologies), but there are only a few general ones (known in information science as upper or foundation ontologies) that are used frequently to build the former. For example FOAF [15] (Friend Of A Friend) is used to describe actors and their real world information, activities and relations, SIOC [16] (Semantically Interlinked Online Communities) to describe online communities and the interactions in them, SKOS [17] to describe terms of controlled vocabularies, OPO [18] (Online Presence project Ontology) to provide portability and visibility of an actor's profile between different social platforms etc.

3.1 Unified Description of Actors

One of the basic requirements is a unified and rich description of all actors to form as a basis for their social presence and their interactions within the social environment. This description includes two main aspects. The first aspect is a domain specific description of the profile for both humans and nonhuman entities. Such a social profile can be described with a variety of domain specific schemata or even ontologies.

For example, the profile of humans can be based on the FOAF (Friend Of A Friend) [15] ontology, mainly used to describe people, the links between them and the things they create and do. Actually, the first core class in FOAF is the 'agent' referring 'to things that do stuff' including persons, groups, software or physical artifacts. However, most often the sub-class 'person' is used to describe humans. Based on this basic description, one can also add more domain specific fields to provide the means for a rich description of a person. For example, in the case of education, one could also include fields such as "courses that I am teaching", "teaching interests/subjects" or "learning interests/subjects" [19].

Regarding the profile of a non-human actor, again a number of domain specific vocabularies and ontologies can be employed. For example, an educational content item can be described using the IEEE LOM (Learning Object Metadata) XML scheme seems the most prominent standard for describing learning objects [20]. Other, more elaborate and educational oriented schemata can also be used, for example the mEducator metadata scheme [21] developed to focus on medical education and stress educational aspects such as educational objectives, expected learning outcomes, etc. In the healthcare domain there is a plentitude of formal controlled vocabularies and ontologies, for example see the BioPortal [22] for an indicative list. Finally, in the scientific knowledge management field, there is also a thriving number of related ontologies, ranging from the comprehensive CERIF data model (the Common European Research Information Format) [23],[24], a formal model to setup Research Information Systems and to enable their interoperation, to the recently proposed VIVO ontology [25] which aims to integrate researcher information from disparate, largely authoritative, sources into a common format establishing interrelationships and to make it publically available.

On the other hand, one needs to describe information about the interactions between the various actors. Recently a new ontology based model has emerged targeting specifically the social networks that are object centered. OCSO [26] (Object Centered Sociality Ontology) is an ontology that describes the interactions between actors using FOAF (Friend Of A Friend), SIOC [16] (Semantically Interlinked Online Communities) and OPO [18] (Online Presence Project) properties. These actors are defined following the FOAF 'agent' core class, thus encompassing all types of entities.

3.2 Building the Social Profile of Actors

The second challenge in such a heterogeneous network where humans and non-human actors are equally treated is to provide the means for the non-human entities to somehow build their social profile and connections in an autonomous, independent and proactive way.

In general, the social aspect of non-human actors can be created in a variety of ways, including (a) the obvious connections via common tags that are used in their profile description; (b) connections based on collective usage and other related interaction of human users, i.e. what human users do with the nonhuman entities; (c) social connections based on some type of inheritance, i.e. non-human entities that are generated or are the product of other resources, in the sense of the genealogy tree; and (d) semantic connections and similarities that can be built based on the wealth of information available in the linked data cloud. These different ways of enriching the social profile of a non-human entity can be clarified with the following proof-of-concept example from the field of education.

4. AN EXAMPLE FROM THE DOMAIN OF EDUCATION

Continuous advances in medicine and life sciences lead to an ever expanding core knowledge relevant to the medical practice. Thus, medical academic institutions are increasingly required to invest in order to enrich their curricula by developing overspecialized courses and corresponding educational content. Educational content in medicine includes a broad range of learning object types that address both the theoretical as well as the clinical aspects of medical education. Its unique nature lies along with the fact that it is produced by both academics and clinical teachers, in a variety of places like hospital wards, healthcare practice units, laboratories, classrooms/lecture theaters, and recently the collaborative web and virtual reality spaces. In contemporary education, educational resources can be of a variety of different types. Considering the state-of-the-art nature, the complexity and, consecutively, the cost of state-of-the-art educational content, it is imperative that such content can be repurposed, enriched, and embedded effectively into respective curricula and continuing education, as well as public dissemination and awareness. This need for sharing, re-using and repurposing educational resources actually makes them a natural candidate for social objects in professional educational social networks.

This is addressed in the MetaMorphosis+ [19] semantic social network which aims to provide an environment for resource publishing, sharing and repurposing in medical education. The MetaMorphosis+ semantic social network is a heterogeneous network of persons (including authors, potential authors and final users of learning objects, e.g. students, teachers, educational managers, etc) and educational resources of any type. Educational resources in MetaMorphosis+ can be resources residing in a Learning Management System (LMS), in another educational repository, or merely available on the Web.

4.1 Building a Social Profile for Educational Resources

The most straightforward social dimension of an educational resource as a social object in a network can be realized in the conventional way of connections among profile tags. This requires a standardized metadata set to describe concisely an educational resource and thus create its social profile. Standardizing metadata for describing digital educational resources constitutes one of the main research topics in the e-learning community.

Educational resources in MetaMorphosis+ are primarily described by the mEducator RDF metadata scheme for describing medical educational resources [21],[27]. This includes a number of fields addressing different aspects of the educational resource: (a) general fields: resource title, unique identifier, URL, URN, intellectual property rights clearance/license, quality stamp (if any); (b) fields related to a general resource description: resource authors, creation date, citation (i.e. how the resource should be formally cited), keywords, content description, technical description (including any technical requirements to access and use the resource); (c) fields related to the educational aspect of the resource: educational context (for which the resource is intended), teaching/using instructions, educational objectives, expected learning outcomes, suggested assessment methods, educational prerequisites; (d) fields related to classification/taxonomy information: resource language, type, discipline, discipline subspecialty, educational level; and (e) fields addressing repurposing: resource parents, repurposing context, repurposing description. These user generated description metadata, when treated as social tags, create a complex and dynamic organization of educational resources in a similar fashion as in any conventional social network, thus realizing the resources' social network.

4.2 Resource Sociality based on Collective Usage Interaction

As it has been established, the basic function of a social network is to provide the environment for users to interact with each other promoting the communicator role. When social objects are introduced in these networks the interactions extend to include these objects which in this scenario are educational resources. These are accessed, used, shared, repurposed, and also rated, commented upon, and can be organized in a number of user specified ways in collections.

Capturing and sharing information about the attention that users spend on resources in specific contexts can provide a different aspect of sociality based on the personal views and mental models of the users. This way one can build the profile of a resource as it appears to the external user, as opposed to the profile of the resource according to the view of its creator, as depicted in the description metadata. The perspective and attention is normally captured via recording contextual attention metadata [28]. This includes data about the users' attention and activities that relate both to semantically rich actions on and interactions with educational content items as well as data on indirect interactions amongst content items. Additionally, basic interaction metadata can also be considered which includes all other basic user-system interactions that provide some kind of basic attention information (not necessarily semantically and contextually rich).

Apart from creating a better user experience in an individual environment, the motivation is that these interactions can give more information about the user's habits, likes, dislikes and interests that can be applied everywhere following the model of the Semantic Web. In order for these attention metadata to be able to be shared or aggregated in a meaningful way researchers have produced formats and uniform ways to represent them. For example the Attention Profiling Mark-up Language (APML) [29] has introduced a portable file format that describes user's interests and interactions in ranking order.

4.3 Resource Family Trees based on Repurposing History and Inheritance

The term 'repurposing' refers to changing a learning resource initially created and used for a specific educational purpose in a specific educational context in order to fit a different new educational purpose in the same or different educational context. Although not formally addressed as such, educational content repurposing is what any educator is routinely engaged in when preparing a new educational experience, including preparing the educational content itself. Customarily, when an educator sets the context and goals of a new educational experience, he/she will overview existing content and/or search for new relative content and then repurpose and re-organize content to fit the purpose of the new educational experience.

There can be a variety of situations where repurposing educational content is desired. These situations, referred to as "repurposing contexts", can be of a pedagogical nature, a technical nature or both, and include the following [30],[31]: repurposing (1) in terms of the actual content; (2) to different languages; (3) to different cultures; (4) for different pedagogical approaches; (5) for different educational levels; (6) for different disciplines or professions; (7) to different content types; (8) for different content delivery media and/or technology; (9) to educational content from an initial content type that is not intended for education; and (10) for people with special needs.

In MetaMorphosis+ repurposing is addressed as a means to provide a different kind of sociality for the educational resources. Thus repurposing history and inheritance are used as basic social relationship among educational resources in order to cluster resources into families. Each repurposed resource declares its parent(s) resource(s). Following iteratively the 'parents' in a chain of repurposing ancestors, the entire 'family' tree of the particular resource can be compiled. A force-directed graph is used to depict the specific resource's family and inheritance patterns. Each node in the graph represents a resource, while the directed edges represent repurposing relationship, with the arrows pointing from the "source" objects to their "repurposed" descendants. The nodes also state the 'repurposing context', while they are active links to the resource profile where more information on the repurposing description can be obtained. For the entire resource collection, a circular directed graph representation is used which depicts all the resources with the various individual inheritance trees, usually not interconnected amongst them. A resource inheritance tree is a group of resources that have a relationship based on repurposing – this can also be viewed as resource 'family'.

4.4 Semantic Links between Resources by Harvesting the Linked Data Cloud

Finally, the social dimension of educational resources can be further expanded and enriched by harvesting semantically rich information available in the Linked Data cloud. The Linked Open Data (LOD) approach is simply about "using the Web to create typed links between data from different sources. These may be as diverse as databases maintained by two organisations in different geographical locations, or simply heterogeneous systems within one organisation that, historically, have not easily interoperated at the data level [12]. The goal of the Linking Open Data project is to extend the Web with a data commons by publishing various open data sets on the Web, and making links between data items from different data sources. Since its inception in June 2007, the size of the cloud has rapidly exploded and already includes a large variety of open data sets including several research and medical data sets. This wealth of information can be used to automatically enrich educational resources metadata with references to external vocabularies, and in particular domain specific vocabularies, thus creating a rich domain specific profile and extending the resource's social connections to other web objects.

The architectural framework for semantic data and service linking and federating of disparate educational resource pools that powers the social environment is described in detail elsewhere [32]. At the lower level of this semantic technology framework, a Web data and service layer employs distributed Web services that harvest educational resource metadata from heterogeneous data sources on the Web. In the upper layer, semantic data and service integration is achieved based on the Linked Services approach and on semantic technologies such as iServe [33] and SmartLink [34]. An RDF repository exposes harvested educational resource metadata as triples (http://ckan.net/package/meducator). Metadata as harvested by Web sources can also be enriched with existing LOD vocabularies).

This is of particular importance to extend rather unstructured metadata, such as keywords or free text subject and discipline descriptions with structured data based on well-known vocabularies. This is achieved by exploiting a variety of medical domain ontologies and the expanding LOD cloud to semantically annotate the existing RDF description of a resource and then expose its metadata back to the LOD cloud for further exploitation by third parties which make use of the web of LOD. Biomedical ontologies provide essential domain knowledge to drive data integration, information retrieval, data annotation, natural-language processing and decision support. BioPortal (http:// bioportal.bioontology.org) is an open repository of biomedical ontologies that provides access via Web services and Web browsers to ontologies developed in various formats including OWL, RDF, OBO format and Protégé frames [35].

In MetaMorphosis+ we have utilized the NCBO BioPortal's RESTful Web services programming interface to access and incorporated terms and concepts from the more than 260 ontologies provided to this day, corresponding to more than 4.5 million medical and life sciences terms. This way the MetaMorphosis+ user can annotate an educational resource with suggested standardized terms and concepts from a variety of ontologies, enriching the RDF output with dereferencable standardized terms as values for the various fields, e.g. keywords, discipline, specialty, etc. The ontologies used include, amongst others, prominent medical ontologies such as SNOMED-CT (Systematized Nomenclature of Medicine – Clinical Terms), ICD9/10 (International Statistical Classification Diseases and Related Health Problems), Body System (body system terms used in ICD11), MeSH (Medical Subject Headings), NCI (Meta)Thesaurus, Galen (the high level ontology for the medical domain), HL7 (the Normative RIM model v2), Biomedical Resource Ontology (BRO, a controlled terminology of resources to improve sensitivity and specificity of Web searches).

As an example, suppose a user intends to describe an educational resource by using the term/concept Telemedicine, in the list of 'Keywords' or in the 'Discipline' and 'Specialty' fields of the metadata description of the educational resource. Semantic annotation in MetaMorphosis can suggest a number of related standardized terms from the available ontologies.

5. DISCUSSION

The specific implementation of MetaMorphosis+ presented in the previous section is only an example of the various different ways one can combine object sociality and semantic annotation and linking to create powerful heterogeneous networks of humans and non-human entities.

5.1 Towards Patient Empowerment Services

Another interesting domain is that of the healthcare services environment. The first decades of applications of information technology in medicine had targeted the health care enterprise and services provided therein. Thus a major technological challenge has been the integration (control, data, presentation, and semantic integration) of various information systems and services to support the healthcare enterprise with emphasis on the tertiary level (e.g. hospitals). Towards this goal, a number of standards and standard communication protocols have been developed and implemented, with variable, albeit considerable, success [36].

Recently, patient empowerment has emerged as a new paradigm that can help improve medical outcomes while lowering costs of treatment by facilitating self-directed behavior change. The concept seems particularly promising in the management of chronic diseases [37],[38] and it is directly connected with personalized patient services and preventive measures. A recent review [39] shows that patient empowerment services mainly aim at educational programs patient reinforcement, with goals usually predefined by the health-care professional, thus in practice contradicting the very notion of empowerment [40].

At these early days of the citizen-centered paradigm, most of patient empowerment services and systems are offered as autonomous modules not directly integrated with each other or with healthcare enterprise information systems. Thus the challenge is to work towards integration efforts of patient centered services and especially semantic integration, which requires a basic agreement for the understanding and description of the respective environment. And, although a lot of work has been conducted towards a common understanding of the healthcare enterprise, even in the special case of the provision of home care, e.g. [41], an analysis and definition of the personal environment of the healthy citizen and the patient is still missing.

Following the line of thought presented in this paper, the health environment for the patient and/or the healthy citizen comprises of various coexisting and strongly interlinked entities: (a) individuals, including patients, healthy citizens and healthcare professionals; (b) organizations, including any institutional or organizational entity involved in any way in the healthcare process, e.g. healthcare providers, social services, health insurances, medical research institutions, research projects, pharmaceutical companies, well-being and fitness clubs, etc; (c) health conditions, i.e. any health or medical condition; and (d) health interventions, including diet, life-style, dialysis or other therapy, drugs, supporting devices, etc. All these can be viewed as actors within a heterogeneous social structure.

The co-existence of multiple networks of individuals, organizations and health conditions/interventions is exploited in order to create different views of the healthcare environment, thus creating variable impact. For example, an individual-centered linking visualization enhances integrated personal management of healthcare, collaboration and expert finding services. On the other hand, an organization-based linking visualization supports administrative, strategy and financial oriented goals, at an institutional, national and international level. Finally, resource oriented linking visualization/organization may serve a variety of goals. For example, visualization based on health conditions and interventions places focus on epidemiology and generation of new evidence on a large scale.

5.2 Towards Scientific Knowledge Management

Another area of application could be the management of scientific knowledge. In more details, conducting research implies the following steps: (1) after a research idea/proposal is generated, (2) in general, an enabling infrastructure may be used, (3) to carry out repeated and reproducible observations or to collect relevant data in authentic contexts, (4) that produce raw data, (5) which may then be processed and possibly transformed using appropriate processing tools (6) into research outcomes; (7) the entire process is briefly described against existing evidence (i.e. published works), and (8) this is subject to peer review and (9) finally published; (10) at a different level, such peer-reviewed work is then incorporated into scholar works and books, and in the formal (and public) educational process, while it may be linked with patents, and/or be commercially exploited.

This research process is usually supported by funding agencies and is carried out in various organizational research settings. Moreover, research is an open, collaborative process, based on communication and often collaboration at an international level. Many research projects are now collaborative endeavors spanning a number of research groups and organizations, even across nations. Well-known examples include the human genome and climate change, but there are many others, especially where expensive infrastructure is utilized such as particle physics or space science. Furthermore, knowledge of the research activity in one group or organization may influence the strategy towards research – including priorities and resources provided –in another group or organization.

Research information is used by researchers (to find partners, to track competitors, to form collaborations); research managers (to assess performance and research outputs and to find reviewers for research proposals); research strategists (to decide on priorities and resourcing compared with other countries); publication editors (to find reviewers and potential authors); intermediaries/brokers (to find research products and ideas that can be carried forward with knowledge/technology transfer to wealth creation); educators and learners (to take up state-of-the-art information and produce learning experiences and thus knowledge); the media (to communicate the results of R&D in a socio-economic context) and the general public (for interest). Thus, there is a need to share research information across organizations and countries, and between different funding agencies, and manage research information in a unified way. This becomes even more pressing if one considers the growing need/trend for multidisciplinary research. Such research process is typically more complex and 'painful' than research in a well defined discipline, while it usually plays a catalytic role in major science and technology breakthroughs.

Following the line of thought presented in this paper, the concept of a virtual scientific community can be explored by a heterogeneous social network where researchers (and non-researchers), research institutions (including research facilities and other stakeholders such as libraries and publishers), and research resources (ranging from raw data to published results to processing tools and beyond) are all participating as distinctive social entities. These diverse actors (humans, resources, organizations) are interlinked in a graph-like approach based on their relationships, which can be built by semantically linking data via a semantic data federation/linking layer. In this way, non-human entities may acquire a degree of 'personality' and 'intelligence' and turn into more realistic 'social entities'.

5.3 Epilogue

Following the approach of a heterogeneous network to organize information objects and humans alike and record their variable interactions one can further exploit notions and concepts of the actor-network theory to analyze the social structures and thus eventually gain more insights on the organization and communication of information.

Following the ANT perspective, actors in such an organization enter into networked associations, which in turn define them, name them, and provide them with substance, action, intention, and subjectivity. In other words, actors are considered foundationally indeterminate, with no a priori substance or essence, and it is via the networks in which they associate that they derive their nature. ANT is interested in the ways in which networks overcome resistance and strengthen internally, gaining coherence and consistence; how they organize and convert network elements; how they prevent actors from following their own inclinations; how they grant qualities and motivations to actors; how they become increasingly transportable and "useful"; and how they become functionally indispensable.

As such an ANT perspective into constructing and studying a heterogeneous semantic social network may give alternative insights for information organization and management on the web in a variety of different application domains.

6. ACKNOWLEDGMENTS

Notions and concepts underlying this work as well as the example from the domain of education presented here have arisen from work partly funded by the mEducator project (Contract Nr: ECP 2008 EDU 418006 mEducator) under the eContentplus programme, a multiannual Community programme to make digital content in Europe more accessible, usable and exploitable.

7. REFERENCES

[1] O'Reilly, T. 2005..What is Web 2.0: design patterns and business models for the next generation of software. http://www.oreillynet.com/pub/a/oreilly/tim/news/2005/09/30/what-is-web-20.html

[2] Berners-Lee, T., Hendler, J., and Lassila, O. 2001. The semantic Web – a new form of Web content that is meaningful to computers will unleash a revolution of new possibilities. *Sci. Am.* 284, 34–43.

[3] Latour, B. 2005. *Reassembling the Social: An Introduction to Actor-Network Theory*, Oxford University Press, Oxford.

[4] Dolwick, J. S. 2009. The social and beyond: introducing actor-network theory, *J Mari Arch.* 4, 21-49.

[5] Cole, G. D. H. 1920. *Social Theory*. Frederick A Stokes Co, New York.

[6] Pinch, T., and Bijker, W. 1987. The social construction of facts and artefacts: or how the sociology of science and the sociology of technology might benefit each other. In: Bijker W, Hughes T, Pinch TJ (eds) *The Social Construction of Technological Systems: New Directions in the Sociology and History of Technology*. MIT Press, Cambridge.

[7] Scott, J. 2007. Sociology and the social: a qualified defence of sociological imperialism. In: Urry, J., Dingwall, R., Gough, I. (eds). What is 'Social' about Social Science? *21st Century Soc.* 2 , 1, 95–119.

[8] Knorr-Cetina, K. 1997. Sociality with objects: social relations in postsocial knowledge societies. *Theory, Culture & Society.* 14, 4, 1–30.

[9] Engeström, J. 2005. Why some social network services work and others don't. The case for object-centered sociality. http://www.zengestrom.com/blog/2005/04/why_some_social.html

[10] Breslin, J., and Decker, S. 2007. The future of social networks on the Internet. The need for semantics. *IEEE Internet Computing.* 11, 87-90.

[11] RDF, http://www.w3.org/TR/rdf-syntax/

[12] Bizer, C., Heath, T., and Berners-Lee, T. 2009. Linked Data – The story so far. *IJSWIS*, 5, 1-22.

[13] LOD, http://www.w3.org/wiki/SweoIG/TaskForces/CommunityProjects/LinkingOpenData

[14] Gruber, T. R. 1993. A translation approach to portable ontologies. *Knowledge Acquisition*, 5, 2, 199-220.

[15] FOAF (Friend Of A Friend), http://www.foaf-project.org/

[16] SIOC (Semantically Interlinked Online Communities), http://sioc-project.org/

[17] SKOS (Simple Knowledge Organization System), http://www.w3.org/2004/02/skos/

[18] OPO (Online Presence Ontology), http://online-presence.net/ontology.php

[19] MetaMorphosis+, http://metamorphosis.med.duth.gr

[20] LOM working draft v4.1 (2000) http://ltsc.ieee.org/doc/wg12/LOMv4.1.htm

[21] mEducator Schema, http://purl.org/meducator/ns

[22] The National Center for Biomedical Ontology, http://bioportal.bioontology.org/

[23] Jorg, B., Jeffery, K., van Grootel, G., and Asserson A. 2010. (Eds), CERIF 2008 – 1.1 Full Data Model (FDM) Introduction and Specification, euroCRIS, March 2010 http://www.eurocris.org/fileadmin/cerif-2008/CERIF2008_1.1_FDM.pdf

[24] Jorg, B. 2010. "CERIF: The Common European Research Information Format Model", *Data Science Journal*. 9, Special Issue : CRIS for European e-Instrastucture, (Jul. 2010), CRIS24-31.

[25] Gewin, V. 2009. Networking in VIVO: An interdisciplinary networking site for scientists. *Nature* 462, 123.

[26] OCSO (Object Centered Sociality Ontology), http://ns.inria.fr/ocso/

[27] mEducator Linked Educational Resources, http://linkededucation.org/meducator.

[28] Wolpers, M., Najjar, J., Verbert, K., and Duval, E. 2007. Tracking Actual Usage: the Attention Metadata Approach. *Educational Technology & Society* 10, 106-121.

[29] APML (Attention Profiling Mark-up Language), http://apml.areyoupayingattention.com/

[30] Kaldoudi, E., Dovrolis, N., Konstantinidis, S., and Bamidis, P. D. 2009. Social networking for learning object repurposing in medical education", *J. Inform Techn Healthcare* 7, 233–243.

[31] Balasubramaniam, C., Poulton, T., and Huwendiek, S. 2008. Repurposing Existing Virtual Patients; an Anglo-German Case Study. Bio-Algorithms and Med-Systems, 5, 91-98 (2009) Bojārs U., Breslin, J. G., Finn, A., Decker, S. Using the Semantic Web for Linking and Reusing Data across Web 2.0 Communities. Web Semantics: Science, Services and Agents on the World Wide Web, 6, 21-28

[32] Yu, H. Q., Dietze, S., Li, N., Pedrinaci, C., Taibi, D., Dovrolis, N., Stefanut T., Kaldoudi, E., and Dominque, J. 2011. A Linked Data-driven & Service-oriented Architecture for Sharing Educational Resources. In the *Proceedings of the Linked Learning 2011: 1st International Workshop on eLearning Approaches for the Linked Data Age, ESWC2011* (Heraklion, Greece, May 29, 2011).

[33] Pedrinaci, C., Liu, D., Maleshkova, M., Lambert, D., Kopecky, J., and Domingue, J. 2010. iServe: a Linked Services Publishing Platform. In the Proceedings of The 7th Extended Semantic Web Conference (ESWC2010), (Heraklion, Greece, May 30 0 03 June, 2010).

[34] Dietze, S., Yu, H. Q., Pedrinaci, C., Liu, D. and Domingue, J. 2011. SmartLink: a Web-based editor and search environment for Linked Services, in the Proceedings of *The 8th Extended Semantic Web Conference (ESWC2011)*, (Heraklion, Greece, May 29 – June 2, 2011)

[35] Noy, N. F., Shah, N. H., Whetzel, P. L., Dai, B., Dorf, M., Griffith, N., Jonquet, C., Rubin, D. L., Storey, M. A., Chute, C., G., Musen, M.A. 2009. BioPortal: ontologies and integrated data resources at the click of a mouse. *Nucleic Acids. Res.* 1, 37.

[36] Lenz, R., Beyer, M., and Kuhn, K.A. 2007. Semantic integration in healthcare networks, *Int J Med Inform.* 76, 201-207.

[37] Chatzimarkakis, J. 2010. Why patients should be more empowered, *J Diab Science Technol.* 4, 1570-1573.

[38] Anderson, R. M., and Funnell, M. M. 2010. Patient empowerment: myths and misconceptions, *Patient Educ Couns.* 79, 277-282.

[39] Ajoulat, I., d'Hoore, W., and Deccache, A. 2007.. Patient empowerment in theory and in practice: Polysemy of Cacophony, *Patient Education & Counseling.* 66, 13-20.

[40] Traynor, M. 2003. A brief history of empowerment, *Primary Health Care Res & Devel.* 4, 129-136.

[41] Valss, A., Gibert, K., Sanchez, D., and Batet, M. 2010. Using ontologies for structuring organizational knowledge in home care assistance, *Int J Med Inform.* 79, 370-387.

On the Effect of Visual Refinement Upon User Feedback in the Context of Video Prototyping

Miroslav Bojic, Areti Goulati, Dalila Szostak and Panos Markopoulos
Eindhoven University of Technology
Den Dolech 2, 5612AZ
Eindhoven, the Netherlands
{m.bojic, a.goulati, d.szostak, p.markopoulos}@tue.nl

ABSTRACT

There has been extensive discussion and research surrounding fidelity or refinement of prototypes in paper and software form, especially focusing on how the nature of prototypes influences the feedback that this prototype can help elicit during user testing. We extend this debate to the domain of video prototypes, where use scenarios are acted out on video. This study examines how the visual refinement (a.k.a. visual fidelity) of design representations presented in such videos impacts user feedback. An experiment was performed where two video prototypes were compared, one where the product is portrayed with high visual refinement and the other looking rough and sketchy. Our results could not identify any significant effects upon the number or type of comments returned by users. This finding contrasts widely held contentions relating to fidelity of software and paper prototypes, though it agrees with similar experiments done with non video prototypes. In practice our results support the validity of testing with low fidelity videos and suggest that the choice of visual fidelity in video prototypes should be based on pragmatic project concerns, e.g., whether the video should be used also for communication and the resources that are available for prototyping.

Categories and Subject Descriptors

D2.1 [**Requirements / Specifications**]: Elicitation Methods – video prototyping

General Terms

Design, Human Factors

Keywords

Video prototyping, fidelity, visual refinement.

1. INTRODUCTION

Video prototyping is a widely used technique to prototype interaction design that can be used as means to visualize

interaction and interactive experiences prior to the system implementation or even before availability of technology required to build such interaction [10]. This enables gathering of early feedback by user representatives and other stakeholders. Furthermore, it can be used as a participatory design technique, allowing stakeholders who are not very skilled in creating other types of prototypes to represent ideas, situations, and experiences [8].

When creating a video prototype, a designer stands before a number of important decisions that have strong influence on how the interaction is portrayed. Some of these refer to the general qualities of the filming and the video production more generally. Others refer to the representation of the designed artifact or system and correspond to the notion of prototype fidelity as discussed in the field of human computer interaction (HC). McCurdy et al. [3] refined the concept of fidelity and identified five different prototype dimensions that can be varied, affecting the representation of the interaction. These are:

1. Visual refinement; realism and visual polish of the artifact being presented,

2. Breadth of functionality; number of different functions of the artifact in the video,

3. Depth of functionality; detail of functionalities presented in the video,

4. Richness of interactivity; detail of interaction between the artifact and the user including handling of errors and unusual situations,

5. Richness of data model; realism of the data utilized by the prototype, reality of situations and circumstances.

While these have been typically used to discuss paper or software prototypes, they can be described to distinguish between video prototypes as well. For example, if a video portraits only a single functionality of the designed system, but does so in great detail, the prototype can be considered to be of low fidelity (lo-fi) in the dimension of breadth of functionality, but of high fidelity (hi-fi) in the dimension of depth of functionality.

It is widely accepted in the field of HCI that lo-fi and hi-fi prototypes provoke different reactions from evaluators; for example see standard textbooks [6]. A much stated argument by Rettig [5] is that lo-fi prototypes compel viewers to think about content rather than appearance. This favors iterative design and educates developers to have concern for usability and formative evaluation. Similarly, Nielsen [4] shows that user reactions to lo-fi prototypes can give significant insights into usability. Mackay et al. [2] confirm this further, suggesting that lo-fi prototypes make viewers more comfortable in asking questions and pointing out weaknesses in the proposed design. Generally, lo-fi prototypes are faster, easier, and less expensive to produce, a contention that of course depends on the tools available and the skills of the team as well as the idiosyncrasies of the design context in question.

On the other hand, hi-fi prototypes are said to be able to 'set the rules' in a way that is not possible with a lo-fi prototype, effectively narrowing the set of plausible interpretations [1]. When the prototyping medium is video, it is important to note that this comes with a risk of the video prototype being interpreted as rhetorical and persuasive [2].

While there are many publications covering advantages and disadvantages of hi-fi and lo-fi prototypes, there is so far no related methodological approach for designers creating video prototypes. Therefore, this study can be regarded as a first step in this direction. The study aims to confirm claims about effect of fidelity on prototype evaluation in a formal way. The following hypotheses were posed:

H1: Comments about lo-fi prototypes will be more focused on content than appearance, compared to comments about hi-fi prototypes.

H2: Users will be more positively disposed towards high fidelity prototypes (higher scores for user acceptance, usefulness, and usability)

H3: Viewers of lo-fi prototype will provide more comments than viewers of hi-fi prototype.

H4: Viewers of lo-fi prototype will provide comments that are more critical than viewers of hi-fi prototype.

For this particular study all but one fidelity dimension, as identified by McCurdy et al. [3], were kept constant. The dimension varied was visual refinement of the prototype, allowing relevance of the work to a broader body of research that has studied the impact of visual fidelity of prototypes.

2. METHOD

A case study was conducted where a conceptualized product was prototyped in two fidelities with respect to visual refinement. An experiment was set up to evaluate hypotheses H1-H4 above.

2.1 Concept Product: P'eco

A nonexistent, but believable future product was conceived to be the object represented through video prototypes: P'eco, an ecological office printer with a capability of ink and paper recycling by various means. The product was described as being a regular size office printer with all the common functionality of such devices but with the following added possibilities: a possibility to insert used paper for the printer to recycle, to store printed documents for reuse (archiving), and to print with time sensitive fading ink, allowing the same paper to be reused for printing multiple times.

After drafting the scenario involving two office workers going about their day and coming in touch with the printer, two video prototypes were filmed. Everything in the videos was kept consistent with the exception of how the printer was represented.

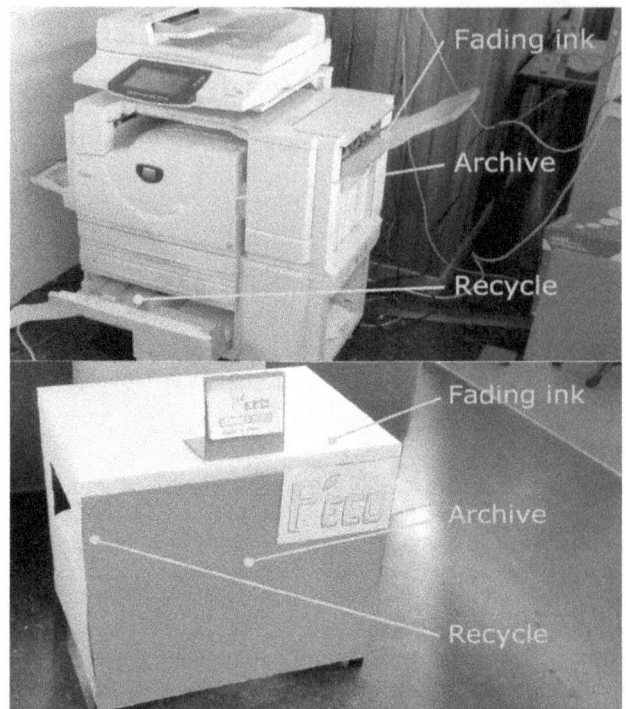

Figure 1: The printer, as it has been represented in the hi-fi (above) and lo-fi (below) video prototype.

In the lo-fi video, the printer was made out of cardboard, and all the interaction through the computer screen was represented with hand-drawn sketches. In the hi-fi version, an existing office printer was used, and the interaction was presented through Flash-based screen mock-ups/animations which were edited in the video. Images of the hi-fi and lo-fi representations of the printer are shown in Figure 1.

Both videos were about three and a half minutes in length. The videos consisted of a short introduction of two characters, followed by a showcase of printer's recycling functions. The video concluded with the discussion of printer's functions by the two office workers

2.2 Experiment Setup

A within-subject design was adopted. Although we aimed primarily to compare the amount of comments between subjects after viewing a single video, we also decided to give the participants the opportunity to also view a second video prototype in a different fidelity in order to probe them directly as to whether their attitude towards the product changed after seeing the same product in a different fidelity.

Upon welcoming the participants, the researchers explained the procedure of the experiment and both parties signed a consent form. Next, the participant viewed the first video. The order of the videos was counterbalanced; half of the participants viewed lo-fi video first, while the other half viewed hi-fi video first. After the participants had just seen their first video, they were asked to fill in a UTAUT based questionnaire [9]. The questionnaire was adjusted to this specific study by taking out two sections: voluntariness and anxiety, because they were not considered relevant to the interaction shown in the videos. The adapted questionnaire included six constructs: attitude, performance

Table 1: Coding of the comments provided by the participants after seeing the lo-fi video prototype.

Comment Type	Positive	Neutral	Negative	Suggestion	Total
Content	15	3	4	1	23
Appearance	8	0	1	0	9
Usability	15	2	12	3	32
Feasibility	4	11	9	0	24
Functionality	13	13	25	13	64
Total	**55**	**29**	**51**	**17**	**152**

Table 2: Coding of the comments provided by the participants after seeing the hi-fi video prototype.

Comment Type	Positive	Neutral	Negative	Suggestion	Total
Content	30	4	3	5	42
Appearance	9	2	2	3	16
Usability	14	3	13	5	35
Feasibility	3	13	3	0	19
Functionality	15	9	18	5	47
Total	**71**	**31**	**39**	**18**	**159**

expectancy, effort expectancy, social influence, and facilitating conditions and behavior influence. The order of the questions in the form was randomized. Additionally, the participants were asked to list as many keywords as possible to describe the prototype that they had just seen.

After the participant.completed the questionnaire, a short, semi-structured interview followed. The participant would then view the second video, and fill in the UTAUT questionnaire and keyword list for the second time. The second semi-structured interview assessed only if the participant changed his/her opinion or attitude about the printer. Finally, the participant was debriefed and given an opportunity to ask any additional questions about either the prototype or the study.

Twenty participants were recruited for the study, 11 female and 9 male. The participants were recruited among university employees and students and were blind to the experimental hypotheses. The recruitment method was direct; the researchers approached potential participants, introduced the study and inquired whether they would be interested in participation, either immediately or at a later time. Participation was voluntary.

The experiments were conducted in an office setting. Two researchers were present, one guiding the participant through the procedure and another observing and taking notes. The equipment used in the experiment consisted of a laptop with the two videos and the questionnaires in paper form. On average, each experiment took about 45 minutes.

3. RESULTS

The answers that the participants provided to the UTAUT questionnaires were summed up per construct and standardized. The Mann-Whitney test was performed to evaluate if the scores were different for participants who have watched lo-fi video first versus the participants who have watched the hi-fi video first. No significant difference was found between these two populations.

Next, a regression analysis was performed for each condition and each construct score in order to see whether there is a significant correlation between particular constructs depending on the fidelity of the video watched. For the hi-fi video, no significant correlations were found between the constructs. For the lo-fi video, significant correlations have been found between the scores assigned to performance (P) and attitude (A) ($p < 0.001$; P = 0.782 * A), and social influence (SI) and self efficacy (SE) ($p = 0.007$; SI = -0.634 * SE).

The UTAUT scores were compared within persons as well, using Wilcoxon signed pair test. Overall no effect of fidelity was found on the UTUAT scores. There was only one significant finding: the behavioral intention (BI) of participants who saw hi-fi video first and lo-fi video second increased significantly ($p = 0.026$, median lo-fi = 19, mean lo-fi = 18.5; median hi-fi = 18, mean hi-fi = 16.9).

The information gathered from the participants during the interviews was transcribed and coded by two independent coders. The comments made by the participants were subdivided into categories that were in line with the hypotheses: content (behavior, interaction and concept), appearance (size and color), usability insights (ease of use and ease of learning), feasibility (perceived credibility and possible problems in implementation), and functionality. The comments were further coded as either positive (commending some aspect of the prototype), neutral (pure observations without personal opinion attached), negative (doubts or not being able to understand a particular aspect of the prototype) or a suggestion (recommendation on how to change or improve an aspect of the prototype). The coding of the comments to the lo-fi and hi-fi videos can be found in Table 1 and Table 2 respectively.

These quantitative results were checked for significance with a two-tailed t-test. Significant difference was found for the total number of comments regarding content of the video ($p = 0.039$, lo-fi: 23 comments, hi-fi: 42 comments). There were no significant differences for the other types of comments provided by the participants.

4. DISCUSSION

The study was motivated by the general aim to examine how fidelity or refinement of video prototypes impacts user perceptions and feedback regarding the concepts shown. In order to keep the study focused, only the visual refinement of the prototype, which is the fidelity dimension most extensively studied in non-video prototypes, was manipulated. The hypotheses of this experiment were not confirmed, something that is surprising considering the widely held and published views regarding prototype fidelity. Several notions about prototyping in other mediums such as paper vs. computer based make clear distinctions not only with regards to audience and funding, but also with regards to the extent of information that can be extracted from participants when using them for evaluations. It is suggested by this study that these might not apply to video. While this finding goes against literature, other fidelity dimensions need to be considered before a conclusive remark can be made as the results only display information regarding one of the five dimensions of fidelity.

There is a chance that the fidelity dimension that was manipulated in the prototype does not have a high influence on how the specific prototype is perceived. An explanation for this might be that the participants, while watching the video, were able to suspend belief in such a way that the actual visuals of the artifact presented did not matter in its overall perception. Another reason could be that there was an interaction effect between different fidelity dimensions. While the video prototype presented quite a broad view of functionality, the depth of the presented functionality was quite shallow. It is possible that the effect of visual refinement fidelity on how the artifact is perceived only becomes apparent if depth of the presented functionality is substantial.

On the other hand, several experimental studies such as those reviewed by Sauer [7], also failed to find any effects on fidelity, suggesting that the widely held beliefs regarding the differences in outcomes from different fidelity prototypes may not be justified. On the basis of research until now one could argue that low fidelity video prototypes allow valid feedback to be elicited during user testing. Further, it can be argued that the choice of prototype refinement needs to be based on broader project constraints than just the expected feedback from user representatives in evaluation sessions.

5. REFERENCES

[1] Kindborg, M., 2001. How Children Understand Concurrent Comics: Experiences from LOFI and HIFI Prototype. In: *IEEE 2001 Symposium on Human Centric Computing Languages and Environments*, Washington, DC (2001)

[2] Mackay, W., Ratzer, A., Janecek, P., 2000. Video artifacts for design: Bridging the gap between abstraction and detail. In: *DIS '00 Proceedings of the 3rd conference on Designing interactive systems: processes, practices, methods, and techniques*, pp. 72--82. ACM, New York (2000)

[3] McCurdy, M., Connors, C., Pyrzak, G., Kanefsky, B., Vera, A., 2006. Breaking the fidelity barrier: an examination of our current characterization of prototypes and an example of a mixed-fidelity success. In: *CHI '06 Proceedings of the SIGCHI conference on Human Factors in computing systems*. ACM, New York (2006)

[4] Nielsen, J., 1995. Using paper prototypes in home-page design. *IEEE Software*. Volume 12 Issue 4 pp.88--89, 97 (1995)

[5] Rettig, M., 1994. Prototyping for tiny fingers. *Communications of the ACM*. Volume 37 Issue 4, pp.21-27 (1994)

[6] Rogers, Y., Preece, J., Sharp, H., 2002. *Interaction Design: Beyond Human-Computer Interaction*. John Wiley & Sons, New York (2002)

[7] Sauer, J., Sonderegger, A., 2009. The influence of prototype fidelity and aesthetics of design in usability tests: Effects on user behaviour, subjective evaluation and emotion. *Applied Ergonomics*, vol. 40, no. 4, pp. 670--677 (2009)

[8] Sefelin, R., Tscheligi, M., Giller, V., 2003 Paper Prototyping - What is it good for? A Comparison of Paper- and Computer-based Low-fidelity Prototyping. *CHI '03 extended abstracts on Human factors in computing systems*. ACM New York (2003)

[9] Sundaravej, T., 2010. Empirical Validation of Unified Theory of Acceptance and Use of Technology Model. *Journal of Global Information Technology Management*. Volume 13 Issue 1, pp. 5--27 (2010)

[10] Tognazzini, B., 1994. The "Starfire" video prototype project: a case history. In: *CHI '94 Human factors in computing systems: celebrating interdependence*, Beth Adelson, Susan Dumais, and Judith Olson (Eds.). ACM, New York, NY (1994)

Augmenting the Learning Experience
with Virtual Simulation Systems

Lucia Pannese
Imaginary srl
via Mauro Macchi 52
20124 Milano Italy
lucia.pannese@i-maginary.it

Sonia Hetzner
University of Erlangen
Nägelsbachstraße 25b
91052 Erlangen
sonia.hetzner@fim.uni-
erlangen.de

Roland Hallmeier
University of Erlangen
Nägelsbachstraße 25b
91052 Erlangen
roland.hallmeier@fim.uni-
erlangen.de

ABSTRACT

The described half day workshop introduces all participants in a very interactive way into the activities of the ImREAL FP7 project which wants to augment the learning experience with the use of highly adaptive simulators. Real world activities will be integrated with the simulation environment by means of intelligent semantic services and a novel approach to digital and interactive storytelling. Researchers as well as practitioners are invited to interact with the simulation under development, discuss and participate to the definition of potential further development.

Categories and Subject Descriptors: H.m

General Terms: Human Factors

Keywords: Augmented learning experience, dialogue simulation, semantic services, multicultural interpersonal communication, user model, adaptive simulator.

1. INTRODUCTION

The creation of effective Virtual Reality training simulation tools that adapt to trainees' past experiences or preconceptions is extremely challenging. Researchers working in ImREAL, an FP7 ICT project are aiming at closing the gap between the 'real world' and the 'virtual world' by developing a simulated learning environment focusing on interpersonal communication in multicultural environments that responds to users' behavior and adapts accordingly to the user model.

2. INTEGRATION OF REAL AND VIRTUAL WORLDS

The proposed workshop is focused on the integration of real world activities with the simulation environment by means of intelligent semantic services and a novel approach to digital and interactive storytelling. The proposed event presents the European FP7 project ImREAL and its innovative approach to the augmentation of training simulations with real life information. ImREAL aims at augmenting the experience in virtual simulation systems with the help of software services which are able to draw real world experiences from actual application contexts into the simulators. These services are designed to work independent of the simulation. This means that they can be used in any existing system and with any existing simulation content. The project proposes to use storytelling as a method to capture real life experiences from work scenarios that match the topic of the learning content in the simulations. Storytelling is conceived as a suitable tool to harvest procedural knowledge and feed it into the simulations as additional enriching material. In order to enrich the simulation experience and to draw in experiences from the real world, additional materials apart from the contents of the simulations are needed. ImREAL aims to provide users, i.e. the learners using the simulators, with the possibility to submit media that document their own experiences related to the concepts they are going to learn. For this purpose, an online web 2.0-platform is developed where material can be collected in a user-friendly way. Additionally, the ImREAL software services will be able to extract relevant information from social media accounts the learners are using, i.e. information posted to Facebook, Twitter, BibSonomy, Delicious or other web applications. All the different information elements must be annotated semantically to allow for retrieval of matching contents and to create a relevant ontology that maps real-world input to simulator learning content. With the help of the online system and contributions by users themselves, training simulations for vocationally relevant soft skills can be enriched with information of high quality which enables the simulators to adapt to the target group's learning needs. This is possible through the computer-generated real world model and ontologies derived from information provided by users.

3. WORKSHOP STRUCTURE

The proposed Workshop shows and discusses in a very interactive way the possibilities in using storytelling as source for information that augments the learning experience in virtual simulation systems. Also, evaluation results of a first version of the online storytelling environment will be discussed. Participants of the workshop will be introduced to the main concepts of the ImREAL project and have the opportunity to work with the storytelling environment and contribute to its further development. The half-day workshop will be led by imaginary, partner of the ImREAL consortium and developer of the simulator used in the session. Researchers and practitioners interested in the topic as well as learning experts with academic or business interest are all invited to join the workshop.

ACKNOWLEDGMENTS: The research leading to these results has received funding from the European Union Seventh Framework Programme (FP7/2007-2013) under grant agreement no ICT 257831 (ImREAL project).

Work through the Web:
A Typology of Web 2.0 Services

Doug Divine
University of Washington
423 Sieg Hall
Seattle, WA 98195
206-369-7317

rddivine@uw.edu

Toni Ferro
University of Washington
423 Sieg Hall
Seattle, WA 98195
503-360-7226

tdferro@uw.edu

Mark Zachry
University of Washington
423 Sieg Hall
Seattle, WA 98195
206-616-7936

zachry@uw.edu

ABSTRACT
To better understand how publicly available online services (PAOSs) are used by knowledge workers on the web, we devised and tested a classification scheme for Web 2.0 services. This classification scheme focuses on genres of services and types of interactions associated with PAOSs. Our experiment, which involved a double-coded assessment of 238 unique sites, demonstrates that our definition of Web 2.0 and our defined genres and associated user interaction types are recognizable. In addition, this study suggests that genres of services can be a valuable instrument in the analysis, discussion, and design of sites used by knowledge workers.

Categories and Subject Descriptors
K.4.3 [**Organizational Impacts**]: Computer-supported collaborative work

General Terms
Design, Experimentation, Human Factors, Standardization, Theory, Verification

Keywords
Web 2.0 services, publicly available online services, genre, collaborative work, survey, knowledge transactors.

1. INTRODUCTION
New forms of cooperative interaction made possible by network-based applications on the web have rapidly changed how people work together to get things done. This change is partly evident in the growing use of publicly available online services (PAOSs), an ever-changing set of tools through which individuals are mediating knowledge to connect with peers, collaborate on projects, and even coordinate world changing protests. These services fall under the broader category of Web 2.0 services, which in varied forms facilitate read-write functionality through browser interfaces. Many of these services are specifically designed to support interactions among multiple users connected to one another, and are thus commonly labeled as social networking technologies. For the purposes of our study, however, we focus instead on the use of such services in work, particularly in the emerging forms of distributed work wherein activities are coordinated using web-based services. Through an exploration of work facilitated by PAOSs, we offer a typology through which services can be tracked and investigated over time, setting the stage for future explorations of their evolving designs and implementation.

The varied PAOSs available today enable knowledge workers to accomplish tasks ranging from collaborative authoring to schedule coordination; from webcasting to co-designing. Some PAOSs are well known while many others compete for recognition and wider adoption. Both the variety, volume, and the rapid pace of change in the technical space of PAOSs (wherein new services are constantly being introduced, modified, redesigned, combined, and abandoned) present challenges for researchers and designers who seek to understand the new ways in which knowledge work is being mediated through services on the web. Our study explores a potential framework for ordering the technologies and associated work in this space, offering a typology of service genres and of the interactions supported by such services.

We begin with a brief discussion of the rationale for our approach, which relies on genre classification based in activity theory. We then report on the results of our research study, including the development and verification of our classification scheme. We conclude with a discussion of our results and an exploration of future research directions.

2. BACKGROUND
Researchers have recently explored possibilities for creating a typology of Web 2.0 services (e.g., [2], [3]). Beer [2] argues that identifying categories of online services is important for researchers to develop an understanding of the current cultural shift toward online collaboration and user-generated content. He also notes that an "umbrella term like Web 2.0 allows for a series of categories to be fitted in it" [2, p. 519]. Genre theory—with its focus on classifying typified forms of communicative interaction—offers a potential scheme for classifying the kinds of services represented under the broad heading of Web 2.0. We recognize that the use of genre theory, rooted in rhetorical studies of texts, might pose some confusion for current theorists, given that our focus is on the categorization of online services and not the texts that are generated by them. We are confident, however, that a reasonably grounded foundation of service genres might in fact help bridge the gap that seems to exist between the study of form and function of online genres of text. A review of the literature finds little consistency in current taxonomies of online

text genres. Those genres receiving somewhat consistent attention from a rhetorical view include homepages, wikis, and blogs. Döring [6] has written a review of research on personal homepages and Poole & Grudin [12] have provided a genre based taxonomy for enterprise wikis. Herring et al. [8] have conducted research focused on the genre antecedents of blogs and the position of blogs in the genre ecology of the Internet. These studies, however, highlight questions about boundaries between genres, sub-genres, and genre sets. Given the fact that a valuable taxonomy requires the ability to identify consistent forms, it is not surprising the study of online genres remains taxing given that the focus of genre theory has been based in social action rather than form for several decades.

Miller [10], for example, was instrumental in refocusing current genre theory on the social action of communicative texts. She argues that genres of text have social significance because they allow people to better understand their own, shared social contexts:

"A genre is not just a pattern of forms or even a method of achieving our own ends. We learn what ends we may have: we learn that we may eulogize, apologize, recommend one person to another, instruct customers on behalf of a manufacturer … We learn to understand better the situations in which we find ourselves and the potentials for failure and success in acting together" (p.165).

Following this line of argument, examining communicative interactions as they are enacted through genres, entails not just considering generically recognizable forms of communication, but—more importantly—the social actions that people recurrently accomplish with one another through those forms.

With our focus on publicly available online services (PAOSs) used for work purposes, we value Miller's perspective on genre based in social activity. Miller's genre-classification lens invites us to examine, "what ends we may have," in relation to today's professional online collaboration using PAOSs. For example, what types of professional collaboration and communication are happening using PAOSs? What PAOSs are knowledge workers relying on to collaborate professionally? What professional collaboration situations lend themselves to the use of PAOSs? And what do PAOSs that are used for professional collaboration have in common? The implications for understanding the answers to these questions are far reaching. An understanding of the professional situations that lend themselves to collaboration via PAOSs may impact how PAOSs are developed and implemented on specific sites and may impact our approach to professional communication education.

Devitt, however, believes that current theories of genre, based largely on social action, have tended to neglect important aspects of form [4]. She posits that theorists like Miller have not rejected form as a vital component of genre study, but instead have rejected formalism wherein the study of a genre's form overshadows the purpose and activity of the genre. Devitt makes this claim to encourage researchers to begin focusing on "contextualized form," which takes into account the action of a genre, but also its substance and form. The current focus on social action might be occluding important elements responsible for the development of forms within genres of text.

We believe genres of services can help influence the study of form within online texts. Herring et. al. [8] note that the structural features of blogs are in part determined by the blog creation software the author uses. Therefore, the affordances and constraints of the online services play an important role in shaping the text-based genre of a blog. A recent exploration by Miller seems to concur with this assessment; however, she takes it one step further. Miller claims that a blog, once studied as a genre of text through her own research, is actually "a technology, a medium, a constellation of affordances - and not a genre" [11, p. 283].

Extending this ongoing discussion about the nature of genres, Huckin [9] and Bauman [1] discuss the importance of emerging genres of text to pedagogy and education. Huckin suggests that genres are not necessarily strictly agents or tools and instead that there is a continuum between agents and tools and some genres are closer to agents on the continuum and other genres fall closer to tools on the continuum [9]. Similarly, Bauman notes that in the midst of the sea change caused by the introduction of computers, texts fall "somewhere between being flotsam and jetsam on the surface and being the turbine driving the turbulence" [1, p. 272].

This research and analysis seems to support the notion that forms of online texts are in fact impacted by a larger sense of structure. We believe that genres of online services, defined and recognized based on technical formations of user actions, could be providing this structure. Our approach to classifying PAOSs into genres of services is built on the assumption that PAOSs serve as mediating tools within a larger activity system, but are not necessarily technologies or mediums as Miller might claim. The structures of services are more flexible and malleable than technologies or mediums. Their structures are recognizable but rooted directly in the evolving activities of users. They are in fact the bridge between technology and texts. This approach to genres of service, builds on Russell's [13] combination of genre with activity theory in which he argues that genres are socially flexible constructs used to mediate the objective of a given activity system. He defines an activity system as:

"Any ongoing, object-directed, historically-conditioned, dialectically-structured, tool-mediated human interaction… mutually (re)constructed by participants using certain tools and not others" (pp. 4-5).

Russell quotes Bazerman in his shared opinion that genres are not best described as textual forms, but rather, "forms of life, ways of being, frames for social action" [13, p. 7]. Russell claims that, "As forms of life, genres and the activity systems they operationalize are (temporarily) regularized, stabilized, through routinized, typified tool-use within and among (sub) groups/genres." (p. 7).

While most genre theorists consider genres as they are enacted through varied textual-symbolic forms associated with recurring rhetorical situations, our focus here is different. Because there has been relatively little systematic study of the social actions in which people engage while working through the web, we are taking an initial step in that direction by first attempting to understand the genres of *services* used to mediate knowledge work. Thus, instead of focusing on the genre by looking at individual communicative acts, we look at commonalities among the many services employed by professionals to complete their work. Our categorization of these services, as well as the interactions that they facilitate, are all oriented toward understanding recurring communicative performance types; however, a formal analysis of performance type is a future goal of this ongoing project. The more immediate problem addressed by this study is developing a systematic way of classifying the kinds of web-based services available to knowledge workers and the kinds of interactions those services facilitate. To achieve this goal, our use of genre must incorporate not only an understanding of the use and interaction of services, but also the forms through which the services are recognized.

Ferro and Zachry [7] introduced the idea of genres of services in an attempt to map the online spaces that knowledge workers report as important. This work extends that idea by considering such genres in terms of the larger technical activity systems in which these services are embedded. Specifically, this study begins to consider the online sites through which such services are rendered. To better understand the recurring situations in which professional actions are taken, we contend that a necessary first step is to understand the activity systems in which different genres of services are used.

We take an empirical approach to develop this mapping of services, interactions, and sites. As we describe below, our investigation begins with an attempt to verify the ability of individuals to identify the presence of Web 2.0 services across a sampling of sites used by knowledge workers. This first step of identifying services within sites helps determine the social validity of the constructs defined for each service genre. We also attempt to determine how individuals apply a list of defined user interactions across the same collection of sites. Understanding how unique individuals apply a list of interactions to their interpretation of the site helps illuminate associations between genres of services and user interactions within the confines of each unique site as an activity system. Finally, we explore the relationship between the complexity of a site, defined primarily through the number of potential service genres recognized within the system, and a user's ability to agree on the presence and use of those services as the complexity increases. With this information we can begin laying the foundation for future research that examines the evolution of services in the rapidly changing domain of Web 2.0 technologies used for work.

For the purposes of this study we use Web 2.0 as defined by Ferro and Zachry:

> "A software-driven system that allows users on the Internet to write data that persists and is shareable with other Internet users, who may, in turn, be able to manipulate that data."

In addition, while the terms *site* and *service* are used in a variety of ways in Internet studies, for our purposes a site is defined as a set of related and connected web pages that are available on the Internet and typically identified through a common domain name, for example Amazon.com or twitter.com. We define service as an offering available to the users of a site. For example, Amazon.com offers services such as a product search, a wish list, and a shopping cart. A site can include one service or many services. In addition, a site that contains multiple services may have services with properties that meet our definition of Web 2.0, and other services that do not. For our research, we discuss Web 2.0 services and genres of Web 2.0 services.

3. METHODS
The data set used for this study is based on a set of 300 unique and valid URLs collected from an annual survey of technical knowledge workers between 2008 and 2010 [7].

Using this data set, three annotators participated in a multi focused assessment of each URL's content. Six lists, containing 50 URLs each, were created and loaded into a tool called Qbox, which supports multi-party, inline annotation of digital web content [5]. Each set of 50 URLs was assigned to two annotators,

so that every URL within a given set could be double coded. The annotators were provided with a codebook that defined terms necessary for each step of the study and were asked to record their assessments in Qbox.

To test the comprehensibility of the codebook as well as the annotators' ability to interact with the Qbox technology, the first set of 50 URLs was coded with periodic comparison of results and discussion among all members of the research team. During these early discussions the annotators and researchers realized the instructions asked annotators to provide assessments for each site, though a thorough examination of the site's services were required in order to meet this request. A site can offer multiple services, but users often identify a single service as the primary reason for using the site. The original coding instrument, for example, asked whether a site was Web 2.0 using a yes / no classification. The annotators felt that the choice was too limiting because although some sites had Web 2.0 services by definition, these services did not represent the primary service or reason that a user would interact with the site. This led some annotators to disqualify certain sites as Web 2.0 when in fact they possessed Web 2.0 services.

The annotation options for this analysis were therefore modified. Due to the changes in the recording instruments, the first set of 50 URLs was dropped from the study. After this adjustment, 250 URLs remained in the formal study. During the annotation process 12 additional URLs were eliminated due to html rendering issues within Qbox. This brought the total number of URLs assessed within this study to 238. All data was downloaded to a spreadsheet and analyzed focusing on Web 2.0 services, service genres, site complexity, and user interaction types.

3.1 Step One: Web 2.0 Service Identification
The initial focus of our research was to determine whether blind agreement could be obtained among annotators using a single definition of Web 2.0 services across our list of URLs. We used the definition of Web 2.0 service offered by Ferro and Zachry [7].

Each annotator was asked whether the site qualified as:

- Primary Web 2.0– the site's primary purpose is facilitated by Web 2.0 service(s),
- Secondary Web 2.0 - the site offers Web 2.0 services; however these services do not adequately represent the primary purpose of the site,
- Web 2.0 services not offered – the site does not offer Web 2.0 services and therefore should not be coded for the purposes of this study.

Obtaining agreement on this particular dimension was important because only sites that contained Web 2.0 services would be analyzed in subsequent steps. An independent analysis of the data revealed that after the first coding pass of 238 sites, annotators agreed on 167 of the sites (70%) but disagreed on 71 (30%). To determine whether the disagreement was based on confusion over the definition of Web 2.0 services or difficulty in identifying a Web 2.0 service, each annotator was provided a list of the sites they had identified as having Web 2.0 services that another annotator identified as not having Web 2.0 services. Each annotator was asked to review the sites on their list again and provide written justification indicating that Web 2.0 services were in fact present. The justifications were collected, reassembled into new lists, and shared so that the second annotator failing to reach initial agreement could reassess their finding. Annotators reached agreement on 64 sites through this comparative review while 7 sites had to be adjudicated by the research team to reach agreement. Through this process 100% agreement was reached for all sites regarding their qualifications under the definition of Web 2.0 services.

3.2 Step Two: Service Genre Identification

To gain further insight into the publicly available online services employed by workers on the web, a genre analytical approach was introduced by Ferro and Zachry [7]. Our initial goal for this step of the study was to determine whether this typology of service genres could be verified based on blind agreement between annotators for the presence of genres across our list of URLs. The annotators were presented with a codebook containing the genres (see Table 1) and were asked to determine their application against the sites coded as having Web 2.0 services. Because each site could potentially contain more than one service, the annotators were asked to indicate all service genres applicable to the site as well as their choice for the primary service genre that best represented the site as a whole.

In addition, we analyzed each site's complexity based on the total number of Web 2.0 services available on the site. The combined number of service genres reported between the annotators for a site was used to establish this complexity. Agreement trends were used to determine the relationship of the site's complexity to the level of the annotators' agreement on service genres and interaction types.

Table 1. Definitions for Genres of Services

Genre of Service	Definition
Asynchronous Forum	An online space to which contributors can contribute individual postings.
Blog	A journal through which a designated individual or group of individuals can publish ideas.
Knowledge Transactor	A service through which people can submit primarily alpha-numeric information and have it transformed to be shared with others.
Media Sharing Tool	A service through which people can submit primarily visual / audio material to be shared with others.
Microblog	Application through which users can enter free form text of constrained length, broadcasting via the Internet.
Network Creator	An application through which individuals identify other online individuals with whom they have a relationship.
Social Marking Tool	An online tool allowing individuals to tag, classify, index, or mark information in a form that can be aggregated and shared with others.
Synchronous Interaction Tool	An online tool through which people engage in real-time exchanges via text, audio, and/or video.
Wiki	A webspace that publishes pages that can be read by individuals and edited / supplemented collaboratively by contributors

3.3 Step Three: Interaction Type Identification

In addition to coding the service genres present on the sites, annotators were asked to identify the types of interactions users are likely to perform on the sites. The types of user interactions were provided in the codebook (see Table 2). The annotators were asked to indicate all interaction types applicable to the site as well as the primary interaction that best represented the site as a whole.

Table 2. Definitions for Interaction Types

Interaction Type	Definition
Publishing/ Sharing	The user is using the service to share original content or personal information with other users of the service.
Classifying/ Rating	The user is interacting with the service for the purpose of weighting opinion in favor of their experiences or views.
Conversing	The user is interacting with the service to engage in a dialogue (synchronous or asynchronous) with other users of the service.
Manipulating Data	The user is interacting with the service to alter or manipulate data or content visible to other users of the service.
Coordinating	The user is interacting with the service to plan / coordinate actions or work with other users of the service
Associating	The user is interacting with the service to develop or strengthen associations with people, groups, or organizations.

4. Results

Of the 238 sites included in the study, 151 sites were found to have Web 2.0 services, thus qualifying them for further analysis. The following results show that the definition for Web 2.0 service was recognized by annotators and applied successfully across a diverse population of sites. The service genres and interaction types all had high levels of agreement among annotators, however levels of agreement were lower for complex sites (where multiple Web 2.0 services existed on the site).

4.1 Web 2.0 Identification Results

With 100% agreement between double coded results, the results showed that of the 238 sites analyzed, 151 (63%) of the sites possessed Web 2.0 services, while 87 (37%) lacked Web 2.0 services (see Table 3). Though annotators did not always agree whether the primary purpose of the site was Web 2.0, there was unanimous agreement between sites that contained Web 2.0 services and those that did not.

Table 3. Results of Web 2.0 Analysis

Annotator Agreement on Web 2.0	# of Sites	Percent
Primary Web 2.0	73	48%
Secondary Web 2.0	47	31%
Mixed Primary and Secondary Web 2.0	31	21%

4.2 Genre Identification Results

Of the 151 sites found to contain Web 2.0 services, 27 were not coded by two independent annotators on the genre dimension and were therefore eliminated from the study. This left 124 sites in this step of the analysis.

As shown in Table 4, relatively strong agreement was found for the service genres when examined across the sample of sites. Annotators were able to identify genre categories consistently across 93 unique sites, therefore 75% of the sites annotated had agreement for at least one service genre. Of the 93 sites where agreement occurred, 31 sites (25%) had exact agreement between all services genres reported. Among these 31 sites, all service genres, with the exception of microblog, were uniquely identified by two annotators. Agreement by genre is presented in Table 4.

Table 4. Number of Site Agreements by Annotators per Service Genre

Genre of Service	Did not agree	Agree present	Agree not present	Total agree	Percent agree
Asynchronous Forum	42	37	45	82	66.13%
Knowledge Transactor	40	31	53	84	67.74%
Blog	32	6	86	92	74.19%
Media Sharing Tool	28	16	80	96	77.42%
Wiki	26	3	95	98	79.03%
Network Creator	21	10	93	103	83.06%
Synchronous Interaction Tool	19	6	99	105	84.68%
Social Marking Tool	15	3	106	109	87.90%
Microblog	9	0	115	115	92.74%

4.3 Site Complexity Results

Of the 124 sites included in the service genre analysis, 93 sites (75%) were recorded as having three or fewer genres of service. 27 sites (22%) were recorded as having only one service genre. In these cases, annotator agreement was 100%. However, for sites reported to have more than one genre of service, the agreement level dropped drastically to 37%. Exact agreement was not obtained for a single site reported as having more than three service genres. As expected, annotator agreement continued to drop as the number of service genres on a site increased, staying at or below a level of 30% agreement for sites with three or more service genres.

Table 5. Number of sites indicating annotator agreement based on the total number of service genres reported per site

Total # of reported service genres	Sites	Sites with agreement for all reported genres	Sites without agreement for all reported genres	Average % agreement for reported genres
1	27	27	0	100.00%
2	35	3	12	37.14%
3	31	1	9	30.11%
4	14	0	7	16.07%
5	6	0	1	23.33%
6	9	0	1	25.93%
7	2	0	1	7.14%

4.4 Interaction Type Results

Similar to what was seen with genres of services, a large percentage of agreement was found for the interaction types when examined across the sample of sites. Annotators were able to identify interaction types consistently across 111 unique sites, therefore 90% of the sites annotated had agreement for at least one interaction type. Of the 111 sites where agreement occurred, only 23 sites (19%) had exact agreement between all interaction types reported. Among these 23 sites, all interaction types were uniquely identified by two annotators. Agreement by interaction type is presented in Table 6.

Table 6. Number of Site Agreements by Annotators per Interaction Type

Interaction Type	Did not agree	Agree present	Agree not present	Total agree	Percent agree
Conversing	46	45	33	78	62.90%
Coordinating	45	20	59	79	63.71%
Associating	36	10	78	88	70.97%
Data Manipulation	31	9	84	93	75.00%
Classifying / Rating	22	6	96	102	82.26%
Publishing / Sharing	22	90	12	102	82.26%

5. DISCUSSION

While this study is an early foray into PAOSs used by knowledge workers, we have identified key findings that enhance the understanding of work in online spaces. We have found that it is possible to characterize the nature of a site as well as its complexity through the analysis of its services. Our results consistently point to the notion that the purpose and value of a specific site pivots on the professional- rhetorical situation of the knowledge worker.

Annotators were able to identify sites that include Web 2.0 services and sites that do not. In addition, for sites with only one Web 2.0 service, annotators agreed 100% of the time on the genre of Web 2.0 service available through the site. Where exact agreement was achieved, all but one of the service genres were covered, which illustrates that the genres of services presented in this study are recognizable. This shows that characterizing sites and services, using the category of Web 2.0 and service genres, is possible and has the potential to provide insights into the new ways knowledge workers are collaborating and communicating.

Consistent with the individual use of genre, based on social action promoted by Miller [10] and Russell [13], individual annotators were unable to reliably determine whether the primary purpose of the site was related to its Web 2.0 service(s) or not. In 21% of cases where a site was determined to offer a Web 2.0 service, two annotators disagreed on whether that service was related to the primary purpose of the site. In addition, when two or more genres of Web 2.0 services were available on a site, the annotators were unable to reliably agree on the genres of services available. The interaction types identified by annotators as being applicable to a site were not identified reliably. We suggest that the reason the annotators did not reliably agree is because each approached the site from a unique contextual situation; unique personal histories with each site, histories with comparable sites, unique perspectives on the importance of the different types of work that can be accomplished by the site, etc.

Similarly, we suggest that in cases where more than one Web 2.0 service genre was available on a site, annotators were unable to agree on the presence of genres because they were approaching the site looking for and expecting different elements. It is likely that the annotators' expectations of the site based on their situation caused them to look in some places that the other annotators did not. Finally, the high levels of disagreement on the interaction types for each site illustrate that the use of Web 2.0 services is personal and situational. This is what one might expect based on the individual use of tools within the confines of a larger activity system.

We propose future research to continue this work to characterize the sites valuable to knowledge workers, examine the trends in sites over time, and understand the complex relationships between sites, service genres, and interaction types.

6. FUTURE RESEARCH

This study suggests multiple areas of further research. Specifically, the notion of site complexity (the number of services per site) is an interesting avenue of study and may provide insights into the nature of professional web sites that are popular today with knowledge workers. In the sample used for this study the majority of sites (75%) had between one and three Web 2.0 service genres reported. Only two of the sites had seven service genres reported. Because we are conducting this study annually it may be interesting to analyze the trends in site complexity year over year. For example, we can ask if the sites most frequently reported by knowledge workers as being important to their work are highly complex, or whether they contain only one or two Web 2.0 services. The concept of site complexity also raises the question of whether or not knowledge workers are reporting a site as important because of a specific Web 2.0 service available on the site, or because of all of the services available on the site.

Continued study of the relationship between PAOS genres and the possible use of interaction types on a site is a central area of interest that will strengthen our understanding of PAOS genres serving as mediating tools within activity systems. To truly realize the value of these genres as mediating tools, it is important to understand the recurring and culturally situated ways they are actually used.

Since the proposed list of service genres and user interactions were found to be recognizable between annotators, and across varied online sites, we have increased confidence in their promise to serve as a focal point for further research in the evolution of PAOSs. We propose a more precise examination of each service genre, using the lens of activity theory, to help illuminate the unique and collaborative roles that these tools play in mediating a user's need to interact or communicate within complex online environments. It is our belief that understanding the ways PAOSs work in activity systems associated with Web 2.0 technologies will not only provide insight into their evolution, but will reveal important contextual information that can be used in planning, (re)design, and development of online systems.

A closer look at the service genres and interaction types proposed in this study suggests that they are all involved in the communicative aspects of information, a concept reflected in our definition of Web 2.0. Understanding the service genres as tools within an activity system may actually help bridge the gap in the understanding and definition of genre itself. At what point does a service genre, or tool used in online communication, become an established genre of communication within its own right?

To further test the typology of service genres we advocate a new methodology where a select number of sites are vetted by a group to determine consensus on the presence of service genres. This sample of sites could then be grouped according to complexity and analyzed by a random sample of potential users to determine the percentage of agreement made with the established view of the initial group. If we couple this with the typology of user interactions, we can also illuminate how the sample users' intended use of services influence their recognition of specific service genres. In addition we can attempt to explore more fully the effect of worker experience and background to better understand how specific types of users interact with a given site or in a given activity system to mediate their unique needs for work.

7. ACKNOWLEDGMENTS

We thank the research team of Nathan Bilbao, Joy Palludan, and Zach Lym who performed the annotation work reported in this study. We also thank Jamie Ourada for his assistance with setting up QBox to facilitate the coding experiments.

8. REFERENCES

[1] Bauman, M. L. 1999. The Evolution of Internet Genres. *Computers and Composition*, 16, 269-282.

[2] Beer, D. 2008. Social network(ing) sites… revisiting the story so far: A response to Danah Boyd & Nicole Ellison. *Journal of Computer-Mediated Communication*, 13(2), 516-529.

[3] Boyd, D., & Ellison, N. B. 2007. Social network sites: Definition, history, and scholarship. *Journal of Computer-Mediated Communication*, 13(1), 210-230.

[4] Devitt, A.J. 2009. Re-fusing form in genre study. In J.Giltrow & D. Stein (Eds.), *Genres in the internet: Issues in the theory of genre*, 27-47. Amsterdam/Philadelphia: John Benjamins Publishing Company

[5] Divine, D., Morgan, J.T., Ourada, J., & Zachry, M. 2010. Designing Qbox; a tool for sorting things out in digital spaces. In *Proceedings of the 16th ACM international conference on Supporting group work* (GROUP '10). ACM, New York, NY, USA, 311-312.

[6] Döring, N. 2002. Personal home pages on the Web: A review of research. *Journal of Computer-Mediated Communication*, 7.

[7] Ferro, T., & Zachry, M. (forthcoming). Networked Knowledge Workers on the Web: An Examination of US Trends, 2008-2010. *Handbook of Research on Business Social Networking: Organizational, Managerial, and Technological Dimensions*. Hershey, PA, USA: IGI Publishing.

[8] Herring, S. C., Scheidt, L. A., Bonus, S., Wright, E. 2004. "Bridging the Gap: A Genre Analysis of Weblogs." *Proceedings of the 37th Annual Hawaii International Conference on System Sciences (HICCS)*.

[9] Huckin, T. 2007. Electronic genres and what they mean for genre theory and pedagogy: some thoughts. *Proceedings of the International Symposium on Genre Studies (SIGET)*, 70-80.

[10] Miller, C. R. 1984. Genre as social action. *Quarterly Journal of Speech* 70(May), 151-67.

[11] Miller, C.R., & Shepherd, D. 2009. Questions for genre theory from the blogosphere. In J. Giltrow & D. Stein (Eds.), *Genres in the internet: Issues in the theory of genre*, 264-290. Amsterdam/Philadelphia: John Benjamins Publishing Company.

[12] Poole, E.S. & Grudin, J. 2010. A taxonomy of Wiki genres in enterprise settings. In *Proceedings of the 6th International Symposium on Wikis and Open Collaboration* (WikiSym '10). ACM, New York, NY, USA, , Article 14 , 1-4.

[13] Russell, D.R. 1997. Rethinking Genre in School and Society: An Activity Theory Analysis. *Written Communication* 14 (4), 504-554.

Support for Remote Usability Evaluation of Web Mobile Applications

Tonio Carta
CNR-ISTI, HIIS Laboratory
Via Moruzzi 1, 56124 Pisa, Italy
Tonio.Carta@isti.cnr.it

Fabio Paternò
CNR-ISTI, HIIS Laboratory
Via Moruzzi 1, 56124 Pisa, Italy
Fabio.Paterno@isti.cnr.it

Vagner F. de Santana
Institute of Computing, UNICAMP
Albert Einstein Av., 1251,
Campinas, São Paulo, Brazil
vsantana@ic.unicamp.br

ABSTRACT
Usability evaluation of Web sites is still a difficult and time-consuming task, often performed manually. This paper presents a tool that supports remote usability evaluation of Web sites accessed through mobile devices. The tool considers client-side data on user interactions and JavaScript events. In addition, it allows the definition of custom events, giving evaluators the flexibility to add specific events to detect and consider in the evaluation. The tool supports evaluation of any Web site by exploiting a proxy-based architecture and enables the evaluator to perform a comparison between actual user behaviour and an optimal sequence of actions.

Categories and Subject Descriptors
H.5.2 **[Information Interfaces and Presentation]**: User Interfaces – Evaluation/methodology. D.2.2 **[Software Engineering]**: Design Tools and Techniques – User interfaces.

General Terms
Experimentation, Human Factors.

Keywords
Tools for Usability Evaluation, Remote evaluation, Log analysis.

1. INTRODUCTION
Although usability has long been addressed and discussed, when people navigate the Web they often encounter a number of usability issues. This is also due to the fact that Web surfers often decide on the spur of the moment what to do and whether to continue to navigate in a Web site. Usability evaluation is thus an important phase in the deployment of Web applications. For this purpose automatic tools are very useful to gather larger amount of usability data and support their analysis.

Remote evaluation [2] implies that users and evaluators are separated in time and/or space. This is important in order to analyse users in their daily environments and decreases the costs of the evaluation without requiring the use of specific laboratories and asking the users to move. In addition, tools for remote Web usability evaluation should be sufficiently general so that they can be used to analyse user behaviour even when using various browsers or applications developed using different .toolkits. We prefer logging on the client-side in order to be able to capture any user-generated events, which can provide useful hints regarding possible usability problems. Moreover, the tool allows the usability experts to analyse through some graphical representations of the logged data how users interacted with the user interface (UI).

Ivory and Hearst [4] provided a good discussion of tools for usability evaluation according to a taxonomy based on four dimensions: method class (the type of evaluation); method type (how the evaluation is conducted); automation type (the evaluation aspect that is automated); and effort level (the type of effort required to execute the method). According to this classification our solution is for usability testing, it captures logs generated client-side, supports automatic analysis and a number of visualizations to ease the identification of the usability issues, and only requires that users perform some predefined tasks specified by the evaluators.

Google Analytics [1] has the potential to be configured to capture custom events at client-side and it offers a number of statistics information and reports, but it is rather limited in terms of number of events that it captures for each session. Model-based approaches have been used to support usability evaluation. An example was WebRemUsine [6], which was a tool for remote usability evaluation of Web applications through browser logs and task models. Propp and Frorbrig [7] have used task models for supporting usability evaluation of a different type of application: cooperative behaviour of people interacting in smart environments. A different use of models is in [5], in which the authors discuss how task models can enhance visualization of the usability test log. In our case we do not require the effort of developing models to apply our tool. We only require that the designer provides an example of optimal use associated with each of the relevant tasks. The tool will then compare the logs with the actual use with the optimal log in order to identify deviations, which may indicate potential usability problems.

Costa et al. [8] used a logger to collect data from a user session test on a Web interface prototype running on a PDA simulator in order to evaluate different types of Web navigation tools and identify the best one for small display devices. Users were asked to find the answer to specific questions using different types of navigation tools to move from one page to another. A database was used to store users' actions, but they logged only the answer given by the user to each specific question. Moreover they stored separately every term searched by the user by means of the internal search tool.

Our approach is also based on a "question-answer" paradigm, but we log every user's interaction with the Web sites. The answer is often implicit and can be inferred by the page in where the user finished the interaction. Moreover, Web Usability Probe allows the evaluator to create tests based on real Web sites instead of prototypes, giving the possibility to observe the user's interaction in a real environment. While some general preliminary results were introduced in [9], in this paper we provide a description of a novel tool able to address usability evaluation of mobile Web applications.

In the paper, we first introduce our approach, then we describe how setting up a usability test with our tool, and its support for the analysis of user tests. To better present our approach we present an evaluation of a mobile Web application. Lastly, we draw some conclusions and provide indications for future work.

2. THE APPROACH PROPOSED

The approach proposed is based on an intermediate proxy server whose purpose is to annotate the accessed Web pages in order to include JavaScripts that will carry out the logging of the actual user behaviour (see Figure 1). The tool does not require use of plug-in installation or specific client configuration. The scripts used by the tool are stored in the proxy server and thus there is no security conflict when the page is accessed from the client since the page appears as coming from the proxy server. The server also acts as a usability server in which the evaluator can enter information useful to guide the usability test, such as the list of tasks to perform, what events to log, etc. All such information is stored in a database. Once users have carried out their test tasks, the logs can be accessed by the evaluators, who can customize their representations by selecting what actions to be represented in the reports in order to ease the identification of usability issues.

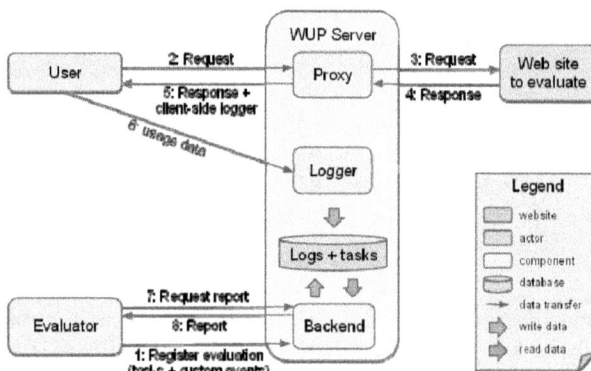

Figure 1. Overview of the approach proposed in the Web Usability Probe.

When a new user test is to be started, the evaluator can access the tool to provide users with the information required to carry out the test. The evaluator then plays the role of user by performing the tasks in an optimal way, without errors (which are actions useless for the current task). Users only need to start using the Web site to be evaluated through the proper link available at the proxy. Then,

when users start the test they are informed about the task to accomplish. When they complete it they have to indicate this by accessing the dialogue box automatically generated with the controls related to the task. Next, a new task to perform will be indicated until the end of the test is reached.

The scripts that are injected by the server in order to log usage data and always redirect navigation through the proxy are implemented in JavaScript and use jQuery[1]. All the logged data are sent asynchronously to the server while the user is interacting with the page and when the user moves from one page to another; the server stores the logged data in a database, thus it is possible to extract all data in multiple formats to meet the evaluator's needs.

This approach satisfies a number of requirements about evaluation tools: it works in different configurations of hardware and software; it does not depend on specific configurations; it does not impact on the Web site usage; and it does not interfere with the Web page.

The development of a proxy-based tool considering client-side data encounters different challenges regarding the identification of the elements that users are interacting with, how to manage element identification when the page is changed dynamically, how to manage data logging when users are going from one page to another, amongst others. The following are some of the solutions we adopted in order to deal with these issues.

When logging data at the client-side, identification of the target element is an issue if the target element of a certain event does not have a name or the id attribute. In this case, two main approaches can be followed: either ignore events involving unidentified elements or assign an id according their position in the Web page structure (Document Object Model Tree). The first approach does not allow the evaluator to know exactly the elements referenced by the trigged events if any usability problem is identified, which complicates its correction. The second approach, on the other hand, can cause some overhead. The approach used in the Web Usability Probe generates ids according to the XPath[2] syntax, and thereby allowing the id attribute to be computer and human readable. This provides the possibility of mapping back an id to the Web page element being analysed.

Another issue that a client-side logging tool should address is how to inform evaluators that only a certain part of the page has been changed dynamically. This can occur, for instance, via AJAX, which can result in new UI elements. Our tool addresses these cases by detecting the events triggered when the DOM Tree is changed, which can then be reported in the timeline, allowing the evaluators to verify where and when they occurred.

3. SETTING UP A REMOTE USABILITY TEST

The evaluators can create the settings for a remote usability test at any time. In the administrator part of the usability tool there is an item for each test indicating the name, a description, the evaluator and the number of tasks that should be performed. The tool provides dynamically the indication of the number of sessions that have been logged for that test.

---

[1] http://jquery.com

[2] http://www.w3.org/TR/xpath/

Associated with each test there is an editable list of tasks (an example in Figure 2). For each task there is the indication of the name, a description, the indication of the URL where the task should be started, whether it can be skipped, and if its performance depends on some other task. A dependency means that the other task should be performed first than the current one.

Figure 2. An example of task list for a user test.

These features allow remote participants to clearly understand what they should do: the name and description are the texts that users will see through automatically generated dialogue boxes. The starting URL provides flexibility in the evaluation setup, since allows evaluators to define that certain tasks have to start in different parts of the evaluated Web site, or even start in another Web site, allowing evaluations to perform comparison among Web sites.

Finally, the dependency feature among tasks is provided in order to make possible to define evaluations where one tasks is mandatory (e.g., login) in order to perform others (e.g., creation of content in a login protected Web site).

Our tool supports logging any standard event[3], jQuery Events[4], touch, gestures, and accelerometer events present at the Safari API[5]. The set of events observed by the tool is shown by grouping them by their type, mainly the device that can generate them: accelerometer, keyboard, mouse, touch. We also consider form-related events (e.g., *change*, *select*, and *submit*), system related events, and customizable events. The evaluator can define custom events, which can be various types of composition of basic events in terms of their ordering or standard events on specific parameters (e.g. a *pageview* event is triggered when a page is shown to the user), and it is possible to associate them with specific events names that can then be visualized in the reports.

4. ANALYSIS OF A REMOTE USABILITY TEST

Once some users have actually performed the user test, the evaluator can access graphical representations of such logs. Hilbert and Redmiles [3] indicated that timelines can be useful for this purpose. We follow this approach: there is one timeline for

[3] http://www.w3schools.com/jsref/dom_obj_event.asp

[4] http://api.jquery.com/category/events/

[5] http://developer.apple.com/library/safari/#documentation/apple applications/reference/safariwebcontent/HandlingEvents/Handli ngEvents.html

each task performed by a user (see Figure 3). The first timeline is dedicated to the optimal log. The graphical representation is interactive and allows the designers to line up logs according to some important event using the 'scroll lock' UI control. In this way the evaluator can compare the optimal behaviour with that of the actual users in order to see whether there was some particularly long interaction, due, for example, to difficulty in understanding how to proceed, or some errors that indicate some usability issue. The zoom level of timelines can be interactively set in order to identify the optimal representation scale.

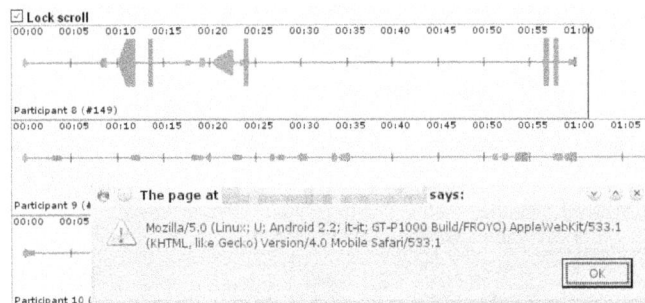

Figure 3. Example of timelines generated by the tool in order to represent usage data.

In addition, the evaluator can easily select the types of events to display on the timelines according to the needs of each analysis. Figure 4 shows the event selection tool of the accelerometer and touch event types, both typical of mobile devices.

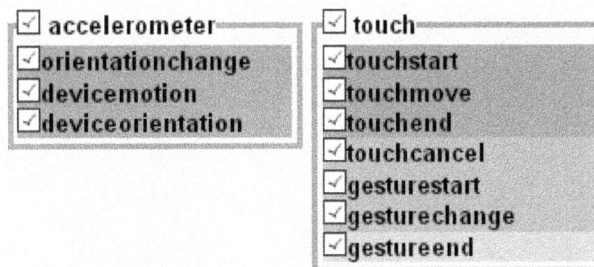

Figure 4. A detail of the event selector feature.

For each timeline the evaluator can also access the User Agent string sent by the user's browser, to easily identify the browser and the device. This is essential information since different devices may lead to a very different user experience and thus a different way to interact with the same page. This information is available clicking on the label "Participant X" (where X is the participant's number) on the bottom left corner of each timeline, and is shown in a popup window (Figure 3).

Our proposal for representing event streams in timelines also uses the height of the time markers present in the timelines to represent the repetitions of a certain event in an element. This allows evaluators to identify useless actions as well as to check repetitive mouse movements over poorly designed links, misguided clicks on non-clickable elements, among others.

When visualizing the timelines of a certain task it is possible to zoom in and out in such representations and visualize them at the very basic event level or at the categories level. In the case of the categories visualization, the timeline uses different colours for different sets of events, for instance, mouse-related events are indicated with the same colour, keyboard-related events in a different colour and so on.

5. AN EXAMPLE APPLICATION

In this section we illustrate an application of our tool and show how an evaluator can infer usability issues from the visualizations provided by the tool. We report on a usability test of the Dallas / Fort Worth, Texas airport Web site (http://www.dfwairport.com/mobile/index.php) for mobile devices.

The tasks to be performed at the airport Web site, which were specified in the configuration of the Web Usability Probe tool, were the following:

- Check the United Airlines departure flights to Chicago

- Find the United Airlines terminal / gate

- Find the list of the shops located in the United Airlines terminal

The mobile version of the Web site has a considerably simplified content with respect to the desktop version. Figure 5 left shows the home page.

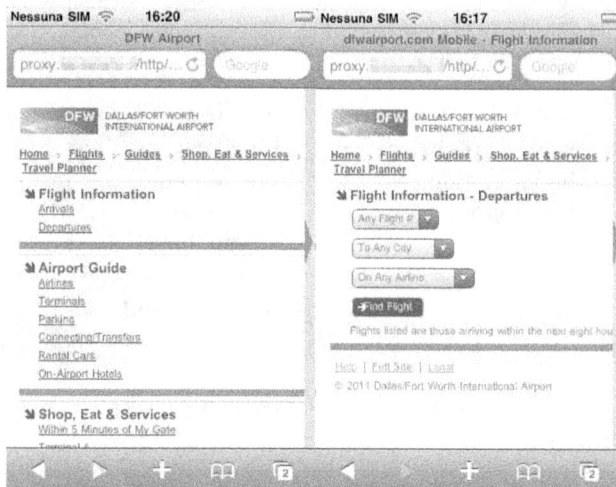

Figure 5. The application considered in the case study.

5.1 Check departure task

The Web site allows users to access all the departure flights but there is no page that contains such information accessible through a specific link. Users must use a form with three pull-down menus (see Figure 5 right), which allow them to filter the relevant flights. The menus also provide the possibility to filter no content. Thus, to find the United Airlines flights to Chicago the users should find the page with the form, and then select Chicago and United Airlines in the corresponding pull-down menus. In order to better analyse the logs we decided to define some custom events:

- *clickOnDeparture* is generated when the user selects the link pointing to the page with the form

- *citySelected* is generated when the user selects an arrival town

- *airlineSelected* is generated when the user selects an airline

- *formOk*, is generated when the user sends the form, only if the preconditions are satisfied: *citySelected* and *airlineSelected* must occur at least once before *formOk* is generated, which means that the user has to first select arrival town and airline;

- *formSubmitted*, is still associated with the form submitted event but it has no precondition.

Figure 6 shows an optimal sequence, obtained through an Apple iPod with iOS 4.2.1 and Safari browser. It is possible to note a high presence of accelerometer events generated by a mobile user. The GPS was turned off in this session.

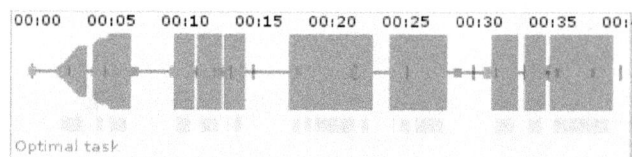

Figure 6. Visualization of Timeline with many accelerometer events.

The visualization tool allows evaluators to hide irrelevant events and thus, if we hide the accelerometer events, we obtain the representation in Figure 7, which is more readable.

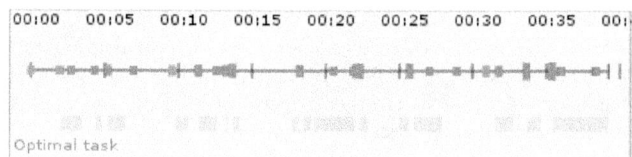

Figure 7. Visualization of Simplified Timeline.

The Safari browser detects the interactions carried out using the touch screen as normal mouse events, represented by purple markers. In addition, whenever users rotate the device to change the orientation from horizontal to vertical or conversely, the browser generates a resize event, with width and height values of the window exchanged, which falls within the System category, whose events are marked in red. The evaluator, in the recording of the optimal session for this first task, visited three pages and for each of them changed the device orientation, a clear sign of the utility of such a feature when you are using a screen of small dimensions.

One of the goals of Web Usability Probe is to ease the comparison between various user sessions in order to better identify behaviours that diverge from the optimal performance. If in the optimal session there is an event whose absence in the user session highlights an error in the task performance, then it is sufficient to appropriately configure the event selector to show that event (and eventually other relevant events) in the timeline.

Consider Figure 8, where the registration of the first participant in the evaluation is compared with the optimal session. The filter has been configured to show the events *pageviews*, *change*, *finishtask* and *formOk*. The latter, as described above, indicates that the user has interacted with both drop-down boxes needed to successfully complete the task. However, in the second timeline this event (marked in light green in the first timeline) is not present. Nevertheless, at the end of the timeline there is the event *finishtask*, thus the user has erroneously considered the task as successfully completed.

Observing the events preceding the end of the task, it is clear the absence of the event change on the drop-down menu associated with the destination city. If the user had realized the error in the search results, he could have used the browser functions to return to the previous page and fill in the form properly. There are two possible explanations for the decision to consider the task as successfully completed: the task was not expressed clearly enough; the page containing the results of the search does not show the search parameters used properly.

It is not possible to verify the first case, but the fact that most other participants correctly selected an item from both drop-down menus tends to discount this hypothesis.

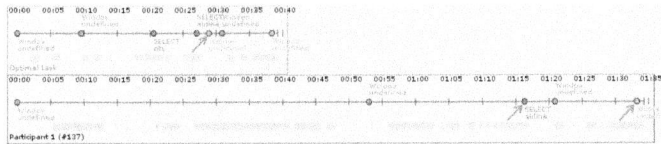

Figure 8. The first user made an error filling in the form.

Instead, we can analyse the second case. Figure 9 shows a comparison of search results in both cases: on the left the result of proper research, on the right the results of a search in which the filter on the destination city was omitted.

The two pages are very similar. The difference is that the page on the left shows only the top three results of a longer list, which can be seen by scrolling the page down, but unfortunately the display size of the device used by the user (an Apple iPhone, as shown by the User Agent string) allows users to see immediately only the first three, which coincidentally are exactly the flights to Chicago. Moreover the absence of visual indications of the page height (which in a desktop browser is done by the vertical scroller, not visible on the iPhone until the user "taps" on the screen) prevented the user from understanding the amount of information contained in the page.

This page has clearly a usability problem, since it does not provide adequate feedback to the user about the operation

performed, and it would be appropriate to show in the top of the page a summary of the parameters used for the search clearly stated.

5.2 United Airline Location Task

The second task has no specific starting page, so when users start its performance they should be on the page where they concluded the previous task. If this is done properly, this page is the one containing the research results of the United Airlines flights leaving for Chicago. The purpose of this task is to check the usability of the Web site concerning the search for generic information.

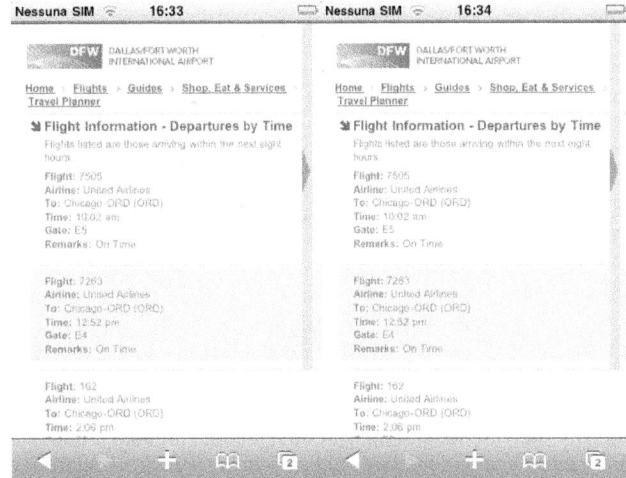

Figure 9. Search result comparison.

The evaluator - of course - successfully completed the first task, and thus begins the course of the second task from the page containing the results of the flights search. The site provides information about each airline by devoting to each of them a small information page. The shortest path to reach this page from the point where the evaluator starts is to follow the link "Guides" in the header, and then use the link "Airlines" on the next page. This link takes the user to a list of all the airlines, the last of which is United Airlines. Following the link leads to a page containing information about the company, including the information sought: the United Airlines is based in Terminal E. In Figure 10 you can see the sequence of pages visited by the evaluator to find the information sought in the most efficient way.

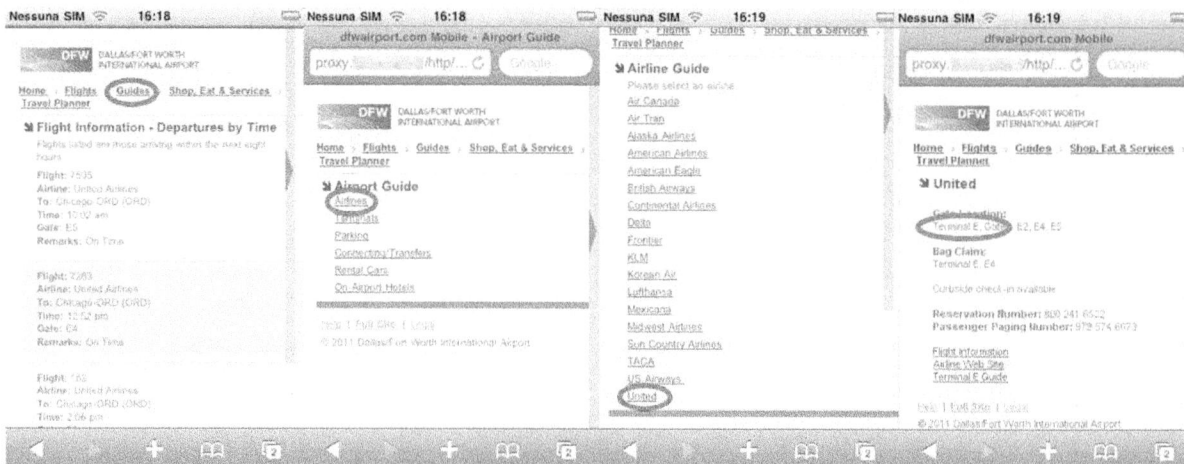

Figure 10. Sequence of pages visited by the evaluator.

The actions taken by the evaluator allow him to complete the task in about thirty seconds, as seen from the timeline shown in Figure 11. The three blue markers represent *pageviews* events, and are exactly the three page changes made. The green marker represents a semantic Custom event (*clickOnAirlines*) that was prepared for this task, and that is generated at the event click on the link that leads to the list of air companies. We chose this combination because such link is present in several places of the Web site and represents the minimum step to access the information sought and conclude that task successfully.

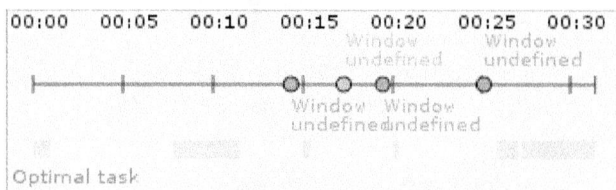

Figure 11.Timeline relating to the evaluator's performance for the second task.

It should be noted that the timeline in Figure 11 shows only four events simply because, as a mere matter of readability, it was decided to display the most relevant information for understanding the shortest path.

In the following we will analyze one timeline different from that generated by the evaluator. The first user successfully completed the first task, then, like the evaluator, started from the page containing the results of the flight departure search. Just like the evaluator, this user decided to follow the link "Guides" included in the page header, and the path is identical to the page containing the information sought.

When he reached this page, he unexpectedly decided to skip to the homepage from which, after about a minute, he again used the link to the page with the list of airlines and repeated the same steps, until completing the task. The entire sequence is illustrated in the timeline of Figure 12, which shows that the two *clickOnAirlines* events (which are the green markers) indicate the two times when the user decided to access the list of airlines. The question is: what caused the user to go to the home page and

repeat the same path first to convince himself that he had found the information sought? It seems that the first time he considered the information in the page unsatisfactory or inadequate to the task proposed.

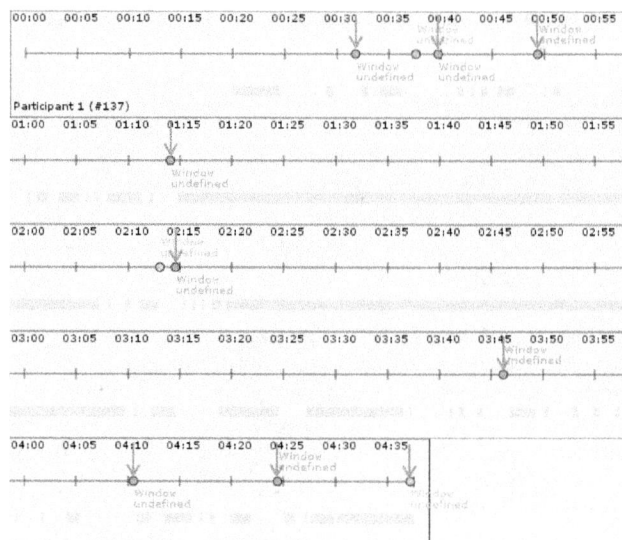

Figure 12. The user followed two different paths.

5.3 Shopping Task

In this case the optimal performance recorded by the evaluator consists of just two steps. The evaluator had concluded the previous task on the page containing the information on United Airlines, including information about the terminal (Terminal E). The evaluator then clicked the link in the header of all pages labelled "Shop, Eat & Services", which leads to a page where users can choose from one of these five terminals or access a search engine that helps users to find the services within five minutes of their gate.

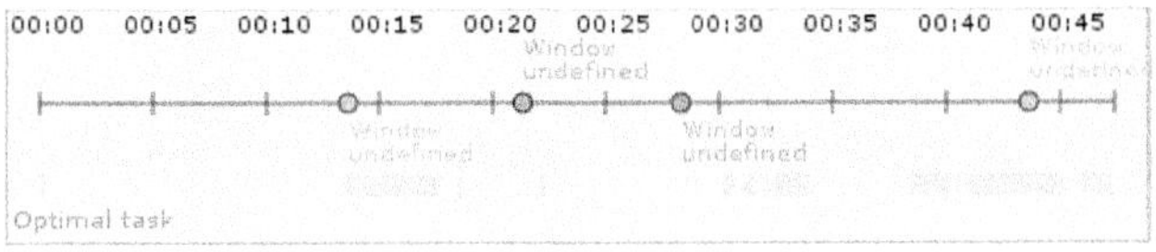

Figure 13. The evaluator's performance for the third task.

The evaluator correctly selected the link "Terminal E", as associated with United Airlines, and this led to the corresponding page with the link "Shops", which allows users to access the list of stores in Terminal E.

The timeline of the evaluator's performance is shown in Figure 13. The event selector has been configured so as to show only *pageviews*, *startTask* and *finishtask* events, as the other events were not considered relevant for this analysis.

We now analyse the timeline of a user who successfully completed the task. He started performing this task from the same page as the evaluator.

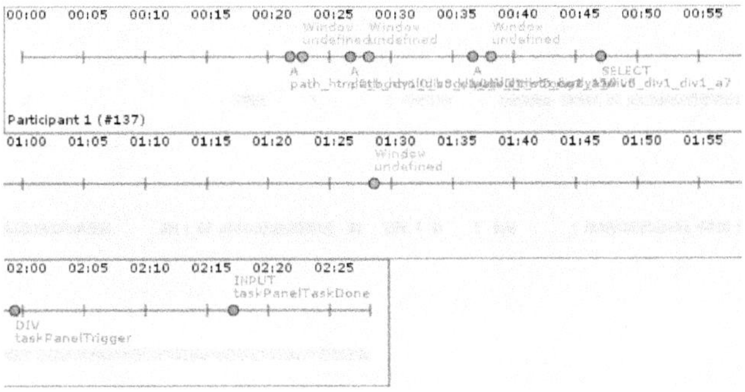

Figure 14. The pageview sequence of the first user performance.

His first two choices of the links to follow were the same, then the user reached a page where, instead of choosing the link "Shops", preferred to follow the link labelled "Within 5 Minutes of My Gate". The page loaded by following this link contains a form that allows users to search for services within five minutes from the Terminal / Gate selected. There is a drop-down menu to select the Terminal, and optionally users can enter the number of the desired Gate in the text field (see Figure 15).

This page has an obvious usability problem: the user in fact reached this position after clicking the link "Terminal E", and accessing first another page. The fact that this page shows a form that allows users to select a Terminal disorients the user, who had already "selected" the desired Terminal via the link previously.

From the timeline shown in Figure 14 one can see that once the user arrives in the page containing the form (*pageviews* event, third blue marker) he uses the drop-down menu to select a terminal (event with SELECT label). The form is not sent, however - in fact there is no submit event - and about a minute and a half after there is a *pageview* event (another blue marker) without any click before. The details not visible in the picture show that the page loaded is the same that the user was already seeing, for which it is likely he did a reload using the browser button. After the page reload the user decided to open the tool's control Panel and declare the task complete.

Figure 15. The service search page.

6. CONCLUSION AND FUTURE WORK

This paper presents a tool that allows evaluators to decide what tasks users should perform, and gather many types of data related to user interaction. The tool provides some graphical representations, which allow evaluators to analyse the data collected from a usability perspective. The tool also allows the end users to freely access the Web applications with any browser-enabled mobile device without any constraint regarding where and when to perform such accesses during the test sessions. The case study reported indicated that the visual reports provided by the tool in form of timelines summarize event streams and highlight useless actions, allowing evaluators to identify usability problems, easing the task of mapping back events to actual actions occurred during user sessions. The experiment reported provided us with encouraging feedback, even if more validation will be carried out in the near future.

The extensive events vocabulary, including events typically generated by mobile devices, allows the evaluator to identify usability problems that can occur when using Web applications with devices other than the traditional desktop computer.

As future work we plan to extend the tool in order to better support the possibility of automatically identifying and highlighting potential usability issues. We also plan to investigate the use of the optimal sessions as a training set in data mining processes in order to find similar behavioural sequences and thus isolate those that are very different.

ACKNOWLEDGMENTS

We would like to thank *Fundação de Amparo à Pesquisa do Estado de São Paulo* (grant #2009/10186-9) for the support to the last author.

REFERENCES

[1] Google: Google Analytics. http://www.google.com/analytics/index.html. (2009)

[2] H. R. Hartson, J. C. Castillo, J. T. Kelso, W. C. Neale: Remote Evaluation: The Network as an Extension of the Usability Laboratory. CHI 1996: 228-235.

[3] D. M. Hilbert, D. F. Redmiles: 2000. Extracting usability information from user interface events. ACM Comput. Surv. 32, 4 (Dec. 2000), pp. 384-421.

[4] M. Y. Ivory, M. A. Hearst: The state of the art in automating usability evaluation of user interfaces. ACM Comput. Surv. 33(4): 470-516 (2001)

[5] I. Malý, P. Slavík: Towards Visual Analysis of Usability Test Logs Using Task Models. TAMODIA 2006: 24-38

[6] L.Paganelli, F.Paternò: Tools for Remote Usability Evaluation of Web Applications through Browser Logs and Task Models, Behavior Research Methods, Instruments, and Computers, 2003, 35 (3), pp.369-378, August 2003

[7] S. Propp, P. Forbrig: ViSE - A Virtual Smart Environment for Usability Evaluation. HCSE 2010: 38-45

[8] C. J. Costa, J. P. Novais Silva, M. Aparicio: Evaluating Web Usability Using Small Display Devices. SIGDOC 2007: 263-268

[9] T. Carta, F. Paternò, V. F. de Santana: Web Usability Probe: A Tool for Supporting Remote Usability Evaluation of Web Sites, INTERACT 2011 Proceedings, LNCS, Volume 6948, pp. 349–357, Springer, Lisboa, September 2011

Cognitive Load and Usability Analysis of R-MAP for the People who are Blind or Visual Impaired

G. Hossain
Department of EECE
The University of Memphis
Memphis, TN 38152, USA
ghossain@memphis.edu

Akbar S. Shaik
Department of EECE
The University of Memphis
Memphis, TN 38152, USA
asshaik@memphis.edu

M. Yeasin
Department of EECE
The University of Memphis
Memphis, TN 38152, USA
myeasin@memphis.edu

ABSTRACT

The ultimate goal of this work is to understand the confluence of cognitive load and usability studies in evaluating the performance of fully integrated assistive technology solutions. The platform used for this study is called, Reconfigured Mobile Android Phone (R-MAP). The focus of this study is to measure the cognitive load and perform usability analysis and use them as a guide to refine the design and improve the usability of the R-MAP. A "secondary task performance" based procedure for measuring the cognitive load was used to study the R-MAP. The score of the secondary task performance was found to have strong relationship with the cognitive load, usability of the R-MAP and also the differences in performances among various categories of users.

Categories and Subject Descriptors

H.5.2 [Information Interfaces and presentation]: User Interfaces—Evaluation/methodology, Input devices and strategies, User-centered design, Voice I/O ; K.4.2 [Computers and Society]: Social Issues—Assistive technologies for persons with disabilities

General Terms

Design, Experimentation, Human Factors.

Keywords

Assistive technology; android phone; OCR; usability; cognitive load; working memory load; cognitive load theory; sonification; virtual sound.

1. INTRODUCTION

Let us consider a "typing competition" between two people: one user can type without seeing the keys on the keyboard and the other needs to see the keys all the time. In this scenario, it is pertinent to ask "who uses more cognitive resources?" Let us take it a step further, between these two people, one is blind or blind from birth and the other is sighted but blindfolded. Is there any

difference in cognitive processing of a sighted but blindfolded people and blind people? The granularity of the answers to such questions will help in re-designing a system with better feedback, improved functionalities, enhanced usability, lower cognitive load and adaptive to the needs and level of a user.

To answer granular questions in the context of performance evaluation of assistive technology, it is imperative to study the confluence of cognitive load and usability study. Hence, the main research goal of this paper is to measure the cognitive load of a person who is blind or visually impaired while using an assistive technology system. In particular, called R-MAP [1] was used to perform a number of experiments at various levels of granularity. The R-MAP is a fully integrated, stand-alone system that has an easy-to-use interface to reconfigure an Android mobile phone. The product was designed and developed to facilitate day-to-day activities of people who are blind or visually impaired. The key services offered by the RMAP include (but are not limited to): (i) reading out loud "printed text" on various types of surfaces such as "printed letter", "medicine bottle", "street sign" and etc. just to name a few, (ii) providing a sense of direction in an open space, (iii) enhancing shopping experience through integrated barcode reading service, and (iv) assistance for indoor navigation.

The R-MAP has different types of sound feedbacks for the user to make them aware of the state of the application in the process of reaching the user's goal. An extra sound feedback, wherein sound produced was random and different from the one used in the instruction sound. This is a secondary task [2] based on virtual sound feedback. The feedback on secondary task by direct observation of participants' reaction was mapped using a subjective score. A subjective rating system with five levels: 1 = very low, 2 = somewhat low, 3 = medium 4 = high, and 5 = very high, was used for the study. In addition, three subjective load related questionnaires similar to [3, 4] were used along with usability study to measure three types of cognitive loads: intrinsic, extraneous, and germane load.

The objectives of this study is to research three conditions: (i) differences in cognitive load between expert participants (who have prior smart phone use experience) vs. non-expert (no prior experience) while using assistive technology (R-MAP); (ii) differences in cognitive load and usability between blind folded participants and participants who are blind or visual impaired; and (iii) the impact of visual mapping capability of blind folded people over visual impaired.

Based on the empirical analyses, it was observed that significance for the first hypothesis that signifies expert blind people over expert blindfolded smart phone users. It was evident in both cases of cognitive load measurements as a subjective study or secondary feedback task response. During the experiment it was observed that expert blind people can work with partial virtual sound which could be made in certain form that we would not understand its rhythm. That is the special sound makes someone feel bored but someone else is motivated and more inspired to work smoothly. It was researched earlier that blind people have a different cognitive map [18]. They lack the visual mapping but their auditory mapping is stronger which helps them work in different situation. As the blindfolded non-expert people already has a picture in their mind about the smart phone and its buttons (during practice), they perform better than the blind people.

The rest of the paper is organized as following. Section 2 describes some related work in cognitive load measurement and usability analysis besides the reason for choosing R-MAP as an assistive tool. In section 3, we explain a brief description of Experimental design and data collection with R-MAP user interface and secondary task operation. Section 4 discusses about usability and cognitive load evolution results. Finally in section 5 a brief discussion and conclusion with some direction of farther possible research is discussed.

2. LITERATURE REVIEW

A number of assistive technology solutions for people with disabilities available to access print are Braille devices, screen readers (HAL [7] etc.), screen magnification software, and scanning and reading software (GOCR [6] etc.), just to name a few. Most of these devices and software often require custom modification, or are prohibitively expensive. Many people with disabilities do not have access to custom modification of the available devices and other benefits of current technology. While some applications made effort to use the usability study but the reported literature have not considered users' cognitive load and usability based modification to make the device adaptive and more user friendly. The ultimate aim of such modifications is to develop systems that satisfies requirements (but are not limited to): accessibility, affordability, compatibility, expandability, ergonomics, flexibility, learnability, portability, reliability, utility and usability based on users level of expertise, dexterity and cognitive load.

Cognitive Load

Cognitive load refers to the amount of working memory load imposed on the human cognitive capacity when performing a particular task. Measuring cognitive load in ordinal cognitive load scale is important in designing an optimal interaction approach between humans and assistive technology systems in order to produce the highest task performance. These loads deal with mental processes of learning, memory and problem solving. Mayer [8] explains human cognitive capability by a magic number seven plus minus two. Sweller [9] defines the Cognitive Load theory, "The quality of instructional design will be raised if greater consideration is given to the role and limitations of working memory." There are three types of cognitive loads [10, 11], namely intrinsic, extraneous and germane. *The Intrinsic cognitive load* represents the inherent difficulty associated with any problem. Example: "2+2" or "solving a differential equation". *The extraneous cognitive load* is considered as how the information is presented to the learners. It is under the control of instructional designers. For example: Defining a "square shape" literally or showing a picture takes different cognitive load. The

cognitive load devoted to the processing, construction and automation of schemata is known as *germane cognitive load*. The cognitive load theory suggests increasing the germane load while decreasing intrinsic and extraneous load.

There are a number of cognitive load measures. These are broadly categorized as subjective load measure, combination measure and objective load measures. Table 1 shows the types of existing cognitive load measure with sub categories. We used a secondary virtual sound feedback based objective measure and subjective rating scale. Our approach provides an opportunity to objectively detect small variations in cognitive load, in real-time, as desired in assistive technology design.

Table 1: Cognitive load measures

Objective Measures	Task and Performance Measurement	Example: Task completion time, efficiency etc. [34]
	Secondary Tasks	Example: Defining game with difficulty levels, dual-task [32,35]
	Psycho-physiological	Example: different dependent behavioral data (e.g. heart rate, eye movement, pupil dilation, and brain fMRI, EEG or ECG etc.) [34, 35]
Combinational methods	Behavioral Models into a performance model.	Cognitive Load Model, in intelligent agents like ACT-T, Soar, LIDA [20]
Subjective Measures	Rating Scale	Example: Scoring between the range very low mental effort to very high mental effort.

Among the number of available load measurement techniques, the reason we used a secondary virtual sound feedback based objective measure to impose dual-task method as a novel way to cognitive load measures incorporated with assistive technology for blind people.

Usability study

One of the main reasons of usability study is to find out how to improve the developed system for user satisfaction and usefulness. There are two types of usability tests [14]: formative usability and summative usability study. Formative usability is an iterative usability study that works as a part of continuous development process. The formative usability evaluates the design, identifies its short comings and makes recommendation. The summative usability works on deployed product, to check whether it meets the usability requirements and goals.

To measure formative usability, the most popular and effective method with five attribute is proposed by J. Nielsen [15] [16]. These five usability attributes are: Learnability, Efficiency, Memorability, Errors, and Satisfaction. We analyzed three types of cognitive loads [10] by subjective study and compared their additive score with the secondary feedback performance to justify the hypotheses described above. Based on Nielsen's definition we studied users' evaluation and achieved 70% average usability score that substantiates the acceptability of the system to the people who are blind.

3. EXPERIMENT AND DATA
3.1 Subjects

This study was conducted between two groups of participants. In the first group there were four blind people, two are non-expert and two are expert. The expertness is considered based on their experience in using smart phone for more than a year. The second study group contained twenty blindfolded participants; ten of them are considered expert and the other ten participants are non-expert. Participants were trained and were asked to use the R-MAP to read different objects, documents that have text in it (eg. texts from a text book).

Figure 1 shows blindfolded (a) and blind people (b) participating in this experiment.

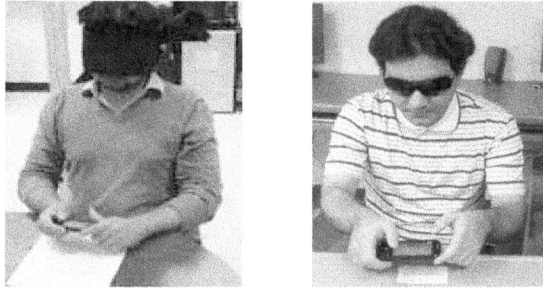

Figure 1. a) Blindfolded   b) Blind person

3.2 Task

All subjects had first a quick tutorial to learn how to use the system. In each session, the R-MAP and a text book is provided to the subject. The primary task was to read a text from the book. They are asked to open the book and to reach any text location.

3.2.1 The Secondary Task with R-MAP operation

The R-MAP operation for capturing a text and reasoning takes four steps:

Step-1: Open application,

Step-2: Enter into capture mode.

Step-3: Capture image,   Pause for 5-20 sec.

Step-4: Speech (Voice o/p).

In secondary task, R-MAP operation is changed a little with guidance of two virtual sounds (VS$_1$ and VS$_2$) following speech based cognitive load measurement technique [9][10]. A special shift of first push location in figure 2 ('a' to 'b' or 'b' to 'a') in R-MAP is made with VS$_1$. The second virtual sound VS$_2$, instructs subject to push the reset button to cancel secondary task mode. The task performance is scored by the examiner in 0-5 range. The more mistakes means subjects are cognitively overloaded. The highest score 5 out of 5 indicates the subject were fully overloaded with secondary task. The usability scores and cognitive load scores are then computed separately.

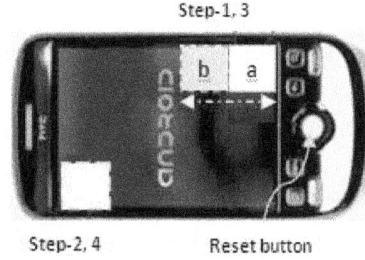

Figure 2: RMAP with virtual sound feedback for secondary task

Step-1: Open application, // *Virtual sound alert (VS1 or VS2)*, **Step-2:** Enter into capture mode. **Step-3:** Capture image,   // *Virtual sound alert (Vs1 or VS2)*, Pause for 5-20 sec. **Step-4:** Speech (Voice o/p).

3.3 Measurement Metrics

The task load measurement metrics are followed from Xie and Salvendy [13]. Table 2 explains an example of different task levels that resemble to intrinsic, extraneous, and germane load category. The short notation IL means intrinsic load, EX for extraneous load and GL for germane load. In low load cases, users don't have any type of load, average workload user faces only intrinsic load, whereas, a high load user faces both extraneous and germane loads. In task description, decision task involves different form of Boolean or fuzzy based decisions; for example, selecting the reset button or next push location; the cognitive or memory retrieval task involves query and information retrieval from main memory or secondary memory; for example, in our case memorizing the operation instructions.

Table 2: Task level vs. cognitive load

Task level	Task description	Comment
Low Load Task	-No decision task -No memory retrieval task -Good presentation	IL→NO GL→NO EX→NO
Average Load Task	-given a decision task - No memory retrieval task - Good presentation	IL→YES GL→NO EX→NO
High Load Task	-No decision task -Memory retrieval task -Bad presentation	IL→NO GL→YES EX→YES

*IL-Intrinsic load, EX-extraneous load and GL-germane load

3.3.1 Usability and Subjective load

Subjective cognitive load measurement is followed within usability studies. Three load sensible questioners representing three types of cognitive load index (intrinsic load, extraneous load and germane load)[4] is merged with the subjective rating of formative 10 (5 x 2) usability questioners [15] of Nielsen's five attributes: learnability, efficiency, memorability, errors, and satisfaction as explained in table 3.

The intrinsic load scale was asked *"How difficult was the learning instruction content for you?"*. The extraneous load was asked *"How difficult was it for you to learn with the instruction format?"* and the germane load scale was asked *"How much did you concentrate during learning process?"*.

Table 3: Usability and subjective Cognitive load questioners

Description By Nielsen (1992)	Usability Questionnaires considered for Blind Person/Person with blind fold.
Learnability: How easy it is for a user to accomplish basic tasks at the first time?	It is easily learnable after first few attempts. It is easy to understand the audio based feedback.
Efficiency : How quickly the user can perform tasks?	I am able to perform task quickly after I learnt how to use it. The user interface and audio feedbacks help me in minimizing mistakes in operating it.
Memorability: How easily users reestablish the proficiency when performing task in next time?	I'll be able to recall how to perform task without instructions after some period of not using R-MAP. I recommend that the feedbacks and User interface is easy to remember
Error: How many errors the users make, and how easily they can recover from the errors?	Very few attempts are made to accomplish task completely for first time. R-MAP has few frequencies of serious errors while operating.
Satisfaction: Freedom from discomfort and positive attitude to use the product.	Considering the experience, I'm comfortable with R-MAP. I find R-MAP useful in daily life.

3.4 Dat

A sample representative data of eight users (four blindfolded and four blind) are shown in table 4. This data contains some demographic information, namely: age, ethnicity and gender. In our earlier study we noticed the differences of R-MAP use between male and female participants. In this study we consider age, gender and ethnicity independent user interaction with smartphone with skill (experience) and performance (less error) in confluence of assistive technology use.

Table 4: The Sample data

UsersID	Age	Ethnicity	Blindness	Gender	Smart Phone use Exp	Error
User-1	29	Asian	BF	M	n	5
User-4	31	American	BF	F	y	2
User-7	30	African	BF	F	y	2
User-10	30	American	BF	M	n	5
User-24	40	American	BP	F	n	4
User-6	35	American	BP	M	n	5
User-23	27	American	BP	F	y	3
User-25	42	American	BP	M	y	2

*n- non-expert user, y- expert user, M- Male, F- Female, BF-Blind-folded, BP- Blind People

4. RESULTS

In this section a details of usability and cognitive load scores among blindfolded and blind people are explained with difference of performance observed between blindfolded and blind subjects.

To see most similar observation and the cluster of observation with contemplation of outliers, we used a radar chart of usability analysis. Figure 3 explains the radar diagram of five variables of usability scores among 20 blindfolded participants. The red

marked line that is nearest to center among all other indicates a less satisfaction by the most of the blindfolded user. More specifically, dissatisfaction is dominant in this small observation suggesting that the system should be redesigned based for user satisfaction. The green line indicates they made less error with the technology as they expected. The other three variables learnability, efficiency and memorability indicate relatively higher cognitive loads of average participants.

In case of blind subjects we considered simple bar chart to see their comparative usability score that is shown in figure 4.

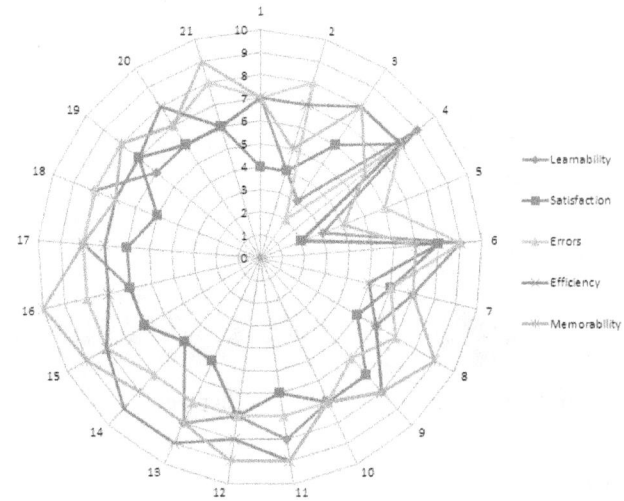

Figure 3. Radar Diagram of R-MAP usability

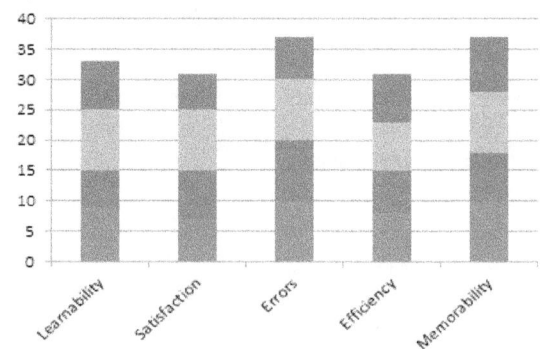

Figure 4. Combined usability scores of four blind subjects.

The experiment includes the dependent variable "experience". Based on experience, subjects are divided in to novice/non-expert and expert subgroups. Another dependency is the visual capability; sub-group types are blindfolded (BF) and visual impaired (VI). Source of dependent variable for performance measure in secondary task is the number of errors a subject made during experiment.

We considered Welch's *t-test* for non-parametric testing and performed with 95% confidence interval with standard error calculation. The results are shown in table 5 for expert vs. non-expert participants and table 6 for blindfolded vs. visual impaired participants.

Table 5: Usability and Cognitive Load comparison between Non-expert and Expert group of participants

	Usability Score		Cognitive Load (Subjective)		Cognitive Load (Secondary Task)	
	M	SD	M	SD	M	SD
Non-Expert (N=12)	32.80	5.96	6	2	3.73	0.79
Expert (N=12)	38.83	1.40	3.33	0.65	2.73	0.90
t-value	3.81		4.391		0.361	
p-value	0.0024		0.0007		0.0123	

Table 5 shows the t values during error calculation and two-tailed p-value for significance judgment. As non-expert subjects do not have prior smart phone use experience, the result shows that in all case of usability and cognitive load measure, difference between non-expert and expert are statistically significant.

We applied same test on blind folded versus visually impaired people (table 6). The result also shows significant difference in case of usability score.

Table 5: Usability and Cognitive Load scores between Blind folded and visually impaired participants

	Usability Score		Cognitive Load (Subjective)		Cognitive Load (Secondary Task)	
	M	SD	M	SD	M	SD
Blind Folded (N =20)	34	5.34	5.2	0.95	3.65	0.93
VP (N =4)	42.25	4.65	6.312	0.77	4.25	0.96
t-value	3.158		2.5193		1.1489	
p-value	0.0342		0.0532		0.3146	

In case of subjective cognitive load, the difference is considered to be not quite statistically significant. The secondary task performance also suffices that, this difference is considered to be not statistically significant.

Box-and-whisker plots are also considered to see differences between populations without making any assumptions of the underlying statistical distribution. Figure 6 graphically depicts the usability score between blindfolded and blind participants. Similarly, figure 9 shows usability comparison between expert and non-expert sub-groups.

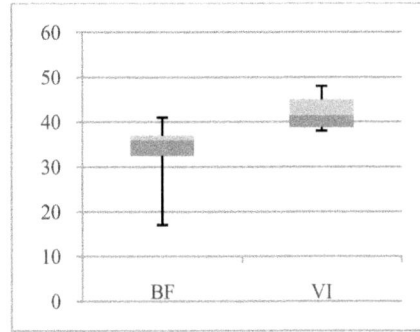

Figure 6: Usability score Box-and-whisker plot between blindfolded (BF) and visual impaired (VI)

Figure 7 and figure 8 explains the differences between cognitive load assessments between blindfolded subjects and the people who are visual impaired. Dissimilarity is found in subjective rating of blindfolded people and their corresponding task performance scores. This is because of their less patience to completion of all tasks provided to them.

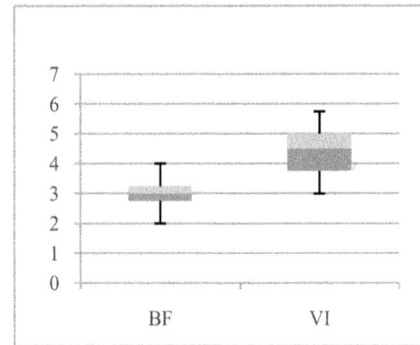

Figure 7: Cognitive Load (secondary task) Box-and-whisker plot between blindfolded (BF) and visual impaired (VI).

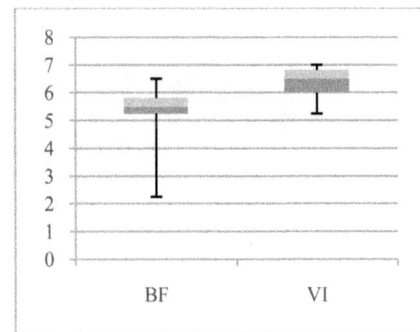

Figure 8: Cognitive Load (Subjective rating) Box-and-whisker plot between blindfolded (BF) and visual impaired (VI)

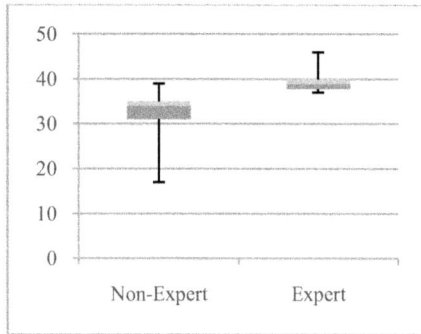

Figure 9. Usability score Box-and-whisker between Expert and Non-Expert users

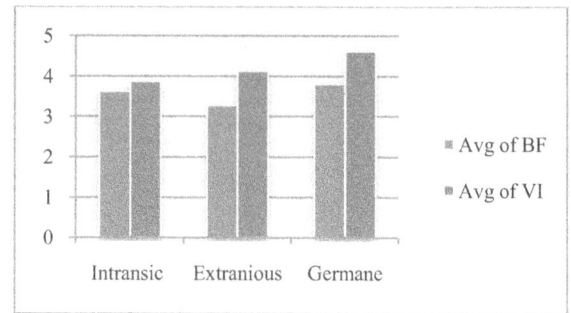

Figure 12. Comparison of the three types of cognitive load : intrinsic, extraneous and germane

In case of expert and non-expert groups in cognitive load performance and subjective rating, it is observed that although expert blind people completed all tasks with a reasonable load performance (less error) and being in the group of expert blindfolded they show overload kind of assertiveness. Figure 10 and figure 11 shows these incompetence of performances showed by expert and non-expert groups.

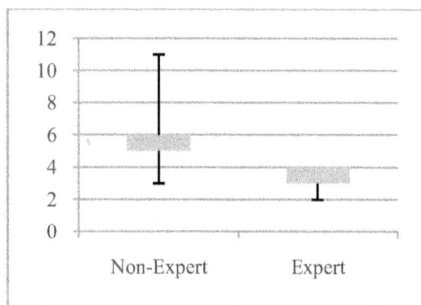

Figure 10. Cognitive Load (Subjective rating) Box-and-whisker **between Expert and Non-Expert users**

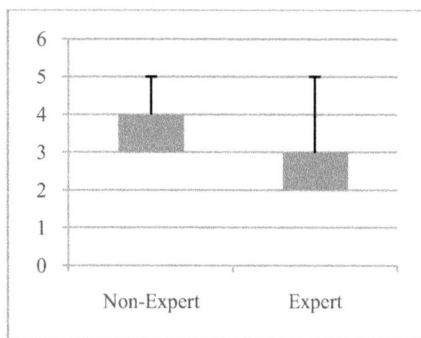

Figure 11. Cognitive Load (secondary task) box plot between Expert and Non-Expert users

A simple average cognitive load comparison of three types of cognitive load (that is found from three separate cognitive load questioners) between blindfolded and visual impaired is shown in figure 12.

In this study we used R-MAP as a tool to explain three hypotheses we discussed in the beginning:

H1: Expert blind people have the capability to understand and work efficiently with only virtual sound feedback as guidance and found the device useful.

H2: Compared to the self-reporting and secondary task performance, expert blind people feel lower load than a non-expert blind people using smart phone based assistive technology.

H3: Compared to the self-reporting and secondary task performance, blindfolded feel more load than blind subjects.

5. CONCLUSION AND FUTURE WORK

An assistive interaction system should be aware of the user's current cognitive load so that it can be more responsive. Assessing cognitive load for people who are blind or visually impaired and using mobile phones for day to day activities is more challenging.

In this paper, we performed usability and cognitive load measurement with R-MAP, to provide mobile access to printed texts for people who are blind or visually impaired. For usability measurement, we used the most popular attributed introduced by Nielsen. We performed subjective rating scale and found the evidence of the hypothesis we were thinking of.

In cognitive load measurement, we adopted virtual sound based feedback system, as a new form of secondary task using auditory feedback. This new task for objective measurement is especially for blind people. The result of cognitive load measure shows interesting similarities and differences for blind people to use assistive technology and assistive technology simulated by a blindfolded person. Another finding is that the cognitive load of blind people also biased by their skill and knowledge. As it is observed that expert blind participants are most prominent user, can perfectly use assistive technology with minimum guideline.

The main limitations/Implications of this research is the small population, the only four blind participants in this study, and is relatively small. Also, in both group there were not the same number of participants. This is because; limited access to people who are blind or visually impaired and also use smart phone.

In our future study we are considering more number of blind subjects, variant of measurements using physiological sensors for real time cognitive load measurement of blind people acting with assistive technology systems. We are also working on some sonification techniques for real time auditory feedback design in R-MAP.

Integration of such services will make the system more effective to use for blind people. The preliminary results of cognitive load in the overall system are exceptionally satisfying and promising.

6. ACKNOWLEDGMENT

This project was partially funded by National Science Foundation (NSF-IIS-0746790), USA.

7. REFERENCES

[1] Shaik, A., Hossain, G., and Yeasin, M. 2010. *Design, development and performance evaluation of reconfigured mobile Android phone for people who are blind or visually impaired.* Proceedings of the 28th ACM International Conference on Design of Communication (SIGDOC '10). ACM, New York, NY, USA, 159-166. DOI=10.1145/1878450.1878478

[2] Ohuchi1, M., Iwaya, Y., Suzuki, Y., and Munekata, T., *Cognitive-Map Formation of Blind Persons in a Virtual Sound Environment*, Proceedings of the 12th International Conference on Auditory Display, London, UK June 20 - 23, 2006

[3] Klatzky, R. L., Marston, J. R., Giudice, N. A., Golledge, R. G., and Loomis, J. M., *Cognitive load of navigating without vision when guided by virtual sound versus spatial language*, Journal of Experimental Psychology: Applied, vol. 12, pp. 223-232, 2006.

[4] Cierniak, G., Scheiter, K.., and Gerjets, P., *Explaining the split-attention effect: Is the reduction of extraneous cognitive load accompanied by an increase in germane cognitive load?* Computers in Human Behavior, 25 (2009) 315–324.

[5] Android TTS - http://android-developers.blogspot.com/2009/09/introduction-to-text-to-speech-in.html.

[6] GOCR - a free OCR program. http://jocr.sourceforge.net/.

[7] HAL Screen Reader and Cicero-http://www.dolphinuk.co.uk/index dca.htm.

[8] Ohbuchi, E., Hanaizumi, H., and Hock, L. A., *Barcode readers using the camera device in mobile phones.* Cyber World CW 2004, pages 260–265, IEEE Computer Society.

[9] Mayer, R. (1981), *The psychology of how novices learn computer programming.* ACM Computing Surveys. 13, 121-141.

[10] Sweller, J., and Chandler, P. (1994), *Why some material is difficult to learn.* Cognition and Instruction, 12(3), 185-233.

[11] Paas, F. , Tuovinen, J.E., Tabbers, H.K., and Van Gerven, P.W.M., (2003) *Cognitive load measurement as a means to advance cognitive load theory,* Educational Psychologist, 38(1): 63-71.

[12] Paas, F., and.Merriënboer, J.J.G, (1994) *Instructioqnal control of cognitive load in the training of complex cognitive tasks.* Educational Psychology Review, 6, 51-71.

[13] Xie, B. and Salvendy, G., *Prediction of Mental workload in Signal and Multiple Task Environments,* International Journal of Cognitve Ergonomics, 2000, 4(3), 213-242, Journal of visual Impairment and Blindness, 90(3):287, May -June 1996.

[14] Dicks, R. S., (2002). *Mis-usability: on the uses and misuses of usability testing.* Proceedings of the 20th Annual International Conference on Computer Documentation (1st ed., pp. 26-30). New York, NY: ACM Press. N. Efron. Optacon - a replacement for Braille? Australian Journal of Optometry, (4), 1977.

[15] Nielsen, J., 1992 *The Usability Engineering Life Cycle*, Computer, vol.25 no.3, pages.12-22.

[16] Nielsen, C.M., Overgaard, M., Pedersen, M.P., Stage, J., and Stenild, S., It's worth the hassle!: the added value of evaluating the usability of mobile systems in the field, Proc. 4th Nordic CHI 2006, pages.272 - 280.

[17] Taub, E. A*., The blind lead the sighted: Technology for people with disabilities finds a broader market*, The New York Times, October 1999.

[18] Chen , M., Huang , C., and Wang, C., *Difference on Spatial Working Memory between the Blind and Sighted People*, APIEMS 2008 Proceedings of The 9th Asia Pasific Industrial Engineering & Management Systems Conference.

[19] Eye Doctor Guide.com, *Blind People And Their Memory,* http://www.eyedoctorguide.com/eye_general/blind_people_a nd_memory.html

[20] Pylyshyn, Z., *Return of the mental image: are there really pictures in the brain?* Opinion, TRENDS in Cognitive Sciences , Vol.7 No.3 March 2003.

[21] Ritter, F.E., and Young, R.M., (2001*), Embodied models as simulated users: introduction to this special issue on using cognitive models to improve interface design.* International Journal of Human-Computer Studies, 55(1): 1-14.

[22] Yin, B., Chen, F., Ruiz, N., and Ambikairajah, E., (2008), *Speech-based cognitive load monitoring system.* In Proc. IEEE ICASSP 2008, 2041-2044.310

[23] Murphy, E., Bates, E., and Fitzpatrick, D., 2010. *Designing auditory cues to enhance spoken mathematics for visually impaired users.* In Proceedings of the 12th international ACM SIGACCESS conference on Computers and accessibility (ASSETS '10). ACM, New York, NY, USA, 75-82. DOI=10.1145/1878803.1878819

[24] Yoshida, T., Kitani, K. M., Koike, H. , Belongie, S., and Schlei, K.., *EdgeSonic: image Feature Sonification for the Visually Impaired*, AH '11 Proceedings of the 2nd Augmented Human International Conference ACM New York, NY, USA 2011, doi>10.1145/1959826.1959837

[25] Su, J., Rosenzweig, A., Goel, A., De Lara, E., and Truong, K.N., *Enabling the Visually-Impaired to Use Maps on Touch-Enabled Devices*, In Proceedings of MOBILECHI, 2010.

[26] Luis Francisco-Revilla and Jeff Crow. 2010. Interpretation of web page layouts by blind users. In *Proceedings of the 10th annual joint conference on Digital libraries* (JCDL '10). ACM, New York, NY, USA, 173-176. DOI=10.1145/1816123.1816148 http://doi.acm.org/10.1145/1816123.1816148

[27] Peter Schmutz, Silvia Heinz, Yolanda M\&\#233;trailler, and Klaus Opwis. 2009. Cognitive load in ecommerce applications: measurement and effects on user satisfaction. *Adv. in Hum.-Comp. Int.* 2009, Article 3 (January 2009), 9 pages. DOI=10.1155/2009/121494 http://dx.doi.org/10.1155/2009/121494

[28] Andreea Niculescu, Yujia Cao, Anton Nijholt: Manipulating Stress and Cognitive Load in Conversational Interactions with a Multimodal System for Crisis Management Support. COST 2102 Training School 2009: 134-147

[29] Brunken, R. Plass, J. L. Leutner, D., Assessment of Cognitive Load in Multimedia Learning with Dual-Task Methodology: Auditory Load and Modality Effects, Journal of INSTRUCTIONAL SCIENCE, Kluwer Academic Publishers, Netherlands 2004. ISSN 0020-4277.

[30] Weidong Huang, Peter Eades, and Seok-Hee Hong. 2009. Measuring effectiveness of graph visualizations: a cognitive load perspective. Information Visualization 8, 3 (June 2009), 139-152. DOI=10.1057/ivs.2009.10 http://dx.doi.org/10.1057/ivs.2009.10

Usability Evaluation of Horizontal Navigation Bar with Drop-down Menus by Middle Aged Adults

Eduardo P. B. dos Santos
Institute of Mathematics and
Computer Sciences,
University of São Paulo
400, Trabalhador
São-carlense Avenue - Center
São Carlos/SP, Brazil
epbsanti@icmc.usp.br

Silvana M. A. de Lara
Institute of Mathematics and
Computer Sciences,
University of São Paulo
400, Trabalhador
São-carlense Avenue - Center
São Carlos/SP, Brazil
silvana@icmc.usp.br

Willian M. Watanabe
Institute of Mathematics and
Computer Sciences,
University of São Paulo
400, Trabalhador
São-carlense Avenue - Center
São Carlos/SP, Brazil
watinha@icmc.usp.br

Mario C. A. Filho
Institute of Mathematics and
Computer Sciences,
University of São Paulo
400, Trabalhador
São-carlense Avenue - Center
São Carlos/SP, Brazil
mario@icmc.usp.br

Renata P. M. Fortes
Institute of Mathematics and
Computer Sciences,
University of São Paulo
400, Trabalhador
São-carlense Avenue - Center
São Carlos/SP, Brazil
renata@icmc.usp.br

ABSTRACT

The Web has become an extremely important source of information and services, that have been made widely available. Navigation is an important aspect in designing a Web site in order to make the information easy to find, however the task of organizing and structuring information from a website can become complex as the set of information and services provided increases. The aim of this study is to investigate the effect of eight different types of menus while performing two tasks for each menu. The target for the experiment was of people aged over 40 and some experience in using the Internet. The experiment revealed that menus which presented properties more commonly found in web applications, the task completion time and number of errors was lower, during the sessions.

General Terms

Human Factors

Categories and Subject Descriptors

H.5 [**Information Interfaces and Presentation**]: H.5.2 User Interfaces H.5.4 Hypertext/Hypermedia User Issues

Keywords

Web Accessibility, Interaction, User Interface

1. INTRODUCTION

Menus provide a contextual and structural model for the logical organization and functional interface as well as a means of communication between users and the system [10, 11, 14, 15]. Menus on Web pages can have three functional roles of great importance, which are navigation through the links, suggestions for structural support and contextual support while searching for information. Although research in the area of HCI design aim to improve the navigation menu, it is still difficult to develop hypertext systems that are able to effectively support the task of searching for information and help users navigate seamlessly from disorientation or cognitive overload.

The problem of menu design is also subject of research in the areas of information retrieval systems [12], hypertext systems [8, 13, 18] and computer-based applications [20], as the menu design plays an essential role not only in the performance of information retrieval, but also in the learning activity of hypertext systems.

According to Vera Hollink [9], despite all the efforts for building menus that allow users to navigate the web site efficiently, often the initial design of these menus is far from ideal because designers do not know the goals and the strategies of usage for future users. In practice, the design of web sites is often based on the structure containing the organization that owns the site, instead of how users access the web site.

The present study highlights the importance of determining how to present information in a way that the activation and speed of horizontal menus influence user perception and usability, both from the point of view of analysis of records of interactions as well the comments of the users. Users who took the test were mostly people over forty years old and who have used the computer at least once, these features were prioritized because this research fits into a larger project, which aims to identify the accessibility barriers considering the age of users [1].

In Section 2 the work related to studies on menus and navigation are presented; Section 3 presents the case study developed to analyze the properties of the menus, and describes the eight menus implemented, the tests, the profiles of participants and limitations found; in Section 4 we discuss the results of case study; in Section 5 the concerns regarding the results previously presented are shown and in Section 6 the final remarks are presented.

2. RELATED WORK

Menus are the main form of navigation in web pages and should be designed to allow intuitive, efficient and effective navigation, according to the user's perception and to encourage the exploration of the site. In the literature, few studies have investigated what are the best types of menus for specific user profiles and these studies are not conclusive.

The study performed by Burrell & Sodan [4] used six different kinds of menus contained in the pages of institutions. The aim was investigate which styles were preferred by users who had little experience using computers. Factors such as clarity of information, layout, ease of use, ease of learning and motivation were assessed. The results showed that the navigation styles consisting of tabs, followed by the navigation bar at the top and vertical menus on the left were more appreciated by users.

Cockburn & Jones [6] and Fleming [7] investigated the influence of properties in navigation, such as size and color in the presentation of the link, type of presentation structure (hierarchical, sequential, or networks), the need for meaningful names in the entries of Menu, among others.

Although Shneiderman [19] and Borges et. al [3] focus the importance of using separate index pages of content pages, such as the use of the site map, tables of contents and alphabetical list of pages per issue, Bernard [2] concluded that the search times of information on menus organized by category are faster than the alphabetic index searches.

In a study conducted collaboratively by the Poynter Institute and Eyetools Inc. showed that users prefer the navigation bars at the top instead of the sidebars (left or right) and then the left side navigation instead of navigation at the bottom of the screen [16].

There is still a great need to determine which menu arrangement is the most appropriate or preferred by certain groups of users, but a good direction is to tailor the design of the menus according to the actual users usage.

3. CASE STUDY

The experiment consists of users performing two predefined tasks for each of the eight types of horizontal implemented menus. The contents of the Web page which contains the navigation menu is always the same and these are texts related to travel. To prevent the effects of learning on the use of one type and another menu, the order of presentation of the eight menus used was generated randomly. Thus, if there was a passive participant viewing the test of another active participant at the time that passive participant would perform the test, he/she would visualize a new order of presentation of the eight menus.

To conduct the study we invited, preferably, participants aged 40 years, aiming the middle-aged adults and older people who had some experience using computers. We also allowed participants under the age of 40 year conduct the tests in order to obtain a control group.

Test participants received a message via email requesting that carried out the test by accessing the server where the pages containing the menus were available. In the web address, the system presented the participants information to clarify the test objectives. Then, the participants were redirected to a form webpage that was to be filled with their profile information.

After completion of initial registration, whose information was provided date of birth, educational level, frequency of Internet use and the main purposes of their use, the participant was led to start your test with the menus. The following shows a brief description of the main features of each of the eight types of menus implemented.

3.1 Description of the menus

The eight menus presented were developed using HTML tags to manage the hierarchy of options. The appearance and the properties of the menus were implemented using CSS and jQuery. For the eight menus, seven major properties were observed:

1. **Disposition:** describes in which position the submenus are displayed. The arrangement may vary depending on the level of submenu. The values are: Down (▼), Up (▲) and Right (➡);

2. **Speed:** is the property that represents the time for presenting the submenu. This property has been classified into three values: fast, with time of presentation of the submenu below or equal to 0.3 seconds; medium, time of presentation between 0.3 to 0.6 seconds; slow, with a presentation time greater which 0.6 seconds [5]. The representations of values are: Fast (❶), Medium (❷) or Slow (❸);

3. **Activation interation:** describes if the submenu activation requires a click event or a mouse over event to be performed by users. Values are: Yes (✔) or No (✘);

4. **Identification of continuity:** property which describes the existence of a visual element to show the existence of submenus for a particular suboption menu. Values are: Yes (✔) or No (✘);

5. **Color Contrast:** this feature is activated when the pointer is over the activation area and shows the changing colors or font size to improve the identification of the menu to be fired. The major changes are normally smooth exchange of background color of the activation area, underlining the text or incrementing the contrast of the font and background. Values are: Yes (✔) or No (✘);

6. **Presentation of the hierarchy:** describes the way it is presented the hierarchy inherent in the menu. The hierarchy can be divided with the levels of submenus or even spacing in a block of content. Values are: Levels (❙) or Block (■);

7. **Tip presence:** describes the presence of informative text at the beginning of a particular submenu option. Values are: Yes (✔) or No (✘).

Table 1 summarizes the main characteristics of eight types of menus selected, identified by M [i] where i ranges from 1 to 8, representing **menu i**.

Table 1: Properties of the eight menus

P	M1	M2	M3	M4	M5	M6	M7	M8
1	▼➡	▼	▼	▼➡	▼	▲	▼	▼➡
2	❷	❸	❶	❶	❷	❷	❷	❶
3	✗	✗	✗	✗	✓	✗	✗	✓
4	✓	✓	✗	✗	✓	✗	✓	✗
5	✓	✓	✓	✓	✓	✓	✓	✓
6	▮	■	▮	▮	▮	▮	■	▮
7	✗	✗	✗	✗	✗	✗	✗	✓

Menu 1 (http://goo.gl/5krI1) is a horizontal menu widely used in Web pages presents signaling submenus (down arrow to the right of text) and its area of activation corresponds to the entire menu box, and each division between the options is marked by a vertical line. The submenus are presented below the main option the submenus are presented bellow the main option with a fade-in effect and has a slight contour shading. Arrows are not displayed to the second level submenu, which is presented to the right of first level. The menu navigation key for <tab> keyboard navigation is possible to follow visually.

Menu 2 (http://goo.gl/bQZK6) shows the links horizontally but without division among them graphic. The activation area is bounded by the link text more submenu arrow indicator, so the sub can be activated by the text and the arrow which is attached to identify the menu option. The options in this menu are organized in large groups and their subgroups are presented all at once, in each subgroup where the options are presented as links side by side.

Menu 3 (http://goo.gl/7TDzy) has no visual division between the menu and the area of activation is the text identification of the option plus a small space around the text. Its features are the presentation of the name or logo of the site as their first option, rounded look to every corner of the menu and its placement at the top of the page, which often causes confusion in their own identification as a menu for users. This type of menu was first employed in the service site video publishing personal Vimeo.

Menu 4 (http://goo.gl/UF3iU) presents its suboptions under the main option and the second level submenu is displayed to the right of first level. The activation area is bounded by the box containing the textual identification of the option and its border area. It features a vertical bar to delimit each menu option and at the time a particular option is pointed with the mouse pointer a different color is displayed. Its distinguishing feature is the indication of the next levels of options by means of arrows and the option to view that all categories of the submenu are open, but this option must be implemented by the developer of the site which want to use this menu.

Menu 5 (http://goo.gl/3dgXF) provides high contrast between the background color and text options. It's area of activation is composed of the box containing the text. By overlaying the navigation pointer on one of the options, it is presented with a soft lighting effect. The main feature of this menu is the activation of the submenus, the submenu in which a particular option is only enabled when the user clicks at arrow to the right of the text of the option and not the text itself. This different activation of the submenus become a complicating factor for most users.

Menu 6 (http://goo.gl/jgoxY) suboptions to the main menu are displayed above the menu, causing a shift in the presentation of the same, with different motion and change of the default behavior. The area of activation of the options has a high color contrast between background and text, although there is no vertical bar to the delimit of each menu option.

Menu 7 (http://goo.gl/Himaz) creates columns for grouping information in submenus. The submenus can be triggered by identifying the option as indicative of the arrow. The area of activation involves the text of the existing option and the area around it, characteristic valid for submenus. Items within submenus are displayed with an arrow in the right of the text of the option.

Menu 8 (http://goo.gl/1bz7B) does not present indication of the submenus on the first level, however, presents a visual change when the mouse pointer is positioned above each horizontal menu option. To activate the submenus you must click with the mouse pointer over the option. From the fist level submenu, each option that has an associated submenu presents an arrow icon and requires only a mouse over event to display its submenu. The activation area consists of the identifier of the option plus the area around him, a characteristic also valid for submenus. Each option in the submenus may contain an icon to the left of their texts.

3.2 Test performance

The case study conducted with the participation of each user through a single Web session, whose maximum estimated time to complete took around 25 minutes. Initially the participant was asked for providing information regarding age, educational level, frequency and purpose of using the Internet, which took around three minutes to be filled.

Next, participants looked at the first menu that has been assigned randomly and the first task associated with this menu. For each menu two tasks were prepared, which were presented one each time and the participant took an average of slightly more than 1 minute each to be performed (reading task and perform the action).

For each of the eight types of menus used, a participant should complete the two required tasks, the goal of with task was to look for a predefined information, that is, before the participant look at a menu he should read carefully the specified task. After completing the reading, the participant should mark a checkbox agreeing that have read the job and felt confident to start it, he would click the button labeled with text "Continue". As an example, one of the tasks requested to the menu 1 was "select a trip to **Paris**".

At the moment a participant began the task a automatic registration of interaction is done in the log file. Next, a screen containing the menu and its options was presented to the participant. In the middle of the screen, the same content of the travel's theme, containing informative essays about three tourist cities in Brazil, was always presented.

When the participant selects any menu option, even it was correct or not, the record of interaction was made in the log file until he finishes up the task. When the participant selects the correct option, a screen containing a positive message and the option to continue the test were presented to him. If a participant chooses any other option, a screen with an error message was presented and the participant could choose to return to the previous screen and try to complete the task correctly, or give up that job and move to the next task.

To record the sequence of interactions of each participant, a logging mechanism was applied, in which every step of the participant interaction during the tasks, both in text and file in the database were stored. Automatic registration of interaction is important because it allows to recover all the steps of the interaction, favoring the identification of the moments of disorientation of the participant.

Furthermore, it was possible to obtain measurements relating to time of completion of the tasks by the participants and to extract several parameters regarding to the types of menus used, such as: time to complete each task, number of errors logged, total dropouts, menu and number of attempts before the discontinuance.

There was no time limit for completion of tasks. After doing the two tasks on each menu, a page where he could record his impression by using the menu, the difficulties, a score from zero to ten and some suggestions for how such a menu could be improved was presented to the user.

The period of data collection was between 26th. July and 22nd September of 2010, 244 people participated, but only 135 people finished the test, ie, interacted with all of the 8 menus, completing all required tasks. The profile of participants who completed the test is shown below.

3.3 Profile of participants

From the data collected from participants at the start of the test, it was possible to identify the following profiles:

- The ages of participants ranged from 18 years to 69 years old, and the largest number of people concentrated in the age group of 40 to 49 years old, 39 people (28.9 %) as well the people of 20 to 29 years old, the third largest group was of 50 to 59, 29 people (21.5 %) and the fourth largest group was aged 30 to 39 years old, 19 people (14 %);

- Of the 135 people who finished the test, 57 (42 %) were female and 78 (58 %) male;

- 48 people (36 %) have completed higher education level and 39 people (29 %) had completed a doctorate;

- People from 10 different Brazilian states[1] took a test, and the most representative state was Sao Paulo with 92 people (68 %), followed by the state of Parana, 25 people (19 %).

3.4 Limitations

During the test run we found some difficulties and problems that were noticed only after the collection of user data. One of the main difficulties observed was the small number of elderly users, since only eight participants aged more than sixty years old.

Another difficulty was the lack of justification for withdrawals during the tests. Of the 252 participants who started the trial, 115 participants (45%) did not perform all tasks. Since the tests were run remotely, there may be multiple causes of interruption of the test, such as power outage, closing the Internet browser, interrupting the test execution to another task, among others.

---

[1]They are: SP, PR, RJ, MG, EP, BA, MS, MT, RS and SC.

4. RESULTS

To perform a comparative analysis of results, the total users were divided into two groups. The division was related to age, forming the group of users with **forty years old or less** (G1) and the group with **more** than forty years old (G2). The characteristics of both groups are: The number of users in the group G1 contains 63 persons, of which 17 are women and 46 are men. The number of users in the group G2 are 72 people, comprising 40 women and 32 men.

It is worth noticing that G2 has a higher number of people compared to G1. Another factor that separates both groups is the educational achievements, represented in Figure 1.

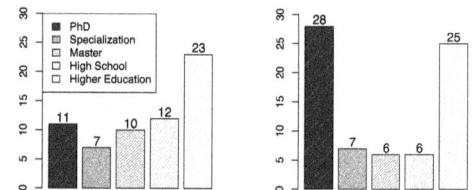

Figure 1: Scholarity in G1 (left) and G2 (right)

For both groups the following data were analyzed: number of errors and the average running time of tasks. Figure 2 shows the number of errors for each task in both groups.

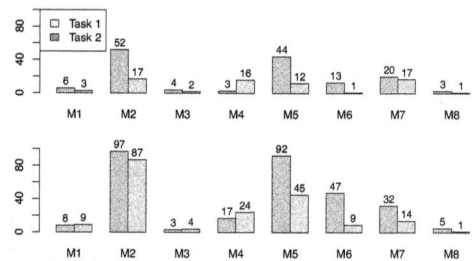

Figure 2: Number of errors made by the task group G1 (top) and the group G2 (bottom)

Figure 3 shows the average time of completion for each age group.

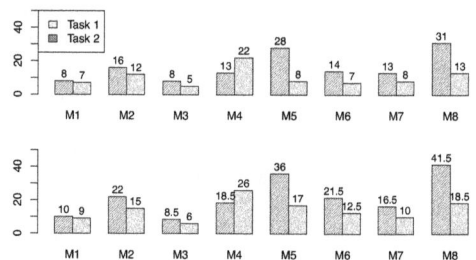

Figure 3: Mean time for the realization of tasks G1 (top) and G2 (bottom)

Figure 4 presents the application of survival analysis to the golden age of sixteen tasks performed by users. You can verify that the curves which decay more rapidly represent tasks that were performed more quickly, on average, by users.

Survival analysis is a term used to designate the statistical analysis of data when the study variable represents the time from a well-defined initial time until the occurrence of certain event of interest. For the application of survival analysis in the times collected via the logging mechanism was used statistical language R [17].

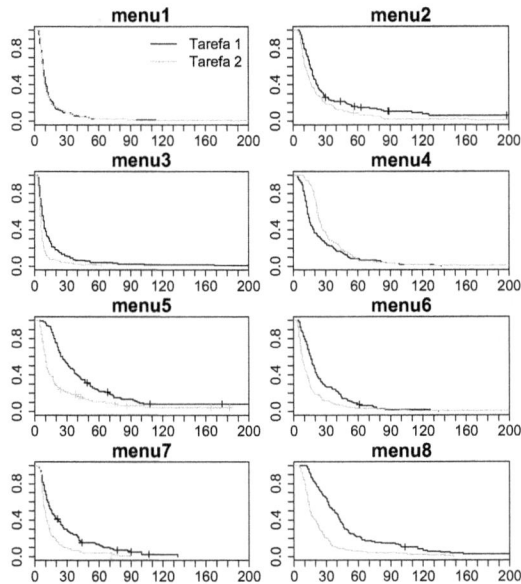

Figure 4: Kaplan-Meier estimates of time to accomplish tasks

showed the highest number of withdrawals were menus 2 and 5.

Another factor that helped to measure the performance of various menus was the time required to perform each task. The mean times for each group of people is presented in Figure 3. G2 presented a higher average completion time than G1 for all menus, which was expected due to the higher average age observed in G2.

However, for menus 1 and 3, the difference between G1 and G2 in average of time for performing tasks 1 and 2 was small. For the menu 1 the difference was of two seconds for the two tasks and for menu 3 the difference was of half a second for a task 1 and a second for the task 2.

The only menu that had the highest average of time for performing the task 2 than the task 1, was the menu 4, showing the poor performance of this menu, when considering that for task 2 the user is already familiar with its interaction mechanisms thus the completion time should be reduced.

Table 2: Compared using the log-rank test

Menus	Chi-Sq	p-Value
M1	0.1	0.762
M2	8.7	0.00323
M3	22.6	2.02e-06
M4	9	0.0027
M5	35.6	2.4e-09
M6	19.7	9.22e-06
M7	21.4	3.74e-06
M8	50.1	1.43e-12

5. DISCUSSION

In Figure 1, it can be observed that more than 39% of the participants of G2 present doctoral degrees (the highest education degrees considered), while 35%, present higher education degrees (the lowest education degrees). These numbers denote a great variety of user profiles that compose G2. The high number of doctoral degrees observed in G2 participants, can be justified by the fact that a great deal of the participants were recruited in the University of São Paulo.

Considering the learning outcomes between menu interactions, it can be observed that most menus showed a lower rate of errors in task 2 in comparison to task 1, considering that task 2 was realized after task 1. The exception for this behaviour is the Menu 4, which presented a higher rate of errors for task 2 in comparison to task 1.

When analysing the number of errors per interaction, menus 1, 3 and 8 presented the lowest rates. It is worth noticing that these menus presented a fast (menus 3 and 8) and medium (menu 1) presentation speed for the submenus. They feature a good amount of activation area for each option, while menus 1 and 8 present a hight time for the disappearance of submenus as the mouse leaves the activation area. These defining features assisted the interaction for the older and participants who presented lack of accuracy in using the mouse device.

The number of withdrawals was small compared to the number of errors and were not represented graphically, while only two menus (menu 1 and menu 3) had a higher number of withdrawals in task 2 than in task 1. The menus that

Another factor to be ascertained is the completion time difference between the tasks. It can be observed that in menu 1 and 3, this difference is small compared with the other menus. This shows that menus 1 and 3 presented a very fast learning behaviour for the users. Table 2 presents the data analysis of the completion time difference between tasks 1 and 2 for each menu in Figure 4, using the log-rank test. It can be observed that only menu 1 does not present differences between the completion time for task 1 and 2 (with p-value equals to 0.762), while all other menus present different performance rates for tasks 1 and 2.

6. CONCLUSION

After identifying the barriers to accessibility in Web interfaces, we selected eight horizontal menus with sublevels, also known as drop-down menus in the literature. The eight menus have different properties and were chosen based on menus used on sites with high popularity. After choosing, implementing the test environment and defining the tasks to be performed by users, the evaluation system of menus was sent to the participants, primarily to persons aged over 40 years old.

After the analysis of logs acquired with user interactions through the menus, it was found that the best menus are the first and third. The average completion time for the first menu was of 9 seconds for task 1 and 8 seconds for task 2. The average completion time for the menu 3 was of 8 seconds for task 1 and 6 seconds for task 2, the latter being the lowest median value among all the menus.

We conclude that menus 1 and 3 represent best suit navigation tasks for users who present profiles similar to the groups that participated in the experiment.

The third menu is served in commercial use in video distribution Vimeo. The third menu is a good alternative for sites that have little need to sublevels, otherwise many links to the menu 3 will tend to require a lot of options in the first menu level, and may hinder navigation.

The first menu was created using the jQuery library and was based on the drop-down menus using only CSS. In the current version, it is a menu with various settings and features that are rarely found in commercial sites. The main feature that helps to access the menu is the keyboard navigation (in all the menus you can access the content via keyboard), but only menu 1 presents this navigation mechanism which is perceived visually, that is, you can navigate through keyboard directly to the menu and see which option is selected.

Acknowledgment

We thank all the participants who voluntarily performed the experiments and the body National Council for Scientific and Technological Development (CNPq), CAPES and FAPESP (project number 2010/05626-7) for the financial support.

7. REFERENCES

[1] S. M. Affonso de Lara, W. M. Watanabe, E. P. B. dos Santos, and R. P. M. Fortes. Improving WCAG for elderly web accessibility. In *Proceedings of the 28th ACM International Conference on Design of Communication*, SIGDOC '10, pages 175–182, 2010.

[2] M. L. Bernard. Criteria for optimal web design (designing for usability), 2003.

[3] J. A. Borges, I. Morales, and N. J. Rodríguez. Page design guidelines developed through usability testing. In *In Forsythe*. Publishers. Mahwah, 1998.

[4] A. Burrell and A. C. Sodan. Web interface navigation design: Which style of navigation-link menus do users prefer? In *ICDE Workshops'06*, 2006.

[5] S. K. Card, A. Newell, and T. P. Moran. *The Psychology of Human-Computer Interaction*. L. Erlbaum Associates Inc., Hillsdale, NJ, USA, 1983.

[6] A. Cockburn and S. Jones. Which way now? analysing and easing inadequacies in www navigation. *International Journal of Human-Computer Studies*, 45:105–129, 2000.

[7] J. Fleming. *Web Navigation: Designing the User Experience*. O'Reilly Media, 1 edition, 9 1998.

[8] G. H. Frank. Reflections on notecards: seven issues for the next generation of hypermedia systems. *Commun. ACM*, 31(7):836–852, 1988.

[9] V. Hollink, M. Someren, and B. J. Wielinga. Navigation behavior models for link structure optimization. *User Modeling and User-Adapted Interaction*, 17(4):339–377, 2007.

[10] Y.-R. Lai and M. L. Waugh. From information searching to learning: A comparison of contrasting hypertextual menu designs for computer-based instructional documents. Apr. 1994.

[11] A. Laverson, K. Norman, and B. Shneiderman. An evaluation of jump-ahead techniques in menu selection. *Behaviour & Information Technology*, 6(2):97–108, 1987.

[12] G. Marchionini. *Information Seeking in Electronic Environments*. Cambridge University Press, Mar. 1997.

[13] J. Nielsen. *Hypertext and hypermedia*. Academic Press Professional, Inc., 1990.

[14] K. Norman and J. Chin. The effect of tree structure on search in a hierarchical menu selection system. *Behaviour & Information Technology*, 7(1):51–65, 1988.

[15] J. L. D. Oliveira, M. A. Gonçalves, and C. B. Medeiros. A framework for designing and implementing the user interface of a geographic digital library. 1999.

[16] S. Outing and L. Ruel. Navigation placement on news homepages, 2004.

[17] R Development Core Team. *R: A Language and Environment for Statistical Computing*. R Foundation for Statistical Computing, Vienna, Austria, 2010. ISBN 3-900051-07-0.

[18] B. Shneiderman. Designing menu selection systems. *Journal of the American Society for Information Science*, 37(2):57–70, 1986.

[19] B. Shneiderman. Designing information-abundant web sites: issues and recommendations. *International Journal of Human-Computer Studies*, 47:5–29, 1997.

[20] B. Shneiderman and G. Kearsley. *Hypertext hands-on?an introduction to a new way of organizing and accessing information*. Addison-Wesley Longman Publishing Co., Inc., 1989.

Effects of Self-Conscious Emotions on Affective and Behavioral Responses in HCI and CMC

Jinghui Hou
University of Southern California
3502 Watt Way, ASCJ G6
Los Angeles, CA 90089-0281, USA
+1 608 258 2852
jinghuih@usc.edu

Kwan Min Lee
University of Southern California
212 Kerckhoff Hall, 734 W. Adams Blvd
Los Angeles, CA 90089, USA
+1 213 740 3935
kwanminl@usc.edu

ABSTRACT

It remains unsettled whether the design of humanlike interfaces is the gold standard in HCI. This study tested how the degree of humanness of the interfaces and the perceived interactants (HCI vs. CMC) might impact individuals' affective and behavioral responses in text-based interactions of a trivia game. The results showed that although users liked the computer agent more than the "other person," human-like representation, as manipulated by self-conscious emotions, only affected likability in the CMC context. And the "machine-like" interface actually appeared more expert. Our findings suggest humanlike interfaces should be applied with caution and within the right context. Important implications for user experience, as well as design for including emotions in HCI are discussed.

Categories and Subject Descriptors

H.5.5 [**Information Interfaces and Presentation**]: User Interface – *evaluation/methodology, interaction styles.*

General Terms

Human Factors.

Keywords

HCI and CMC, self-conscious emotions, humanness, fair offer.

1. INTRODUCTION

In the field of human-machine interaction (HMI), we have a primitive urge to compare the quality of HMI to human-human interactions, as human interaction is often seen as the gold standard to be reached. Much effort has been invested in human-computer interaction (HCI) design to increase the saliency of computers' "humanness." Today's perfect implementation of technologies mimicking human characteristics makes it hard for users to distinguish the interactions with people (CMC) from those with machines (HCI). Nevertheless, some scholars [30, 32] are concerned with the possible negative impacts brought about by human mimicry in HCI. This concern is perhaps best upheld by the failure of the "intelligent" interface agent - Microsoft Office Assistant. Instead of sticking to a still questionable standard, a more direct approach, and perhaps a more valid one, to judge success of human computer interactions is simply to ask: does the

interactions satisfy the users equally, or even better, do its outward representations objectively match a human?

This criterion is two-fold in nature. First, it asks whether people respond more positively towards the machine as the HCI interface becomes increasingly human-like. Second, and perhaps part of greater interest, it asks if it is possible that people react more favorably to a human being than to a computer no matter what.

Under the "computers as social actors (CASA)" paradigm, Nass and his colleagues [8, 21, 23, 26] demonstrate that HCI parallels human-human interaction in many circumstances. Humans are evolutionarily programmed to treat computers as real social actors. That being said, however, will people look at computers through rose-colored glasses? It is part of human nature to stereotype, and to impose expectations accordingly [11]. By placing stereotype-based expectations on social beings, we routinely adjust our judgment standards and corresponding behaviors. Do we adjust our judgments and behaviors once we realize that we are dealing with a machine? The CASA studies focus mainly on the equalities between human-human and human-computer interactions; however it is likely that users responding to HCI or CMC exhibit enormous variety in their assessment dimensions and behavioral responses.

This study aims to evaluate how (a) the degree of human-likeness of the interface, as manipulated by self-conscious emotions, and (b) the perceived interactants (HCI vs. CMC) might impact individuals' affective and behavioral responses in text-based interactions.

1.1 Social Responses to Computers

It is well-established that humans, as a result of evolution, are hard-wired to respond to computers as people [26]. Empirical studies have consistently demonstrated that individuals unconsciously and automatically apply social rules in their responses toward computers. For example, previous studies have revealed that individuals attribute gender stereotypes to computers [22], can identify with a computer as a teammate [19], can be influenced by politeness or flattery from a computer [8], provide socially appropriate responses to a computer [17], and are influenced by ethnic cues [6]. The equality has been shown to apply to all modern media, such as television, films, computers, robots, etc. Reeves and Nass [26] used the umbrella term "media equation" meaning media equal real life to embrace the studies on this phenomenon. Nevertheless, even though this approach reveals similarities in responses, we may still want to ask precisely how similar or different the responses are, when similarity or difference happens and why [18, 20].

Some studies have shown that media equation may not be a consistent effect. Bartneck et al. [3] mimicked Milgram's obedience experiment using a robot in the role of the student. All subjects went through up to the maximum voltage compared to only 40% subjects who reached that level in the original experiment. They imply that humans feel empathy for the robot, but not up to the level of real human beings. Morkes et al. [18] examined the effects of inclusion of humor in solving the Desert Survival Problem with either a computer or another person. Their results showed HCI subjects felt less similar to their interaction partner, demonstrated less mirth, and spent less time on the task. Morkes et al. [18] conclude that the CMC condition elicits stronger social responses than the HCI condition. Weibel et al. [34] examined users' experience when playing online games against other users in comparison with playing against computer-controlled opponents. They found that subjects in CMC condition reported more experience of presence, flow, and enjoyment. Lim and Reeves [16], using psychophysiological measures, showed that players exhibited greater physiological arousal when they believed that they were playing with other people than with computer-controlled characters when the interactions were identical.

In an fMRI study, Sanfey et al. [29] investigated the brain activities of players of the Ultimatum Game, in which subjects were given the opportunities to split a sum of money (in their experiment $10). Each subject was proposed to as to how the money should be split (i.e., $5:$5, $7:$3, $8:$2, $9:$1). The subject could either accept or reject the offer. If it was accepted, the money was split as proposed, but if the subject rejected the offer, then neither received anything. The study found that unfair offers made by human partners were rejected at a significantly higher rate than those made by computers, with subjects showing stronger emotional reactions to unfair offers from humans than from computers. The fMRI data reported that one brain region, the anterior paracingulate cortex (bilaterally), showed significantly greater activation when subjects believed they were playing against a person than against a computer. The anterior paracingulate cortex is known for mentalizing, which refers to our ability to place ourselves in the mind of another person and predict their intentions [5]. This finding suggests that people are sensitive to "whom" they are interacting with. Believing that they are interacting with another person activates a distinctive set of brain responses. In other words, people's processing of HCI and CMC interactions may depend on two distinctive sets of mechanisms. Such a finding could challenge the CASA paradigm, suggesting a more nuanced investigation when comparing peoples' responses in HCI and CMC.

1.2 Self-conscious Emotions as a Manipulation of Human-likeness

Self-conscious emotions are emotions such as shame, guilt, embarrassment, and pride. Unlike the basic emotions such as fear, anger, sadness, and joy that are present in early infancy [7], self-conscious emotions are more complex and they emerge later in life [15]. The elicitation of self-conscious emotions requires that individuals must have a sense of self, a set of social norms or moral rules, and the ability to evaluate their behaviors according to those norms. Self-conscious emotions function to protect people's social well-being. The motives to self-enhance, self-verify, and self-expand are partly rooted in people's concerns with social approval and acceptance, and self-conscious emotions are believed to facilitate people's social interactions and relationships. Thus, self-conscious emotions are related to our social self, and serve intrapersonal-interpersonal and behavior-regulatory functions for the individuals [2].

Self-conscious emotions are thought to be unique to humans and certain great apes [9]. They require a sophisticated level of cognitive skills, which many argue that computers will never be able to capture. Thus, it is plausible to suggest that self-conscious emotions reflect humanity. And a high degree of personhood of a computer, therefore, was manipulated by inducing self-conscious emotions to the interactions in this study.

1.2.1 Human-likeness and Affective Responses

Research on anthropomorphic machines suggests that human-like representations evoke more positive affective reactions from users [1, 12, 14, 25, 33]. For example, Gong [10] manipulated four levels of anthropomorphism (low, medium, high, and real human images) in a choice dilemma task, and found that as the agent became more human-like, it received more positive responses from the users in terms of social judgment, perceived homophily, competency, and trustworthiness. Bartneck and Hu [4] observed that the more intelligent a robot was, the more hesitant people were to perform destructive behaviors on it.

The present study varied the degree of humanness manifested in HCI and CMC by manipulating the presence of self-conscious emotions in the interaction. Based on the findings above, it is hypothesized that individuals will evaluate the interaction more positively as their interactant shows higher level of humanness.

H1a-c. Individuals will perceive the interactant showing self-conscious emotions as (a) more likable, (b) more trustworthy, and (c) more expert than the interactant showing no such emotions.

1.2.2 Human-likeness and Behavioral Response

According to the previous studies, it seems that people are less sympathetic to computers than to other people in their actions. Individuals demonstrated less mirth when they heard jokes from a computer than from another person [18]. Individuals went through up to the maximum voltage when executing electric shocks to robots [3]. They executed more hits to "smart" robots than to "stupid" robots [4].

The present study tested how the degree of humanness manipulated by the presence of self-conscious emotions would affect individuals' likelihood of social treatment of their interactant in a money splitting task. As suggested by the studies above, it is hypothesized that individuals will split the points more fairly as their interactant shows higher levels of humanness.

H2. Individuals will propose fairer splitting with the interactant showing self-conscious emotions than with one showing no such emotions.

1.2.3 Human-likeness in HCI vs. CMC

As discussed above, evidence from CASA studies demonstrates that there is no "on-off" switch in the brain that allows one to process machines differently from real people [26]. However, data from neuroscience studies indicates that believing that one is interacting with another person versus with a computer actually activates two distinctive sets of brain areas. It is still unclear whether individuals are sensitive to "whom" they are interacting with and to what extent. Therefore, this study aims to test how individuals' perception of the interactants might influence affective and behavioral responses. Thus, we address the following two questions:

RQ1: Does the belief that one is interacting with a computer agent as opposed to another person influence an individual's perception of the interactant?

RQ2: Does the belief that one is interacting with a computer agent as opposed to another person influence how an individual splits the money?

2. METHOD

2.1 Participants
Subjects were 60 college undergraduates enrolled in a large introductory communication course. They were invited to play a trivia game with a computer agent (HCI) or with an actual person (ostensible CMC) as their teammate, while in fact the interactions were identical and preprogrammed. The conversations were structured with scripted responses. The trivia game interface was designed using the VB.net 3.5 program. During the game, subjects were asked to cooperate with their teammate on twelve trivia questions (e.g., "Which animal has fingerprints that are almost impossible to tell apart from a human fingerprint?"). Inspired by previous studies [13], we asked the subjects to choose a set of questions ranging from 1 to 10 to enhance a sense of interactivity. All subjects were actually presented with identical questions in the identical order.

2.2 Experimental Design
This study used a 2 (perception of interactant: HCI vs. CMC) × 2 (humanness answers: with vs. without self-conscious emotions) between-subject design. Subjects were randomly selected into one of the four conditions. In the CMC condition, each subject was told that his or her teammate was in another room and they were connected through the network. Each subject was then told that the two players would be randomly assigned a role in the game: one would be a dominant player (Player 1), and the other would be an assisting player (Player 2). Player 1 was in charge of deciding a final answer to each trivia question, using Player 2's answer as a reference. In the end of the game, Player 1 needed to decide how to split the team score, i.e., game points they earned, between the players. Player 2 only needed to submit answers to Player 1, and would get individual game points assigned to him or her by Player 1. In fact, there was no random assignment of Player 1 and Player 2; all subjects were assigned as Player 1. Subjects received assignments from the game interface, which took 4 seconds. The purpose was to make subjects believe that they *were* randomly assigned.

In the HCI condition, Subjects were told that their teammate was a computer agent located in another room and they were connected through the network to play the Trivia game. Each subject was then told that he or she would be a dominant player (Player 1), and the computer teammate would be an assisting player (Player 2). Each subject was also told to split the game points with the computer teammate at the end of the game. To enhance their involvement in the experiment, subjects were told before the game

that they would be evaluated on the final answers as well as team performance and receive game points accordingly, and a cash prize would be offered to the person who earned the highest score.

2.3 Procedure
Upon arrival at the laboratory, subjects first read the trivia game questions and the answers. After a brief delay, they saw the answers provided by their teammate (computer or human) on the screen. And finally the subjects were asked to choose the team answers. Subjects were explicitly told that they could use their teammates' answers as reference and determine the final team answer accordingly, but their teammates' answers might be right or wrong. We repeated this procedure for 12 different questions. After the game, subjects were given the same amount of points (i.e., 88), but they were told that the amount of game points they received was based on their final answers as well as the team performance in the game. Then they were asked to split the point amounts between their teammates and themselves. A cash prize would be offered to the person who earned most points, thus assigning more points to oneself was more beneficial to the subject.

Subjects in the control condition received generic answers without self-conscious emotions. In the humanness condition, subjects, in addition to the generic answers, received additional comments containing self-conscious emotions five times (e.g., I know this! Very proud of myself!!). We also added corresponding emoticons to enhance the manipulation. To enhance the credibility of the CMC condition, we showed a real person's profile photo and that person's nickname. In addition, a random 20-sec to 40-sec delay in response time of the "other person" was preprogrammed, while the random delay in HCI condition was ranged from 3-sec to 5-sec. The interface of this experiment was similar to that of a typical instant messaging. Finally, we asked the subjects to describe the interaction they had. We excluded those subjects from the analysis if they did not mention that they had been working with another person. After the game, the subject filled out a questionnaire. Next, the subjects were thanked, debriefed, and informed about the deception.

2.4 Measurement
Both attitudinal and behavioral dependent variables were measured. For likeability, perceived trustworthiness, and perceived expertise indices, subjects were asked to rate to what extent they agreed with each item on a 7-point scale (1 = very strongly disagree, 7 = very strongly agree), using a paper-and-pencil questionnaire. The index mean and standard deviation represented the average of the scaled value. Their behavioral responses, i.e., the game points splitting, were collected through the trivia game software.

Table 1. Descriptive Statistics for Variables by Conditions

	HCI		CMC (ostensible)	
	Humanness *M (SD)*	Control *M (SD)*	Humanness *M (SD)*	Control *M (SD)*
Likeability	5.20 (.64)	5.13 (.64)	5.04 (.82)	4.33 (.85)
Perceived Trustworthiness	3.98 (.90)	4.36 (.80)	3.87 (1.00)	4.04 (1.07)
Perceived Expertise	3.88 (.80)	4.28 (.54)	3.89 (.72)	4.23 (.76)
Splitting score	60.00 (16.38)	58.08 (15.83)	59.47 (18.15)	55.80 (19.25)

Table 2. Effects of Humanness and Perceived Interactants

	Main Effect for Humanness $F(1, 56)$	Main Effect for Perceived Interactant $F(1, 56)$	Humanness × Perceived Interactant $F(1, 56)$
Likeability	4.10*	6.19*	2.81*
Perceived Trustworthiness	1.29	.74	.17
Perceived Expertise	4.02*	.01	.03
Splitting score	.13	.23	.21

2.4.1 Affective Responses

Likeability. Likeability was measured using the 3 items adapted from Reysen Likeability Scale[28]: "My teammate is approachable," "My teammate is friendly," and "My teammate is likeable" ($M = 4.93$, $SD = .91$, $\alpha = .81$).

Perceived trustworthiness. Perceived trustworthiness was measured using the 3 items adapted from [27] Reysen Honesty Scale: "My teammate is trustworthy," "My teammate is reliable," and "I would seek my teammate's advice" ($M = 4.06$, $SD = .94$, $\alpha = .82$).

Perceived expertise. Perceived expertise was measured using the 5 items adapted from [27] Reysen Expertise Scale: "My teammate is intelligent," "My teammate is not experienced (reverse coded)," "My teammate is knowledgeable," "My teammate is an expert," and "My teammate is not well qualified to the Trivia game (reverse coded)" ($M = 4.07$, $SD = .71$, $\alpha = .83$).

2.4.2 Behavioral Response

Splitting score. Splitting score was measured by how many game points, out of the team game points (i.e., 88), subjects assigned to themselves. Obtained values of splitting score ranged from 35 to 88 ($M = 58.72$, $SD = 17.02$). As mentioned above, the number of final points assigned to the subjects themselves was linked to a corresponding cash prize. Therefore, a higher splitting score meant that the subject offered less to his or her teammate, and a lower splitting score indicated a relatively fairer offer.

3. RESULTS

Table 1 presents descriptive statistics for the variables in the treatment and control groups. Kolmogorov-Smirnov tests of normality were conducted on the dependent variables, and the results supported the normality assumptions. Then a two-way full-factorial ANOVA was performed on all measures to test the hypotheses and research questions (Table 2).

3.1 Hypothesis and Research Question Tests

H1a-c proposed that individuals would perceive the interactant showing self-conscious emotions as (a) more likable, (b) more trustworthy, and (c) more expert than the interactant showing no such emotions. There was a significant main effect of humanness on perceived likeability, $F(1, 56) = 4.10$, $p = .048$, partial $\eta^2 = .07$. Subjects rated their teammate as more likable when their teammate expressed self-conscious emotions in the interaction.

The ANOVA analyses also yielded a significant main effect for humanness on perceived expertise, $F(1, 56) = 4.10$, $p = .048$, partial $\eta^2 = .07$. Subjects perceived their interactants providing generic answers as more expert than those providing answers with self-conscious emotions, contrary to our expectation.

The results showed no significant main effect of humanness on perceived trustworthiness. Thus, H1a was supported. H1c was not supported. H1b was not supported but the effect was significant in the opposite direction.

H2 predicted that individuals would propose fairer splitting with the interactant showing self-conscious emotions than with one showing no such emotions. The results shown that participants in the humanness condition did not engage in significantly fairer splitting to the computer agent or "the other person" than did participants in the control group. It was not supported.

RQ1 pertained to the effect of perceived interactant (HCI vs. CMC) on affective responses. The results indicated a significant main effect for perceived interactant on likeability, $F(1, 56) = 6.19$, $p = .016$, partial $\eta^2 = .10$. Participants liked the computer agent more than "the other person." This main effect, however, could be qualified by a marginally significant interaction effect between humanness and perceived interactant, $F(1, 56) = 4.02$, $p = .050$, partial $\eta^2 = .07$ (see Fig. 1). Decomposition of the interaction effect suggested that although users liked the computer agent more than the "other person," human-like representation, as manipulated by self-conscious emotions, only affected likability in the CMC context.

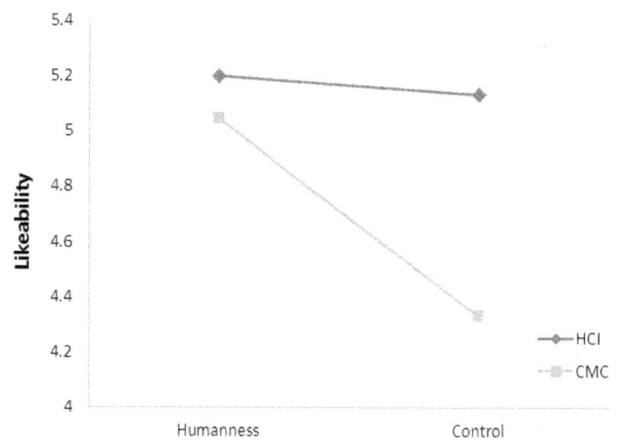

Figure 1. Likeability by humanness and perceived interactants

No significant difference was found between HCI and CMC conditions in how participants thought of "the other person" in terms of trustworthiness, and expertise.

RQ2 concerned how perceived interactant might influence the way an individual split the money. The result failed to find a significant difference between the HCI and CMC conditions in term of splitting scores.

3.2 Additional Analyses

In addition to the main analysis, we concerned how gender would influence subjects' affective and behavioral responses. Four separate 2 (perception of interactant: HCI vs. CMC) × 2 (humanness: with vs. without self-conscious emotions) × 2 (gender: male vs. female) ANOVAs were run on each of the dependent variable measures: likeability, perceived trustworthiness, perceived expertise, and splitting score. Two-tailed significance tests were used.

Our results indicated that male subjects ($M = 65.55$, $SD = 17.45$) assigned significantly more game points to themselves than female subjects ($M = 54.76$, $SD = 15.66$), $F (1, 52) = 6.00$, $p = .018$, partial $\eta^2 = .10$.

Our results also found a marginal significant interaction between gender and perceived interactant, $F (1, 52) = 3.19$, $p = .060$, partial $\eta^2 = .07$, on perceived trustworthiness (see Fig. 2). Female subjects rated the "human" interactant ($M = 4.25$, $SD = .75$) as more trustworthy than the computer agent interactant ($M = 4.10$, $SD = .94$), while male subjects rated the agent interactant (M = 4.30, SD = .69) as more trustworthy than the human interactant ($M = 3.50$, $SD = 1.23$).

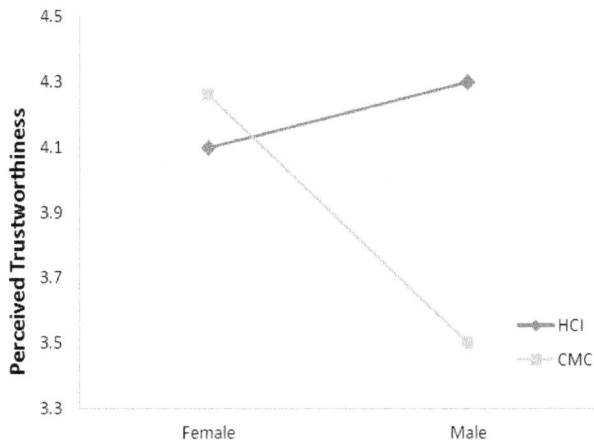

Figure 2. Perceived trustworthiness by perceived interactant and gender

4. DISCUSSION AND CONCLUSION

This study shows some interesting findings that are uncommon in previous research. According to our results, human-like representations do not necessarily evoke positive affective reactions or behavioral responses from the users in HCI, suggesting a more nuanced investigation of the anthropomorphism hypothesis. Our direct test of the Computers as Social Actors paradigm also leads to speculation about to what extent HCI and CMC approximate and where the boundaries of the equalities are. In general, this study raises the question of how varying contexts and user factors may influence people's responses in HCI and CMC.

The present study uses self-conscious emotions (shame, guilty, embarrassment, and pride) to manipulate the degree of human-likeness. Such high level emotions are believed to facilitate people's social interactions and relationships. Contrary to our expectations, the data indicated that the use of self-conscious emotions in a text-based interaction actually detracted from an interactant's perceived expertise. It is possible that emotions like shame, guilt, embarrassment, and pride may not be beneficial in task-oriented interactions. In our experiment, participants were encouraged to do well in the trivia game. Their final performance was linked with a cash prize. Seeing their teammates showing shame, guilt, and etc. did not help the task-performance in the game. Actually off-task activities, such as joking, being playful, or being emotional, are considered diversions from completing the task and even a waste of time [31]. Users who are focusing on their task may resent too many irrelevant distractions, as it is advised that productivity software in workplace should be "business-oriented and ... as realistic as possible"[24]. Self-conscious emotions are essential for us to protect our social well-being. However, being emotional may not be a good practice in task-oriented contexts. It is our suggestion that anthropomorphism approach is appropriate but we should be careful about its operationalization and test settings. Future studies could examine self-conscious emotions in entertainment-oriented context, such as socializing, and gaming. The results also imply that we should be cautious when deciding on the inclusion of emotions in the design of interactive interfaces.

Another surprising finding proposes that people may prefer "talking" to a machine to talking to a person under some circumstances. Computers may be better liked than humans to some people during some interactions. This suggests that the psychological effects of interactive interfaces are complex and are context-dependent. We may turn to families and friends when we want to have fun, to socialize, or to seek comfort. Previous studies testing the CASA hypotheses in entertainment-oriented context do suggest that people enjoy playing video games with other people more than with computers [16, 34]. However, when we are handling tasks or work problems, we might prefer a computer, because we expect it to be reliable, efficient, and productive. The results may therefore reveal some possible boundary conditions of the CASA paradigm. In addition, it also indicates that the design of interactive applications should consider the nature of the context (task vs. entertainment) as well as the source of the interactant (e.g., computer controlled agents vs. human controlled avatars).

Our additional analysis on gender differences speaks to the potential effects of user factors on interactions in HCI and CMC. Female users tend to respond more positively in CMC than in HCI, while male users gave more credit to computers in a task context. This is somewhat consistent with the social stereotyping of gender roles; women are often pictured to excel in social relationship and networking, while men are more likely to show interests in mechanism and machinery. In addition, all the perceived "interactants" in our experiment were presented as "male." There could be a same-sex and opposite-sex influence on interactions. We recommend taking users' gender impact into account for HCI designs, especially for social interfaces.

It is also worth noting that we briefly interviewed the CMC subjects after the trivia game, asking them to describe the interactions they had. The original purpose was to exclude the responses from the analysis if the subjects suspected that they had been working with another person. No subject expressed doubt that his or her teammate was not a person in the CMC condition, suggesting a successful design. However, interestingly, some subjects (2 out of 24) in the HCI condition did ask the experimenter whether their teammates were actually computers, suspecting that they had been working with a human being instead. It is hard to conclude how many subjects had doubts in the HCI conditions, as we did not intentionally interview them. It appeared to us that many subjects enjoyed teaming up with a computer as they thought their partner was "cool" and "awesome." The results may indicate that people relish interacting with computers if they surprise them. We believe that it is necessary and worthwhile to further validate this hypothesis, and future investigation could benefit from some qualitative data.

In conclusion, our results suggest that HCI researchers should consider a more nuanced examination of the context and user factors when assessing something so general as how people respond to computers.

5. REFERENCES

1. Bailenson, J.N., Blascovich, J., Beall, A.C. and Loomis, J.M. Equilibrium theory revisited: Mutual gaze and personal space in virtual environments. *Presence: Teleoperators & Virtual Environments*, 10 (6). 583-598.
2. Barrett, K.C. A functionalist approach to shame and guilt.
3. Bartneck, C., Chioke, R., Menges, R. and Deckers, I. Robot Abuse–A Limitation of the Media Equation.
4. Bartneck, C. and Hue, J. Exploring the abuse of robots. *Interaction Studies*, 9 (3). 415-433.
5. Chaminade, T., Hodgins, J. and Kawato, M. Anthropomorphism influences perception of computer-animated characters' actions. *Social Cognitive and Affective Neuroscience*, 2 (3). 206.
6. Dotsch, R. and Wigboldus, D.H.J. Virtual prejudice. *Journal of Experimental Social Psychology*, 44 (4). 1194-1198.
7. Emde, R. Development terminable and interminable - Innate and motivational factors from infancy. *The International Journal of Psychoanalysis*, 69. 23-42.
8. Fogg, B.J. and Nass, C. Silicon sycophants: The effects of computers that flatter. *International Journal of Human-Computer Studies*.
9. Gallup Jr, G.G. Self awareness and the emergence of mind in primates. *American Journal of Primatology*, 2 (3). 237-248.
10. Gong, L. How social is social responses to computers? The function of the degree of anthropomorphism in computer representations. *Computers in Human Behavior*, 24 (4). 1494-1509.
11. Hamilton, D. A cognitive-attributional analysis of stereotyping. in Berkowitz, L. ed. *Advances in experimental social psychology*, Elsevier, New York: NY, 1979.
12. Hinds, P.J., Roberts, T.L. and Jones, H. Whose job is it anyway? A study of human-robot interaction in a collaborative task. *Human-Computer Interaction*, 19 (1). 151-181.
13. Lee, E.J. I like you, but I won't listen to you: Effects of rationality on affective and behavioral responses to computers that flatter. *International Journal of Human-Computer Studies*, 67 (8). 628-638.
14. Lee, K.M., Park, N. and Song, H. Can a robot be perceived as a developing creature? *Human Communication Research*, 31 (4). 538-563.
15. Lewis, M. Self-conscious emotions: Embarrassment, pride, shame, and guilt. in Lewis, M. and Haviland, J. eds. *Handbook of emtions*, 1993.
16. Lim, S. and Reeves, B. Computer agents versus avatars: Responses to interactive game characters controlled by a computer or other player. *International Journal of Human-Computer Studies*, 68 (1-2). 57-68.
17. Moon, Y. and Nass, C. Are computers scapegoats? Attributions of responsibility in human-computer interaction. *International Journal of Human-Computer Studies*, 49 (1). 79-94.
18. Morkes, J., Kernal, H.K. and Nass, C. Effects of humor in task-oriented human-computer interaction and computer-mediated communication: A direct test of SRCT theory. *Human-Computer Interaction*, 14 (4). 395-435.
19. Nass, C., Fogg, B.J. and Moon, Y. Can computers be teammates? *International Journal of Human Computer Studies*, 45 (6). 669-678.
20. Nass, C. and Moon, Y. Machines and mindlessness: Social responses to computers. *Journal of Social Issues*, 56 (1). 81-103.
21. Nass, C., Moon, Y. and Carney, P. Are People Polite to Computers? Responses to Computer Based Interviewing Systems1. *Journal of Applied Social Psychology*, 29 (5). 1093-1109.
22. Nass, C., Moon, Y., Fogg, B.J., Reeves, B. and Dryer, C. Can computer personalities be human personalities? *Conference companion on Human factors in computing systems*, ACM, 1995, 228-229.
23. Nass, C. and Steuer, J. Voices, boxes, and sources of messages. *Human Communication Research*, 19 (4). 504-527.
24. Nielsen, J. *Usability Engineering*. Academic Press, San Diego, CA, 1993.
25. Parise, S., Kiesler, S., Sproull, L. and Waters, K. Cooperating with life-like interface agents. *Computers in Human Behavior*, 15 (2). 123-142.
26. Reeves, B. and Nass, C. *The media equation: How people respond to computers, television, and new media like real people and places*. Cambridge University Press, 1996.
27. Reysen, S. Construction and validation of measures of perceived honesty and perceived expertise *the 54th annual meeting of the Southwestern Psychological Association Conference*, Kansas City, MO, 2008.
28. Reysen, S. Construction of a new scale: The Reysen likability scale. *Social Behavior and Personality*, 33. 201-208.
29. Sanfey, A.G., Rilling, J.K., Aronson, J.A., Nystrom, L.E. and Cohen, J.D. The neural basis of economic decision-making in the ultimatum game. *Science*, 300 (5626). 1755.
30. Schaumburg, H. Computers as tools or as social actors? The users' perspective on anthropomorphic agents. *International Journal of Cooperative Information Systems*, 10 (1-2). 217-234.
31. Shneiderman, B. *Designing the user interface: strategies for effective human-computer-interaction*. Addison Wesley Longman, 1998.
32. Shneiderman, B. and Plaisant, C. *Designing the user interface: strategies for effective Human-Computer Interaction*. Pearson Addison Wesley, London, 2004.
33. Sproull, L., Subramani, M., Kiesler, S., Walker, J.H. and Waters, K. When the interface is a face. *Human–Computer Interaction*, 11 (2). 97-124.
34. Weibel, D., Wissmath, B., Habegger, S., Steiner, Y. and Groner, R. Playing online games against computer-vs. human-controlled opponents: Effects on presence, flow, and enjoyment. *Computers in Human Behavior*, 24 (5). 2274-2291.

Keynote Talk

Natural Interaction in Ambient Intelligent Environments

Constantine Stephanidis
Institute of Computer Science
Foundation for Research and Technology - Hellas (FORTH)
Heraklion, Crete, GR-70013 Greece
and
Department of Computer Science
University of Crete, Greece
cs@ics.forth.gr

ABSTRACT

Ambient Intelligence (AmI) constitutes an evolution of Information and Communication Technologies which responds to the current increasing demand for anytime anywhere availability of information and electronic services. AmI technologies integrate sensing capabilities, processing power, reasoning mechanisms, networking facilities, applications and services, digital content, and actuating capabilities distributed in the environment. While a wide variety of different technologies is involved, the goal of AmI is to either entirely hide their presence from users or to smoothly integrate them within the surrounding context as enhanced environment artifacts, rather than as technological gadgets. The pervasiveness of interaction in AmI environments requires the elaboration of new interaction concepts that extend beyond the current user interface concepts like the desktop metaphor and menu driven interfaces. AmI will therefore bring about new interaction techniques, as well as novel uses and multimodal combinations of existing advanced techniques, such as, for example, gestures and localisation. Additionally, interaction is embedded in everyday objects and smart artifacts. This concept refers to interfaces that use physical artifacts as objects for representation and interaction, seamlessly integrating the physical and digital worlds. Interaction in AmI environments inherently relies on multimodal input, implying that it combines various user input modes, such as speech, pen, touch, manual gestures, gaze and head and body movements, as well as more than one output modes, primarily in the form of visual and auditory feedback. In this context, adaptive multimodality is prominent to support natural input in a dynamically changing context-of-use, adaptively offering to users the most appropriate and effective input forms at the current interaction context.

The ICS-FORTH Ambient Intelligence Programme is an on-going horizontal interdisciplinary RTD Programme aiming to develop and apply pioneering human-centric AmI technologies and Smart Environments, capable of "understanding" and fulfilling individual human needs. This Programme constitutes a systematic effort towards addressing the challenges which arise in the context of AmI, by providing natural forms of interaction and access to information and communication. In this context, a wide variety of AmI applications and services have been developed for various environments and domains, including home and everyday living, office work, culture and museums, exhibitions and public spaces, education, and health. These developments constitute showcases for demonstrating in practice AmI technologies and their potential and benefits in different aspects of everyday life and activities. Some of them have been deployed "in vivo" and are available and used in real environments, such as, for example, the exhibition of AmI artifacts "Macedonia from fragments to pixels" deployed at the Archaeological Museum of Thessaloniki. The new ICS-FORTH AmI Research Facility, due to be completed by the end of 2011, will comprise simulated AmI-augmented environments and their support spaces, laboratory spaces for developing and testing related technologies, and will provide an appropriate environment for the pilot deployment and user-based evaluation of the developed AmI technologies under conditions very similar to real life.

Categories & Subject Descriptors:
H.5 INFORMATION INTERFACES AND PRESENTATION

General Terms: Design, Human Factors

Bio: Constantine Stephanidis, Professor at the Department of Computer Science of the University of Crete, is the Director of the Institute of Computer Science, Foundation for Research and Technology - Hellas, Head of the Human - Computer Interaction Laboratory, and of the Centre for Universal Access and Assistive Technologies, and Head of the Ambient Intelligence Programme of ICS-FORTH. Over the past 25 years, he has been engaged as the Scientific Responsible in more than 50 European Commission and nationally funded projects in the fields of Human-Computer Interaction, Universal Access and Assistive Technologies. He has published more than 500 technical papers. He is the Editor-in-Chief of the Springer international journal "Universal Access in the Information Society". He is the Editor and (co-)author of many chapters of the book "User Interfaces for All - concepts, methods and tools" (LEA 2001), and of "The Universal Access Handbook" (T&F 2009). Since 2001 he is the Founding Chair of the International Conference 'Universal Access in Human-Computer Interaction' and since 2007 the General Chair of the HCI International Conference series. Since October 2010 he is member of the Academia Europaea.

Necessary and Neglected? An Empirical Study of Internal Documentation in Agile Software Development Teams

Christoph Johann Stettina
stettina@liacs.nl

Werner Heijstek
heijstek@liacs.nl

Leiden Institute of Advanced Computer Science, Leiden University
Niels Bohrweg 1, 2333 CA Leiden, the Netherlands
http://www.liacs.nl/home/{stettina,heijstek}

ABSTRACT

When compared to traditional development methods, agile development practices are associated with more direct communication and less documentation. However, few empirical studies exist that investigate the role of documentation in agile development teams. We thus employed a questionnaire to measure the perceptions of a group of agile practitioners with regard to the documentation in their projects. We obtained responses from 79 agile software development professionals and 8 teams in 13 different countries. Our findings include that over half of developers in our data set find documentation important or even very important but that too little documentation is available in their projects. Agile practitioners do not seem to agree with the agile principle that "The most efficient and effective method of conveying information to and within a development team is face-to-face conversation." We were able to validate this result for a set of dissimilar agile teams in various domains.

Categories and Subject Descriptors

D.2.1 [**Software Engineering**]: Requirements/Specifications—*Methodologies*; D.2.7 [**Software Engineering**]: Distribution, Maintenance, and Enhancement—*Documentation*; K.6.1 [**Management of computing and Information Systems**]: Project and People Management—*Management techniques*

General Terms

Documentation, Management, Human Factors, Measurement

Keywords

Documentation, Agile software development, Empirical study

1. INTRODUCTION

Scrum [18] is an often applied software development methodology [1, 6]. In the spirit of lean manufacturing, Scrum emphasizes a focus on working software and direct communication rather than written documentation [1,3,6,17]. Based upon the mental attitude of value-oriented utilization of resources, lean manufacturing considers the expenditure of resources for any goal other than the creation of value for the end customer as wasteful. In agile development, these attitudes can be found in the agile manifesto [9] which considers heavyweight processes and comprehensive internal documentation of no direct use to the end customer. Internal documentation in software engineering may include requirement specifications, design specifications and technical documentation of program code. While such might be of no direct use to the end-user of consumer products, technical documentation in software projects such as embedded comments within the source code, descriptive and/or explanatory notes of APIs, interfaces and algorithms are thought to be beneficial to project initiators as well as to the engineers who are to maintain or expand the software in the future. Originating from practice [18] and reflected in theory [14], the advantages and limitations of Scrum as an agile development method and agile teamwork in particular [21] have been widely discussed in literature (e.g. [1, 6]). However, although companies using agile methods have been found to be more customer-centric and flexible than document-driven ones [20], little has been reported on use of documentation within agile teams. While the strictly defined Scrum method with its subsequent phases aids in reducing uncertainty, there is surprisingly little to no anchorage of documentation within the process. In this contribution we therefore aim to improve the understanding of internal documentation in agile software development teams in general, and how agile practitioners perceive this documentation in particular.

2. RELATED WORK

The term Scrum depicts cross-functional team characteristics and overlapping phases similarly to those in rugby. It is a lightweight, agile development method, aiming to strip the process of software development to its bare minimum and putting emphasis on direct communication and self-managing teams [6,21]. As an adaptive rather than predictive model [17] it does not depend on heavy documentation written upfront. Relying on constant collaboration among the team members and stakeholders, however, literature points at the dangers of general loss of undocumented knowledge (e.g. [1, 17]) when members leave the team or when the project is delivered. In distributed software development projects, which are increasingly common, software documentation is thought to play a more central role due to the absence of face-to-face communication. The common "transfer by development stage" [13] approach to global software development (GSD) where design and implementation activities take place at different geographical locations, complicates matters further. In this situation, offshore developers are often not able to directly contact a member of the architecture team due to geographical separation. Synchronous communication is often difficult due to time zone differences. In such a scenario documentation plays a more central role in intra-project knowledge sharing processes. In addition, complete and detailed documentation is essential to software maintenance as this typically involves different engineers from the ones who developed the system. Studies reporting on the use of software documentation during software development are few and deliver mixed results. In studies researching developers' preferences regarding documentation, Lethbridge et al [8,10] find a preference for simple and powerful documentation and conclude that documentation is an important tool for communication, even if it is not up to date. In their literature review on empirical studies addressing the scientific level of evidence behind agile software development methodologies, Dybå and Dingsøyr [6] address "documentation" in just one of the identified contributions [20]. In one of the few contributions to understanding of documentation in agile projects, Clear [3] points at the behavior of students and observes documentation being seen as something external. Instead of being produced in-line with the system as natural part of the development process, documentation was often hurriedly pieced together at the end of a project.

3. OBJECTIVES

There is a commonly assumed antipathy of agile practitioners towards internal documentation. This assumption stems not in the last place from the agile manifesto, which states that *"[Software documentation is] important, but we need to understand that customers don't care about documents, UML diagrams or legacy integration."* [9]. With the increasing number of integration projects and changing team setups, however, the transfer of development knowledge becomes increasingly important. In this paper we are interested in understanding the role of documentation in agile development projects, and how the amount and importance of documentation is perceived from the perspective of an agile team. We therefore pose the two following research questions:

1. *How do team members in agile software development projects document their work?*
2. *How do they perceive the amount and importance of their internal documentation?*

4. METHOD

In order to be able to attain a level of external validity, data from a wide range of agile practitioners is needed. In order to uniformly obtain a sizable sample and to promote objective answers we developed an anonymous questionnaire.

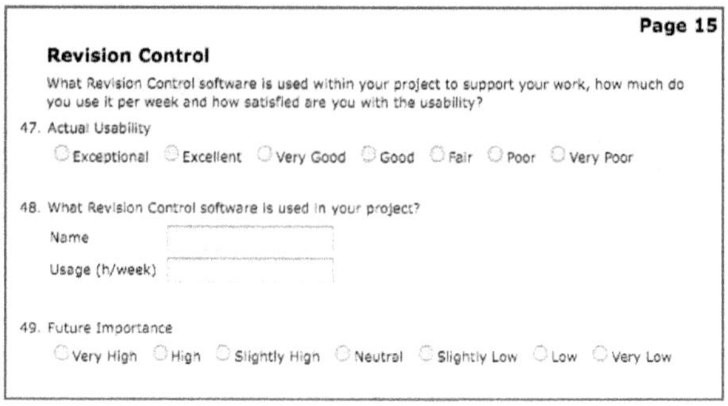

Figure 1: Online Questionnaire: Technology

Surveys are easy to deploy and when self-administered through a computer, their use minimizes the effect of socially desirable responding [15] due to the impersonality of the computer. To reduce bias we encouraged the respondents to provide their honest opinions by emphasizing the anonymous treatment of data. While we provided personalized links for each team member to ensure the consistency of input, no personal details were stored or used within the examination. An example of the format of the questionnaire is displayed in Fig. 1. Additionally, Miles and Huberman [12] propose linking quantitative and qualitative data to provide a deeper picture for the research. We thus asked each ScrumMaster (i.e. (agile) project leader) of an interested Scrum team a set of open-ended interview questions regarding the project environment at the end of the data collection. These qualitative questions (compare Tab.1) aimed to learn about the background of the project and details not covered by the quantitatively collected data.

4.1 Questionnaire Design

In line with our objective, we want to understand how agile teams produce their documentation and how satisfied they are with it. To reach this two-fold goal we divided the questionnaire into two parts. Part one was geared towards collecting the perceptions of team members regarding their documentation. Part two was designed to inquire about the software tools applied to manage that documentation. The questionnaire was part of a bigger study on agile teams and was developed with software developers including input from practitioners and fellow researchers working in the field of agile software development. To minimize possible flaws in the questionnaire design and to ensure appropriate scales applied, we reviewed the questions with colleagues from the faculty of psychology at the NTNU Trondheim which was the original site of this study.

4.1.1 *Perceptions Regarding Documentation*

The data collected from the teams was coded according to a five-point Likert scale. The questions have been administered in the following order:

1. *How much time do you spend on writing documentation daily?*
2. *How do you feel about documentation at work?*
3. *How effective do you consider finding internal documentation?*
4. *How important do you consider documentation for your project?*

Next to the questions regarding documentation, the following question was included to probe the usage of physical artifacts within the agile environment:

- *How important do you consider physical artifacts like story cards or "the wall" for your project?*

4.1.2 Supportive Software

In addition to developers' perceptions of documentation we also needed to inquire about the software tools supporting the development work. To cover a wide range of documentation tools within the survey we agreed upon including 6 categories of tools, namely: (1) *issue tracking*, (2) *revision control*, (3) *electronic discussion*, (4) *Scrum support*, (5) *document management* and (6) *calendar & scheduling*. As we needed to measure the usage of software packages applied, we first asked the participants if a certain tool category is being used within their project. We then asked for the perceived usability from the perspective of the developer. To optimally collect an objective measure of software usability, we applied a method adopted from the European Software Institute's (ESI) 1995 Software Excellence Survey [5] as discussed by Dybå and Moe [7]. We assessed the usability by placing two opposing subjective rating scales accompanying each question: the *actual usability* and the *believed future importance* as depicted in Fig. 1. The gap between believed importance and usability can be regarded as a measure for disaffection with a given solution. This gap is visualized in Fig. 7b. The perception of each team member was gathered for the respective categories as depicted in Fig. 1. To prevent inconsistency among the rating items we used two Likert scales consisting of 7 items: *Very High* = 7, *High* = 6, *Slightly High* = 5, *Neutral* = 4, *Slightly Low* = 3, *Low* = 2 and *Very Low* = 1.

4.2 Team Agreement

Variance (σ^2) is a measure of how far each value in a set of responses is from the mean. We calculated the variance of the collected values on a team basis to obtain insight in inter and intra-team agreement. A lower variance corresponds with a greater level of agreement within a team. The maximum variance in a team is the variance of the maximum and minimum values that can be given in response to an answer. The minimum variance is 0, denoting complete agreement. On a Likert scale ranging from -2 – 2, the maximum variance is

$$\sigma^2 = \frac{\sum(X - \mu)^2}{N} = \frac{\sum X^2}{N} - \mu^2$$
$$\text{MAX}(\sigma^2\{1, 5\}) = \frac{1^2 + 5^2}{2} - \left(\frac{1 + 5}{2}\right)^2 = 4.$$

4.3 Data Collection

To collect data, the questionnaire has been presented as a set of online survey questions to a group of international project teams, practitioners and experts applying the Scrum methodology. The participants had to be actively involved in a Scrum development team. Only completely filled questionnaire were considered for analysis. To look for international Scrum teams interested in the study Scrum and agile oriented groups within business related networks were targeted. After identifying related individuals from different online community platforms, user groups as well as agile practitioners originating from direct and indirect contacts,

invitations to participate were sent to 150 potential participants. Those who expressed their interest in participation, received an anonymized link allowing identification of teams within the online survey system. In addition, each ScrumMaster then received the set of open-ended questions regarding the project environment (Tab. 1).

5. RESULTS

After data collection all obtained answers were collected into a *global sample*. In addition to this sample, where at least four agile practitioners of a single team provided a valid survey response, data was also divided into *team samples*. These team samples provide a second perspective on the collected data set by enabling analysis on a team level. The total number of valid data responses comprises 79 software engineers from eight teams located in 13 different countries. Most of the engineers are software developers (47%) and ScrumMasters (18%). Other groups, however, emerged within the data collection phase. These groups are: *Product Owner* (8%), *Quality Assurance* (6%), *Agile Coach* (6%), *Consultant* (9%), *Interaction Designer* (1%) and *CTO* (5%). Their data has been taken into evaluation as long as the individuals were committed to a *"Pig role"* within the Scrum project, thus, being directly involved in the production in a formal and frequent way while referring to internal documentation. The gross amount of relevant working experience among the participants is situated around a work record of 1–5 (38%) and 6–10 (29%) years. Eight teams were analysed in detail. The teams consisted of at least four members and at least two-thirds of all teams have answered the survey. We therefore feel that a consistent representation of a group image was attained for all eight teams. We first present our results from the global sample and then switch to the team perspective.

5.1 Global Sample

5.1.1 Documentation

In Fig. 2, an overview can be found of the time the participants spend on writing documentation in their project daily. We find that the majority of participants spend less than 15 minutes on writing documentation daily. In line with this finding, we observe that almost half of the participating software experts perceive the existing documentation in their project as *too little* (Fig. 3). Fig. 4 presents an overview of developers' perceived effectiveness of finding existing documentation in their project. The diagram depicts a balanced distribution. This balanced distribution implies that a substantial group of participants does not find availability in line with agile practices in which documentation must support the development process. Fig. 5 depicts an overview of participants' responses with regards to their perception of the importance of documentation. Here, we observe that majority of the participants define documentation as being *important* or *very important*. This observation is remarkable as we would have expected that agile practitioners would rate documentation as not so important. According to Sharp et al., while relying heavily on direct, face-to-face communication, agile teams use simple physical artifacts to support interaction [19]. This is confirmed by our findings as the majority of participants think physical artifacts are important in their project (Fig. 6).

Table 1: ScrumMaster Interview Questions

- Please describe your project shortly. What is the product? What is its size (e.g. man months, lines of code)?
- Please describe your team shortly.
- What is the team's spatial distribution? Is it physically separated?
- What changes did you had to adapt to while switching to Scrum?
- Which aspects of communication do you consider the most salient for the project?
- Does the communication differ to the projects you had before Scrum? How?
- How do you report to your manager? Do you have separate reports to Project Owner and to "Chickens"?
- How do you document the work you do? What is the structure of the project documentation?
- How do you prioritize documentation tasks within the project?
- Are you happy with the current process to handle communication in general (Documentation, Requirements, Meetings etc.)?
- Are you using additional tools to those shared by the rest of the team to improve your productivity?

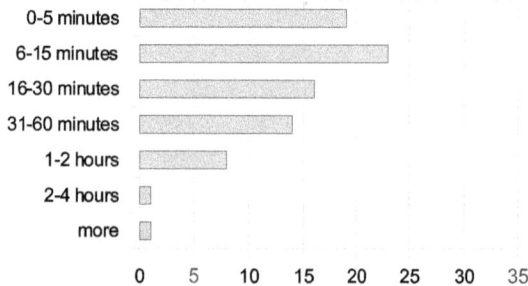

Figure 2: Time spent on writing documentation

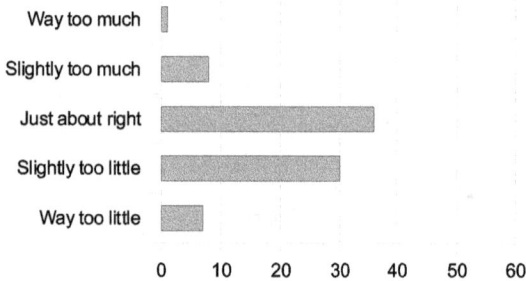

Figure 3: Perceived amount of documentation

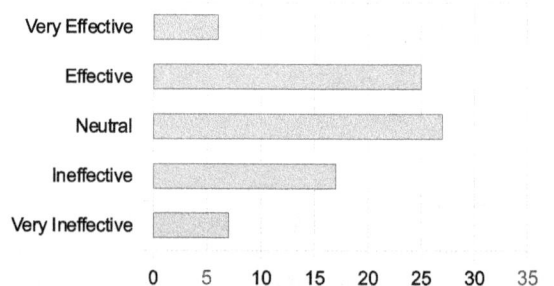

Figure 4: Perceived effectiveness in finding documentation

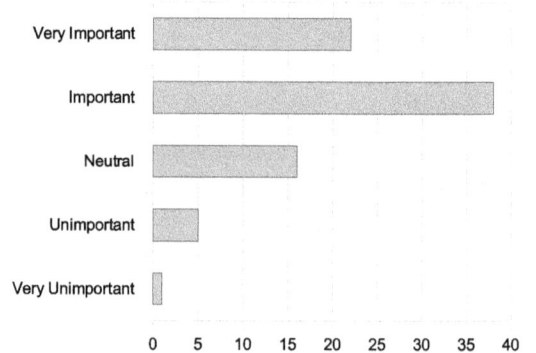

Figure 5: Perceived importance of documentation

5.1.2 Supportive Software

In Fig. 7, we present an overview of the software categories applied by the agile practitioners in their projects. We observe that issue tracking and revision control are used by most participants. The common use of this technology might well be explained by the notion that, next to their employees, source code and knowledge are among the most valuable assets of a software company. Calendar and scheduling tools are used by 62% of the participants. Software supporting electronic discussions and Scrum are similarly distributed with 47% and 48%. Document management is the least applied tool category. Interestingly, document management is reported to be used least by the respondents. In the survey, *document management* was explained to entail the storage of

requirements, design papers, used interfaces, created functions and sub-functions.

While looking at the deviation of usability and importance we observe that revision control, issue tracking and Scrum support have the biggest gap. This means that the participants perceive the highest disaffection for these three categories. The use of Scrum support tools seems surprising. Although one might think that the need for applications supporting a rather direct and physical development method would be rare, there indeed seems to be a demand for supplementary software tools. The perceived usability of solutions for electronic discussion shows the smallest gap among all categories. The most applied software packages

162

Software Usage

Issue Tracking	83%
Revision Control	84%
Electronic Discussion	47%
Scrum Support	48%
Document Management	37%
Calendar & Scheduling	62%

0.00%   50.00%   100.00%

(a) Usage

Software Usability

Issue Tracking	4.8	5.77
Revision Control	5.4	6.38
Electronic Discussion	5.32	5.82
Scrum Support	4.97	5.81
Document Management	4.54	5.18
Calendar & Scheduling	4.94	5.43

0 2 4 6 8 10 12 14

☐ Importance
☐ Gap
☐ Usability

(b) Usability

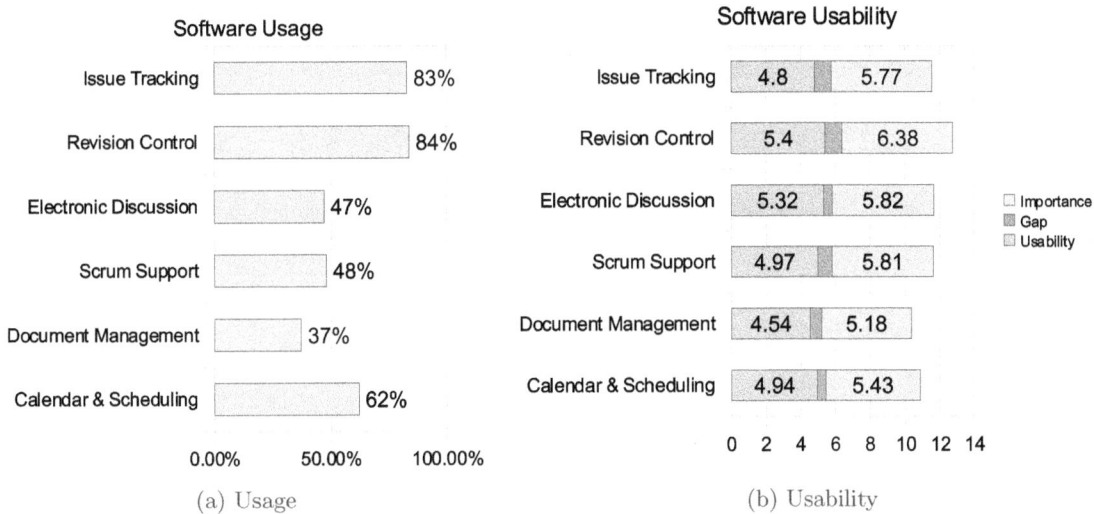

Figure 7: Software usage, perceived usability and believed importance

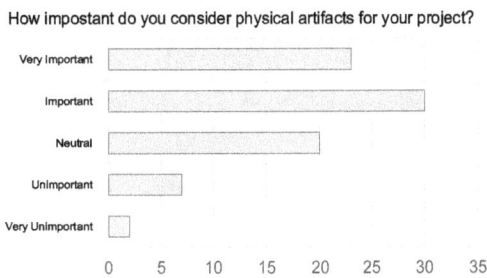

How impostant do you consider physical artifacts for your project?

Very Important	
Important	
Neutral	
Unimportant	
Very Unimportant	

0   5   10   15   20   25   30   35

Figure 6: Perceived importance of physical artifacts

for the respective categories were: (1) issue tracking: *JIRA*, (2) revision control: *Subversion*, (3) electronic discussion: *Skype*, (4) Scrum support: *JIRA and Microsoft Team Foundation Server (Scrum plug-in)*, (5) document management: *Wikis and Google Docs* and (6) calendar & scheduling: *Microsoft Outlook*.

5.1.3   Correlation Analysis

Due to non-normality, we resort to non-parametric tests. Using a Mann-Whitney test on the global sample of 79 participants, we find, not surprisingly, that those who identify as software engineers are significantly younger and have significantly less experience than people in managerial roles such a project leader, director or chief technology officer. The latter group notes that they spend significantly more time on conversations at work and writing documentation. This contrasts with the claim by software engineers that they find that too little documentation is available. However, when we compare software engineers to those in senior technical roles such as architects, we find that this latter group also spends significantly more time writing documentation. So in the teams in our data set, top down dissemination of documentation seems prevalent from the perspective of who writes the documentation.

Interestingly, we find no difference between the answers given by the ScrumMasters and those that identify themselves as 'normal' project leaders. When compared to 'traditional' technical leads, ScrumMasters note that they write significantly less documentation but that they spend significantly more time in conversations. Again, this does not seem to correspond with agile developer's requirements regarding the availability of documentation in their projects.

We find that the more experienced agile team members are, the more efficient they find documentation in their project ($\tau = -0.294$ at $p = 0.018$). A possible explanation could be that developers only learn to understand the importance of documentation as they progress in their careers.

We find that those that spend much time creating documentation are significantly more positive about the amount of documentation available in their jobs ($\tau = 0.555$ at $p = 0$). This could simply mean that these people justify their labor or that this group is simply more aware of the documentation that is available. It might, however, also indicate that this group is given the time to write documentation and are therefore happier. We are unsure whether teams in which these engineers work were more efficient as a result of this, though.

5.2   Team Sample

Data sets consisting of sufficient interrelated team members have been aggregated into team samples and are presented in Tab. 2. Team T1 (UK) provided a back-end software for a major Massive Multiplayer Online (MMO) game publisher. Team T2 (US) developed a collaborative solution to support building design and construction-related tasks for a major American software company. Team T3 (UK) developed software for digital media and mobile platforms concentrating on software development, interaction and visual design. Team T4 (Norway) was employed by a company providing smart card based public key solutions for security transactions, consisting of developers from 2 separate locations running several parallel projects. T5 (The Netherlands) was in charge of corporate websites and web shops. Team T6 (Sweden) developed and maintained a Swedish news guide and community website. Team T7 (India) worked on an e-commerce solution. Team T8 (New Zealand) consisted of a business analyst, a quality assurance specialist and two developers working for a state insurance agency.

Between the teams, the team members agree most on the fact that too little documentation is available. This consistency between dissimilar teams strengthens our earlier finding that agile practitioners find that too little documentation is available.

5.2.1 Documentation

As presented in Tab. 2, the perceptions on the amount of documentation, effectiveness in finding internal documentation and importance of artifacts are accumulated from the data. According to the respective Likert scale, the values are distributed on a scale from "−2" to "+2". A "0" thus corresponds to *"just about right"*, a "+1" to *"slightly too much"* and a "+2" to *"way too much"* while a "−1" and a "−2" correspond to *"slightly too little"* and *"way too little"*, respectively. The value of "1" therefore means that the team perceives documentation as *"slightly too much"*, while the value of "−2" would represent a team perception of documentation as *"way too little"*. Consistently with the global sample Tab. 2 reveals that more than half of the researched teams reported perceived a deficit in the amount of documentation. Note that none of the teams perceive their documentation as *"too much"*.

5.2.2 Supportive Software

We observe that Wiki solutions are prominent within the researched teams: five of the eight groups specifying to use a document management solution name a Wiki system as the tool used. The two Wiki solutions in brackets, mentioned in row "documentation tool" in Tab. 2, mark the two cases where the team ScrumMaster mentioned the particular application used by the team in the open questions. Team members of those same teams, however, did not specify the use of these specific tools. This might imply that these Wiki solutions were introduced but not adapted in practice by the team: *"[W]e have a wiki that we are supposed to use,"* comments the ScrumMaster of Team T6.

After the Wiki, the most commonly used artifact seems to be the "user stories". A user story is the agile equivalent of a use case. The distinction between the Wiki and user stories seems to be fluid, as one ScrumMaster (Team 1) notes, *"Work is documented on the company wiki where required. If it is a small addition then it will be part of a task, but if it is a larger addition then it may have it's own user story."*. Software tracker JIRA[1] was mentioned several times, *"We use JIRA with the Greenhopper plug-in. This provides virtual equivalents to for a wall, User Story cards, burndown,"* says a ScrumMaster (Team 2). Also Team seven was positive about JIRA, *"Jira is our "source of truth". Confluence [A Wiki] is the repository for collaborative documentation. We also required sensible comments in commits. We ran Clover for test coverage, Crucible for collaborative code reviews, CruiseControl for Continuous Integration. Most of the project documentation was divided between the product backlog (in Jira) and shared documents in Confluence,"* noted its ScrumMaster.

Team three makes use of a combination of Google Docs and a whiteboard, *"We have a sprint backlog for each team as a Google docs, editable by the whole team. Our release*

---

[1] http://www.atlassian.com/software/jira/

plan is on a whiteboard, and we have per-client product backlogs for individual products - again, in Google Spreadsheets. [...] Beyond that the main documentation we produce is user experience design docs. I think we're a bit heavyweight here right now but we're working for some clients who demand this stuff for their internal sign-off procedures," according to the ScrumMaster.

Team five works with a combination of an advanced change and configuration management system and post-it notes: *"We have a Story Board with progress using post-its next to the team. I add the burndown-chart there every morning. The team keeps the StoryBoard up to date. For estimating we use Planning Poker (with cards). [...] As the ScrumMaster I don't have a lot of documentation to do. The Product Owner will provide the documentation for the team, creates User Stories for them in Microsoft Team Foundation Server (TFS) and decides the prioritization,"* says the ScrumMaster.

6. DISCUSSION

In this section we discuss our findings in line with our research questions. There seems a natural antipathy of software engineers towards activities not directly linked to the creative process of writing code, many engineers indeed prefer writing code instead of drafting their ideas in text [3]. Agile software development methods concentrate on direct communication emphasizing that comprehensive internal documentation is of no direct use to the end customer [9]. In line with existing concerns [1, 17], however, the findings of this study point out that direct communication alone seems insufficient.

6.1 Documentation Amount and Importance

Agile practitioners in our multinational sample perceive documentation as important for their projects and find there is too little internal documentation available in their projects. Documentation seems neglected by original Scrum literature. It is mentioned but not anchored in the original process [18] which relies heavily on verbal communication. But verbal communication is susceptible to lapses of memory and after some time it get progressively harder to recall design rationale. This problem is compounded by team turnaround. As a member of T6 comments, *"Code comments are used in an effective manner. During project development any needed documentation is generally available. However, finding documentation for older projects is not always easy, and sometimes this documentation is missing."*

The correlation analysis confirms a predominant top-down dissemination in agile settings where practitioners in senior technical roles spend significantly more time on writing documentation. As mentioned in the interviews, product owners usually write requirements and user stories. From there on it is up to the team, it takes care of the implementation and controls what is documented.

Some agile scholars propose documentation to be *"light but sufficient"* [4]. Sufficient, however, it doesn't seem to be, as none of the researched teams noted that they perceive documentation as such. Writing less than 15 minutes (Fig. 2) of documentation daily seems not enough for the produced software and is surely not enough to sustain a co-developed artifact, produced in-line with emerging code. Surprisingly, the vast majority of respondents perceives documentation as important or very important.

Table 2: Descriptive variables, team results (x) and agreement (σ^2)

		T1	T2	T3	T4	T5	T6	T7	T8	avg. agr.
country		UK	US	UK	NO	NL	SE	IN	NZ	
team size (*pers.*)		4	9	5	12	6	4	8	6	
collected answers		4	6	5	6	5	3	8	4	
avg. exp. (*yrs.*)		7.75	13.7	6.6	12.7	2.6	10	7	3.5	
spacial distribution		co-loc.	co-loc.	co-loc.	distrib.	co-loc.	co-loc.	distrib.	co-loc.	
documentation tool		Wiki	Con-fluence Wiki	Google Docs	-	-	Wiki	Con-fluence Wiki	-	
perceived doc. amount	x	-0.25	-0.50	-0.40	-1.30	-1.00	-0.75	-0.13	0	
	σ^2	(0.19)	(0.25)	(1.44)	(0.89)	(0.40)	(0.67)	(0.61)	(0)	(.56)
perceived eff.. finding doc	x	0.65	0.76	0.44	0.60	0.52	0.50	0.75	0.45	
	σ^2	(0.69)	(0.47)	(0.16)	(1.33)	(1.44)	(0.89)	(0.69)	(0.69)	(.80)
perceived importance artif.	x	1.00	0.70	0.76	0.57	0.72	0.75	0.7	0.85	
	σ^2	(0)	(2.25)	(0.16)	(0.47)	(1.04)	(0.67)	(0.50)	(0.69)	(.72)
average agreement	σ^2	(.29)	(.99)	(.59)	(.90)	(.96)	(.74)	(.60)	(.46)	(.69)

6.2 Software, More Than a Backchannel

The teams in our study predominantly adopt collaboration tools to document and share agile artifacts such as user stories or sprint backlogs. An interesting finding is the perceived importance and application of software that directly aim to support Scrum. This is surprising to that extend that one could expect the sufficiency of direct communication and physical artifacts. Convenient handling of agile artifacts and distributed settings seems to be one reason here. *"We have good experience using physical artifacts for local projects, but most of our projects are multi location and require an electronic solution."*, says the ScrumMaster of Team T4.

The perceived usability of solutions for electronic discussion showed the smallest gap among all categories, meaning that the participants find the current solutions very usable. According to comments from team members, the solutions surpass the expectations of a pure *"backchannel"* (Team T3). The growing instant messaging culture seems to make a contribution here and Skype has been the most named tool in this category. A quote from the ScrumMaster of Team T7: *"Communication with the team and our client worked very well when we decided to move away from "voice" conversations (accents, network latencies, time wasted setting up conference phones) to text chats. Even though they can take substantially longer, logs are permanent and we found it easier to share documentation, make decisions and stick to them."*.

7. CONCLUSIONS

In this paper we present the results of an empirical study on documentation in agile Scrum software development teams. Executed in a multidimensional manner we analyze the collected data sets consisting of quantitative team and global samples as well as qualitative interview questions. Our findings stem from a representative data set of agile practitioners and international teams and warrant further study.

One of our main findings is that documentation alone is insufficient. While agile methods recommend to make "lean"

documentation, suggesting that documentation should only include information that is used, we found that agile software development practitioners perceive their internal documentation as important but that they feel that too little documentation is available. Analogously to the observations of Clear [3], we found that documentation is rather seen as a burden than a co-created (core) artifact and found support to the perceptions in literature that without ensuring a proper documentation process agile methods can cause major knowledge loss during or after system development [1,17].

We found that agile teams adopt collaboration tools to share and work on agile artifacts and that Scrum dedicated software is perceived as important and helpful to support the method. We found that instant messaging is perceived as a helpful "backchannel" and supports documenting decisions. We can conclude that integration of software tools into the process is crucial. Lightweight solutions such as Wikis or Google Docs are prominent, their adoption however needs further research (compare Tab. 2).

When interviewing practitioners the authors often found abroad interest for agile methods. Discussing their tools and routines it was the first time developers would address a software development process with passion. This, however, seems not yet true for agile documentation, and future research needs to address an appropriate incorporation within the process to make knowledge transfer truly agile *and* sufficient.

7.1 Validity Considerations

Due to the low amount of data sets containing 79 individuals conclusions were drawn carefully. As we base our evidence on small team data sets, we have improved the transparency of data by adding the variance of given answers among the team members. Throughout the whole process of data collection, we encouraged participants to give realistic answers and emphasized the anonymous treatment of data to establish a reasonable level of trust and to reduce bias. No results other than the processed outcome for the whole team would be distributed or given to their superiors.

While we provided personalized links for each team member to ensure the consistency of input, no personal details were stored or used within the examination. We address the bias of participants towards positively perceived answers (socially desirable responding (SDR) [15]) by anonymous self-administration of questions through a computer, meaning that when the subjects' personal details are not required the person does not feel directly and personally involved in the answers he or she is going to give. This effect is further neutralized through the impersonality of the machine. To validate the perceptions collected via quantitative questionnaire we collected open-ended interview responses from ScrumMasters as proposed by Miles and Huberman [12]. We must be careful to make conclusions regarding the reported time spent documenting as we are unsure what the quality of the resulting documentation was. Furter conclusions can only be drawn when we review the documentation itself.

8. FUTURE WORK

The results of this study point to a number of directions to pursue future research. First, our study in a reality-check manner collects how agile practitioners perceive internal documentation in their projects, further in-depth studies thus are necessary to address the quality of created documentation along with the process and team routines. Second, it has been argued that the lack of architectural focus leads to suboptimal design-decisions [11] in agile methods. UML has been found useful during the design phase but is considered as heavyweight by many practitioners. Further research on incorporation of lightweight modeling methods such as the ICONIX process [16] or the Active Documentation Software Design (ADSD) [17] is recommended. Physical artifacts are widely accepted in the agile community, perhaps there are also possibilities for a more physical extension of UML. Third, previous studies [2] found that Wiki systems have been successfully applied to improve internal documentation efficiency, and have been found widely applied in this study. Further research on the adoption of lightweight documentation systems such as Google Docs or a Wiki is necessary.

9. REFERENCES

[1] P. Abrahamsson, J. Warsta, M. T. Siponen, and J. Ronkainen. New directions on agile methods: a comparative analysis. In *Proceedings of the 25th International Conference on Software Engineering*, ICSE 2003, pages 244–254, Washington, DC, USA, 2003. IEEE Computer Society.

[2] A. Aguiar and G. David. Wikiwiki weaving heterogeneous software artifacts. In *Proceedings of the 2005 international symposium on Wikis*, WikiSym 2005, pages 67–74, New York, NY, USA, 2005. ACM.

[3] T. Clear. Documentation and agile methods: striking a balance. *SIGCSE Bulletin*, 35(2):12–13, 2003.

[4] A. Cockburn and J. Highsmith. Agile software development: The people factor. *Computer*, 34:131–133, November 2001.

[5] S. Dutta and L. N. van Wassenhove. Report on the 1995/1996 software excellence survey. Working Paper 96/52/TM, INSEAD, Boulevard de Constance, 77305 Fontainebleau, France, 1996.

[6] T. Dybå and T. Dingsøyr. Empirical studies of agile software development: A systematic review. *Information Software Technology*, 50(9-10):833–859, 2008.

[7] T. Dybå and N. B. Moe. Rethinking the concept of software process assessment. In *Proceedings of European Software Process Improvement Conference (EuroSPI 1999)*, Pori, Finland, 1999.

[8] A. Forward and T. Lethbridge. The relevance of software documentation, tools and technologies: a survey. In *ACM Symposium on Document Engineering*, pages 26–33, 2002.

[9] J. Highsmith and M. Fowler. The agile manifesto. *Software Development Magazine*, 9(8):29–30, 2001.

[10] T. Lethbridge, J. Singer, and A. Forward. How software engineers use documentation: The state of the practice. *IEEE Software*, 20(6):35–39, 2003.

[11] P. McBreen. *Questioning Extreme Programming*. Addison-Wesley Longman Publishing Co., Inc., Boston, MA, USA, 2002.

[12] M. Miles and A. Huberman. *Qualitative Data Analysis : An Expanded Sourcebook*. Sage, Thousand Oaks, 2. edition, 1994.

[13] A. Mockus and D. M. Weiss. Globalization by chunking: A quantitative approach. *IEEE Software*, 18(2), 2001.

[14] S. Nerur and V. Balijepally. Theoretical reflections on agile development methodologies. *Communications of the ACM*, 50:79–83, March 2007.

[15] D. L. Paulhus. *The role of constructs in psychological and educational measurement*, chapter Socially desirable responding: the evolution of a construct, pages 46–69. Mahwah NJ: Lawrence Erlbaum, 2002.

[16] D. Rosenberg and K. Scott. *Use case driven object modeling with UML: a practical approach*. Addison-Wesley Longman Publishing Co., Inc., Boston, MA, USA, 1999.

[17] E. Rubin and H. Rubin. Supporting agile software development through active documentation. *Requirements Engineering*, 16:117–132, 2011.

[18] K. Schwaber and M. Beedle. *Agile Software Development with Scrum*. Prentice Hall PTR, Upper Saddle River, NJ, USA, 1st edition, 2001.

[19] H. Sharp, H. Robinson, and M. Petre. The role of physical artefacts in agile software development: Two complementary perspectives. *Interacting with Computers*, 21:108–116, January 2009.

[20] A. Sillitti, M. Ceschi, B. Russo, and G. Succi. Managing uncertainty in requirements: A survey in documentation-driven and agile companies. In *Proceedings of the 11th IEEE International Software Metrics Symposium*, Washington, DC, USA, 2005. IEEE Computer Society.

[21] C. J. Stettina and W. Heijstek. Five agile factors: Helping self-management to self-reflect. In *Proceedings of European Software Process Improvement Conference (EuroSPI 2011)*, Roskilde, Denmark, 2011.

Maintaining Islands of Consistency
via Versioned Links

Andrea Kohlhase
Jacobs University Bremen
Campus Ring 1
28759 Bremen, Germany
a.kohlhase@jacobs-university.de

Michael Kohlhase
Jacobs University Bremen
Campus Ring 1
28759 Bremen, Germany
m.kohlhase@jacobs-university.de

ABSTRACT

One of the core tasks of technical communication and knowledge management is maintaining the internal and external consistency of document collections. The design of (technical) communication infrastructures has to take this into account from the start. Consistency of static collections is enforced by format constraints (e.g. specified in a schema and validated grammatically). Recently, consistency in mutable knowledge collections can be supported by change management systems, that draw on specified semantics for knowledge objects and their relations. But even with machine support a seemingly minor change can easily cascade into a major adaptation task. In this paper we argue that the practice of maintaining "islands of consistency" in mutable knowledge collections can be supported by versioned links: Links as first-class elements defined by a triple of versioned elements (subject/predicate/object). The main idea explored here is that changes need not be propagated to linked elements, if those still reference the originally linked object. With this concept a major adaptation task can be put under user-friendly impact management. We give a model for versioned links that is easy to embed in existing systems and show how this concept supports impact management workflows.

Categories and Subject Descriptors

I.2 [**Artificial Intelligence**]: Knowledge Representation Formalisms and Methods

General Terms

Documentation, Theory, Management

Keywords

Change Management, Consistency Management, Knowledge Management, Links, References

1. INTRODUCTION

The generally accepted model for knowledge management (KM) assumes that explicit knowledge is represented in some form of document collections, which we will call **knowledge base**s. These knowledge bases range from a project's collection of documents in various formats as used in [13], over semantic DITA [5] files, to organizational wikis as suggested in [19]. It is an implicit assumption that each knowledge base $\mathcal{K}$ is **consistent**, i.e., satisfies validity conditions of the representation format and additional semantic conditions. In particular, knowledge in $\mathcal{K}$ may not lead to contradictions. In a semantic format like DITA some of the integrity conditions involved in determining consistency may be expressed in $\mathcal{K}$ in the form of links between document fragments. In contrast, a knowledge base $\mathcal{K}$ is a **correct** description of a situation $\mathcal{S}$, iff all statements that can be derived from $\mathcal{K}$ hold in $\mathcal{S}$. The consistency assumption for $\mathcal{K}$ is largely independent of the notion of correctness, since it cannot be defined as a property of $\mathcal{K}$ alone. Clearly, correctness is a very strong desideratum for a knowledge base, but consistency is a precondition, since inconsistencies in $\mathcal{K}$ render the very notion of correctness and must therefore be maintained at all times.

However, knowledge management processes naturally involve changes — either because the situation $\mathcal{S}$ changes or to improve correctness and/or completeness. Changes can range from addition of new material, over correction of errors and refactoring of concepts, to formalization, and deletions (see e.g. [11]). In the presence of the validity and semantic constraints mentioned above, even small changes may induce the necessity to adapt other (related) knowledge items (possibly in other documents) to restore consistency. This process can cascade a seemingly minor change into a major adaptation task. As a consequence the KM community has developed elaborate mechanisms for "change management" to maintain consistency. These make use of the fact that semantic formats often explicitly represent the relations between objects to compute related objects and predict the way changes affect them; see [12, 15, 3] for recent progress in this field.

But even with such systems in place, establishing consistency after each change in the collection remains a daunting prospect, which we will elaborate on in Sect. 2. To enable the conservation of consistency within typical workflows nevertheless, we explore in this paper the new concept of 'versioned links' (introduced and discussed in Sect. 3). We assume that document collections are stored in a revision control system as a concession to change, inducing a notion of 'versioned object'. Next we elevate the relations between versioned objects to first-class citizens and obtain versioned links as triples (`subject/predicate/object`) in Sect. 3. Naturally, they are versioned as well, so that links and their components carry an independent revision number. The main idea explored in this paper is that changes *need not* be propagated to linked objects, but can continue to reference the originally linked object. Moreover, in Sect. 4 we argue along a DITA use case that versioned links are closer to current authoring practices with "islands of consistency" that allow for a more flexible change management in actual workflows. Sect. 5 concludes the paper.

2. CHANGE MANAGEMENT AND CONSISTENCY

Change management (CM) comprises all the knowledge management tasks that are concerned with the consequences of modifications, particularly with respect to the consistency of the underlying knowledge base. For the purposes of this paper we assume that it is organized in three recursively applicable (and possibly empty) phases:

Change Impact Analysis (CIA) For a given change of an artifact A, a change impact analysis draws on dependency information for artifacts and results in a set of affected items. A CIA may be used for multiple purposes. For example, it can be consulted in order to assess the acceptability of a change by predicting the size of its impact (e.g. with a change propagation index as in [8]). This becomes relevant e.g. in software production or migration. Other purposes consist in acting on found impacts via impact management processes.

Automatic Impact Management builds on propagation rules and change patterns afforded by the underlying ontology and can be automatically executed by the system. Note that distinct underlying ontologies supply different relationships between objects and thus distinct notions of dependency.

Manual Impact Management Here, the user decides for each potentially affected object found by the CIA whether they need to be modified or not. This process needs to be supported by the system and user interfaces to be feasible in practice, e.g. with services that present the relationships leading to this point as in [6].

Typically, a change management process performs a CIA for an artifact first, then an automatic and thereafter manual impact management are applied iteratively on the CIA data (see for example [9, 175ff.]). Note that links are made heavy use of, but it is not clear what happens if a link itself was changed: Is the CIA based on the old or the new link or even both links? We see directly that change management for links as versioned objects is not sufficient, they rather need to be treated as first-class objects. The process by which a change of an artifact yields sequential changes (as well as its product) is often called **propagation of change** in the literature (e.g. [9, 8, 3]).

To get a feeling for the consistency issues involved consider a document collection $\mathcal{K}$ of DITA files, which formalize the scenario "Getting Ready for the Day" as in Fig. 1. In particular, there are concepts `coffeeMachine`, and `coffee`, which are used in a task `morningProcedure`, that describes the suggested procedure for getting ready for the day.

In Fig. 2 we consider three changes with distinct propagation consequences:

- **"id" changed:** Here, we consider the case where an author of $\mathcal{K}$ changed the value of the `id` attribute of the concept `coffeeMachine` e.g. to "coffeeMaker". Then the change results via an automatic impact management in automatic updates from all references to `coffeeMachine` to `coffeeMaker`. This process of **automatic propagation** yields a consistent document collection.

- **"link" changed:** Now, let us look at the consequences if the related `link` (in the concept `coffeeMachine`) to the Wikipedia entry for "Coffeemaker" `http://en.wikipedia.org/wiki/Coffeemaker` is changed to "Coffeepreparation". The automatic impact management can determine that changes in `related-links` do not have consequences for tasks using the changed concept, but it cannot decide automatically whether the corresponding `linktext` element needs to be updated or not. Here, we speak of **semi-automatic propagation**, which leaves $\mathcal{K}$ in a possibly inconsistent state.

- **"xref" changed:** Finally, we envision a modification of the reference to the concept `coffee` within the concept `coffeeMachine` to a concept `decaf`. This means that the coffee machine is modified into a decaf machine, which might have consequences for the task `morningProcedure`. Moreover, the informal descriptions within `conbody` might also need to be adapted. Here, the author herself has to decide on necessary updates, that is a **manual propagation** of change is asked for. As the state of $\mathcal{K}$ is unclear, it may or it may not be consistent.

Note that impact management can easily become more and more complex as new change events are triggered by propagated changes. In general, there are the following concerns about change management of collections:

- Most changes are rather informal (i.e., concerning informal text "tweaking a bit here and there") and must be treated manually (automation would be an AI-hard problem). As a consequence the triggered (manual) impact management cascade can easily outgrow the user's cognitive limits: Giffin et al. reported for example a maximum of 2579 linked changes [8, p. 16] in a Software Engineering study over an 8-year course. Fortunately though, they found *"the majority [. . . to be . . .] comprised of less than 10 changes"*.

- Even in formal systems rules for automatic modification after certain types of change are hard to conceive.

- Automatic impact management might be explicitly objectionable in many workflows; for instance, in cooperative mathematical processes different (e.g. evolving) assumptions in theorems occur frequently and have distinct consequences. Thus a global consistency may be cumbersome and even harmful in the creative process. An author might willingly commit an inconsistent document collection, as long as the document in question or some part of it stays consistent, and global consistency can be achieved for publication.

- Storage with version management alone does not make consistency management tractable if commit policies assume semantic validity requirements. In [13] for example we resorted to a relaxed formalization tool to

```
HotDrinks.dita
<concept id="coffee"><title>coffee</title>
    <shortdesc>A hot drink based on brewing coffee beans</shortdesc>
</concept>
<concept id="coffeeMachine">
    <conbody> A coffee machine produces <xref href="#coffee">coffee</xref>.</conbody>
    <related-links>
        <link format="html" href="http://en.wikipedia.org/wiki/Coffeemaker" scope="external">
            <linktext>Coffeemaker</linktext>
        </link>
    </related-links>
</concept>

morning.ditamap:
<map>
    <topicref keys="HotDrinks" href="HotDrinks.dita/>
    <keydef keys="coffee-machine" href="HotDrinks#coffeeMachine"/>
    <keydef keys="coffee" href="HotDrinks#coffee"/>
    <topicref href="morningProcedure.dita" type="task"/>
</map>

morningProcedure.dita:
<task id="morningProcedure">
    <title>Get ready for the day</title>
    <taskbody>
    <prereq>Alarm is on and you wake up.</prereq>
    <steps>
        <step><cmd>Set alarm off.</cmd></step>
        <step><cmd>Get out of bed.</cmd></step>
        <step><cmd>Start <keyword keyref="coffee-machine"/>.</cmd></step>
        <step><cmd>Take shower.</cmd></step>
        <step><cmd>Enjoy the sniff of <term keyref="coffee">coffee</term>.</cmd></step>
        <step><cmd>Enjoy the cup of <conref href="HotDrinks#coffee"/>.</cmd></step>
```

Figure 1: Our CIA Scenario in DITA Format: "Getting ready for the day"

overcome consistency requirements in early development phases.

This leaves us with the questions where consistency management has its rightful place in collection workflows, and what a sensible scope of it would be. We recommend that this should be left to the user; the next section provides us with the necessary tools.

3. CHANGE MANAGEMENT WITH VERSIONED LINKS

We have seen that inconsistency issues often arise because changes in one place in a knowledge base $\mathcal{K}$ affect linked objects in other places, which if adapted to the original change trigger affects at yet another set of linked objects in yet other places in $\mathcal{K}$ and so on. The idea for improved handling of changes is that changes need not be propagated to linked objects if the original link itself continues to exist. Instead of resolving links late, i.e., resolving links according to current objects, one can resolve links early, i.e., resolving links according to the objects one started out with.

Termed this way, one can see easily that the technique of "late binding" (also called dynamic/name binding) in programming languages in Software Engineering, where the method being called upon an object is looked up by its name at runtime, is used in a similar situation. Indeed, it comes with similar problems of inconsistencies, which often lead directly to compiler errors. There, late binding problems are treated e.g. by links to versioned packages. Packages are collections of inter-related files intended for re-use in other packages, their internal references are kept in sync. When a new version of a package is released, dependent packages may be ported to it. In the packages approach links are treated as package metadata and deployment problems are mitigated by specialized package management systems building on this metadata. The introduction of versioned links to a document collection $\mathcal{K}$ can be seen as a carry-over of a late-binding-problem solution developed in Software Engineering extended by a finer granularity.

Concretely, we suggest to make use of two facts: *i)* Revision control systems (RCS) give access to old revisions, in particular, access to objects in old revisions to which other objects are consistently linked.[1] *ii)* The advent of versioned query interfaces like [21, 7] enable access to versioned objects. In particular, the (platonic) concept of "the" object with identifier $\mathcal{O}$ is refined to the set of (concrete) objects $\mathcal{O}$ with distinct revision numbers, therefore links can point to such versioned objects.

To make the discussion more precise, we will now define the concepts involved more formally, starting out with a simplified version of the notion of *fs*-trees and version control systems developed in [15], which we will review now.

3.1 *fs*-Trees and RCS Repositories

We will use *fs*-trees as a unifying notion of file system trees and semi-structured (XML) documents that abstracts from particular file system implementations and encodings.

In a nutshell, an *fs*-**tree** is an ordered, typed, labeled tree, whose edges are labeled with (directory/element) names and its leaves with strings (which either correspond to text files

---

[1]In this paper we assume a concept of global revisions as employed e.g. in the Subversion system [17]. There, any commit to the repository increments the revision number.

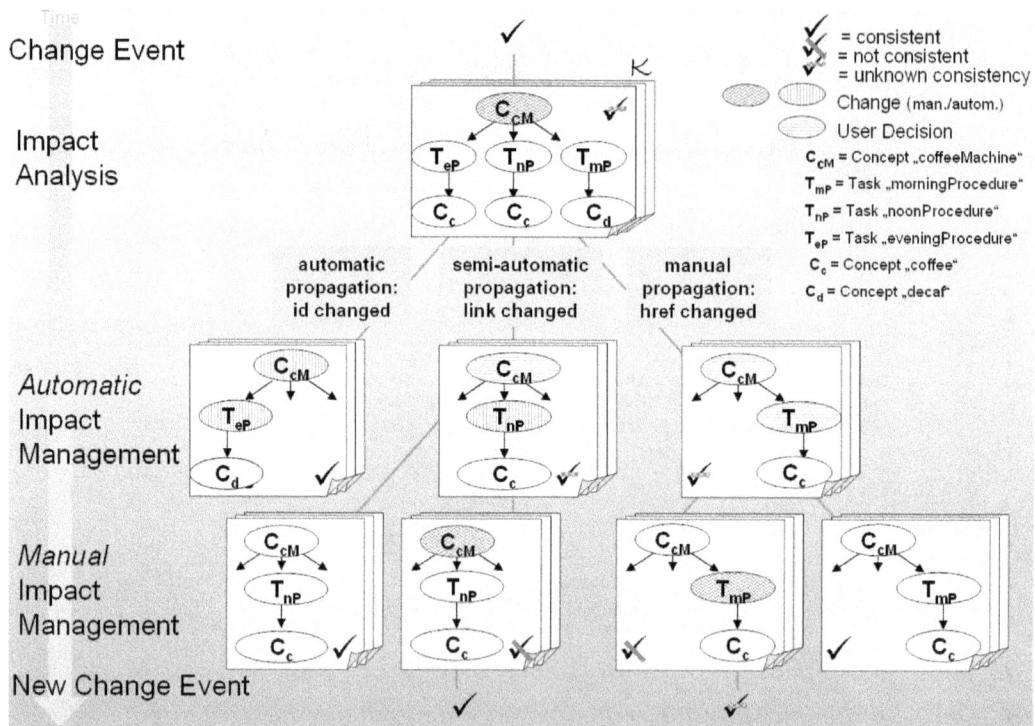

Figure 2: Change Management and Consistency

or text nodes in XML)[2]. The node types distinguish nodes into directories, files, XML elements, and XML attributes, and carry constraints that make them faithful models of file systems and XML files.

The main property we will use in this paper is that any node/subtree in an *fs*-tree $\mathcal{T}$ can be addressed by a unique **name path**, i.e., a sequence $\pi = a_1/\cdots/a_k$ of names a_i. We write $\mathcal{T}/\pi$ for the *fs*-subtree of $\mathcal{T}$ rooted at π. Note that for a given *fs*-tree $\mathcal{T}$, a subtree $\mathcal{T}/\pi$ is either a directory, a file, or an XML fragment/subtree. Note furthermore, that name paths in *fs*-trees directly map to (file) URIs with XPath fragment identifiers. Thus any name path π is of the form δ/ρ, where δ is a **directory path** (i.e., a name path where all names are directory names) and ρ is a **fragment identifier** (i.e., a name path, where all names are XML element names).

If we denote the set of all *fs*-trees by $\mathcal{FS}$, we can represent a version control **repository** as a partial function $\mathcal{R} \colon \mathbb{N} \rightharpoonup \mathcal{FS}$ that maps **revision identifiers** (without loss of generality an initial segment of $\mathbb{N}$) to *fs*-trees. For a repository $\mathcal{R}$ and $n \in dom(\mathcal{R})$, where $dom(\mathcal{R})$ is the domain of $\mathcal{R}$, we call the *fs*-tree $\mathcal{R}(n)$ the **revision** n of $\mathcal{R}$; this notion extends to *fs*-subtrees: We say that a subtree of $\mathcal{R}(n)$ is **at revision** n. Finally, we say that $\mathcal{D}$ is a **document in** $\mathcal{R}$, if $\mathcal{D} = \mathcal{R}(n)/\delta$ for some directory path δ and revision n.

Given this vocabulary, the correspondence to knowledge management in the large can be seen as in Fig. 3. We employ repositories to model the development of document collections over time, where the collection $\mathcal{K}$ at a concrete time point corresponds to a revision $\mathcal{R}(n)$ of the repository $\mathcal{R}$,

and document collections, documents, and objects are realized as *fs*-tree fragments (subtrees of the revision) $\mathcal{R}(n)/\pi$. From now on we will use the concepts in Fig. 3 modulo the correspondence relation given by the dotted lines.

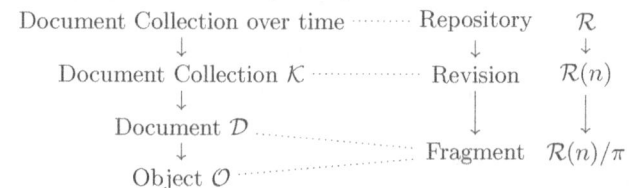

$$
\begin{array}{ccc}
\text{Document Collection over time} \cdots\cdots & \text{Repository} & \mathcal{R} \\
\downarrow & \downarrow & \downarrow \\
\text{Document Collection } \mathcal{K} \cdots\cdots\cdots\cdots & \text{Revision} & \mathcal{R}(n) \\
\downarrow & \downarrow & \downarrow \\
\text{Document } \mathcal{D} \cdots\cdots\cdots\cdots\cdots\cdots & & \\
\downarrow & & \text{Fragment} \quad \mathcal{R}(n)/\pi \\
\text{Object } \mathcal{O} \cdots\cdots\cdots\cdots\cdots &
\end{array}
$$

Figure 3: A Realization of Document Collections over Time

3.2 Versioned Links

Before we can define the concept "versioned link", we need to think about the status of links in semantic representation formats.

Definition 1 Let $\mathcal{T}$ be an *fs*-tree, then we define an (unversioned) **link in** $\mathcal{T}$ to be an RDF triple (see [14]) where subject, predicate, and object are name paths in $\mathcal{T}$. We distinguish **intra-document links**, where subject and object are in the same document, from **inter-document links** where they are not.

For the time being we will disregard links outside of a document collection $\mathcal{K} = \mathcal{R}(n)$ for some n; as all practical revision control systems encode file paths as URIs, our notion of links is a special case of RDF triples, if we assume that the predicates are documented in the collection, which we can without loss of generality.

---

[2]The original *fs*-trees had the notion of symbolic links and repository externals which we do not need here.

The set of links induced by a document collection $\mathcal{K}$ is determined by the representation format of the documents in $\mathcal{K}$. Instead of making this formal, we will appeal to the intuition of the reader by giving some examples:

i) `conref` links in DITA files induce document links for a predicate "input", which tells the formatting engine to replace the value of its `href` attribute (which resolves into a URI to a specific DITA object) with the title of its `object`.

ii) Similarly, `\input` statements in TeX/LaTeX induce document links for the predicate "input", which tells the formatting engine to replace `\input{⟨⟨fileURI⟩⟩}` with a file referenced by ⟨⟨fileURI⟩⟩.

iii) `<a href=''⟨⟨URI⟩⟩''⟨⟨attribs⟩⟩>⟨⟨label⟩⟩</a>` in HTML induces a link for the predicate "display", which tells the browser to display the fragment referenced by ⟨⟨URI⟩⟩ in the browser when the user left-clicks ⟨⟨label⟩⟩ (details specified by ⟨⟨attribs⟩⟩).

Note that all of these links rely on name paths in $\mathcal{K}$ (realized as URIs) for identification of resources (nodes in $\mathcal{K}$). Note furthermore, that all of these induce links whose predicate is pre-determined by the document format, i.e., given by the special syntax and induces a URI referencing a relation from the document ontology and whose subject is the resource containing the syntax that induces the link. We will call such link-inducing syntax in a format $\mathcal{F}$ an $\mathcal{F}$-**reference**. Even though $\mathcal{F}$-references dominate in semantic formats, we will also cover proper links represented in any RDF representation format; they sometimes exist as standoff markup in KM systems.

Let $\mathcal{R}$ be a repository, $n \in dom(\mathcal{R})$ a revision identifier, and $\pi \in \mathcal{R}(n)$ a name path, then we call a pair $\langle \pi, n \rangle$ a **versioned name path** in $\mathcal{R}$. Note that $\langle \pi, n \rangle$ identifies a resource in a repository $\mathcal{R}$. Building on this, we can finally define the concept of a versioned link.

Definition 2 For a given repository $\mathcal{R}$ we call an RDF triple a **versioned link in** $\mathcal{R}$, iff its subject, predicate, and object are versioned name paths in $\mathcal{R}$. **Versioned** $\mathcal{F}$-**references** are defined accordingly. We distinguish versioned links into **inter-revision** links/references, iff they involve at least two different revisions, and **intra-revision** links/references otherwise.

The purpose of versioned links and references is to avoid situations, where the *meaning* or *functionality* of an object changes unintentionally due to a change in an object it references; e.g. a mathematical theorem may be invalidated, if the definition of a concept it uses is changed. Intuitively, a versioned link to the definition insulates the theorem against the change.

Note that versioned links generally involve four revisions: The revisions of the subject, predicate, and object as well as the revision of the link itself (e.g. given by the revision of the file that contains the representation of the RDF triple). For versioned $\mathcal{F}$-references this revision variety is restricted by their special syntactic structure. In particular, the revisions of subject and link are necessarily identical, and the revision of the predicate is given by the format $\mathcal{F}$, it is therefore uniform over the document. Note that this observation has an implication on the design of document formats: If we want to escape the version identifications of links, we need to use standoff links.

Versioning systems usually reserve a special, intensional "revision identifier" for the respective youngest revision (cal-

led the **head revision** and denoted with ↑). Therefore, we define a versioned name path as **head path**, iff it is of the form $\langle \pi, \uparrow \rangle$ for some name path π. To formally differentiate between versioned and unversioned links, we call a versioned link a **head link**, iff all of its three versioned name paths are head paths.

Wikipedia, for example, uses an underlying versioning system. It strongly advises using versioned references for citing articles (see [20]), on the other hand all links between articles are head links. To understand the advantages and disadvantages of using versioned links, we discuss and exemplify workflows with and without versioned links in the next section.

4. ISLANDS OF CONSISTENCY WITH VERSIONED LINKS

Consider the following situation: Author Mike of the "Getting Ready for the Day" DITA scenario (Fig. 1) wants to update `morningProcedure.dita` to reflect his personal habit change from brewing only real coffee in the morning to also brewing decaf for his girl-friend. He realizes that the concepts in file `HotDrinks.dita` do not yet distinguish between coffee and decaf. He modifies the concept `coffee` to include only 'real' coffee and adds a concept `coffee-generic` to hither relink all present `coffee` references (see Fig. 4 in the propagation phase). The transformation of concerned links into versioned links means, that these links are frozen to point at the object versioned last. Without the use of versioned links, the whole set-up is now inconsistent as the relinking changes are not yet propagated to `morningProcedure.dita`. Note that consistency restraints (with respect to reality reflection wrt. Mike's changed habit) were fulfilled before the refinement. If Mike were in a hurry now and if he thus checked the file into a version management system, then this inconsistency were manifested which might yield consequences for collaborators. But let's say, Mike still has time to follow up on consequential changes.

The change impact analysis (if present and enabled) returns a list of potential conflict locations. In this small example the CIA already contains the concept `coffeeMachine` in `HotDrinks.dita`, the `keydef` element `coffee` in `morning.ditamap`, and a `conref` element in `morningProcedure.dita`. For use of DITA Priestley suggests to "*factor out any context-specific elements*" [18], which is practically done by using a DITA map for defining `keydef` and the (`keys`/`href` attributes in the) `topicref` elements to contain context-specific information and to reference hither from everywhere else. To achieve broadest possible consistency Mike thus starts propagating the change with modifying the `keydef` element in `morning.ditamap`. Note that he probably oversees that `term` elements are only interpretation help for a locally set string (here: "coffee") and therefore need further attention to keep consistency. If this new change triggers a new CIA yielding a list of all parents of affected `term` nodes, then transforming them into versioned links would allow Mike to work the remnant propagation requirements first. Again, without versioned links Mike has to hope that he can finish the entire propagation before check-in into the version management system, otherwise he starts to manifest rather complex (i.e., more and more dependent and interrelated) consistency issues. We also like to point out, that without versioned links the original CIA needs to include all potential subsequent changes as it is supposed to show the

```
HotDrinks.dita
<concept id="coffee"><title>real coffee</title>
    <shortdesc>A caffeinated, hot drink based on brewing coffee beans</shortdesc>
</concept>
<concept id="decaf"/>
<concept id="coffee-generic"><title>coffee</title></concept>
<concept id="coffeeMachine">
    <conbody> A coffee machine produces <xref href="#coffee">coffee</xref></conbody> ...
</concept>
<concept id="decafMachine">
    <conbody> A decaf machine produces <xref href="#decaf">coffee</xref></conbody>
</concept>

morning.ditamap:
<map>
    <topicref keys="HotDrinks" href="HotDrinks.dita/>
    <keydef keys="coffee-machine" href="HotDrinks#coffeeMachine"/>
    <keydef keys="coffee" href="HotDrinks#coffee-generic"/>
    <topicref href="morningProcedure.dita" type="task"/>
</map>

morningProcedure.dita:
<task id="morningProcedure">
    <title>Get ready for the day</title>
    <taskbody>
    <prereq>Alarm is on and you wake up.</prereq>
    <steps>
        <step><cmd>Start <keyword keyref="coffee-machine"/>.</cmd></step>
        <step><cmd>Enjoy the sniff of <term keyref="coffee">coffee</term>.</cmd></step>
        <step><cmd>Enjoy the cup of <conref href="HotDrinks#coffee-generic"/>.</cmd></step>
```

Figure 4: Our CIA Scenario 1 with Propagation of Change (marked grey)

impact of a change. Therefore, the use of versioned links reduces the overall-complexity of changes to a step-by-step complexity. This propagation would have been easier for Mike, if he had consistently used `conref` elements for referencing as the resp. string is generated from the title of the link target. Here, he will realize only after controlling all the items found by the second CIA, that no further change is needed. Generally, we envision that using CIA as a tool will drastically change DITA best practices.

Before Mike started the whole process, he talked about his plans to Andi by which Andi was motivated to create her own `morningProcedureAndi`. As the communicated idea was to refine the old generic concept `coffee` to a new specific concept `coffee` and otherwise to relink `coffee` references to `coffee-generic` ones, she assumed the concept `coffeeMachine` to become generic as well. Therefore, in order to write her own task, she added the concept `decaf` to `HotDrinks.dita` and copied and modified the original task `morningProcedure` accordingly into `morningProcedureAndi`. Unfortunately, Mike thought it obvious that with the refinement of `coffee` comes along the refinement of `coffeeMachine`. If he has not transformed the links of his first CIA into versioned links (updating *her* task document by that), this misunderstanding now hinders collaboration on the document collection as the concept `coffeeMachine` is used inconsistently in Andi's task. Unfortunately, if Andi is authoring her reference after he refined `coffee`, then the misconception might live on anyway.

To sum up, versioned links allow new, much more flexible workflows. In particular, the complex recursive propagation of change becomes time- and order-independent.

4.1 Islands of Consistency

This example exhibits many typical aspects commonly found in the human, informal development and change process of technical documents. Conceptually, we can divide this into two phases:

- **Knowledge Exploration** In this phase knowledge items are created, In particular, concepts are formed and put down in definitions, conjectures about the concepts are proven, and local narrative structures that motivate and connect all of these are established. Note that the consistency of inter- and intra-document links is not the foremost concern here.

- **Codification** Published knowledge, however, certainly should aim for consistency. The exploration phase thus is followed by a codification phase, when the practice of reorganizing knowledge in documents to streamline the elegance and beauty of arguments happens. In particular, in the codification phase documents are brought into the form of a coherent document (collection) addressed at a particular audience.

Actually, in real life, document development and change usually proceed in multiple phases, interleaving the exploration and codification phases, gradually shifting emphasis from the former to the latter, and from local codification to global coherence concerns, but the conceptual division of these two phases remains useful. Even in the knowledge exploration phase, a (possibly temporary) document form is usually chosen to write down the knowledge items. Note that in these "development documents", global consistency is usually not a primary concern in the early exploration-heavy stages, since this is deferred to the codification phase. In the middle phase of the document development and modification process, when concepts, definitions, and links start stabilizing and attention shifts to detail and codification, we observe that authors start establishing document fragments that are internally consistent, but may be inconsistent with other parts of the document collection under development. We call such document fragments **islands of consistency** and observe that much of the codification proceeds by enlarging these islands and merging them until a globally consistent document (collection) is reached.

We claim that humans implicitly use versioned links in the development and change of technical documents, since they *allow* us to organize consistency in mutable document collections by fixing revisions and thus insulating against the effects of changes in linked objects. In our elaboration of the "Getting Ready for the Day" scenario, this was also evidential. Explicit versioned links (as presented in Sect. 3) enable the process of maintaining and developing islands of consistency without time or order constraints. Additionally, Haramundanis reports a new modularization paradigm for the information engineer in [10]. This means in particular, that the amount of links is dramatically rising and with it the number of potential inconsistency issues. The underlying reason for this modularization is a growing need for collaboration on document collections. We have outlined in our use case how islands of consistency come in here especially handy.

But maintaing islands of consistency has hidden costs: It introduces inter-revision links – which finally have to disappear – in a document collection and thus weakens its coherence.[3] Therefore, in a sense all what the introduction of versioned links does is that it allows to move parts of the problem of *consistency management* in the exploration phase into one of *coherence management* in the codification phase. In this respect versioned links are closer to current scientific publication behavior where we almost only reference archival papers which never change. In particular, new versions of publications are considered as distinct entities with different "URIs"[4].

5. CONCLUSION

We have presented the concept and practices of using versioned links as a tool for managing change in document collections including knowledge repositories, particularly as a tool for maintaining "islands of consistency". Essentially the introduction of versioned links allows to move parts of the problem of consistency management in the exploration phase into one of coherence management in the codification phase. However, we contend that this allows for much more flexible and natural workflows, and is thus well worth the (minimal) effort in extending the representation formats to versioned links.

We loosely built our discussion on the model of a *centralized RCS* like Subversion. At first glance, one may be tempted to think that *distributed RCS* (**DRCS**) like Git or Mercurial already support the "islands of consistency" practices versioned links are designed for (to get an overview of their differences see e.g. [16]). Indeed, one can see and use each local repository in a distributed network as such an island, and the practice of pulling changes from local

---

[3]We could define/measure the "revision coherence" of a document collection as the number of intra-revision links.

[4]In situations, where this practice is lax (e.g. in editions of books), this has been known to lead to problems, see [4] for an example, where the loci of branch cuts in definitions of special functions vary between editions of [1].

repositories as a coherence management process. But note that this approach only supports the equivalent of *file-level versioned links* and is therefore too course-granular for technical knowledge which requires *object-level links*. Incidentally, programming languages mainly support file-level links, so DRCS fit the versioned packages development model in Software Engineering. We conjecture that in this case, a repository network is essentially isomorphic to a flattened repository with versioned links. It seems possible to mimic versioned links in DRCS, if we are willing to break apart documents into object-size files using an inclusion technique like XInclude, but this seems a larger intervention than the introduction of versioned links we propose. We used the centralized model in this paper, since we have the TNTBase system [21], that offers efficient access to versioned XML objects, given a similar XML-fragment-access-enabled DRCS, studying the interaction of versioned links with distribution will probably lead to even more natural workflows.

In this paper we have defined the concepts and looked into the workflows afforded by versioned links. The eventual practicability of the extension will of course only become apparent when versioned links are supported in editing and knowledge management environments. For instance, editors could have a configuration option that allows to specify the default behavior when no revision is given, that is either we assume head revision or the current revision. Similarly, the underlying revision control system could be extended to automatically introduce versioned links; Consider a situation, where an object b is referenced by an object c. In this case, the RCS can change the head link in c to a versioned link to b at the last revision before the change. It is easy to see that versioning all such references to b conserves consistency. This behavior is essential in multi-author situations, for example, if the author of b does not have write access to c and only its authors can propagate the changes to upgrade the reference on c to b to a head link again. So in this case, the RCS would probably notify the authors of c of a coherence enhancement opportunity. For the codification phase we wish for a coherence management module in editors. It could step through inter-revision links and jointly present difference-marked up versions of `subject`, `predicate`, or `object`, for instance. Then it might offer the author the choice between upgrading the link revision or copying the object. For collective authoring situations in larger document collections we could imagine a notification system for revision updates.

6. REFERENCES

[1] M. Abramowitz and I. A. Stegun, editors. *Handbook of Mathematical Functions (with Formulas, Graphs, and Mathematical Tables)*. Applied Mathematics Series. National Bureau of Standards, 1964.

[2] ACM Special Interest Group for Design of Communication. *Proceedings of the 28th ACM International Conference on Design of Communication*, SIGDOC '10, New York, NY, USA, 2010. ACM Press.

[3] S. Autexier and N. Müller. Semantics-based change impact analysis for heterogeneous collections of documents. In M. Gormish and R. Ingold, editors, *Proceedings of the 10th ACM symposium on Document engineering*, DocEng '10, pages 97–106, New York, NY, USA, 2010. ACM.

[4] R. Corless, J. Davenport, D. Jeffrey, and S. Watt. According to Abramowitz and Stegun. *SIGSAM Bulletin 2*, 34:58–65, 2000.

[5] OASIS Darwin Information Typing Architecture (DITA).

[6] DocTIP.

[7] G. Fourny, D. Florescu, and D. Kossmann. A time machine for XML. Technical report, ETH Zürich, Switzerland, 2011. available at `http://www.dbis.ethz.ch/research/publications/timemachinexml.pdf`.

[8] M. Giffin, O. de Weck, G. Bounova, R. Keller, C. Eckert, and P. J. Clarkson. Change propagation analysis in complex technical systems. *Journal of Mechanical Design*, 131(8):081001, 2009.

[9] J. Han. Supporting impact analysis and change propagation in software engineering environments. In *Proceedings of the Eighth IEEE International Workshop on Software Technology and Engineering Practice*, pages 172–182. IEEE Computer Society, 1996.

[10] K. Haramundanis. Experience report: modularization - the new paradigm for the information engineer. In B. Mehlenbacher, A. Protopsaltis, A. Williams, and S. Slatterey, editors, *Proceedings of the 27th annual ACM international conference on Design of communication (SIGDOC)*, pages 151–154, New York, NY, USA, 2009. ACM Special Interest Group for Design of Communication, ACM Press.

[11] K. Haramundanis. Modularizing in glossaries: an experience report. In *Proceedings of the 28th ACM International Conference on Design of Communication* [2], pages 131–134.

[12] D. Hutter. Semantic management of heterogeneous documents (invited talk). In *Proceedings of the Mexican International Conference on Artificial Intelligence (MICAI-2009)*, number 5845 in LNAI, pages 1–14. Springer, 2009.

[13] A. Kohlhase, M. Kohlhase, and C. Lange. sTeX – a system for flexible formalization of linked data. In A. Paschke, N. Henze, T. Pellegrini, and H. Weigand, editors, *Proceedings of the 6th International Conference on Semantic Systems (I-Semantics) and the 5th International Conference on Pragmatic Web*. ACM, 2010.

[14] F. Manola and E. Miller. RDF Primer. W3C Recommendation, World Wide Web Consortium (W3C), Feb. 2004.

[15] N. Müller. *Change Management on Semi-Structured Documents*. PhD thesis, Jacobs University Bremen, 2010.

[16] B. O'Sullivan. Making sense of revision-control systems. *Communications of the Association for Computing Machinery (CACM)*, 52(9):57–62, 2009.

[17] C. M. Pilato, B. Collins-Sussman, and B. W. Fitzpatrick. *Version Control With Subversion*. O'Reilly & Associates, Inc., Sebastopol, CA, USA, 2 edition, 2008.

[18] M. Priestley. Scenario-based and model-driven information development with xml dita. In *SIGDOC '03: Proceedings of the 21st annual international conference on Documentation*, pages 45–51, New York, NY, USA, 2003. ACM.

[19] F. Sousa, M. Aparicio, and C. J. Costa. Organizational wiki as a knowledge management tool. In *Proceedings of the 28th ACM International Conference on Design of Communication* [2], pages 33–39.

[20] Wikipedia. Citing wikipedia — Wikipedia, the free encyclopedia, 2011. [Online; accessed 05-Jan-2011].

[21] V. Zholudev and M. Kohlhase. TNTBase: a versioned storage for XML. In *Proceedings of Balisage: The Markup Conference 2009*, Balisage Series on Markup Technologies. Mulberry Technologies, Inc., 2009. available at `http://kwarc.info/vzholudev/pubs/balisage.pdf`.

Lost in Transition:
Issues in Designing Crossmedia Applications and Services

Gert Pasman
Faculty of Industrial Design Engineering
Delft University of Technology
Landbergstraat 15, 2628 CE Delft, The Netherlands
g.j.pasman@tudelft.nl

ABSTRACT

Crossmedia communication, in which content is spread over multiple platforms and the user is required to cross over from one medium to another to acquire the full experience, has until now been mainly the domain of the marketing, game and entertainment industry. However, now that more and more 'serious' applications and services, such as online banking or multichannel shopping, are becoming distributed through multiple platforms as well as used at various times and locations, its specific characteristics are becoming increasingly relevant for other design domains as well. This paper will reflect on the process of designing crossmedia applications and services by describing experiences from teaching a course in crossmedia interaction design to industrial design students. It is argued that, in order to create seamless, interactive experiences, real crossmedia design should go beyond a pragmatic mix of the principles and characteristics of the design disciplines that constitute the individual platforms.

Categories and Subject Descriptors

H.5.2 [**Information Interfaces and Presentation**]: User Interfaces – *Graphical User Interfaces (GUI), Theory and methods, user-centered design.*

General Terms

Design

Keywords

Crossmedia design, service design, crossmedia applications.

1. Introduction

In recent years the media landscape has rapidly been transformed into an increasingly complex mix of applications, platforms and devices, in which the previously clear distinction between producers/designers of content and consumers of content has become a rather blurry one. More and more people are getting involved through websites, games, social networks, blogs etc. in creating, communicating and distributing all kinds of media content to others in the world. Homemade movies are put on YouTube, relationships are maintained through Facebook or LinkedIn and personal opinions are ventilated through Twitter. At the same time, media properties, services and experiences are increasingly distributed across multiple platforms using a variety of media forms. Think, for example, of newspapers that offer extra articles or news videos on their website, TV shows like Big Brother which are also broadcasted on the Internet, web games that are also played on mobile phones etc. Moreover, all this content can be produced as well as consumed 'anytime, anywhere' using a range of devices, such as personal computers, smart phones, game consoles, MP3 players etc.

These developments have given way to new forms of communication that are increasingly labeled as 'crossmedia' [1,2] or 'transmedia' [3]. In crossmedia communication, content is spread over multiple platforms and the user is invited to cross over from one medium to another, usually by means of a common theme or story. Each medium has its specific qualities which ideally should be used in such a way that they contribute in a optimal way to the overall goals of the intended experience [4]. Especially in the marketing, game and entertainment industry, crossmedia communication has become very popular. Using various media and platforms, increasingly complex and engaging stories or campaigns have been created, like for example the TV-shows Lost and Heroes, that demand a high level of involvement in order to get the full experience. By making use of strong narrative structures or special incentives, a user is persuaded to cross over to a different platform or device, where the journey can be continued [5,6]. Moreover, the user is often actively involved by contributing user-generated content, thereby adding personal value to the actual experience [7].

These characteristics are becoming increasingly relevant now that more and more 'serious' applications and services, such as online banking or multichannel shopping, are becoming distributed through multiple platforms as well as used at various times and locations by means of various devices. The principles of crossmedia communication might therefore be applied beyond the domain of marketing and entertainment into the realm of product design and service design. How to maintain identity and coherence across platforms, how to design the transitions from one platform to another, how to prototype and evaluate a crossmedia concept etc., thus become important considerations in the process of designing new, crossmedia-like applications and services.

However, because crossmedia communication is a relatively new area, an established process for designing crossmedia experiences seem not yet to be in place. As a consequence the current design process will most likely be a pragmatic mix of the principles and characteristics of the design disciplines that constitute the individual platforms, such as web design, mobile design, game design, or graphic design. Real crossmedia design, however, should go beyond the individual disciplines and platforms in order to create fully integrated interactive experiences. Smooth, meaningful and logical transitions from one platform to another should take place, stretching and blurring their respective boundaries. Ideally, the interaction design of a crossmedia application or service should seamlessly be tailored to the desired user experience, supporting the user to such an extent that he can fully concentrate on this experience.

This paper addresses the process of designing crossmedia applications and services by reflecting on experiences in teaching a course in crossmedia interaction design to industrial design students. The context and structure of the course are described, followed by discussing how a number of specific crossmedia issues were integrated. The results of the course are subsequently presented and discussed in relation to these specific issues.

2. CONTEXT

Crossmedia Interaction Design (CMID) is a 3rd year elective in the Bachelor program at the Faculty of Industrial Design Engineering. In the course, which has a total workload of 210 hours, students work in teams of four on the design of a crossmedia application. At the start of the project a design brief is given by an actual client. Each week the teams have a meeting with a design tutor in which the progress of the project is presented and discussed. Weekly lectures are given by regular staff or guest lecturers and workshops are conducted on special topics, such as usability and user experience, visual design and prototyping. Three plenary presentations are scheduled, in which the teams present their work to each other. The final presentation is also attended by a representative of the client.

Mediamatic (http://www.mediamatic.nl/) is a Dutch design agency, that creates and develops social networks, communities and connections with the physical world. Most of their clients are organizations which want to make a professional domain more transparent for the organizations in that domain and more visible to the outside world. Mediamatic tries to achieve this goal by providing infrastructures where people and organizations can publish about themselves and their activities. Social network tools like contacting people, sending messages, 'who knows who' and many more are standard features of their solutions. Example projects are Creative African Network, a social networking website and growing cultural directory connecting the creative world within and outside of Africa; The Memory of East Amsterdam, a story site that contains personal descriptions and stories on the everyday life of the inhabitants of District East of Amsterdam and is maintained by the residents themselves; and

Symbolic Table, an interface-free media player, that can be used for a wide range of applications.

One of Mediamatic's clients is PICNIC, an annual three day festival and conference in Amsterdam that brings together and disseminates the ideas and knowledge of creators and innovators (www.picnicnetwork.org), through a top-class conference, a broad selection of participative sessions, interactive experiences and matchmaking events, all wrapped in a highly interactive festival experience. Its visitors are coming from a wide range of disciplines, such as media, film and television; art and design; advertising and marketing' and education. They are not only there to hear about and experience new developments, but also for networking and meeting new, interesting people. Mediamatic has designed the accompanying website, which next to information about the conference, the program and the speakers, includes an online social network with profiles of over 11.000 speakers, partners and visitors who keep contact with each other before and after the PICNIC conference.

The brief given to the students was to design a crossmedia concept that would make use of the idea of an elevator pitch as a means to help visitors of PICNIC to meet interesting new people. An elevator pitch is "a logical and concise overview of a product, service, or business that can be delivered quickly (the time of an average elevator ride)". By creating an elevator pitch a PICNIC-visitor could introduce or 'sell' himself to others before or during the conference in order to eventually meet these people in person. Additionally, the concept should fit in the existing infrastructure that Mediamatic has put into place for PICNIC and should be operated without any human assistance from PICNIC or Mediamatic. Wireless internet is available at the venue and the online network is available for new applications, for all kind of data about PICNIC and the visitors.

To stress the crossmedia aspects, (part of) the concept should be specifically authored to drive its users to make a journey across various media devices. Thus, the concept should at least run on two different platforms, for example a website and a mobile application, and should also make use of the ikTag, a physical badge containing a RFID-chip, which links to a profile on the PICNIC website. Content placed on the different platforms should be critical to stay in touch with the experience and narrative bridges should tease towards investigating or moving to other media forms or platforms.

3. CROSSMEDIA ISSUES

Throughout the course the teams followed a basic process of designing interactive applications, consisting of an analysis phase, a design phase and an evaluation phase. Besides regular interaction design techniques, such as scenarios, personas, paper prototyping, interactive prototyping and usability testing, in each phase special attention was paid to issues specific for crossmedia design.

First, in the analysis phase each team was asked to develop a personal vision on crossmedia design by exploring and analyzing existing crossmedia systems. Aspects that were to be addressed in the analysis were, for example, how consistency and identity are maintained in the various media; whether the designers have considered different types of usage goals and/or situations for the various platforms; what levels of crossmedia are incorporated; and how the interaction and user experience of one medium is related to the interaction and user experience of another medium.

Based on the analysis the students were to develop a vision on crossmedia design, which should direct them further in their own design process.

Secondly, in the design phase it was explicitly required to create a strong and unique identity for the concept, that would make it recognizable and give it a consistent look and feel across the different media. Graphic and interactive variables that could play a role here were typeface, typography, lay out, color, shapes, frames, icons, pictures, background, animations, etc. On a more conceptual level, the identity should define the user experience and character of the system. For example, the user might experience the system as the equivalent of a dating site, or as a good friend that brings him in contact with others or maybe (more neutral) as a box of useful and enjoyable information.

Finally, in the evaluation phase the main focus was on prototyping the concept in such a way that it could be evaluated. Since a crossmedia system by definition spans more than one platform, testing the entire system using one single prototype seemed not feasible. Thus it was decided to have the students built (at least) two types of prototypes. The first type would be an interactive, vertical prototype of the user interface of one individual platform, such as the website or the mobile application, in which some key features of the system should be worked out in full detail. The second type should then be a non-interactive, horizontal prototype, which showed a full overview of the whole system by means of a linear presentation. The first prototype was then to be used in a simple user test to address the usability of the system, while the second prototype served to demonstrate the overall user experience.

4. RESULTS

At the end of the course all teams presented their concept during a final presentation for their tutors and the representative of Mediamatic. As was to be expected from industrial design students, a large number of concepts included, beside a website and a mobile application, one or more physical products, such as a key cord with a nametag, which you would receive prior to the conference to get 'warmed up'; several booths, in which you could record your elevator pitch; paper flyers, that give more information about the concept etc. One of the more interesting ideas was called the ikCube, consisting of a small cube on a key cord, which can be activated by means of somebody else's ikTag.

Several groups used QR codes in their concept. A QR code is a two-dimensional bar code, which can be scanned by the camera of a mobile phone. Reader software will then launch the phone's browser and direct it to a programmed URL. QR codes can be created and printed by users themselves and can be put on any physical object, creating so called physical world links. Thus they become a powerful tool for designers to make users cross over from the physical to the virtual domain.

One concept that incorporated QR codes is called Picniconnect (Figure 1). It makes use of a specially designed QR-reader, which is distributed at the event to each visitor that has previously created an elevator pitch on the PICNIC website. Together with the reader comes a roll of personal QR-tags, which can be put on designated places, which in turn have been marked with an RFID tag. If a visitor then scans a QR-tag, the corresponding elevator pitch is displayed on the device. If the pitch is liked, a message can be sent to the device of its creator with the request to meet in person and exchange profiles through using their devices.

The concept that was valued most for its design was called PitchBooth (Figure 2). It consist of a cabin for recording pitches and a video wall for watching pitches. The cabin (PitchBooth) is an old-fashioned English telephone booth, where you can record a 30-second elevator pitch and which can be found at various locations on the conference venue. The PitchBooth is activated by the ikTag. Inside is a multitouch screen combined with a video camera and an old-fashioned telephone receiver, which is used to give voice instructions how to create the pitch and functions as a microphone to record audio. Through the multitouch screen the recording process is controlled, displaying a live image of the videos that are being created. It is also possible to import pictures and drag and resize these while recording the pitch, giving the opportunity to create a lively presentation.

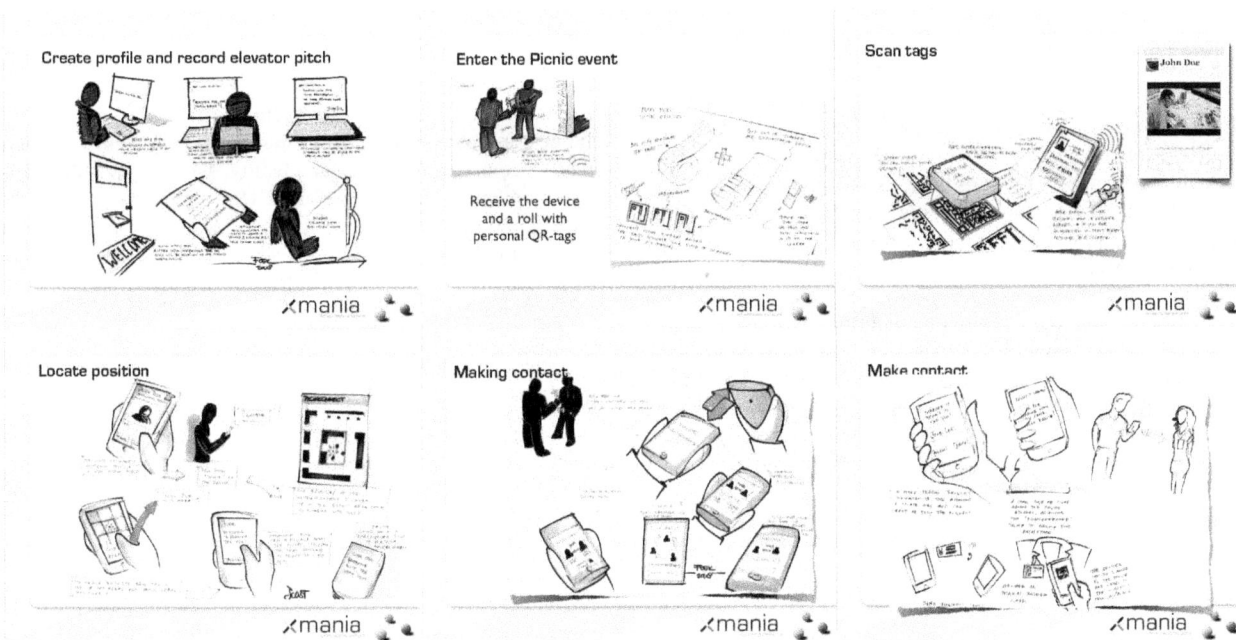

Figure 1

Figure 2

The second part of the concept is the VideoWall, which is also located at the conference site. At the VideoWall you can listen and respond to the pitches created in the PitchBooth. The wall consists of several screens, housed in old televisions. All pitches are color-coded in categories, such as Games, Software and Graphic Design. The wall is operated through a number of old telephones, which again can be activated by means of the ikTag. It was felt that the old-fashioned, retro look and feel, which was consequently used in both the aesthetics and the interactions gave the concept a very clear identity as well as a refreshing contrast to the high-tech context of the PICNIC event itself.

5. LESSONS LEARNED

Although all design teams ended up with a concept which involved the use of multiple platforms, only few of them succeeded in (partly) creating a true crossmedia experience, which had its users actively engaged and involved on various levels and at various moments. Many teams seem to struggle to integrate the functionalities, which they identified in the analysis phase, into one coherent story, resulting in rather fragmented user experiences. While scenarios and storyboards were generated extensively, in almost all of these the focus was on the use of the concept's functionalities by one individual user, on one individual platform, and at one moment in place and time. Crossmedia design, however, seems to benefit more from an overall, more holistic concept development, which first addresses the user experience as a whole by describing the complete narrative that is leading the user through the entire concept. So, a story describing the use of the concept by multiple users, on multiple platforms, and at various moments in place and time. This would call for more attention on story development and narrative techniques early in the design process as well as other ways of creating scenarios and storyboards than the traditional linear, single-user type.

Regarding the specific crossmedia issues which we build into the course, it can be concluded that having students develop a vision on crossmedia design proved to be somewhat over-ambitious. Although the students learned a lot by analyzing existing crossmedia campaigns and experiences, it seemed too hard for most of them to translate this into a personal statement regarding the design of such applications. As a consequence their design visions turned out to be rather superficial, being more of a summary of their findings than a reflection of their own perspective on crossmedia design. This could be caused by the fact that our students are not trained as media designers or communication specialist and that they therefore lack the knowledge, experience and overview needed to abstract from their exemplary findings to a more general understanding of crossmedia communication.

The second issue dealt with creating a strong and unique identity, which should result in a better overall consistency. The teams that did best in this respect, such as the Pitchbooth team, were indeed able to come up with a clear identity, which they subsequently applied over the various platforms. However, even in those cases concessions had to be made due to the specific characteristics of each platform. While the visual aspect of the concept's identity could usually be maintained through the use of the same logo, colors, fonts etc, consistency in other aspects, such as interaction style or the flow and dynamics of the interface, turned out to be much harder to achieve.

It might be questioned, though, what consistency actually means within the context of a crossmedia concept and to what extent it should be applied [8]. Should the designer strive for maximum consistency over all platforms, for maximum consistency within each platform, or should the intended experience of the concept be the decisive factor in determining the overall level of consistency? And if the latter is indeed the main factor, how then should be designed for this, considering that a typical crossmedia experience can start and end on various platforms at various moments and locations, while the actual experience itself could be short or long, linear or non-linear, task-oriented or playful etc.?

So, while it seems obvious that within one platform users will benefit from having things look and behave in the same way, it could be that the overall concept calls for a different experience on each platform. For example, a mobile application that will be used at various locations during short instances might require an interaction style that is very direct, short and visual, while an accompanying website which will be mainly used in the comfort of one's own home for much longer periods of time, will benefit more from a more 'laid-back' style of interaction, which is less task-oriented and responsive. Again, this calls for a top-down approach that values the overall crossmedia experience over the experiences of each individual platform.

However, users should not be uncertain or unaware about why, how and when they should traverse to another platform, which might result in a discontinuation of their process, leaving them 'lost in transition' between platforms. Clear signals, either explicit or implicit, should therefore be incorporated into the design to have people continuously involved. Dena [9] refers to these signals as "Call to Actions" and states that such a Call to Action (CTA) should consist of three phases: 1) Primer: to prepare and motivate the audience to act; 2) Referral: provide the means and instructions on how and when to act; 3) Reward: acknowledge and reward action. One possible way of incorporating these Call to Actions into the process of designing the overall user experience could be to incorporate them explicitly into storyboards and scenarios as pivotal elements in the storyline.

Finally, creating both an interactive, vertical prototype in which some key features of the user interface of the concept were fully implemented, and a linear, non-interactive prototype that showed the intended storyline and flow of the overall concept, proved to be a useful technique. With the first prototype possible usability problems could be identified, while the latter prototype served to elicit opinions about the concepts' user experience. By separating these issues clearly over the two distinctive prototypes, both evaluation studies could be more focused and controlled.

This approach has it's drawbacks, though. In real life usability and user experience are two sides of the same coin that clearly influence each other. Bad usability can contribute very much to a bad user experience, while a good overall user experience can make people forgive certain usability problems. A prototype which is used to evaluate a real crossmedia experience, would thus have to incorporate aspects of both usability and user experience in ways that closely resemble the actual concept. This would call for a prototype that has interactive parts on various platforms, in which the user actively controls the path taken, as well as linear, non-interactive parts, in which the storyline is taken further or brought to a different platform. Such a prototype would thus clearly have strong game-like qualities and designers and developers of crossmedia prototypes might therefore turn to game design as a possible source of inspiration.

6. CONCLUSION

Teaching the CMID course to industrial design students has shown that designing crossmedia applications or services is not simply an extension of or variation on a regular product design or interaction design process. Its complex mix of various media,

platforms, devices and contexts requires a dedicated process, which seems to benefit more from a more top-down approach in which the overarching concept is first defined, rather than a bottom-up approach, which starts by defining specific functionalities.

Good crossmedia communication should enhance the value of communication by making the level and depth of (message) involvement more personal and therefore more relevant and powerful, triggering the curiosity of its users in such a way that they will engage with others. Now that the field of user experience design and service design are quickly coming of age, it is felt that the need for a crossmedia-specific design process, with a dedicated set of tools, methods and techniques, is becoming more and more important. Hopefully the issues that have been put forward in this paper, will contribute to further research into and development of this particular kind of design process.

7. REFERENCES

[1] Saffer, D. *Designing for interaction: creating smart applications and clever devices.* Berkeley CA: New Riders, 2007

[2] Segerståhl, K. 2009. Crossmedia Systems Constructed around Human Activities: A Field Study and Implications for Design. In Proc. INTERACT 2009.

[3] Jenkins, H. Transmedia Storytelling, *Technology Review*, January 15, 2003. Retrieved May 2, 2011.

[4] Minna Wäljas, Katarina Segerståhl, Kaisa Väänänen-Vainio-Mattila, and Harri Oinas-Kukkonen. 2010. Cross-platform service user experience: a field study and an initial framework. In *Proceedings of the 12th international conference on Human computer interaction with mobile devices and services* (MobileHCI '10). ACM, New York, NY, USA, 219-228.

[5] Soares de Oliveira Neto, J., Roussel, N. and Filgueiras, Lucia V.L. 2009. User's issues in crossmedia applications. In *Proceedings of the 27th ACM international conference on Design of communication* (SIGDOC '09). ACM, New York, NY, USA, 119-126.

[6] Soares de Oliveira Neto, Filgueiras, Lucia V.L. 2008. Crossmedia application design: exploring linear and non-linear narrative abilities. In *Proceedings of the 26th annual ACM international conference on Design of communication* (SIGDOC '08). ACM, New York, NY, USA, 225-234.

[7] Löwgren, J., Designing for collaborative crossmedia creation. In Drotner, K. & Schrøder, K. (eds), *Digital content creation: Perceptions, practices & perspectives*, pp. 15–35. New York: Peter Lang, 2010

[8] Kai Richter, Jeffrey Nichols, Krzysztof Gajos, and Ahmed Seffah. 2006. The many faces of consistency in cross-platform design. In CHI '06 extended abstracts on Human factors in computing systems (CHI EA '06). ACM, New York, NY, USA, 1639-1642.

[9] Dena, C. 2007. Patterns in Cross-Media Interaction Design. It's much more than a URL. In *Proceedings of the 1st International Conference on Crossmedia Interaction Design*, Hemavan, Sweden.

Towards a Flexible Notion of Document Context

Andrea Kohlhase
Jacobs University Bremen
Campus Ring 1
28759 Bremen, Germany
a.kohlhase@jacobs-university.de

Michael Kohlhase
Jacobs University Bremen
Campus Ring 1
28759 Bremen, Germany
m.kohlhase@jacobs-university.de

ABSTRACT

Much of the scientific, technical, engineering, and mathematical knowledge that enables modern society is laid down and communicated in technical documents. Due to their static presentation presentation of the complex issues involved, they remain inaccessible to most readers and pose formidable barriers even for experts. To enable advanced interactions which would support understanding, software systems will have to incorporate machine-understandable (formal) information, while retaining the informal nature of the documents, which allows efficient communication of ideas and methods between humans. The simplistic dichotomy between "formal" (as expressed in a logic) and "informal" (everything else) is not helpful as a guide for designing representation formats for context. As a step towards a remedy we propose the notion of flexibly formal representations (*flexiforms*) based on the analysis of document content and its context in the Software Engineering project SAMSDocs where we elicited a formal context for an informal document collection.

Categories and Subject Descriptors

I.2 [**Artificial Intelligence**]: Knowledge Representation Formalisms and Methods

General Terms

Documentation, Theory, Design

Keywords

Flexiforms, Formality, Formalization, Knowledge Mgt.

1. INTRODUCTION

Advances in science, technology, engineering, and mathematics (STEM[1]) are driven by the communication of specialized, often mathematically founded knowledge and its

---

[1]In the following, we treat mathematical documents as

appropriation and application in new situations. It is clear that for mastering this, humans need a deep understanding of the complex issues involved as well as a wide overview over the field(s) and literature. The idea of enlisting computer support in this endeavor is obvious, but has been stymied by the fact that natural language is inaccessibility to machine understanding: computers need syntactic representations of the knowledge to operate on.

Document Commons ¦ Content Commons

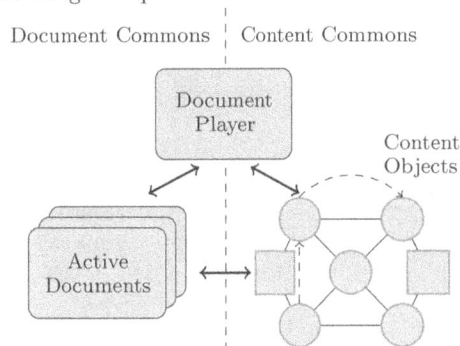

Figure 1: The Active Documents Paradigm

Semantic Interaction with Technical Documents.

An idea that is currently gaining traction in the scientific/technical community is to embed machine-actionable syntactic information into documents. In *semantic document formats* this is provided by making explicit in a formalization process the otherwise implicitly given content and context structure of the documents that convey this knowledge. In *semantic publishing* (see [7] for a recent workshop focusing on this topic), this information is exploited for additional user-level services. An example of this is [14], where text fragments in scientific papers are annotated with references to an ontology of scientific argumentation and experimentation, to help information retrieval. Our **Active Documents Paradigm** (ADP; see Figure 1) goes a step further, it uses formal representations to make the semantically enhanced documents interactive, to embed semantic services, or to validate them. In the ADP, active documents are generated by a **document player** from the **content commons**, a background ontology that organizes content objects (formal representations and document fragments) by their internal structure, their relations amongst each other and to context structures. In the ADP documents become flexible, adaptive interfaces to the domain objects and their contextual inter-relationships in the content commons.

---

paradigmatic representatives for technical documents with STEM content.

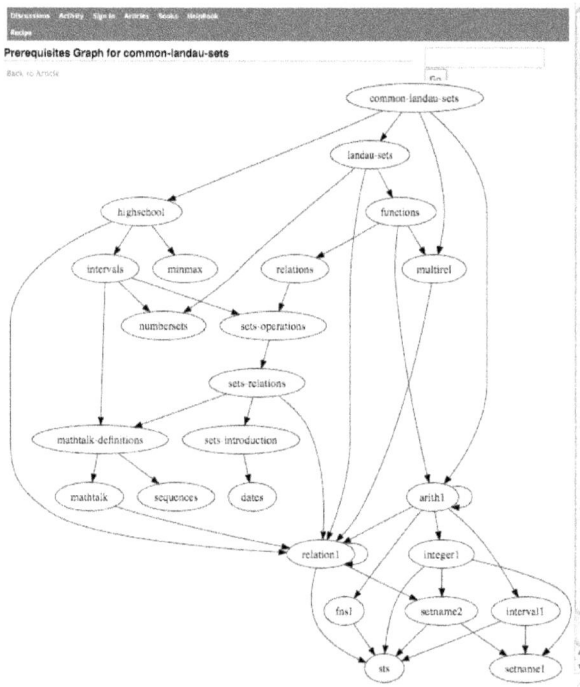

Figure 2: Navigating Prerequisites

The Planetary system [13, 5, 1] is an ADP-based semantic publishing system for scientific/technical documents that uses the OMDoc format [12] for representing the content commons. The context is explicitly represented as a theory graph, which governs visibility and scoping of concepts and and model assumptions. The format also allows to mix formal (i.e., represented as formulae or in a logical system) and informal (i.e., represented in natural language) element in arbitrary nesting levels. These representations can be aggregated and transformed into dynamic HTML+MathML+RDFa documents, which are presented for interaction by a browser. The theory/context graph can be directly used to visualize the logical context of a document fragment and operationalize it for navigation (see Figure 2 based on [9]). The dependency information in this graph can be further used for aggregating from the content commons targeted documents (guided tours) that introduce the necessary prerequisites (the text in the lower half of Figure 2).

Another semantic service that explicitly makes use of the context induced by the OMDoc formalization is the definition lookup service in Figure 3. Still others include unit conversion, program execution, semantic folding of subformulae and text fragments, formula search, information retrieval, change impact analysis, and project management. All feed on different aspects of the structures, relations, and context links made explicit in the semantic annotations in the content commons. A general observation we make in the active documents paradigm is that we see a variant of the "garbage in – garbage out" principle: the more fine-grained and specific the classifications of semantic objects and their relations become, the more services they afford. This suggests a process of iterative formalization of documents to reach a sweet spot defined by the tradeoff between the envisioned level of semantic interaction and the available (human) resources for semantic annotation.

But we also observe from our work in the Planetary system

and the formalization of SAMSDocs described in Section 3.1 that formalization and formality are not as simple as they seem. As the main topic of investigation in this paper we will study in Section 2 the notion of formality and formalization processes with a focus on mathematical knowledge, since mathematics has a long tradition of discussing this, and mathematical models and argumentation play a crucial role in technical documents. In Section 3 we propose two new concepts: flexiformality and flexiformalization to alleviate the conceptual difficulties with absolute formality and formalization identified in Section 2. We defend our new terminology as useful in Section 3.4. The discussion in these two sections is supported by two case studies of technical documents. Finally, in Section 4 we conclude that flexiforms allow to upgrade the practice of "reading a document" into an experience of "communicating with the knowledge the document conveys".

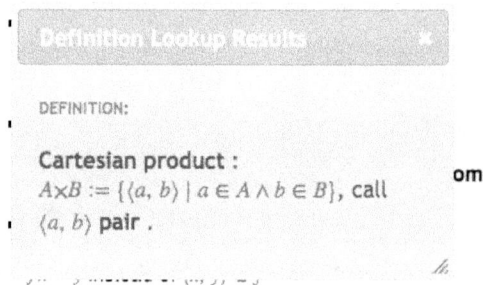

Figure 3: Definition Lookup Service

2. WHAT IS FORMALITY?

We can already see that the notion of formalization and formal representations seem to be much more flexible and less clear than we were told in the introductory logic or AI courses. Those identify the notion of formal representations with logics; i.e., systems that are built on a formal language, a model theory, and a proof calculus. This is a fundamentalist view, as it only allows us to distinguish between "formal" (representations in logics) and "informal" (all other representations), and thus is insufficient for analyzing formalization as an incremental process. Moreover, informality is contagious: A long, complex, and fully formalized proof can be made informal by adding a single informal term like "obviously" or "trivial" — a concept important for the efficient communication of (informal) argumentations that is not supported by logical systems (though one could argue that the integration of fully automated proof procedures into proof checkers is an expression of this in the formal world). Philosophically oriented foundational analyses of mathematical practice like [2] also recognize the level of *informal rigour* as a level of efficient communication of mathematics, but avoid a precise definition of what constitutes it.

2.1 Formalization in Mathematics

A lot has been written about (formal) representations of mathematics, much less about languages and tools that support stepwise formalization of unstructured natural language into formal representations, but very little about the *process* of formalization — probably, since formalization is at heart a cognitive process that seems hard to tackle with the tools of our trade. Social media based approaches strive for collaboration to motivate formalization (e.g. [19]), but have mostly disregarded the need for communicating mathematics therein. But if we relax the problem of understanding formalization a little, then we can make use of the mathematical practice of developing formalization products as a sequence of documents (resulting in a collection $\mathcal{S}$), e.g.

  i) an informal proof sketch on a blackboard, and
  ii) a high-level run-through of the essentials of a proof in a colloquium talk,
  iii) and the speaker's notes that contain all the details that are glossed over in
  iv) a fully rigorous proof published in a journal, which may lead to
  v) a mechanical verification of the proof in a proof checker.

The motivation for this paper is grounded on taking a document-view *versus* a collection view on formality in [10]. Here, we apply both perspectives to the *process of formalization*. Concretely, we drill down on (in)formality by using the document perspective on a formalization process (see Section 2.2 for a first requirements analysis) yielding a partial ordering relation "more formal than" on documents. In Section 3, particularly Subsect. 3.1, we consider documents as elements in a collection and what that means for their formality within their formalization process.

In our exemplary set $\mathcal{S}$ of documents the process of formalization can be taken as the transformation of a (less formal) document to a more formal one. But note that all but the last documents mentioned above are equally *informal* by the classical definition, which takes formality as "*rigidity of form (and thereby unambiguous precision of a particular logic representation)*" [15, p. 55]. In particular, the notion of "formal" is so confined, that the term "informal" becomes inflated and thus both unpractical. Therefore, a *scientific notion of (in)-formality that captures notions of mathematical rigor in documents* is needed.

The main problems in the conceptualization of formality are that we have to understand the space of reifications of technical/scientific knowledge and at the same time capture the intuitively clear notion of "degrees of formality" in formalization processes (see [17] for an interdisciplinary view). To understand the central issues of a conceptual model for formality and informality, let us look at intra-document issues in a paper on Turing machines.

2.2 The Document View Case Study

Intuitively, we speak of different 'degrees' of formality in mathematical documents. Take for instance this introduction of an accelerated Turing machine[2]:

An accelerated Turing machine (sometimes called Zeno machine) is a Turing machine that takes 2^{-n} units of time (say seconds) to perform its n-th step. from[3]   (1)

This is a very informal definition, which leaves open many aspects, for instance, which of the many (equivalent) notions

of Turing machine is referenced. This situation is common in the high-level introduction of a research paper, which is intended to 'remind' the reader of the definition rather than introducing the concept. In a sense, it can be seen as a reference to a more rigorous definition in the background (e.g. in the original paper this one builds upon). Indeed in our formalization of [3] we made the underlined fragment a typed link (shown as underlined in (1)) to the following definition, which in turn links to similar definitions.

> **Definition 1.3**: An **accelerated Turing machine** is a Turing machine $M = \langle X, \Gamma, S, s_o, \Box, \delta \rangle$ working with with a computational time structure $T = \langle \{t_i\}_i, <, + \rangle$ with $T \subseteq \mathbb{Q}_+$ ($\mathbb{Q}_+$ is the set of nonnegative rationals) such that $\sum_{i \in \mathbb{N}} t_i < \infty$.   (2)

Intuitively, (2) is more "formal" than (1) in two ways: It details the components of an accelerated Turing machine explicitly, and it links to a rigorous definition of a "Turing machine" and a "time structure". If we think of these two formalization actions in terms of formalization in logic, the first one extends the signature (set of concept names), and the second one imports axioms of the referenced definitions. Much to the retroactive surprise of the authors, (2) is not only more formal/specific than (1), but also more general: It allows any sum-bounded step size sequence not just $(2^{-n})_{i \in \mathbb{N}}$. Again, this is a rather typical situation: We realize and take advantage of generalization potential in formalization. To be fully faithful to the original, we would have had to instantiate (2) to a (2′) which imports (2) and specializes the step size sequence. But there is another aspect: A vague introduction like (1) has another purpose, which runs counter the notion of formalization ("the more formal the better"[3]): An underspecified introduction of the concepts signals that the results of the paper apply to "any formalization/concretization", which makes the paper more applicable.

2.3 What is Informal Mathematical Knowledge?

A good starting point for a definition of "formality" and "informality" that is useful for markup techniques is that in the semantic markup process documents are 'intended to be formalized' in some way, so we take the 'meaning' of a document to be the set of its formal representations. But even the space of fully formal reified mathematical knowledge is large and difficult to grasp — it contains all well-formed expressions in all logics, so we conceptualize it as a two-dimensional space $\mathcal{F}$ on the right: Let $\mathcal{S}$ be the set of all logical systems and for any $S \in \mathcal{S}$ let $\mathcal{L}(S)$ be the language of S, i.e., the set of well-formed expressions in S. Now, the space $\mathcal{F}$ of formalization products can be constructed as $\mathcal{F} := \{\langle S, e \rangle \mid S \in \mathcal{S}, e \in \mathcal{L}(L)\}$, and any formal representation is a point in $\mathcal{F}$.

We are deliberately liberal in what we understand as a logic. We include logics that allow a formalization of mathematical

---

[2] The examples in this section are taken from a case study of marking up the content of a paper on accelerated Turing machines [3] together with the required background knowledge. We conducted this study to evaluate the adequacy of the nascent concept of flexiformalization for typical mathematical documents.

[3] Indeed, in our formalization case study, we were initially motivated by the possibility of formalizing the argument [3] for a logic-based proof checker; see [4] for a precedent and discussion.

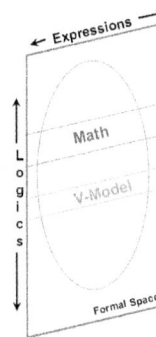

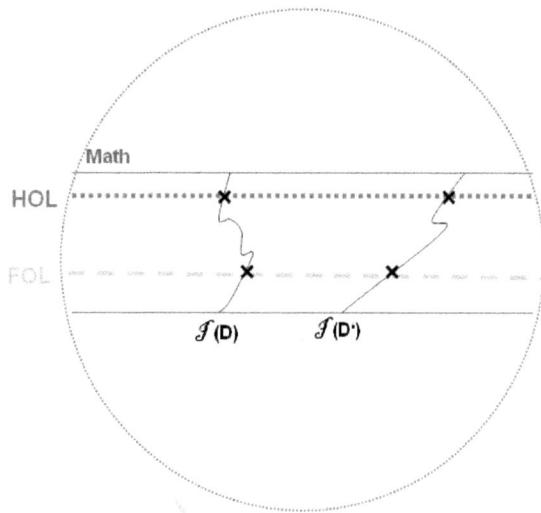

Figure 4: Formal Space Detail

concepts like first-order logic (FOL) or Higher-Order Logic (HOL), but also modal logics or description logics that describe relational structures like the V-Model relations (see Section 3.1) between document fragments. In the Formal Space picture above we have indicated these different kinds of logics as horizontal bands in the space of formalization products.

We will now work towards a conceptual model for the 'meaning of informal mathematics'. For this we need to understand the structure of the space of informal mathematics, which we look at from an abstract point of view first. We consider documents as underspecified representations of formalization products, so for any document D, there is a set $\mathcal{I}(D) \subseteq \mathcal{F}$ it could be formalized as. Note that $\mathcal{I}(D)$ is non-empty, since we postulate documents to be formalizable (in principle) and indeed $\mathcal{I}(D)$ is usually quite large, since even rigid mathematical documents omit many aspects and details of the formalization products.

In particular, mathematical objects (e.g. the definition of an accelerated Turing machine in (1)) can be formalized in different logics, and in a given logic as different expressions — these include different concretizations of the concept as well as logically equivalent formulations of a concretization. In Figure 4 we show a detail view of $\mathcal{F}$, where each document or object D corresponds to a cross-section $\mathcal{I}(D)$ of logical expressions.

In Figure 5 we have depicted the space $\mathcal{F}$ as a plane on the right hand side, and a sequence of documents with their interpretations depicted as cones based in $\mathcal{F}$. We understand this sequence as a *stepwise formalization* process, beginning with a document D. In our example, each successive formalization steps will fix certain formal aspects, restricting the set of possible formalization products further and further. Following this intuition we can define that a document D is **more formal than** D' (write $D' \lll D$), iff $\mathcal{I}(D) \subseteq \mathcal{I}(D')$. This relation on documents and objects is a partial ordering relation (because the subset relation is) and provides an answer to the question of graded formality raised by the case study. Fragments of a document D correspond to sub-formalization products of $\mathcal{I}(D)$, so we can extend the 'more

formal than'-relation to document fragments and the objects of formalization.

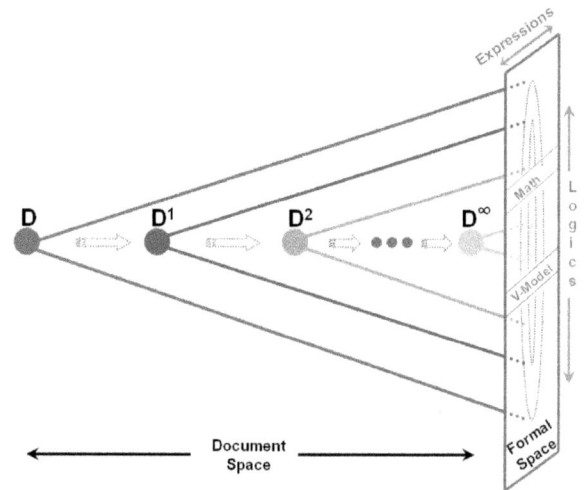

Figure 5: Formality and Informality

3. FLEXIFORMS AND FLEXIFORMALIZATION

A consequence of this notion of "more formal than" must be that the formalization "steps" metaphor implicit in the sequence $\mathcal{S}$ has to be refined: A study of formality structures of a document collection in a Software Engineering scenario showed that "formalization steps" can only be identified within the scope of marked "dimensions of formality" [10] (see Section 3.1).

Intuitively, in contrast to 'degrees of formality' from the document perspective, we assign different 'levels of formality' to documents in a collection, e.g. $\mathcal{S}$ consisting of a proof sketch, a colloquium presentation, the speaker's notes, a published proof, and its verification. Here, the *purpose of formality* varies from document type to document type. For instance, a proof sketch serves insight, whereas a presentation communicates insights. In both document types underspecification is important. In contrast, it is regarded harmful in a published proof and a fatal flaw in input logic for a theorem prover in a verification document. Nevertheless, the objects within such a set are related, even though we cannot use the "more formal than" relationship.

As we already have a case study on the relationships between documents resp. document fragments in a Software Engineering scenario [10], we only report the results with respect to formality here.

3.1 The Collection View Case Study

In [10] we studied the classifications and relationships of **"objects"**, i.e., autonomous meaningful text units, within a collection of documents, which were created within the lifecycle of a Software Engineering project. The **V-Model** governed the development process. It resulted in a collection of documents SAMSDocs, which are presented according to the V-Model in Figure 7. Document formats ranged from MS Word over LaTeX to specific theorem prover input documents. Interestingly, many of the inter-document relationships of objects involved the notion of formality but did

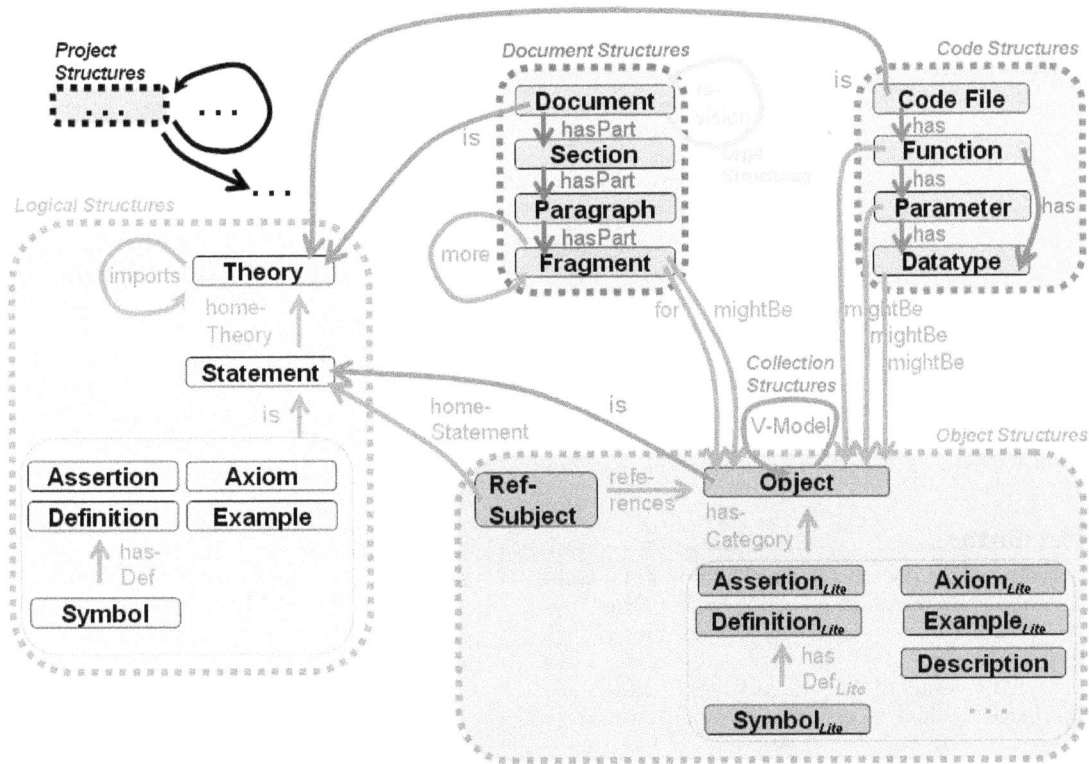

Figure 6: The SAMSDocs Domain Model

not adhere to the sequentiality of $\mathcal{S}$. An object in the contract for example became more formal when implemented and more informal, but rigidly so, when communicated in the manual for customer approval. Another example was some object in the module specification, which became more formal in the implementation, but when in the verification process it was discovered that it needed a slight change, the module specification was updated accordingly.

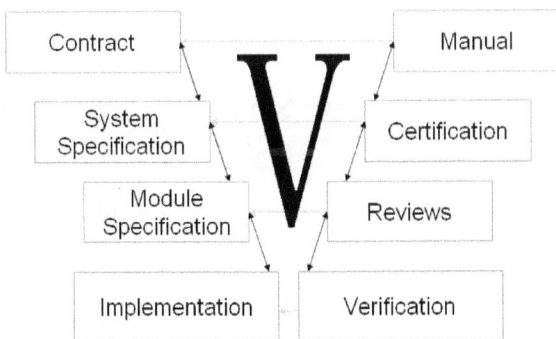

Figure 7: A V-Model for Documents

In more detail, we analyzed distinct formality structures, e.g. the logical structures of a document (like definitions and theorems about them) versus the organizational management of documents or specific document fragments (like a refinement via the V-Model). All these primary and secondary classifications and relationships build a **multi-dimensional space of formality** — if made explicit in the formalization

process. In particular, we cannot speak any longer of "the formality of an object", as there might well be more than one at one point in time.

Kirsh notes in [8, p. 276] that *"how agents frame a problem, how they project meaning into a situation, determines the resources they see as relevant to its solution"*, which adequately describes the formalization process in this project. Depending on the respective domain ontology in focus, document fragments were **spotted** (coined as - classified - objects or references to specified other objects), **chunked** (connected to structural items like assigned to theories) and **related** (i.e., relationships between objects or structures were made explicit). Note that the 'formality' depended on the concerned dimension of the domain ontology and progress of formalization was always done with respect to one of those dimensions.

Figure 6 shows an extract of the elicited collection domain model of SAMSDocs. It consists of several independent domain ontologies and document models, every component has its own characteristics. The most formal one consists of the *logical structures* (here, the OMDoc ontology), the most informal one of the *object structures*. Note that the informal structures can copy formal ones, but their objects and relationships are not as rigid as in the logical structures, thus they can be considered as "lite" elements. This is important in the formalization process where we often have a time gap between the spotting of an object and its assignment to a chunk. But in the ontology this property has to be existent right away, otherwise the document is invalid and cannot be parsed. Some structures depend on the document type. For example, a software file might provide functions with parameters (*code structures*), whereas a Word document is hierarchically structured into sections which in turn consist of paragraphs and so on (*document structures*). In the SAMSDocs collection we also found *organizational structures*, in particular revision descriptions within each document. Some reoccurring *project structures* like project-specific definition tables were identified and supported. Additionally, the project development process was mirrored in the objects spotted. In particular, the semantic objects were developed over the creation of the document collection, so a link of one object instance in two distinct documents could be described by the V-Model. Such relationships we called *collection structures*. The objects of all the distinct structures could be connected via informal "inter"-links. The linearity of the document structures e.g. made it necessary to be able to concatenate document fragments (with different locations) to build a complete object element.

3.2 Flexiforms

We have shown that documents sensibly are formal (supporting syntax-driven reasoning processes) and informal (appealing to a human reader) at the same time, that is they are of *flexible formality*. Moreover, they can be more or less formal in each dimension of the formality space at the same time. In order to be able to express this quality, we introduce the adjective "**flexiform**" to describe the fact that a representation is of flexible formality in any of the adequate dimensions of formality.

A good example for a flexiform document is a mathematical text, which contains informal representations — e.g. historical remarks or proof sketches — as well as formal definitions *and* version management information. We understand the term "flexiform" in an inclusive sense. In particular, we include fully formal representations like algebraic specifications of software properties and in principle also fully informal documents like e-mails into the set of flexiform documents. See [16] for an exploration into the structure of documents we now call flexiform documents. We are also interested in

- **flexiform theories**, i.e., mathematical theories that are represented with flexible formality (within the mathematical formality dimension). Flexiform theories tend to be formal objects that make use of informal representations for documentation.

- **flexiform digital libraries**, i.e., collections of flexiform documents whose relations may be marked up with flexible degrees of formality, ranging from the 'source' relation pointing from a derived to an original resource, as defined by the Dublin Core metadata vocabulary, to theory morphisms.

- **flexiform fragments**, i.e., self-contained fragments that make up the flexiform objects or collections above. Good examples for small-scale flexiform fragments are given by parallel markup of formulae in MathML, where an (informal) representation in presentation MathML and a (formal) one in content MathML are combined in a joint fragment and interlinked by cross-references that mark up corresponding subformulae.

We will use the noun "**flexiform**"[4] to denote an arbitrary

---

[4]The term "flexiform" is also used independently by DMR

flexiform object, fragment, or collection as exemplified above. This concept of the class of flexiforms is useful, since it has very good closure properties: Flexiform fragments can be composed to flexiform documents, which can be collected to flexiform libraries, which in turn can be formalized to flexiform theory graphs or excerpted to flexiform documents. In particular all of the knowledge management processes mentioned above can now be described in terms of flexiforms.

The class of flexiforms, as defined here, is very broad; it includes arbitrary (informal) documents, datasets, and logical axiomatizations. We restrict the set of completely informal representations to those that are intended to or could in principle be formalized, excluding e.g. poetry, which are outside our interest in this paper. The class of flexiforms particularly includes all mathematical documents; indeed, since the foundational crisis of mathematics, mathematicians contend that all mathematics can in principle be formalized e.g. the ZFC set theory, even though this is almost never executed in practice. Note furthermore, that the question of mere formalizability is quite independent of 'truth' or provability in mathematics, as even false conjectures can be formalized and — given sufficiently liberal logics — even 'faulty' proofs. Concretely, the class of flexiforms includes specifications from program verification, semantically annotated course materials, textbooks in the "hard sciences", etc.

3.3 Flexiformalization

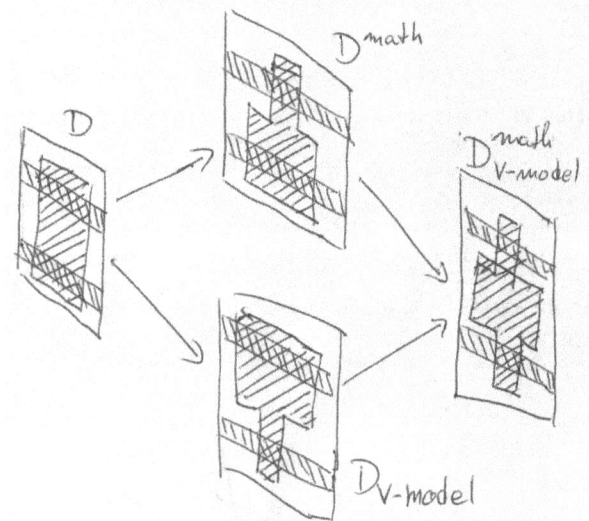

Figure 8: Document Diamond

The most salient aspect diagnosed in [10] is that real world collections contain a multi-dimensional space of classifications and relations. Of course our flexiformalization model must be able to account for this. In Figure 8 we have sketched the situation. A flexible formalization process begins with a document D, which is informal with respect to its mathematical and V-Model aspects (we depicted this by having a large intersection of $\mathcal{I}(D)$ with the logics that talk about math and V-Model aspects, given by the shaded bars, see also Figure 5). Now, D can be independently formalized into D^{math} and $D_{\text{V-Model}}$ (reducing the intersection of

---

Limited and InterDev Pty Ltd, but in both cases it describes unrelated technical concepts.

186

$\mathcal{I}(D)$ with the math and V-Model bars respectively). But as the mathematical and V-Model relations do not interact, we make the diagram in Figure 8 commute as a diamond by going to $D^{\text{math}}_{\text{V-Model}}$.

We have seen in Section 2.3 that the term formalization is as difficult to get as the term formalization product even applied to an object. The latter is now defined to be a flexiform fragment, but can we supply a helpful replacement for "formalization"? Shipman and McCall suggested *"incremental formalization, in which, first, users express information informally and then the system aids them in formalizing it"* [18, p. 199], which is based on having a notion of progressive formalization. The document view of formality in section 2.3 lead us to the definition of a partial ordering of documents. So the term "incremental formalization" can be used, but has to be specialized to take into account the multi-dimensionality discussed in the collection view section.

Whenever we can find such a relation among flexiforms we can speak of a transformation process from one into another, which we call **flexiformalization**. As a side note we observe that the pair of terms flexiformalization/flexiform behaves differently than the pair formalization/formalization product discussed above: mathematical documents cannot be formalization products because the formalization process is almost never completed (formalization products usually only cover part of the knowledge in a document). It is one of the advantages of our new conceptualization that flexiformalization of flexiforms to more formal flexiforms does not have to be complete to be meaningful.

A semantic markup process of a collection can be viewed as flexiformalization as the informality of marked-up objects changes in the process. Moreover, authoring documents within a collection can be seen as flexiformalization as well if the collection structure is (naturally) explicated in the process. For instance, we can study SAMSDocs as a flexiformalization result since the objects/documents are connected within the collection via the V-Model. In [11] we made a point that authoring is different from formalizing. Flexiformalization dissolves this contrast too.

3.4 Yet another New Buzzword?

The introduction of new terminology has to be undertaken with care. Buzz words for selling science to the public or colleagues are dangerous as they devaluate publishing as market strategy and moreover, they prevent readers from realizing new from hot ideas. We believe that "flexiformalization" is a new idea, which will not only help to digitalize more knowledge resources, but also will allow to add more, user-centered services. In this section we try to convince you too.

In a nutshell, we have argued in Section 2 that the term "formalization" interpreted as formalization product describes an end product of a *complete* formalization process, but as such is not flexible enough to support the "more formal than" order on documents/document fragments. In Section 3 we looked at the extension of this order to a total order on the multi-dimensional formality space. Here, the term "formalization" interpreted as formalization process is flawed, as "more formal than" is only adequate in one formal dimension. In contrast, the notion of "flexiformalization" backs up the "more formal than" relation within a document in any formal dimension. In the following we like to cue you in to the advantages of the new terminology.

Precision: The formalizing process builds on multiple formality levels and dimensions, therefore we oversimplify the process description when we talk about "formalization" because it is de facto a *"flexi*formalization". With precision come all the well-known advantages of deep understanding.

New Services: Note for example that with understanding the formalizing task as "flexiformalization" comes the opportunity for innovative support services. For instance, formalizing different dimensions conceptually require different people/demons. Studying the intention of formality in terms of flexiforms may lead to a new appreciation of formality per se as the efficiency of formalizing, particularly over- or sub-formalization with respect to a certain task, can be discussed much more precisely.

New Knowledge Documents: Moreover, if we understand documents as flexiforms, then more documents come into focus for knowledge management, that is: We gain knowledge sources.

Dimensions of Formality: In the course of the SAMSDocs project we frequently experienced that people were curious to know the progress of formalization. This was inherently hard or even impossible to answer as 'the' formalization was not yet 'formal'. If it were recognized that there are distinct dimensions of formality as analyzed in [10, sec. 2], then progress of formalization could be appropriately evaluated. In other words, if formalization were recognized as flexiformalization, then communication and appreciation is alleviated.

Levels of Formality: In [11] we differentiated between spotting, chunking and inter-relating to describe the development within the formalizing process. If we understand documents as flexiforms, then we acknowledge the impreciseness of formalization or the informality of knowledge dissemination. This is important, because every level of formality can be exploited by machines, what is necessary though is that it *is* explicated.

Degrees of Formality Some SAMS project members expected a 'full' semantic preloading of SAMSDocs, whereas others wanted to be pragmatic about formality depth, i.e., only to the point where pre-determined management services were enabled. Here, implicit "degrees of formality" were addressed without being able to express it explicitly. On the one hand the flexiform model gives us a notion of "more formal than" among the stages of a flexiformalization process. On the other hand the relation $\lll$ is not a total ordering (because $\subseteq$ isn't), so a critical aspect of intuitive "degrees of formality" understood across unrelated documents is still not captured.

4. CONCLUSION

In this paper we have tried to understand a crucial, foundational aspect of semantic publishing, an emerging paradigm for making scientific/technical documents interactive and thus upgrading the practice of "reading a document" into an experience of "communicating with the knowledge the document conveys". As interactivity requires machine-actionable representations, preparing documents for semantic publishing, requires a process of reifying technical, particularly mathematical, knowledge into representations that are amenable to knowledge management technologies. We have analyzed this formalization process from a perspective of authors' practices (what do authors do when they reify knowledge: They write documents in collections) and from a theoretical perspective (what is the meaning of such document collections: Formal representations). We have found "document- and collection-inherent flexibility of formality" as well as "application-induced flexibility", therefore we propose the notion of flexiforms for reifications and flexiformalization for the process of reification of knowledge.

We contend that this new conceptualization contributes to the understanding of semiformal knowledge repositories, as far as they are created by (flexi)-formalizing informal ones. Our practical experiences with the various (flexi)-formalization projects cited above has shown that our OMDoc format can be used for all flexiformalization products and thus for all stages of the formalization process. We have just not seen it as a flexiformalization format in the past.

Also, there is more conceptual work to be undertaken, we have looked at the formalization process in this paper, but not at the dual "verbalization process", which generates less formal representations from more formal ones in the new context of flexiforms. Such processes have been studied in general under the heading of "natural language generation" in computational linguistics and specialized e.g. for the mathematical domain as "proof presentation" for formal, machine-found proofs (see [6]). We conjecture that our notion of flexiforms may add some clarity to the discussion there.

Acknowledgements. We gratefully acknowledge that the ideas presented in this paper have been shaped by intensive discussions with Cris Calude working on the Turing Machine case study. We are grateful for the support and the stimulating environment he provided in the six months the authors spent on sabbatical at the University of Auckland. An equally important influence was the collaboration with Christoph Lange with whom we discussed the influence of multi-dimensional metadata, needs and services in our SAMSDocs case study. Finally, we also want to thank the reviewers for their helpful comments and pointers.

5. REFERENCES

[1] Planetary developer forum.
http://trac.mathweb.org/planetary/.

[2] H. Barendregt and A. M. Cohen. Electronic communication of mathematics and the interaction of computer algebra systems and proof assistants. *Journal of Symbolic Computation*, 32:3–22, 2001.

[3] C. Calude and L. Staiger. A note on accelerated turing machines. CDMTCS Research Report 350, Centre for Discrete Mathematics and Theoretical Computer Science, Auckland University, 2009.

[4] C. S. Calude and S. Marcus. Mathematical proofs at a crossroad? In J. Karhumäki, H. Maurer, G. Paun, and G. Rozenberg, editors, *Theory Is Forever*, LNCS, pages 15–28. Springer-Verlag, Berlin, 2004.

[5] C. David, D. Ginev, M. Kohlhase, B. Matican, and S. Mirea. A framework for modular semantic publishing with separate compilation and dynamic linking. In García Castro et al. [7].

[6] U. Egly, A. Fiedler, H. Horacek, and S. Schmitt, editors. *Proceedings of the Workshop on Proof Transformation, Proof Presentations and Complexity of Proofs (PTP-01)*. Universitá degli studi di Siena, 2001.

[7] A. García Castro, C. Lange, E. Sandhaus, and A. de Waard, editors. *Proceedings of the 1ˢᵗ Workshop on Semantic Publication, Extended Semantic Web Conference*, number 721 in CEUR Workshop Proceedings, Aachen, 2011.

[8] D. Kirsh. Problem solving and situated cognition. In P. robbins and M. Aydede, editors, *Handbook of Situated Cognition*, pages 264–306. 2009.

[9] A. Kohlhase and M. Kohlhase. Semantic transparency in user assistance systems. In B. Mehlenbacher, A. Protopsaltis, A. Williams, and S. Slatterey, editors, *Proceedings of the 27ᵗʰ annual ACM international conference on Design of communication (SIGDOC)*, pages 89–96, New York, NY, USA, 2009. ACM Press.

[10] A. Kohlhase, M. Kohlhase, and C. Lange. Dimensions of formality: A case study for MKM in software engineering. In S. Autexier, J. Calmet, D. Delahaye, P. D. F. Ion, L. Rideau, R. Rioboo, and A. P. Sexton, editors, *Intelligent Computer Mathematics*, number 6167 in LNAI, pages 355–369. Springer Verlag, 2010. http://arxiv.org/abs/1004.5071.

[11] A. Kohlhase, M. Kohlhase, and C. Lange. sTeX – a system for flexible formalization of linked data. In A. Paschke, N. Henze, T. Pellegrini, and H. Weigand, editors, *Proceedings of (I-Semantics)*. ACM, 2010.

[12] M. Kohlhase. OMDoc – *An open markup format for mathematical documents [Version 1.2]*. Number 4180 in LNAI. Springer Verlag, Aug. 2006.

[13] M. Kohlhase, J. Corneli, C. David, D. Ginev, C. Jucovschi, A. Kohlhase, C. Lange, B. Matican, S. Mirea, and V. Zholudev. The planetary system: Web 3.0 & active documents for stem. *Procedia Computer Science*, 4:598–607, 2011.

[14] C. H. Marcondes. A semantic model for scholarly electronic publishing. In García Castro et al. [7].

[15] D. E. Millard, N. M. Gibbins, D. T. Michaelides, and M. J. Weal. Mind the semantic gap. In *HYPERTEXT '05: Proceedings of the sixteenth ACM conference on Hypertext and hypermedia*, pages 54–62, New York, NY, USA, 2005. ACM.

[16] C. Müller. *Adaptation of Mathematical Documents*. PhD thesis, Jacobs University Bremen, 2010.

[17] L. Radford. The seen, the spoken and the written: a semiotic approach to the problem of objectification of mathematical knowledge[1]. *For the Learning of Mathematics*, 22:14–23, 2002.

[18] F. M. Shipman III and R. J. McCall. Incremental formalization with the hyper-object substrate. *ACM Trans. Inf. Syst.*, 17(2):199–227, 1999.

[19] F. Sousa, M. Aparicio, and C. J. Costa. Organizational wiki as a knowledge management tool. In *Proceedings of the 28th ACM International Conference on Design of Communication*, SIGDOC '10, pages 33–39, New York, NY, USA, 2010. ACM Press.

Assisting Users in a Cross-cultural Communication by Providing Culturally Contextualized Translations

Bruno Akio Sugiyama
Federal University of São Carlos
Rodovia Washington Luís, km 235 - SP-310
São Carlos - São Paulo - Brazil
+55 16 3351 8615
bruno_sugiyama@dc.ufscar.br

Junia Coutinho Anacleto
Federal University of São Carlos
Rodovia Washington Luís, km 235 - SP-310
São Carlos - São Paulo - Brazil
+55 16 3351 8615
junia@dc.ufscar.br

Helena de Medeiros Caseli
Federal University of São Carlos
Rodovia Washington Luís, km 235 - SP-310
São Carlos - São Paulo - Brazil
+55 16 3351 8615
helenacaseli@dc.ufscar.br

ABSTRACT

In this paper, we present a web-chat application called Culture-to-Chat (C2C). The purpose of this chat is to help users to produce messages in a English as a Second Language - ESL. Regarding this task, C2C has two resources that we named Cultural Translator and Machine Translator. The Cultural Translator uses a Brazilian Portuguese cultural knowledge base (from the Open Mind Common Sense – Br Project in collaboration to Media Lab - MIT) that works with the sender's vocabulary expression in order to provide alternative suggestions that can have the same colloquial meaning. The Machine Translation converts texts from a source language to a target language. The process that we used to combine these features and develop the application was based on an user-centered design approach with a focus on prototyping. We used different types of fidelity-levels (low, mid, high) before developing the functional web prototype version of C2C. User tests were then applied to evaluate usability issues. After collecting data from questionnaires and observation, problems were corrected and now we are heading to a larger user study regarding the C2C functionality. We have been performing a study case involving Brazilian and Canadian users. There are some initial results available from this study that will be discussed further. These data show that users appreciate the resources that help them design messages for cross-cultural communication.

Categories and Subject Descriptors

D.2.2 [**Software Engineering**]: Design Tools and Techniques - *evolutionary prototyping, user interfaces;* H.1.2 [**Information Systems**]: User/Machine Systems - *human factors, human information processing;* H.5.2 [Information Interfaces and Presentation]: User Interfaces - *graphical user interface, natural language, prototyping, screen design, user-centered design;*

General Terms

Design, Human Factors, Experimentation, Languages.

Keywords

Cultural Translation, Communication mediated by technology, Human Computer Interaction, Natural Language Processing.

1. INTRODUCTION

Computer has been used to learn foreign languages since the 60's . In the first generation of this kind of learning, the computer was a tutor that repeatedly trained the students. The second generation (end of 70's) was the time where the personal computers were being used for individual work. It is related to the learning process of discovery, expression and development focusing more on the interaction among students than between student and machine. In the beginning of the 90's, the third generation allowed the integration of many media types: text, sound, image and video. Combining these resources, teaching a foreign language can be more dynamic thus the study will be focused in the study.

The growth of the Internet contributed to advances in the learning methods provided by the computer: students can learn whenever and wherever they want. Many technologies such as instant messaging, games, social network are emerging as new learning tools . Although some people consider that these technologies are not worth for students, many educators and researches argue that the technologies help people building communicative skills, community and collaborative learning. In particular, chat communication is a common and popular form of communication.

Users are easily exposed to a cross-cultural experience through these advances on the Internet. The communication between users that speak different languages can be affected due language barrier and cultural factors. The way the sender uses the language affects directly the understanding of the receiver .

In this context, this paper focus on the design of a web-chat called Culture-to-Chat or C2C that intends to help users in the process of creating a message in a foreign language. For the time being, this project is working with translations from Brazilian Portuguese to English. Different from other chats, the C2C has resources that consider the users' culture to perform its task. Applications that use cultural knowledge, also known as culture-sensitive computer applications , improve the Human-Computer Interaction (IHC) providing a more natural interaction to the users.

In addition, we have been following a user-centered design approach based on . It allows designing a project focusing on the users' need. The design of C2C has been guided by an evolving model of prototype which can help us to get the requirements before start coding.

The paper is organized as follows: section 2 discusses some related work that helped us to design and develop our project; section 3 present the design process of C2C; in section 4, it is described the interaction between users and C2C; section 5 and 6 describes a study case and some initial results involving our tool; finally, section 6 presents some conclusion remarks and points to future works.

2. RELATED WORK

2.1 Cultural Knowledge

In other to develop a culture-sensitive computer application, we adopt the cultural knowledge database from the Open Mind Common Sense in Brazil (OMCS-Br) Project. Common sense is a kind of cultural knowledge that can be defined as the knowledge of every-day things based in life experience or beliefs of a group considering time, space and social aspects. Examples of common sense knowledge are: "a lemon is sour", "when you receive a gift you may be happy" or "a pineapple is a kind of fruit". OMCS-Br is a project based on the American OMCS , which has been developed since August 2005.

The common sense collection is made through a website[1]. A fill-in-the-gap mechanism, called template, is used to collect the Brazilian's common sense. Examples of templates (written in English in this paper just for clarification) are:

A **buck** is also known as _____.

A ____ is also known as **Canadian one dollar coin.**

Snowboarding is a ____.

The templates are made of three parts: a dynamic part, a static part and a blank part (the horizontal line). The dynamic part, represented by the bold words, is filled automatically by the website; the static part is a fixed query structure; the blank part is the field where users write their knowledge. The complete sentence is stored in a database and then is processed by some NLP mechanisms (a lemmatizer, a Part-of-Speech tagger, etc.) that break it in interconnected concepts.

For the knowledge representation, these concepts are linked by a relation forming a semantic network called ConceptNet. Currently twenty relation types are used to build the OMCS-Br ConceptNet. Those relation-types are organized in eight classes, presented by . They were defined to cover all kinds of knowledge that compose the human common sense – spatial, physical, social, temporal, and psychological. Some of the relation-types, the K-Line relation-types, were adopted from Minsky's theory about the mind. In that theory, K-Line is defined as a primary mechanism for context in memory . Example of relations that can be mapped from the previous templates:

```
(defined-as "buck" "dollar" "f=3; i=0")

(defined-as   "loonie"   "Canadian   one
dollar coin" "f=4;i=0")

(is-a "Snowboard" "sport" "f=2;i=1")
```

The parameters f (frequency of uttered sentences) and i (frequency of inferred sentences) are part of the semantic relations. The f represents how many times a relation was generated directly from the sentences stored in the knowledge base, through extraction rules. The i represents how many times a relation was generated indirectly from the sentences.

2.2 Machine Translator

Machine Translation (MT) is one of the oldest and most important areas of Natural Language Processing (NLP). It is the application of computer programs to generate a translated equivalent version of a source text, in a target language. From its beginnings we have witnessed some changes in the proposed MT paradigms ranging from the basic level —in which MT is performed by just replacing words in a source language by words in a target language— to more sophisticated ones —which rely on manually created translation rules (Rule-based Machine Translation) or automatically generated statistical models (Statistical Machine Translation - SMT). SMT is considered the state-of-the-art according to the automatic evaluation measures BLEU and NIST [2].

The availability of some toolkit (such as Moses, Google Translate and Bing Translator) to train, test and evaluate SMT models has helped the wide employment of this MT approach to perhaps almost any language pair and corpus type. In fact, SMT is an inexpensive, easy and language independent way for detecting recurrent phrases that form the language and translation models.

3. DESIGNING C2C

Based on , the design process of the C2C can be divided into stages pointed by a prototype. For each stage, the design process uses a design, prototype, analysis cycle where we begin with design strategies, followed by the questions to be addressed in that cycle, then a prototype that incorporates the strategies to answer the questions (PT), and then the evaluation/analysis. Stakeholders were involved in each cycle to help in answering the questions. Because we have already discussed part of the prototyping process in , we present a quick overview of each C2C

Figure 1: Prototypes of C2C

prototype (Figure 1) .

Stage 1: The first prototype (PT1) was a paper prototype considered a low fidelity-level prototype. This kind of prototype

[1] http://www.sensocomum.ufscar.br

[2] BLEU and NIST are two automatic measures widely applied to evaluate the target MT output sentence regarding one or more reference sentences.

is a good choice in early stages of a project because of the low cost and flexibility in design.

Stage 2: Still using paper prototyping, we modeled another prototype (PT2) of our application (named at that time 2-Chat). We added new functions and focused on the sender's mental model. The idea was to present the translated message to the user before he/she sends it. For the words that could not be translated, a cultural translator (using the ConceptNet) would provide synonyms to those words. This idea is pretty close to the one of the final prototype, thus we will give more details in the fifth stage.

Stage 3: In this stage, we started to use a medium fidelity-level prototype (PT3). The name of the application was changed to Culture-to-Chat (C2C). This kind of prototype improved the look-and-feel of the application and still kept some characteristics of the low-fidelity prototype: it was fast to build and easy to make changes. The prototyping was built with the help of Balsamiq Mockup[3] and Microsoft Office PowerPoint 2007[4]. This prototype was shown to a committee of stakeholders that validated our idea.

Stage 4: In order to test our idea, we need to connect two existing resources: SMT Moses and ConceptNet. Because it is hard to connect the medium fidelity-level prototype with these resources, we built our first high fidelity-level prototype (PT4) using Java (J2SE). This prototype illustrates the process of creating messages in a foreign language but cannot be used for communication between users. The development of the project up to this stage was presented with more details in .

Stage 5: Migrating from the desktop prototype to a web one (PT5) we adopted Google Translate, instead of Moses, to increase the size of the *corpus* (set of texts that impacts the quality of translation) available for us . The next section presents the web prototype of C2C and describes the interaction between users.

4. INTERACTING WITH C2C

Migrating from a desktop application to a web one, we could develop some requirements more easily. While the desktop prototype uses SMT and ConceptNet that need to be running in the client machine, the web prototype uses these resources from a web server. In addition, this new prototype allowed people to send and receive messages. The C2C has been developed using Ruby on Rails. The interface of a Brazilian user of C2C[5] is shown in Figure 2.

The top left box (item I) represents the area where the conversation will be displayed. The lower left box (item II) is where the original message will be written in the source language (Brazilian Portuguese) and, once finished, the button "Traduzir" (item III) must be clicked to process the message. The cultural knowledge output will be displayed in the upper right box (item IV - Cultural Translator) and the translated message will be shown in the lower right box (item V - Machine Translator). Item VI identifies the button "Enviar" that sends the translated message to its destination. In order to illustrate

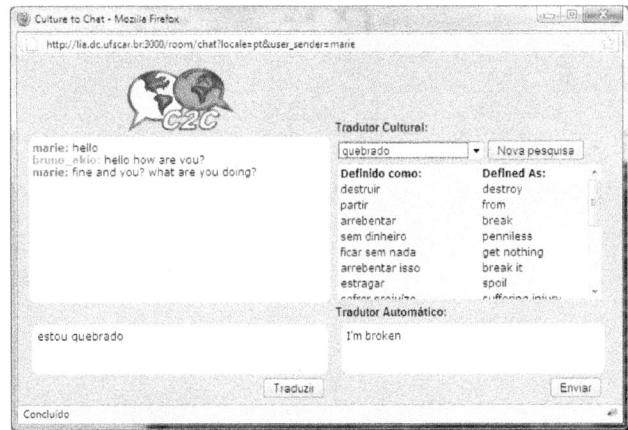

Figure 2: Brazilian Interface of the C2C web prototype

this process, we describe below an example of the process of creating a message in the communication between a Brazilian and an English speaker.

The Brazilian user sees the interface of Figure 2. He receives a message of a foreign user (item I). He wants to show her that he is short of money. After writing a message in his own language and vocabulary (item II), he clicks the "Translate" button (item III). The Machine Translate shows him a verbal translation for his sentence (item V) - "I'm broken" - while the Cultural Translation shows a list of words (and their translations) related with his sentence (item IV). He can also perform a search about other terms. In this list, it is possible to notice that the word "*quebrado*" (broken) can have other meanings in his culture, for instance, penniless or very tired. Thus, the user can edit the translate message in order to make it easier before sending to the receiver. It is also possible to rewrite the original message and translate it again.

For clarification, an example of how it would work for messages in English to Portuguese could be the sentence "Look at her shirt! It's so tired.". The word "tired" can have several meanings (weary, outdated or boring[6]) but in this case it has the same meaning as tacky. The Cultural Translation can warn the user about these different meanings since the automatic translation cannot figure out the real one (it was translated as exhausted). With those suggestions the user can change his/her sentence to a Portuguese sentence with the same meaning as "Look at her shirt! It's so old fashioned".

For the time being, the interface of the English speaker users consists of an ordinary chat that sends and receives messages. This interface is shown in Figure 3. We assumed that the entire communication between the users is in English.

---

[3] http://www.balsamiq.com/builds/mockups-web-demo/

[4] http://office.microsoft.com/pt-br/downloads/CD010200683.aspx

[5] http://lia.dc.ufscar.br:3000/c2c

[6] http://onlineslangdictionary.com/meaning-of/tired

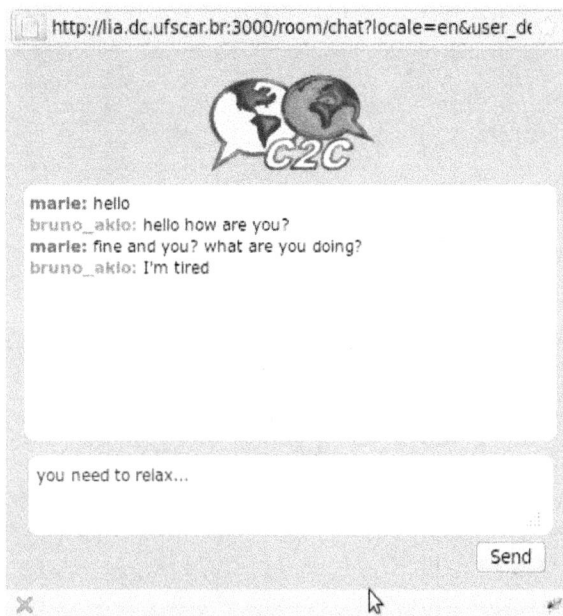

Figure 3: English Interface of the C2C web prototype

From a Brazilian perspective, C2C is different of other chats because its contains the Cultural Translator that uses the commonsense knowledge from the ConceptNet. The user can perform his own searches in this resource and in order to motivate and help him/her we develop an algorithm to automatically identify words that can be colloquialisms. We have chosen to work with such terms because they are words whose meaning can be different depending on the user's culture. Thus, the ConceptNet can help us to provide some synonyms. The algorithm is described below:

```
For each word 'W' of the original
sentence do:

        Search in the ConceptNet all 'X'
where 'X' in (is-a "W" "X" "f=;i=")

        If 'X' is equal to 'gíria'

                Search in the ConceptNet all
'Y' where 'Y' in (defined-as "W" "Y"
"f=;i=")

                Return "Y"
```

The algorithm tries to identify if any word of the sentence in the source language is connected through an 'is-a' relation with the word "*gíria*" (slang, in Portuguese). This means that the word can be a colloquialism. For this word, we try to find all others that have the same meaning using the defined-as relation. All the synonyms are translated and shown to the user. It is a simple algorithm and can warn the user that some of his vocabulary can have meanings which the receiver may not know. Thus, the suggestions help the user by providing a more contextualized translation.

The process of creating messages in a foreign language also helps to populate the OMCS-Br database. It is a process of positive feedback. When the sender uses one of the suggestions of the

Cultural Translator, it creates a 'define-as' relation that will be added to the ConceptNet. It will increase the frequency of utterance sentence (f) described in the topic 2.1. Relations with a higher f appear at the top of the synonym list provided by the Cultural Translator. To identify if the sender used a suggestion of translation word, a trigger is activated when he/she sends a message:

```
For each expression searched or word
automatically identified by the Cultural
Translator 'W' do:

        For each synonym 'S' do:

                If its translation were used in
the sent message

                        Create        the        relation
(defined-as "W" "S")

                        Insert  in  the  database  of
the OMCS-Br Project
```

Figure 4 shows a general representation of how each component is attached. A Brazilian user through the interface in Portuguese accesses the ConceptNet and Google Translate. When he/she sends a message, a Server dispatches it to the interface in English. A foreigner user doesn't have access to additional resources and just sends messages to the Server.

5. CASE STUDY

We performed a case study involving Brazilian and Canadian users, to analyze C2C as a chat tool and how the conversation is affected by its extra resources. The case study consists of a chat session of about 30 or 45 minutes where a Brazilian and a Canadian exchange messages using C2C. All the interaction and computer screen of the Brazilian user is recorded.

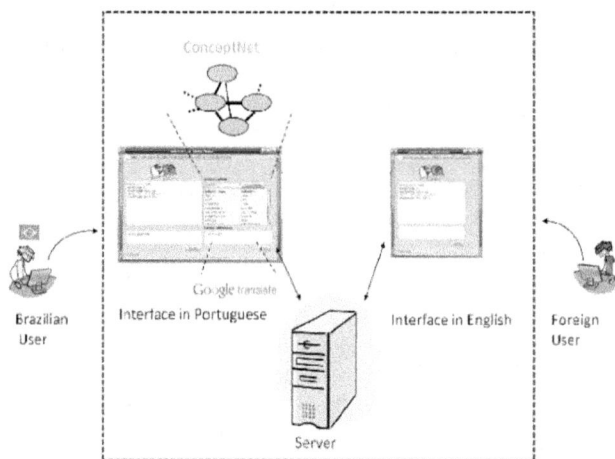

Figure 4: C2C infrastructure

Before the session we present the C2C interface to the users and explain how it works. We emphasize that the information provided by both Cultural Translation and Machine Translator are only suggestions and they can use it or not. After that, the user fills up the first questionnaire of our case study. This first questionnaire contains different questions that depends on the user's nationality. For Brazilian users, we asked questions regarding how they evaluate their English level: "What is your level? Have you been in a English course? How long?". We also asked about the user's experience with computers and chats. For the Canadian users, we asked questions regarding their experience with foreigners or Brazilians using a computer.

During the session, each user was provided with a document containing warm-up questions. These questions are only suggestions in case they run out of ideas to communicate with each other. They are always encouraged to create their own subjects and develop the conversation by themselves.

After the session, each user needs to complete the last questionnaire of our case study. In the Brazilian user's questionnaire, we asked about the interaction with C2C and the experience with a foreigner user. In the Canadian user's questionnaire, we asked them to evaluate the level of English of the Brazilian user. This information is useful for comparison with the answers in the Brazilian questionnaire.

6. RESULTS
6.1 Users' profile
We recorded 5 chat sessions involving 2 people in each (10 users in total). The users are between 22 and 29 years old. While the Canadian users are university students (master's and PhD), the Brazilians users had recently finished their undergraduate courses.

Regarding Brazilian users and the questions in the first questionnaire, we have three users that considered themselves as having basic level of English, one user with intermediate level and one with advanced level. They were interested in learning ESL and very often use a computer to communicate with other people. Some environment that they have used include social networks (Livemocha), internet videos, websites (provided by English schools) and chats (Microsoft Messenger and Skype). Table 1 shows the level of English of the Brazilian users.

Table 1. Brazilian users' profile

User	English Level	Years studying English	Writing/Reading
A	Basic	3 months	5
B	Advanced	5 years	7
C	Intermediate	3 years	8
D	Basic	3 years	7
E	Basic	1 year	4

For Canadian users and the questions of the first questionnaire, all of them had used a computer very often to communicate with other users. None of them had used a computer to communicate with a Brazilian user but three users had used it in another cross-cultural experience. Only one user answered that he/she was not interested in interacting with foreigners. Some tools that they had used to chat with someone were Facebook, Skype and Microsoft Messenger.

6.2 Chat Analysis
From the recorded web-chat sessions, we extracted data presented in Table 2. This table contains information about the number of messages sent by the Brazilian users, the number of

times that they used the Cultural Translator and the Machine Translator, the duration of the session and the relation between the sent messages and duration of the session.

Table 2. Session data

User	Messages	CT	MT	Duration (min)	Average (msg/min)
A	48	1	12	31	1.55
B	96	0	92	45	2.13
C	66	2	11	25	2.64
D	53	2	27	45	1.18
E	24	1	30	35	0.69

We noticed that users with a higher level of English (B and C) produced more messages (in the same amount of time) than users with a lower level. Also, all users used the Machine Translator to translate some messages. For instance, users B and E used it in almost all messages sent.

The number of times that the Cultural Translator was used seems low compared with the number of messages. In this analysis, we did not consider the automatic suggestions provided by the Cultural Translator. This number refers to direct searches performed by the users. Records from users' screen did not enable us to count the number of Cultural Translator suggestions.

6.3 Users' evaluation

In the questionnaire applied after the sessions, both Canadian and Brazilian users have a few questions regarding about the interaction with C2C and its performance. Regarding the interaction, five users answered that it was very easy, four users answered that it was easy and one user (Brazilian) said that it was hard. Regarding to the performance, three users answered that it was very fast, four users said that it was fast, one said that it was neutral and two said that it was slow.

The Canadian users evaluated their partner's level of English (see Table 3).

Table 3. Brazilians' evaluation by Canadians

User	English Level	Writing/Reading
A	Basic	6
B	Intermediate	5
C	Intermediate	7
D	Intermediate	7
E	Intermediate	5

The evaluation shows that, for users with low level of English (A, D and E), the Canadians consider their level slightly higher than they expected (considering the English level and the writing/reading skills). However, for the users with high level (B and C), they were considered slightly lower. It is not possible to ensure that the resources of C2C contribute to these results, but by asking the users about their usefulness we have interesting results.

Regarding the Machine Translator, two users said that it was very useful, two said that it was useful and one said that it was neutral.

Although the user E considered that the Machine Translator was neutral, he/she used it many times during the conversation. When we asked the Canadians if they would like to have a resource to translate sentences to Portuguese, four said that it would be useful and one said that it would be useless.

Regarding the Cultural Translation, one user said that it was useful, two considered it neutral, one considered that it was useless and user B said that he/she could not decide. When we asked Canadian users if they would like to have a resource to help with the identification of colloquialisms, two said that it would be very useful, two considered that it would be useful and one considered that it would be useless.

Users reported that their searches in the Cultural Translator did not return any result. One users stated that it is definitely an important resource. Another stated that he/she would use it more in other sessions. User B said that he/she was engrossed in the conversation and because of that did not use it.

We can conclude that the size of the cultural knowledge database of the OMCS-Br still needs to be increased. The algorithm that automatically identifies colloquialism needs also to be improved to make it more useful. Thus, improving its efficiency will also improve its usefulness.

7. CONCLUSIONS and NEXT STEPS

This paper presented a work-in-progress web-chat tool called Culture-to-Chat or C2C. It helps the user in the process of creating messages in a foreign language (for the time being, English) using two resources. The Machine Translator provides initial translations for the messages while the Cultural Translator provides suggestions of related words using the ConceptNet of the OMCS-Br. Following a user-centered design approach focusing on a prototype was worthwhile since we could develop better the idea of C2C before the start of coding. We performed a case study involving users from different cultures (Brazilians and Canadians) that provided some initial results. In general, most users did not have trouble or difficulties using C2C. This can indicate that our strategy of prototyping helped us design a tool focusing on users' need. The Machine Translator was considered a useful resource for C2C users but they also pointed out that the quality of the translations needs to be improved. Although the Cultural Translation was not so useful to the users in this case study, we conclude that the users still need it. We have been planning another set of session with Brazilians and Canadians. Hiding resources from the Brazilian interface and applying the same case study we can compare how effective C2C resources are. Other future work includes improving web-chat, adding more multimedia resources like video and voice.

8. ACKNOWLEDGMENTS

We thank CAPES and FAPESP for research support. We also thank the students that participated in tests with the application.

9. REFERENCES

[1] Anacleto, J. C., Carvaho, A. F. P. de. 2008. Improving Human-Computer Interaction by Developing Culture-sensitive Applications based on Common Sense Knowledge. In Advances in Human-Computer Interaction. Vienna

[2] Anacleto, J. C., Fels, S., and Villena, J. M. 2010. Design of a web-based therapist tool to promote emotional closeness. In Proceedings of the 28th of the international Conference Extended Abstracts on Human Factors in Computing Systems (Atlanta, Georgia, USA, April 10 - 15, 2010). CHI EA '10. ACM, New York, NY, 3565-3570. DOI= http://doi.acm.org/10.1145/1753846.1754019.

[3] Caseli, H.M. and Nunes, I.A. 2009, Statistical Machine Translation: little changes big impacts, In Proceedings of the 7th Brazilian Symposium in Information and Human Language Technology. São Carlos, SP, Brazil., pp. 1-9.

[4] Doddington, G. 2002. Automatic evaluation of machine translation quality using n-gram co-occurrence statistics. In Proceedings of the Second international Conference on Human Language Technology Research (San Diego, California, March 24 - 27, 2002). Human Language Technology Conference. Morgan Kaufmann Publishers, San Francisco, CA, 138-145.

[5] Godwin-Jones, B. Emerging technologies messaging, gaming, peer-to-peer sharing: Language Learning Strategies & Tools for the Millennial Generation. Language Learning and Technology (2005), 17-22

[6] Haiyan Huang and Eileen M. Trauth. 2007. Cultural influences and globally distributed information systems development: experiences from Chinese IT professionals. In Proceedings of the 2007 ACM SIGMIS CPR conference on Computer personnel research: The global information technology workforce (SIGMIS CPR '07). ACM, New York, NY, USA, 36-45

[7] Herbsleb, J.D. and Moitra, D. (2001). Global software development. IEEE Software, 18(2): 16-20.

[8] Liu, H.; Singh P. (2004). ConceptNet: a practical commonsense reasoning toolkit, BT Technology Journal, v. 22, n. 4, p. 211-226, October 2004, - .

[9] Minsky, M. (1988). The Society of Mind, Simon and Schuster, ISBN: 0671657135, New York.

[10] Papineni, K., Roukos, S., Ward, T., and Zhu, W. 2002. BLEU: a method for automatic evaluation of machine translation. In Proceedings of the 40th Annual Meeting on Association For Computational Linguistics (Philadelphia, Pennsylvania, July 07 - 12, 2002). Annual Meeting of the ACL. Association for Computational Linguistics, Morristown, NJ, 311-318.

[11] Rymes, (2008). Language Socialization and the Linguistic Anthropology of Education. Encyclopedia of Language and Education, 2(8, Springer), 1

[12] Singh, P. (2002) The OpenMind Commonsense Project, KurzweilAI.net, - , - , January 2002, - , - . Available on: http://www.kurzweilai.net/meme/frame.html?main=/articles/art0371.html. Last access in: May 2008.

[13] Sugiyama, B. A. ; Anacleto, J. C. ; Fels, S. ; Caseli, H. M. . Using cultural knowledge to assist communication between people with different cultural background. In: 28th ACM International Conference on Design of Communication (SIGDOC 2010), 2010, São Carlos. Proceedings SIGDOC. New York : ACM Order Department, 2010. p. 183-190.

[14] Warschauer M. (1996) "Computer Assisted Language Learning: an Introduction". In Fotos S. (ed.) Multimedia language teaching, Tokyo: Logos International, p. 3-20

An Approach and Tool Support for Assisting Users to Fill-in Web Forms with Personal Information

Marco Winckler, Vicent Gaits
ICS-IRIT, University Paul Sabatier
118 route de Narbonne
31062 Toulouse, France
winckler@irit.fr, gaits@irit.fr

Dong-Bach Vo
Telecom ParisTech
46, rue Barrault
75013 Paris, France
dong-bach.vo@telecom-paristech.fr

Sergio Firmenich, Gustavo Rossi
Universidad Nacional de La Plata
La Plata, Argentina
sergio.firmenich@lifia.info.unlp.edu.ar
gustavo@lifia.info.unlp.edu.ar

ABSTRACT

Web forms are massively used as a very effective way for user interaction with information systems. Notwithstanding, filling in forms with personal data can be tedious and repetitive. Due to legal and technical constraints, full interoperability of information systems is not a straightforward solution. So that several client-side techniques have been developed in the last years to automate the task of filling in forms; for example, auto-filling and auto-complete are very well-known techniques that employ contextual information to fill in automatically Web forms. However, the accuracy of these techniques is limited by the contextual information available on the Web browser. Some information systems can record users' personal information on the server side and use them to provide pre-filled forms to returning users. The problem with such as an approach is that users must keep updated records of personal information in remote servers; legal and technical issues prevent from sharing personal data among different applications, thus users must maintain multiple accounts. Interestingly enough, the analysis of data requested in forms reveal a pattern in the set of pieces of personal information that are often required (e.g. names, affiliations, billing address, home address, bank account, etc). In this paper we propose a new approach for automating filling in form that relies on these patterns of personal information. Our ultimate goal is to provide means for supporting the exchange of data between user's Personal Information Management Systems (PIMS) and Web forms. The approach is supported by a tool called PIAFF (which stands for Personal Information Assistant for Filling Forms) and illustrated by a case study concerning forms used for student applications.

Categories and Subject Descriptors

H.5.3 [**Information Systems**]: Group and Organization Interfaces - Web-based interaction. H.5.2 [**Information Systems**]: User Interfaces - Graphical user interfaces (GUI), Interaction styles.

General Terms

Design, Documentation, Human Factors, Standardization.

Keywords

Web forms, personal information systems, Web-based interaction, form filling in interaction techniques, *Microformats*.

1. INTRODUCTION

Currently, a large amount of data users provided to Web application is supplied through forms. Notwithstanding, filling in forms with personal data can be tedious and repetitive [4][6]. This problem becomes even more evident when they occur in a same application domain. For example, in the context of the project ANR PIMI we have carried out the analysis of 40 administrative Web forms that students have to fill in to accomplish 7 administrative applications along their undergraduate courses. The procedures are related to the student life including registration at undergraduate/graduate programs, residence booking inside the campus, scholarships requests, internships applications, student exchange programs such as ERASMUS. We have found out that the most frequent pieces information requested thought Web forms concern personal information (e.g. name, contact information, home address, bank account, etc).

Jones and Teevan (2007) [18] argue that grouping related information is a central personal information management systems (PIM) activity currently hindered by the artificial separation imposed by the different applications. Indeed, from the users' point of view it is not clear why they should provide the same information several times. The reason is that each form is used by an independent administrative unit (e.g. university, bank, student associations) that due to legal and/or technical constraints cannot share user's personal records. The problem is not easily solved even when administrative units are allowed to make their databases interoperable because internal organization will ultimately occur over time (e.g. data structure is updated, roles and hierarchy might change into the organization, access rights can be added/suppressed by new policies, etc) and constraint previous agreements for data exchange.

The example above is revealing of the complexity of making different information system interoperable. One might argue that the barriers inside of an application domain (e.g. university and interdependent organizations) could be removed at some point. However, even so, users will face similar problems with other Web applications (e.g. e-commerce, e-banking, e-government, social networks, etc.) that might also request personal information. Thus, in a general case, it is not possible to carry out a standardization of all exchanges between existing information systems [21][27].

In more recent years several techniques such as auto-completion and auto-filling emerged to assist users to fill in forms [14]. These techniques are implemented on client-site (i.e. Web browsers) and work independently of the back-end information system. Auto-complete [30] is very well-known technique implemented nowadays by many applications (not only Web browsers) that involves a program predicting a word or phrase that the user wants to type in without the user actually typing it in completely. Whilst useful in some situations, auto-complete is error-prone (prediction is not 100% accurate) and it is not directly connected with user's personal information. Auto-filling is driven by contextual information made available by the Web browser [7]; usually the browser can "remember" which values were entered by the users in a given form in a previous visit to the Web site. Several tools implement the Auto-filling strategy. For example, the plug-ins Google Toolbar Auto-Fill [12] and Auto-fill Forms Mozilla Firefox [2] are able to auto-fill forms with information previously recorded by users; however it requires users to login and record Web forms requesting personal data. Safari Web browser [26] implement by default an auto fill form mechanism that reuses previously filled form for automatically filling out different forms with data; however the matching is based on the field labels which may differ across Web applications.

All these tools provide undeniable help to users but they suffer of at least one of the following drawbacks:

• Limited data mapping: data exchange requires exact string matching of form fields (e.g. Safari auto fill);

• Lack of support for collecting data: users have to create their personal data record before filling in forms (e.g. Google ToolBar and Autofill forms);

• Dependency of a particular browser and/or plug-in: this is particularly tricky when users are not in front of the computer that contains their personal data;

• Little user's control on the automation process of filling in forms: currently available tool will automatically fill-in form fields with pre-defined information (e.g. address) but they do not allow users to chose a data set among those available in their information space (ex. home address, professional address, school addressee, billing address, …);

• No clear connection with personal information systems. Another particularly pervasive problem of personal information management is the information fragmentation, i.e., the fact that information related to a single task is often scattered across several different applications and environments.

In this paper we propose a new approach for automating fill in form with personal information. Our ultimate goal is to investigate data schemas and interaction techniques for supporting data exchanges between user's personal information space and applications based on Web forms. Section 2 presents our approach. Section 3 presents the tools we have developed to support the approach. These tools are duly illustrated by the means of user scenarios. Section 4 presents related work and section 5 presents conclusion and future work.

2. OUTLINE OF THE APPROACH
Our approach relies on following premises:

• A single pervasive information space for storing user's personal data is needed to prevent information fragmentation and for making information fully accessible to the users;

• Data interoperability is supported by recognized standards allowing data sharing between user's personal information space and Web forms;

• User should have full control on the diffusion of personal data space to Web forms. This means that users can choose which personal data forms will be filled with.

2.1 Distribution of the Information Space
In order to create a pervasive information space, our approach relies on a set of independent Web applications that are be able to cooperate and execute independently of the Web browser as shown by Figure 1:

• The **Personal Information Space** is a piece of software whose main task is to store users' personal data. It also allows users to organize personal information in meaningful structures (e.g. address, bank account…). Such as personal information is deployed into a cloud computing platform thus ensuring that users' data is ubiquitously available;

• There is a set of **third-party Web applications** whose main interaction technique with user is based on Web forms; These application are not (necessarily) connected to each other but require similar information from the user's personal space;

• A **Personal Assistant for filling forms** is a piece of software that intermediates the communication with the users and ensure the interoperability of data between the personal information space and the Web applications.

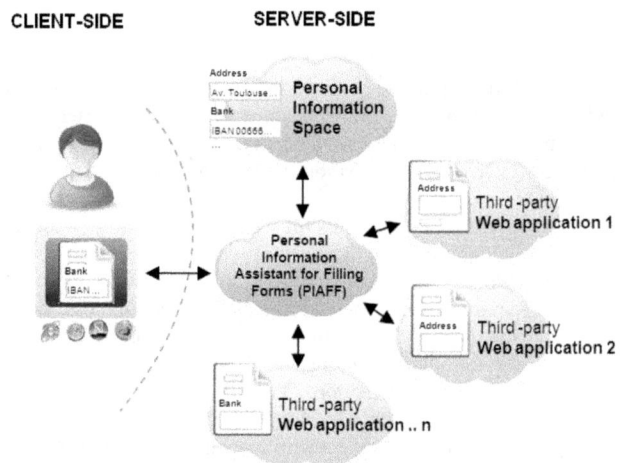

Figure 1. Overview of the approach for ubiquitous assistant for filling in Web forms.

2.2 Data interoperability
The Web forms provided by third-party applications may have different structure and inner organization. For example, form fields can have diverse labels such as city, town, locality, etc; an address can include (or not) the state and mailbox; and so on. So that a mapping process is required to ensure that data can be exchanged between applications. In our approach data operability is ensured by complying form fields with an emerging standard called *Microformats*, which can be defined as 'a set of simple, open data formats built upon existing and widely adopted standards' [19]. *Microformats* are used to describe data with semantic by the means of a markup language (e.g. semantic (X)HTML). This makes them easily readable by humans.

The Figure 2 shows the structure of the *Microformat* hcard. The tag *vcard* indicates the class of the *Microformat*; the *hcard* was originally proposed upon the standard vCard RFC 2426 (Card MIME Directory Profile) to identify individuals. The tag *fn* is used for full name and it is the only mandatory element. The tags *org*, *adr*, *street-address*, *locality*, *region*, *postal-code*, and *country-name* are some of other 29 optional tags can be used to identify a person.

```
<div class="vcard">
<span class="fn">Marilyn Monroe</span>
<div class="adr">
<div class="street-address"> Pennsylvania Avenue</div>
<span class="locality"> Brentwood</span>,
<span class="region">CA</span>,
<span class="postal-code"> 90049</span>
<span class="country-name">United States</span>
</div>
```

Figure 2. Excerpt of the *Microformat hcard*.

Microformats are defined in a similar way as design patterns, which mean that they have to be discovered rather than created. Moreover, *Microformats* must be agreed by a community of users. Currently there are only 9 stable, widely recognized *Microformats* such as *hCalendar* (for calendar-based events), *hCard* (for people contact) and *XFN* (for expressing human relationships using links). However, the community is very active and other 17 *Microformats* such as *tgeo* (for geographic coordinates), *hRecipe* (for cooking recipes) and *hResume* (for publishing CVs) are currently available as drafts. The interested reader can access the full list at http://Microformats.org/.

Data encoded using *Microformats* are suitable to be embedded into other data formats such as (X)HTML, Atom, RSS, and arbitrary XML. Currently, there are several online tools for encoding user data according to *Microformat* structures. There is also some plug-ins that can detect automatically the presence of data into Web pages encoded accordingly to *Microformats* [19]. The use of *Microformats* is spreading fast on the Web so that is not difficult to field Web page that are built over this pattern.

Current use of *Microformats* is often limited to flat text that is going to be published on Web pages. Our approach requires that *Microformats* should also be used to encoded form fields. In this context, we should consider two possible scenarios for third-party Web applications:

a) Forms fields are created according to *Microformats* structures;

b) Forms fields do not embed *Microformats*.

In the first case (a) Web forms already integrate *Microformats* so that forms can be used as such with the personal assistant for filling forms. In the second case (b) the original Web forms have to be annotated with *Microformats*. These scenarios are illustrated by Figure 3. The annotation is done by using an annotation tool and stored as external files into the personal assistant for filling forms. Therefore, the annotation process needs to be done only once. If known annotations for a Web form exist, they are added to the original Web form to produce a modified form featuring *Microformats*. Notice that Web forms are not modified on the third-party Web server making the solution independent of the Web form provider.

The annotation process can be done in many ways either manually coding the annotations into a text file or by using several annotation tools such as Greasemonkey scripts [11] and open annotation services [28][29]. We consider that annotation should be done by web developers, but the use of annotation tools require little training and can be mastered by experienced Web users. Moreover, the efforts of annotating are reduced by the collective effort. So that most of users will not need to annotate forms before using them. The process for modifying Web pages using external annotations is supported some tools such as [15] [16].

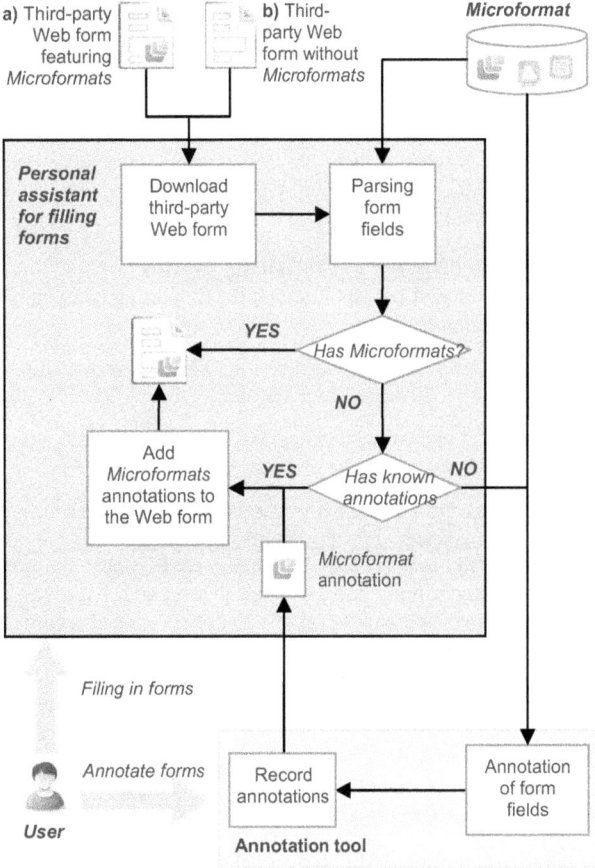

Figure 3. Embedding *Microformats into Web forms*.

2.3 User's Control

Most of available techniques will fill in forms with data without prompting users. As users do not know beforehand which data will be automatically entered, they have to cross-check all form fields. Wrong predictions of data put into form fields might cause frustration and ultimately reduce user performance. Moreover, users' confidence on the system may decrease if they do not fell in control of the data transfer.

In other to prevent these drawbacks, our approach defines user's control on automatic form fill in as follow:

- It should be possible to create as many records of personal information as needed, for example multiple personal addresses (e.g. home address, secondary house, etc);

- Users have to select the data going from their personal information space to Web forms;

- The personal information space can be update at any time;

- Users must be allowed to modify partially/totally the content of form fields even after the personal assistant has previously filled them in with data chose by users;

- Personal data have to be accessible from everywhere so that users can keep control of their personal data regardless the browser and/or the computer they are using.

3. TOOL SUPPORT AND CASE STUDY

In this section we present the tools we have developed to support our approach. Section 3.1 and 3.2 are concerned by the tools for filling in forms; these tools are aimed to be available for any Web users. Section 3.3 presents a tool for annotating Web forms; such as tool was develop to help developers (or at least experienced Web users) to annotated third-party Web forms that do not originally include *Microformats*.

3.1 Tools support for filling forms

We have developed two applications for supporting automatic fill in Web forms, as follows:

- A personal data server application, which is responsible for providing secure access to users' data;

- A client application tool called PIAFF which stands for Personal Information Assistant for Filling Forms.

In order to ensure a pervasive access to users' personal data, the data server is hosted into a clouding computing network from where users can manage their personal records. Users can create their own information space, manage their personal records and make these records available on a Web page. Personal records are organized in the form of cards that can be pilled up and managed as digital posts-it. The inner structure of these cards is based on existing *Microformats*. The personal information server is implemented as a simple database secured by a login. So far, the personal data server is only accessible via PIAFF. However, in the future we are planning to deploy the personal data server as a standalone application.

The main goal for PIAFF is to provide users with means for transferring personal data from the personal information space to third-party Web forms. In order to accomplish this task, PIAFF implements a parser that is able to detect form fields encoded using *Microformats*. These features are implemented using AJAX [8] technology which is necessary to ensure that he can run in most currently available Web browsers. The communication between the client and the server application is implemented under an architecture REST [9] that allows the client to fetch data on the server using the protocol HTTP without having to refresh the page in the client. Under this architecture users can access and modify their personal records using any Web browser including those embedded into Smartphones.

PIAFF is organized in four graphical zones inside the Web browser as shown by Figure 4.a. The numbers indicate the ordering on which users are supposed to start using the tool. The zone ❶ provides support to login and it also is used to display the items of personal information, which are depicted as small cards. Then, the zone ❷ is used to provide the URL of the Web form that have to be filled in with personal data. The zone ❸ presents the Web form after client application has finished parsing it. The zone ❹ is reserved for user interaction with form fields encoded with *Microformats*. Figure 4.b features a screen shoot of PIAFF.

Our parser was conceived to modify the structure of original Web forms using a client-side Web adaptation technique [10]. When the parser detects a *Microformat* in a Web page, the corresponding fields are highlighted using a blue box (see zone ❹ at Figure 4); other fields are presented without change (e.g. form fields 3 and 4). Inside the blue box, i.e. zone ❹, a button **R** is added to allow used to *record* filled in data in Web forms into the personal information space.

The main purpose of the tool PIAFF is to allow users to automatically fill in the form with personal information. In order to accomplish this tasks, users have to select items of personal information available at the zone ❶ and move them to the zone ❸. PIAFF implements a drag & drop interaction techniques for moving items of personal information from a zone to another. This is only possible because the technology of Rich Internet Applications (RIAs) we are using, i.e. AJAX [8] and REST [9]. Using Drag & Drop, users manipulate entire blocks of personal information (e.g. home address encoded using *hcard*) instead of individual fields (e.g. street address). When the user releases the bloc of personal information item into a zone ❹ containing the corresponding *microformat*, the form fields are automatically filled in. The process is flexible enough to fill in forms with data available leaving the other form fields empty. After PIAFF has filled in the form fields, users can decide to modify these fields locally without changing the data stored in the personal information space.

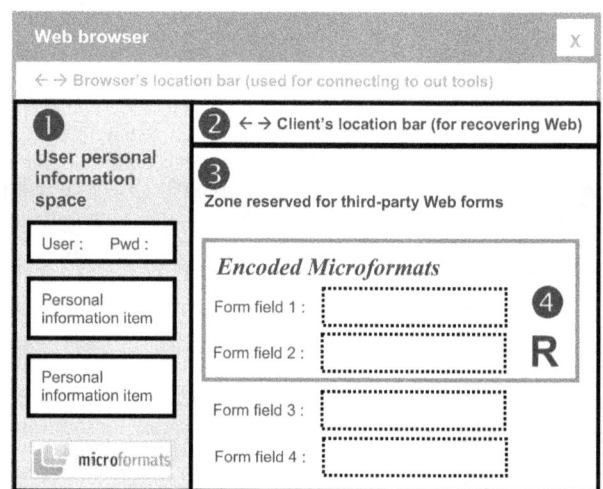

a) Graphical schema of the user interface.

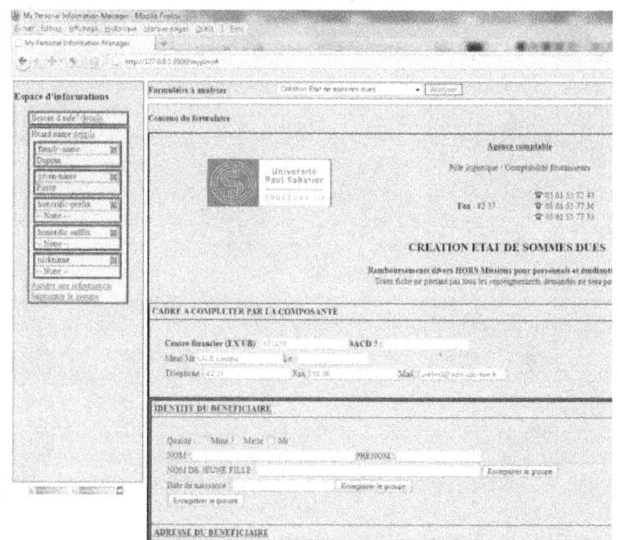

b) Screenshot of the application in a Web browser.

Figure 4. The organization of PIAFF inside of a Web browser.

3.2 Scenarios of filling in Web forms

The sequence of scenarios below concern a *personas* named *Pierre Dupont* who is a student applying for two scholarships. The main goal of Pierre is to fill in the Web forms necessary for scholarship applications. Our aim is to show how the tool PIAFF can assist Pierre to record personal information filled in Web forms, how to manage such as personal records and then reuse previously recorded information to fill in other Web forms.

3.2.1 Initializing PIAFF

We assume that our user Pierre never used PIAFF before. So at first he starts by visiting the PIAFF web site and create an account for his personal information space. After that, Pierre is presented with an empty information space as shown by Figure 5. Notice that on the top-right site the combo box which offer the list of forms available for scholarship applications. From this point user can populate their personal information space.

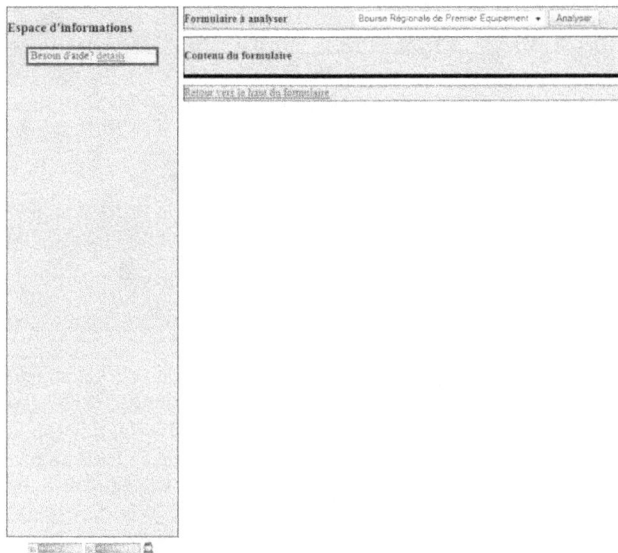

Figure 5. PIAFF after the creation of a user account.

3.2.2 Populating users' information space with data from Web forms

We assume that users would prefer to populate his personal space whilst filling in forms rather than to setup all information before starting using the tool. This scenario describes therefore how PIAFF assists users to record information into their personal information space with data from the filled in Web forms. Using a Web browser Pierre open the Web site of PIAFF, create an account and then he gets logged into it for his very first time. Once he is connected to PIAFF, he can open the Web sites containing the Web form required for scholarships applications. PIAFF parses the application form and identifies form fields that were encoded as *Microformats*.

As shown at Figure 6, these form fields are surrounded by a blue box; data inside the box can be manipulated as blocs of information rather than individual form fields. Inside each box there is a button named "*record information*" (i.e. **R**, see Figure 4.a) that can be used to transfer data from forms to the personal information space. Notice that several buttons (**R**) have been added to allow users to interact with different groups of information (i.e. contact, address, etc). An addition button allows users to record all information at once.

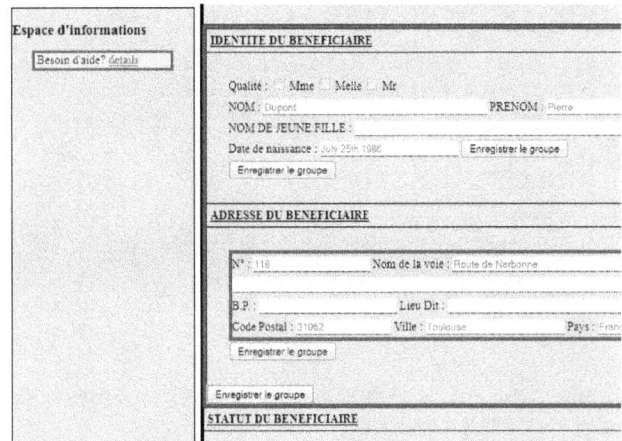

Figure 6. Presentation of the user's personal information space (at left) and the parsed Web form (right) highlighting form fields containing personal data by blue box.

As his personal information space is empty, Pierre should fill in the form manually. However once fields form have been populated, Pierre can click on the button next to the blue box to record this information into his information space. Recorded information appears in the information space as shown by Figure 7. By repeating this task, Pierre can gradually populate his information space. Notice that only fields containing valid values are recorded (i.e. *name/Nom, firstname/Prénom*). These blocs of information can be completed and revised latter on. It is noteworthy that blocs of information are recorded as independent entities and they are not specific to a particular Web form. So that Pierre will be able to reuse these blocs of information in other Web forms.

Figure 7. User's personal information space presenting data recorded by the user (i.e. yellow box at left).

3.2.3 Using the information space to fill in forms

In this scenario Pierre applies for a complementary scholarship and for that he needs to fill in another application form. Some of the information requested in the application form is already available from his personal information space so that he starts by connecting to PIAFF and then chose corresponding application form. The Web form is parsed by PIAFF that highlights the form fields encoded with *Microformats*. Such form fields can be populated by performing a *Drag & Drop* operation from the information space (at left) the Web form (at right) as shown by Figure 8. During the *moving* action (preceding the *drop*) form fields that match to the *Microformat* are colored in green, so when the users *release* the data the form fields are automatically filled in with the corresponding information. Notice that users can modify the entries to form fields afterwards if needed.

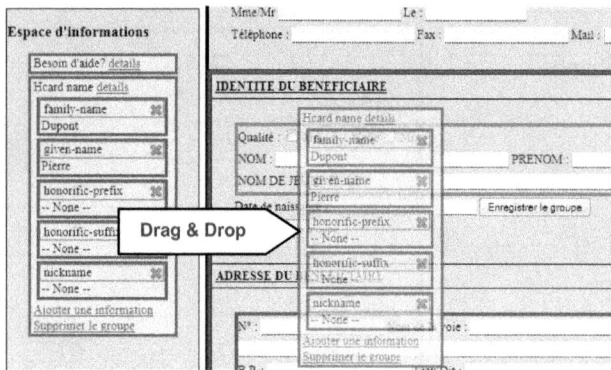

Figure 8. Use of *Drag & Drop* to populate Web forms (at right) from personal information space (at left).

3.2.4 Managing the information space

PIAFF allows the manipulation of personal information records as either in condensed or detailed view modes as shown Figure 9a. Condensed view presents just the label of the information (see *Hcard name* at Figure 9a) whilst detailed view show details and enable the edition mode (Figure 9b). Users can modify pre-filled information, add/remove new fields in the bloc, delete the entire bloc of information or just change its label. They can also create new records by selecting the green boxes of *Microformat* in the bottom part of the information space; after selecting the creation of a new record our user Pierre is prompted to give a name to it (see Figure 9c). In real world, users may have different records for similar information. So that, Pierre is allowed to create as many record of a same type as needed (ex. mama's birthday, dad's birthday …).

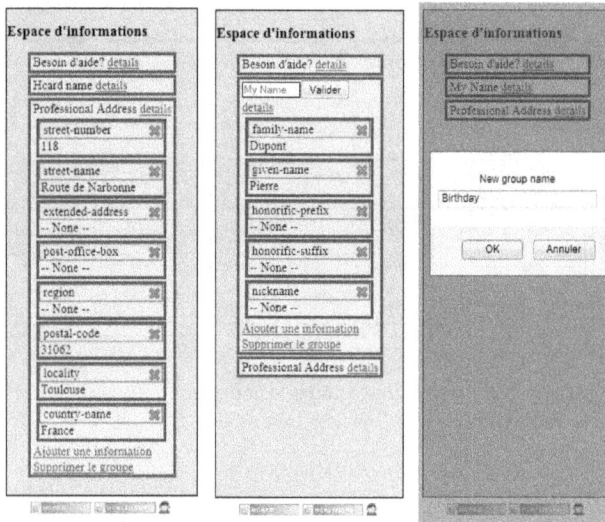

a) Visualization mode   b) Edition mode   c) creation mode

Figure 9. Visualization, edition and creation modes in PIAFF.

3.2.5 Publishing the information space

Most of information stored in personal information spaces is for private use only. However, users could decide to share non-sensible information in their own Web sites or personal networks. For that, PIAFF implements an additional feature that allows users to publish selected pieces of information. Once the user has selected their personal data, the tool can export personal either in the format of a publically available Web page or a piece of (X)HTML code that can be embedded by the users in own Web

pages. It is noteworthy that the publication of the information space follows the structure of *Microformats*, which may facilitate its integration in order personal information space. For example, *Pierre* could visit his father's public personal space and the collect there the home address as a *Microformat* (e.g. *hcard)* that can be immediately integrated to Pierre's information space for filling in applications forms.

3.3 Annotation of Web forms

In order to allow the annotation of third-party Web forms that do not originally include *Microformats* we have developed a plug-in shown by Figure 10. Once activated, this tool highlight in red form fields that do not use *Microformats* and places next these fields a button (see the green cross). By clicking of this button, a pop-up dialog opens guiding the user along the annotation process. Annotations are stored in the PIAFF Web site and are made available for whoever requests the annotated third-party forms as shown by Figure 3.

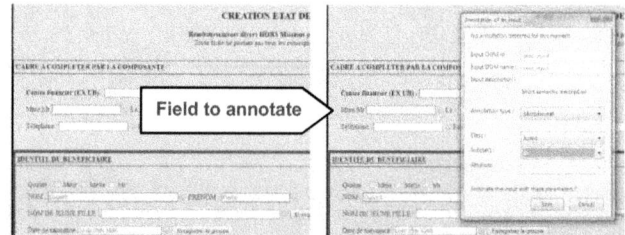

Figure 10. Annotation of Web forms with *Microformats*.

4. RELATED WORK

As presented in the introduction, currently available techniques implemented on the clients (i.e. for *Auto-complete* [30] and *Auto-filling* [7]) for automating that task of filling in Web forms are not perfect solutions. The diversity of structure and organization of Web forms is major constraint that still prevents the development of a seamless solution for automating filling in Web forms. The lack of standardization in data entry forms is not a new problem as pointed out by Sankar (1984) [27], however, it is still standing one. Some recent work [1][31] try to tackle the problem by using similarity functions to predict which personal information is expected for each form fields. Their results are very promising [1] but it is not always accurate. Moreover, such as prediction techniques fail to provide users with full control of their own data exchange; this issue might have an impact on trust and potential of user adoption of the final solution.

Other authors [4][33] investigate the use of Semantic Web technology for developing data bindings schemas. Data binding patterns are established techniques that help to connect user interface elements and data objects of applications [15]. The main drawback with such as techniques is that one needs an Ontology describing third-party applications before to perform the data integration. The creation of Ontology is time consuming and only can be afforded by large companies.

OpenID [24] technology allows users to provide certified identification and share information with trusted Web sites. Personal records can then be used to automatically fill in Web forms of trusted Web sites. One of the inconvenient of such as approaches is that it requires the agreement of third-party web sites to operate. Despite the fact OpenID has been around for some years, his use is still limited to a few specialized Web sites. Moreover, the reinforced user identification promoted to OpenID is not always a mandatory requirement for user interaction with most Web forms.

Instead on focusing on custom Ontology for particular Web applications, some binding schemas relies on the emergence of open standard data types such as *Microformats* [19] and *Microdata* [13]. *Microdata* is an under development standard of the World Wide Web Consortium whose aim is to integrate complex data as native types in XML-like technologies. The structure and underlying approach of *Microformats* and *Microdata* is pretty similar. However, *Microformats* have the advantage of an open community and already existing tools to support it.

We strongly believe on the emergence of open, standard, data formats giving more semantics to content available over the Web [17], which may ultimately include content provided via Web forms. The entire approach discussed in this paper relies, indeed, on the premise that *Microformats* can be used in personal data exchanges with Web forms. *Microformats* [19] are indeed a promising solution to the problem of data interoperability. The number of existing stable and widely agreed *Microformats* is still limited (9 so far), but several drafts are in discussion. More and more Web sites are using *Microformats* to enrich their data with semantics. We should say that due to the need of large agreement to define the characteristic of *Microformats,* they are more likely to cover only common persona data types (e.g. contacts, geographical position, addresses, etc). Notwithstanding, it is worth notice that most repetitive data exchange through Web forms concerns personal data for which *Microformats* are indeed available. So that, the universal use of *Microformats* to support interaction with all data possibly available in Web forms can be dismissed.

This work is also closely related to the emergence of Personal Information Management Systems (PIMS) [18]. PIMs studies have mostly focused on very large data sets, such has the whole content of a user hard drive, and therefore has mainly concentrated on search/ retrieval issues, with some findings about the great variability in which people search their own information (see for instance [3]). However, in more recent years some authors start to investigate the management of personal information over the Web [20][23][25]. For example, Norrie (2008) [23] proposes a complete architecture based on Web 2.0 technology enabling users to manage their personal records on the Web and synchronize them with other Web applications, in particular social networks. Notwithstanding, these efforts are mainly related to textual flat data and do not take into account interactive users tasks such as filling in forms. Our approach is another motivating example for promoting the development of pervasive PIMS [34].

The approach introduced in this paper also made use of client-side adaptation techniques for modifying third-party applications [10]. Indeed, the tool PIAFF add new *interactors* on third-party Web forms (i.e. highlight, new buttons and drag & drop interaction techniques) for supporting users tasks. The adaptation on the client of Web pages is an emerging topic of research. Our tool demonstrates that client-side adaptation is feasible from a technical point of view. As far as the adaptation occurs in the client-side, neither the information system hosted in the server-side or the Web forms it provides need to be changed to that our approach has virtually no impact on the sever-side. However, client-side adaption is not very known of the large public so that more research is required to investigate the effect of such as technology on the user experience.

5. CONCLUSIONS AND FUTURE WORK

More than a definitive solution to the problem of filling forms, this paper aims at raising questions of both scientific and practical significance such as the integration of information spaces in Web applications, the automation of common user's tasks with the Web applications, composition of distributed applications, the evolution of the Web technology allowing use of more advanced interaction techniques (e.g. drag & drop), the development of possible uses of emerging data patterns such as *Microformats*.

In this paper we introduce a new approach for assisting users to filling in Web forms with personal information. Our solution combines different existing technologies and proposes a new usage for them. The approach is validated by a prototype tool that proves the concept. The tool is fully operational and can be used as a demonstrator. However, despite a few beta-users that demonstrate a vivid interest on the tool [32], no proper usability testing has been organized yet. As part of our future work, we are planning to test the prototype with real users to investigate several dimensions that may have in impact on the efficiency, usability, trust, security on data transfer, felling of user control, and overall satisfaction.

We have found that currently available tools for annotation satisfy the basic technical requirement of encoding *Microformats* into Web forms. Notwithstanding, they still required a user with some basic programming skills. Currently we are working on the development of tools for making the annotation process suitable available for end-users. Indeed, the annotation process is the bottleneck of our approach as it is very unlikely that all organizations will create their Web forms using *Microformats*. We believe, however that some end-users would be keen to annotate the Web forms they use the most and they would like to share their annotations with other users.

6. ACKNOWLEDGMENTS

This work is supported by the ANR project MyCitizSpace and ANR PIMI.

7. REFERENCES

[1] Araujo, S., Gao, Q., Leonardi, E., Houben, G. J. 2010. Carbon: domain-independent automatic Web form filling. In Proceedings of the 10th international conference on Web engineering (ICWE'10), Boualem Benatallah, Fabio Casati, Gerti Kappel, and Gustavo Rossi (Eds.). Springer-Verlag, Berlin, Heidelberg, 292-306.

[2] Autofill Forms - Mozilla Firefox add-on. Available at: http://autofillforms.mozdev.org/

[3] Blanc-Brude, T., Scapin, D. L. : What do people recall about their documents? Implications for desktop search tools, in : IUI (10th Intelligent User Interfaces Conference), Honolulu, HI, USA, January 28-31 2007. pp. 102-111) (2007).

[4] Bownik, L., Gorka, W., Piasecki, A. Assisted Form Filling. Engineering the Computer Science and IT. Safeeullah Soomro (ed.) Publisher: InTech, October 2009. ISBN 978-953-307-012-4

[5] Brabrand, C., Møller, A., Ricky, M., and Schwartzbach, M. I. 2000. PowerForms: Declarative clientside form field validation. World Wide Web 3, 4 (Dec. 2000), 205-214.

[6] Camenisch, J., Shelat, a., Sommer, D., and Zimmermann, R. 2006. Securing user inputs for the Web. In Proceedings of the Second ACM Workshop on Digital Identity Management (Alexandria, Virginia, USA, November 03 - 03, 2006).

[7] Chusho, T., Fujiwara, K., Minamitani, K. 2002. Automatic Filling in a Form by an Agent for Web Applications. In *Proceedings of the Ninth Asia-Pacific Software Engineering Conference* (APSEC '02). IEEE Computer Society, Washington, DC, USA, 239-.

[8] Crane, D., Pascarello, E., James, D. (2005) Ajax in Action. Manning Publications, 680 pages. ISBN-10: 1932394613

[9] Fielding, R. T. 2000 Architectural Styles and the Design of Network-Based Software Architectures. Doctoral Thesis, University of California, Irvine.

[10] Firmenich, S., Winckler, M., Rossi, G. A Framework for Concern-Sensitive, Client-Side Adaptation. In Proc. of International Conference on Web Engineering (ICWE 2011), Paphos, Cyprus, June 20-24, 2011. Springer, LNCS 6757, pages 198-213.

[11] Greasemonkey, At: http://www.greasespot.net/

[12] Google Toolbar Autofill. At: http://toolbar.google.com

[13] Hickson, I. HTML Microdata – W3C Working drafy (2011), http://www.w3.org/TR/microdata/

[14] Hartmann, M., Muhlhauser, M. 2009. Context-Aware Form Filling for Web Applications. In Proceedings of the 2009 IEEE International Conference on Semantic Computing (ICSC '09). IEEE Computer Society, Washington, DC, USA, 221-228.

[15] Heinrich, M., Gaedke, M. WebSoDa: A Tailored Data Binding Framework for Web Programmers Leveraging the WebSocket Protocol and HTML5 Microdata. In proc. of International Conference on Web Engineering (ICWE 2011), Paphos, Cyprus, June 2011, Springer, LNCS Vol. 6757, pp. 387-390, DOI: 10.1007/978-3-642-22233-7_32

[16] Hori, M., Kondoh, G., Ono, K. 2000. Annotation-based Web content transcoding. In Proc. of the 9th int. World Wide Web conference. North-Holland Publishing Co., Amsterdam, The Netherlands, 197-211.

[17] Holzinger, W., Kruepl, B., Baumgartner, R. 2008. Exploiting semantic Web technologies to model Web form interactions. In Proceeding of the 17th international conference on World Wide Web (WWW '08). ACM, New York, NY, USA, 1145-1146.

[18] Jones, W., Teevan, J. Personal Information Management. University of Washington Press. Seattle, WA, USA. 2007. 334 p.

[19] Khare R., "Microformats: The Next (Small) Thing on the Semantic Web?," IEEE Internet Computing, vol. 10, no. 1, pp. 68-75, January/February, 2006.

[20] Leone, S., Grossniklaus, M., de Spindler, A., Norrie, M. C.-Synchronising Personal Data with Web 2.0 Data Sources. WISE 2010 411-418.

[21] McGuinness, D. L.,van Harmelen, F. (eds.) OWL Web Ontology Language. W3C Recommendation 10 February 2004. http://www.w3.org/TR/owl-features/

[22] Maret, P., Rubel, P., Beney, J. 1999. Multimedia Information Interchange: Web Forms Meet Data Servers. In Proceedings of the 1999 IEEE International Conference on Multimedia Computing and Systems - Volume 02 (ICMCS '99), Vol. 2. IEEE Computer Society, Washington, DC, USA.

[23] Norrie, M. C. PIM Meets Web 2.0. ER 2008 15-25.

[24] Recordon, D., Reed, D. 2006. OpenID 2.0: a platform for user-centric identity management. In *Proceedings of the second ACM workshop on Digital identity management* (DIM '06). ACM, New York, NY, USA, 11-16.

[25] Rukzio, E., Noda, C., De Luca, A., Hamard, J., Coskun, F. 2008. Automatic form filling on mobile devices. *Pervasive Mob. Comput.* 4, 2 (April 2008).

[26] Safari - Auto Fill: Personal Information. Available at: http://www.apple.com/safari

[27] Sankar, C. S. 1984. A method to simplify filling data entry forms. *SIGDOC Asterisk J. Comput. Doc.* 10, 4 (December 1984), 15-21.

[28] Signer, B. and Norrie, M.C. A Model and Architecture for Open Cross-Media Annotation and Link Services, Information Systems 36(3), Elsevier, May 2011

[29] Signer, B., Norrie, M. C. An Architecture for Open Cross-Media Annotation Services. WISE 2009. p. 387-400.

[30] Stocky, T., Faaborg, A., and Lieberman, H. 2004. A commonsense approach to predictive text entry. In CHI '04 Extended Abstracts on Human Factors in Computing Systems (Vienna, Austria, April 24 - 29, 2004). CHI '04. ACM, New York, NY, 1163-1166.

[31] Toda, G. A., Cortez, E., da Silva, A. S., de Moura, E. 2010. A probabilistic approach for automatically filling form-based Web interfaces. *Proc. VLDB Endow.* 4, 3 (December 2010), 151-160.

[32] Vo, D.-B., Winckler, M. 2009. PIAFF: un outil d'aide à la saisie d'informations personnelles pour les formulaires éléctroniques. In Proc. of the 21st International Conference on Association Francophone d'Interaction Homme-Machine (IHM '09). ACM, New York, NY, USA, 355-358.

[33] Wang, Y., Peng, T., Zuo, W., Li, R. 2009. Automatic Filling Forms of Deep Web Entries Based on Ontology. In *Proceedings of the 2009 International Conference on Web Information Systems and Mining* (WISM '09). IEEE Computer Society, Washington, DC, USA, 376-380.

[34] Zhou, D., Chander, A., Inamura, H. 2010. Optimizing user interaction for Web-based mobile tasks. In Proceedings of the 19th international conference on World wide Web (WWW '10). ACM, New York, NY, USA, 1333-1336.

Usage of and Satisfaction with Online Help vs. Search Engines for Aid in Software Use

Charles J. Welty
University of Southern Maine
Department of Computer Science
96 Falmouth Street
Portland, ME 04104-9300
Tel: 1.207.780.4240
welty@usm.maine.edu

ABSTRACT

Computer users have long been frustrated by software problems. It is unusual that the Help menu actually helps with the software problems they have. At the same time, computer science students and professionals have been using search engines to get help with the complex software they use. The use of search engines to get help with software by both computer scientists and students in other disciplines is investigated. Students from all disciplines tested were found to use and be more satisfied by search engines than Help. Further investigation showed that, generally, students went to other people more than Help or search engines but found search engines and people to be the most satisfactory sources of help. Recommendations are made to improve Help systems by incorporating aspects of search engines.

Categories and Subject Descriptors

H.1.2 [**Information Systems**]: User/Machine Systems– *Human factors*

General Terms

Documentation, Experimentation, Human Factors

Keywords

Help systems; search engines; statistical study.

1. INTRODUCTION

In the early 1970s a school in California had an annual faculty-student sports day. Neither the students nor the faculty were very good athletes. One student, a talented systems programmer, always made a dismal showing at cricket, lacrosse, baseball or any sport involving a bat or stick. A faculty member said, "Give him a manual, he can do anything with a manual." Everyone seemed to get the picture of him swinging a big heavy systems manual and winning the game. Laughter ensued.

This student had the ability to read, understand and use manuals to find solutions to difficult programming problems. Manual use is rare now [11, 12, 18, 16, 5].

With the advent of graphical user interfaces, software houses no longer routinely generated and distributed these massive manuals[1]. Instead, they now include the Help menu item and put the documentation directly at hand. In many ways this is an improvement over paper documentation. It is searchable and it automatically comes with any new version of the software. On the other hand, various aspects of Help dialogs are frustratingly poorly conceived, implemented [14, 1] and accepted [15, 2] by users. Also, the Help system usually does not contain nearly as much information as the manuals it replaces. This is not an argument for returning to paper manuals but for rethinking Help. All the above cited papers deal with approaches to alleviate computer-related user frustration but others have addressed this frustration more directly [3, 4, 6, 13, 9]. Help systems have not made significant progress since the early and embarrassing efforts with Microsoft Bob and Clippy [8]. Help systems were problematic then and continue to be problematic.

Anecdotal evidence implies that computer scientists are now using search engines for software help almost exclusively in place of Help systems. Has the use of search engines supplanted Help not only for computer scientists but for people in other disciplines? What long term direction will Help take? Also, due to its problems, could Help be changed so that Help in its current form ceases to exist?

The basic hypotheses that will be investigated here are:

HA. Computer science students use search engines for software help more than students from other disciplines.

HB. Computer science students are more satisfied with search engines than students in other disciplines.

HC. Students in diverse disciplines use search engines for help more than they use Help.

HD. Students from diverse disciplines are more satisfied with search engines than Help.

HE. Students from diverse disciplines are more satisfied with search engines than with any other source of help.

The following conjecture, although not statistically analyzed, is of interest:

CA. Students in diverse disciplines use search engines for help more than they use any other source of help.

---

[1] Of course, many bookstores have large sections devoted to texts on how to use software. This will be discussed briefly later.

Confirming or rejecting these hypotheses will lead to recommendations for improving help systems.

2. THE CASE FOR SEARCH ENGINES

When finding the answers to a multitude of questions, people no longer go to physical libraries or encyclopedias; they now go to the search engine, especially the Google [TM] search engine. The popularity of search engines is due to the excellence of their responses to search queries. At the same time many more users with diverse backgrounds, and few computer skills, have become involved with office software such as word processing, spreadsheets, presentation builders and many others. Each of these software products contains a Help[2] menu attempting to supply the user with much needed help. Help systems have limited search capabilities and their navigation often conforms to the structure of the associated software. They also bring only the support documentation supplied by the software house to bear in finding answers to software questions. There are many other available resources of help they do not reveal.

Faculty and student experience points to computer science students and professionals using search engines to obtain help in using software such as .NET and Java nearly to the exclusion of Help. Search engines allow the use of multiple terms, including terms that may not be part of the Help vocabulary but make sense to the user. If these terms are also used by others, a search engine will find the relevant sites. The search engine will find forums, blogs and individual web sites that Help would never find. The search engine also usually does a better job of indexing into the product's online Help than the software product itself. Thus, even if a search uses the same terms that the Help builders used, search will index into their documentation better than Help. The user will also benefit from other sources of information. In addition, much open source software is only detailed in forums and blogs, which lend themselves to search engines.

Several of the above points result in it being much easier to navigate using a search engine than Help (Novick and Ward, 2006b). The hierarchical organization of the Help system is often problematic. The flatness of the Web eliminates this problem.

Another advantage that a search engine brings is that it presents a single, often familiar, interface. If several pieces of software are used, each will have its own Help structure. The search engine's interface is always the same. Recreational experience with a search engine can transfer to searching for help with a much reduced learning curve. This is an aid to new users of a software system.

3. POPULATION DEMOGRAPHICS AND REPRODUCIBILITY OF RESULTS

The University is an urban, comprehensive university. Its urban setting results in a large number of commuter students although the majority are full-time students. The average age is 25. The term "comprehensive" means that it is mainly an undergraduate institution with several master's degree programs but few doctoral programs. Participants in this questionnaire were not randomly chosen; they were whatever students chose to take the surveyed classes.

Reproducibility would depend on the population demographics of a future study as well as any changes to software and web usage that could affect the results.

4. THE SURVEY

The questionnaire went through several pilot tests with faculty and 56 students. The resulting one-page questionnaire was distributed to students in different majors: arts and humanities (Arts, 94 students), business (Bus, 92 students), computer science (CS, 62 students) and sciences and engineering (Sci, 85 students). Questionnaires were distributed in first year through fourth year classes in a variety of subjects including physics, chemistry, introduction to business, market research, political science, criminology, philosophy, English, and the entire range of computer science courses offered in that semester. The students were given approximately 10 minutes to complete the questionnaire at the beginning of each surveyed classes.

The first question determined the major, year in school, years of computer use and favorite search engine of participants. Question two served to introduce participants to what sorts of software we were discussing, from social networking through programming. To encouraging their thinking fairly deeply about their use of each software category, participants were asked to rate their expertise in each area. This data was not found to be useful for analysis.

Question 3., asking how frequently they used Help or search engines and how satisfied they were with the results, is shown in Fig. 1; it uses a Likert scale.

The final question (Q.4., also in Fig. 1.) asked what resources students used to get help with software and how satisfied they were with those resources. In both the following question statement and the brief oral introduction to the questionnaire, participants were told that the use of human resources, text and any other sources were of interest, not just search engines and Help.

---

[2] Microsoft eliminated the Help menu in Office 2007, using a question mark icon instead. Other manufacturers use function keys. Both the question mark and function keys have the same functionality as Help. Thus, in the following, the term Help refers to any of these mechanisms.

*3. **Please write down the response to the following questions that most accurately reflects your use and satisfaction with using Help and search engines to aid in using software.***

1	2	3	4	5	6	7	0
Strongly disagree	Disagree	Mildly disagree	Neutral	Mildly agree	Agree	Strongly agree	I do not use this method

***A.** I frequently use Help when getting help in using software: ______ (1 – 7 or 0)*

***B.** I am very satisfied with Help when getting help in using software: ________ (1 – 7 or 0)*

***C.** I frequently use a search engine when getting help in using software: ________ (1 – 7 or 0)*

***D.** I am very satisfied with this search engine when getting help in using software: ________ (1 – 7 or 0)*

*4. A. **From what 3 source(s) do you usually get help in using software?** (e.g., Google, Help, friends, teachers, user guides, help desk ...) If you use fewer than 3, just leave the others blank.*

1.__________________ 2.__________________ 3.__________________

*B. **How satisfied are you with each of the sources specified in question 4 A.?** (1 – 7 where 1 is totally unsatisfied to 7, which is totally satisfied.) If you use fewer than 3, just leave the others blank.*

1.____ 2.____ 3.____

Fig. 1 Questions 3. and 4. from the survey.

5. OVERALL SURVEY RESULTS

The survey was run using the above questions and the four groups of participants. Questions Q1 and Q2 were not statistically analyzed. Q1 did show that 86% of participants preferred Google: 79% of arts students preferred Google, 86% of business students, 95% of computer science students and 89% of science and engineering students.

Detailed analysis of Q3 and Q4 is given in the following section.

Questionnaire question Q3. gathered data on participants' use and satisfaction with Search and Help. The participant groups were statistically compared (see below) to each other to see if there were any differences between them in their use and satisfaction with Search. While there were no statistically significant differences between the non-CS groups, computer science participants used and were satisfied by Search significantly more than all other groups. Thus hypotheses HA and HB were confirmed.

Also in questionnaire question Q3, the paired responses of participants evaluating their use and satisfaction with Help and Search were statistically tested, see below. The overall group and the individual groups all showed that they used and were satisfied by search significantly more than Help. Thus, hypotheses HC. and HD. were confirmed. The results are graphed as percentages in Figures. 2 – 5. (If these figures are seen in black and white, the bars are shown in the order Arts, Bus, CS, Sci, starting from the left.)

When Fig.'s 2 and 3 (Help) are compared to Fig.'s 4 and 5 (Search), the higher usage and satisfaction with Search over Help is immediately noticeable. This seems to be true for all groups, especially CS. These differences will be statistically analyzed in the next section.

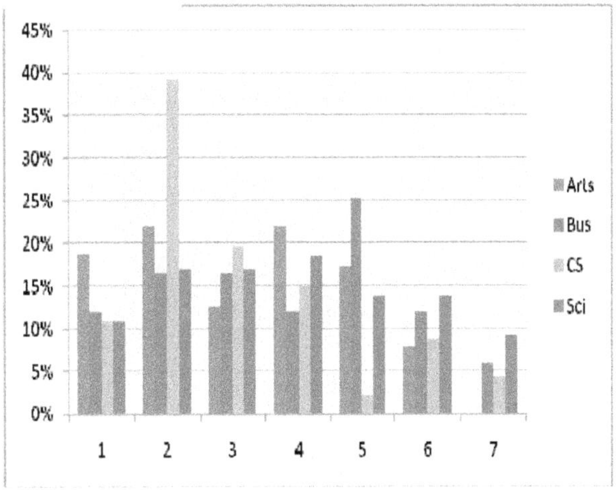

Figure 2. Frequency that participants used Help. Survey question Q3.A.

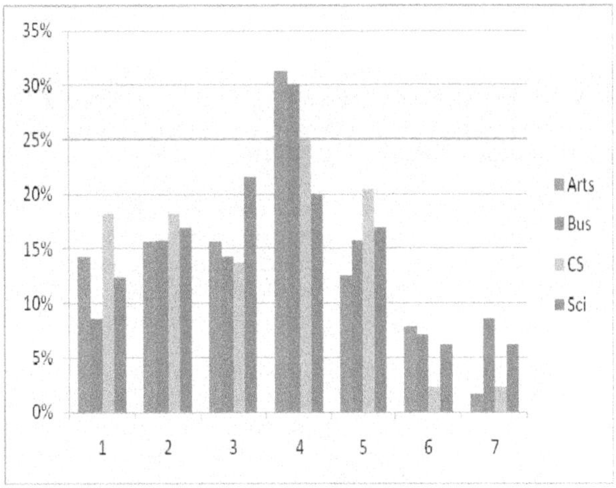

Figure 3. Frequency that participants were satisfied with Help. Survey question Q3.B.

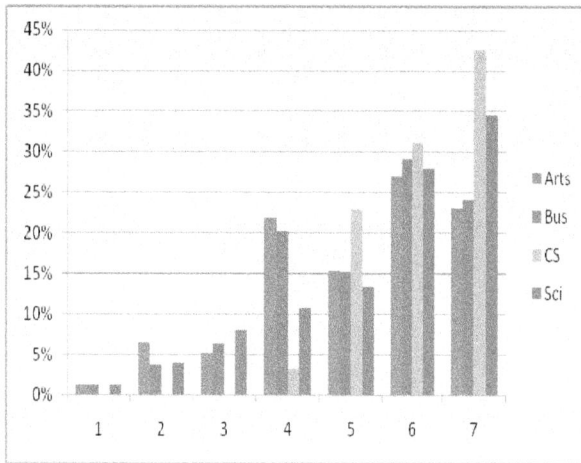

Figure 4. Frequency that participants used Search. Survey question Q3.C.

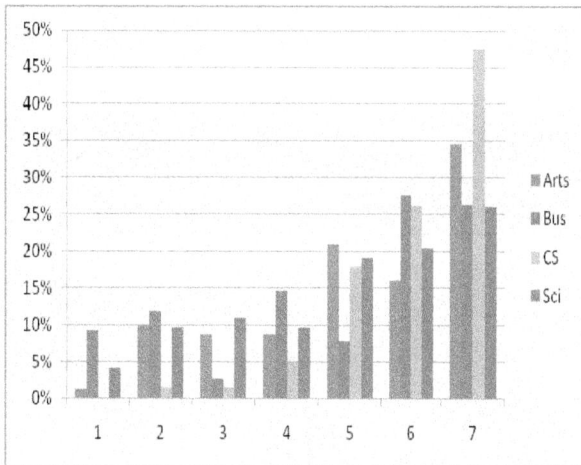

Figure 5. Frequency that participants were satisfied with Search. Survey question Q3.D.

Questionnaire question Q4.A. was concerned with sources of help that participants used in addition to search engines and Help, see Fig. 6. Responses to Q4.A. were categorized as being from Person (friend, family, teacher, help desk, etc), Search (Google, Yahoo, Blackle, etc.), Help, and Text (books, manuals, user guides, etc.). Figure 6 summarizes the result of Q4.A. These results were not statistically analyzed as discussed below. Overall, Person was the most cited source of help (37%). Thus, conjecture CA is not supported.

In question Q4.A., participants were not asked to state their help preferences in any order. Therefore choice order is not analyzed. Asking for choice order caused problems in the pilot studies, see below.

Questionnaire question Q4.B. assessed satisfaction with the help sources found in part Q4.A. These results are not as amenable to graphic representation and will be presented thoroughly in the next section. Overall, there were significant differences between the levels of satisfaction with the four help sources. Further investigation showed that Arts, Business and CS each showed statistically significant differences in satisfaction between the help sources.

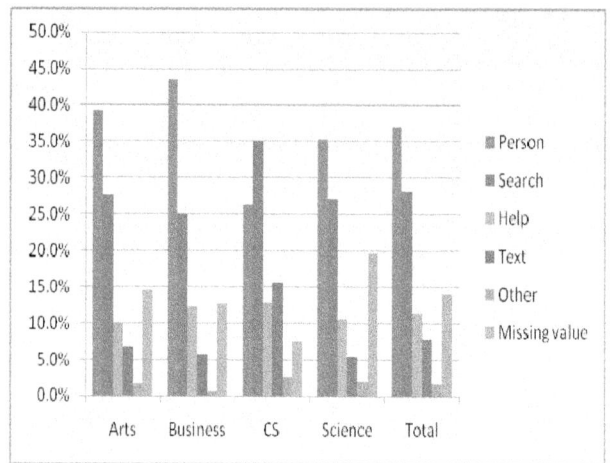

Figure 6. Participant's choices of help sources by group and source. Survey question Q4.A. Choice order is ignored.

The results for Science were not significant. Drilling down one more level shows that Arts, Business, CS and Sci were significantly more satisfied with Search than Help. Overall, Person was favored over Search. Only CS participants were statistically more satisfied with Search than Person. Also, only the CS group found Help significantly less satisfying when compared to any other help source. See below for the analysis. HE. is not supported.

Details of the statistical analysis are given in the next section. A test was significant if the p value was less than 0.01. Testing with 3 or 4 groups was done using the Kruskal-Wallis test. Tests of two separate groups used Mann-Whitney. Paired tests used the Wilcoxon-Test [7]. All are non-parametric tests, as discussed below.

6. DETAILED SURVEY RESULTS
Each of the following sections will address pairs of the 5 hypotheses and one conjecture formulated above.

6.1 Hypothesis HA. Computer science students use search engines for software help more than students from other disciplines.

Hypothesis HB. Computer science students are more satisfied with search engines than students in other disciplines.

For hypothesis HA. the medians and means from questionnaire question Q3, parts A. through D. are reported in Table 1. While the means are useful in many comparisons of experimental effects, they do not lend themselves to the description of the ordinal Likert scale values. Medians are the more appropriate measure or these ordinal values. Means are supplied just as reference points.

The medians and means show that all participants used and were satisfied by Search more than by Help, that computer science students used and were satisfied by Help less than any other group and that computer science students were satisfied by Search more than any other group.

Table 1. Median and mean values of responses to statements Q3.A., Q3.B., Q3.C.,Q3.D. A seven point Likert scale was used with 7 being the highest score, corresponding to most used and most satisfied. See also Fig.'s 2 - 5, above.

	Q3.A. Help Used	Q3.B. Help Satisfied	Q3.C. Search Used	Q3.D. Search Satisfied
	Median (mean)	Median (mean)	Median (mean)	Median (mean)
Arts	3 (3.20)	4 (3.43)	6 (5.25)	5.5 (5.17)
Bus	4 (3.82)	4 (3.77)	6 (4.81)	6 (5.20)
CS	2.5 (3.02)	3.5 (3.27)	6 (6.08)	6 (6.13)
Sci	4 (3.86)	3 (3.55)	5 (4.96)	6 (5.53)
All	3 (3.52)	4 (3.53)	6 (5.23)	6 (5.47)

Are these differences statistically significant? As stated above, participants in this survey were not randomly chosen. Also, the values on the Likert scale (1 to 7) are ordinal, not cardinal, values and do not allow the arithmetic operations required to find means, standard deviation, etc. For both of these reasons, the standard parametric statistical tests (e.g., analysis of variance) cannot be used. Instead, the non-parametric Kruscal-Wallis test is used.

Table 2. summarizes the results of the Kruskal-Wallis test. Given the 4 participant groupings used, the test had 3 degrees of freedom. The null hypothesis (that the distribution of the various population medians were equal) was rejected if the test statistic, p, was less than 0.01. This will be the form of the null hypothesis and its rejection whenever Kruskal-Wallis is used.

Table 2. Statistical significance of the dependent variables on the combined discipline groups using the Kruskal Wallis Test. Cells in bold, italic face type show significant differences, those in plain face are not significant.

	Q3.A. Help Used	Q3.B. Help Satisfied	Q3.C. Search Used	Q3.D. Search Satisfied
p	0.018	0.470	*0.0007*	*0.0008*

The Mann-Whitney test, another non-parametric test comparing medians of two groups at a time, was used to drill down into the data. These tests were run on dependent variables that showed significant differences in the Kruskal-Wallis tests, see Table 2. This pursuit of the source of statistical significance is generally deprecated due to the dependent variables probably not being linearly independent of each other. These results are reported anyway but the increased probability of error must be noted. The null hypotheses were that the CS group's median distributions are less than or equal to that of the compared group and were rejected with $p < .01$. These results are in Table 3.

The only significant results between groups of two were for CS versus each of the other groups; none of the non-CS groups (Arts/Business, Arts/Science and Science/Business) showed significant differences. This shows that the statistically significant overall results (Table 2.) were entirely due to CS students and, thus, CS students used and were satisfied with search significantly more than students in other majors. Hypotheses HA and HB are accepted.

Table 3. The first 3 rows show the statistical significance of the comparisons of the CS group with each of the non-CS groups using the Mann-Whitney test. A Kruskal Wallis test (last row of Table 3.) summarizes the 3 Mann-Whitney tests that showed the differences between the non-CS groups were not significant. Cells in bold, italic face type show significant differences, those in plain face are not significant.

	Q3.C.Search Used	Q3.D. Search Satisfied
	p	p
CS/Sci	*< 0.0001*	*0.0069*
CS/Arts	*< 0.0001*	*< 0.0001*
CS/Bus	*< 0.0001*	*0.0003*
Sci/Art/Bus	0.4488	0.1948

6.2 Hypothesis HC. Students in diverse disciplines use search engines for help more than they use Help.

Hypothesis HD. Students from diverse disciplines are more satisfied with search engines than Help.

Further investigating Question Q3 (level of use and satisfaction with search and Help); the pairs of responses for each participant on their use and satisfaction are tested using the non-parametric Wilcoxon test, with $p < .01$. This investigates whether or not each individual participant used and/or was satisfied more with Search or Help. The following results were found.

Table 4 shows the paired use and satisfaction data for all (column All) participants were statistically tested first and the results were significant. Drilling deeper, the tests showed a significant difference in each group's use and satisfaction with Search and Help. Thus, these overall results are not due to just a subset of the groups as was found earlier (see Tables 2. and 3.) with computer science participants skewing the results for all the groups. Students from all disciplines used and were satisfied with Search significantly more than they were with Help, confirming hypotheses HC. and HD.

6.3 Conjecture CA. Students in diverse disciplines use search engines for help more than they use any other source of help.

Hypothesis HE. Students from diverse disciplines are more satisfied with search engines than with any other source of help.

Table 4. Statistical comparison of use and satisfaction with Help and Search using the Wilcoxon test. The paired responses for each participant to question Q3.A./C. (Use) and Q3.B./D. (Satisfaction) were tested. Cells in bold, italic face type show significant differences; note, all cells are in bold, italic face.

		All	Arts	Bus	CS	Sci
Use (Help vs. Search)	p	*< 0.0001*	*< 0.0001*	*0.0046*	*< 0.0001*	*0.0036*
Satisfaction (Help vs. Search)	p	*< 0.0001*	*< 0.0001*	*0.0001*	*< 0.0001*	*< 0.0001*

Table 5. Percentages (and counts) of participants in each group choosing a source of help in question Q4.A. See also Fig. 5 above.

	Arts	Business	CS	Science	Total
	% (count)	% (count)	% (count)	% (count)	% (count)
Person	39% (111)	44% (120)	26% (49)	35% (90)	37% (370)
Search	28% (78)	25% (69)	35% (65)	27% (69)	28% (281)
Help	10% (28)	12% (34)	13% (24)	11% (27)	11% (113)
Text	7% (19)	6% (16)	16% (29)	6% (14)	8% (78)
Other	2% (5)	1% (2)	3% (5)	2% (5)	2% (17)
No response	15% (41)	13% (35)	8% (14)	20% (50)	14% (140)
Total	100% (282)	100% (276)	100% (186)	100% (255)	100% (999)

Table 6. Median and mean satisfaction of participants with the various help sources in question Q4.B.

	Arts	Bus	CS	Sci	Overall
	Median (mean)	Median (mean)	Median (mean)	Median (mean)	Median (mean)
Person	6 (5.44)	6 (5.53)	5 (4.93)	6 (5.27)	6 (5.36)
Search	6 (5.55)	6 (5.58)	6 (5.82)	6 (5.44)	6 (5.59)
Help	4 (4.30)	4.5 (4.47)	4 (3.50)	4 (4.63)	4 (4.28)
Text	5 (4.37)	6 (5.60)	5 (5.24)	5 (5.21)	5 (5.09)
Other	7 (6.4)	6.5 (6.5)	6 (6.20)	6 (5.80)	6 (6.18)

Question Q4.A. asked each participant to state three actual sources from which they get help using software. The responses were varied, but were classified as being from Person (e.g., teacher, tutors, friend, family, help desk, help line), Search (e.g., Google, Yahoo, and other software with a search feature, such as YouTube), Help, Text (books[3], user manuals) or Other (not easily classifiable sources). The results are shown in Table 5.

The data show that in all groups, except CS, the Person count was higher than the Search count. Help was third for the non-CS groups but was fourth for CS. This shows that three of the four groups preferred Person to Search. No appropriate statistical tests were found that fit this situation without stretching the limits of statistical credulity. The percentages have to speak for themselves. Conjecture CA is apparently, but not statistically, contradicted because Person was the most used help source, not Search. (Note: The original test design had the students rate their three help sources in order of preference. This caused a variety of

problems. It was decided just to have them list the top three, not in order of preference.)

The final question, Q4.B., asks participants to rate their satisfaction with each of the help sources listed in their response to Q4.A. Both medians and means are reported in Table 6 as discussed above.

Although Table 5 shows that participants listed Person most often as the source of help, the medians in Table 6. show Search and Person to be very close in level of satisfaction. Both Person and Search were more satisfactory than Help or Text. Help is the least satisfactory for all groups; it is the only row with 4 or 4.5 as the medians. Computer scientists were most satisfied with Search and the least satisfied with Help of all groups.

---

[3] The primary text source was an assigned class text. Students did not seem to buy books specifically to aid in the use of software.

Table 7. Results of the Kruskal-Wallis statistical test first show that the distribution of the medians for all participants differed in their satisfaction with the four sources (Person, Search, Help, and Text). This was followed by the tests within each major. Cells in bold, italic face type show significant differences, those in plain face are not significant.

		Overall	Arts	Bus	CS	Sci
Satisfaction with sources	p	*< 0.0001*	*< 0.0001*	*0.0009*	*< 0.0001*	.078

Table 8. Statistical results using the paired Wilcoxon test of satisfaction within majors and between help sources. Cells in bold, italic face type show significant differences, those in plain face are not significant.

	Person/Search	Person/Help	Person/Text	Search/Help	Search/Text	Text/Help
Arts	0.9210	0.0362	0.4223	*0.00706*	*0.0041*	0.7983
Bus	0.2040	*0.0012*	0.7226	*0.000914*	0.8454	0.4237
CS	*< 0.0001*	*0.0005*	0.9192	*0.000132*	0.0186	*0.0003*
Sci	0.5153	0.1925	0.8597	*0.0051*	0.1557	0.7276

Table 7. First shows the results of statistical testing of the overall participant satisfaction with the help sources. For this, Other was eliminated due to the few respondents and the variety and ambiguity of the sources classified as Other. The overall test was significant so the component majors were then compared. Again, the Kruskal-Wallis test is used with significance at $p < 0.01$.

All majors except Science showed significance differences in their overall satisfaction with the help sources. Arts, Business, CS and Sci were further investigated using the paired Wilcoxon test to see where any differences occurred. The results, in Table 8, show that Search significantly dominates Help for all groups. CS participants significantly preferred all other sources of help to Help. No group other than Computer Science significantly preferred Search to Person. All pairings other than Search/Help are inconclusive for some groups of participants. These results do not reject the null hypothesis. Thus, hypothesis HE is rejected. Search is not significantly more satisfactory than any other source of help.

7. CONCLUSIONS AND RECOMMENDATIONS

Three hundred and thirty three undergraduate students were surveyed about their sources of help in using software. The participants were placed in 4 groups, based on their major: arts, business, computer science, and science (with engineering). When use and satisfaction with a search engine was compared directly with the use of the standard software help mechanism, every group used and was satisfied significantly more with a search engine. Computer science students used and were significantly more satisfied with a search engine than any other group. Thus, Search was perceived by the study participants as superior to Help for aid in software use.

The results are much less conclusive when comparing Search and Help with other help sources (People and Text) used by the participants. Each tested group still significantly preferred Search to Help but results were mixed for other help pairings. Thus, Search is not the preferred help mechanism when compared to the other mechanisms that participants reported using: Help, People and Text.

Given the above, how might software companies provide better support to users? The obvious recommendation is to augment the Help mechanism with a tailored search engine. In order to implement this recommendation, all applications, whether web-based or not, would have searchable online help documentation supported by more in-depth, manual-like, online, searchable documentation. The search should be tailored to allow users to also access trusted forums, blogs and other relevant sites. The included sites could be expanded as more are found relevant. The user could also choose to search additional specific sites or the entire web.

Adobe Creative Suite 5 uses Google Site Search to power its Adobe Community Help Centre system [10]. Google Site Search allows Adobe to index into its own content as well as specific community-recommended sites. These sites include blogs, forums, etc. This application almost fully embodies the above recommendation.

It is interesting that, while participants went to other people for help more than to any other resource (Table 5), they were not consistently more satisfied with people than any other source (Table 8). In a campus setting, people are usually available and often helpful. As computing has become more ubiquitous, people have the web available wherever they go. This could drastically affect where people go most often for aid.

In conclusion, more complex software has made its use more and more difficult. People need tools to easily find solutions to their software problems. User satisfaction is the key to successful software. People are not satisfied with current Help systems. Therefore, Help must be actively reviewed and changed by both new and established software enterprises.

7. ACKNOWLEDGEMENTS

Many thanks are due to the students and faculty that participated in this study.

8. REFERENCES

[1] Andrade, O., and Novick, D. 2008. Expressing help at appropriate levels, *Proceedings of SIGDOC 2008*, Lisbon, Portugal, September 22-25, 2008, 125-129.

[2] Andrade, O. D., Bean, N., and Novick D.G. 2009. The macro-structure of use help. In *Proceedings of the 27th ACM international SIGDOC conference on Design of communication* (Bloomington, Indiana, USA, October 5-7, 2009). DOI= http://doi.acm.org/10.1145/1621995.1622022.

[3] Baecker, R., Booth, K., Jovicic, S., McGrenere, J. and Moore, G. (2000). Reducing the gap between what users know and what they need to know. *Proceedings of the ACM 2000 International Conference on Intelligent User Interfaces*, January 9-12, 2000, New Orleans. 17-23.

[4] Bessiere, K., Ceaparu, I., Lazar, J., Robinson, J., and Shneiderman, B. 2003. *Social and psychological influences on computer user frustration*, CS Technical Report 4410, Department of Computer Science, University of Maryland.

[5] Carroll, J., Smith-Kerker, P., Ford, J., and Mazur-Rimetz, S. 1987. The minimal manual. *International Journal of Human-Computer Interaction,* 3(2), 123-153.

[6] Ceaparu, I., Lazar, J., Bessiere, K., Robinson, J., and Shneiderman, B. 2004. Determining causes and severity of end-user frustration, *International Journal of Human-Computer Interaction*, 17(3), 333-356.

[7] Hays, W. 1994. *Statistics, fifth ed.* Wadsworth Publishing, Belmont, CA. ISBN-13: 978-0030744679

[8] Markoff, J., Elliott, S. 2001. Humor Is at Center of Microsoft's New Campaign. The New York Times, Wednesday, April 1.

[9] Mendoza, J. and Novick, D. 2005. Usability over time. *Proceedings of SIGDOC 2005*, Coventry, UK, September 21-23, 2005, 151-158.

[10] Nicholson, M., 2010. Adobe Community Help and Google Site Search: Making search come alive in CS5. Official Google Enterprise Blog, April 30, 2010. http://googleenterprise.blogspot.com/2010/04/adobe-community-help-and-google-site.html, last accessed May 16, 2011.

[11] Novick, D., and Ward, K. 2006. Why don't people read the manual? *Proceedings of SIGDOC 2006*, Myrtle Beach, SC, October 18-20, 2006, 11-18.

[12] Novick, D., and Ward, K. (2006). What users say they want in documentation *Proceedings of SIGDOC 2006*, Myrtle Beach, SC, October 18-20, 2006, 84-91.

[13] Novick, D., Elizalde, E., and Bean, N. 2007. Toward a more accurate view of when and how people seek help with computer applications, *Proceedings of SIGDOC 2007*, El Paso, TX, October 22-24, 2007, 95-102.

[14] Novick, D., Andrade, O., Bean, N., and Elizalde, E. 2008. Help-based tutorials, *Proceedings of SIGDOC 2008*, Lisbon, Portugal, September 22-25, 2008, 1-8.

[15] Novick, D, Andrade, O., and Bean, N. 2009. The micro-structure of use of help, *Proceedings of SIGDOC 2009*, Bloomington, IN, October 5-7, 2009.

[16] Rettig, Marc. 1991. Nobody reads documentation. *CACM* 34, 7, July 1991, 25-29

[17] Rieman, J. 1996. A field study of exploratory learning strategies. *ACM Transactions on Computer-Human Interaction 3*, 198-218.

[18] Smart, K., Whiting, M., and De Tienne, K 2001. Assessing the need for printed and online documentation: A study of customer preference and use, *Journal of Business Communication* 38, 285-314.

A Cognitive Perspective on Developer Comprehension of Software Design Documentation

Hugo H.
Schoonewille[1]
hschoone@liacs.nl

Werner Heijstek[1]
heijstek@liacs.nl

Michel R.V.
Chaudron[1]
chaudron@liacs.nl

Thomas Kühne[2]
thomas.kuehne@
ecs.vuw.ac.nz

[1]Leiden Institute of Advanced Computer Science
Leiden University, Niels Bohrweg 1, 2333 CA Leiden, the Netherlands
[2]School of Engineering and Computer Science
Victoria University of Wellington, P. O. Box 600, Wellington 6140, New Zealand

ABSTRACT

Software design documentation is an important aid for communication during software development and maintenance. Nevertheless, little empirical evidence exists regarding the use of software documentation, and effective software design representation in particular. In an experimental setting, we used documentation from industry in which aspects of a software design were modeled in both a (UML) diagram and text. We recorded and analysed how participants used these media to answer various design-related questions and collected additional information in various questionnaires. By having participants think aloud, we set out to understand the underlying cognitive processes of developer design comprehension by applying the grounded theory method. We validated the results with concepts from the cognitive theory of multimedia learning. Results show a positive correlation between *developer certainty* and *correctness of answers*, whereas the opposite was not found. Also, *self-rated experience* and *self-rated skill* coincide with higher levels of certainty. We found that participants rated information based on perceived importance and that their "common sense" plays a significant role. Surprisingly, more than 60 percent of the answers were based on the consultation of a single medium. These results clearly ask for further investigation. We propose corresponding future work.

Categories and Subject Descriptors

D.2.7 [**Software Engineering**]: Distribution, Maintenance, and Enhancement—*Documentation*; D.2.11 [**Software Architectures**]: Languages—*description*; D.2.10 [**Design**]: Representation

General Terms

Documentation, Design, Experimentation, Human Factors

Keywords

software design comprehension, cognitive theory of multimedia learning

1. INTRODUCTION

Unambiguous communication is always beneficial during software development [12, 19] but of even greater importance in software maintenance and Global Software Development (GSD), when physically separated teams work on a project [15]. Due to the limited possibilities for direct communication in these situations, documentation plays a more fundamental role. The degree to which Software Architecture Documentation (SAD) is intelligible can then be crucial to the success of the development effort. Software design documentation is only effective if it allows designers and developers to understand the intended design [28]. Supporting this process of understanding by tailoring the methods used to convey the design in a way that fits human cognitive processing [23] could increase the efficiency of communication – and thus benefit the development process [1, 29]. As Mayer [27] expounds, we should not perceive "understanding" as passive information acquisition but rather as active knowledge construction. In order to ease this knowledge construction, the *integration* of information communicated through multiple media should be facilitated to build up a mental model. We argue that a more complete mental model decreases error and mistake sensitivity, increases development speed and reduces the amount of training a developer requires [7]. Supporting the construction of comprehensive and accurate mental models is thus of great importance. In this work, we aim to develop an understanding of the development of these mental models at a fundamental level [22]. In particular, this research aims at obtaining a better understanding of the relationship between human cognition and methods of documentation. Therefore, our research question is:

> *How do software developers comprehend software architecture representations?*

The structure of this paper is as follows: Sections two and three elaborate on the background and methodology of the study. In sections four and five, results are presented and discussed. Finally, sections six and seven outline our conclusions and future work.

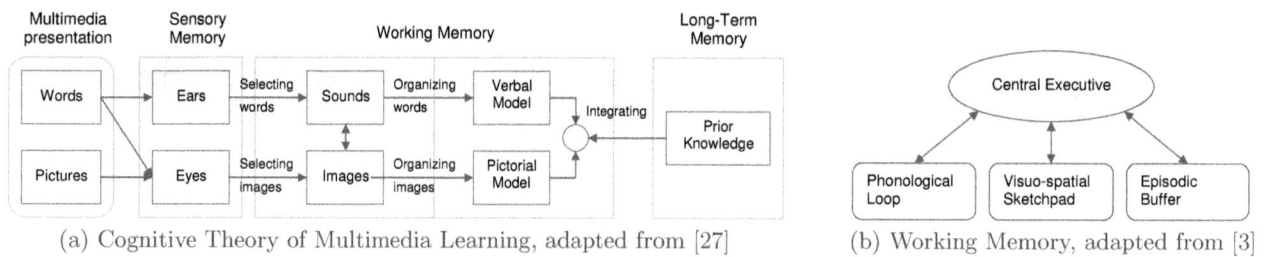

(a) Cognitive Theory of Multimedia Learning, adapted from [27]   (b) Working Memory, adapted from [3]

Figure 1: Diagrammatic representations of the working of human cognition

2. BACKGROUND

2.1 Communication

Development of software highly depends on collaboration, which raises the potential issue of coordinating activity hindrances [20]. The coinciding increase in stress on communication is diverted through the *informal* and *formal* channels [20]. The combination of communication tools and proper modularisation ameliorates the quality of informal communication and (or) decreases its necessity [16, 33]. Still, in certain settings such as GSD or maintenance, more formal methods of documented communication constitute an indispensable complement to informal communication [6, 25]. In practice, it appears that developers in general avoid using design documents when possible [20, 16, 30]. In addition, in a GSD setting, developers have no choice but to use documentation, as direct communication to certain team members is hindered by temporal, geographical and socio-cultural distances [16, 24, 36]. This implies that some problems inherent to GSD could be mitigated by improving documentation quality. The utility of SAD depends on two documentation properties: what the author embeds in it and what the developer extracts from it. Ideally, the latter would coincide with the former, but various factors influence the efficacy of this process. Four factors could be focused on to improve this:

- **Personal and Organisational**: It is acknowledged that people's background influences the perceived content [21]. Important to these backgrounds are the organisational aspects constituted by common ground, a shared knowledge base and shared technologies [6, 32].
- **Technological**: Technological aids for communication in Software Development. Media choices belong to this area.
- **Process**: Development processes and methods (like RUP, XP, Scrum etc.) facilitate software development. They impact on the type and amount of documentation required.
- **Representation**: Documentation may or may not fit human cognition. Modeling styles or notational conventions [28] may play a role on top of fundamental paradigm choices.

The research presented in this paper focuses primarily on the last point.

2.2 Human cognition

Both the visual and textual representations of a system should befit human cognitive processes to ensure correct understanding. This section construes a fundament for basic understanding of the human cognition.

2.2.1 Human Memory & Understanding

The path from stimulus acquisition to cognitive understanding can be divided into the processes of *selecting*, *processing*, *storing* (or encoding), and *retrieving* information. Research into the cognitive foundations of these processes has resulted in several models of which Baddeley and Hitch's appeared to be best able to explain a wide variety of phenomena [2, 3, 13]. As can be seen in Figure 2, Baddeley and Hitch's model subdivides human memory into three major components. The Working Memory (WM) is most interesting in software development context because this system is used to keep information active while performing complex tasks such as reasoning and comprehension [3]. In here, the mental model resides, comprising attended information, available for consultation during cognitive tasks. The WM can be divided into several subsystems, depicted in Figure 1b. The total capacity of WM is limited, but each subsystem could be loaded more or less independently [2, 3]. Storing information from WM into Long Term Memory (LTM) occurs through encoding. During encoding, information is organised and structured into a schema (or *knowledge construct*) and linked to existing schemas residing in LTM. Comprehension occurs as a result of selecting the right information and combining it with apt existing knowledge [18].

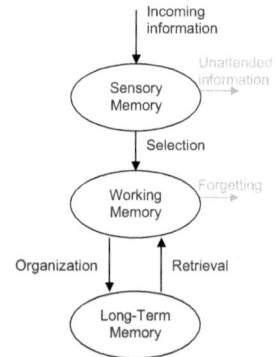

Figure 2: Human memory systems, adapted from [4]

2.2.2 Cognitive Theory of Multimedia Learning

The basis of the cognitive theory of multimedia learning is the idea that the design of multimedia messages should be consistent with the way people process information. A hypothesis is that learners are able to create a better, more complete mental model using multiple types of media. Such an enhanced model in turn enables them to obtain a deeper understanding of the presented material. Three principles from the cognitive sciences found this assertion [27]:

- the Dual-Channel assumption;
- the Limited Capacity assumption;
- the Active Learning assumption.

The *Dual-Channel* assumption suggests that it is advantageous to simultaneously use multiple channels for communicating information; the *Limited Capacity* assumption asserts that there is a limitation on the amount of information humans can process per channel at a time; and the *Active Learning* assumption supposes the idea that humans need to actively construct knowledge rather than just absorb presented material. The *Active Learning* assumption is subdivided into three separate processes:

- Selection;
- Organisation;
- Integration.

These processes are represented by the annotated arrows in Figure 1a and all take place in the working memory. Information enters through the eyes or ears into the sensory memory. Then, one selects interesting information out of all stimuli. Subsequently, the learner constructs separated verbal- and pictorial models and finally, the models are integrated into one mental model. It hence becomes clear that the integration of verbal and pictorial models is indispensable for attaining understanding. However, it is important to minimise the cognitive load during these processes. Mayer proposed several guidelines for instructional design to improve the transfer of information and construction of knowledge by decreasing unnecessary cognitive load [27].

3. METHODOLOGY

The following subsections describe the experimental setup used to obtain knowledge about the way developers use software documentation. Also, the methods of analysis are described here. This experiment is also reported on by Heijstek et al. [14].

3.1 Sample

We applied quota sampling [37] to obtain at least one professional developer for every three students who participated in the experiment. For both groups, we applied convenience sampling. In Wellington, students participated voluntarily and went into a draw for a prize of NZ\$50. In Leiden students participated both voluntarily and through a mandatory part of a course – most students were more than happy to participate, though. Industrial organisations in Wellington participated voluntarily. All students, but not all professionals, had used the UML during their studies. All participants had previous experience with the UML. A total of 47 subjects participated in the original experiment of which 35 were male and 12 female. The average age was 27, ranging between 21 and 41. The participants came from two Universities and four different organisations. Participants include BSc., BSc-hons., MSc. and Ph.D. students at the School of Engineering and Computer Science (ECS) at Victoria University Wellington (VUW), MSc. students and Ph.D. candidates at the Leiden Institute of Advanced Computer Science (LIACS) at Leiden University (UL) and developers from the field of custom software development at various different organisations in New Zealand and the Netherlands, including Capgemini the Netherlands, Infoprofs and ASR Insurances. From the above described pool, 11 of the most articulate participants were drawn to ensure that enough relevant data could be collected.

3.2 Data Collection

Participants were presented with a series of different software systems. Each description comprised of a text and a diagram – separated on different sheets of paper respectively. We defined a set T that holds all design information described in the text sheet and a set D that holds all design information described in the diagram sheet. All design information is then described by $T \bigcup D$. We designed the questions so that the answer to some questions can be found in the intersection $T \bigcap D$, some answers can only be found in the complement $T \setminus D$ and some answers can only be found in the complement $D \setminus T$. Finally, some questions are not to be found in either set ($\sim (T \bigcup D)$). Dividing the two types of information (see Figure 3) enabled us to obtain information regarding media use.

3.3 Material Design

We used five text-diagram pairs that were inspired by authentic industrial SADs. We focused on the ability of participants to extract design information from both grammatically and syntactically correct diagrams and texts. All diagrams represented structural views of a system. We used UML 2 component and deployment diagrams. An example diagram is shown in Figure 3a.

Texts consisted of a natural language description of the architectural component. An example is shown in Figure 3b. Texts were designed to be in concordance with texts found in industrial SADs as much as possible. The non-verbose versions contained fewer details regarding the architectural design and were about half as long as the respective verbose versions. Questions and design documents were carefully tuned to each other to allow a multitude of subsequent analyses to be performed. Examples of questions are: *"Is component X the only component that may modify attribute Y?"* and *"Through what node does system X connect to system Y?"*. When designing questions, we limited ourselves to questions that could be answered with information that could be described in text or diagrams. We made sure not to rely on detailed knowledge of UML notation/semantics. The experiment design process involved determining and listing the most important information conveyed in the design, creating a set of questions relating to this information and validating the questions by means of trials. For each architecture two descriptions were created. One version contained a verbose diagram and non-verbose (content reduced) text and the second version contained verbose text and a non-verbose diagram. We refer to the former as a diagram-dominant representation and the latter as a text-dominant representation. We created non-verbose versions of diagrams and text by removing elements or sentences from the more complete ones.

3.4 Experiment execution

Each participant was presented two diagram-dominant representations and two text-dominant representations. The location of the verbose diagrams was alternating between left and right. The questions were the same for diagram- and text-dominant representations of the architecture. The participants were asked to think-aloud during problem solving and were encouraged to keep verbalising when they fell silent, all following the rules of Think out Loud (ToL) from Protocol Analysis [8, 9]. For further analysis of their behaviour, audio and video were recorded. In addition to the architecture representation documents we devised two questionnaires: a pre-questionnaire to collect the participant's background information, and a questionnaire following the experiment to see how they evaluated the experiment: how they think they used the documentation and what their thoughts were about its utility.

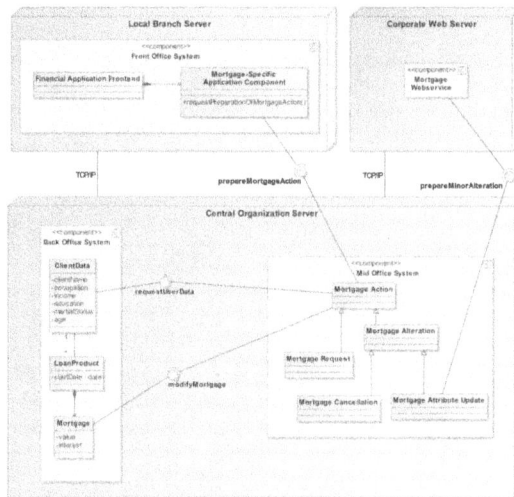

(a) verbose diagram

The system described in this diagram provides support for creating new mortgages and alteration of existing mortgages.

The design aims to separate the complexities of the business logic from the Financial Application Frontend by bundling all mortgage-related services on a central Mid Office System. This system provides services for the setup of all `mortgage actions'.

The Front Office Component hosts a Financial Application Frontend which contains a Mortgage-specific Application Component. Due to concerns regarding decreased Back Office availability, mortgage action requests may have a maximum size of 300 kilobytes.

The Mortgage Webservice provides an additional method to update mortgage attributes. This service only connects to an interface provided by the Mortgage Attribute Update specialization.

(b) non-verbose text

Figure 3: Example design

3.5 Analysis

We used the videos and audio recordings to analyse how subjects used the architecture representations while trying to answer questions.

3.5.1 Grounded Theory: Data-driven coding

Grounded Theory (GT) was used during analysis. GT is an inductive form of qualitative research that claims to construct theories that remain grounded in observations rather than being generated in the abstract [10, 11, 26]. With GT, one does not establish hypotheses prior to performing research; the researcher creates them during analysis. With GT, one first transcribes the data and divides it into segments containing one answer per unit. Second, the process of coding commences. To remain open to every (unexpected) pattern of behaviour, no preconceived coding scheme (data-driven coding) is applied. Third, the emerged codes are categorised according to their content and relations. The final stage of theory or hypothesis construction bases itself on the outcomes of the previous phases, combined with the concurrently produced memos containing rudimentary conceptualisations and ideas that came to mind while analysing. The result of the whole process, from enquiry to writing, is a theory that theorises about the meaning of actions and relations between them [5].

4. RESULTS

During the coding stage, 20 different codes emerged, which could roughly be divided into two separate categories: *behaviour* and *attitude*. The first category captures the actual behaviour expressed by the participant, whereas the *attitude*-category captures the "attitude" with which the participant gave his answer. The latter is most interesting in this analysis, largely because the behaviour-codes can be assessed quantitatively as well, as has been shown by Heijstek et al. [14]. Four of the codes – all from the *attitude* category – will be discussed in this section, alongside with examples They were chosen based on value and evidence available.

4.1 Codes 1 & 2: "Certain" and "Uncertain"

The first codes explored are *uncertain* and *certain*, referring to the attitude of a participant towards an architecture and related questions. A typical example of an *uncertain* answer is the one given by participant 29 to question δ3 ("Is the communication between system x and system y secure?"):

> *"The only thing I see is SQL, and that doesn't give me anything about security. So I would say it's not secure."*

Answers coded as *certainty* were concise and given with confidence. The codes are especially valuable because a developer's assessment of their own answer might be indicative for its correctness and/or developer skill. Any conclusive results could be used to be alerted of potentially incorrect answers (e.g., in the form of misreadings) in an early stage and deal with them proactively. A first hypothesis that comes to mind is a positive relation between *certainty* and *correctness*. As can be seen in Figure 4, the majority of the answers is correct, regardless of the level of certainty. However, over 70 percent of the answers coded as *certain* are correct - almost 20 percent more than answers coded as uncertain. However, the correlation between *certainty* and *correctness* is not significant. Some participants displayed a high propensity in being either certain or uncertain. Figure 5 shows this clearly for participant 16 and 33. Note, however, that their correctness score was not above average. In contrast, consider participant 19: 10 of his 13 answers were coded as *uncertain* of which only five were correct. In general, a balanced self-assessment of a developer regarding their certainty coincides with better answers albeit not statistically significant. Combining the above with the self-rated experience, skills and education obtained from the questionnaire yields Figure 6. It shows a (non-significant) correlation between higher experience and certainty.

4.2 Code 3: "Common Sense"

The third code that emerged was *common sense*. This code is useful to understand a participant's reaction to am-

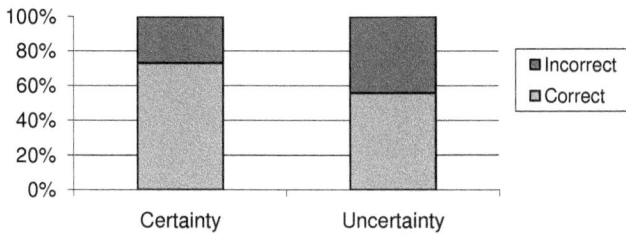

Figure 4: Answers correct or incorrect per code

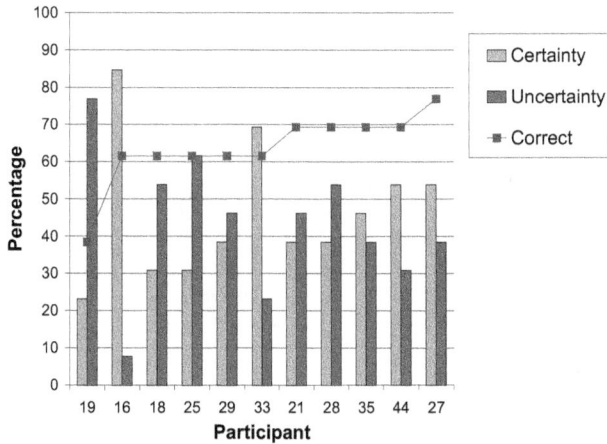

Figure 5: Correlation between certainty, uncertainty, and correctness. Sorted according to correctness

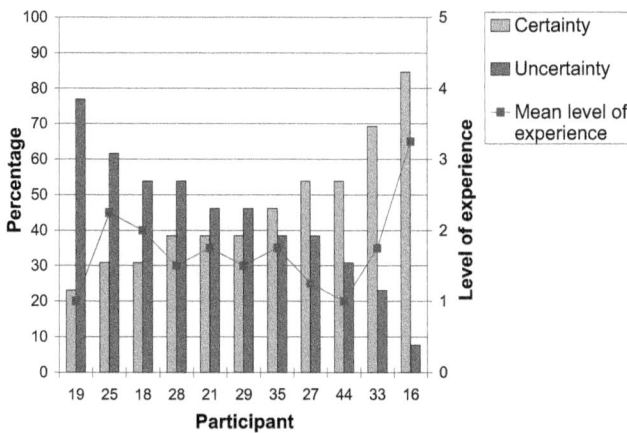

Figure 6: Correlation between certainty and level of experience. Sorted according to certainty

biguous or absent information. Does a developer acknowledge that they cannot make a decision, or do they use common sense to fill in absent information? A first observation is that participants make assumptions of the importance of information. When they think their own knowledge surpasses the presented information, they tend to prefer their own common sense: some developers are happy to base their decision on what essentially is speculation. An incorrect form of reasoning is demonstrated in the following answer given by participant 21 to question β3 ("Can message type x be ignored by system y?"):

"There's no special thing about this one. Messages can be ignored is a general [sic] (...) It's unclear about this one so I guess yes, they can be ignored."

He probably assumes that allowing to ignore a message is the safest option, but what if that is not the case? Of course the developer's assessment may be correct in this or another particular case, but in general they should not base decisions on assumptions. Of all participants, 4 answered question β3 in a way we categorised as using *common sense*. This relatively high percentage can probably be explained with the type of question. We classified question β3 as difficult: it cannot be answered with the information provided and we furthermore included as "false friend" – a property that could be expected to mislead someone. Many developers assume familiarity with system β – a booking system for flights – and hence feel confident to fill in specificities using *common sense*. Except for participant 16's answer on the first (example) question, every other *common sense* answer was coded *uncertain* as well. So, at least developers acknowledged that their answers were based on some level of speculation.

4.3 Code 4: "Single Medium Based Answer"

The last code analysed was *Single Medium Based Answer* (*SMBA*). Answers were coded as SMBA when the participant:

1. only looks into one of the two media and comes up with an answer,
2. explicitly mentioned that his answer was based on a single medium or
3. only peeks shortly (presumably too short to see anything valuable) into another medium.

This code is useful for understanding how developers make use of information provided in both textual and visual media and, in particular for understanding whether there is a correlation between correctness and use of media. If we only take into account (1), i.e., where the participant looked (and thus disregard the think aloud analysis), we find that the use of a single medium has a negative impact on the amount of correct answers given ($\tau = -.279, p = 0.02$). For our wider definition of use of a single medium (*SMBA*), we find that 64 percent all given answers belong to this group. Of this total, 57 percent was correct (Figure 7) compared to 74 percent correctness for answers given based on both media. The use of both representations is indeed associated

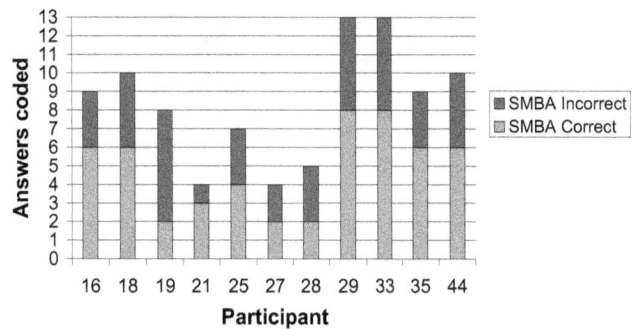

Figure 7: Answers coded *SMBA* per participant

with the amount of correct answers. We can therefore assert that the participants seemed to have gotten a better understanding of the presented architecture when both documents were used. This finding is in line with what could be expected based on the cognitive theory of multimedia learning.

Combining the results from section 4.1 with this code yields Figure 8. Participants answering less than nine answers using *SMBA* are more often *uncertain*. In addition, they were more often incorrect than average. These observations might be explained by the fact that participants unsure about their current answer are likely to consult both diagram and text in order to look for further evidence.

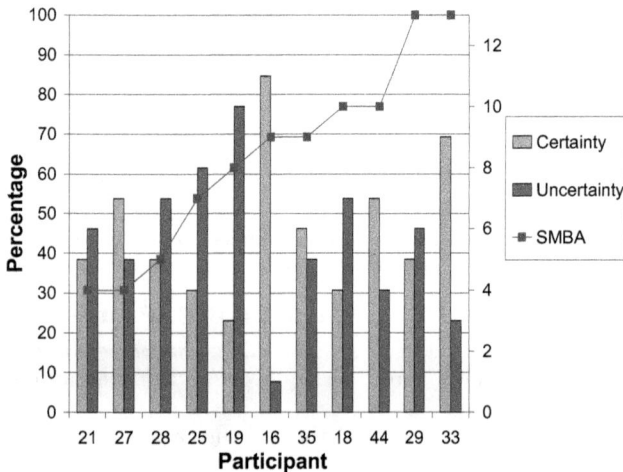

Figure 8: *Certainty* and *uncertainty*. The left five participants are constituted by the participants in the 'less than nine answers *SMBA*' group; the right six in the category of 'nine or more answers *SMBA*'

Another interesting observation emerges when taking the questions as viewpoint rather than the participants. Questions $\gamma 1$ through $\gamma 3$ are all coded as *SMBA* one or two times *more* often than average; questions $\alpha 3$, $\delta 1$, and $\delta 2$ are coded *SMBA* one time *less* than average. Combining this observation with the correctness of the answers on these groups of questions in Figure 9, we see that answers given in the 'less than average'-category are correct more often. Questions that make a participant more susceptible to answer it using only one medium, increase the amount of errors as well. The present research however cannot provide conclusive thoughts regarding this distinction.

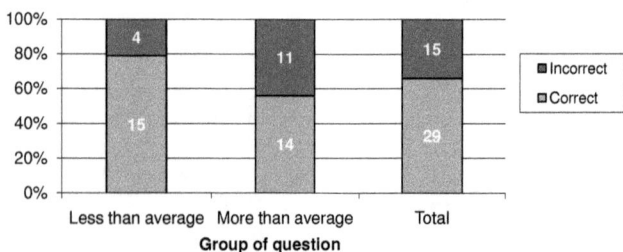

Figure 9: Results of questions coded *SMBA*. The category 'less than average' is constituted by questions $\alpha 3$, $\delta 1$ & $\delta 2$; 'greater than average' contains questions $\gamma 1$, $\gamma 2$ & $\gamma 3$. 'Total' consists of only answers coded *SMBA*. The numbers represent the actual amounts

5. DISCUSSION

5.1 Certain and Uncertain

Holmes identified that second language learners could experience difficulty in expressing modal meanings [17]. As most of our participants were non-native English speakers, their expression of their understanding of the documentation could be distorted. In turn, this could result in the absence of a clear relation between *uncertainty* and (in)correctness. The positive correlation between *certainty* and correctness might be explained by participants taking educated guesses based on scarce cues combined with experience and skills that turn out to be correct. Our results indicate that a propensity towards extreme positions regarding the self-assessment of one's abilities is undesirable. High overall uncertainty might indicate that the developer is less knowledgeable; high overall certainty might indicate that the developer has an overrated self-image regarding their work. Any such low correlation between the *perceived* abilities and the actual abilities is potentially problematic. In our experiment, balanced self-assessments correlated with better quality answers. Another useful observation we made is the positive correlation between the level of experience and correctness of answers.

5.2 Common Sense

In general, the ability of developers to speculate about the importance of information is not bad in itself. Experience and skill may often lead to correct assumptions. For example, developers sometimes implicitly use the Level of Detail in a UML diagram to successfully assess the importance of a component [31]. However, developers sometimes err in their judgment, as partly confirmed by our experiment. They could be helped by emphasising important parts of the system in the textual and pictorial description, hence reducing extraneous processing. To avoid developers being forced to fill in missing information more or less successfully, the authors should be aware of the guidelines proposed in the cognitive theory of multimedia learning. Documentation should be **concise** – so developers can actually find the relevant information and are willing to check the whole documentation [34]. It should be designed to reduce extraneous and manage essential processing by facilitating integration of both textual and pictorial representations. Besides, it should also be **up-to-date** so it contains the correct information. Ideally, knowledgeable colleagues can be consulted by a developer but this is not always possible, in particular in off-shore development scenarios. This experiment simulated such a situation. Gaps in documentation are less problematic if the author and recipient share some *common ground*. Common ground refers to the knowledge that different people have in common and that they are aware of the fact they do [32]. Common ground can thus decrease the chance of miscommunication: when some detail was omitted from the documentation by the designer – maybe even intentionally so – every developer sharing the same common ground is then able to fill in the correct answer. A decrease in surface completeness could hence be complemented with this common ground.

5.3 SMBA

Our observation that answers coded *SMBA* are slightly more often correct than average may not be generalisable to all sorts of documents since our software designs did not contain any inconsistencies. The behaviour of participant 19, for instance, might simply be the result of a lower level of experience and hence less correct answers overall. In general, participants answering less answers based on a single medium are more uncertain. As mentioned before, a possible explanation for this could be that they more often chose to consult both media to come up with an answer while being uncertain about their current answer candidate. This in turn could be due to the absence of data in one medium, but then every participant would have been expected to show roughly the same pattern. A more likely cause therefore is an inability to extract the requested information or the desire to double check answer candidates using all available information because of a general level of uncertainty. Either way, our results clearly indicate that using multiple media in forming an answer and uncertainty are positively correlated.

Answers to a few questions were noted to be coded as *SMBA* one time more or one time less than average. In the 'answers coded as *SMBA* less than average'-question category, more answers were correct. This apparently contradicts earlier results, which suggested that correctness increases with an increase in *SMBA*, but note that we are only considering the subset of SMBA answers here. Questions that make a participant susceptible to answer it using only one medium, increase the error rate. Causes for this effect might be found in the architecture at hand, but that only holds for the 'answers coded as *SMBA* more than average'-category, as all these questions came with architecture γ. The 'less than average'-category shared a different common denominator: their topological nature. Apparently, people struggled less with questions of such nature.

Most importantly, over 60 percent of the answers were coded as *SMBA*. This SAD usage pattern raises some major questions regarding the creation of such documentation. Is it even advantageous to use multiple media simultaneously or should the focus be on improving single-media documentation? This shows a use for the hypothesis of the cognitive theory of multimedia learning: *SMBA*-amounts could be decreased and performance increased by facilitating integration. The hypothesis states that a better, more complete mental model of a system to-be-build can be obtained by using both pictorial and textual models, *but* emphasis should be placed on ease of integration. Using the same words for the same components in both documents for example, simplifies selection and integration. Hence, both documents would be used more often and deeper understanding of the model could be reached.

6. CONCLUSION

The research presented in this paper provided a peek into the developer's mind: we saw how extreme self-assessments can be an indicator of problematic performance and that developers are happy to fill in missing information without necessarily having the common ground with the author of the documentation that justifies such a step. Being certain about one's findings is good, but only if the certainty is justified. Hence, even more important than being right most of the time is the ability of a developer to successfully self-assess whether a perceived certainty is justified or not. Such critical, meta-cognitive thinking is the prerequisite for stopping developers to make unjustified assumptions or incorrect interpretations but consult further sources instead. In part the research presented here shows the suitability of the Grounded Theory method to improve Software Architecture Documentation. We believe it was successful in that it produced a number of emergent codes that revealed interesting developer characteristics. Together with the guidelines proposed within the cognitive theory of multimedia learning, textual and pictorial representations could be aligned better. Using the same words for the same components, highlighting important parts and showing linked parts near each other are only a few examples of how integration of the two representations could be improved. This analysis resulted in a number of promising directions for future work.

7. FUTURE WORK

Potential future research based on this work includes investigations addressing the following directions and questions.

The tendency of developers towards being certain or uncertain, their justifications, and the effects thereof should be further examined. As proposed by Holmes [17], developer certainty could be expressed using a quantitative scale. Such a quantitative measure could subsequently be related to the effect size, e.g., to defect density.

The self-awareness of developers about their attitude, e.g., regarding filling in missing information, could be assessed. We hypothesise that increased self-awareness results in better software, as the developer is then expected to more often ask for elucidation when necessary. Results confirming this hypothesis could then be used to create self-awareness training for developers to increase their performance.

The relation between *uncertain* and *common sense* should be looked into. Does an inherent uncertainty of the developer imply an increased use of common sense or is it the other way around? In the presented research, common sense implies uncertainty in most cases, but not to a statistically relevant extend. Does a perceived familiarity with a system domain automatically imply an increased use of common sense and if so, why? Is the problem that authors (intentionally or unintentionally) leave out details they expect to be known by developers, or is it that developers are inclined to use knowledge that is most readily available to them – i.e., in his memory rather than in the documentation (an effect known as the *availability bias* [35])?

Further research should address the correctness and completeness of the mental model. The contents of it are usually a mixture of perceived and retrieved information from Long-Term Memory, but there is no guarantee that it is a healthy mixture. We hypothesise that increased application of common sense generally implies a mental model that excessively relies on Long-Term Memory information, hence increasing the error rate.

How do inconsistent and/or incomplete SADs affect the quality of the resulting software? The effect of inconsistent architectural documentation in software development is unknown. We hypothesise that scenarios that make developers susceptible to consulting only part of the available documentation have a detrimental effect on software quality because inconsistencies in the documentation that could have been picked up by a comprehensive consultation slip through unnoticed. In some cases, this will lead towards inconsistencies in the developed system [31]. As a result, it may not always be a good idea to distribute information across different media if it is known that some developers have an adversity to one media type (e.g., UML) and/or are known to excessively rely on another media type (e.g., text).

Finally, thus another interesting question is: what makes developers choose only one medium? Is it too burdensome to integrate information from different sources? Are their personal preferences, such as past bad experiences with certain types of media (e.g., sub-standard UML diagrams)? Is it even advisable to use multiple media at all, or should one rather focus on improving the quality of single-media documentation?

8. ACKNOWLEDGMENTS

The authors would like to thank all participants and Craig Anslow, John Hine and Jason Low for their support during the experiment.

9. REFERENCES

[1] AGARWAL, R., AND SINHA, A. Object-oriented modeling with UML: a study of developers' perceptions. *Communications of the ACM 46*, 9 (2003), 248–256.

[2] BADDELEY, A. D. Is working memory still working? *European Psychology 7*, 2nd (June 2002), 85–97.

[3] BADDELEY, A. D. Working memory. *Current Biology 20*, 4 (February 2010), 136–140.

[4] BADDELEY, A. D., KOPELMAN, M. D., AND WILSON, B. A., Eds. *The Essential Handbook of Memory Disorders for Clinicians*. John Wiley and Sons, 2004.

[5] CHARMAZ, K. *Constructing Grounded Theory*. Sage Publications, 2006.

[6] CURTIS, B., KRASNER, H., AND ISCOE, N. A field study of the software design process for large systems. *Comm. of the ACM 31*, 11 (November 1988), 1268–1287.

[7] DONAHUE, G., WEINSCHENK, S., AND NOWICKI, J. Usability is good business. *from http://www.yucentrik.ca/usability.pdf (02/06/2011)* (1999).

[8] DUMAS, J. User-based evaluations. In *The Human-computer Interaction Handbook* (2002), J. Jacko and A. Sears, Eds., L. Erlbaum Associates Inc., Mahwah, pp. 1093–1117.

[9] ERICSSON, K. A., AND SIMON, H. A. *Protocol Analysis: Verbal reports as data*, 2nd ed. MIT Press, 1993.

[10] GIBBS, G. R. *Analyzing Qualitative Data*. Sage Publications, 2007.

[11] GLASER, B., AND STRAUSS, A. *Grounded Theory: The Discovery of Grounded Theory*. New York: De Gruyter, 1967.

[12] HAYES, J. H. Do you like piña coladas? How improved communication can improve software quality. *IEEE Software 20*, 1 (2003), 90–92.

[13] HEALY, A. F., PROCTOR, R. W., WEINER, I. B., FREEDHEIM, D. K., AND SCHINKA, J. A., Eds. *Handbook of Psychology: Experimental psychology*. John Wiley and Sons, 2003.

[14] HEIJSTEK, W., KÜHNE, T., AND CHAUDRON, M. R. V. Experimental analysis of textual and graphical representations for software architecture design. *ESEM* (2011).

[15] HERBSLEB, J. D. Global software engineering: The future of socio-technical coordination. In *FOSE* (2007).

[16] HERBSLEB, J. D., AND MOITRA, D. Global software development. *IEEE Software 18*, 2 (March/April 2001), 16–20.

[17] HOLMES, J. Expressing doubt and certainty in english. *RELC Journal 13*, 9 (1982), 9–28.

[18] KALYUGA, S. Knowledge elaboration: A cognitive load perspective. *Learning and Instruction 19* (2009), 402–410.

[19] KOTLARSKY, J., VAN FENEMA, P. C., AND WILLCOCKS, L. P. Developing a knowledge-based perspective on coordination: the case of global software projects. *Information and Management 45* (2008), 96–108.

[20] KRAUT, R. E., AND STREETER, L. A. Coordination in software development. *Comm. of the ACM 38*, 3 (March 1995), 69–81.

[21] KUHN, T. S. *The Structure of Scientific Revolutions*, 3rd ed. The University of Chicago Press, 1996.

[22] LANGE, C. F. J., AND CHAUDRON, M. R. V. Managing model quality in UML-based software development. In *Int. Workshop on S.Tech. and Eng. Practice* (2005), pp. 15–23.

[23] LARKIN, J., AND SIMON, H. Why a diagram is (sometimes) worth ten thousand words. *Cognitive science 11*, 1 (1987), 65–100.

[24] LATOZA, T. D., VENOLIA, G., AND DELINE, R. Maintaining mental models: A study of developer work habits. In *ICSE* (2006), pp. 492–501.

[25] LEE, G., DELONE, W., AND ESPINOSA, J. Ambidextrous coping strategies in globally distributed software development projects. *Comm. of the ACM 49*, 10 (2006), 35–40.

[26] LYONS, E., AND COYLE, A., Eds. *Analysing Qualitative Data in Psychology*. Sage Publications, 2007.

[27] MAYER, R. E. *Multimedia Learning*, 2nd ed. Cambridge University Press, 2009.

[28] MOODY, D. The "physics" of notations: Toward a scientific basis for constructing visual notations in software engineering. *IEEE Trans. on Soft. Eng.* (2009), 756–779.

[29] MOODY, D. L., AND VAN HILLEGERSBERG, J. Evaluating the visual syntax of UML: An analysis of the cognitive effectiveness of the UML family of diagrams. *Software Language Engineering 5452* (2009), 16–34.

[30] MÜLLER, M., AND TICHY, W. Case study: Extreme programming in a university environment. *ICSE* (2001), 537–544.

[31] NUGROHO, A. Level of detail in UML models and its impact on model comprehension: A controlled experiment. *Information & Software Technology 51*, 12 (2009), 1670–1685.

[32] OLSON, G. M., AND OLSON, J. S. Distance matters. *Human-Computer Interaction 15* (2000), 139–178.

[33] PARNAS, D. L. On the criteria to be used in decomposing systems into modules. *Comm. of the ACM 15*, 12 (December 1972), 1053–1058.

[34] ÅGERFALK, P. J., AND FITZGERALD, B. Flexible and distributed software processes: Old petunias in new bowls? *Communications of the ACM 49*, 10 (October 2006), 27–34.

[35] TVERSKY, A., AND KAHNEMAN, D. Judgements under uncertainty: Heuristics and biases. *Science 185* (1974), 1124–1131.

[36] VAN VLIET, H. *Software Engineering: Principles and Practice*, 3rd ed. Wiley, June 2008.

[37] WOHLIN, C., RUNESON, P., HÖST, M., OHLSSON, M. C., REGNELL, B., AND WESSLÉN, A. *Experimentation in Software Engineering: An Introduction*. Kluwer Academic Publishers, Norwell, MA, USA, 2000.

Why Use Screen Captures? – An Experience Report

Katherine Haramundanis
Hewlett-Packard Company
ESSN Technical Documentation
Westford, MA 01886
kathy.haramundanis@hp.com

ABSTRACT

Why do users want or need screen captures in documents? Is there a different need for screen captures if the document is accessed by the user as an online pdf or as online help? Are there ways to improve the user experience with high quality screen captures? Is there a benefit to using screen captures? Are there things to avoid when using screen captures? This paper addresses these questions and provides some examples of the use of screen captures.

Categories and Subject Descriptors

I.7.1 [**Computing Methodologies**]: Document and Illustration Editing

General Terms

Documentation, Design, Standardization, Illustration

Keywords

Information design, Translation, Writing Standards, Development Process, Design of Communication, Graphics, Screen Captures

1. INTRODUCTION

In creating technical documentation, whether for online display or pdf creation, screen captures can be effective if used appropriately. Too many screen captures that do not add to the content can be burdensome for the reader or user. Inaccurate screen captures or those with poor resolution so that details are obscured can impede the reader's use. But crisp, meaningful, and correctly placed screen captures can be very useful to the reader and assist following a process or learning a tool.

1.1 What is a screen capture?

A screen capture or screen shot is a figure created by capturing a working screen or part of that screen that is visible to the user as they follow a procedure. A user on a Microsoft Windows system can capture a full screen by pressing the Print Scrn key or a partial screen by pressing both the Alt and the Print Scrn keys simultaneously. Either of these actions saves a single screen capture in the Clipboard, from which it can be pasted into a graphics tool such as MS Paint or GIMP for cropping or editing.

1.2 What documents use screen captures?

There are many technical documentation types, addressing the needs of marketing, reporting and instruction. This paper addresses only instructional documentation that can include: customer manuals, user manuals, instruction manuals, site preparation, installation, owner's manuals, reference manuals, service manuals, system manager's manuals, administrator's manual, operator's manual, technical descriptions, functional specification, user interface specification, glossaries, training manuals, quick-start guides, course materials, online tutorials, online help, online procedures, online instructional presentations, wizard text, and interactive procedures or processes. Most of these will include procedural descriptions that are quite likely to need screen captures. Most will not contain screen captures showing the level of detail observable in the statistical works of Tufte [15], but some will have screens equivalent in detail to some of the fine and informative graphics in the newspaper *USA Today*.

2. WHY USE SCREEN CAPTURES?

Use screen captures for several reasons:

- To help explain something that is difficult to describe briefly in words, such as where on a busy screen to find a key piece of information. This is a targeted screen capture (see Figures 1 and 2).

- To eliminate descriptive verbiage that does not add to the procedural content.

- To show displays on physical equipment.

- To focus your reader on key information.

- To make your text more memorable to the reader.

- To build confidence in your reader that they are at the correct step in a procedure.

Things that we recall are often visual. For example, "the book (whose title I forget) is red," "the information I am looking for was just above a picture or at the top right of a page." Screen captures assist this type of search as they may be the few visual artifacts in a largely text document. They can serve to prime the reader's memory in the context of the task at hand and help them return there later if necessary. Memory is modeled today as having two broad types, declarative or explicit and non-declarative or implicit. Explicit memory includes all the facts we know such as that Paris is in France; implicit memory includes knowledge such as how to ride a bike, recognize faces, and motor functions such as typing[1].

Just as we follow the suggestions of Tinker [14] for effective typography, Miller [10] for lists, the observations of Chase and Simon [3] are useful when considering the patterns and mental models stored in long-term and short-term memory and how these models are used differently by experts, intermediate and novice users.

3. SCREEN CAPTURES IN PDFS OR ONLINE HELP

Screen captures are more likely to be useful in pdfs, files that contain information in book form to be viewed online or printed, than in online help. However, sometimes it can be useful to include a cropped screen capture in online help to ensure that the reader connects the text with a specific part of the tool being described. In either case, selecting only the essential screens to capture is crucial to helping the reader use a procedure successfully.

Screen captures are less likely to be useful on hand-held devices such as cell phones or other electronic communication tools with small screens. As hand-held devices for monitoring systems proliferate, alert icons may supplant the use of screen captures for providing certain types of information such as status [11].

3.1 Screen capture figure titles and numbering

Traditionally, figures in technical communications have titles and are numbered sequentially throughout a document. Many academic documents adhere to this style, recommended by the Chicago Manual of Style (which calls figure titles captions that may be augmented by a legend), although variations are possible. Experience and experiment have shown that particularly in procedural documents where instructions are numbered sequentially, screen captures inserted in the numbered steps without figure titles reduce clutter and are easier for the user to assimilate than numbered figures [5,6, 13, 16].

4. BENEFITS IN USING SCREEN CAPTURES

Screen captures, like all illustrations, are one of the Great Attractors in technical documentation. They attract the eye and attention of your reader, introduce a change of pace and convey ideas or concepts that are difficult to convey only in words. How you place screen captures affects the look of your document, its readability and usability. Too many screen captures, gratuitously included, can make an enormous, unwieldy, and forbidding document.

The goal of any document, whether in a pdf or online form, is to help the user complete the task described in the shortest amount of time without errors [2,12]. Judiciously placed and appropriately described, screen captures can assist this. Using a highlight, a red oval or rectangle, or a directed arrow can additionally aid the user to find the relevant information on a large screen with many elements.

For example, Figure 1 shows a busy screen with the salient information highlighted in yellow.

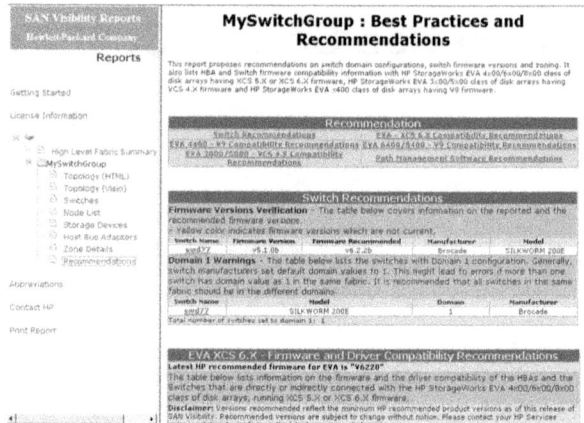

Figure 1. Highlighted text in a screen capture

Another busy or dense screen shot (Figure 2), shows key information identified with red ovals.

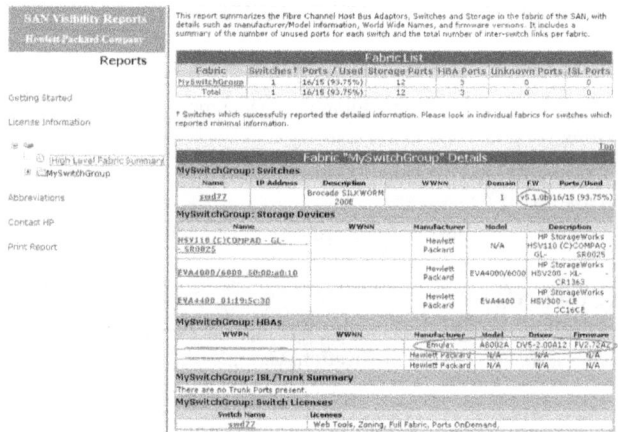

Figure 2. Key information marked with red ovals

Both these ways of marking a screen capture help the reader focus on a specific area of a screen that contains the key piece of information the user needs to find. Screen captures can also be prime candidates for reuse in a modularized system where figures are accessible as individual modules [7,8].

Google Chrome's help information (Google Chrome→Help articles→New to Google Chrome?) is based on a screen capture, where the user clicks visible features such as a tab or icon (folder, tab, arrow, and so on) to obtain explanatory text. Google Chrome's user manual, modeled on a comic book, uses no screen captures at all; effective in describing details of the implementation in a narrative, it may challenge the reader to find a key piece of information more easily sought in the online help.

5. GETTING HIGH QUALITY SCREEN CAPTURES

It can be difficult to obtain high quality screen captures. You may not have access to the software that displays the screens you need, you may not have the tools needed to make changes to the screens, or the tools used to create your final output may not render the screen captures you have with reasonable fidelity.

In addition to Microsoft Print Srcn/Alt Print Scrn, several other tools [4,9], some of them free, enable you to take screen shots and edit them. For example, GIMP, Snagit, Paint Shop Pro and Adobe Photoshop can help with screen capture work. (Both GIMP and Snagit are available as free downloads.)

Assuming that you have even a simple tool, such as MS Paint or GIMP, to make changes to your screen captures, you can often prepare screen captures that serve your purpose. To improve the chances of getting a crisp screen capture using the software you are documenting, follow these suggestions:

- Use as large a monitor as possible, not just a laptop screen. A 17 in. (43 cm) monitor is a good start, 24 in. (61 cm.) would be better. This enables you to capture as many pixels as possible. The more pixels, the better the resolution of your screen captures.

- Do not enlarge a screen capture, but improve it by making it smaller. Many graphics, not only screen captures, can be improved by making them smaller.

- Crop your screen capture to display only the crucial information – eliminate extraneous edges.

- When scaling a graphic down in a tool, pull it from the corner to ensure that it scales proportionally.

- To improve the details in your screen capture, reset your screen resolution to a higher one while you take your screen captures. Reset it back to your normal screen resolution when you are done.

6. FILE FORMATS FOR SCREEN CAPTURES

When you capture a screen, the tool you use will provide a default file format, .bmp, .png, .jpg, .gif, or some other. You may need to change this file format to conform to the requirements of the tools you are using. Each file format has its advantages and disadvantages:

- .bmp (bitmap) – can give very high resolution but is very large, producing very large document files; avoid when storage is limited.

- .png – a lossless file format, so can provide better resolution for some details.

- .jpg – a lossy file format, so some details may be lost. Often used for photographs.

- gif (graphics interchange format) – less detail than the others

Note, however, that if you are using a system that takes your xml source file and graphics, transforming your document into a printable form such as a pdf, the transform can alter the quality of your screen captures in the resulting document. If this occurs, check with your local experts on the transforms to establish the correct way to prepare your screen captures and what are the best formats to use.

7. CONCLUSION

Use screen captures judiciously with consideration for how users will interpret them. Reduce clutter by careful choice of which screen captures to provide and by highlighting key information the user needs to check.

8. ACKNOWLEDGEMENTS

My thanks to Hewlett-Packard Co. for the opportunity to present this information, and to reviewers and colleagues who provided valuable comments.

9. REFERENCES

[1] Buonomono, Dean, *Brain Bugs: How the Brain's Flaws Shape Our Lives*, W.W. Norton & Co., New York, NY, 2011.

[2] Carroll, John, *The Nurnberg Funnel,* MIT Press, Cmbridge, MA, 1990.

[3] Chase, William G., Herbert A. Simon, "The Mind's Eye in Chess," *Visual Information Processing*, Academic Press, NY, 1973.

[4] Cox, Joyce, Joan Preppernau, *Microsoft Office Word 2007 Step by Step*, Microsoft Press,Redmond, WA, 2007.

[5] Gellevij, Mark and Hans van der Meij, "Screen Captures to Support Switching Attention," *IEEE Transactions on Professional Communication*, vol. 45, No. 2, June 2002.

[6] Gellevij, Mark and Hans van der Meij, "Empirical Proof for Presenting Screen Captures in Software Documentation," *Technical Communication*, vol. 51, No. 2, May 2004.

[7] Haramundanis, Katherine, "The new paradigm for the information engineer," *Proceedings of the 27th ACM International Conference on Design of Communication*, SIGDOC 2009, pp. 151-154.

[8] Haramundanis, Katherine, "Modularizing in Glossaries – an Experience Report," *Proceedings of the 28th ACM International Conference on Design of Communication*, SIGDOC 2010, pp. 131-134.

[9]http://www.dmoz.org/Computers/Software/Shareware/Windows/Graphics/Screen_Capture/

[10] Miller, George A., "The Magical Number Seven, Plus or Monus Two: Some Limits on Our Capacity for Processing Information," *The Psychological Review,* 63, no. 1, March 1956, pp. 81-07.

[11] Mohommed, Iqbal, Jim Chengming Cai, Sina Chavoshi, Eyal de Lara, "Context-Aware Interactive Content Adaptation," *Proceedings of the 4th International Conference on Mobile Systems, Applications, and Services*, MobiSys 2006, pp. 42-55.

[12] Redish, J., "Minimalism in technical communication: Some issues to consider," *Minimalism beyond the Nurnberg funnel*, ed. J.M. Carroll, Cambridge, MA: MIT Press, pp. 219-245.

[13] Stuur, Addo, *Internet and E-mail for Seniors with Windows XP*, Visual Steps B.V., Netherlands, 2005.

[14] Tinker, Miles A., *Bases for Effective Reading*, University of Minnesota Press, 1965.

[16] Tufte, Edward R., *The Visual Display of Quantitative Information*, Graphics Press, Cheshire, Conn., 1983.

[17] van der Meij, Hans, Mark Gellevij, "Screen Captures in Software Documentation," *Technical Communication,* Fourth quarter 1998, pp. 529-543.

Working from Home in a Globally Distributed Environment

Robert Pierce
Advisory Information Developer
IBM Corporation
Alfred, ME, USA

robertp@us.ibm.com

Kirk St. Amant
Technical and Professional Communication
East Carolina University
Greenville, NC USA

stamantk@ecu.edu

ABSTRACT

This experience report provides an overview of working in globally distributed teams and the role communication technologies and protocols play in the successes of such teams. It describes technical and social aspects for interacting in such teams.

Categories and Subject Descriptors

D.2.7 [**Software Engineering**]: Topic-based content, Distributed development, Globalization, Best practices, Configuration management, Asset management, Topic types – documentation.

General Terms: Documentation, Design, Globalization

Keywords: Distributed development, Global support, Computer documentation, Information development, Best practices.

1. INTRODUCTION

The concept of the workplace is increasingly shifting from a physical location to a state of mind. Today, over 17 million Americans rely on information technology (IT) to collaborate across distances and away from a physical company office/headquarters. [7] Such practices are also increasing globally as organizations in more nations are trying distributed models of work. [2, 6, 14] The 21st century workplace has thus become increasingly distributed and global.

The distributed work process has advantages and limitations, and both are connected to the opportunities and pitfalls resulting from interacting in virtual groups [13, 16, 27, 28]. Individuals working within such contexts must therefore be aware of such items to participate successfully in globally distributed projects.

The objectives of this experience report are to provide:

- An overview of communication tools affecting information sharing in globally distributed teams.

- Strategies for interacting effectively in globally distributed projects.

These strategies should not be considered definitive. Rather, they provide a framework from which readers can develop communication best practices for globally distributed teams.

2. Distributed work environments

A number of individuals have cited the following advantages of distributed work – particularly in global contexts [25, 28]:

- Reducing the environmental impact of the home office.

- Making the home as a communication and information hub.

- Enhancing efficiency and productivity by the home as a place for work and education.

- Improving privacy and security with the home as a private and secure space for working with data.

This paper focuses on aspects that companies prioritize (e.g., communication and information, network technologies, efficiency and productivity, and privacy and security). [1, 8, 17, 23]

2.1 An information development workflow

Figure 1 illustrates information development tasks that individuals can complete from any location based on connectivity.

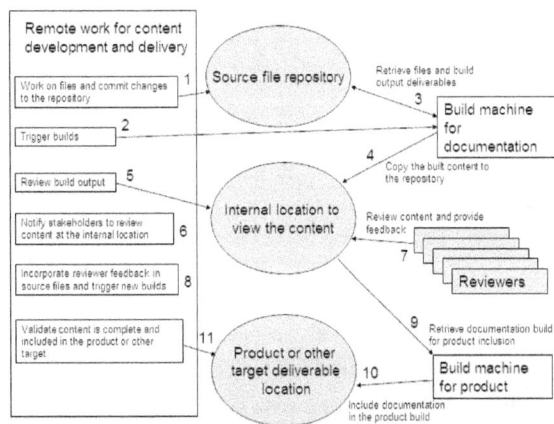

Figure 1. Information development example

The numbered steps cover a common sequence where:

1. Writers do content work and transform source file content to documentation deliverables (e.g., online help).

2. The build machine fetches source files and generates output.

3. The build machine copies and makes output available on a target machine.

4. Writers review the output for correct results.

5. Writers notify reviewers provide feedback.

6. Reviewers provide feedback on the documentation content.

7. Writers incorporate the reviewer input.

8. The build machine copies content for product inclusion.

9. The build machine generates product bits and documentation deliverables.

10. Writers/testers confirm product includes documentation.

Each part involves effective communication to complete a step and generate an effective product. This focus on communication also has important implications for how and why such processes can be expanded to global contexts.

2.2 An information development workflow for delivering multiple languages

The global distribution of work offers a number of key advantages – particularly in product translation and the localization. As employees in other nations participate in the development process, they can identify and address prospective items that could affect the translation and localization processes related to that product. [26] Moreover, addressing such factors during product development can be more efficient and cost effective than trying to do so after a product is ready for market release. [4, 12]

Figure 2 shows a workflow process for delivering a product in multiple languages for domestic and international release.

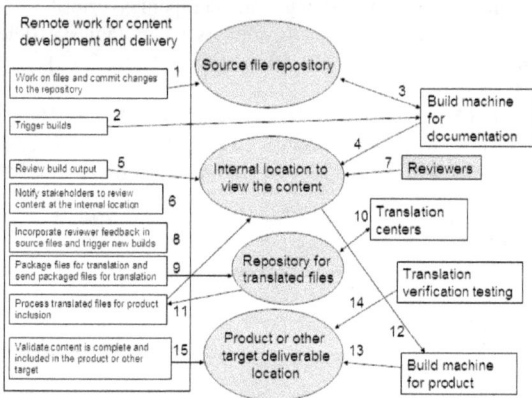

Figure 2. Information development and translation

As this image illustrates:

- Translators translate the packaged files and then send the translations back to the information development team.

- Translation verification testers review content and test translated content quality and completeness.

All of the processes are enabled by tools that can be used from remote work sites.

The complex and varied nature of such works means the communication and collaboration process can be particularly challenging when working remotely. [17, 23, 28] The global distribution of such work can, however, allow organizations to develop effective international products more quickly and effectively. [24, 26]

3. Tooling and connectivity

In distributed work contexts, participants need to communicate regularly to exchange needed and current project information. Such exchanges are essential to assure all involved individuals continue to move toward the same goal. Communication tools that foster such interaction and collaboration are thus essential. Such tools fall into two main categories:

- *Collaboration tools* are the technologies that allow co-workers to interact regularly and quickly throughout a project. They are also the tools used to ask questions, request clarification, and share recent developments (e.g., phone, email, instant messaging, wikis, etc.). [13]

- *Software development and information development tools* are technologies used to track the development of a project over time and facilitate version control during the development process (e.g., change management and version control systems with shared database access). [16]

For the members of a distributed team to interact effectively, they need to understand the nature and uses such tools. [21]

3.1 Collaboration tools

Collaboration and communication skills are as critical in successful working from home as any requirements. [22] Thus, effective use of collaboration tools is an ongoing requirement and should never be a roadblock in day-to-day work. [11, 13]

Figure 3 shows a desktop with an online conference sharing a computer screen, an instant messaging utility, two web dashboards – similar to wikis – for work management (one for the documentation team and one for the development team).

The online conferencing tool might include audio or the worker would be using a telephone as well.

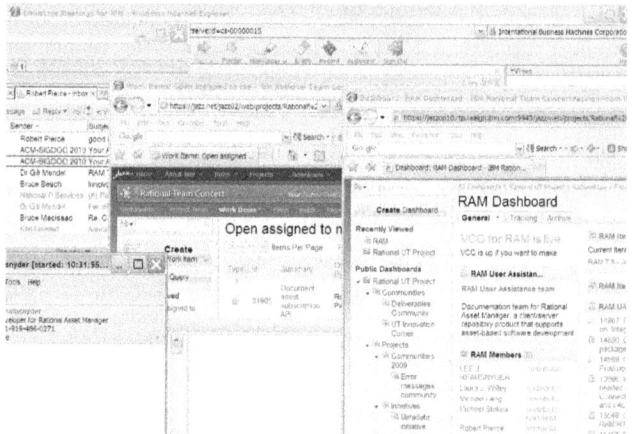

Figure 3. Collaboration tools

As Figure 3 illustrates, a constant part of information development and certainly for doing it remotely is managing complexity – both for managing information and for managing the tools and processes that are part of the day to day job. However, most of the complexity in tools, processes, and information apply to all workers and by being remote, it might actually be easier to focus on the information without having the distractions common in workplace office settings. [10]

Ironically, there are many times when an internal network or firewall is down, and on-site colleagues having connectivity issues while the remoter worker with local internet connection and tunnel to the corporate servers has no issues at all.

3.2 Software and information development tools

Many organizations incorporate software development tools, processes, and best practices, into their information development efforts. [21] As noted in the previous section, managing tools and engaging in processes while working remotely requires dependable connectivity. Given the connectivity, there are no barriers to being highly productive while working with tools for information development. [29]

By using a web client interface to trigger an automated documentation build and then using a web browser that points to the output on an internal web server to view the build output, a remote worker can perform release engineer tasks and validate documentation content.

The effective use of these tools, however, is connected to a common understanding of use across the members of a distributed project team. [22] Certain information-sharing strategies can, in turn, facilitate such understanding.

4. Strategies for effective tool use in globally distributed development teams

The situation created by distributing work over a number of locations is a complex one. By focusing on certain communication-based strategies, individuals and organizations can use collaborative tools to create effective practices for sharing information across distributed teams. The key is to provide team members with access to the information needed to participate effectively on distributed projects.

4.1 Protocols for access

Effective project communication involves access to information. [22, 24] Thus, the project-related work individuals produce should not be stored on local hard drives. Rather, it needs to be backed up to a common location (e.g., an organizational server) to which all parties have access. Participants must, in turn, use a common set of practices for addressing: [22, 24]

- Where to back up information (e.g., to what server).
- How often to back up work (e.g., every 30 minutes).
- How to title materials and versions of files so they can be found quickly and easily by other team members.
- What notes or comments to include when final backups are done at the end of each work cycle.

Such protocols can make it easier for team members to find needed information quickly and effectively while avoiding communication pitfalls that could plague such processes.

5. Establishing trust in distributed teams

Perhaps the single most important factor related to the success of distributed teams is trust. In a distributed team, however, conventional FTF meetings designed to forge such trust are often not an option. Rather, organizations need to find new methods to create and maintain such trust throughout a project. [19] To do so, organization can use certain communication-based strategies.

5.1 Initial biographies

Distribute team member biographies and position descriptions prior to any formal project-related interactions. Providing an initial introduction to team members can help identify and clarify the roles of team members and help avoid discussions of who is responsible for doing what.

5.2 Initial project meeting

Have an initial introduction meeting where team members are introduced by the overall project manager. [19] Each individual can discuss their background, area of expertise, and role (and related activities and responsibilities) in relation to the project. Such a meeting allows team members to get to know each other, to gain an understanding of what each person will do, and to learn how to communicate effectively with each other – all of which contribute to an initial sense of trust among these individuals.

5.3 Conduct regular project team meetings

Have regular project team meetings where the project manager reviews what team members have completed to date and notes what members need to complete by the next meeting as well as clarifies roles in relation to completing those activities. Team members can also raise questions or discuss issues. Such interactions maintain a common understanding of the project and re-enforce trust among individuals. [19]

6. Professional development and technical vitality

Working remotely offers a model of giving choice and control to individuals, but it also requires greater personal challenges. It takes independence and fortitude to grow in the areas of developing the communication skills, independence, leadership, and collaboration skills essential to success. [18]

Some companies offer online training and other resources for ongoing professional development (e.g., internal lectures, online articles, recording, and self-paced courses). Types of learning might also be available as online training, articles, and webcasts, or as self-paced explorations of working with a tool and reading its existing product documentation.

Learning new and enhancing existing interpersonal skills and gaining experience with new work-related technologies enhance one's value and help justify the work from home model. [8, 10]

7. SUMMARY

All of the tasks involved in information development can be successfully completed from a remote work location. [9, 10] Thanks to the high availability of fast internet connections, tools with web user interfaces for connecting to remote servers and source repositories, there are no real barriers to working from home. [3, 4]

Whereas older misconceptions of work from home viewed remote workers as lower-achievers, the work from home model has been validated as supporting a high level of productivity at a lower cost to support the employees and provide them with more flexibility. [10, 23] Additionally, companies are continuing to support the work from home model as long as workers demonstrate successful time management and maintain high productivity rate in completing work. [15, 20] Studies, moreover, indicate that the work from home model benefits both individuals and companies. [5, 8, 20]

In sum, presenting a winning model for efficient and effective working from home requires a skill set that helps dispel any preconceived notions about working from home by some on-site colleagues and demonstrates productivity and success. [10]

8. REFERENCES

[1] Atkinson, S. R., & Moffat, J. (2005). "The agile organization: From informal networks to complex effects and agility." February 3, 2006, http://www.dodccrp.org/publications/pdf/Atkinson_Agile.pdf

[2] "Australia moving toward carbon pricing over telecommuting." (2010). Telecommute News. Retrieved June 1, 2011, from http://www.telecommutenews.com/international_telecommuting/australia-moving-toward-carbon-pricing-over-telecommuting/

[3] Bertot, Juan Carlos, "Public Libraries and the Internet 2002: Internet Connectivity and Networked Services." Retrieved April 8, 2005, http://www.ii.fsu.edu/publications/2002.plInternet.study.pdf

[4] Bikson, Tora K., Panis, Constantijn W.A., 2000. "Citizens, Computers, and Connectivity: A Review of Trends." Rand Corporation, Santa Monica, CA.

[5] Brown, Jeffrey R., Goolsbee, Austan, 2002. "Does the internet make markets more competitive? Evidence from the life insurance industry." The Journal of Political Economy 110, 481–507.

[6] China: Telecommuting to decrease carbon emissions. (2010). Telecommute News. Retrieved June 1, 2011, from http://www.telecommutenews.com/international_telecommuting/china-telecommuting-to-decrease-carbon-emissions/

[7] Deringer Research Group, Inc. (2009). Telework Trendlines: A Survey Brief by WorldatWork. Scottsdale, AZ: WorldatWork.

[8] Cooper, C.L. and Jackson, S. (1998), "Creating Tomorrow's Organizations," Wiley, Chichester.

[9] Lewis, S. and Cooper, C.L. (2005), "Work-Life Integration," Wiley, Chichester and New York, NY.

[10] Cary L. Cooper, "The future of work: careers, stress and well-being, Lancaster University Management School," Lancaster, UK, Career Development International, Vol. 10 No. 5, 2005, pp. 396-399, Emerald Group Publishing Limited

[11] Dimaggio, Paul, Hargittai, Eszter, Celeste, Coral, Shafer, Steven, 2004. "Digital inequality: from unequal access to differentiated use." In: Neckerman, K. (Ed.), Social Inequality. Russell Sage Foundation, New York, pp. 355–400.

[12] Esselink, B. (2000). A practical guide to localization. Philadelphia, PA: John Benjamins.

[13] Gopalakrishnan, Gopakumar, Pillai, Sreekumar, and Dhanju, Nidhi, "Collaboration in offshore software projects: practices and challenges," Proceeding of the 2009 International Workshop on Intercultural Collaboration, February 2009, ACM Press, pp. 225-228.

[14] Implementing Canadian national work from home day. (2010). Telecommute News. Retrieved June 1, 2001, from http://www.telecommutenews.com/international_telecommuting/workopolis-promoting-canadian-national-work-from-home-day/

[15] Sara Nephew Hassani, "Locating digital divides at home, work, and everywhere else," Department of Sociology, Princeton University, USA, 2006 Elsevier B.V., j.poetic.2006.05.007, http://www.learning-works.org/moodle/file.php/34/Digital_Divide_-_access_points_article.pdf

[16] Herbsleb, J.D and Moitra, D., "Global software development," IEEE Software, March-April 2001, pp. 16-20.

[17] Johnson-Eilola, J. (2005). "Datacloud: Toward a new theory of online work." Cresskill, NJ: Hampton Press.

[18] Christine Koh, Damien Joseph, Soon Ang. "Cultural intelligence and collaborative work: intercultural competencies in global technology work teams," Proceeding of the 2009 International Workshop on Intercultural Collaboration, February 2009, ACM Press, pp. 261-264.

[19] Kotlarsky, J. and I. Oshri. (2005). "Social ties, knowledge sharing and successful collaboration in globally distributed system development projects." European Journal of Information Systems, 14, 37-48.

[20] Malone, T.W. (2004). "The future of work: How the new order of business will shape your organization, your management style and your life." Boston: Harvard Business School Press.

[21] Pierce, R., "Leveraging Technology Affinity – Applying a Common Tools and Practices to Information Development," SIGDOC '05, October, 2005, Coventry, UK. ACM Press, pp. 123-130.

[22] Ramasubu, N. M. S. Krishnan, and P. Kompalli. (2005, May/June). Leveraging global resources: A process maturity framework for managing distributed development. IEEE Software, 80-86.

[23] Robinson, John P., Kestnbaum, Meyer, Kestnbaum, Alan, Alvarez, Anthony S., 2002. "The Internet and other uses of time." In: Wellman, B., Haythornwaite, C. (Eds.), The Internet in Everyday Life. Blackwell, Oxford, pp. 244–263.

[24] St.Amant, K. (2009). Understanding IT outsourcing: A perspective for managers and decision makers. In K. St.Amant (Ed.), IT outsourcing: Concepts, methodologies, tools, and applications Vol. I (pp. xxxii-lix). Hershey, PA: IGI-Global.

[25] St.Amant, K. (2008). Virtual office communication protocols: A system for managing international virtual teams. In G. Hayhoe & H. M. Grady (Eds.), Connecting people with technology: Issues in professional communication (pp. 219-228). *Amityville, NY: Baywood Publishing Company.*

[26] St.Amant, K. (2006). Open source and outsourcing: A perspective on software use and professional practices related to international outsourcing activities. In H. S. Kehal & V. P. Singh (Eds.), Outsourcing and offshoring in the 21st century: A socio-economic perspective (pp. 229-247). Hershey, PA: Idea Group Publishing.

[27] Clay Spinuzzi, University of Texas at Austin, TECHNICAL COMMUNICATION QUARTERLY, 16(3), 265–277, Copyright © 2007, Lawrence Erlbaum Associates, Inc.

[28] James Stewart, "The social consumption of information and communication technologies (ICTs): insights from research on the appropriation and consumption of new ICTs in the domestic environment," 21 February 2003, Springer-Verlag London Limited.

[29] Wallace, Patricia, 2004. "The Internet in the Workplace." Cambridge University Press, Cambridge, MA.

Explosive Ordinance Disposal: Motion Sensor Simulator in Nintendo Wii

Markos Mentzelopoulos
and Mihai Tanasa
School of Electronics and
Computer Science
University of Westminster,
New Cavendish Street
W1W 6UW,London, UK
+44 (0)20 7911 5000 ext
64552
mentzem@westminster.ac.uk
m.tanasa@my.westminster.ac.uk

Aristidis Protopsaltis
Serious Games Institute
Coventry University Tech Park
Cheetah Road, Coventry
CV1 2TL, UK
+44 2476 158252
aprotopsaltis@gmail.com

Daphne Economou
School of Electronics and
Computer Science
University of Westminster,
New Cavendish Street
W1W 6UW,London, UK
+44 (0)20 7911 5000 ext
64506
d.economou@westminster.ac.uk

ABSTRACT

Simulation based games attempt to replicate real life or fiction scenarios for the purposes of learning, training, investigating or predicting results. This paper presents a case study of a simulation based on terrestrial which are primarily used by Explosive Ordinance Disposal Units (E.O.D.) in the investigation and disposal of bomb threats in Nintendo Wii, to examine different methods and techniques of player immersion, adaptation and learning. The paper presents background research that has been conducted for the design and implementation of the E.O.D. simulator. The simulated environment demonstrates its usefulness over a number of real bomb scenarios where player has to actively inspect the environment to locate and dispose of any potential bomb threats in an efficient manner.

Categories and Subject Descriptors

D.1.5 [**Object-oriented Programming**]: Miscellaneous; H.5.2 [**User Interfaces**]: Input devices and strategies, Screen design; I.2.1 [**Applications and Expert Systems**]: Games

General Terms

Algorithms, Documentation, Performance, Design, Experimentation.

Keywords

Game Engine, Object Oriented, SDK (Software Development Kit), AABB (Axis Aligned Bounding Box), OOBB(Object Aligned Bounding Box) , SIVET (Simulated Infrared/Visible Engagements with Targets), AVT (Automatic Video Tracking), PEO STRI(Program Executive Office for Simulation, Training and Instrumentation), IGs (Image Generators), VR (Virtual Reality), XNA Pipeline.

1. INTRODUCTION

Simulation is the attempt to replicate a real life or a hypothetical scenario so that it can be studied to see how it works and behaves. The sole purpose of simulators are to capture the essential workplace environment in a way that allows participants to apply new skills, try different approaches and explore the implications of decision making without worrying about their actions. They are able to provide real time feedback allowing users to assess their current situation, analyse options for moving forward and measure results of past decisions and actions. The aforementioned qualities make simulation simulator games ideal environments for learning.

One can argue that despite the advancement in technology the basic interface interaction between humans and computer systems regarding games has been slowly catching up. This is evident with numerous gaming input hardware devices still greatly in use such as; Keyboard and Mouse (1868), Light Gun (1966) and Joystick/Control Pads (1981) where the basic core methodology of user interaction has remained steadily unaltered throughout the years.

With the release of the 'Nintendo Wii' in 2005, a new way of user interaction was introduced. It uses a combination of built-in accelerometers and infrared detection to sense its position in 3D space when pointed at the LEDs within the Sensor Bar. This design allows users to control the game using physical gestures as well as traditional button presses. The controller connects to the console using Bluetooth and features rumble as well as an internal speaker. The Wii Remote can connect to expansion devices through a proprietary port at the base of the controller. The device bundled with the Wii retail package is the Nunchuk unit, which features an accelerometer and a traditional analogue stick with two trigger buttons [6]. This technology can be utilised in real life situations where we can now use new means of interaction with application software and 3D simulated environments. This is possible with simple hand gestures or body movements tracked by the controller which offer users a more compelling way to actively learn.

Nowadays, the use of robots in difficult and high risk tasks, especially when dealing with explosives is a common practice. One example is the Explosive Ordinance Disposal (E.O.D.) robots which are remote controlled robots used by bomb disposal units in the investigation of suspicious packages or vehicles which may contain explosives devices.

It is of great importance that E.O.D. trainees are able to perform under pressure and have adequate training to adapt to various real time situations. Since the initiation of the E.O.D program robotic systems have helped save countless lives by wiping away the threat of improvised explosive devices and vehicles. Sgt. Gregory Carroll who currently serves in Iraq states the following: *"The cost of losing a robot is not nearly as close as losing a trained EOD person"* [4]. Therefore, a safe practice environment which eliminates such risks will be an ideal training tool.

The aim of this project was to create an Explosive Ordinance Disposal (E.O.D) robot simulator. The simulation features an interactive 3-dimensional environment where player's movements are primarily dependent on hand gestures, tracked by the accelerometers of the controllers (wiimote and nunchuk). The gameplay is focused on creating a realistic simulation environment heavily dependent on collision and physics functionalities.

The rest of the paper is organized as follows. Section 2 gives a theoretical background over simulation games and their current trends. Section 3 describes the implementation of the proposed game simulator. In section 4 an evaluation of the proposed model is given over some real scenarios developed for users to test their abilities. Finally section 5 concludes with final outcomes and future work.

2. THEORETICAL BACKGROUND

Simulation games are frequently used in the training of civilians and military personnel [3]. They are used in situations that replicate real world situations when it is too expensive or too hazardous to allow trainees to use real equipment. Simulations are able to enumerate through a number of different states allowing the trainee to adapt to a number of training scenarios which may occur in real life. This procedure offers invaluable experience in a 'safe' virtual environment. "The military has a long and rich history of using models and simulation. The US military alone spends hundreds of millions of dollars acquiring, designing, fielding, and operating simulation systems. These systems have been categorized by the Department of Defense into training, analysis, and acquisition applications." [7].

Starting from three basic types of strategic, planning and learning exercises: games, simulations and case studies, - a number of hybrids may be considered, among which are simulation games used as case studies [1]. Training simulators can be broken into three main categories: virtual, constructive, and live simulations each with its own benefit. They are as follows:

- *Virtual Training*: The trainee is immersed in a virtual world where physical actions such as driving a vehicle or firing a weapon are visible on the synthetic world they are in.

- *Constructive Training*: Also known as war games. Tests the player's tactical and strategic choices by analyzing the position of military formations on the field. A way of observing how players use their forces effectively.

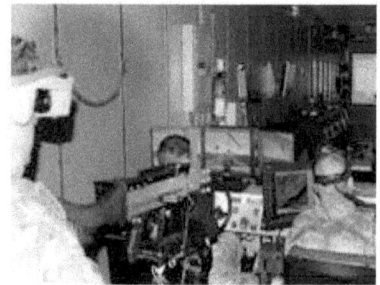

Figure 1: "DARWARS Ambush" equipment Virtual Training Environment.

Figure 2: "DARWARS Ambush" In game screenshot.

- *Live Training*: The application of real equipment in mock combat scenarios or firing ranges. These allow pilots, tank drivers, and other soldiers to practice the physical activities of war with their real equipment.

2.1 Constructive Training

DAWARS Ambush! Is a military-based training simulation developed by the U.S. Defence Advanced Research Projects Agency to teach and train military personnel on the rules of engagement [2]. Players engage in real-life combat situations, infantry tactics, and other areas of military training (Figure1/2). The system focuses on troop level experiences and convoy ambushes as well as dismounted forces, allows for field authoring so that new experiences can be added to the system easily, and provides support for capturing, sharing, and discussing incidents. The goal of "DARWARS Ambush!" is nothing short of saving soldiers' lives in Iraq and Afghanistan by capturing, analysing, and disseminating lessons learned experiences.

2.2 Live Training

Navy submarine simulators are different from typical simulators since there are no windows to the outside world on a submarine meaning there is little need for realistic graphics. Submarine simulators instead require accurate and advanced tool readings as the crew navigates though the simulation. Some submarines are stationary which can diminish the user's sense of immersion. Others are mounted on a set of pneumatic arms that can replicate the motion of diving or surfacing (Figure 3).

2.3 Virtual Training

An impressive naval application of virtual environments is the virtual bridge. The navigation, seamanship and ship-

Figure 3: Live Cabin simulator for Submarine navigation.

Figure 4: Naval Virtual Bridge.

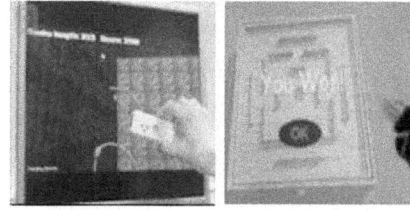

Figure 5: (Left): the player is able to control the snake's angular velocity by using the accelerometer in the Wiimote to obtain the directional gravity relative to the controller. (right): The player is using the accelerometer in the wiimote controller to alter the angle of the board, thus tilting it.

Figure 7: BCI - Lifting a heavy stone in a Stonehenge game designed by Emotive Systems.

handling trainer (NSST) accurately replicates the bridge of a large Navy ship. The simulator has dozens of computer monitors, some that serve as the bridge's windows and some that serve as ship monitors. Navy bridge teams can train together through various scenarios, building teamwork and ship-handling skills in the process." [8].

Another form of Virtual Training is the Advanced Concepts Flight Simulator (ACFS). The ACFS is a unique tool that was developed at Ames specifically for research with advanced aircraft. This highly customizable aircraft was conceived and scaled on the basis of projected air traffic usage requirements in the 21st Century.

The ACFS simulates a generic commercial transport aircraft [The visual systems closely match those of the B747-400 simulator and offer a 180-degree horizontal / 40-degree vertical field-of-view] and employs advanced flight systems including many features from the newest aircraft being built today. The cab is mounted on a six-degree-of-freedom synergistic motion system and uses side-stick controllers for aircraft control in the pitch and roll axes. Among its many advanced technologies, the ACFS includes fly-by-wire flight controls, touch-sensitive electronic checklists, aircraft systems schematics, a customizable flight management system, and cutting-edge graphical flight displays including head-up displays.

2.4 Game Consoles for Human Computer Interaction in Games

In 2005 Nintendo released 'Nintendo Wii' as part of the 7th generation gaming console with the ability to track movement depending on the players actions. This was achieved with the use of accelerometers inside the wiimote and nunchuk controllers able to sense the player's position in 3-dimensional

space. Furthermore the wiimote allows connectivity to external hardware devices such as PC's via bluetooth device.

Game enthusiasts are utilising the Nintendo Wii controllers to create new game innovations. The combination of a classic game with new generation technology adds a new gameplay aspect where players are more conscious of their actions.

The Brain Computer Interfacing Institute (BCI) is researching and developing the intensity in brain patterns in order for users to control a virtual environment [10]. "BCI users are patients that do not have control, or full controls, of their muscles and that have to learn to control a prosthetic device, a communication device, or a mobility device (e.g., a wheelchair) by thought" (Figure 6).

3. IMPLEMENTATION

Simulation games require a concise game story with clear objectives for the player to follow. The game story acts as the initial form of contact between the player and the game. To ensure that the player is fully immersed it is important that there is a realistic scenario that the player can connect with.

The scenario that the game will follow will be in accordance to the story which is as follows: "The player takes control of player character Mark Swain, a highly skilled retired bomb disposal operative. In light of the recent bomb threats in London, Mark was selected as the prime candidate for the E.O.D. training simulation program for the prevention of future bomb attacks. Mark must use the technology at hand to locate and dispose any potential bomb threats in a safe manner, testing his ingenuity, speed, control and effectiveness in any given environment".

3.1 Model Creation

The aim of the project is to create a realistic simulator

Figure 6: (a) Original Hardware Manufactured machine Robot- "SuperRobot" - (b) Wireframe Model - (c) Plain Texture Model.

for trainees to experience and it is crucial that the graphics and functionality of the robot are relatively similar to one they might experience in real life. The decided E.O.D. model which will be used in the game is 'SuperRobot HD2 SWAT' (Fig 7a). To achieve a level of realism the model was created using reference pictures from the real Robot and altered slightly to accustom special features incorporated in the model. The model was created in Maya, using basic primitive shapes which were then altered with the appropriate polygon tools to achieve the desired shape (Fig 7b/c).

3.2 Camera

The game has been developed from a third person view camera angle that allows the player to easily observe and track the robots movements within the environment. The robot is also equipped with an additional camera that is mounted on-top of the robot's arm for added view support. The camera has the ability to alter between states: *Normal*, *Infrared* and *Sound Mode*.

- Normal mode: Displays a clear and sharp image of the current environment. It can be used with the camera 'zoom' to read items which are unreachable or too small to read clearly without the use of zoom.

- Infrared state: Gives the player the unique ability to see-through walls, this state allows users to easily locate items within the level.

- Sound Mode: Allows the player to locate bombs which emit a signal. The robot itself will beep faster depending on the initial distance between itself and the bomb location.

The player will have to altern between states in order to successfully complete the game.

3.3 Game Engine Core

The game was programmed using an object oriented approach in accordance to the XNA framework as shown in Figure 8. The XNA framework offers users a simple process to initialize, load, update and draw graphics within the game window. At the beginning of the program the 'Constructor()' initializes a new instance of the class which provides the basic graphics device initialization, game logic, rendering code and a game loop. The 'Initialize()' function is then called which enumerates through any game components that have been added to Game components and call their Initialize methods. As the game components are initialised the 'Loan()' function is called which is used to load assets that have been processed by the content pipeline (audio, models etc.).The 'Update()' function is called when the

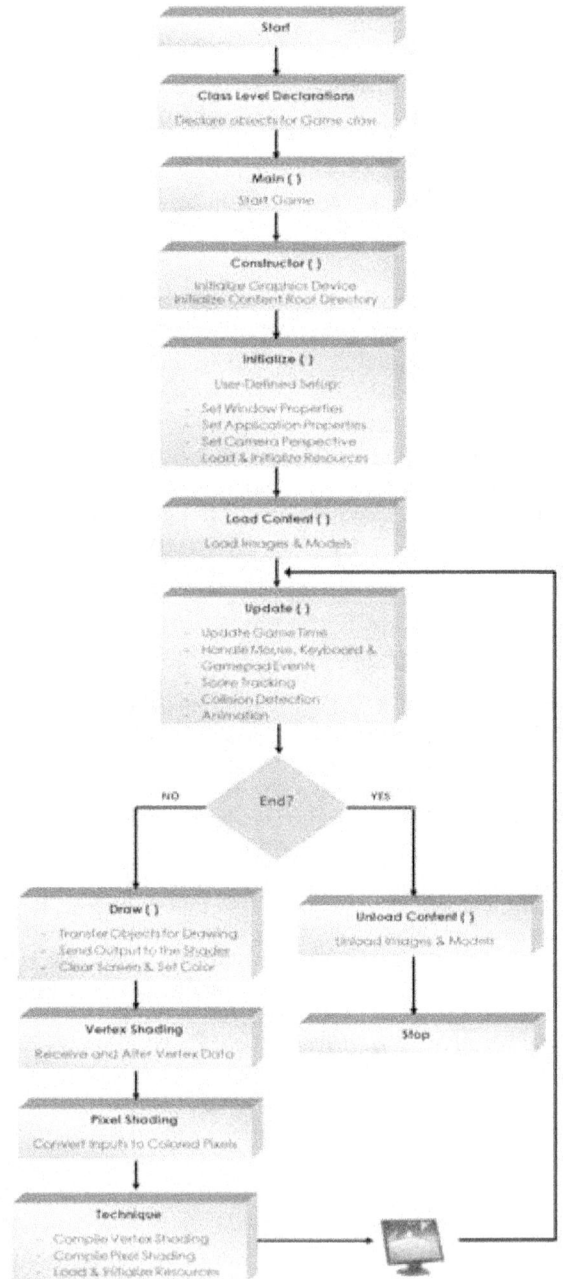

Figure 8: XNA Framework.

game has determined that game logic needs to be processed. This might include the management of the game state, the processing of user input, or the updating of simulation data. Furthermore it gets called approximately 60 times per second. Lastly, the 'Draw ()' function is called which renders objects onscreen [5].

3.4 Collision

Collision is one of the most important factors in gaming and simulations by creating a playable scenario for the user to interact with in a 3-dimensional world. It creates the illusion of a dense world where players are unable to transpire through solid objects such as walls. There is a number of different collision methods available however each with their pros and cons depending on their use and implementation within games.

Further investigation was required in analysing different types of collision detection for real-time gaming applications to determine which method is best applicable to the E.O.D. Simulation game scenario. Given the dynamic nature of the model mesh, conventional collision methods such as; creating simple rectangle bounding box which engulfs the whole model is too simplistic and a more accurate system needed to be developed.

The game will utilise different types of collision implementations depending on the colliding situation. These are:

- i. *Axis Aligned Bounding Box* (AABB) it provides a quick way of determining if collision has occurred where the size of the bounding box is dependent on the minimum and maximum points of the model. One disadvantage that this method poses is its inability to accurately rotate (if needed) since AABB require shapes to be aligned in accordance to its axis. AABB is best applicable in static level designs, ensuring fast collision with the robot.

- ii. *Object Orientated Bounding Box* (OOBB) is created and primarily dependant on the vertex points of the model. This allows the bounding box to actively rotate with the model without the need of recreating the bounding box. It also means that this method will provide a more accurate fit around the model in comparison with AABB (if rotation is required). The locations of the object's vertices relative to the box never change. It means you are able to pre-calculate the shape of the box for every object within the game. Calculating the shape of the box is the most costly part of the algorithm, and it makes an oriented bounding box check better than an axis aligned bounding box check because of its increased accuracy and ability to pre-calculate the size and shape of the box, allowing for fast collision checks. OOBB collision is best applicable for objects which orientation will be altered.

- iii. *Bounding Spheres* they offer a fast response for testing collisions. They do not generally provide the best approximation of an object's extents. This method of collision is best applicable on spherical shaped objects for a better space approximation.

Because bounding spheres are used on spherical shaped objects or simple objects which do not require precise collision to perform fast collision checks it was decided to build the foundation for collision detection in the E.O.D. robot

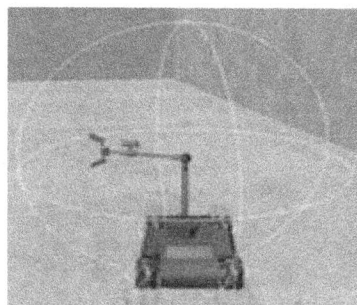

Figure 9: Bounding Spheres on E.O.D. Model.

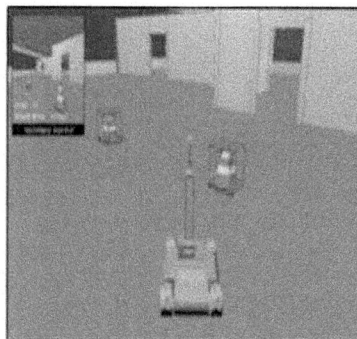

Figure 10: AABB Collision Implementation.

model using them. Spheres are attached to main parts of the robot that are likely to collide with the environment (claw, wheels, etc.) shown in Figure 9. The robot is composed of a number of bounding spheres using a hierarchical order where collision is first performed against the largest bounding sphere (Figure 9 - White Sphere). If collision returns true then bounding sphere collision checks are performed for the robot claw and wheels respectively. This approach saves processing memory as it only performs collision checks for the wheels and claw only if collision is recorded against the largest sphere.

AABB Collision was used in the development of the game levels due to its efficient and fast processing capabilities. Although OOBB collision would be better suited because of its ability to create a bounding box depending on vertices giving it the ability to rotate, it is slower than AABB. The level itself is static therefore there is no need for rotate objects, making AABB collision a better candidate in this instance.

To avoid creating a level where there are a large number of mesh files joining each other dependant on code is time consuming and not practical. As a result a custom content pipeline was added to the project. Originally based on the implementation by 'Nemo Krad' [9] and altered to meet the projects specifications it is able to handle mesh extraction from (.fbx) files created in a 3D modelling package such as Maya. Creating the level design in Maya offers complete control over the aesthetic appearance of the level itself where the accuracy of the level in accordance to the level design and texturing can be created to a realistic standard.

As seen in Figure 10 the assets are first read in by an 'Importer' used as a primary method to read data from the file which is then utilised in the 'design time cycle'. The 'Content Processor' read in the data in a raw format and

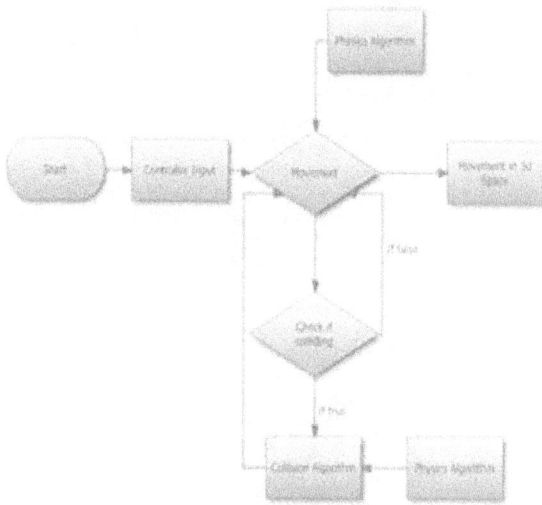

Figure 12: Player Interaction Flow Chart.

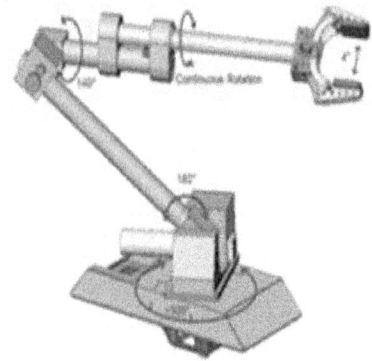

Figure 13: E.O.D Rotation Movement.

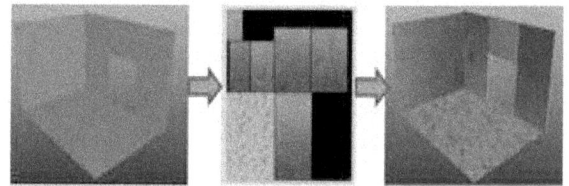

Figure 14: (a) Lift Mode - (b) UV Texturing - (c) Model Texturing.

converts it into 'processed data'. The final step is when the Content loader reads in the compiled asset file and turns it into an object that XNA can utilise.

When the game is initialised, the custom model processor is able to loop through the model file meshes, creating a custom tag which is later used in a for-loop for the creation of AABB. Each bounding box is dependent on the minimum and maximum mesh shape. The game model file (.fbx) is loaded into the content processor and is then updated accordingly as shown below: This creates bounding boxes of the models using the minimum and maximum points gathered from the content pipeline as shown in Figure 11.

The content pipeline is able to generate bounding boxes around the level itself however, for non-static objects such as: doors, pickup items, crates and bombs further expansions on these methods were needed - each requesting its own individual approach based again on combinations of Bounding Spheres and AABB.

3.5 Movement and Control

To add realistic impact in the simulator extra care was given to different application of forces and object behaviour in gaming environment such as: orientation in 3-dimensional spaces, inertia, torque, angular momentum, force, acceleration and integration of quaternion rotation was necessary to create accurate movement. To replicate real life movement appropriate physics were also implemented when the user hits certain objects by exerting energy and gradually decreasing its speed depending on the objects weight. Furthermore to create the illusion of an object being moved, the use of rotation also needs to be applied appropriately on non-static objects.

Control movement plays a crucial role in the overall player gameplay immersion and it is imperative that the controls are easily accessible. For this case we used the wiimote and nunchuk controllers which were able to sense the player's position in 3-dimensional space. The game controllers can be connected to any PC via bluetooth connection.

If the wiimote is tilted on the 'X' or 'Y' axis whilst holding 'A' the robot will respond by movement of its arm in the same direction. Further research into modelling techniques

and animation was required since XNA does not provide built in animation library support. The model animation needs to coincide with the players input actions and act accordingly.

The method of implementation required specific target of each object mesh within the model file, where the corresponding transformation or rotation is then applied on the X, Y or Z axis. With this way it was given to the robot the ability to twist/turn over 4 rotation axis for more user flexibility within the simulation as indicated in Figure 13.

3.6 Game Interactive Objects

3.6.1 Lift

The lift model was created in Maya composed of rectangular shapes. To create more accurate texturing UV mapping was performed by exporting the UV texture as a .jpg image and importing it into Adobe Photoshop to create the textures. This creates a more realistic environment ultimately, creating a better player experience.

3.6.2 Bombs

There are different set of bombs based on scenario requirement. The player will need to find a way to disarm the explosive device by use of items or puzzle solving.

3.6.3 Collected Keys

When the game starts all doors are locked and the player is required to search and collect the corresponding key to unlock the door.

3.6.4 Camera Motion

The model has a camera attached on the gripping arm. A separate class was created to handle the secondary camera, giving it the ability to zoom in/out and alter between

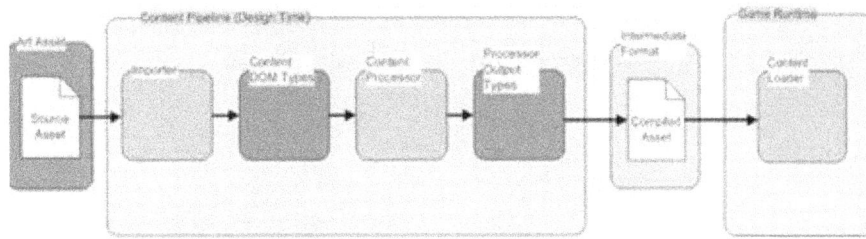

Figure 11: Content Pipeline diagram.

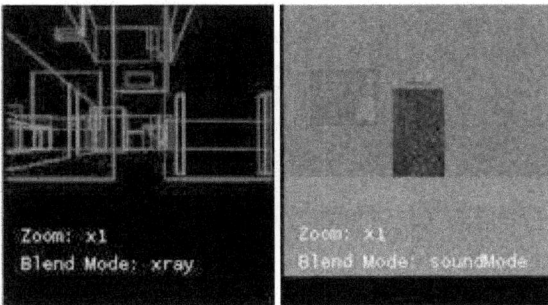

Figure 15: (a) Infrared Mode (Left) - (b) Sound Mode (Right).

states. A custom class was created to handle the positioning and rendering of objects within the world. To create a 3rd person camera, the position of the camera is placed behind the targeted object (being the robot in this case).

Infrared Mode: Altering the rendering states, colour and background buffer it is added to the game playability the option the pickup items to be visible (shown as white spheres) except the bombs which remain invisible (Figure 15a) *Sound Mode:* One of the in-game bombs is able to emit a certain frequency which is detected by the E.O.D robot. Depending on the distance between the robot and bomb the 'beep' sound is played faster. To add to the realism, the camera image is partially distorted when this mode is activated (Figure 15b) *Normal Mode:* The normal mode was created originally to give the player a secondary camera source. Rotation to the camera is applied when the user rotates the E.O.D.'s extending arms. As the game is initialised the camera is pushed forward to give the effect that it is looking though the E.O.D. camera mesh The zoom in/out feature was achieved by modifying the cameras field of view (as performed with real cameras when they zoom in/out). As in real life the E.O.D. robots have a certain rotation limit on the pivoting arms. This was done by 'clamping' the rotation values of the model, giving a minimum and maximum degree of rotation.

4. EVALUATION: CASE STUDIES

To evaluate the simulation we created 2 game scenarios of bomb thread attack which take place in an abandoned military warehouse. This game has been designed to last for a maximum of 30 minutes depending on the player's skill in successfully finding and disarming the bombs. Upon successful disposal of each bomb the 'bomb counter' will go down accordingly. If it reaches zero or the game's count-

down timer reaches zero, the simulation will end. The levels contain obstacles that the player has to maneuver around to get to the checkpoint component. Other levels may require movement of objects and successful navigation though the given environment. The level has been split into several sections where each section contains its own set of challenges and items. The player has an active inventory where he will be required to find and collect special items to either unlock doors or defuse bombs (dependant on scenario).

Players will be subjected to alternate threats where puzzle solving is crucial for the progression. Upon failure to dispose of all bomb threats in an efficient manner the simulator will terminate. Depending on the players difficulty a time element will be incorporated.

4.1 Design and Level Objectives

The level design was done using Maya 2011, a 3D modelling package created by Autodesk. The model is created and exported as an .fbx file and imported into the XNA Framework. The level design is composed of a series of objectives/tasks that the player needs to achieve in order to progress to other sections. The complete game level design can be seen in Figure 17. Enumerated are the collectable items or tasks that the user will have to encounter.

The game necessitated the use of sliding doors that would stop the player from progressing further unless certain ingame objectives are completed. To progress to the next level the user will need to collect the appropriate keys scattered around the Factory.

4.2 First Bomb Scenario

The first bomb scenario requires the player to disarm the explosive device by collecting a special item (screwdriver). If the item has not been collected and the bomb is armed, moving it too much will trigger an explosion. This is the easy level for the user to become familiar with the E.O.D simulator movement and how to transverse through the environment.

4.3 Second Bomb Scenario

The player needs to disarm a total of 5 bombs, all interconnected with each other (Figure 17). The bombs can be disarmed by placing the correct coloured objects onto their corresponding circle thus disconnecting the bomb on the posing circuit. The player needs to successfully disconnect the green, yellow and red circuit which automatically triggers and disconnects the blue circuit.

The user had to investigate the surrounding area to discover the necessary pattern he/she will have to follow in order to deactivate the bombs. There are hidden locations for the keys and pictures that the player had to discover

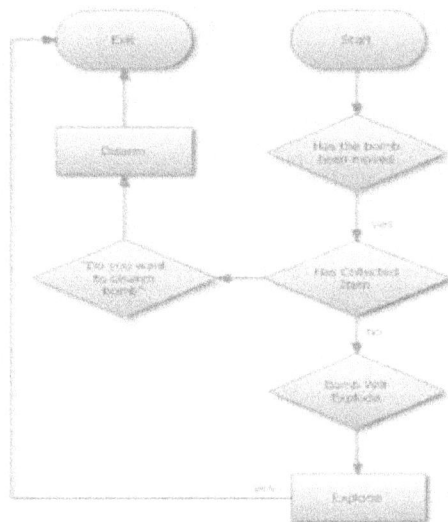

Figure 16: Bomb Scenario 1 - Flow Chart .

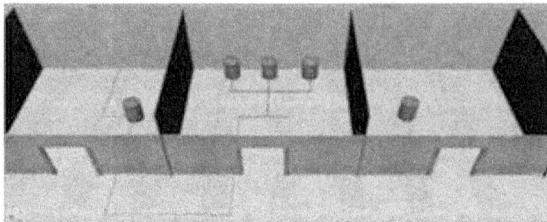

Figure 17: Bomb Scenario 2.

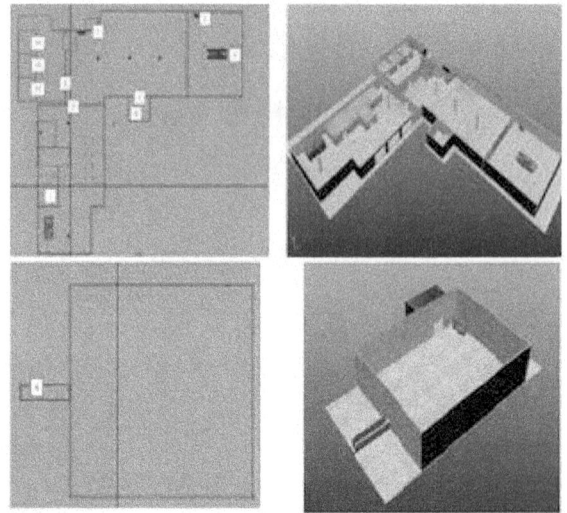

Figure 18: From top left to bottom right: 1) Level 1 Top Down view , 2) Level 1 Maya Render , 3) Level 2 Top Down view, 4) Level 2 Maya Render.

within set limited time. Therefore options like Infrared Mode/Sound mode and zoom in/out were essential.

5. DISCUSSION AND FUTURE WORK

In this paper a prototype for Explosive Ordinance Disposal game simulator has been introduced using motion sensors. The accelerometers in the wiimote and nunchuk controller offers new means of user interaction by making players more aware of their action and ultimately improving their concentration and level of skill when conducting the simulation. Simulation projects require a lot of time and a number of skilled individuals each with their area of specialization (design and programming and evaluation). From research conducted in the analysis stage it was evident that simulators require a high level of detail in all areas of implementation to achieve a realistic scenario where players can assimilate the virtual environment with the real world.

The gameplay and realism can be greatly enhanced by the addition of finger tracking. Although the technology is still under development, significant progress has been made, where players are able to track the position of their finger onscreen. Using this idea, players are able to control a robot (in particular its arm) by finger movement. This would allow players to interact and complete tasks with great precision. 'Head Mounted Displays' can also be utilized in conjunction with built-in accelerometers. This technology would offer players a unique experience allowing a 360 degree view of the 3-dimensional environment complimented by accelerom-

eters in the helmet that pans as the player looks around. In addition the simulation can expand on collision and physics elements by creating pin point accuracy and adding particle effects such as: fog and rain into the level design which would reduce the player's field of view. It can also benefit from having multiple categories of robots to choose from during simulation for: air, ground or water units where each robot would have its unique features and equipment.

6. REFERENCES

[1] M. Carrie. History of military gaming. *Soldiers Magazine*, September 2008.
[2] DARWARS. Darwars ambush!raytheon bbn technologies. *http://www.bbn.com/technology*, 2011.
[3] K. Jones. *A Handbook for Teachers and Trainers*. 1995.
[4] S. J. Montgomery. Eod robots performing tech wonders in iraq. *Army News Service*, January 10 2005.
[5] MSDN. Game method. *http://msdn.microsoft.com/en-us/library/ microsoft.xna.framework.game.update.aspx*,2011.
[6] Nintendo. Wii accelerometer. *http://en.wikipedia.org/wiki/WiiWii$_R$emote.April*, 2011
[7] R. D. Smith. Essential techniques for military modeling and simulation. In *Proceedings of the 30th conference on Winter simulation*, WSC '98, pages 805–812. IEEE Computer Society Press, 1998.
[8] T. Solutions. Stisim. *http://www.stisimdrive.com /our-solutions/training-solutions/professional-drivers/police-drivers.htmlben.*,2010.
[9] X. U. UserGroup. Bounding box xna. *http://xna-uk.net/blogs/randomchaos/archive/2010/08/09/ boundingbox-s-in-xna-4-0.aspx*,2011.
[10] Vallabhaneni, Anirudh, Wang, Tao, He, and Bin. Brain-computer interface. *Bioelectric Engineering, Springer US*, pages 85–121, 2005.

Tweeting Disaster: Hashtag Constructions and Collisions

Liza Potts
CeME Lab
Old Dominion University
Norfolk, Virginia U.S.A
lkpotts@gmail.com

Joyce Seitzinger
Eastern Institute of Technology
Napier, New Zealand
joyce@cats-pyjamas.net

Dave Jones
CeME Lab
Old Dominion University
Norfolk, Virginia U.S.A
dljone01@gmail.com

Angela Harrison
CeME Lab
Old Dominion University
Norfolk, Virginia U.S.A
aharr094@odu.edu

ABSTRACT

In this paper, we describe the issues surrounding the use of various hashtags by Twitter users who are attempting to exchange information about recent natural disasters. During these disasters, hashtag usage was somewhat mired by inconsistent formats, spellings, and word ordering. This paper argues for systems that can help bridge this issue by creating participant-centered data streams that can collect and re-route these conversations.

Categories and Subject Descriptors

H.5.2 [**Information Interfaces and Presentation**]: User Interfaces—*Interaction styles, User-centered design.*

General Terms

Design, Human Factors, Standardization

Keywords

Social Web, Social Media, Twitter, Communication Design, Information Design, Information Architecture, Hashtags, Disasters

1. INTRODUCTION

In the past few years, the information network Twitter has been used as a communication tool during times of disasters. As a tool for participants, Twitter has allowed people to share information and redistribute knowledge across countries, time zones, and cultures [20]. In doing so, participants are working to locate data and validate information about these events. Such details about the disaster zone, missing persons, and possible hijackings have been shared across this network.

For many reasons, not the least of which is an attempt at organizing content, participants use hashtags to communicate within the Twitter stream. In this paper, issues concerning the

distribution of information through twitter is discussed. In the cases reviewed here, hashtag usage was somewhat mired by inconsistent formats, spellings, and word ordering. This paper calls for systems that can help bridge this issue by creating participant-centered data streams that can collect and re-route these conversations.

2. DEFINING HASHTAGS

Twitter content is largely public. Unless a Twitter participant has protected his or her account, updates posted to Twitter are publicly visible. Because Twitter content is public, participants have used the service in numerous contexts to communicate and distribute information quickly [23]. Police departments use the service as a way to notify citizens of recent crimes, raise awareness of events hosted by the police department, or to publicize achievements by the department or its members [10]. Twitter has proven a popular tool to facilitate both public and "backchannel" communication during events, such as academic conferences [15, 16]. In other cases, Twitter has been used as a communication tool in the workplace [27, 35]. Journalists use Twitter to publicize news stories or post quick newsworthy notices for followers, raising questions about the service's role in journalism and news media [5]. And Twitter has proven an extremely useful crisis communications tool in response to various natural and human-made disasters [20, 36].

2.1 About Twitter

Twitter participants post updates, called tweets, which are limited to 140 characters. Any Twitter participant can follow the tweets of any other participant. And because tweets are public, they are also searchable using either Twitter's own search feature or the search function of numerous third-party applications that connect through Twitter's application programming interface (API) [12]. Participants see the updates of any other participant they are following, and their updates are visible to any of their followers. A post on Twitter's blog claims that participants "now send more than 140 million Tweets a day" [29]. All tweets are displayed on a "timeline," which Twitter describes as a "a collected stream of Tweets listed in real-time order" [31].

Participants use several different tools to direct tweets at other participants, or to direct tweets to specific aggregations of tweets. Participants can respond to other participants by using a text command called an "@reply" (pronounced *at-reply*). The text command includes the recipient's username preceded by the @

symbol. These commands appear as "@username," and once they are sent they appear in the recipient's "mentions" timeline. If participants look at their mentions timelines, all tweets directed at them using an @reply are visible, even from participants they may not follow. The mentions timeline also displays "retweets," which occur when one participant republishes another's tweet by posting it to his or her own timeline. Retweets are created using an "RT @username" text command. Retweets can be published by either copying the original tweet exactly as is, or by copying it and then adding a modification to it, such as a comment, a link, or an additional information. As long as the total number of characters in the tweet do not exceed 140, any text-based content can be transmitted, including links to other sites or links to digital images and videos collected on services such as Flickr, Twitpic, or YouTube (digital photo- and video-sharing services).

2.2 Hashtag Use

Hashtags are another tool used by Twitter participants. These tags emerged as a convention invented by Twitter participants as a way to tag tweets [30]. They are tags added to tweets and preceded by the # symbol, so that they appear as "#tag." By searching Twitter content using Twitter's search feature or that of a third-party application, hashtagged tweets can be viewed in a separate timeline that displays them as a chronologically organized aggregation. This aggregation is updated in real-time, displaying new tweets in which participants have attached the necessary hashtag. Though hashtags were first created and used by Twitter participants, the site has since more robustly integrated hashtags into the Twitter experience by making them hyperlinks. Clicking on a hashtag will automatically take participants to the timeline for the tag, showing them the aggregation of tweets using that tag.

Hashtags are a form of social tagging, or "folksonomy" [17, 18, 32]. Folksonomies are "*ad hoc* labeling and tagging systems" used in "a social environment" where multiple people can use the tag [32]. Folksonomies such as hashtags connect bits of information based on the ways social participants understand and use that information, rather than the way it would imposed on a space by an information architect. These are bottom-up systems, derived from the keywords used by participants and online communities. Tags are supposed to "weave a disparate collection of objects together" [17]. They can further be viewed as a form of knowledge work emerging from the writing performed by collectives of participants within specific social contexts. Writing makes knowledge work visible [9], and folksonomies such as hashtags make the collective knowledge work of social web participants visible by leveraging the mobility of content [23].

Due to their potential as folksonomies, hashtags have been the subject of numerous scholarly studies. McNely studies the ways an organization attempted to establish conventions for using Twitter hashtags during an academic conference, only to see conference attendees using Twitter reject the organization's plan and establish their own folksonomy [16]. Potts traces the ways hashtags were used as "a major conduit through which participants shared information" about the Mumbai Terror Attacks of 2008 [20].

Yet, because folksonomies emerge from use by participants within the social web, several problems can occur, as well. Previous research by Potts points to other folksonomies and their uses in response to crisis situations [19, 21]. During the London Bombings of 2005, social web participants, including victims of the terror attacks, turned to numerous social web tools to chronicle their experiences, including Flickr. Flickr is a photo-sharing site that allows participants to tag uploaded photos, creating a folksonomy intended to catalogue similar photos into groups from across the site. However, in many cases tags were inconsistent. Single participants would inconsistently vary between tags such as "bomb," "bombs," and "bombing" in order to describe the images they were uploading. In addition, the terms "blast" and "blasts" became popular tags for content related to this disaster [19]. The lack of consistency in tags in these spaces becomes a problem with making such content more easily searchable and findable across the site itself, as well searchable and findable across the broader social web.

Similar problems mark the use of hashtags in Twitter. In some instances, a hashtag's widespread usage and ability to draw large audiences has lead its exploitation by spammers advertising websites, or even companies advertising products to participants tweeting about the Iran Elections crisis of 2009 [36]. In other cases, a problem similar to that of the London Bombings and Flickr occurs. Hashtags related to the same event or discursive context proliferate, creating potential problems in maintaining "sustainable" communication contexts [16], or leading to issues in finding relevant and necessary Twitter-based content [12, 23]. So, while hashtags possess enormous potential as folksonomic tools for distributing information in contextually-aware ways, participants also encounter issues in these information streams. The volume of content moving through a particular hashtag timeline can become overwhelming, and the participants must often sort through large amounts of social media content in order to identify legitimate information that is relevant to them and the contexts in which they are communicating [21, 23].

2.3 Twitter's Search

Twitter's approach to making the site's content searchable is unfortunately inadequate. The site uses a dedicated search page to allow participants to find Twitter-based content. The site does support Boolean operators on the main search page. And using Twitter's advanced search page, participants can search for keywords, hashtags, user accounts, full phrases, tweets that contain links, or even filter search results by "attitude," which will search for tweets with either happy or sad emoticons. Search results are returned in reverse chronological order, showing the most recent tweets first and proceeding towards the oldest tweets.

Due to these limitations, Twitter participants can encounter problems in finding relevant or much needed content. Specific tweets can be extremely difficult to find in timelines indexing popular or widely used hashtags. In other cases, older tweets may not be visible at all. This problem is compounded by recent decisions by Twitter to shut down tools that might facilitate the mining of Twitter streams for data, including the popular archiving platform Twapperkeeper [8]. This lack of access creates major problems finding content. In addition, if multiple hashtags are used to respond to the same event, participants may be searching multiple hashtag timelines, creating a number of usability problems for participants trying to manage information [12, 23].

3. RECENT DISASTERS

Recent disasters demonstrate the utility of services such as Twitter as communication platforms while also highlighting the problems participants encounter when using such systems to find, organize, and distribute information. New Zealand suffered two major earthquakes in less than a year—September 2010 and February 2011. Both events saw widespread use of Twitter and hashtags to distribute information to victims seeking assistance in their wake. The March 2011 earthquake and tsunami that struck Japan also saw victims, families, and many others turn to Twitter and other social media platforms for many of the same reasons. All these events saw similar issues: proliferation of hashtags that did not cross-pollinate and a lack of usability in the tools necessary for managing massive amounts of streaming information for participants who needed it.

The tweets discussed in this section were collected using the archiving service TwapperKeeper.com. In the case of the Japan disaster, some tweets were found through online news services that used other systems, such as Storify.com, in order to collect tweets during the event. Many of these tweets were also captured within Twitter itself.

3.1 New Zealand

On 4 September 2010 at 4:35 in the morning, the Canterbury region of New Zealand was rocked by a magnitude 7.1 earthquake [7]. There were no human casualties but the level of destruction was massive, estimated at 3 billion New Zealand dollars, including the damage caused by aftershocks [2]. This disaster was the first major crisis in New Zealand since the advent of social media. With telephones lines destroyed and no electricity, each smartphone or laptop became a communication hub while its battery lasted.

After the 2011 New Zealand quake, the All Hazards disaster blog posted a brief summary of the event followed by some phone numbers, and a list of Twitter hashtags that included #eqnz and #chch. Also listed was an #eqnzcontact hashtag that was to be used for finding missing relatives [33]. Aside from suggested hashtags, the post included instructions and examples of how to tweet and provided links to Twitter posts that were near Christchurch. One blogger who identified himself as living about 200 miles from Christchurch posted about his experiences trying to get information on the disaster. He stated that he discovered the event via Twitter and that most of the tweets he saw were from local media sites such as TV, newspaper, and radio. He also highlighted which hashtags were being used, which included #eqnz and #eqnzcontact [1].

As shown to commonly be the case in prior research on disasters and social media [19, 20, 21], the information for the September 2010 New Zealand quake was coming from Twitter and other social media, not from major media outlets. The information participants distributed via Twitter also included commentary that varied from the appropriateness of what was being broadcast to outright frustration with media outlets and government agencies. At 6:48am @radiowammo tweeted: "Oh. So Radio NZ is playing 'Good Vibrations' by the Beach Boys. ummm. huh. #eqnz". And at 6:49am, more than 2 hours after the earthquake, @glynnfoster tweeted, "You think it might make sense to get someone from the national defense crisis center on the airwaves? (like now) #eqnz #radionz #fail". He was not the only Twitter participant airing frustrations concerning media and government responses. The media and the governmental agencies were slow to react with relevant and needed information, particularly when compared with the instantaneous ground reports from Twitter (see Figure 1).

One interesting side note - we gave been relying on Twitter for ALL info since it happened. Much faster than radio etc
#eqnz

Figure 1. A tweet from @kalena indicating the reliance on Twitter for information after the 2010 New Zealand earthquake. From http://twitter.com/#!/kalena/status/22909823819.

Since many media outlets and government agencies responded to the earthquake more slowly than many social web participants, hashtags for the crisis were chosen by the first Twitter participants on the scene, or those participants who turned to their Twitter streams for information, whether they were in Christchurch or somewhere else around the world. It also meant that these tags were instigated and spread in a networked manner rather than dictated by major nodes such as might happen in the case of scheduled events, like conferences or royal weddings.

How did this fledgling community manage its choice of a common hashtag? Immediately after the earthquake, Twitter "exploded with tweets mentioning 'new zealand', 'earthquake' and 'christchurch'. And pretty soon the first hashtags started forming: #earthquake, #quakenz, #nzquake, #nz, #christchurch and combinations of these. And of course there was the inevitable question after Indonesia, would there be a #tsunami? By around 5am one hashtag began emerging: #eqnz" [25] (see Figure 2).

#earthquake Apparently the official hashtag is #eqnz; #doingitwrong. Glad someone's got priorities sorted.

Figure 2. @adzebill tweeting regarding the #eqnz hashtag. From http://twitter.com/#!/adzebill/status/22905414859.

Hashtags are the primary way to effectively pool information in a Twitter conversation. Pooling of information was essential for those seeking assistance, shelter, or loved ones. Rapidly, experienced Twitter participants began guiding other participants to the common hashtag #eqnz, when at 5:17am @adzebill posted: "#earthquake Apparently the official hashtag is #eqnz; #doingitwrong. Glad someone's got priorities sorted." @tristamsparks said, "thanks megan! RT @harvestbird Try tag #eqnz. Power out in much of Chch, water mains damaged.

237

#nzquake." And some participants used gentle admonishment as at 6:16am @morealtitude: "@louis_press Note ur tweeting on Christchurch earthquake, fyi official hashtag = #eqnz (not sure who makes it 'official', but...)." Comparing the usage of several commonly used hashtags to date shows #eqnz emerged as the clear favorite (see Figure 3).

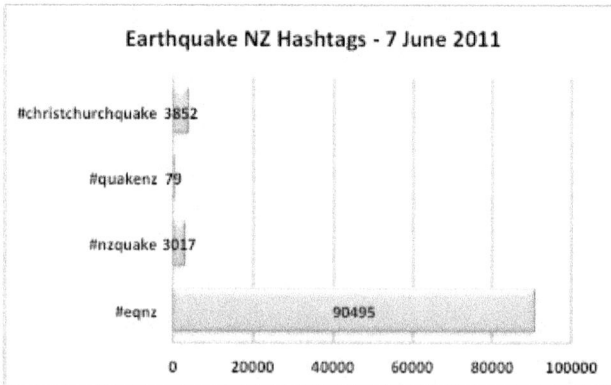

Figure 3. Comparing the use of #eqnz to other hashtags.

Further analysis also shows that the hashtags most commonly used in combination with #eqnz were chch, nz, christchurch, fb, shareanidea, eqnzpositives, tedxeqchch, cera, earthquake. This demonstrates Twitter participants using combinations to talk about #eqnz related topics. However, many of these hashtags were used either infrequently or quickly fell out of use. For instance, @harvestbird uses the "Chch" abbreviation, but does not include the # symbol needed to make it a functional hashtag.

An example of a hashtag that fell into disuse by many participants was #christchurchquake. It was first used around 6 am [25]. By 10:30am its lack of popularity was evident, as @stevevoisey tweeted, "Lol '@catspyjamasnz: update 6 hrs in: #eqnz tweets 2936 v #christchurchquake tweets: 330 #incrisisdonotgoforlongesthashtagever'." Why did the #christchurchquake hashtag fail? It is difficult to assess the reasons for the choices of online communities. And the research presented here examines the technical and social constraints of technologies available to those responding in the immediate aftermath of a crisis.

To this end, some practical difficulties are evident with the #christchurchquake hashtag [25]. At 18 characters, it was too long. The tag took up a substantial portion the 140 characters Twitter allows for every tweet. Even #ccquake would have been better. This also meant that the hashtag could take longer to type, a significant usability hurdle for a participant using a mobile phone to access Twitter. The hahstag also emerged after other tags were already established.

On the other hand, the #eqnz hashtag quickly gathered a following and prevailed not only in the aftermath of the 2010 quake, but also returned during the 2011 event that struck the same area of New Zealand. But why did the #eqnz hashtag prevail? Just as practical difficulties appear with the #christchurchquake hashtag, the shorter #eqnz hashtag reveals several key benefits for participants using Twitter to communicate and organize information [26]. It was short, using only 5 characters of the 140 characters allotted. This left more room in a tweet for necessary information. It was also descriptive while being concise, using "eq" to reference earthquake and "nz" to specify its location in New Zealand at a time when it was not quite clear where exactly the epicenter of the quake was located. The combination of brevity and descriptiveness helped participants remember the tag and its meaning more easily. It was quick to type, especially on mobile devices.

3.2 Japan

On 11 March 2011, an earthquake with an 8.9 magnitude struck Japan. The quake has been documented as the fifth largest worldwide and 8,000 times stronger than the quake that hit New Zealand [3]. The quake spawned a tsunami that hit northern Japan and swept away houses, buildings, cars, and boats. Also affected were a number of nuclear plants that brought forth fears of a meltdown in the days after the quake. Twitter is credited as one of the main sites of communication following the disasters, used by both individuals and organizations alike [4].

Participation on Twitter, always high in Japan, hit a frenetic pace after the initial quake. One blogger noted that the number of tweets coming from Tokyo reached about 1,200 tweets per minute less than an hour after the quake struck [28]. Since the quake knocked out phone lines and television feeds, many turned to their mobile devices in order to send information. [4, 34]. #Japan and #earthquake emerged as the most prominent hashtags, followed by ones like #prayforjapan, #japanquake and #tsunami [4, 6]. One tweet, sent from the account of the United States ambassador to Japan, John Roos (@AmbassadorRoos), gave information on how to find missing loved ones: If you have friends or loved ones in #Japan that you've been unable to reach, email japanemergencyusc@state.gov." [13]. Here, @AmbassadorRoos used the #Japan hashtag to make sure that his information would receive maximum viewing. The information shared included what was going on, inquiries of friends and family, what places were affected, and where to go in the event of an emergency [4].

In another example, a photographer for the American newspaper *USA Today* traveled to Japan following the crisis and tweeted about his experiences. His tweets included crucial information, such as gas shortages and food rationing, as well as more positive events such as reconstruction [14]. However, he did not use hashtags in any of his tweets, suggesting that those who needed it most may not have easily found his critical information. Other participants shared practical, learned information. For example, one tweeter passed on information he learned about radiation and public baths [34]. However, like the previous example, there is no mention of hashtags, thus it is hard to ascertain how much the information spread. What both examples suggest is that though helpful, hashtag use is not always common among participants closest to events such as the Japan earthquake and tsunami.

In other cases, participants quickly and efficiently banded together in order to push updates and information through Twitter and other social media services. Hashtags were established fairly quickly in both English and Japanese among many of these participants. However, as discussed earlier, there is a fair amount of misuse and misinformation that makes its way into tweet streams [36]. In the case of Japan, there were a few rumors that made their way into the various hashtag streams, including one about the possibility of toxic rain following a refinery fire near Tokyo [11]. One blogger collected the rumors on Twitter and posted them onto his site, including good practices for retweeting information [24]. The list of some rumors that were found on

Twitter included the toxic rain, looting by foreigners, conspiracy theories, deaths of famous people (example: *"The creator of Pokémon died today in the #tsunami, #Japan. RIP: Satoshi Tajiri. #prayforjapan")*, requests to distribute relief supplies, and, like the New Zealand quake, misleading information about donations [24].

4. CALL TO ACTION

The inefficiencies in Twitter use in these two crises can be attributed to two factors. One is a human factor and the other is a technical factor. First, inexperience on the part of Twitter participants with the service's hashtag features is combined with a lack of experience with the ways hashtags can be used by different Twitter-based communities. This resulted in the proliferation of multiple hashtags of widely varying lengths and ability to effectively contextualize information. Second, participants faced inadequate systems and tools to easily detect patterns in tweets and the information they contained. The volume of tweets and the speed with which they can be posted by thousands (or, in the case of the Japan quake, even millions) of participants created significant hurdles for participants trying to manage streams of information.

This paper is a call to action for communication design researchers to critically examine the ways social web participants engage with massive streams of information. People cannot and should not be replaced by automated systems, but we can better understand and design participatory experiences that enable people to manage information. In the wake of crises and disasters, better empowering people to find, sort, and understand information is a crucial step for future research.

4.1 Conventions and Usage

As our research indicates, in the wake of major disasters and similar to the issues documented using other social media platforms [19, 20, 21], hashtags on Twitter proliferate, become popular, fall into disuse, are misused to spread inappropriate or misleading information, and can be a burden to participants due to usability problems in managing information [23]. These systems rely largely on folksonomies, or the categorization methods that emerge from within the communities where information originates. As a result, they do not follow rigid, well-defined rules for use that can be effectively monitored and enforced. Instead, people step forward in these spaces to find and distribute relevant information using their own practices. Communication researchers and designers must account for these differences in conventions and usage among participants, and help build systems that facilitate people-powered moderation of content.

For those who assume the role of finding, organizing, and distributing information, tools should be flexible and adaptable to these situations. Those tools must be able to trace the multiple conventions among online communities and allow for the widely varying characteristics in usage that will occur. Our call to action is not to argue for the imposition of top-down hierarchies in information categorization, but to leverage within social media the folksonomies that emerge in response to disasters. This way, people can respond to events and direct critical information in the ways they see necessary.

4.2 Systems

To support these folksonomies, systems for managing massive information streams, such as those that form around hashtags in Twitter, we must present useful and usable information management and data visualization options for participants. Third-party applications that access social media services through APIs already provide some suggestions for how to do this [12]. However, stronger research and design is needed to build systems that can flexibly find and adapt to the changes in conventions and usage among participants. Communication researchers and designers must support those participants who step forward as moderators that find, sort, and distribute information. Systems must leverage the language of categorization that participants create, not impose categories on them that may be difficult to understand, lack necessary context, or potentially create cross-cultural issues among participants. By allowing folksonomies to play well with taxonomies, we can help build support structures and allow information to flow freely to those who need it most.

5. REFERENCES

[1] Abdul, D. 2011. #eqnz: the web mobilizes for New Zealand earthquake. *The Word of Awahid*. Available from http://blog.awahid.net/2011/02/eqnz-the-web-mobilizes-for-new-zealand-earthquake/.

[2] Bennett, A. 2011. EQC "could deal with another big one"—Business. *NZ Herald News*. Available from http://www.nzhearld.co.nz/business/news/article.cfm?c_id=3&objected=10709579.

[3] Buerk, R. 2011. Japan earthquake: tsunami hits northeast. *BBC News*. Available from http://www.bbc.co.uk/news/world-asia-pacific-12709598.

[4] Crump, I. 2011. Using Twitter to cover the earthquake in Japan. *BBC News*. Available from http://www.bbc.co.uk/blogs/5live/2011/03/using-twitter-to-cover-the-ear.shtml.

[5] Farhi, P. 2009. The Twitter explosion. *American Journalism Review* (June/July 2009), 27-31.

[6] Farivar, C. 2011. Social media, web provide Japan quake sources. Deutsche Welle. Available from http://www.dw-world.de/dw/article/),,149056400,00.html.

[7] GNS Science. 2010. *GeoNet—New Zealand Earthquake Report*. Available from http://geonet.org.nz/earthquake/quakes/3366146g.html.

[8] Godry, P. E. 2011. Twitter shuts down TwapperKeeper. *Business Insider*. Available from http://www.businessinsider.com/twitter-twapperkeeper-2011-2.

[9] Grabill, J. and Hart-Davidson, W. 2010. Understanding and supporting knowledge work in everyday life. *Language at Work* (February 2010), 1-4.

[10] Heverin, T. and Lisl, Z. 2010. Twitter for city police department information sharing. In *Proceedings for ASIST 2010* (Pittsburgh, PA, October 22-27). ASIST 2010. ACM, New York, NY. 1-7.

[11] Hosaka, T. 2011. Japan disaster sparks a social media innovation. *2News Today*. Available from http://www.kjrh.com/dpp/news/science_tech/japan-disaster-sparks-social-media-innovation-wcpo1301917492825.

[12] Jones, D. and Potts, L. 2010. Best practices for designing third party applications for contextually-aware tools. In *Proceedings of the 28th ACM International Conference on Design of Communication* (Sao Paolo, Brazil). SIGDOC '10. ACM, New York, NY, 95-102.

[13] Kessler, M. 2011. Japan: Twitter earthquake and tsunami updates from the ground. *USA Today*. Available from http://content.usatoday.com/communities/ondeadline/post/2011/03/japan-twitter-updates-from-the-ground/.1.

[14] Kessler, Michelle. (2011). Japanese tsunami reaction from Twitter, Facebook. USA Today. Available from http://content.usatoday.com/communities/ondeadline/post/2011/03/japanese-tsunami-reaction-from-twitter-facebook/.1.

[15] McNely, B. J. 2009. Backchannel persistence and collaborative meaning-making. In *Proceedings of the 27th ACM International Conference on Design of Communication* (Bloomington, Indiana). SIGDOC '09. ACM, New York, NY, 297-303.

[16] McNely, B. J. 2010. Exploring a sustainable and public information ecology. In *Proceedings of the 28th ACM International Conference on Design of Communication* (Sao Paolo, Brazil). SIGDOC '10. ACM, New York, NY, 103-108.

[17] Morville, P. 2005. *Ambient Findability*. Sebastopol, CA., O'Reilly.

[18] Panke, S. and Geiser, B. 2009. "With my head up in the clouds": Using social tagging to organize knowledge. *Journal of Business and Technical Communication* 23, 3, 318-349.

[19] Potts, L. 2009. Designing for disaster: Social software use in times of crisis. *International Journal of Sociotechnology and Knowledge Development* 1, 2, 33-46.

[20] Potts, L. 2009. Peering into disaster: Social software use from the Indian Ocean earthquake to the Mumbai bombings. In *Proceedings of the International Professional Communication Conference*. Hawaii: IEEE.

[21] Potts, L. 2009. Using actor network theory to trace and improve multimodal communication design. *Technical Communication Quarterly* 18, 3, 281-301.

[22] Potts, L. 2010. Consuming digital rights: Mapping the artifacts of entertainment. *Technical Communication* 57, 3, 300-318.

[23] Potts, L. and Jones, D. 2011. Contextualing experiences: Tracing the relationships between people and technologies in the social web. *Journal of Business and Technical Communication* 25, 3, 338-358.

[24] Sasaki, T. 2011. Japan: Toxic rain, earthquake weapons and other false rumors. *English Global Voices*. Available from http://globalvoicesonline.org/2011/03/13/japan-toxic-rain-earthquake-weapons-and-other-false-rumors/.

[25] Seitzinger, J. 2010. Social media use in crisis—#eqnz—wich hashtag prevails. *Cat's Pyjamas*. Available from http://www.cats-pyjamas.net/2010/09/social-media-use-in-a-crisis-eqnz-which-hashtag-prevails/.

[26] Seitzinger, J. 2011. #eqnz: which hashtag prevails? Presentation at *the IRGO Conference* (Dunedin, New Zealand).

[27] Stolley, K. 2009. Integrating social media into existing work environments. *Journal of Business and Technical Communication* 23, 3, 350-371.

[28] Taylor, C. 2011. Twitter users react to massive quake, tsunami in Japan. *Mashable*. Available from http://mashable.com/2011/03/11/japan-tsunami/.

[29] Twitter. 2011. *Happy birthday Twitter!* (March 21, 2011). Available from http://blog.twitter.com/2011/03/happy-birthday-twitter.html.

[30] Twitter. 2011. *What are Hashtags ("#" Symbols)?* Available from http://support.twitter.com/articles/49309-what-are-hashtags-symbols.

[31] Twitter. 2011. *What is a Timeline?* Available at http://support.twitter.com/groups/31-twitter-basics/topics/109-tweets-messages/articles/164083-what-is-a-timeline.

[32] Vander Wal, T. 2007. Folksonomy. *Vanderwal.net*. Available from http://vanderwal.net/folksonomy.html.

[33] Wild, D. New Zealand Christchurch earthquake. *All Hazards Blog*. Available from http://allhazards.blogspot.com/2011/02/feb-2011-new-zealand-christchurch.html.

[34] Winn, P. 2011. Japan tsunami disaster: As Japan scrambles, Twitter reigns. *Global Post International News*. Available from http://www.globalpost.com/dispatch/news/regions/asia-pacific/japan/110318/twitter-japan-tsunami.

[35] Zhao, D. and Rosson, M. B. 2009. How and why people twitter: The role that micro-blogging plays in informal communication at work. In *Proceedings of GROUP '04* (Florida). ACM, New York, NY.

[36] Zhou, Z., Bandari, R., Kong, J., Qian, H., and Roychowdhury, V. 2010. Information resonance on Twitter: Watching Iran. In *Proceedings of the 1st Workshop on Social Media Analytics* (Washington, DC). SOMA '10. ACM, New York, NY, 123-131.

Google News: How User-Friendly is It for the Blind?

Barbara Leporini
ISTI – CNR
Via G. Moruzzi, 1
56124 – Pisa, Italy
+39-050-3152034

barbara.leporini@isti.cnr.it

ABSTRACT

Being able to read text, find out information and know about the latest news has always been a challenge for those who cannot access the printed version, such as the visually-impaired. The advent of the Web has been a big step in the right direction for blind people to obtain up-to-date information on the internet. Many portals and Web sites offer online services for up-to-date news. In this paper our aim is to evaluate how easy and rewarding it is for blind people to access this. For this purpose, we are focusing on the well-known online service provided by Google, i.e. Google News as a case study. In order to truly benefit from access to the information available on the Web, the page interface must be simple and easy to use by everyone, including people who have to use assistive technologies. In this work we analyze not only the accessibility of the service offered by Google for its News, but also in particular the usability when interacting via screen reader.

Categories and Subject Descriptors

H.5.2 (User Interfaces): Auditory (non-speech) feedback, Evaluation/methodology, Graphical user interfaces (GUI), Interaction styles, Screen design, Voice I/O.

General Terms

Design, Human Factors.

Keywords

News service, user interfaces, accessibility, usability, blind users, screen reader.

1. INTRODUCTION

Being able to read text, find out information and know about the latest news has always been a challenge for those who cannot access the printed version, such as the visually-impaired. The advent of internet and advancements in User Interfaces (UIs) as well as in assistive technologies make this challenge increasingly feasible. Reading and retrieving information from several sources

are important research subjects widely studied in the accessibility and usability field for people who have difficulty in accessing the printed version. To have books and documents in electronic format, as well as platforms for supporting distance education usable by all, is certainly a big step towards a more inclusive community. Accessing information of any type is not only possible from reading books or using distance-learning systems, but it includes other opportunities such as obtaining information on recent events or up-to-date news. Therefore, the information services should not only be accessible, but especially simple to use, so that it possible to read the latest news with little effort. To ensure that all available resources, on the Web or for desktop applications, are truly usable via assistive technologies (such as screen readers), the interfaces should be designed according to specific principles.

In this paper we analyze blind user interaction with an information service (on-line news) in order to understand the main accessibility and usability issues related to it when using a screen reader. We consider the news pages offered by the well-known Google service as a case study to identify the main issues encountered by the blind when accessing the information. Google News is a computer-generated news site that collects headlines from more than 4,500 English-language news sources worldwide, groups similar stories together and displays them according to each reader's personalized interests (http://news.google.co.uk/intl/en_uk/about_google_news.html). For this kind of service, we consider the accessibility and usability issues for the two main functionalities "Reading the news" and "News personalization". Google has been considering accessibility properties (http://www.google.com/accessibility/), especially for its search engine. The aim of this study is to understand the main accessibility and especially usability issues encountered by blind people when reading the news. The results can be useful to focus on the most important functionalities related to an information service in order to identify specific aspects to be considered when developing a similar portal for on-line news.

This paper is organized as follows: after a short introduction to other studies in the field, the main functionalities offered by Google News are evaluated and discussed in section 3. A short discussion and some possible suggestions based on the results conclude the paper.

2. RELATED WORK

2.1 Screen Reader Interaction

A screen reader is a software that attempts to identify and interpret what is being displayed on the screen. Then, the content reported on the screen can be presented to a blind user as speech through a voice synthesizer or as a braille display.

For the Web, as well as for some other applications, screen readers are not reading the screen any more; instead, the screen reader is using the DOM to provide a speech rendering of data that is a web page. A screen reader must present the two-dimensional graphical web page to a user who is blind as a one-dimensional stream of characters, which is usually fed to a speech synthesizer. It is very important to be aware that this screen-reading process is converting a twodimensional page to a one-dimensional text string, whether spoken or displayed in Braille. Another way to picture the linearization process is to read the page from left to right and from top to bottom. The resulting text file is the linearized version of the page. The screen reader JAWS for Windows (http://www.freedomscientific.com/jaws-hq.asp) uses the Virtual Cursor in Web pages, which allows the user to read as if it is a word processing document. It seems that those users who are blind rarely listen to a page in full. Often, they navigate to the content and controls of the page. Tab and Shift+Tab move forward and backward through the active elements of the page—that is, through the links and form controls. Screen readers have key commands to read by characters, by words, by lines, and by sentences, as well as HTML features like headings, paragraphs, tables, and lists. It is in this linearized world that some of the accessibility and usability requirements begin to make better sense [9]. Thus, generally speaking, there are many different ways to use a screen reader [11]. Users can move to the next or previous lines, jump over a number of lines, or skip to items of a certain type such as headings, links, or form fields. There are also search commands which can be used to go directly to a given phrase within a page. In [1] there is an overview of the browsing strategies which screen reader users employ when faced with challenges, which range from unfamiliar web sites and complex web pages to dynamic and automatically-refreshed content.

In brief, the main problems for a blind person interacting through screen reader are: (1) Lack of context, (2) Information overload, (3) Excessive sequencing in reading (4) Keyboard navigation, and (5) Screen reader interpretation. So, based on these key aspects, possible principles and criteria have been proposed to enhance the interaction in terms of usability for people who use screen readers. Several studies have already proposed a set of guidelines or alternative solutions for the usability of accessible pages [6] and [10].

2.2 Web accessibility

In order to be truly satisfying and effective for users with disabilities, a Web service or page must not only be well organized and appealing but also accessible and usable. Accessibility and usability are two important aspects that are increasingly combined in order to improve user interfaces. In literature there are many studies that propose and discuss possible principles, approaches and solutions aimed at simplifying interaction for all users. In the context of the Web, several accessibility guidelines and recommendations have been proposed, such as the renowned W3C WCAG 1.0 and the new version WCAG 2.0 [12]. Several investigations show that focusing only on accessibility is not enough to ensure a satisfactory user interaction when using a screen reader [6] and [10]. Usability plays a key role because even when pages meet accessibility standards, they can still be difficult to traverse [4]. A study which evaluated 100 Websites with 51 users who had a disability [8] reports that 45% of difficulties encountered were on pages which complied with accessibility requirements. With

reference to services offered by Google, some accessibility and usability investigations have been conducted mainly for the blind [5]. The authors propose and evaluate a set of suggestions aimed at improving Google search user interfaces when interacting via screen reader. In this work we analyze the accessibility and especially usability aspects for the Google News service in order to identify the main issues for news services.

3. GOOGLE NEWS EVALUATION
3.1 Method

The Google News service has been selected as a case study of online news and information pages in order to analyze and identify potential problems encountered by people with visual disabilities when reading the news. To evaluate the main aspects related to a news service, we consider the two activities mainly involved when accessing a news service:

Reading the news: the page is opened by clicking on "News" on the Google home page (http://news.google.co.uk), which is available for each Google local version (i.e. English, French, Spanish, Italian, etc.);

News personalization: the "Add a new section", "Remove a section" as well as "section arrangement" features.

For our purposes we considered the browsers IE (Ver. 8.0) and Mozilla Firefox (Ver. 3.6), and the screen reader Jaws (version 11.0). The JAWS screen reader has been chosen based on the fact that it is widely used by several blind people [3], [6] and [7]).

In relation to the methodology, advanced familiarity with the interaction with the UI of the system through a screen reader, as well as some specific principles and criteria proposed in the literature [6], especially when interacting via screen reader, were the basis for analyzing the main features offered by the news service. Thus, to test the UI usability through a screen reader, an inspection evaluation method by an expert in accessibility and usability topics (the author of this paper, who is herself blind) has been applied. In particular, we based our accessibility and usability evaluation on the principles such as "Content structuring" (e.g., Logical partition of interface elements, Number of links, etc.), "Content appropriateness" (e.g., Proper link content, Proper names for tables and images, etc.), "interactivity" (e.g., operability via keyboard, Messages and dynamic data management, etc.) and so on. In brief we considered those aspects which can greatly influence the pleasure of reading. The screen reader interprets the Web contents sequentially. So, it is important to understand whether the contents have been properly designed to evaluate the correctness of their linearity and operability via screen reader and keyboard. The methodology herein used is based on the simulation of exploration of the web page in sequence (arrows and Tab keys) or using advanced Jaws commands (Insert + F6 for the list of headers, Insert + F7 for the links, "h", "l" or "t" for navigating the content, etc.). The two sequential and advanced interaction modalities have been considered in order to simulate both beginner and skilled users, and to evaluate the perception and ease of interaction with the interface via keyboard and screen reader. This method could therefore be used and applied by developers to test their Web pages.

3.2 Reading the News

While the Google News home page looks very accessible and simple to use, when interacting via screen reader some usability issues may be encountered. The main goal of the page is to provide the latest news. Several different sources are made available by the service for each news item. So, the user can read part of the news item (i.e. just the headline and a small block) and then choose the preferred source to read as the full article. In this context, we analyze how a blind user perceives the content and how they move from one news story to another.

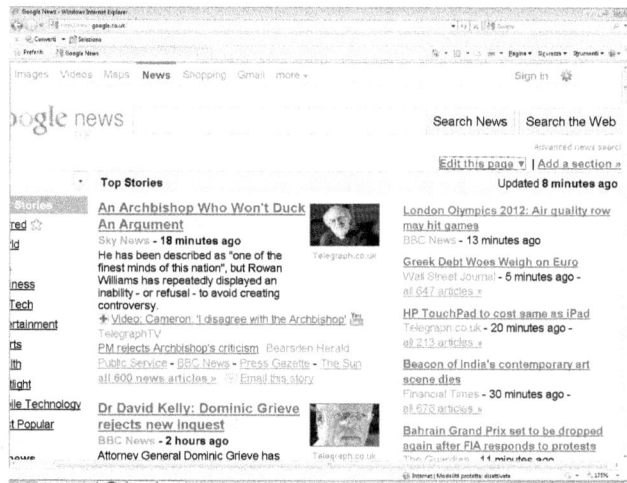

Figure 1. Google News Home Page.

According to the criteria mentioned in section 3.1, the main usability and accessibility issues observed are:

Content structure and layout (columns and Sequential Order).

The contents, including even those arranged on two or more columns, are well sequenced. The screen reader first detects the title of a section, it reads the items in the section, and afterwards it moves on to the next section that may be in the other column.

Sections and Articles (Headings).

A frequently observed strategy for "Logical partitioning of UI elements" is to use landmarks for orientation and navigation within the content [1] or headings obtained with the <Hn> tags [6], which offer several benefits [13] including being able to have "on the fly" a specific table of contents (JAWS command Insert + F6). On the Google News home page, headings are associated both to the sections and news headlines. All headings are at the same level "2" (<H2>) and therefore no hierarchical arrangement is used to structure topic sections and news items. As a result, the user is not able to quickly understand the main sections (i.e. world, health, sports, etc.) since the list of headings (Jaws command F6) shows both sections and headlines (more than 40 items). So the user has to read all the headings sequentially with no distinction between sections and headlines.

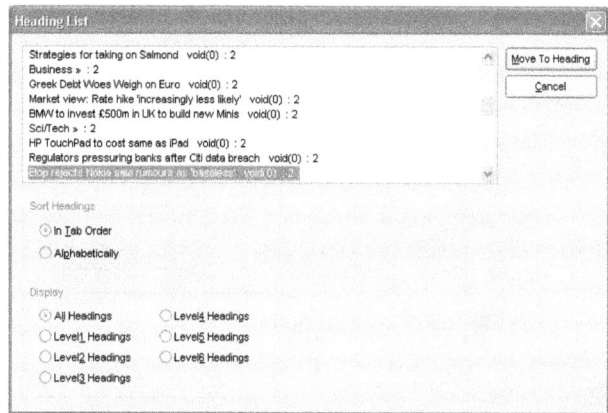

Figure 2. Google news: list of headings captured by Jaws.

Sources of Information (links).

For each news item several links related to various information sources are available (i.e. more than one article for each specific topic). The links can clearly affect the UI perception and operability in terms of accessibility and usability. Here below are some aspects related to the links which affect the user interaction via screen reader:

Number of links - The page contains more than 350 links. This makes scrolling via Tab key or scrolling through the list of all the links (Insert + F7 Jaws command) difficult and frustrating. The number of links or the negative effects derived from the interaction via Tab key should be reduced (e.g. by removing the links from the Tab key navigation order) (see below for more details). Using headings reduces only in part the undesired effects when exploring the UI via screen reader. User interaction should be enhanced also in terms of links.

Graphical links - The large number is not the only drawback regarding links. In fact, several graphical links have no alternative text, making it difficult to understand the associated content. The Tab. 1 shows portions of the Google News page read by Jaws and highlights how the screen reader sequentially interprets the content via the virtual cursor. The links associated with section titles in the table are an example of graphical links without alternative text. In particular, the links related to the titles of articles, which are identified by Jaws as "Void (0)" and graphically represented by the symbol "star", could cause confusion because neither its importance nor the resource linked by them is clear. The word "Void (0)" appears right next to each news headline, as shown in Fig. 2, which reports the list of the headers associated with the news (See the list of news headlines).

Unclear references - Links to external resources that are associated with each title of the article (i.e. the link located on the left for each headline) are not detected by Jaws in the correct way in relation to the sequenced content. In fact, as can be seen in Tab. 1, the link pointing to the information resource seems to be related to the previous article, because it is detected by the screen reader before the news headline. Indeed since Jaws sequentially interprets the content, the link related to the current news is located near the links for the previous news (i.e., the content is not appropriately linearized). Thus, in this way the user can notice that the link is associated with the previous news and not the right one.

Section index - The list of links on the left of the page is a kind of "table of content" for the sections available on the page. By clicking on one section of these links the corresponding page is opened. However, as the links are coded, the blind user might have some difficulty in perceiving correctly the content as a result of: (1) the graphical links without alternative text (see above); (2) the links are not local links within the page, but they point to external resources, although they are labeled with the names of the sections available in the current page; (3) the links are listed in a table without the summary attribute (see Tab. 1).

News Updating (dynamic messages).

When the Google News Page is automatically updated with the latest news (every few minutes), this change is not notified to the screen reader user. There is only a very short sound, but the user needs to explore all the contents in order to perceive and find the updates.

3.3 Content Personalization

Through Google personalization features it is possible to set up the personal news page to show just the preferred stories. In this perspective, the interface can be simplified by removing the unwanted sections, thus reducing the page complexity. In particular the personalization functionality offers the opportunity to add and remove sections, as well as to rearrange the whole News page by giving a preferred order to the news sections. In this way, the interface should be more suitable for a screen reading user. In this section we consider if the procedures used for personalizing the page are truly accessible via keyboard and using a screen reader.

3.3.1 Removing a section.

The procedure to delete a section highlights some accessibility and usability issues related to the interaction via keyboard and to the feedback notification for dynamic messages. To remove the section "Sports", for instance, it is necessary to click on the link "Edit this page". As a consequence a small portion of the page changes and the message "Drag to rearrange page. Click to edit" appears within the content, but it is not automatically announced by the screen reader. The user might perceive that nothing has changed. To find the new message, it is necessary to sequentially explore the page content with the arrow keys. This could take a large amount of time and effort by the user. Then, to choose the section to be removed, the user has to click on its name (e.g. World, Business... Sports, etc.). Unfortunately the screen reader detects each section name as a static text and no indication of the clickable item is announced. This makes the action practically inaccessible and the user cannot proceed. However, if the user could select the section name, the next step (i.e. personalization options) would be more feasible and accessible. To remove a section, a specific checkbox needs to be selected and confirmed with the "Save changes" button. Also in this case small portions are updated without reloading the entire page. The screen reader does not announce those changes, so exploration of the surrounding area is needed. After clicking on the "Save Changes", a short confirmation message is displayed briefly, but the user does not have time to read it, because it almost immediately disappears without notifying the screen reader. Thus this kind of dynamic feedback is inaccessible to screen reader users. This makes the procedure inaccessible for some required actions, and unusable for other activities especially by beginner users.

...

Link Edit this page

|

Link Add a section »

Other News Editions

Combobox U.K. 1 of 71

table with 2 columns and 12 rows

Link img/cleardot

Link Top Stories

...

Link img/cleardot

Link Sports

...

table end

Heading level 2   Updated 8 minutes ago

Heading level 2   Top Stories

...

Heading level 2 Link Sci/Tech »

Link msnbc.com

Heading level 2 Link HP TouchPad to cost same as iPad

Link void(0)

Telegraph.co.uk -

Link Matt Warman

 - 35 minutes ago

The TouchPad, HP's...

Link HP TouchPad to cost the same as the iPad 2 in the UK upon mid-July arrival

CNET UK

          Link HP TouchPad available in UK from mid-July

Mobile News

Link T3

-

Link Reuters

-

Link The Guardian (blog)

-

Link BGR

Link all 219 news articles »

Link Email this story

...

Table 1. Google News: fragment read by Jaws.

3.3.2 Adding a Standard or Personalized section.

Google News User Interfaces have different versions (e.g., English, French, Spanish, Italian, etc.). However, generally speaking, the procedure used to add a new section is in practice feasible, although it is not particularly usable. After clicking the link "Adding a section", the next steps requested are basically accessible. The main issues are related to usability aspects. The main difficulties are related to the page focus, which does not automatically highlight the main and appropriate content. The user is asked to explore via arrow keys or Tab.

Just to give an example, Fig. 3 shows the page directory of the news found by looking for the string "assistive technologies". The results are visualized using tables, one for each identified section, according to the performed search (in our example the two sections "Disability" and "assistive technologies"). As shown in the portions interpreted by the screen reader (Tab. 2), the layout of the results was obtained with tables without "summary" attribute and graphical links with no alternative description (i.e. two important accessibility properties are missing). After confirming the addition of the new section, the user is redirected to the page related to the section that has been just added. So, this may confuse the blind user who does not understand what is happening due to the lack of content overview. To go back to the news page, the user needs to click on the link "Google News". So, in terms of usability, the risk is that the users become confused.

However, despite some usability problems, the user can choose the section to add. Therefore, we can conclude that the procedure was successful, even though more steps were required of the user. Moreover, for each section to be added, the entire procedure must be repeated.

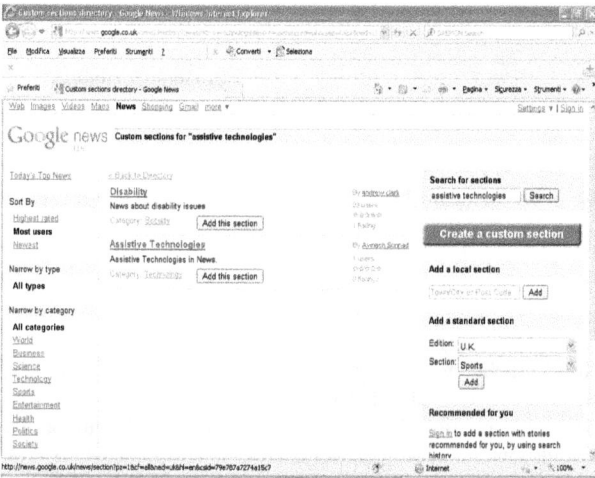

Figure 3 - Adding a new section: results found for "assistive technologies".

3.3.3 Rearranging the news sections.

To better personalize the contents of standard and customized sections in the personal News page, a Google function allows the user to move sections in any preferred order. To do it, it is necessary to click on the link "Edit this page" and then work on the available sections in a similar way as introduced in the previous paragraphs. Unfortunately, this specific function cannot

...

Link graphic Google News

Custom sections for

"assistive technologies"

Link Today's Top News

Sort By

list of 3 items

...

Link « Back to Directory

table with 3 columns and 3 rows

Link Disability

By

Link andrew clark

23 users

1 Rating

News about disability issues

Category:

Link Society

Add this section Button

table end

table with 3 columns and 3 rows

Link Assistive Technologies

By

Link Avinash Sonnad

1 users

0 Ratings

Assistive Technologies in News.

Category:

Link Technology

Add this section Button

table end

Heading level 3 Search for sections

Edit assistive technologies

Search Button

Link Create a custom section

Heading level 3 Add a local section

Edit

Add Button

Table 2 . Portion of Google Personalization page.

be performed via keyboard and screen reader because the drag-and-drop is required. The blind user cannot fully customize their news page. So, this feature is fully inaccessible.

4. DISCUSSION and DESIGN SUGGESTIONS

In this study we analyzed the main aspects of interaction via screen reader with the Google News service. The choice of Google News is based on the identification of a case which has the basic functionalities commonly available in an online news service, such as "Reading the news" or "Service personalization". In this perspective, the results reported in this study represent a starting point for identifying possible principles and guidelines for developers of information and news services.

On the whole we can say that the Google News service is accessible for "reading news". The main difficulties are related to usability issues, while severe accessibility problems result from some steps in the personalization procedure. In short, the main issues observed by analyzing the Google News service can be summarized as follows:

Unusable layout and messages: Unsuitable logical partitioning of contents, pages with too many links and lack of appropriate feedback on updating and dynamic messages make the interaction difficult and frustrating.

Inaccessible and non-flexible procedures: Personalization is difficult and sometimes inapplicable. Adding or removing more than one section implies repeating the whole procedure from the beginning for each section.

Inapplicable section rearrangement: Although the personalization page can be reached in just a few clicks, the section reorganization in a preferred order is not in practice feasible via keyboard and screen reader.

According to usability principles, in order to have a satisfactory interaction, it is necessary for the user to be able to achieve the goal (i.e. easily reading the news) effectively and efficiently. Indeed the user should be able to concentrate on the news without any type of technological interference. Thus the user should be easily able to read (1) the latest news, (2) the available information topics and (3) the listed news for a specific subject. In addition, it would be important to avoid undesired information as well as to arrange the news in a preferred order and position. In short, a news service should offer a powerful personalization function to allow the user to customize their preferences independently of their abilities (i.e. including people with disabilities).

Based on the main issues herein identified as possible difficulties affecting the interaction via screen readers and keyboard, some first suggestions to keep in mind when designing an information service can be identified:

Logical partitioning and clear structure for sections and headlines: the user should be able to quickly obtain an overview of topics and to easily move between both sections (topics) and articles.

Proper content for headlines and sources: the title of articles should be descriptive and include a clear reference to the main source the link points to.

Simple layout and agile navigation: if numerous links related to several information sources or additional references are available for each news item, an agile sequential navigation via keyboard should be made available (e.g. by excluding secondary links from the navigation order).

Easy and flexible personalization: an accessible procedure for layout and content personalization should be offered to simplify the user interface; removing, adding or rearranging sections should be easily possible including via keyboard. Other advanced personalization features (e.g. saving preferred articles, organizing by category, etc.) might greatly facilitate using the system and user interaction as well.

For Web-based information systems, W3C ARIA (Accessible Rich Internet Applications) suite [2] could represent a valuable solution to enhance user interaction through assistive technologies. In order to overcome the partitioning issues, for example, ARIA "landmarks" roles could be used for sections; or, alternatively, each section could be embedded in a DIV block included in a navigation order via Tab key. In this way a screen reader user could obtain the list of subject sections and choose one of them, or can move from one section to the next using the Tab key, and then it is possible to explore the section in a sequential way or move between the headlines using the Jaws command " H " (or Insert+F6 for the list of the News). In addition, ARIA could positively affect the interface regarding the usability issues for the links. The graphical links could be made available either by assigning the standard alternative content (i.e. alt =""), or by assigning the role "link" to the images while maintaining the same look-and-feel. Moreover, for each article there are a group of links pointing to other resources referred to the same news (i.e. the links listed below the news). Those links contribute to making navigation frustrating. So, they could be excluded from the order of keyboard navigation through specific ARIA properties; so that those links are detected when exploring the page in a sequential way, but they are not reachable by the focus when moving via Tab key. Consequently the user could move via Tab key article header by header, and they can explore sequentially via arrow keys when reading a desired news story.

5. CONCLUSION

In conclusion, the user interaction could be made not only accessible but especially satisfactory for those who use assistive technologies. Using ARIA through roles and specific attributes, the user interface via screen reader could be made accessible and more usable, especially for those functions that are currently difficult or impossible to use. Currently ARIA-based solutions are partially supported. Just some ARIA roles or properties work well with the screen readers and Web browsers. So, in order to have a really simplified user interaction for people with disabilities, both Web designers as well as user agent and assistive technologies should take into account and make practical use of the new recommendations and indications.

Future work includes a prototype for evaluating possible ARIA-based solutions to enhance user interaction via screen reader when using News Google service. Guidelines for news and information services will be more refined. Also accessibility and usability of reading news from mobile devices will be considered.

6. REFERENCES

[1] Borodin, Y. P., Bigham, J., Dausch, G. and Ramakrishnan, I. V. 2010. More than Meets the Eye:A Survey of Screen-Reader Browsing Strategies. In *Proc. of the 2010 international workshop on Web Accessibility (W4A)*, Raleigh, NC (USA), April 26-27, 2010

[2] Craig, J. and Cooper, M. 2011. Accessible Rich Internet Applications (WAI-ARIA) 1.0, W3C Candidate Recommendation, 18 January 2011 at http://www.w3.org/TR/wai-aria/

[3] Donker, H., Klante, P. and Gorny, P. 2002. The design of auditory user interfaces for blind users. In *Proc. of the second Nordic conference on Human-computer interaction*, ACM, New York, NY, USA, 2002

[4] Lazar, J., Allen, A., Kleinman, J., and Malarkey, C. 2007. What Frustrates Screen Reader Users on the Web: A Study of 100 Blind Users. *International Journal of Human-Computer Interaction*, 22(3), 2007, pp. 247-269.

[5] Leporini, B., Andronico, P., Buzzi, M. and Castillo, C. 2008. Evaluating a modified Google user interface via screen reader. In *the Universal Access in the Information Society (UAIS)*, Vol. 7(3), 2008, pp. 155-175.

[6] Leporini, B. and Paternò, F. 2008. Applying web usability criteria for vision-impaired users: does it really improve task performance? In *"International Journal of Human-Computer Interaction" (IJHCI)*, Vol. 24, issue 1, January 2008, pp. 17-47.

[7] Mankoff, J., Fait, H. and Tran, T. 2005. Is your web page accessible? a comparative study of methods for assessing web page accessibility for the blind. In *Proc. of the SIGCHI Conf. on Human factors in Computing Systems*, CHI '05

[8] Petrie, H., Hamilton, F. and King, N. 2004. Tension, what tension?: Website accessibility and visual design. In *the 2004 international workshop W4A*, pp. 13 – 18.

[9] Tatcher, J. 2006. Assistive technology: screen readers and browsers. Chapter in the book *"Web Accessibility: Web Standards and Regulatory Compliance"*, Rutter et al. (ED), Springer, 2006. Pp. 103-124.

[10] Theofanos, M.F. and Redish, J. 2003. Bridging the gap: between accessibility and usability, ACM *Interactions magazine*, ACM Press, Nov.-Dec. 2003 issue, pp.36-51.

[11] Trewin, S., John, B.E., Richards, J., Swart, C., Brezin, J. Bellamy, R. and Thomas, J. 2010. Towards a tool for keystroke level modeling of skilled screen reading. In *Proc. of the 12th international ACM SIGACCESS conference on Computers and accessibility* (ASSETS '10), Orlando, Florida (USA), October 25-27, 2010

[12] W3C. Web Content Accessibility Guidelines (WCAG) available at http://www.w3.org/WAI/GL/

[13] Watanabe, T. 2007. Experimental evaluation of usability and accessibility of heading elements. In *Proc. of the 2007 international-disciplinary workshop on Web accessibility (W4A)*, Banff. New York, May 7-8, 2007. ACM Press; 2007 pp. 157-164.

The Evolution of Communication Design: A Brief History of the ACM SIGDOC

Brad Mehlenbacher

Department of Leadership, Policy & Adult & Higher Education
College of Education, North Carolina State University
Raleigh, NC 27695-7801
1.919.515.6242
brad_m@gw.ncsu.edu

ABSTRACT

This paper provides an abbreviated history of the Association for Computing Machinery's Special Interest Group for the Design of Communication (ACM SIGDOC). The ACM SIGDOC has a relatively short history as special interest groups go (1975 to the present), but not in terms of the brief history and explosive growth of computer science, interface design, and the design of systems that support computer users. Indeed, interest in forming a special group focusing on systems documentation began to develop in the early 1970s. At the time, few technical writers (or few computer professionals who recognized themselves as technical writers) existed. Most systems documentation was being developed for military applications and large mainframe computer systems (such as those developed by IBM Corporation). Similar to the history of ACM SIGDOC, the field of communication design has burgeoned while simultaneously allowing increased fragmentation and distributed research initiatives across other developing fields.

Categories and Subject Descriptors

K. [**Computing Milieux**], K.7. [**The Computing Profession**], K.7.2. [**Organizations**], ACM.

General Terms

Design, Documentation.

Keywords

Communication Design, Computing Profession, History of Computing.

INTRODUCTION

This paper relies on conference proceedings from 1982 to the present as well as issues from the ACM SIGDOC journal, *ACM Journal of Computer Documentation* (JCD), dated 2000-2002 and, before that, named *ACM SIGDOC Asterisk Journal of Computer Documentation* (1975-1999).

My major goal is to capture a spirit of the history and development of the ACM SIGDOC in a few pages. This is no mean feat given that the SIG has a rich and creative history that

mirrors developments in the fields of technical communication, computer science, rhetoric and communication, engineering, technology studies, and information design. As well, after Brockmann [1], I believe that understanding our rich history as an organization affords us both perspective and a deeper sense of what our professional and organizational future may hold.

NAMING OUR COMMUNITY

Tracing the history of the Association for Computing Machinery Special Interest Group on the Design of Communication (ACM SIGDOC) is much more challenging than one would expect, especially given that the group has a history of less than four decades. To begin with, the acronym, ACM SIGDOC, stands for a name that is several names removed from the original Special Interest Group on Systems Documentation (1982-1996). After that, SIGDOC stood for Special Interest Group on Computer Documentation (1997-2002), Special Interest Group on Documentation (2003) and, finally, the current Special Interest Group on the Design of Communication (2004-present). Changing the name of the SIG, as well, reveals the evolving nature of our objects of study.

Whereas early interest in documentation emphasized the documentation that computer programmers and engineers developed to support, describe, and share their code, researchers and practitioners interested in communication design now span diverse disciplines and industries. In the 1980s and 1990s, the audience for documentation had shifted with the audiences that used documentation. End-user documentation occupied a considerable amount of ACM SIGDOC members' attention although technical specialists were still very much engaged in building systems for other technical specialists and for helping technical writers and editors produce usable manuals and online information. By the late 1990s, Web applications and online information design and evaluation had become a reality and ACM SIGDOC drew interface designers, graphic designers, marketing specialists, and information architects to its annual conferences. The Special Interest Group on Documentation seemed a much more appropriate name. And, finally, with the new century, "documentation" clearly did not capture the myriad of research interests and practical issues that members were bringing to the organization. SIGDOC was rebranded in 2004 as the Special Interest Group on the Design of Communication.

THE BEGINNINGS OF ACM SIGDOC

Halfway through the 1970s, Joe Rigo (ACM SIGDOC founder and first chair) observed, "There were few computer-related jobs outside IBM and the other manufacturers" [19]. To put the computing context of the mid-1970s into perspective, Microsoft Corporation had just been established in 1975 with the mission of selling the Altair 8800 microcomputer, a technology so new that its primary consumer base was the audience of magazines such as *Popular Electronics* and *Radio-Electronics* [14]. During the decade, the computer world grew dramatically (or got smaller, depending on your perspective) from mainframe (e.g., DEC PDP-1, IBM 360/370) and minicomputers (e.g., DEC PDP-8, DEC PDP-11) to microcomputers (e.g., Apple II, TRS-80 and a host of early software applications, including WordStar, VisiCalc, and dbase II) [17]. The late 1970s and 1980s, incidentally, was when I was introduced to my first microcomputer (the TRS-80 using VisiCalc) and although I was familiar with mainframe computing and minicomputers—and inevitably would become much more familiar with them over the next several years while a student at the University of Waterloo—I was largely unfamiliar with the 1970s computing world that Joe Rigo inhabited professionally.

Feeling motivated to make that computing world feel a little less "lonely," Joe Rigo submitted a brief request to the *ACM forum* of the *Communications of the ACM*. His request read

> I would like to hear from persons interested in forming a Special Interest Committee concerned with computer documentation. The group would consider matters of technical writing, system documentation, and communicating with nontechnical associates. This is strictly an exploratory move. I will report the results of the exploration to anyone who contacts me. We can then determine where to go next, if anywhere [18].

He was excited to receive thirty-three responses, letters from University of Scranton, the Canadian government, Texas Christian University, Lockhead Aircraft, and so on. Rigo compiled the responses into a sixteen-page document entitled "SI*DOC—Special Interest * on System Documentation Newsletter." A petition was also sent to the ACM SIG/SIC Board requesting the "establishment of a Special Interest Committee in the area of computer systems documentation" [19, p. 32].

That same October, Rigo went on publish the first issue of an informal newsletter focusing on documentation and to organize a tutorial and panel discussion entitled "SIGDOC: Experiences with HIPO and other documentation techniques" for the ACM '74 conference being held in San Diego, CA. The panel speaker was Joan Rennaker (Productivity Marketing, IBM) and the panelists included N. C. Jurgens (Project Manager, Sperry Univac), J. A. Morin (Regional Computer Support Manager, NCR), R. D. Olson (Principle Programmer, Sperry Univac), and J. R. Glick (Project Manager, Documentation, Health Application Systems) [23]. Joan Rennaker's career path at the time was representative of professionals interested in technical communication, beginning in productivity marketing and culminating in senior product administration. She had authored a manual on HIPO (a design aid and documentation technique) and would later become an innovator in organizing HUB-based writing centers [2].

The response to the 1974 panel was, in some respects, not entirely surprising. Audience members encouraged an interest in documentation but some wondered why a separate group was needed. This is a common response of the larger ACM Special Interest Group (SIG) Board to emerging disciplines or sub-disciplines, where developing SIGs argue for their uniqueness and viability and larger, established SIGs argue that what they do already addresses issues being raised by the developing SIGs.

Rigo continued to engage volunteers (as treasurer and newsletter contributor) and more people signed petitions and submitted letters for submission. These contributions were published in a second issue of the SI*DOC newsletter and, shortly after, Jean Sammet, President of the ACM, asked that he avoid using ACM SIGDOC or SI*DOC in the publication until formal review had occurred [19, p. 32].[1]

One of the earliest contributors to the *ACM SIGDOC Asterisk Journal of Computer Documentation, 2* (6) [1975]—as well as Diane Patterson and Joe Rigo—was Jonathan Sachs, an MIT graduate who majored in mathematics and was doing work for the Jet Propulsion Lab and several centers at MIT including the Center for Space Research and the Biomedical Engineering Center. It was Sachs (1976) who contributed the first "Comments on Comments" article for the *ACM SIGDOC Asterisk Journal of Computer Documentation*. This innovative feature became a regular part of the journal's organization, where authors contributed articles, other authors commented on those articles, and the original authors were provided with the opportunity to comment on those comments. By 1977, Sachs was at Data General, working for employee #14 and, by 1982, he co-founded Lotus 1-2-3 with Mitch Kapor. Sachs left Lotus three years later and, since 1994, has run his own company, Digital Light & Color, developers of Picture Window, a photo-editing application.[2]

Another early contributor to the journal was Martin A. Goetz, founder (1959) and President of Applied Data Research. In addition to receiving the first U.S. software patent in 1968, he was elected in 1989 to the Infomart Computer Hall of Fame and, in 2000, to the New Jersey Inventors Hall of Fame. His expertise at the time and now is in patent law, unfair competitive practices, and copyright issues; in 1976, for ACM SIGDOC, he was writing about automated documentation challenges [8].

Things moved very quickly in those early days. Rigo submitted 120 signatures to the ACM Board in January 1975 with a request to be officially recognized. One-hundred-and-thirty-eight people were subscribed to the (unofficial) SIGDOC listserv at the time. The ACM Board approved the SIG application in March 1975 and, in April 1975, * (Asterisk) became the first official publication of ACM SIGDOC. By 1977, ACM SIGDOC had, according to Joe Rigo, "Almost 2000 members in 42 states, 8 Canadian provinces, and 11 other countries" (e.g., Australia, Hong Kong, and Switzerland) [19, p. 33]. Rigo also reports that ACM SIGDOC had five local chapters (e.g., in Toronto, Washington, DC, and New York) although when these local

---

[1] As a humorous point of interest, Rigo published Jean Sammet's letter in January, 1975, in the third issue of the monthly newsletter, which he had renamed appropriately as "* Systems Documentation Newsletter."

[2] For more detail on Jonathon Sachs' history as co-founder of Lotus 1-2-3, see Campbell-Kelly [5].

chapters dissolved has not been documented.[3] That same year, 1977, Tom D'Auria (Columbia University) became ACM SIGDOC Chair and Joe Rigo became newsletter editor.

ACM SIGDOC IN THE 1980s

Patterson [16] describes in detail the painful process involved in producing the ACM SIGDOC newsletter (*) in the 1980s. After being mailed to the ACM home office,

> It was assembled on large sheets, provided by ACM, by pasting strips of galley-printed stuff on anyone's printer. The best printers in those days were the daisy-wheel ones. Titles were added using adhesive lettering, such as Letraset. We usually received material printed on whatever machine the author had available. There was little chance to edit the material unless we wanted to retype the stuff (no scanners then for the common writer). The large sheets were then reduced and printed by ACM headquarters [16, p. 36].

The newly minted ACM SIGDOC conferences were still held as part of the larger ACM Conference and, in 1982, the first joint conference of SIGDOC and SIGOA[4] was held Los Angeles, CA. The second conference of ACM SIGDOC was held in Seattle, WA, the third in Mexico City, Mexico, the fourth in Ithaca, NY, and SIGDOC '86 was held in Toronto, Canada, along with a special workshop conference of ACM SIGIR, hosted by Michael Lesk, in Snowbird, Utah.[5]

In 1986, the Joseph T. Rigo Award for contributions to the field of documentation was created by Diana Patterson, and supported by the ACM SIGDOC Board. One year later, the first recipient of the award was Sergio Figueroa Balderez who, in Patterson's words, "brought our conference and the concerns of documentation as a serious subject to Mexico, particularly to his university, Univesidad Automata Metropolitana in Mexico City" [16, p. 39]. The second recipient of the Rigo Award was Edmond H. Weiss and the third was R. John Brockmann. Winners of the now prestigious Rigo Award are listed in Table 1.

In addition to being the third recipient of the Rigo Award, R. John Brockmann (1989-1993) was also the fourth ACM SIGDOC Chair, after Joe Rigo (1975-1977), Tom D'Auria (1977-1980), and Diana Patterson (1980-1989). Brockmann [1]

---

[3] It is unclear how many of these members were paying SIGDOC membership dues, although the numbers are still very impressive.

[4] ACM SIGOA stood for the Office Information Systems and then for Organizational Computing Systems, holding seven conferences between 1984 and 1995 before it became SIGGroup (Supporting Group Work).

[5] The ACM Digital Library houses ACM SIGDOC proceedings dating from 1982 to the present (http://portal.acm.org/). No ACM SIGDOC conference was held in 1987.

Table 1: Recipients of the Rigo Award for "an individual's lifetime contribution to the field of communication design" (after 2004, awarded every other year).

Year	Recipient(s)	For
1987	S. F. Balderez	Bringing documentation to Mexico
1988	E. H. Weiss	*How to write a usable user manual* (1985)
Year	Recipient(s)	For
1989	R. J. Brockmann	*Writing better computer user documentation: From paper to online* (1986)
1990	B. Horton	*Designing and writing online documentation: Help files to hypertext* (1990)
1991	J. D. Chapline	Author of original ENIAC and UNIVAC user manuals
1992	E. Tufte	*Envisioning information* (1990)
1993	J. Bolter	*Writing space: computers, hypertext, and the remediation of print* (1991)
1994	J. M. Carroll	*The Nurnberg Funnel: Designing minimalist instruction for practical computer skill* (1990)
1995	J. Redish	*User and task analysis for interface design* (1998)
1996	B. Shneiderman	*Designing for user interface: Strategies for effective human-computer interaction* (1987)
1997	T. Landauer	*The trouble with computers: Usefulness, usability, and productivity* (1996)
1998	P. Wright	*Information design: Writing for information users* (1992)
1999	T. Winograd	*Understanding computers and cognition: A new foundation for design* (1986)
2000	B. Mirel	*Interaction design for complex problem solving: Developing useful and usable software* (2003)
2001	D. Norman	*The design of everyday things* (1998)
2002	S. Doheny-Farina	*Rhetoric, innovation, technology: Case studies of technical communication in technology transfer* (1992)
2003	J. Hackos	*Managing your documentation projects* (1994)
2004	A. Cooper	*About face: The essentials of user interface design* (1995)
2006	D. Goswami & C. R. Miller	Editors of *Writing in nonacademic settings* (1986) and *Writing in nonacademic settings* (1986)
2008	S. Bodker & P. Ehn	Co-authors of *Computers and democracy* (1987) and *Work-oriented design of computer artifacts* (1988)
2010	M. C. Baraneuskas & C. S. de Souza	Contributions to HCI, participatory design, and semiotic engineering in Brazil

writes that, "When I began as President after Diana, SIGDOC was still pretty much THE only game in town if you wanted to discuss the communication aspects of computers, but already other SIGs such as SIGLINL and SIGUCS were beginning to tear off some of the most interesting elements of our originally unified approach to computer documentation" [p. 40]. But by the mid-1990s, Brockmann laments, "… the sense of computer documentation as a unified whole had ended" and "… the days of single book coverage … or single SIG coverage were gone forever" [1, p. 40].

During Brockmann's term as ACM SIGDOC Chair, a second important award was instituted, the Diana Award, given to an organization, institution, or business for their long-term contribution to the field of communication design. Since 2005, the Diana Award has been given every other year, to organizations that have been or are groundbreaking in terms of their contribution to communication and technology processes and products (see Table 2).

Table 2: Recipients of the Diana Award for "an organization, institution, or business for their lifetime contribution to the field of communication design" (after 2005, awarded every other year).

Year	Recipient
1994	Xerox PARC
1995	Carnegie Mellon's Communications Design Center
1996	Seybold Publications and Seybold Seminars
1997	Adobe Systems, Inc.
1998	Netscape Communications Corp.
1999	Rensselaer Polytechnic Institute (RPI)
2000	MIT Press
2001	Information Mapping, Inc.
2002	World Wide Web Consortium (W3C)
2003	IBM Corporation
2004	The Society for Technical Communication (STC)
2005	The British Computer Society (BCS)
2007	Laboratory for Usability Testing and Evaluation at the University of Washington
2009	Apple, Inc.

ACM SIGDOC IN THE 1990s

The 1990s were a watershed decade for the field of documentation. Nina Wishbow (1993-1997) followed R. John Brockmann as ACM SIGDOC Chair and, in many ways, represented the first generation of documentation professionals to find a natural home in the technical and computing industry. To begin with, the 1990s had already seen the advent of the direct manipulation interface, of WYSIWYG document design, and contemporary personal computing as we currently understand it [22]. Wishbow was educated at SUNY, NY, in rhetoric and communication, received a MA in Communications at Purdue, and a PhD in Rhetoric (with a concentration in Cognitive Psychology) at Carnegie Mellon University (CMU). At CMU, she was introduced to document design and evaluation, usability testing of documentation and user interfaces, experimental design, and general human problem solving, skills that she took into the successful professional

career that spanned various roles (as writer, documentation, usability, and project manager) and companies, including Legent, Nortel/Bell-Northern Research, Entrust Technologies, Oracle, Citrix Systems and, now, Openware.[6]

Kathy Haramundanis (1997-2003) became ACM SIGDOC Chair after Nina Wishbow and, for me, represents the chair who managed SIGDOC during its most dynamic years. With an educational background in computer science and Russian, she represented the perfect blend of organizational leadership, academic curiosity, and professional expertise in information development. Her industry experience began with technical writing and now involves information engineering management, an expertise she has brought to numerous computer companies, including Digital Equipment Corporation, Compaq, and Hewlett-Packard.

Scott Tilley (2003-2005) followed Haramundanis as ACM SIGDOC Chair and—educated as a computer scientist at Concordia University and the University of Victoria—brought an exciting computer science expertise and focus to the SIG. With an impressive technical background (IBM Canada Ltd., Software Engineering Institute, and the Florida Institute of Technology), Tilley revitalized the engineering documentation and textual analysis and manipulation research strands present in the SIG since its early days.

My first exposure to ACM SIGDOC was in 1988 during its 6th Annual International Conference on Systems Documentation, held in Ann Arbor, MI. I had started my PhD in Rhetoric (with a concentration in Document Design) at CMU in 1987, the same year Nina Wishbow graduated from the program and, before that, the University of Waterloo had prepared me well for the work that I would do as a doctoral student. At ACM SIGDOC 1988, I was presenting a theory of help system design and evaluation and demonstrating a model help system with a fellow PhD student and future co-author, James E. Palmer [6]. Diana Patterson, then ACM SIGDOC Chair, made the following comment about our tutorial in her *Chairman's Corner* field notes [15]: "They built the [help] system based on information they gathered from a survey, and they asked the audience to complete survey forms to help them build their understanding of their model. The system was interesting, but slow, and not very unusual: another CMU toy" [p. 9].

I have always very much appreciated that assessment, in part because the "revolutionary" research that I was doing did not immediately influence the technical communication professionals I thought it would resonate with, and partly because it was quite probably true—I *was* working with "toys," exploring what I now realize was part of the future of the profession and experimenting with systems that would ultimately inform reading and writing in hypertext environments and on the World Wide Web.

But I had also found an intellectual and professional home, somewhere between my interest in writing, reading, rhetorical theory, design, usability theory, and human-computer interaction. ACM SIGDOC appeared to embrace both the complex theoretical challenges presented by information and

---

[6] From http://www.linkedin.com/pub/nina-wishbow/1/ab7/706.

communication design and the fast-moving, edgy world of technology creation and use, what Buchanan [3] refers to as *neotoric*, "the inherently rhetorical dimension of all design thinking" [4, p. 24].

After finishing my PhD at CMU in 1992, I took a position at North Carolina State University as an Assistant Professor of Rhetoric and Technical Communication and, there, I began my career-long professional relationship with ACM SIGDOC. I attended and presented at ACM SIGDOC conferences in 1992 (Ottawa, Canada), 1993 (Waterloo, Canada), and 1994 (Banff, Canada), served as Conference and Program Chair of the 14th annual international conference on systems documentation, ACM SIGDOC 1996, held in Research Triangle Park, NC, created and chaired our Graduate Student Competition (1996-2007), served as Awards Officer (1997-present), as SIGDOC Representative for the Technical Communication Summit meetings in 1998, and as Program Committee Member for eight annual conferences (1993-present). In 2003, I ran for Vice Chair and lost and, in 2005, I ran for Chair and won, my first of four terms as ACM SIGDOC Chair (2005-present).

ACM SIGDOC IN A NEW CENTURY

The new century began with the organizational realization that a new project, entitled the ACM Portal to Computing (a major addition to the ACM Digital Library), would be adding considerable bibliographic references and important computing literature to the portal each year. References would be cross-linked and both past and present materials added quickly. As well, ACM SIGDOC's once informal newsletter had been transformed into the *ACM Journal of Computer Documentation* and its issues were being added to the ACM Digital Library, thanks to the long-term and creative efforts of T. R. Girill (Editor-in-Chief, LLNL) and Susan Jones (Production Editor, MIT).

The new century also began with a downward trend in membership numbers for ACM SIGDOC. As Kathy Haramundanis, ACM SIGDOC Chair (1997-2003), noted in the SIGDOC Newsletter,

> Over the past few years, nearly all ACM SIGs have been losing members (the exceptions being recently established SIGs in new technology areas), and the ACM continues to examine possible reasons for this decreased interest. As your Chair, I would greatly appreciate any comments on this topic and recommendations for new approaches our SIG can take that would convince both academicians and practitioners to join the SIG and participate as volunteers in SIG planning and conference activities [9, 10].

Membership numbers, counted by paying members, have continued to drop since: 350 members (2003), 284 members (2004), 245 members (2005), 259 members (2006), 233 members (2007), 237 members (2008), 211 members (2009), and 197 members (2010).[7]

At the same time, ACM SIGDOC reaches many constituents that may or may not be paying members. In addition to hosting its own organizational website (http://www.sigdoc.org/), ACM SIGDOC shares information through various social media spaces, including Facebook (99 Members), LinkedIn (132 Members), Slideshare (4 Members), Twitter (105 Followers), and Wikipedia (http://en.wikipedia.org/wiki/SIGDOC). As well, ACM SIGDOC's quarterly, online newsletters are archived at http://www.sigdoc.org/newsletter/archives/index.html (thanks especially to Rob Pierce's leadership as editor of the newsletter from 2001-2009).

Definitions of organizational influence are beginning to be much more difficult to establish and, although ACM SIGDOC appears to have gotten smaller over the last decade or more, its reach and influence also reflects the bulkanization of the field of communication design across disciplines, conferences, organizations, and publishing venues.[8] Clearly, ACM SIGDOC research and publications now have a well-established history (35 years) and are downloaded and cited in considerable numbers for use in various fields. Although its conferences are traditionally small (with approximately 60 registrants), the quality of the conference submissions is strong and, with an acceptance rate of approximately fifty percent, the proceedings papers are multidisciplinary and cutting-edge: the last several years have included research emphases on genre theory, interactivity and usability, serious gaming, organizational culture, and social media. Table 3 is an overview of the ACM Digital Library's analysis of ACM SIGDOC's publication history since 1975.

Table 3: ACM SIGDOC bibliometrics: Publication history.

ACM SIGDOC Bibliometrics: Publication history	
Publication years	1075-2010
Publication count	1,974
Citation count	2,746
Available for download	1,865
Downloads (6 weeks)	5,527
Downloads (12 months)	51,188
Downloads (cumulative)	460,351
Average downloads per article	246.84
Average citations per article	1.39

In June 2003, the SIGDOC Board agreed to propose a name change to the Special Interest Group for Systems Documentation to the Special Interest Group for Design of Communication. In Kathy Haramundanis' [11] words, "The new formal name, we believe, more clearly reflects the areas of interest and activity of the SIG that have changed significantly from a time perhaps 20

---

[7] From ACM SIGDOC Viability Review Reports (2003-2010).

[8] Searching for "documentation" in the ACM DL shows papers published in *Journal of Systems and Software*, *Journal of Medical Systems*, *COSC: Proceedings of Conference on Organizational Computing Systems*, etc.; "communication" produces many more journals, including *Computers in Human Behavior*, *Communications and Information Theory*, *Education and Information Technologies*, *International Journal of Mobile Communications*, to name a few.

years ago when the main focus of the SIG was indeed documentation. Today people who attend our conferences address issues of usability, Web information construction and design, course materials, distance education, professional training, knowledge management and so on."

Today's ACM SIGDOC members and conference attendees are also from a wide range of fields (united by a common interest in the relationship between text and technology) and from many countries and institutions. Conferences since 2005 have been located in Coventry, UK, Lisbon, Portugal, Sao Paulo, Brazil and, in 2011, will be held in Pisa, Italy (see http://www.sigdoc.org/conference/). Table 4 lists the top twenty-five institutional affiliations by paper count.

Table 4: ACM SIGDOC top twenty-five institutional affiliations by paper count.

Affiliations by Paper Count	Paper Count
IBM	148
University of Sao Paulo	73
University of Washington	63
Carnegie Mellon University	56
Massachusetts Institute of Technology	50
North Carolina State University	46
Tsinghua University	39
University of Waterloo	38
Hewlett-Packard Laboratories	36
University of Surrey	28
Georgia Institute of Technology	26
University of Text at El Paso	24
University of Memphis	23
Harbin Institute of Technology	22
Microsoft Research	22
University of California	22
Rensselaer Polytechnic Institute	21
University of Maryland	21
Shanghai Jiao Tong University	19
University of Michigan	19
Nanjing University	18
The University of Texas at Austin	18
Michigan State University	17
National University of Defense Technology	17
Xerox Palo Alto Research Center	17

THE FUTURE OF ACM SIGDOC

An increase in journals, professional societies, and the distributed nature of the "field" of technical communication has led to reduced membership in ACM SIGDOC (the "why should I pay for it if it's available on the Web?" effect). But, if long-term influence over a wide-range of research issues of interest to both academic and nonacademic professionals working in the broadly-defined area of communication design is the ultimate mission of ACM SIGDOC, then the thirty-five year old SIG is very healthy and has an exciting future.

During the last three and a half decades, ACM SIGDOC members have witnessed, contributed to, researched and published on early attempts to assist programmers through the explosion in end-user print documentation through the advent of the hypertext documents and the World Wide Web to the social-collaborative support spaces that we design for today.

Rather than concluding with a list of emerging technologies that promise to change the way we design communication over the coming decade (e.g., mobile computing, augmented reality, open source information, gesture-based interfaces, cloud computing, etc.), it may be more illuminating to simply list authors who have published in the ACM SIGDOC journal or proceedings and who have subsequently published books over the last thirty years. Not only have these ACM SIGDOC authors found audiences for their work through our organization they are also leaders in the multidisciplinary field and, indeed, have helped us define, refine, and set its future course (see Table 5).

ACKNOWLEDGEMENTS

The views and conclusions contained in this paper are those of the author and should not be interpreted as necessarily representing the complete history and development, either expressed or implied, of the ACM SIGDOC. I would like to thank, in particular, Kathy Haramundanis and Susan Jones for supporting my early years with ACM SIGDOC and Rob Pierce for serving as a model of creative and committed leadership during my years as ACM SIGDOC Chair.

REFERENCES

[1] Brockmann, R. J. (2001). SIGDOC reminiscences. *ACM Journal of Computer Documentation, 25* (2), 40-41.

[2] Brown, B. (1991-1992). IBM mulls entry into flexible hub market. *Network World, December 30-January 6*, 9.

[3] Buchanan, R. (1992). Wicked problems in design thinking. *Design Issues, 8* (2), 5-21.

[4] Buchanan, R. (1995). Rhetoric, humanism, and design. In R. Buchanan and V. Margolin (eds.), *Discovering design: Explorations in design studies* (pp. 23-66). Chicago, IL: U of Chicago P.

[5] Campbell-Kelly, M. (2004). An Interview with Jonathon Sachs. Needham MA: Charles Babbage Institute. Available online: http://www.cbi.umn.edu/oh/pdf.phtml?id=340

[6] Duffy, T. M., Palmer, J. E., and Mehlenbacher, B. (1993). *Online help: Design and evaluation.* Westport, CT: Greenwood Publishing Group.

[7] Gleick, J. (2011). *The information: A history, a theory, a flood.* NY, NY: Pantheon Books.

[8] Goetz, M. A. (1976). Automated documentation. *SIGDOC Asterisk Journal of Computer Documentation, 2* (8), 11.

[9] Haramundanis, K. (2001a). Notes from the Chair. *SIGDOC Newsletter, 2* (3). Available online: http://www.sigdoc.org/newsletter/archives/sept01members.html

[10] Haramundanis, K. (2001b). SIGDOC reminiscences. *ACM Journal of Computer Documentation, 25* (2), 42-46.

[11] Haramundanis, K. (2003). Notes from the Chair. *SIGDOC Newsletter, 4* (2). Available online: http://www.sigdoc.org/newsletter/archives/june03members.html

[12] Mehlenbacher, B. (2008). Communication design and theories of learning. *SIGDOC'08: The 26th ACM International Conference on Design of Communication Proceedings*. Lisbon, Portugal: ACM, 139-146

[13] Mehlenbacher, B. (2010). *Instruction and Technology: Designs for Everyday Learning*. Cambridge, MA: MIT P.

[14] NewScientist. (2009). March of the outdated machines. *NewScientist.com, 21 September*. Available online: http://www.newscientist.com/gallery/dn17805-computer-museums-of-the-world/4

[15] Patterson, D. (1988). Chairman's corner. *ACM Journal of Computer Documentation, 14* (3), 8-9.

[16] Patterson, D. (2001). SIGDOC reminiscences 1981-88. *ACM Journal of Computer Documentation, 25* (2), 34-39.

[17] Powers, J. (2009). Boomers, Gen Xers and Millenials feel technology differently. *JPowers@IN3.org*. Available online: http://in3.typepad.com/powers/2009/03/boomers-gen-xers-and-millenials-experiencing-technology.html and, especially, http://in3.org/course/Ages3.pdf

[18] Rigo, J. (1974). A SIC on computer documentation? *Communications of the ACM, 17* (9), 543.

[19] Rigo, J. (2001). SIGDOC reminiscences. *ACM Journal of Computer Documentation, 25* (2), 31-33.

[20] Sachs, J. (1975). Proposal for a program support facility. *ACM SIGDOC Asterisk Journal of Computer Documentation, 2* (6), 9-12.

[21] Sachs, J. (1976). Some comments on comments. *ACM SIGDOC Asterisk Journal of Computer Documentation, 3* (7), 7-14.

[22] Shneiderman, B. (1987). *Designing the user interface: Strategies for effective human-computer interaction.* Reading, MA: Addison-Wesley.

[23] Van Duyn, J., Rigo, J., Rennaker, J., Jurgens, N. C., Morin, J. A., Olson, R. D., & Glick, J. R. (1974). Tutorial and panel discussion—SIGDOC: Experiences with HIPO and other documentation Techniques. *ACM '74 Conference Proceedings*, 82.

Table 5: ACM SIGDOC representative authors and books.

Author	Book Title (Year)
Abbott, R. J.	*An integrated approach to software development* (1986)
Akscyn, R. M.	*The ZOG approach to database management* (1984)
Albers, M.	*Content and complexity* (2003), *Communication of complex information* (2004), and *Usability of complex information* (2010)
Barnum, C. M.	Edited *Techniques for Technical Communicators* (1992), *Usability testing and research* (2001), and *Usability testing essentials* (2010)
Barrett, E.	Edited *The society of text* (1989), edited *Sociomedia* (1994), co-edited *Contextual media* (1997), and authored *The MIT guide to teaching Web site design* (2001)
Bernhardt, S. A.	Co-authored *Writing at work* (1997) and co-authored *Metaphor and knowledge* (2003)
Bodker, S.	*Computers and democracy* (1987), *Work-oriented design of computer artifacts* (1988), and *Through the interface* (1990)
Bolter, J.	*Writing space: computers, hypertext, and the remediation of print* (1991)
Borenstein, N.	*Programming as if people mattered* (1994)
Borland, R.	17 *Microsoft Windows* books (1990-1998)
Brasseur, L. E.	*Visualizing technical information* (2003)
Brockmann, R. J.	*Writing better computer user documentation: From paper to online* (1986) and *Twisted Rails, Sunken Ships ...* (2004)
Campbell, B.	Six *Microsoft and PC* product books (1990-1993)
Carroll, J. M.	*The Nurnberg Funnel: Designing minimalist instruction for practical computer skill* (1990)
Chapline, J. D.	Authored original ENIAC and UNIVAC user manuals

Author	Book Title (Year)
Cooper, A.	*About face: The essentials of user interface design* (1995)
Dautermann, J.	Co-edited *Electronic literacies in the workplace* (1996) and authored *Writing at Good Hope* (1997)
Dewhurst, S.	*C++ gotchas: Avoiding common problems in coding and design* (2002)
Doheny-Farina, S.	*Rhetoric, innovation, technology: Case studies of technical communication in technology transfer* (1992)
Duffy, T. M.	Co-edited *Designing usable texts* (1985), *Constructivism and the technology of instruction* (1992), and co-authored *Online help: Design and Evaluation* (1993) and *Learner-centered theory and practice in distance education* (2003)
Ehn, P.	Co-authored *Computers and democracy* (1987) and authored *Work-oriented design of computer artifacts* (1988)
Erickson, T.	Co-edited *HCI remixed* (2007)
Farkas, D. K.	Co-authored *Principles of Web design* (2001)
Goswami, D	Co-edited *Writing in nonacademic settings* (1986) and authored *On teacher inquiry: Approaches to language and literacy research* (2009)
Hackos, J.	*Managing your documentation projects* (1994)
Hallgren, R. C.	*Interface projects for the Apple II* and *for the TRS-80* (1982)
Haramundanis, K.	*The art of technical documentation* (1997)
Hill, C. A.	*Defining visual rhetorics* (2004)
Horn, R. E.	*Mapping hypertext* (1990) and *Visual Language* (1999)
Horton, B.	*Designing and writing online documentation* (1990)
Johnson. R. R.	*User-centered technology* (1998)

Johnson-Eilola, J.	*Nostalgic angels* (1997), *Designing effective web sites* (2001), *Datacloud* (2005)
Krull, R.	*Word processing for technical writers* (1988)
Landauer, T.	*The trouble with computers: Usefulness, usability, and productivity* (1996)
Lesk, M.	*Practical digital libraries* (1997) and *Understanding digital libraries* (2004)
Marcus, A.	*Graphic design for electronic documents and user interfaces* (1992)
Mehlenbacher, B.	Co-authored *Online help: Design and evaluation* (1993) and authored *Instruction and technology: Designs for everyday learning* (2010)
Miller, C. R.	Co-edited *Rhetorics and technologies* (2010)

Author	Book Title (Year)
Miller, G. A.	*Language and Speech* (1981) and *Psychology: The science of mental life* (1998)
Mirel, B.	*Interaction design for complex problem solving* (2003)
Neumann, P.G.	*Computer-related risks* (1994)
Norman, D.	*Things that make us smart* (1994), *The design of everyday things* (1998), *Emotional design* (2005), *The design of future things* (2009), and *Living with complexity* (2010)
Patterson, D.	*The computer documentation kit* (1984)
Perlman, G.	*Unix for software developers* (1987)
Porter, J. E.	*Audience and rhetoric* (1991) and *Professional writing online* (2000)
Ramey, J. A.	*Field methods for software design* (1996)
Redish, J.	*User and task analysis for interface design* (1998)
Rockley, A.	*Managing enterprise content* (2002)
Rogers, W. A.	*Designing for older adults* (2009)
Rubens, P.	*Science and technical writing* (1994)
Schriver, K. A.	*Dynamics in document design* (1996)
Selber, S. A.	Authored *Multiliteracies for a digital age* (2004) and co-edited *Rhetorics and technologies* (2010)
Shneiderman, B.	*Designing for user interface: Strategies for effective human-computer interaction* (1987) and *Leonardo's Laptop* (2003)
Siemens, R.	*A companion to digital humanities* (2008)
Spinuzzi, C.	*Tracing genre through organizations* (2003) and *Network* (2008)
Sullivan, P. A.	Co-edited *Electronic literacies in the workplace* (1996) and *Opening spaces* (1997)
Swarts, J.	*Together with technology* (2007)
Talburt, J. R.	*Entity resolution and information quality* (2010)
Tharp, A. L.	*File organization and processing* (1988)
Tufte, E.	*Envisioning information* (1990), *The visual display of quantitative information* (2001), and *Beautiful Evidence* (2006)
Weiss, E. H.	*How to write a usable user manual* (1985)
Winograd, T.	*Understanding computers and cognition: A new foundation for design* (1986)
Weinberg, G. M.	*The psychology of computer programming* (1998) and *General systems thinking* (2001), Silver Editions
White, J. V.	*Designing for magazines* (1982), *Great pages* (1990), and *Editing by design* (2003)
Wright, P.	*Information design* (1992)
Yourdon, E.	*Object-oriented design* (1991) and *Byte wars* (2002)
Zachry, M.	*Communication practices in workplaces and the professions* (2007)

A Humanistic Approach to the Study of Social Media: Combining Social Network Analysis & Case Study Research

Ashley R. Kelly
Communication, Rhetoric, & Digital Media
North Carolina State University
ashleyrosekelly@gmail.com

Meagan Kittle Autry
Communication, Rhetoric, & Digital Media
North Carolina State University
makautry@gmail.com

ABSTRACT

Humanistic research into social media is presently diverse in approach, but rich in theoretical underpinnings. It is unsurprising that there is some difficulty in translating often text-based approaches to multi-media rich, rapidly-evolving social networking environments. We explore theoretical issues for studying social media with respect to one popular research methodology: case study research (CSR). Here we examine the challenges that social media pose to CSR in the humanities and then advance an approach using social network analysis (SNA) to assist in selecting case studies. This approach, we argue, improves selection of case studies by considering the network structures of social media.

Categories and Subject Descriptors

K.3 [**Computers and Society**]: General

General Terms

Theory

Keywords

social network analysis, case study research, social media, humanities

1. INTRODUCTION

Humanities-based studies, within our articulation of the disciplines, describes studies primarily concerned with a depth of theoretical propositions and not, at least primarily, the empirical qualification or support of claims. Such consideration is difficult when studying social media as individual technologies outpace our ability to join as users, let alone develop a thoughtful, critical, and comprehensive analysis of social media tools. Put simply, the growth and pace seen in social media technologies poses new problems for humanities researchers. Yet questions posed regarding social media, from the public and academy alike, are frequently of a humanistic variety. To say something meaningful about social media technologies, then, we must look past particular tools, particular companies, and fleeting trends to how we understand the underlying characteristics of social media.

The rise of so-called "Web 2.0" or "participatory media" applications seemingly occurred with the shift from static hyperlinked text pages of the old web to a participatory and socially-driven web. Though there were certainly "social" elements and applications of the web, recalling Internet Relay Chats and MUDs, there was some fundamental shift in the way in which the web both engaged and was engaged by users. Mehlenbacher et al. (2010) outline the vast reach of the social media applications, saying "[t]oday, when researchers refer to social networking media, they are usually including self-publishing media such as podcasts, wiki[s], blogs, RSS/XML feeds, mashups, bookmarking applications, and so on"[13, p.65]. Further detailing the ever-growing list of social applications, Poynter (2011) includes microblogging; photo, video, and music sharing; consumer reviews; and virtual worlds and networked games[16, p.160]. The constellation of technologies that constitute social media marks the beginning of the difficulties in selecting a site or object of analysis. In addition to a multitude of technologies, each social media tool may offer numerous internal applications, notes Mehlenbacher et al.,"such as establishing public and private groups, maintaining profiles, tagging, note-taking, summary presentations, commenting, email, real-time posting, instant messaging, and the integration and display of data from other common social media applications"[13, p.65].

Poynter (2011) argues that precise definitions of social media are difficult as scholars define and redefine the scope of the technologies. Social media, then, becomes a broad term surrounding a core concept about the way that the internet and other new technologies are being used to move away from media that was essentially a one-to-many model, for example broadcast, towards a many-to-many model, such as Facebook"[16][p.160]. To avoid reliance upon particular social media tools we expand this definition of social media. Social media describes internet connected and using software applications that facilitate user-generated and user-based content and connections. Connections facilitated by social media are driven primarily by abilities to communicate with a subset of users on the media platform in personally relevant and meaningful ways. The technologies are, more broadly, capable of scaling to large user bases, while allowing for use to be tailored to specific areas of interest (e.g., groups, lists). Most important to this discussion, social media tools often generate and accumulate a large amount of data. Thus, with the rapid evolution of social media tools and the substantial amount of data they generate, new research design methods are required. Here we propose a method that allows for depth of analysis and thoughtful selection of data that is amenable to humanistic scholarship.

2. CASE STUDY RESEARCH

The case study has emerged as favoured methodology for humanities scholars studying social media phenomena, although little attention has been given to why this methodology is appropriate for such research[3]. Furthermore, little justification is offered within publications for the choice of case study methodology. Thus, here we explore previous scholarship about case study research (CSR) and advance a discussion about how humanities scholars can effectively employ CSR to study social media. It is important to note and understand that many subscribe to the idea that case study research is not in and of itself a methodology, but instead, researchers choose methods by which they study a case[11, 9]. Thus, many view case study research as a research strategy to help them select an appropriate subject and later develop methods to study that single case.

Case studies, as a research strategy, are the subject of a wide range of published scholarship. Woodside (2010) offers a conceptualization of the process: "CSR [Case study research] is an inquiry that focuses on describing, understanding, predicting and/or controlling the individual (ie. process, animal, person, household, organization, group, industry, culture, or nationality)"[19, p.16]. Further, he describes the principal goal of case study as deep understanding, and getting to this deep understanding "usually involves the use of multiple research methods across multiple time periods"[19, p.21]. These methods may include archival research, interviews, focus groups, textual analysis, questionnaires, and observations. To accomplished a coherent analysis across multiple data sources both Woodside (2010) and Stake (1995) suggests triangulating points of data. Triangulation of sources is an essential component to providing high quality and consistent interpretations of measurements used in CSR. In order to accomplish this end, protocols and procedures for case studies must be enacted with careful research design to ensure validity across data observation and interpretation. Triangulation protocols may include data sources, investigators, theory, and methods[17]. The latter is perhaps the most valuable triangulation as provides a solution to the problem of researchers approach influencing results, a common problem in the social sciences, according to Stake.

Yin (1989), in his seminal work *Case Study Research*, offers an additional perspective on this research strategy and defines case studies technically based on three main criteria: a case study "investigates a contemporary phenomenon within its real-life context; when the boundaries between phenomenon and context are not clearly evident, and in which multiple sources of evidence are used"[20, p.23]. Furthermore, Yin writes that case studies useful for when "a how or why question is being asked about a contemporary set of events over which the investigator has little or no control"[20, p.13]. Eisenhardt (1989) adds that case studies are "particularly well suited to new research areas or research

areas for which existing theory seems inadequate"[5, p.548]. Thus, case studies can be useful in both establishing new theoretical concepts or exploring how theoretical concepts apply to a particular case.

However, CSR has been the subject of criticism in the past for its alleged lack of rigour and ability to add anything to a scientific body of knowledge. Citing Abercrombie, Hill, and Turner's (1984) definition of "case study" in the Dictionary of Sociology,[1] Flyvbjerg (2006) writes that such definitions are dramatically oversimplified and provide little insight into the value or application of case studies in social scientific research. According to Flyvbjerg, the oversimplification of CSR results from several primary misunderstandings which are worth quoting at length:

> Misunderstanding 1: General, theoretical (context-independent) knowledge is more valuable than concrete, practical (context-dependent) knowledge.
> Misunderstanding 2: One cannot generalize on the basis of an individual case; therefore, the case study cannot contribute to scientific development.
> Misunderstanding 3: The case study is most useful for generating hypotheses; that is, in the first stage of a total research process, whereas other methods are more suitable for hypotheses testing and theory building.
> Misunderstanding 4: The case study contains a bias toward verification, that is, a tendency to confirm the researcher's preconceived notions.
> Misunderstanding 5: It is often difficult to summarize and develop general propositions and theories on the basis of specific case studies.[6, p.221]

Flyvbjerg continues by explaining how each of these misunderstandings can easily be corrected, emphasizing that the case study is a viable and important research method. He argues that "context-dependent knowledge and experience are at the very heart of expert activity"[6, p.222], and that while many great scientific and social scientific findings have been based in CSR, the value of generalization to scientific progress is highly overrated. Yin (2003) also dispels the second misunderstanding, stating that case studies "are generalizable to theoretical propositions and not to populations and universes"[21, p.10]. Flyvbjerg indicates that the third misunderstanding can be corrected in correspondence with the second: once we realize that generalizability is not the only goal of case-based research, we can see how it can indeed offer final conclusions in lieu of merely producing or testing hypotheses. He dispels the fourth misunderstanding, bias toward verification, by indicating that this critique grossly misunderstands case study methods; case study research has vigorous methods of its own, and while it does not follow the scientific method, these methods are nonetheless intensive. Lastly, he resolves the fifth misunderstanding by citing fellow CSR scholar Peattie (2001), who writes, "It is simply that the very value of the case study, the contextual

---

[1]Abercrombie et al. (1984) define case study by saying, "The detailed examination of a single example of class of phenomena, a case study cannot provide reliable information about the broader class, but it may be useful in the preliminary stages of an investigation since it provides hypotheses, which may be tested systematically with a larger number of cases" (p. 34)[1].

and interpenetrating nature of forces, is lost when one tries to sum up in large and mutually exclusive concepts"[15][6, p.238]). He ends by asserting that a strong field of study is one in which scholars have conducted many rigorous case studies.

We argue that the study of social media requires new conceptualization of CSR methods. Vast amounts of data and increasing numbers of connected individuals complicate the first step for CSR, selecting a case or cases for analysis. The value of completed research hinges first on the selection of appropriate and interesting case studies that will allow the research to not only explore theory but to investigate a meaningful phenomenon that will add to the body of scholarship. Here, we suggest that social network analysis can serve an important role in the beginning stages of research. First, we explore social network analysis, offering a review of current literature, and second discuss how this type of analysis can be usefully applied to social media case studies by humanities scholars.

3. SOCIAL NETWORK ANALYSIS

Social media is a technology rooted in a networked society. The idea of the networked society is perhaps most familiar to communication and related fields through the work of Manuel Castells (2000) and Mark Granovetter (1973; 1983). In these theories, the importance of the structure of social relationships is elucidated. These relationships provide important insights into the creation and functioning of groups (nodes) and the connections between groups (forming the larger network). Network analysis, then, offers both an understanding of structures and relationships as well as entities[10]. To advance these modes of analysis in social media spaces, we turn to social network analysis.

Durland and Fredericks (2005) define social network analysis (SNA) as "the study of relationships within the context of social situations"[4, p.9]. It can be used to study the connections between people, organizations, computers, and various other connected entities in both a visual and mathematical way. Social network analysis is a field that can be traced to three primarily disciplinary traditions: psychology, anthropology, and sociology[10]. The field has been becoming increasingly popular with social sciences exponentially accelerated use of the key idea of the "social network"[10]. Growing over the last three decades, the field of social network analysis is becoming increasingly popular and accessible to social scientific researchers. Knoke and Yang (2008) explain that social network analysis relies on three main assumptions: 1) The structure of social relations can be as important (or more important) for understanding behavior than other features, such a race, age, or ideology; 2) Social networks carry influence over a variety of socially constructed social mechanisms, such as opinions and actions; and 3) Structural relations are dynamic processes that are continually evolving. Thus, SNA focuses on the actors and connections between actors to examine more complex issues within a social system, as opposed to collecting average numbers to offer a surface summary of a relationship[10].

Hansen (2011) begins to explore the idea of using social network analysis for internet applications in his article, "Exploring Social Media Relationships."[8] Hansen explains that social media can help explore relationship structures and that as more people begin to use social media tools, the picture they paint will become an increasingly accurate representation of real-life social ties. As well as being an accurate representation of the social ties, the data provided by social media technologies affords access to certain insights about how social relations function independent of a subject's perceptions of those relations. That is, unlike a survey instrument, the data provided by social media technologies escapes some of the biases of self-reporting. Yet, as previously noted, the massive amount of data generated by these technologies requires new methods for gathering, organizing, and analysing. Advancing social network analysis to better respond to these challenges methods for computational social network analysis have began to take shape[2].

To usefully analyze large amounts of noisy information, such as the infrastructures of social media networks produce, SNA has adopted principles from information theory. Information theory offers several important concepts that may be valuable when analysing social media technologies. For example, the idea of path-transfer flow, which describes how information is passed in a node-to-node network structure. In this model there is no parallel information transfer and the centrality of nodes it determined by the likelihood that a given node can pass a message along that will reach every other node in the network[14, 18]. Central nodes, path-transfer flow posits, will be able to further distribute information than peripheral nodes, which becomes an important factor when considering variables such as influence. A variable such as "centrality" might be used to measure individuals within a network as well as relations between individuals within networks (or subnetworks) to determine their influence on one another[14]. But using such theories and models of network information transfer requires some ability to computationally process the large amounts of information. Computational social network analysis describes a variety of methods and tools.

Social network analysis has the potential to be an important research tool for humanities scholars to find relevant and interesting case studies. Scholars in other disciplines have already began to articulate the value of this relationship[12]. While some may be skeptical of the method, the technology used for SNA is easily within reach of humanists. Hansen (2011) reports that while once a highly specialized field of analysis, SNA has gone "mainstream" with open-source network metric tools such as NodeXL and Gephi[7, 8].[2] SNA tools allows researchers to calculate key players in a network, find groups of highly-connected actors, and identify overall patterns in networks.

Social network analysis provides scholars with a tool that provides greater insight about network dynamics during the initial search for cases. SNA can thus help humanities scholars respond to questions of methodological rigour in terms of sampling, allowing them to make the case for having selected representative artifacts in the most appropriate form for the particular variables one is interested in. Using such a systematic approach draws first on the empirical approaches used in information, social, and computer sciences. The wisdom of these fields is employed through the network analysis, a broad approach to search for synthesize information about particular networks and nodes within those networks. These nodes, we argue, provide spaces for deeper humanistic analysis through the case study. Finding a particular node of interest allows it to be traced outside of an indi-

---

[2]NodeXL available at http://nodexl.codeplex.com/ and Gephi available at http://gephi.org/.

vidual network into the larger social media landscape. For example, finding a node, a key player, on Twitter means that once an understanding of their role in that network is at least partially understood that understanding can be further supplemented by a triangulation with information across other networks (e.g., Facebook, blogs, etc.).

4. CONCLUDING REMARKS

While aggregating a large amount of data might yield a useful sample for analysis of some variables, much difficultly arises in situating those variables within larger frameworks. This problem is not new; however, with social media technologies are new and so we must consider how they aid and abet our methodologies. Further, we must distinguish between our initial searches for sites of interest and subsequent research. We argue then that some delineation between the process of searching for a site of interest and data collection and conducting research on that site must be more explicitly acknowledged in humanities research methods.

Humanities-based research finds its value in the depth of analysis. Whether an artifact is an outlier or representative cases does not determine the value of a study, for example. What determines the value is the critical insight offered by the research. What we proposed here does not deviate from this model, but is offered as one possible method to reconcile some of the difficulties facing humanities researchers as we begin to look at particular cases of social media.

Indeed, we believe that humanities scholarship offers great insight into the complexity of artifacts online. For example, in a recent pilot study we examined the merger between Duke Energy and Progress Energy, two major utilities providers in the United States. We attempted to collect data from the popular social networking site Twitter.com and from blogs. Our methods were, at the risk of revealing our scholarly insecurities, problematic. We were not interested in producing the quantitative results we ultimately did through our pilot study. Instead, our interest was in determining how conversations between key players online is occurring–though this was not immediately apparent to us. After sorting through a mass of data we collected from Twitter and blogs we sought a better method for identifying who key players are and how they were using social media to shape the discourse surrounding the merger. It was in this search for a better research strategy that we found SNA. Using this method we would have been better able to identify specific sites of interest, key players, and then triangulate those for analysis in a case study.

Combining Social Network Analysis with Case Study Research, we argue, provides an open-ended research strategy that allows researchers to thoughtfully identify specific artifacts and data of interest on social media sites and then organize the constellation of information through the case study, allowing then for a variety of critical analyses. It is not our aim to offer a formulate, so-called "rigorous approach" or prescribed method, but one strategy that may be useful in navigating the increasingly vast and complex store and network of information found through social media.

5. REFERENCES

[1] N. Abercrombie, S. Hill, and B. Turner. *The Dictionary of Sociology*. Penguin, Harmondsworth, UK, 1984.

[2] A. Abraham, A.-E. Hassanein, and V. Snasal. *Computational Social Network Analysis: Trends, Tools, and Research Advances*. Springer, London, 2010.

[3] C. Cheng. New media and event: A case study on the power of the internet. *Knowledge and Technology Policy*, 22(2):145–153, 2009.

[4] M. Durland and K. Fredericks. An introduction to social network analysis. *New Directions for Evaluation*, 107:5–13, Fall 2005.

[5] K. Eisenhardt. Building theories from case study research. *Academy of Management Review*, 14(4):532–550, 1989.

[6] B. Flyvbjerg. Five misunderstandings about case-study research. *Qualitative Inquiry*, 12(2):219–245, 2006.

[7] Gephi. The open graph viz platform. urlhttp://gephi.org, 2011.

[8] D. Hansen. Exploring social media relationships. *On the Horizon*, 19(1):43–51, 2011.

[9] J. Hartley. Case study research. In G. S. C. Cassell, editor, *Essential Guide to Qualitative Methods in Organizational Research*, pages 323–333. Sage, London, 2004.

[10] D. Knoke and S. Yang. *Social Network Analysis, 2nd Edition*. Sage, Thousand Oaks, CA, 2008.

[11] F. Kohlbacher. The use of qualitative content analysis in case study research. *Forum: Qualitative Social Research*, 7(1), 2006.

[12] A. Martínez, Y. Dimitriadis, B. Rubia, E. Gómez, and P. de la Fuente. Combining qualitative and social network analysis for the study of social aspects of collaborative learning. *Computers and Education*, 41(4):353–368, 2003.

[13] B. Mehlenbacher, S. McKone, C. Grant, T. Bowles, S. Peretti, and P. Martin. Social media for sustainable engineering communication. In *SIGDOC'10: The 28th ACM International Conference on Design of Communication Proceedings*, pages 65–72. ACM SIGDOC, 2010.

[14] D. Ortiz-Arroyo. Discovering key sets of players in social networks. In A. A. et al., editor, *Computational Social Network Analysis*, pages 27–47. Springer, New York, 2010.

[15] L. Peattie. Theorizing planning: Some comments on flyvbjerg's rationality and power. *International Planning Studies*, 6(3):257–262, 2001.

[16] R. Poynter. *The Handbook of Online and Social Media Research: Tools and Techniques for Market Researchers*. Wiley, West Sussex, UK, 2011.

[17] R. E. Stake. *The Art of Case Study Research*. Sage, Thousand Oaks, CA, 1995.

[18] F. Tutzauer. Entropy as a measure of centrality in networks characterized by path-transfer flow. *Social Networks*, 29(2):249–265, 2006.

[19] A. Woodside. *Case Study Research: Theory, Methods, and Practice*. Emerald Group, Bingley, UK, 2010.

[20] R. Yin. *Case Study Research: Design and Methods, 2nd Edition*. Sage, Thousand Oaks, CA, 1989.

[21] R. Yin. *Case Study Research: Design and Methods 4th Edition*. Sage, Thousand Oaks, CA, 2003.

Using Serious Games to Improve Communication: Talking about a Revolution

Pamela M. Kato, Ed.M., Ph.D.
University Medical Center Utrecht
The Netherlands
pamela.kato@yahoo.com

Abstract

Serious games engage users with through video game technology and gameplay mechanics to educate and train. There is promising evidence that serious games can be used as a tool to improve communication. I will present evidence of the impact of serious games on communication especially in the area of games for health for young patients. I will also discuss a recent serious game aimed to improve patient safety skills among young medical doctors. Because communication failure has been shown to be a root cause in a majority of medical errors that result in unintended deaths and injuries in hospitals, improving communication skills was a key aim of the project. I will discuss my insights in why serious games can have an impact on improving communication among difficult-to-reach groups and how that can be done.

ACM Classification Keywords: Computing Milieux, Computers and Education, Computer Uses in Education, Computer-Assisted instruction (CAI), Serious Games

General Terms: Human Factors

Keywords: Serious games, Health care, communication, patients, physicians, biofeedback

Bio

Dr. Kato has an appointment at the University Medical Center Utrecht in the Netherlands and she also teaches Health Psychology at University College Utrecht. Dr. Kato received her masters in Counseling and Consulting Psychology from Harvard University and her Ph.D. in Psychology from Stanford University. She completed her postdoctoral fellowship at the Stanford University School of Medicine. She was the founding president and CEO of HopeLab, a non-profit that focuses on research and innovation to improve the lives of young people with chronic illnesses. At HopeLab she led the efforts to develop and do research on Re-Mission, a game clinically shown to improve adherence to cancer treatment among adolescents and young adults with cancer. She recently completed Air Medic Sky 1, a game designed to improve patient safety among young doctors.

CATS – Using Scenario Dramatization to Rapidly Design Public Displays for Stimulating Community Interaction

Elisa Rubegni
Faculty of Communication
University of Lugano (USI)
6904 Lugano, Switzerland

elisa.rubegni@usi.ch

Nemanja Memarovic
Faculty of Informatics
University of Lugano (USI)
6904 Lugano, Switzerland

nemanja.memarovic@usi.ch

Marc Langheinrich
Faculty of Informatics
University of Lugano (USI)
6904 Lugano, Switzerland

marc.langheinrich@usi.ch

Abstract

The falling cost of display technology has led to a proliferation of large public displays. However, to move beyond simple advertising kiosks and use public displays as a community tool typically requires a lengthy ethnographic approach. In this paper we describe CATS, a rapid UI design methodology that we developed and used to create a public display system for stimulating community interaction during a large university alumni event. The CATS methodology relies on the co-evolutionary process between (C)oncept design, (A)ctivity design, and *(T)echnology design* through (S)cenario dramatization. Each of the three design strands occurs simultaneously and is connected through a central scenario dramatization process, in which study participants selectively enact various aspects of the interaction in order to verify and explore different design issues. In this article, we briefly describe the CATS methodology and report on our use experiences.

Categories and Subject Descriptors

H.4.3. Communications Applications; H.5.2. [User Interfaces]: Interaction styles, User-centered design; H.5.3. [Group and Organization Interfaces]: Theory and Models; J.4. [Social and behavioral sciences]: Sociology

General Terms

Design, Human Factors, Documentation

Keywords

Design methodology, public display design, Interaction design, Human-Computer Interaction

1. Introduction

Public display systems that foster community interaction (in the following called PDSCI) have been the focus of research for over a decade. Already in 1996, Houde et al. [5] developed the "Newspaper" system, which revolved around creating a joint newspaper within a workspace environment and projecting the results on a big screen. Ever since then the number of PDSCI has been increasing:

- in 2001 Greenberg and Rounding designed the Notification Collage [4], a mix of public and private displays with a goal to extended the collaboration between the workgroup members beyond the workspace environment.
- in 2003 Churchill et al. [2] reported on the Plasma Poster Network system that allowed easy content posting to networked displays inside the office space with a goal to increase the social interaction within a working environment.
- in 2006 Taylor and Cheverst [16] designed and deployed the Wray Photo Display which displayed community-generated photos on several locations with a goal to increase the sense of community and belonging.
- in 2008 McDonald et al. [9] deployed two PDSCI installations at a conference, namely Ticket2Talk that showed user interest of conference attendees near the display, and Neighborhood Window that displayed connection between the attendees through the intersection of their interests.
- in 2009 McCarthy et al. [8] deployed the CoCollage system in a café. The system represented an early version of a social networking website and displayed photos and comments from present users on a large screen.
- in 2011 Munson et al. [10] used Twitter as an input method to allow people to post thank you notes and more loose messages on a public display with a goal to increase social interaction among colleagues.

This list is most certainly not a comprehensive one, but captures the increasing interest in PDSCI well. Most of the above mentioned systems were both developed and deployed over a longer period of time, typically involving a significant ethnographic effort.[1] However, while longer development and deployment have their advantages (e.g., achieving a deeper understanding of the user needs and/or providing an opportunity for more design iterations), there are often situations when ad-hoc communities and/or short-term deployments do not allow for such an in-depth approach, such as when designing a display for use at a conference. It is for these situations that we have developed the CATS design methodology. CATS stands for (C)oncept design, (A)ctivity design, (T)echnology design, and (S)cenario dramatization. CATS connects three simultaneous design parts, i.e., concept, activity, and technology design, through the process of scenario dramatization, a method in which the envisioned interaction is enacted with the help of study participants in order to quickly discover challenges and opportunities of the envisioned

---

[1] While Ticket2Talk and Neighborhood Window [9] were only deployed for a few days, they did not describe/follow any specific design methodology.

UI and interaction pattern. The remainder of this article will briefly describe the CATS methodology and describe our experience with using it to develop a PDSCI user interface.

2. CATS design methodology

The CATS design methodology is based on a three-strands co-evolutionary process between *Concept design, Activity design,* and *Technology design*, in which each thread occurs simultaneously and informs the others. This design process is inspired by the approach used within the POGO project that aimed at developing a narrative environment for children [12]. The techniques and methodologies within the co-evolutionary process change according to the design context, such as type of users and activities, team members, budget, or time constraints. The *Scenario dramatization* technique connects the outcomes of the three strands: starting from a concept or an early mock-up the technique supports the prototype development by exploring its features within the context of use.

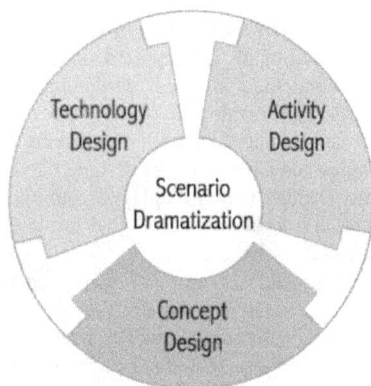

Figure 1 CATS: concept design, activity design, technology design, and scenario dramatization co-evolutionary process.

The first strand concerns the *Activity Design* and aims at understanding the users' needs with respect to the specific activity and situation. The importance of the analysis of the human activity resides in Activity Theory [11] and Cultural-historical psychology [1]. According to these approaches, humans do not simply react to external stimuli but instead interact with the environment through tools. While the artifacts are produced to support a specific human activity, they at the same time modify the activity for which they were made. Thus, in order to design suitable systems we have to take into account the objectives and the tools that regulate user activity. The results of this strand inform the others by *providing user requirements*.

The *Concept Design* strand allows for the analysis of the problem setting, the envisioning of promising ideas, and the exploration of possible alternatives. Several techniques can be used for concept generation, e.g., mind maps, metaphorical thinking, or attribute listing. This strand enlarges the semantics of the project's problem and helps to avoid coming up with solutions that focus solely on facts without additional creative re-elaborations. The final concepts are the result of several sessions during which the problem setting is explored and investigated in several directions. The concept design feeds the other strands by *reinforcing and enlarging the vision for technology design* and by assessing the activity analysis.

The *Technology Design* strand attempts to understand which technologies can be used for development. By both looking at the current state-of-the-art and by projecting current trends into the

near future, suitable technologies are explored in terms of their opportunities and limitations. The result of technology design can be a list of suitable technologies, as well as a design mock up. This strand provides new *insights into what current technologies can be used* and at the same time what opportunities lie in future enabling technologies that can inspire concept design.

The three-strands process converges and produces concepts as well as mock-ups. Nevertheless, a working prototype is necessary for assessing the results of the design process. In CATS, this working prototype is designed and evaluated using *Scenario Dramatization* [15] that offers the opportunity to explore design ideas through an active engagement of participants in using a prototype. Scenario dramatization is based on the idea of using "envisioning scenarios" as a script for enacting and engaging the participants in performing a specific task with a prototype in its real use context. Participants can be designers or final users; it depends on the project context or in the step of the design process in which this practice occurs. For instance, in the early stage of the design process prototype can be tested by the designers and just after its assessment it can be evaluated with end users. Our scenario dramatization approach closely follows Loke et al. [7] who used the enactment of personas and scenarios to explore human movement characteristics. Throughout the session a facilitator takes note of the emerging interaction elements that surface during the enactment. Scenario dramatization has its roots in Iacucci et al.'s *Situated and Participative Enactment of Scenarios* (SPES) methodology [6]. While SPES attempts to involve all stakeholders in the scenarios enactment, others have limited enactment to only designers and developers [3].

In the above examples, dramatization is a process of collaborative brainstorming in which designers and stakeholders are actively involved in experiencing the envisioning scenarios. These methodologies are mostly used in the early phase of the design process, when the team is still exploring the problem setting or generating concepts. In our case the enactment takes place at an advanced stage with the purpose of testing a working prototype. Our scenario dramatization process exploits the benefits of scenario enactment by exploring directly opportunities and issues with the existing prototype. In CATS, sessions are focused around few specific issues in order to collect feedback on the aesthetic and kinesthetic qualities of the experience, including the UI, gesture patterns, and interaction patterns of the prototype. Scenario dramatization allows the convergence of the three design strands and can offer important suggestions for assessing the prototype within real use context. This can be particularly important for gesture or tangible user interfaces because the quality of interaction is a crucial aspect for this type of interfaces: the limitations and opportunities of the UI emerge in real interaction.

3. CATS case study: *USIAlumni Faces*

We used CATS to rapidly design a public display installation called *USIAlumni Faces* that was used during a large university alumni event. The event aimed at establishing and strengthening the contact network among university graduates, faculty, and students, and to create a sense of community among the participants. We therefor envisioned an interactive application that had the purpose of engaging people in getting in touch and socializing. Our final objective was to stimulate and/or improve sense of belonging to the university community among the participants (alumni). Over 200 people used the deployed installation during the course of a 1-day event (see [14] for details).

3.1 Design co-evolution: Activity design, Concept design, and Technology design

The co-evolutionary design process was used to define interaction patterns and corresponding content that would support the users in engaging in social activities with their peers, and to stimulate a sense of belonging to the university community. *The concept design* began by soliciting community needs through focus groups and interviews with the alumni. The initial design was developed over several brainstorming sessions during which team members explored the problem setting and envisioned metaphors for presenting content and innovative strategies for interactions. The content should stimulate discussion around common experiences while the interaction modality should use gesture to make user's actions and intentions publicly visible. *The activity design* analysis helped defining the problem statement along with some key issues for driving the design process. Key issues included, e.g., encouraging the socialization of attendees, stimulating contact exchanges among people, and creating a sense of community. These issues in turn informed the concept and technology design phases. *The concept design* process was stimulated by the technology design analysis, which suggested a series of enabling technologies. In particular, the Nintendo Wii had been demonstrated to be easily modified and flexible enough to create custom input devices as demonstrated in many previous research projects.[2] We decided to adopt this technology and to begin with the development of a series of mock-ups that would stimulate concept generation and user requirement assessment.

3.1.1 Content

We used a 'yearbook' metaphor for *USIAlumni Faces* to present pictures, i.e., facial images, of the university students grouped by faculty. As suggested by the Living Memory project [1], creation of a collective memory can support interpretation and preservation of a community's local culture, as well as strengthening the sense of belonging to a community. Thus, sharing of memories can be used as a motive for encouraging people to talk and socialize. We envisioned that pictures of university alumni could serve as conversational 'ice breaker' and stimulate the participants to reminiscence stories and memories from the past.

3.1.2 Interaction

In *USIAlumni Faces* the interaction patterns are gesture based: user can browse the images by flipping the page with a toy-torch input device. This gesture-based interaction induces a process of *imitative learning* in which an observer attempts to copy the gesture of the other by reproducing the intentional actions of the other [13]. The imitative process implies understanding of a person's goal and it transforms the bodily motion into meaningful intentional action. The design of an interactive system based on gesture and/or physical manipulation of objects should take into account the complex interplay of mind, body and the environment. Thus, the design process requires a careful study of the forms of interaction (including the motor-physical aspects) offered to the user. Indeed, the design process is addressed to define the form of input and output in order to foresee the possible actions including those that are unintentional.

3.2 Scenario dramatization

In designing *USIAlumni Faces*, we conducted two dramatization sessions during which the technology, concept, and interaction patterns evolved. In the first session we involved just the

designers while in the second end-user were also engaged. In both cases a real-size prototype was built as well as a light version of the gesture recognition. For the gesture-based recognition we used the Wii controller (Wiimote) as the input device. The mock-up was installed in the space where the event would happen.

In the beginning of the first session we enacted the scenarios, which revealed an important design improvement: we changed the concept metaphor from a "Picture wall" to a "Yearbook" (Figure 1). This metaphor was much closer to the content provided and it was more inspiring in terms of possible gestures patterns: the gesture of flipping a page for browsing the content promised to be very effective and bound to have an imaginative value for the users. The Wiimote-based input device suggested "page flipping" as the most evocative and appropriate gesture for the context. We also established the technological setting, i.e., the gesture, location of the beamer and of the screen for projection, as well as the minimum and maximum distance of the user from the screen.

Figure 2 Interface inspired by the "Picture wall" metaphor (left) and "Yearbook" metaphor (right).

The prototype was redesigned according to outcome of the first session and was further refined during the second dramatization session. From a technical point of view we decided to change the input device: the Wiimote controller was mounted on the screen acting as receiver, while an infrared pen hidden inside a toy torch casing acted as the input device. The UI changed to fit the Yearbook metaphor and included the previously identified interaction pattern. Second session aimed at assessing the final technological setting and application, as well as looking at the participants' social and collaborative behavior. We tested the group interaction by involving two groups of two university students each, who enacted the scenario in two separate sessions. We also investigated individual usage with another five university students. Second session showed immediately that users were highly engaged in the interaction and were stimulated to discuss the presented content. The interaction model was comprehensible and easy to imitate and the input device was easy to use. However, the individual session showed some limitation in the interaction model comprehension: the time for understanding the pattern was longer than in the group session. However, this issue reinforced the merit of the installation as a social artifact.

The two sessions were strategic for understanding the limitations and opportunities of *USIAlumni Faces*. This first session aimed at assessing:

- the definition of *gesture patterns*,
- the understanding of *perturbing environmental factors* (i.e. elements that can affect the interaction, such as light),
- and the *technology setting* (e.g. the correct positioning of the sensor recognizer).

While in the second we refined:

- the *ease of understanding the interaction model behind*,
- the *intuitivity of the input device*,
- and the *emergence of social behavior*.

---

[2] See, e.g., http://johnnylee.net/projects/

4. Discussion and Conclusion

The design of Public Display Systems for fostering Community Interaction (PDSCI) typically requires an in-depth ethnographic design process that properly takes into account all stakeholders. However, short-term deployments may not have the time nor the opportunity for such an approach. The CATS approach presented in this paper allows designers to rapidly explore the main issues of concern for short-term PDSCI deployments. CATS includes the fundamental steps of a user-centered design process: from activity analysis to the prototype evaluation. The CATS approach is based on three strands – concept design, activity design, and technology design that in parallel explore the different parts of the design process and feed each other during the development. A central scenario dramatization process integrates the three strands and offers a central activity for iterative prototype refinement. We have applied this methodology in the development of a PDSCI based on gesture interaction, called *USIAlumni Faces* [14]. CATS permitted the *USIAlumni Faces* team to investigate and explore the problem setting simultaneously from different perspectives: to analyze human activity, to explore enabling technologies, to envision conceptual solutions, and to create a working prototype. During the (first) divergent phase these threads informed each other in order to produce consistent outcomes. In the next phase, the results converged on a refined prototype that was built and assessed in a real context-of-use.

We believe that CATS can effectively support the design process for the development of PDSCIs from a range of different perspectives:

- *Reduce overall design time:* diverse members of the team (with competences on the specific practice) conduct the activity in parallel sessions,
- *Increase the synergy of the members of the team with different background and expertise*: the constant connection of the members during the process improves their ability of understanding each other and favors co-working,
- *Include the user perspective in every development phase:* the end user is involved in the process from the beginning by the different threads and during the scenario dramatization,
- *Allow envisioning innovative solutions and evocative interaction patterns by direct manipulation with the prototype:* the scenario enactment supports effective exploration of the interaction patterns and evaluation of the concept,
- *Explore technology constraints in the context of use:* the enabling technology identified by one thread is constantly refined in the divergence phase, however a more consistent assessment occurs during the scenario dramatization,
- *Investigate the opportunity and the breakdowns of the user in performing the activity:* the scenario dramatization offers a unique opportunity for understanding the effect of the interactive artifact on human dynamics (e.g. social attitude, creation of innovative interaction modalities). Our contribution to the existing body of research is both epistemological as well as practical: to understand the issues that intervene in the design process for a PDSCI, and try to resolve these issues by providing a suitable methodological approach.

5. ACKNOWLEDGMENTS

The research leading to these results has received funding from the European Union Seventh Framework Programme (FP7/2007-2013) under grant agreement no. 244011. Our thanks to the TEC-Lab team, the university alumni event organizers, and the alumni.

6. REFERENCES

[1] Casalegno, F. 2005. Sharing Communal Memories for a Poetical Existence: Thoughts on Media, Communities and Memories. In Purcell, P. (ed.) *i3 net – Intelligent Information Interfaces, Connected Community Book.*

[2] Churchill, E.F., Nelson, L., and Denoue, L. .2003. Multi-media fliers: Information sharing with digital community bulletin boards. In *Proc. of communities and technologies.*

[3] Cross, N. 2000. Engineering design methods: Strategies for product design, 3rd edition. Chichester: John Wiley.

[4] Greenberg. S., and Rounding, M. 2001. The notification collage: posting information to public and personal displays, In *Proc. of CHI 2001*, ACM, pp. 514 – 521.

[5] Houde, S., Bellamy, R., and Leahy, L. 1998. In search of design principles for tools and practices to support communication within a learning community. In *SIGCHI Bull.*, 30, 2, ACM, pp. 113-118.

[6] Iacucci, G., Kuutti, K., and Ranta, M. 2000. On the move with a Magic Thing: Role Playing in Concept Design of Mobile Services and Devices. In *Proc. of the 3rd Conf. on Designing Interactive Systems: processes, practices, methods, and techniques* DIS'00, ACM, pp. 193 – 202.

[7] Loke, L., Robertson, T., and Mansfield, T. 2005. Moving bodies, social selves: movement-oriented personas and scenarios. In Proceedings of OZCHI '05, pp. 1-10.

[8] McCarthy, J.F. Farnham, D.S., Patel, Y., Ahuja, S., Norman, D., Hazlewood, W.R., Lind, J. 2009. Supporting community in third places with situated social software. In *Proc of the 4th Int. Conf. on Communities & Technologies*, pp. 225–234.

[9] McDonald, D.W., McCarthy, J.F., Soroczak, S., Nguyen, D.H., and Rashid, A.M. 2008. Proactive displays: Supporting awareness in fluid social environments. In *ACM Trans. Comput.-Hum. Interact.*, 14, 4, ACM, pp. 1-31.

[10] Munson, S.A., Rosengren, E. ,and Resnick, P. 2011. Thanks and tweets: comparing two public displays. In *Proc of CSCW 2011*. ACM, pp. 331–340.

[11] Nardi, B. A. 1996. Context and consciousness: activity theory and human-computer interaction. MIT Press.

[12] Rizzo, A., Marti, P., Decortis F., Rutgers, J., and Thursfield P. 2003. POGO world, In. M.A. Blythe et al. (eds.), Funology: From Usability to Enjoyment. Nederland: Kluwer Academic Publishers, pp. 1-12.

[13] Rizzo, A., Del Monte, M., Rubegni, E., Torsi, S. 2009. The interplay between sensory-motor and intentional affordances. In Workshop on Children & Embodied Interaction at IDC09.

[14] Rubegni, E., Memarovic, N., and Langheinrich, M. 2011 Talking to Strangers: Using Large Public Displays to Facilitate Social Interaction. In: 14th Int. Conf. on Human-Computer Interaction (HCII 2011). Springer.

[15] Rubegni, E. 2011. Act it! How to design interaction patterns "beyond the desktop", in Workshop on Designer Experience at CHI 2011.

[16] Taylor, N., and Cheverst, K. 2009. Social interaction around a rural community photo display. *International Journal of Human-Computer Studies*, 67, 12, Elsevier, pp.1037–1047.

[17] Vygotsky, L.S. 1962. Thought and Language. Cambridge, MA: MIT Press.

Come and Join Us!!! Towards the Formation of Homophilous Online Communities to Potentialize Diffusion of Innovations

Fernando Cesar Balbino, Vanessa M. A. de Magalhães, Junia Coutinho Anacleto
Advanced Interaction Laboratory (LIA)
Department of Computing – Federal University of São Carlos (DC/UFSCar)
Rod. Washigton Luis KM 235 – São Carlos (SP) – Brazil
{fernando_balbino,vanessa_magalhaes,junia}@dc.ufscar.br

ABSTRACT

We describe a computational environment which aims the formation of homophilous online communities based on the interest in a same topic, having people's cultural knowledge regarded. Homophily is the degree to which a pair of individuals who communicate are similar; so, it tends to promote more effective communication. The computational environment is the result of: a) a cultural knowledge-based method to identify people who "talks" about the same topic in social media; b) a method to generate culturally contextualized hyperdocuments, adapted and made available according to the level of literacy of a community. Thus, while the goal of method (a) is to improve the chances of "homophilous people" to come together and join the same community, the goal of method (b) is to make "innovative ideas" accessible to them, so that innovation can be seeded and spread among the online community's members. This research is partially supported by FAPESP-MSR (proc.2010/52135-9).

Categories and Subject Descriptors

I.2.4 [**Knowledge Representation Formalisms and Methods**]: Semantic networks – *cultural knowledge as a way to extend access information*; H.3.3 [**Information Search and Retrieval**]: Search process – *semantic search in online social networks*; J.4 [**Social and Behavioral Sciences**]: Sociology – *applying diffusion of innovations theory in computer science*.

General Terms

Human Factors.

Keywords

Social Media; Communication; Homophily; Diffusion of Innovation; Cultural Knowledge.

1. INTRODUCTION

Information and communication technologies (ICTs) have brought us the possibility to expand our relationship network and Web 2.0 has potentialize communication through social media. We can express opinions about diverse subjects, share photos

about great moments, publish videos, meet "offline" friends in social networks sites (SNSs) and also increase our personal and professional networking. In this context, we understand that people can be introduced to each other in the cyberspace, so they can start an "online friendship" which may be extended to real life. Our strategy is to find people with similarity related to the interest in some topic, e.g. politics. According to Rogers [1], a fundamental principle of human communication and its flow through interpersonal networks is that the exchange of ideas occurs most frequently between individuals who are alike, or homophilous. Yet according to him, "homophily is the degree to which a pair of individuals who communicate are similar", and this similarity may be in certain attributes such as beliefs, education, etc. Consequently, the members of a homophilous online community (OC) have the potential to receive the "seed" of some innovation and spread it, so they can try the innovation and hopefully incorporate it to the dynamics of the community's life to its well being. We consider innovation with the same meaning given by [1]: it is "an idea, practice, or object that is perceived as new by an individual or other unit of adoption" and its diffusion is performed by communicating it through certain channels over time among the members of a social system.

Hence, our computational environment described in this paper identifies people that have interest in a same topic, making this attribute the focus of similarity to potentialize the formation of homophilous OCs; besides that, to take advantage of the homophily and improve the chances of promoting changes in a community's members, our computational environment also offers a method which guides the generation of culturally contextualized hyperdocuments, adapted and made available according to the level of literacy of a group or community. This adaptation regarding cultural knowledge and levels of literacy addresses the "complexity" challenge in diffusion of innovations [1], i.e. the degree to which an innovation is perceived as difficult to understand and use; simplified content can reach a higher audience through social media.

This paper is organized as follows: in section 2 we define cultural knowledge and describe the OMCS-Br Project; in section 3 we describe our computational environment and its composition; in section 4, further works are discussed and in section 5 we present our conclusions.

2. CULTURAL KNOWLEDGE

According to Keesing [2], cultural knowledge consists of "conceptions (...) and theories about the world and the way it is viewed and acted in by members of one's community". In other words, it is everything that is learned and shared by individuals from a community and which gives an identity to this community. Cultural knowledge is easily accepted as true by ordinary people, but some of its conceptions and theories are not recognized by scientific community because they are not proved. Nevertheless, unproven beliefs can bring together valuable benefits. We can cite the case of a Brazilian indians tribe which uses some plants for medicinal purposes as part of their cultural knowledge. There were no scientific proofs about the real benefits of those plants when in the 90's years an English chemist granted the patents over compounds from the plants used by the indians [4]. This illustrates how valuable a conception or theory spread as part of the cultural knowledge of a community can be. It also illustrates that ordinary beliefs and practices can hold a scientific truth.

2.1 The OMCS-Br Project

The Open Mind Common Sense Brazil (OMCS-Br) was released in a collaboration between the Advanced Interaction Laboratory (LIA) and MediaLabs. By means of the OMCS-Br site (www.sensocomum.ufscar.br), cultural knowledge is voluntarily collected from from a general public with diverse ages, gender, levels of schooling and different Brazil's regions. To collaborate, an user needs to fill in the blank spaces of a template with concepts (Figure 1), which can be words or sentences.

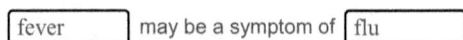

fever | may be a symptom of | flu

Figure 1. A template is a phrase with blank spaces which must be filled in with concepts.

In principle, the words and sentences are stored in a semi-structured form. Thus, it is necessary to process them to make computational systems able to use them. During the 3-stages processing task is created a semantic relation between the words based in the information storage theories defined by Minsky [5]. In the Extraction stage the binary semantic relations are identified between the concepts collected through the templates. There is a set of relations structured in the form (Relation_Type Concept1 Concept2). Considering the example in Figure 1, the relation obtained between the concepts typed by a user is (*EffectOf* "flu" "fever"). The identified relations form the ConceptNet [3], a semantic network of cultural knowledge which can be represented by a graph, where the concepts are represented as ellipses and the relation-type is represented as edges. In the Normalisation stage, a portuguese language parser is used to label each word inside a node syntactically (e.g., flu/SUBSTANTIVE) and then each word is reduced to its canonical form, i.e. adjectives and nouns must be in singular form and verbs must be in infinitive form. In the Relaxation stage, duplicated assertions are merged and an additional metadata field called "f" (frequency) is added to them to indicate how many times each relation was found. Inferences can also be made in this stage to create new relations from existing ones; in this case, a field called "i" (inferred) is also added to track how many times a relation has been inferred from relations explicitly entered by users. The assertion (EffectOf "flu" "fever" "f=82;i=0") indicates that the relation has occurred 82 times in the ConceptNet, i.e. 82 users entered this knowledge. So, starting from sentences collected from OMCS-Br Web site, a cultural knowledge base is gradually obtained; computer applications can use it to a huge number of purposes, including this work.

3. FINDING SIMILAR PEOPLE AND DIFFUSING INNOVATION

Figure 2 illustrates an overview of our computational environment. As mentioned previously, it consists of two methods. To simplify the text, we are going to refer to the methods as PSI (People with Same Interest) and CCH (Culturally Contextualized Hyperdocument); we think that these acronyms represent well the overall idea of each method. PSI identifies people who are "talking" about the same topic in social media, even if they express themselves using diverse cultural background which influences their vocabularies [6]; CCH aids the generation of culturally contextualized hyperdocuments, adapted and made available according to the level of literacy of a group or community [7]. Both methods were developed in our research group and their mechanisms use the cultural knowledge base provided by OMCS-Br Project. The "cloud of innovations" represents the process of formation of one or many homophilous OCs and the process of seeding, trying and adopting innovations which aim the well being of a community. Next subsections briefly describe the methods PSI and CCH.

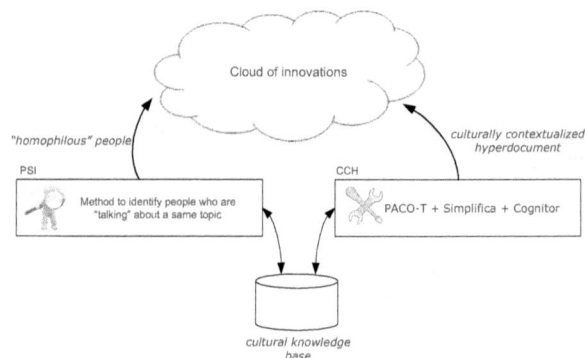

Figure 2. An overview of the computational environment.

3.1 The PSI method

This method consists of 3 steps: i) syntactic extraction from a phrase called "seed", which defines the topic of discussion; ii) cultural translation/expansion of the "seed" phrase; iii) people search in social media. The second step is supported by the cultural knowledge base to expand the "seed" by means of cultural translation, enriching searches in step 3.

The first step consists in extracting syntax from the "seed" phrase, retrieved from any source, e.g. a news headline. Shortly, a "seed" like "Rio de Janeiro continues beautiful" (in Portuguese, "Rio de Janeiro continua lindo") is submitted to a syntactic parser which: a) decomposes the phrase into subject ("Rio de Janeiro"), verb ("continues") and object ("beautiful"); b) normalizes nouns and adjectives to singular and verbs to infinitive form. So, it is generated a semantic relation represented by a meta-relation $mr = v (s, o)$, where v is the verb, s the subject and o the object. Then, from our seed we get the *mr continue (Rio de Janeiro, beautiful)*. The second step consists in performing cultural translation to obtain new meta-relations from the seed *mr*; its components v, s and o are used as parameters to generate parametrized query strings in the Minsky's relations format (first column of Table 1) which are submitted to the cultural knowledge base; the goal is to retrieve all *IsA* and *DefinedAs* relations connected to the seed components so we can obtain the "cultural synonyms" to each of the components (second column of Table 1)[1]. The cultural synonyms are then used to expand the seed *mr* and generate new ones (Table 2).

Table 1. Examples of parametrized query strings.

Search queries	Return in X or Y
IsA (Rio de Janeiro, Y)	*city*
DefinedAs(X, Rio de Janeiro)	*wonderful city*
DefinedAs(Rio de Janeiro, Y)	*marvelous city*
DefinedAs(beautiful, Y)	*gorgeous*
DefinedAs(X, continue)	*keep*

Table 2. Some of the new *mr* generated from the seed "*continue (Rio de Janeiro, beautiful)*" after cultural translation.

continue (Rio de Janeiro, gourgeous)
continue (wonderful city, beautiful)
keep (Rio de Janeiro, beautiful)

Finally, the third step consists in searching text blocks posted by users in social media to seek contents related to the seed topic. For each user post, when a co-occurrence of the values of *s* and *o* components of some *mr* is found in a same phrase (in Figure 3, the phrase is "wonderful city continues beautiful"); this phrase is submitted to a parsing process similar to that in the first step of PSI to also generate a meta-relation which can be called *user-mr*. If *user-mr* is equals to any of the *mr* generated in the second step of PSI, then the user post is retrieved as a matching post, i.e. the method identifies people who are "talking" about the same topic of the seed phrase, even if their vocabularies differ culturally.

> "(...) health, education, security and others (...) they promise to improve these areas but pan was gone and nothing!! (...) people are dying in hospitals (...) and people are dying because urban violence and the wonderful city continues beautiful!"

Figure 3. An excerpt of a post retrieved from a Brazilian SNS. The surrounded words match with *s* and *o* components of *mr* *continue(wonderful, beautiful)*; further, the *v* component is also verified to try to match the whole *mr*.

In [6] we describe the method's evaluation, performed on a very popular SNS in Brazil. The method was completely performed three times, each one of them using a different "seed" topic related to three different subjects: politics, tourism and celebrity. The retrieved posts were analysed by 19 respondents, who answered a 4-questions questionnaire. After tabulating the answers, we could analyze that: i) 81% of the posts retrieved by the method are related to the "seed" topic, i.e. the method can identify people that "talk" about the same topic, even if they use different vocabularies; ii) 95% of the cultural translations performed in step 2 where considered correct, so it indicates a strong evidence that use of cultural knowledge can enrich searches in the Web considering cultural differences; iii) 60% of the participants of the evaluation would agree with making contact with some posts' authors, because they analyzed the posts and considered that the authors had interest in the respective topic. So, these initial results pointed the potential of the method to support the formation of homophilous OCs.

---

[1] *IsA* specializes a concept hierarchically, e.g. (IsA "Rio de Janeiro" "city"). *DefinedAs* uses synonyms to represent the meaning of a concept, e.g. (DefinedAs "Rio de Janeiro" "marvelous city").

3.2 The CCH method

This method establishes a set of tools to generate culturally contextualized hyperdocuments, adapted and made available according to the level of literacy of a group or community.

Firstly, PACO-T [8] is used for planning culturally contextualized learning activities supported by cultural knowledge; in our case, *learning activities* represent the organization of content used to communicate an innovation. PACO-T defines 7 activities: i) to delimit the scope of innovation, defining its theme, goal and the target public to whom it will be communicated; ii) define and organize content topics to form the syllabus of the course; in our case, the course corresponds to a set of information packages which aims a gradual assimilation of the innovation; iii) choose a pedagogical reference to support the content generation; iv) plan the learning activities based on the choice made in previous activity (iii); in our case, activities (iii) and (iv) are optional because people engaged in diffusion of an innovation may not have a pedagogical knowledge background; v) choose textual equivalents, i.e. choose media – like video, images or audio messages – which can substitute text and hence enrich the content and facilitate comprehension; vi) elaborate the content; vii) test the whole generated content; this can be done with a reduced number of people who have the profile of the target public so they can verify the content's quality, e.g. if information is clear enough. Although the step (vii) is part of PACO-T, we recommend it to be performed along all the method. Once the content is elaborated in step (vi) of PACO-T, it is submitted to the Simplifica tool [9], which simplifies a Portuguese text lexically (suggesting some easier synonyms to replace difficult words) and syntactically (simplifying sentences) for people of rudimentary and basic level of literacy. In the CCH method, Simplifica is called Contextualized Simplifica because an adaptation was provided to support simplification through the access to the cultural knowledge base; thus, we can search for cultural synonyms as a rich complement to the suggestions of synonyms based on Simplifica's dictionaries. Contextualized Simplifica is executed iteratively until it indicates that the generated content is in a rudimentary level. After these previous steps, Cognitor tool [10] is used to design and edit quality instructional material in hyperdocuments format. While editing a hyperdocument, it is also possible to locate "cultural synonyms" in the cultural knowledge base, so the author can refine the content a little more to the reality of the target group or community; this is a significant functionality that allows additional adaptations realized during tests performed along the content's generation.

In [12] we describe the method's evaluation. An experiment was conducted with 13 people organized in three groups, according to their specializations in computer science, education and/or milk quality (this last one was because the experiment considered the instantiation of the method to a Brazilian company concerned with the quality of milk production). The participants were given a script to be followed, aiming the goal to transform a text set out in high level of literacy to the rudimentary level, using all the tools available in the method. Hypotheses were formulated to guide the experiment and to observe specially the impacts of using a cultural knowledge base to support contet simplification. It was concluded that lexical and syntatic simplification provided by Simplifica is significantly complemented by searches in the cultural knowledge base, because cultural synonyms can be used according to the target group or community, bringing the content to its "cultural reality". It was also observed the need to run the experiment to different domains in order to obtain a broader validation of the research hypotheses. However, our results were very motivating.

We believe simplified and contextualized content can reach a higher audience through social media; so, here we address one of the challenges in diffusion of innovations: the *complexity*, i.e. the degree to which an innovation is perceived as difficult to understand and use. The CCH method allows a cultural knowledge-based simplification to facilitate an innovation's understanding as a way to improve its adoption.

3.3 The Cloud of Innovations
The cloud of innovations is where we expect great things to happen. We have not formally evaluated the formation of homophilous OCs yet, but, as discussed in subsection 3.1, preliminary results has indicated the potentiality of PSI method to promote them. Rogers states that human communication and the exchange of ideas occurs most frequently between individuals who are homophilous. Hence, we expect to promote the organicity of OCs [11] by means of improving their users' communication. We define organicity as the possibility of diffusing innovations that can "touch" or change people. Considering a community like an organism, we can state that each participant is a cell, each relationship between people a vein, each idea or action the oxygen that feeds a cell and keeps it alive. The cells maintenance, on the other hand, keeps such "organism" wealthy. To guarantee such organic well being, it is necessary to unite cells and provide them a propitious environment to produce and share innovations.

4. FURTHER WORK
Next step is to develop a recommender system based on PSI method. A fourth step will be developed to rank the users identified in the third step of the method. The goal is to count the frequency of posts authored by each user as a way to improve our chances to measure how interested each user really is in the seed topic. If a user posts only a message about that topic, it is very hard to say if s/he is really interested in it. Our common sense says that as more posts a user authors about a topic, more s/he is interested in it. Then, when we apply the method in a recommender system, we will increase the possibilities to analyze "how much interest" is necessary to make people "homophilous". When we say "how much interest", we are considering the measurement of the average of posts a user did about a same topic. This average may be known just when we recommend people to each other in a social network site and investigate the results, i.e. how were the acceptances and rejections and the reasons for each of these actions. Simultaneously, an experiment must be run manually so we can analyze the formation of homophilous OCs. The results may guide us to refine and improve the method.

5. CONCLUSIONS
This paper described a computational environment which aims the formation of homophilous OCs based on the interest in a same topic, having people's cultural knowledge regarded, and also provides a method to guide the generation and diffusion of innovations. Diffusion of innovations is a promising field to the

computer science, especially regarding the challenges of human-computer interaction. Our challenge is to investigate the contributions of this research field, which has been strongly related to traditional social sciences, as a way to explore and use them in computer science, resulting in new contributions from the join of these two worlds. We believe that the connection of (ICTs) and diffusion of innovations theories can contribute to the promotion of sustainable "social phenomena", which means approaching people and making them to clamour: "Come and join us! Let's change the world together!".

6. REFERENCES
[1] Rogers, E.M. *Diffusion of Innovations*. 5th ed. New York, Free Press, 2003.

[2] Keesing, R.M. 1979. Linguistic Knowledge and Cultural Knowledge: Some Doubts and Speculations. IN Darnell, R. 2002. *American Anthropology, 1971-1995: Papers from the "American Anthropologist"*. University of Nebraska Press.

[3] Liu, H., Singh, P. 2004. ConceptNet – a pratical commonsense reasoning tool-kit. IN *BT Technology Journal*, v. 22, n. 4, pp. 211-226. October 2004.

[4] Izique, C. 2003. Fruit of Contention. *Pesquisa Fapesp Online*. <http://revistapesquisa.fapesp.br/?art=832&bd=1&pg=1&lg=en>, last access on June 09, 2011.

[5] Minsky, M. 1986. *The Society of Mind*. New York: Simon and Schuster.

[6] Anacleto, J.C. *et al.* A Cultural Knowledge-based Method to Support the Formation of Homophilous Online Communities. IN *CHI 2011*, Vancouver, CA, 2011.

[7] Magalhães, V.M.A. *et al.* Building contextualized web hyperdocuments taking into consideration readers' culture and literacy in order to allow them to understand these hyperdocuments. IN *IADIS/e-Society 2011*, Spain, 2011.

[8] Carvalho, A.F.P. *et al.* Supporting teachers to plan culturally contextualized learning activities. IN *IFIP Intern. Federation for Information Processing*, v.281, 2008.

[9] Candido Jr, A. *et al.* Supporting the Adaptation of Texts for Poor Literacy Readers: a Text Simplification Editor for Brazilian Portuguese. IN *4th Workshop on Innovative Use of NLP for Building Educational Applications*, Boulder, Colorado, 2009.

[10] Anacleto, J.C. *et al.* Cognitor: a Framework based on Cog-Learn Pattern Language (in portuguese). IN *Rev. Brasil. de Informática na Educação*, v.15, 2007.

[11] Balbino, F.C., Anacleto, J.C. Improving users communication to promote the organicity of online social networks. IN *SIGDOC 2010*, São Carlos, Brasil, p. 261, 2010.

[12] Magalhães, V.M.A. *et al.* e-Rural: a Framework to Generate Hyperdocuments for Milk Producers with Different Levels of Literacy to Promote Better Quality Milking. IN *Interact 2011*, Lisbon, Portugal, 2011. (*to be published*)

"Cognitive Theory of Multimedia Learning" and Learning Videos Design: The "Redundancy Principle"

Dr V. Bouki
Computer Science
University of Westminster
W1W 6UW, United Kingdom
+44 (0)20 7911 5000 ext 64552
boukiv@wmin.ac.uk

Dr D. Economou
Computer Science
University of Westminster
W1W 6UW, United Kingdom
+44 (0)20 7911 5000 ext 64506
D.Economou@wmin.ac.uk

A. Angelopoulou
Computer Science
University of Westminster
W1W 6UW, United Kingdom
+44 (0)20 7911 5000 ext 64508
agelopa@westminster.ac.uk

ABSTRACT

This paper presents an ongoing research project regarding the design of learning videos in relation to Mayer's Cognitive Theory of Multimedia Learning (CTML) and more specifically to the Redundancy Principle (RP). Learning videos have been proved an efficient teaching tool. However poorly designed videos could easily fail if they trigger the RP. The RP is activated when the information parsed through the visual channel consists of animation and on-screen text. This paper presents an experiment that explores the way the RP is related to learning videos and how the type of on-screen visual aid (text, call-outs) affects learners' comprehension. It also discusses preliminary results that derived from a pilot study. The presented work is part of a bigger project that explores several aspects of CTML in relation to learning videos design.

Categories and Subject Descriptors

K.3.1 [K. Computing Milieux]: Computers and Education K.3.1 Computer Uses in Education – *learning videos, multimedia learning theory, split attention effect, redundancy principle.*

General Terms

Design, Experimentation, Human Factors, Theory

Keywords

Learning Videos Design, Multimedia Learning Theory, Redundancy Principle

1. INTRODUCTION

It has been confirmed in several experiments that the use of videos leads to more efficient forms of learning by allowing users to adapt their form and content to their individual cognitive skills and needs [4]. However for a video to have such effect it should be designed for learning purposes. Not all "instructional videos" have a "teaching" potential or can be used for teaching purposes. The standards that a video should satisfy in order to be used for learning purposes are still under investigation and discussion. Many teachers are willing to use any type of video in the classroom – even videos uploaded on "YouTube" – focusing on the information they present. They tend to overlook the design aspects and the fact that a badly designed video could be

unsuitable for teaching purposes and even confuse students. At present, there are not standards on the design of learning videos. What seems to be closer to a generalised model is ISO 14915-1:2002 and ISO 14915-2:2003 ("Software ergonomics for multimedia user interfaces" part 1 and part 2 respectively), however both are quite general models for multimedia applications and not specific for videos. For educators who intend to produce learning videos for their students as well as for companies that are activated in this field, it is very important to have clear instructions on what a "well designed" learning video is and what are the factors that affect students' learning.

Section 2 below presents the main points of the CTML and the RP. Section 3 presents the objectives of this research. Section 4 discusses the challenges we faced by analysing the videos we constructed for the needs of this research and the methods we used to collect data. Section 5 discusses the pilot study; section 6 presents some preliminary results and the last two sections present some final remarks and further work.

2. THEORETICAL BACKGROUND

Mayer's CTML, (based on the "dual-coding theory" – first proposed by Paivio) assumes that humans have separate systems for processing pictorial and verbal material. This is known as the "dual-channel assumption" [6, 7]. Each channel is limited to the amount of material that can be processed at one time (limited-capacity assumption). Meaningful learning involves cognitive processing including building connections between pictorial and verbal representations. The problem with poorly designed videos is that such connections cannot be established. The physical separation of the verbal and the pictorial information leads to the "split attention effect" [6]. A special case of the split attention effect is called the "redundancy principle". This problem becomes apparent when students have to read on-screen text in parallel with the auditory message. According to Mayer, *"students learn better from animation and narration than from animation, narration, and on-screen text"* [5].

Then again most software packages used for the production of learning videos offer teachers the chance to add on-screen text in parallel with the animation as well as subtitles[1].

---

[1] For the needs of this research project we studied three software packages for the production of learning videos: WINK; Demo Builder and Camtasia Studio [1]. All of them allow teachers to add text on the screen. Subtitles can also be added. Camtasia Studio 7 offers a sophisticated 'speech-to-text' tool for the easy production of subtitles.

3. RESEARCH OBJECTIVES

The experiment which is present hereby investigates if the RP applies in the design of learning videos and it examines the role of subtitles. Subtitles differ from any other text because there is a one-to-one correspondence between them and the auditory message. One question that this research addresses is if subtitles cause the RP – thus they should be considered as any other type of on-screen text and their use should be avoided in learning videos – or if they do not cause the RP because of the relation to the auditory message. Furthermore, we try to identify other factors that might trigger RP. In order to achieve our research purposes we investigate the relation between: auditory message; on-screen text; subtitles and activities that take place on the screen.

The rest of the paper presents the design of an experiment that focuses on studying the following issues:

- How RP affects the design of learning videos
- What type of on-screen text triggers the RP in learning videos
- Assuming that no disability is involved how subtitles contribute to RP and if we should distinguish between them and other on-screen text

Furthermore this paper presents preliminary results of a pilot study with a small number of subjects (4).

4. DESIGN OF THE EXPERIMENT

4.1 Learning videos

For the purpose of this research two short learning videos have been designed that present the topic: "how to use a PhpMyAdmin Interface." Each video is approximately 150 seconds, plus 20 seconds for the introductory and concluding titles. The titles were considered important in order to indicate the beginning and the end of each video sequence that deals with a particular topic, as well as to give the subjects the chance to 'relax' among the different tasks of the experiment. The content and design of each video is as follows:

- **Video 1** explains how to **delete data from a table** using PhpMyAdmin interface

Video 1 uses animation, narration and on-screen text in the form of call-outs (see Figure 1). With 'animation' we refer to what happens on the screen. The term refers to visual information only and includes the screen changes as results of instructor's actions as well as the movements of the cursor that might highlight specific parts on the screen. 'Narration' refers to audio description of the actions by the instructor. The on-screen text includes information that is not given in any other format (e.g. narration). The objective of video 1 is to study if the on-screen text causes the RP.

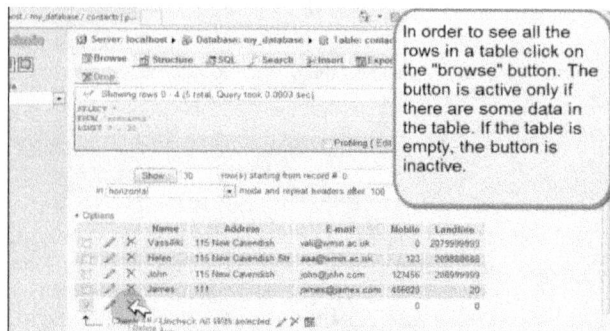

Figure 1: Video 1 with on-screen text in the form of call-outs

- **Video 2** explains how to **update data** using PhpMyAdmin interface.

Video 2 uses animation (same as video 1), narration (same as video 1) and subtitles. Subtitles is a special type of on-screen text (see Figure 2). The difference between the subtitles that are used in video 2 and the on-screen text of video 1 is that there is a one-to-one correspondence and synchronisation between the subtitles and the auditory information in video 2. This is not the case between on-screen text and auditory information in video 1. Subtitles do not carry any information that does not exist in the auditory message. The objective of video 2 is to study if subtitles cause RP.

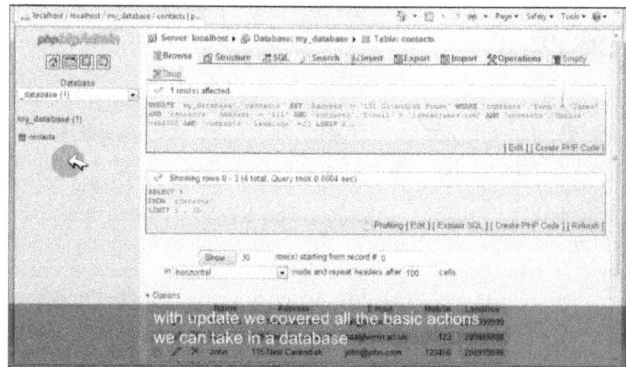

Figure 2: Video 2 with subtitles

4.2 Collecting Data

Data collection was completed with the use of questionnaires and eye tracking.

At the end of each video subjects are asked to complete a questionnaire. The questions that are used aim to evaluate subjects' comprehension of the video content and to identify the type of information they noticed or missed. Table 1, below presents the questions that have been designed for data collection after following video 1 and video 2 respectively and the scope of each question.

Table 1: Questions used for data collection after following video 1 and video 2 and the scope of the questions

	QUESTION	QUESTION SCOPE
Video 1	Q1 & Q3	Asks for a piece of information that exists in the **text call-outs** only – not in narration or animation.
	Q2	Asks for a piece of information that is **visual information only** – not part of the narration
	Q4	Asks for a piece of information that is passed to viewers through the **auditory channel** only
Video 2	Q1 & Q3	Asks for information related to the **auditory message** and **the subtitles**
	Q2	Asks for information related **visual information** only
	Q4 & Q5	Asks for information related information that is **mainly visually and partially related to the narration and subtitles**

A second method used to collect information is eye-tracking. With this method we aim to identify where on the screen subjects focus at and if on-screen visual aids attract their attention. Eye-tracking is a method that has been highly praised for capturing "true" user experience without distorting users' reactions and uncovering the largest number of usability problems. According to a research published by Lancaster University in 2008, eye-tracking helps uncover significantly largest number of usability problems (79% versus 42% in think aloud methodology) [3].

Following the analysis of the questionnaires we relate questionnaires' results with the data provided by the eye-tracking methodology. For example if a certain question has been answered wrongly the visual pattern that has been identified with the eye-tracking will be checked to find out the subject's reaction while the required information was presented (as a verbal or visual message).

For capturing subjects' gaze the TOBII eye-tracking system has been used [2]. TOBII enables to efficiently obtain valid and reliable eye-tracking research results. It is easy to use and it provides highly accurate and precise results. One of the advantages of TOBII is that it is not intrusive for the subjects. No special equipment that users have to use or wear (e.g. glasses) is required. Subjects simply sit in front of the computer screen as they would normally do. The system incorporates an automatic process of being trained to the characteristics of each user's gaze.

The TOBII Studio eye-tracking software provides a comprehensive platform for recording, observation, analysis and visualization in heat maps and gaze plots.

5. THE PILOT

The purpose of the pilot was to evaluate the appropriateness of the prepared material for the experiment and to indicate problems that should be corrected before the final study. The pilot took place in the course of three days and four subjects took part overall. All subjects had good computing skills, but they had no previous knowledge or experience of PhpMyAdmin interface and they wanted to learn how to use it in order to create databases. Subjects were divided in two groups:

- the ones **without computing background** and no previous knowledge or experience of PhpMyAdmin

- the ones that had **computing background** but they had no previous knowledge or experience of PhpMyAdmin

For the first group data has been collected using questionnaires only, while for the second group a combination of questionnaires and eye-tracking has been used. Subjects had to watch the two videos (see Section 4.1) and at the end of each video they were asked to answer a questionnaire (see Section 4.2). For the first group a standard PC has been used and no special hardware has been engaged to record the session.

For the second group the TOBII hardware and software have been used in a specially designed usability lab at the University of Westminster (see Figure 3). The subjects had to watch the videos that have been designed for this experiment (see Section 4.1) and at the end of each video they were asked to answer a questionnaire (see Section 4.2). The moderator was controlling the TOBII system and intervened only to ask the subject to change sitting position in case the system could not capture the subject gaze, which is something that happens if the subject sits too far from the

screen, or to high (see Figure 3). The experiment started with 20 seconds calibration process to teach the system the characteristics of subject's eyes. To a large extent, calibrating TOBII is an automated process. The moderator, who controls the experiment starts the calibration process by clicking the "calibrate button". A pulsating circle moving over the screen is started in subject's monitor. During calibration the subject follows the circle across the screen focusing on the black dot in the middle of the circle.

Figure 3: Subject watching the video on the left; moderator observing that subject's gaze is within the screen (two dots at the screen on the right)

6. RESULTS

Apart from evaluating the prepared material and the experimental settings the pilot provided raw data that had to be related and analyzed in order to grant some understanding about the expected outcomes of the research. The following sections present preliminary results that have been obtained from the pilot study.

6.1 Video 1 – Questionnaires

Initially, the answers collected from the questionnaires are analyzed. As already explained in Section 4.1 video 1 consists of animation (visual information), narration and on-screen text in the form of call-outs. The information presented within text call-outs does not exist in any other format. The video incorporates two different visual pieces of information and the scope of the study is to understand how subjects handle each one. This is done as follows:

- The text call-out related to video 1, question1 (V1Q1) remains on the screen for 30 seconds (approximately for one fifth of the time the video plays – excluding the titles. Total duration of the video: 145 seconds)

- The visual information related to video 1, question 2 (V1Q2) is part of what happens on the screen simultaneously with the text call-out of V1Q1

- The text call-out related to video 1, question3 (V1Q3) remains on the screen for 35 seconds.

- The auditory information that is checked by question4 of video 1, (V1Q4) is given to the subject simultaneously with the text call-out of V1Q3. This intends to study if the subject is able to understand both pieces of information.

Table 2, below presents the questionnaire results for video 1:

- The first column indicates the subject

[2] http://www.tobii.com/

- Columns 2-5 provide the data collected per subject for each question

- The sixth column provides information about the background of the subjects: "NC" stands for "non-computing background" and "C" stands for "Computing' background"

- The last column provides information about the data collection method that has been used. S1 and S2 answered the questionnaires only, while S3 and S4 took the eye-tracking test and they answered the questionnaires.

The symbol "✓" indicates that the subject answered the question correctly, the symbol "X" indicates that the subject answered the question wrongly and the symbol "!" indicates that the answer the subject gave was very ambiguous. In those answers it was not clear what the subject meant. We treat these answers as 'ambiguous – not correct'. Finally, subjects were encouraged to leave a question blank in case they did not know the answer. As a result one cell holds the message "not know". It means that the subject preferred not to answer this question.

Table 2: Results of the questionnaires for video 1

VIDEO 1: auditory & visual information; text call-outs						
	V1Q1	V1Q2	V1Q3	V1Q4	BG	Data
	Text call-out info	Visual info only	Text call-out info	Auditory info only		
S1	!	Not know	X	✓	NC	Q
S2	!	X	✓	✓	NC	Q
S3	!	X	✓	X	C	Q & ET
S4	X	X	X	✓	C	Q & ET

The first thing that becomes apparent from Table 2 is that there is no significant difference in the answers provided by subjects with or without computing background. Especially in questions V1Q2 and V1Q3 the percentages of the correct and wrong answers in each group are identical. No subject answered V1Q2 correctly and 50% of the answers to V1Q3 were correct, 50% wrong, from each group.

The next remark is about the results related to V1Q1 and V1Q2, which indicate that the message conveyed to subjects with the text call-out was not understood at all or clearly. One subject answered this question wrong and the other three gave answers that were very ambiguous. Similar results are obtained for V1Q2. Three subjects answered this question wrongly and one preferred not to answer it. Thus, it is quite safe to say that when subjects are presented with visual information (text and non-textual information) that is not related to the auditory message, none of each was parsed properly and none of each reached the subject.

Subjects did better in V1Q3 and V1Q4. 50% of the subjects answered V1Q3 correctly and 50% answered it wrongly. Finally, V1Q4 was the only one answered correctly by 75% of the subjects. The message that reaches subjects better is the auditory message (results of V1Q4) even when a text message is given to subjects at the same time.

From the above analysis, it could be claimed that the RP is partially confirmed. The subject attention is divided when they are presented with auditory and textual information. It could be added that the auditory message reaches subjects better. A further remark that we consider even more important is that when subjects are presented with two different, unrelated, visual messages it seems that none of them reaches them. This remark is based on the analysis of the answers for V1Q1 and V1Q2. Definitely further research is required in order to confirm those remarks.

6.2 Video 1 – Eye-tracking

The next step was to relate the results that have been obtained from the questionnaires with those obtained from the eye-tracking experiment. It was expected to get more information about subjects' reactions when text messages appear on the screen and as a result to get a better understanding why a message does or does not reach them.

TOBII constructs the "gaze plot" for each subject. The gaze plot displays a static view of the gaze data for each image. It is a useful tool when visualizing scan paths. Each fixation is illustrated with a dot and the radius represents the length of the fixation. Furthermore, TOBII allows us to get a collective picture of how each subject reacted.

Figure 4 below, depicts the gaze plot for S3. The text call-out related to V1Q1 appears on the right hand side part of the screen. The visual message related with V1Q2 appears on the bottom left hand side of the screen.

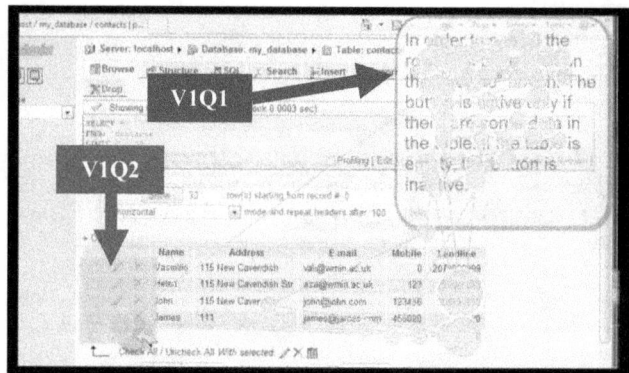

Figure 4: Gaze plot for S3 for video section related to V1Q1 & V1Q2

It is apparent that the text call-out does not go unnoticed – S3 looks at the message for some time. During the 30 seconds, while the message was on the screen, S3 also briefly looked in other parts of the screen. Although this is evidenced in the gaze plot, S3 did not answer V1Q1 correctly. This could be considered as an indication that RP is present here. The attention of the subject is divided between the auditory message and the text. As a result the information in the text does not go through. Additionally, we see that the part of the screen which is related to the V1Q2 goes almost unnoticed by S3. She has a quick look there and she answers V1Q2 wrongly.

The following figure (Figure 5) provides S4's gaze plot. Here we see something similar. Although the subject looks at the text call-out, V1Q1 is answered wrongly – this could indicate the presence of RP again. It is interesting that S4 does not even have a quick look in the other parts of the screen. As expected, S4 answers V1Q2 wrongly.

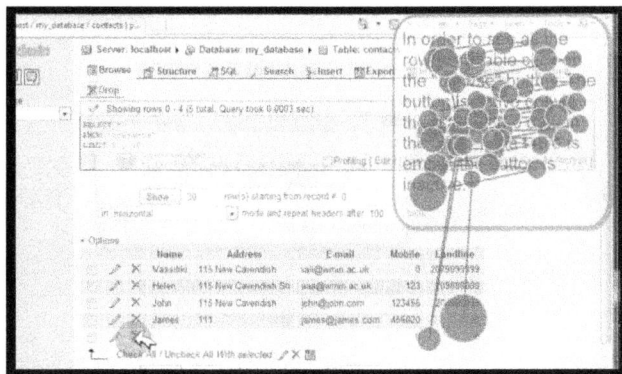

Figure 5: Gaze plot for S4 for video section related to V1Q1 & V1Q2

It is also interesting to mention that both subjects look on the right corner of the screen for some time. The fixation on this part of the screen is evidenced by the dot and the length of the visit by the radius. The right hand side part of the screen is related with the auditory message.

If we compare figures 4 and 5 we see that both subjects followed very similar browsing patterns. This becomes more obvious if we look at the collective gaze plot that is given by the following Figure 6.

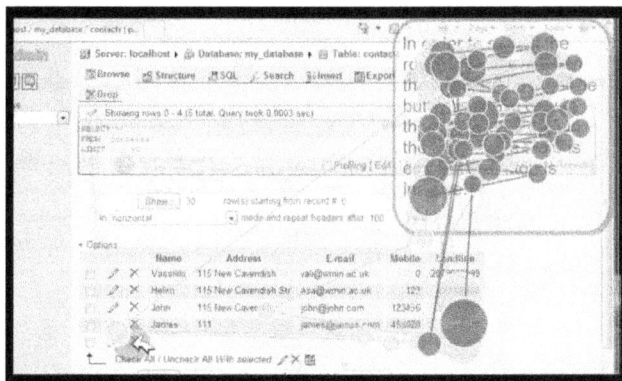

Figure 6: Gaze plot for S3 and S4 for video section related to V1Q1 & V1Q2

Green color shows the gaze plot for subject 3 and blue the gaze plot for subject 4. Both subjects look at the call-out text and both look at the right corner of the screen. The only difference is that subject 3 also has a quick look on the left part of the screen. None of those subjects answered V1Q1 correct and both answered V1Q2 wrong. It seems that the redundancy principle applies here and also that the text is a much stronger visual message than any other part of the screen.

The next two questions related to video 1 (V1Q3 and V1Q4) intend to examine subjects' reactions when they are presented with textual and auditory information respectively. Figures 7 and 8 below depict the gaze plots for S3 and S4 in relation to V1Q3 & V1Q4.

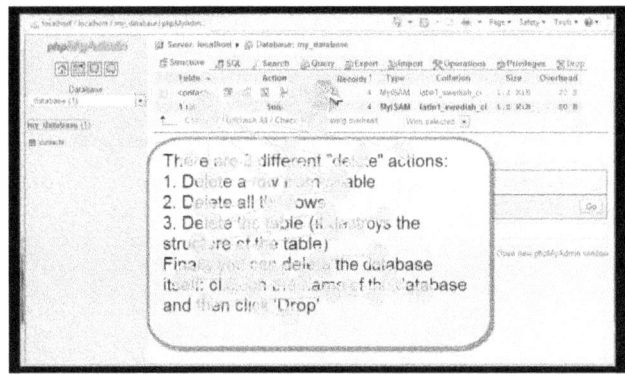

Figure 7: Gaze plot for S3 for video section related to V1Q3 & V1Q4

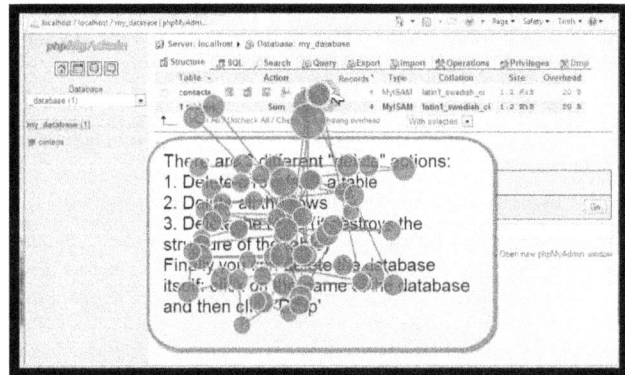

Figure 8: Gaze plot for S4 for video section related to V1Q3 & V1Q4

It is apparent that both subjects look at the text call-out on the screen. It is quite interesting that subject 3 answers question 3 correct and question 4 wrong while subject 4 answers question 3 wrong and question 4 correct. As a result we could claim that in each case it is either the auditory or the visual message that goes through – not both. Which message (auditory or visual) goes through in each subject might depend on other factors such as the type of learner each subject is. The remark that is important for this research is that RP seems to be present here.

Finally, the browsing patterns here are almost identical.

6.3 Video 2 – Questionnaires

Similarly with video 1 the analysis of the results for video 2 was initiated by the data that has been collected from the questionnaire. Table 3 below provides subjects' answers. The same notation with Table 2 is used (notation explanation is provided in Section 6.1).

Table 3: Results of the questionnaires for video 2

VIDEO 2: Auditory & visual information; subtitles				
V2Q1	V2Q2	V2Q3	V2Q4	V2Q5
Narration & subtitles	Visual info only	Visual info only	Visual info partially related to narration / subtitles	Visual info partially related to narration / subtitles
S1 ✓	✓	✓	NOT KNOW	NOT KNOW
S2 !	✓	X	✓	X
S3 ✓	✓	✓	✓	✓
S4 !	✓	✓	✓	✓

An instant observation looking at Table 3 is that subjects answered more questions correctly in comparison to Table 2. Namely, in video 1 only 5 answers out of 16 were correct, – the rest were wrong, "not know" and 'ambiguous'. This means that we have only 31.25% correct answers. While for video 2, 14 answers out of 20 were correct – in other words 70% correct answers. Both videos are supported by auditory, visual and textual information. The main difference between video 1 and video 2 is that in video 2 the textual information corresponds to the auditory message and does not provide additional information as it happens with the textual information which is presented in video 1.

As previously there are no significant differences between subjects with computing and non-computing background. The only considerable difference is in question V2Q5. V2Q5 asks if a database table can be exported in LaTex format. This information is provided as visual information in video 2. The reason that both subjects with non-computing background got it wrong, while both subjects with computing background got it right could be that 'LaTex' means nothing for a person with non-computing background. As a result they do not notice this information on the screen and the visual message was not registered. Apart from V2Q5, we get identical answers from both groups in V2Q1 and V2Q2 and similar answers in V2Q3 and V2Q4.

The message associated to V2Q1 is auditory and it is also presented as textual message in the subtitles. Mixed answers are provided in relation to V2Q1 (50% correct and 50% wrong in each group). In this case the eye-tracking results could provide us with more information about subjects' reactions. V2Q2 and V2Q3 refer to a visual, non-textual, message. Although visual, auditory and text messages are simultaneously provided on the screen (as it happened before in V1Q1 and V1Q2) in this case 75% of the answers were correct comparing to 0% correct answers in the corresponding questions for video1.

The difference between the two videos is not the type of information which is provided, but the relation between the textual and the auditory information. In video 2 the textual information does not conflict with the auditory message. As a result subjects could pay enough attention to understand both the auditory and the visual information. The same applies to the last two questions where the information is visual and only partially related with the text and as a result with the subtitles. The visual message is relatively well perceived.

Comparing the results obtained from the questionnaires for both videos it could be claimed that the textual messages in parallel with visual and auditory messages distract subjects and cause the RP only in the case that the textual message conflicts with the auditory message. If the textual message does not conflict with the auditory, then subjects can easily handle both the visual and the auditory messages. If the textual message conflicts with the auditory message then subjects straggle to follow them. In addition it seems that subjects miss any other visual message that is on the screen (apart from the text) as it has been discussed in Sections 6.1 and 6.2.

6.4 Video 2 – eye tracking
Results of V2Q1 and V2Q2 suggest that when the textual message on the screen is associated with the auditory information it does not reduce subject's attention and does not cause RP. The gaze plots of subjects given in Figures 9 and 10 show that both subjects do not read the textual message on the screen.

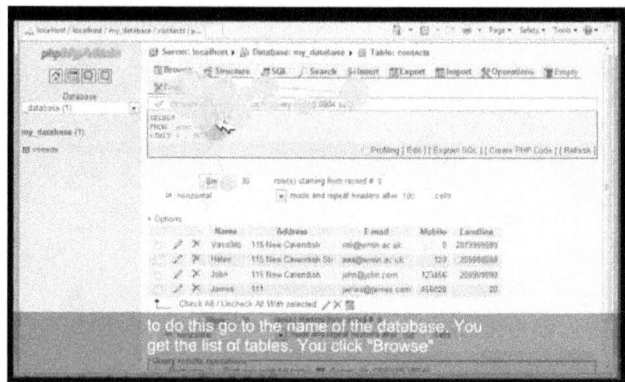

Figure 9: Gaze plot for S3 for video section related to V2Q1

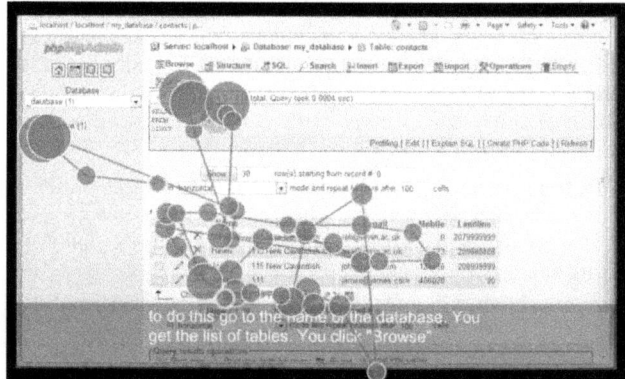

Figure 10: Gaze plot for S4 for video section related to V2Q1

Subject 3 does not even go close to the text while subject 4 has a quick look on top of the subtitles but apparently she does not read them. Contrary to figures 4, 5, 7 and 8 that describe gaze plots for video 1 and indicate that subjects look at the textual message on the screen, figures 9 and 10 show that the text message does not attract subjects' attention.

It is interesting to mention that in video 2 we see different browsing patterns. Subject 3 focuses around the cursor, while subject 4 looks all over the screen. However their behavior in relation to subtitles is the same: none seems to read them.

7. DISCUSSION
Based on the above analysis, it is relatively safe to say that the RP plays a very important role for the design of learning videos. When subjects are presented with text, visual and auditory information not all of those pieces of information go through. Text seems to attract subjects' attention much more than any other part of the screen (e.g. the cursor or other graphical information presented on the screen). Additionally, browsing patterns seem quite similar even when the answers that are given are not the same. The relation between browsing patterns and understanding needs to be investigated further.

The pilot we discuss here gave us the opportunity to reconsider the design of the experiment. Some questions in the questionnaire need to be rephrased in order to be easier for subjects to understand them. Furthermore we decided to make minor changes to the videos in order to slightly reduce their duration and keep the most important information only.

Finally we should mention that this research focuses on the elements that are related to the RP: audio, text and any other visual information on the screen. It does not consider other factors such as the speed of narration.

8. FURTHER RESEARCH

Based on the knowledge we gained from the pilot, we intend to slightly redesign the experiment and complete it by the end of July 2011. In our analysis we intend to focus more on the following issues: a) the text message seems to be stronger than any other visual information that appears on the screen b) the possibility to define browsing patterns for learning videos and finally c) the relation between browsing patterns and understanding.

In this experiment we study only a special case of the 'split attention effect' – the redundancy principle. Our final goal is to investigate further the 'split attention effect' as a whole in relation learning videos design.

9. REFERENCES

[1] V. Bouki, 2009. Using Learning Videos in Classroom: Cognitive aspects and evaluation of software to create learning videos. In International Conference on Education Research and Information (ICERI2009), Madrid, Spain, November 2009, Published by "International Association of Technology, Education and Development" (IATED), pp 005604 – 005608, ISBN: 978-84-613-2955-7

[2] G. Cierniak, K. Scheiter and P. Gerjets 2009. Explaining the split-attention effect: Is the reduction of extraneous cognitive load accompanied by an increase in germane cognitive load? In Computer in Human Behavior, Volume 25, Issue 2, March 2009, Pages 315-324

[3] N. Egar, L. J. Ball, R. Stevens, J. Dodd 2008 "Cueing Retrospective Verbal Reports in Usability Testing Through Eye-Movement Replay" In: People and Computers XXI Proceedings of HCI 2007. The Biritish Computer Society, Swindon

[4] J. Kepler & Department of Media and Information, Fachhochschule Offenburg, University of Applied Sciences, Offenburg, Germany, 2004. Learning and Instruction Volume 14, Issue 3, June 2004, Pages 293-305

[5] R. E. Mayer 2001. *Multimedia learning*. New York: Cambridge University Press. ISBN 0-52178-749-1

[6] R. E. Mayer; R. Moreno 2003. "Nine Ways to Reduce Cognitive Load. Iin Multimedia Learning" *Educational Psychologist*, 1532-6985, Volume 38, Issue 1, 2003, Pages 43 – 52

[7] Moreno, R. 2001. "Designing for understanding: A learner-centered approach to multimedia learning". In the *Human-Computer Interaction Proceedings* (pp. 248–250), Mahwah, NJ: Lawrence Erlbaum Associates

Role of Feedback in Uniform Learning Situation

Hanna M. Olsson
Mid Sweden University
83125 Östersund
Sweden
+4663165768

hanna.olsson@miun.se

Lena-Maria Öberg
Mid Sweden University
83125 Östersund
Sweden
+4663165702

lena-maria.oberg@miun.se

ABSTRACT

In this paper, we explore feedback in a Digital Learning Environment (DLE), based on a study performed in a Swedish military training context. DLEs make uniform learning possible, while allowing interaction (as opposed to a text book). However, it is unclear how interaction should be designed to be beneficial in a uniform learning situation. Feedback is needed in DLE, both for the learning itself, and for the functionality of the system. Through an evaluation framework the uniform learning situation is evaluated and feedback is mapped onto interaction lanes. Balanced feedback has the potential to offer a beneficial DLE for uniform learning. Although the importance of feedback is known in theory, our study shows that practical implementations lack complete feedback. Hence, we propose a design guideline to implement balanced (relative to the framework) feedback in general, and to pay specific attention to Feed-Forward when designing DLEs.

Categories and Subject Descriptors

H.1.2 **[User/Machine Systems]**: Human factors. H.5.1 **[Multimedia Information Systems]**

General Terms

Design, Documentation, Human Factors.

Keywords

Digital learning environments, DLE, interaction, feedback, uniform learning.

1. INTRODUCTION

Digital learning environments (DLEs) are used in various learning situations. Examples of DLEs are distance courses in Learning Management Systems (LMSs) or virtual worlds/simulators used for learning. A motivation for the use of DLEs is that it allows providing uniform training to a large number of learners. This could be especially important in learning situations where critical information is taught. In this paper, we will present an example of

such a learning situation, namely the training of Swedish soldiers who are preparing for an assignment in Afghanistan. The information the soldier needs to assimilate is critical due to the fact that insufficient information accessible on location could lead to severe damage, and in worst-case scenario, to loss of human life. Within military organizations uniform training is valuable since one basic need is the ability to replace any soldier at any point of time.

Another motivation for the use of DLEs is the ability to allow interaction (as opposed to, for example, a textbook). Interaction is often considered an important function when it comes to DLE [1]. However, it is unclear how training in DLEs can benefit from both being uniform and yet allowing a high level of interactivity. Hence, in the following sections we will critically explore two interactive DLEs with the aim of highlighting the agents that interact, and what is necessary to maintain interaction.

2. THEORETHICAL BACKGROUND

Based on three agents, namely learner, instructor and content, Moore [2] describes three types of interaction: learner-content, learner-instructor and learner-learner. Andersson [3] has later extended the perspective to include six types, by adding instructor-content, instructor-instructor and content-content. The extended perspective allows for a more complete, holistic view.

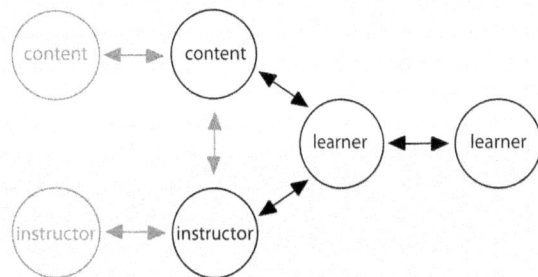

Figure 1. Moore's and Anderson's interactions

We have visualized our interpretation of the six types of interaction in figure 1. The arrows represent lanes of interaction. The learner-content interaction can be thought of as self-evident, as it concerns the subject of study. However, we understand it as being the interaction with the medium of presentation (the system), as well as the learning material. In the study presented in this article, the subject of study is the use and maintenance of a combat vehicle. The medium of presentation is DLE. Interactions in DLEs can be more or less advanced. On a low level, a possibility to press a start and stop button can be considered interaction, while being able to walk freely in a simulated world can be described as a higher level of interactivity. In DLEs, interaction of the learner-instructor type can take place in those cases where the instructor has an active part, as in the case, for example, of distance education through a LMS. However, in other cases, the instructor only participates during the development of the DLE. In that case, the instructor no longer plays an active role after the release or introduction into the organization, once the learner gets into the picture. Learner-learner interaction is also possible through DLE, and can take the shape of concrete collaboration in various ways or the exchange of questions and ideas, for example through a web based forum. Learner-learner interaction tends to be limited to written text [4], even though technology offers diverse forms of communication. Östlund and Svensson [4] voice the need of multimedia communications between learners. Interaction can in this way enable a social dimension. In order for learning to occur, the social dimension has been described as vital, and relates to socio-constructive learning theory [5] based on the ideas of Vygotsky [6]. In blended learning the interaction could be either traditional (face to face) or by use of any digital technology [7].

Feedback is inherent to interaction. In this article, we will follow Hattie and Timperley's [8] definition of feedback as being

"...information provided by an agent (e.g., teacher, peer, book, parent, self, experience) regarding aspects of one's performance or understanding." (p.81)

Feedback within the system is part of interaction, and is also vital for the learning itself [8]. Moore [2] states, regarding learner-instructor interaction

"It is for reality testing and feedback that interaction with an instructor is likely to be most beneficial" (p.22)

Hattie and Timperley [8] relate three questions to feedback, and the first "Where am I going?" deals with the goal of the learning (Feed-Up). The second question "How am I going?" deals with the task or performance carried out (Feed-Back). The third question "Where to next?" involves guidance on how to proceed or directions that will add depth to what has already been reached/achieved (Feed-Forward). Hattie and Timperley state that *"this feed-forward question can have some of the most powerful impact on learning"* [8]. These three questions are interesting for the following discussion, since they help in exploring different kinds of feedback.

Feedback can also allow for the learning experience to be personalized, which is the case of intelligent tutoring systems. A personalized learning system can take into account learning styles through learning performance, previous learner experience, and learning objectives [9].

3. METHOD

We performed an explorative field study in a military training facility. The study has been presented in a Swedish project report [10]. Three soldiers preparing for their assignment in Afghanistan and their instructor took part in a two day test.

The overarching form of the explorative study was a participant observation, in three parts, divided into four steps (see figure 5). The parts were:

1) Think-aloud sessions of 30 minutes per learner (step 1)
2) Quiet observation (step 2)
3) Semi-structured interviews, a group interview (step 3) and an interview with the instructor (step 4)

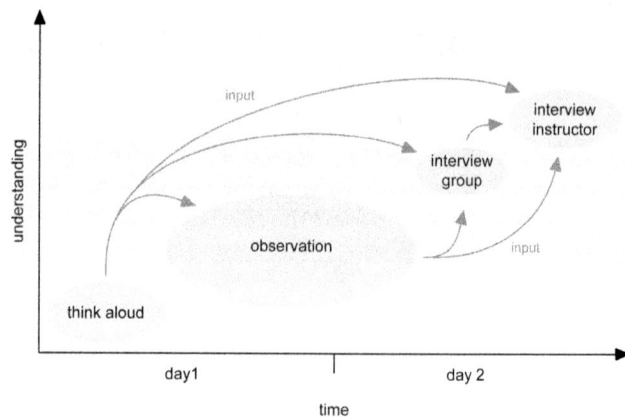

Figure 5. Model of explorative study

A *think-aloud* session is intended to collect the thoughts of users, while they are using an information system [11]. One session per student was performed. Before the sessions, the concept of think-aloud was explained to the users. Furthermore, the fact that it was the system that was to be evaluated, and not the user, was underlined. Likewise, attention was brought to the fact that the users would be anonymous. The session took place while the student was using TTS. During the session the user was asked to speak his thoughts, while using the system. To promote reflection, initial questions were asked. The questions were kept open, while directing the users towards areas of interest for the study: usability, functionality, efficiency and user experience. The whole session had an open structure, and questions were asked if the user became quiet. A session lasted 30 minutes, where the think aloud itself lasted 25 minutes and the 5 minutes remaining were used for summative questions regarding left out areas, or areas that could benefit from being elaborated.

In connection to the think aloud sessions the test leader took a step back, in order to follow the learning situation from a distance in the form of *quiet observation*. The purpose of this was to offer space to the users to use the systems in a more natural and relaxed manner. Observations can also allow users to use systems in unpredictable ways [11]. The quiet observation was also particularly well suited for PTS, since the users' speech often was occupied by communication between users, which made up an important part of the exercises. Hence, think aloud sessions were unsuited for PTS.

Interviews can lead to surprises and new insights, and are thus particularly appropriate for explorative studies [11]. A short summative group interview was performed at the end of the second day. As a round-up activity the instructor was interviewed. This interview offered the opportunity to go deeper into areas brought up by the students and to tie up the study. Both the group interview and the interview with the instructor were semi-structured.

For documentation of image and sound, all four steps were recorded on video. During the two days, our understanding of the issues inherent to the use of DLEs in the learning situation was advanced through the four steps, as visualized in figure 5.

We have analyzed the data collected during the two days through an interpretative approach. For a better overview of the collected data, we transcribed the recordings. We freely translated the statements from Swedish to English. We then used the model presented in section 2 (figure 1) as evaluation framework, by mapping feedback that we identified, onto the lanes of interaction. Where feedback was advanced (elaborated response) and in both directions, we judged it as *satisfactory*. Where feedback was simple (such as a reaction to a request), we judged it as *unsatisfactory*. Where there was no feedback, we labeled it *missing*. The results of the evaluation are presented in section 5.

4. CONTEXT

The learners who took part in the test were male soldiers training in the use of a combat vehicle, as part of their preparation for an assignment in Afghanistan. Together, they make up a complete crew for the vehicle: a driver, a shooter and a coach. Two DLEs were used, where the first was a theoretical training system (TTS) seen in figure 2, and the second was a practical training system (PTS) as in figure 3. The TTS consisted of a self-paced multimedia system where the learner could choose between sections of topics and study through text, images and/or video. Self-tests were offered to the learner for self-verification. The system was built in a LMS.

Figure 2. Theoretical training system

The PTS was a battle simulator, very much like a computer game. The learner acted out his professional role (driver, shooter or coach) in a fictional scenario. In this way the learner could assimilate experiences from diverse situations in a safe and cost effective manner. A specific interface allowed the learner to interact with the simulator through steering and aiming gears identical to those in the actual vehicle. The two systems complemented each other as theory was studied first and then put to practice.

Figure 3. Practical training system

The setting, as seen in figure 4, was a room with several workstations. The learners were placed at three workstations next to each other. The instructor was placed in front of a workstation on the opposite side, so that the learners and the instructor were seated back to back. Each workstation consisted of three screens, one in the middle and one on each side angled inwards, a keyboard, mouse and specific gears as in the vehicle, as described above. Three combat vehicle crews could train simultaneously, but during the days that the test took place only one crew was present.

Figure 4. Soldiers at workstations in the training facility.

The learners had diverse experience of DLEs. Soldier 1, from now on referred to as "Driver", had no previous experience of DLEs. Soldier 2, "Shooter", had only tried a DLE once before. Soldier 3, "Coach", used DLEs during his initial military training, 2 and a half years earlier.

5. EMPIRICAL DATA

For this article only the data of interest for the discussion of interaction are presented. The complete data from the study are presented in a Swedish project report [10]. To start with, the learners have a positive impression of the DLEs, as described for example by the Driver on TTS: *"It is a good complement to being by the machine"* and by Shooter regarding PTS: *"It is a good exercise"*. Some inconsistencies and errors are observed in TTS. For example, passed exercises are sometimes not marked as passed. Driver states *"It is a subject of irritation that I end up in the same exercise that I had already passed"* and Coach *"I have passed all, but some are not marked"*. More images, from different angles, interactive 3D-models and video are requested. *"...3D-models that can be turned around so that all the details can be seen..."* is requested by Driver. Video is appreciated by Shooter: *"It helps a lot. It is much better than just images"*. When Driver finds an error in TTS he is informed about a F2-function that is meant to let users report errors. However he cannot get it to work, but says he would have appreciated such a function.

In PTS, the learners can run exercises in single mode or together as a group. The instructor can follow the exercise on his workstation from a bird's eye perspective. When exercises are run in single mode, the learners get a printed report on their performance from the instructor upon completion of the exercise. The report includes, for example, investigation times such as the time from spotted target until elimination of target. Result images of targets are also provided in the report, with a color scheme for different types of hits. If a detail in the report seems interesting, it is possible to watch the sequence playback. Exercises are recorded, with eventual learner communication. When they run group exercises they communicate continuously through their headsets on what they do and see, etc. After group exercises they watch the exercise playback, with their recorded communication. Thereafter, they evaluate their performance as a group, together with the instructor.

During the interview with the instructor, he explains that DLEs were introduced into the organization in order to facilitate learning, increase motivation, to be able to distribute models, and decrease time spent by the physical machine. He considers that these goals have been met. However, he thinks that the content is not very different from written text in that it gets tedious when studied intensively. Hence, he tries to create a *"classroom feeling"* by interrupting every now and then for evaluations and discussions. He considers that the instructor has an important role in the learning process. The instructor also considers that it is important that the TTS is built in a LMS, so that he can manipulate the material by choosing to present certain sections to the learners. In addition, he would have wished for the ability to add *"quick and dirty"* material such as PowerPoint slide shows that he could produce himself in order to adapt the content. He thinks that flexibility for the instructor is important.

The instructor describes his role as even more important in relation to PTS, since the learners can wander freely, and do almost whatever they want in the simulated world. He explains that there is no *"right or wrong"* as in TTS, and hence, the computer cannot give as good feedback to the learner as can a human being. The instructor, he states, has the possibility to get an overview of the exercise and give the learners valuable feedback. According to the instructor the content can only provide collected data, but cannot judge the collected result as good or bad as can a human in the form of an instructor, or the learners themselves.

6. RESULTS & DISCUSSION

The learning situation presented can be described as blended learning, due to the mix of face to face interaction and interaction in the two DLEs Learning in DLE is dependent on feedback, both for the learning to actually occur, and for the DLE to function properly. When feedback is mapped onto the evaluation framework, it shows to be incomplete in the (blended) learning situation presented in this article. Figure 6 shows where feedback is missing, unsatisfactory, and satisfactory.

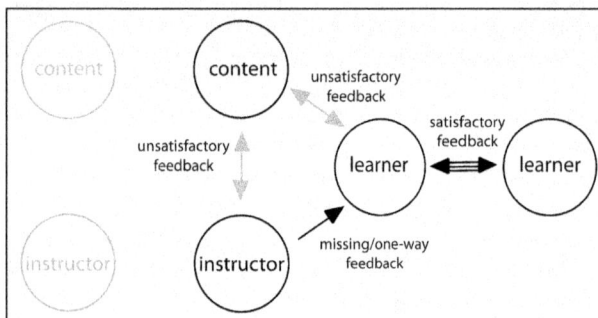

Figure 6. Feedback mapped on lanes of interaction

Learners give feedback to each other during the group evaluations and during the simulation sessions. The feedback during sessions could be of the type such as *"This is not working!"*, *"Well done!"* (Feed-Back) or *"Let's try ..... instead"* (Feed-Forward). Similarly, feedback during group evaluations could be expressed *"We should have ... instead, let's try that next time"*. Communication during sessions is mediated through headsets, while evaluations take place face to face. Hence, it is questionable if the feedback would still have been satisfactory if the learners had been distributed in space. The fact that they are all located within the same physical room could have an impact on feedback, regardless of the use of headsets. As requested by Östlund and Svensson [4], learner-learner interaction in this case does indeed take on other forms than written text, namely speech. Communication that takes place during the PTS group sessions is part of the exercise. Communication is also in a specific language and form, inherit to military organizations. Other types of organizations could take inspiration, and learn from the way verbal communication, and learner-learner feedback is performed

in the learning situation presented, since learner-learner feedback is valuable for the social dimension, and hence for learning [5].

The instructor gives feedback to the learners during the group evaluations and ongoing during sessions. However, learners do not show any feedback towards the instructor. **Content feedback to learners** is limited to "pass or fail" on tasks or sessions (Feed-Back). However, no advanced feedback from the content is offered, such as tips on further directions to take or other personalized actions (Feed-Forward). Learners give feedback to content through their actions. However, the content does not react to this feedback. For example, no suggestions of further directions based on actions taken are offered to the learner. This content feedback would be of great value, considering that Feed-Forward is claimed to have powerful potential [8]. A great deal of information is given regarding learners' preferences, abilities and objectives, and the content could, by using this information, provide a personalized learning experience. However, caution is needed if personalization is provided, in order to keep the learning experience uniform to all learners.

Learners are unable to give feedback to the content regarding bugs/errors or other opinions the learner might have regarding the content. Irritation experienced by the learners could have been avoided if learners could inform those in charge of content maintenance on errors so that they could be corrected. However, there is also the problem of who is responsible for the maintenance of such systems. Improvements in accordance with users' requests would also be possible if the users were able to give such feedback to the content. The agent "content" has a threefold complexity, since it can concern the system, learning material or the maintenance of these two.

The **instructor can retrieve feedback from the content** regarding the learners' performance. This feedback is presented as datasheets of actions at certain points, and results (Feed-Back). The instructor needs to analyze and translate these data to the learners. Thus, the instructor has a position of power, and becomes the filter between the content and the learner. Hence, the competence of the instructors is a key factor as to whether the learning will be uniform throughout the organization. However, the instructor has the ability to give feedback of all three types (Feed-Up, Feed-Back and Feed-Forward) based on the data provided by the content.

The instructor can give feedback to the content, only through actions in the same way as the learners. The instructor can manipulate the content by choosing sessions. Hence, the content responds to those choices by offering requested session, but offers no further suggestions on possible continuation. The instructor wishes more flexibility, which could be at the cost of uniformity of learning within the organization. However, it could as well contribute to a more personalized, or applied learning situation. **Content-content** feedback has not been studied, since the study's main focus was on human factors. **Instructor-instructor** feedback is irrelevant in this case, since only one instructor is involved. As seen in figure 6, there is an imbalance, as more feedback is present on the right side of the figure. This implies limitations in the learning situation, both in terms of learning outcome and functionality.

Due to the claimed potential of Feed-Forward for learning, the DLEs explored in the presented study should be complemented with feedback of this type. For the same reason, we propose a general design advice for DLEs to give attention to this type of feedback. Although the importance of feedback is known in theory [8], this study shows that there are insufficiencies in practical implementations. Regarding personalization, it requires balancing to what extent it should be provided, and yet keep the learning uniform. Equally, the competence of the instructor as a central role of power and filtering could have consequences for the uniformity of the learning. The situation with the instructor in a role of power works rather well in the context presented. In military organizations, roles of authority are common, but it could be possible that it would not work as well in other types of organizations.

7. CONCLUDING REMARKS AND FUTURE DIRECTIONS

A learning situation enhanced by DLEs was explored, and feedback was mapped onto Moore's [2] and Anderson's [3] lanes of interaction. Design, maintenance and redevelopment of DLEs would profit from more complete feedback, which could be described by a balanced framework. Hence, a contribution of this paper is the evaluation framework, which can be used to evaluate feedback in learning situations. We have found in our study that feedback mapped onto the evaluation framework showed to be imbalanced. This implies a limited learning situation, both in terms of learning outcome and functionality. The importance and value of feedback is known in theory [8]. However, as shown in the study presented, practical implementations lack complete feedback. Hence, we propose a design guideline to implement balanced (relative to the framework) feedback in general, and to pay specific attention to Feed-Forward when designing DLEs.

Further directions include exploration of other types of organizations. The design guidelines proposed in this paper should be further assessed through implementation. Furthermore, the complexity of the agent "content" should be explored.

8. ACKNOWLEDGMENTS

Thanks to the European Regional Development Fund of the European Union, for the financial support to the TIC-project, within which this research has been performed.

9. REFERENCES

[1] Davidson-Shivers, G. V. Frequency and Type of Instructor Interactions in Online Instruction. *Journal of Interactive Online Learning*, 8, 1 2009), 23-40.

[2] Moore, M. G. *Three types of interaction*. Routledge, London, 1993.

[3] Anderson, T. Modes of Interaction in Distance Education: Recent Developments and Research Questions. L. Erlbaum Associates, Mahwah, N.J., 2003.

[4] Östlund, C. and Svensson, L. *Authentic learning and multimedia in work-integrated e-learning*. AACE, Quebec City, Canada, 2007.

[5] Fosnot, C. T. *Constructivism : theory, perspectives, and practice*. Teachers College Press, New York, 1996.

[6] Vygotsky, L. S. and Cole, M. *Mind in society : the development of higher psychological processes*. Harvard University Press, Cambridge, Mass., 1978.

[7] Oliver, M. and Trigwell, K. Can 'Blended Learning' Be Redeemed? *E-Learning and Digital Media*, 2, 1 2005), 17-26.

[8] Hattie, J. and Timperley, H. The Power of Feedback. *Review of Educational Research*, 77, 1 (March 1, 2007 2007), 81-112.

[9] Watson, J. and Hardaker, G. Steps towards personalised learner management system (LMS): SCORM implementation. *Campus-Wide Information Systems*, 22, 2 2005), 56-70.

[10] Olsson, H. Utvärdering av multimediasystem i lärandesituation. Mittuniversitetet, Östersund, 2011.

[11] Nielsen, J. *Usability engineering*. Academic Press, Boston, Mass., 1993.

Acquiring Ethical Communicative Tools
for an Online Ethics Training[*]

Montse Serra, David Bañeres, Eugènia Santamaria
Universitat Oberta de Catalunya
Rambla del Poble Nou, 156
Barcelona, Catalunya (Spain)
mserravi,dbaneres,esantamaria@uoc.edu

Josep M. Basart
Universitat Autònoma de Barcelona
Escola d'Enginyeria
Cerdanyola Vallès, Catalunya (Spain)
josepmaria.basart@uab.cat

ABSTRACT

Nowadays, one of the most dynamic areas in applied ethics is professional ethics (e.g. in the areas of medicine, business and engineering). In this paper, we will focus on the online teaching of professional ethics to undergraduate engineering students, mainly in the specialty of Information and Communication Technologies (ICT) [10]. More specifically, the pedagogical structure for the ethical training of future engineers will be designed, within an online context, based on a set of ethical communicative tools. Besides, our proposal will analyze which technological resources are suitable to develop the appropriate ethical communicative competences required by the engineering students, when confronting moral conflicts in their daily professional exercise.

Categories and Subject Descriptors

K.7.4 [**Professional Ethics**]: Ethical dilemmas, Codes of ethics, Codes of good practice. H.4.3 [**Communications Applications**]: Tools. K.3.1 [**Computer Uses in Education**]: Distance learning.

General Terms

Design, Human Factors, Theory.

Keywords

Applied ethics, engineering, online environment, communicative tools, technological resources, forum, OpenStudy, wiki.

1. INTRODUCTION

In society, an engineer and the individual are continually facing situations that must be dealt with a limited set of resources, a particular code and some accumulated experience. The engineer confronts technical problems while the individual finds herself immersed in moral conflicts [21]. For this reason, good education and training in professional ethics are required to take into account the human factor that, very often, is forgotten when analyzing technical difficulties. We expect that designing a good course of applied ethics should help the students to understand how and why their work with technology can affect the life of

(*) An extended version of this article is available under request.

other people [6]. Implementing this kind of course, within a virtual environment involves acquiring moral competences through an adequate set of communicative tools supported by a technological collaborative workspace.

Professors can teach applied ethics, efficiently, making the students understand that different ethical points should be taken into account when resolving a case study [4][12]. Therefore, putting into practice case analysis will promote a discursive approach by means of communicative tools.

Study cases help students to become active and increase their interest towards the subject. Cases are a good vehicle for developing the next competences required in the area of ethics: Ability to analyze and synthesize, resolving conflicts, Adapting to heterogeneous situations, decision-making, critical thinking, writing communication.

However, future engineers need some communicative tools [19] in addition to their professional expertise to persuade others to cooperate, such as dialogue, constructive moral reasoning and judgmental language. These tools will help students to examine reflectively and critically their own thoughts with regard to student's and teacher's opinions. For this reason, training ethics within an online environment [17] requires appropriate technological platforms to promote an experiential and active learning such as the discussion of ideas, the practice of behaviors, or the development of attitudes and skills [20]. Some tools reuses generic web-based resources like forums or wikis to support the courses [2][8][9][16]. All these approaches agree that the selected resources should provide educational experiences that would promote the development of these processes: (1) the students' engagement within a discursive deliberation; (2) the construction of a social interaction to enhance collaboration, (3) the use of communicative tools for a reflective discussion, and (4) peer technological support.

The rest of the paper is structured as follows. Section 2, the communicative tools are, briefly, defined. In Section 3, the students' training activities are presented. In Section 4, the technological resources are justified based on their practical use. Finally, Section 5 presents some conclusions and future work.

2. COMMUNICATIVE TOOLS

In order to understand the moral issues embedded in applied ethics, three communicative tools [19] will be considered to face them: *dialogue, constructive moral reasoning,* and *judgmental language.* Future engineers can not only rely on their professional expertise when they are dealing with moral dilemmas; they also need tools to improve their communication skills to influence rather than instructing or wheedling others in decision-making. However, these tools do not guarantee that the learning process of ethics will be the desirable one. Thus, our ever-present concern from the methodological point of view is to establish a feasible path to follow when resolving a moral dilemma. Mostly, discursive ethics will be used.

3. ACTIVITIES

The objective is to train the future engineering graduates when facing ethical dilemmas through the previous communicative tools. They need to acquire good communicative skills and the ability to articulate decisions with a strong argumentation.

We propose to design a course founded on a case-based approach [7][12]. This method allows us to put in practice these tools. Moreover, the students will cooperate actively to solve a problem instead of passively attending the lectures. We propose two kinds of activities: (1) individual activity related to a case study, (2) teamwork activity related to a particular ethical dilemma.

3.1 Individual Activity

In this initial activity, an ethical dilemma is presented and the activity ends with a deliberation. This activity is a good starting point in the learning process because it allows generating a discussion based on a written dialogue. During this debate, the student trains the inquiry process required to share different approaches when a moral conflict is handled. Autonomy is an essential requirement for the construction of knowledge. It gives the student, as an individual, the capacity to judge, decide and act in accordance with whatever rules he considers to be appropriate. So, this kind of activity is useful to improve self-sufficiency when facing a moral dilemma.

3.2 Teamwork Activity

Teamwork activity considers a case study from several points of view. It incorporates values such as cooperation, collaboration and solidarity. Again, dialogue acts as a main communicative tool to develop the empathy and social perspective. Each team is assigned to a possible conclusion. This kind of activity consists of three exercises: (1) Each team should reach a conclusion on the assigned perspective. The objective is to elaborate a well-built argument to defend. (2) Each team expounds its arguments. (3) A deliberation is, finally, performed taking into account all the presented arguments. In the next section, we present some possible resources to put into practice the proposed activities.

4. TECHNOLOGICAL RESOURCES

This section describes the technological resources that should be suitable for training the communicative tools. Notice that, there are many resources that could be used; however we select a set of them based on the educational benefits.

4.1 Internet Forum

The classical resource used for asynchronous communication among interlocutors within a virtual context is the *Forum*. There are several types of users groups depending on the privileges. In our case, members and moderators are the main groups that will be used. Members will be the students with the rights to post messages. The moderator will be the teacher with the rights to post messages and supervise the forum. Note that, the teacher

should be a good e-moderator [18] in order to manage properly the forum during the activity.

This resource is suitable for individual activities within an online context [9] because students interact by posting new ideas and arguments in the discussion and replaying messages based on their own arguments. This type of deliberation has some benefits in the learning process of ethical skills. The asynchronous communication promotes a deep reflection on the others' words, taking advantage of a momentary delay in the written dialogue for thinking, calmly, before replying [11]. Moreover, teacher and students could take advantage of the asynchronous communication to post more complex questions. The result will be more elaborated answers that will be helpful when trying to reach a consensus during the discussion of ideas. Therefore, one can gain not only insight into the questions, ideas and beliefs of the others, but also in his own [4]. This interaction promotes an intense social network where the standard cultural signifiers do not exist (sex, race, and origin). Virtual communication provides an environment where anonymity is possible and this fact benefits certain social sectors where an interlocutor could be marginalized. Hence, the forum encourages the introduction of new and multiple approaches (interdisciplinary and multiculturalism) through the social network. Simultaneously, it involves a certain commitment to improve the students' personal development such as: the responsibility, knowing how to share, knowing how to listen, the humility to accept mistakes and to change a concrete position when it is not accepted by the rest. In other words, this is personal maturity.

The asynchronous communication has also some drawbacks. The feedback between interlocutors is not immediate and the exchanges of justifications can perpetuate or break the established dialogue. It is also important to emphasize that, within a virtual context, the dialogue should avoid any kind of imperative (commanding, pressing, authoritative, and urgent) because the lack of non-verbal language (gestures, look and tone) can reinforce misunderstandings, confusion and disagreement.

We expect that the forum through the written dialogue will have benefits in the students' training with regard to his moral reasoning by speaking, listening and attending the arguments of the other interlocutors.

4.2 OpenStudy

The objective of the first exercise of the teamwork activity is to reach an agreement or consensus based on a coherent and consistent argumentation that justifies the global position of the team. This exercise demands an intense interaction among students and an effort for mutual comprehension when making decisions. Consistently, teamwork activity, which is a provider of social skills to understand the others' point of view, needs an additional contextual tool between the interlocutors, the *moral imagination*. Moral imagination is a learning tool to carry out applied ethics that allows students to understand the others' moral approaches. The lack of gestures, voice and expression, elements that give us information about a situation in a face to face context, requires looking for a substitute. The moral imagination is proposed to overcome this absence.

Some authors implemented this type of exercise with forums or Wikis [2][16]. In this case, forums and Wikis have an important inconvenient: it is difficult to dialogue in privacy. Virtual worlds allow private messages but it is fundamentally based on synchronous communication. Therefore, another resource is needed to work in groups. At least, the tool should have the option to store information, i.e. a document, and the possibility to communicate. We propose to use a Web-based collaborative tool called *OpenStudy* [15].

OpenStudy is a social learning network where the objective is to interconnect students studying the same topic. Similar to forums, a person posts a question and other people answers it. There are predefined groups (mathematics, physics, finance,…) where questions can be posted. There is also the option to create new groups if existing ones are not suitable for a certain topic or question. OpenStudy has also the feature to create private groups or areas of studying called *Studypads*. These areas are controlled for the owner and a new user can only access with an invitation. In our case, this functionality can be used to create a private group for each team to discuss about their assigned perspective.

Basically, a Studypad is a collaborative word processor combined with an instant messaging tool. The document is written in collaborative mode. The contribution of each member is highlighted in different colors to identify each addition. The instant messaging tool gathers all the irrelevant conversation among members to build the document. Combining these two functionalities, a powerful resource is given with the option to create a document to store the arguments and the option to communicate asynchronously the members of the group. The generation of an argumentation cooperatively is essential in the learning process of the student.

According to [13], six stages in the development of moral reasoning were defined and grouped into three major levels. The progression through the stages reflects cognitive development in the understanding of moral issues. Our educational concern is that students should get past from the first level to the end at the Conventional Level. At this stage, students construct their framework for reasoning about moral issues through their interactions using the technological resource. The intensity of their statements depend on the level of cognitive development. In this way, students are gaining the ability to understand the perspectives of others and the norms and laws that are necessary for society to function effectively. Note that, the emerging moral framework is being developed in an environment where the hindrances that appears during the dialogue coexist (cultural signifiers, prejudgment,…). On the one hand, ethical reasoning becomes a critical subject owing to its level of subjectivity. Our decisions and arguments involve a personal responsibility with regard to the consequences. On the other hand, the learning virtual context leaves only one trace, the written speech, without visual and auditory cues. Therefore, the potential harm caused by the written words is distanced through this environment forcing the students to discern the underlying moral value when a judgment is done.

The dialogue combined with the moral imagination is essential at this stage to reach a consensus. However, communication skills are also crucial to help professionals when handling moral dilemmas and improving their decision-making process under adverse conditions (time pressure, lack of information and budget, technical and social constraints, interests' conflict, etc.).

4.3 Wiki

A forum is still a valid resource for sharing arguments among different groups. However, it could be useful, from an educational point of view, to store the statements of each group together with the debate about a particular case study. This collection of ethical

cases could be a valuable resource to search analogies for new students.

Similar to [2][8][21], we propose to use a *wiki* in order to put in common the arguments of the different groups. Wikis have a user-friendly structure and an embedded editing tool to help non-technical people to edit the content. Wikis also allow adding multimedia resources (images, audio, video) and some newer wikis also allow to add *widgets*. A widget embeds some functionality, i.e. opinion poll, online documents, slide presentation, among others. There is also Sematic Wikis associated to a ontology that could be also used to store a collection of ethical cases similar to [3].

The wiki will be used in the second and third exercise of the teamwork activity. The main objective is to develop the social skills of the students when a study case is discussed. The second exercise involves that each team should post his initial argumentation on the wiki page forcing the students to discern the underlying moral value related to the expounded arguments. A group can use the editing tool to add his defense. Multimedia resources and widget components could help to improve his conclusions. The third exercise is focused on starting a deliberation about the arguments. The discussion panel in the wiki page is perfect for this exercise. The final objective is to refine the arguments of each group using the deliberation to reach a consensus. At this point, essentials requirements of moral reasoning should be requested to complete and polish up the training of the ethical communication.

In accordance with [21], "word choice influences meaning". In this exercise, the teacher will require the use of a careful language when resolving moral conflicts to improve communication competences. In this way, some language strategies that we consider appropriate have to be enforced in the wiki.

When managing ethical issues, students need to know that it is essential to control the meaning of their words because, in every subject they face, a set of pervasive and subjective elements (i.e. opinions, reflections, assessments) are at stake. For instance, expressions such as *ought*, *should* and *must* may be used properly when talking about rules, law, official procedures or technical issues, but not resolving moral conflicts. Note that, interlocutor could feel threatened. Avoiding some forms of intense language will have favorable effects in the communication.

Additionally, constructing the moral reasoning of a virtual speech can be supported by linguistics resources. On the one hand, metaphor improves the intelligibility of a deliberation. In accordance to [21], "the choice of suitable tropes has been found to increase the comprehensibility, emphasis, and credibility of interlocutors and even to make their utterances more persuasive". In every written conversation, the choice of the appropriate words in the arguments influences the interlocutor's interest. On the other hand, "the precise placing of different phrases and clauses within a sentence can itself influence emphasis and comprehension" [21]. In other words, the location of every sentence is essential to increase the effectiveness of the communication.

The previous linguistic strategies are necessary to accomplish a desirable ethical communication. Moreover, the ethical responsibilities inherent to them have to be also taken into account. These responsibilities, called listening and speaking, attention and labeling, and prejudgment, are required to get an understandable and constructive reasoning.

Consequently, paying attention is required within a deliberation. It allows to the interlocutors to think about the different opinions based on a structural and consistent social speech, to recognize differences, construct new arguments and ideas, or simply, promote an appropriate atmosphere for the reflection and mutual understanding. In a sense, wiki promotes all these. The lack of immediate response between questions and answers providing opportunities to reflect, interpret and internalize the argumentations of the several messages.

Finally, it is inevitable that some students cannot escape from their prejudgments, but a possibility arises to realize that their prejudgments are mistaken through the discursive interaction with others students. For this reason, it is essential to set in context all the involved participants to understand the diversity of points of view. Consequently, the only way through which the students can make themselves aware of their own prejudgments is to implement a deliberation, based on moral reasoning.

5.CONCLUSIONS AND FUTURE WORK

When designing a course of ethics, engineering students must be prepared for a leadership role for a successful exercise of their profession. The appropriate moral development, throughout the engineering curricula, starts by exploring moral reasoning through a discursive deliberation. This includes theoretical knowledge, the cognitive domain, language strategies and communicative tools for ethical communication.

Additionally, we utilize web-based technology to improve students' awareness of ethical issues within an online environment and further develop their decision making skills. That technology provides substantial benefits. For instance, it increases sociability which depends on collaboration; it promotes empathic skills by enabling students to see other's point of view; it mediates interactions that depend not only on the explicit exchange of information but also rely on implicit, effective and appropriate modes of communication; and it provides flexible and simple access to repositories of information. Moreover, it has a fundamental capacity to promote communicative tools for a text-based communication.

As future work, we need to define the assessment criteria of the course. A good possibility is to use a method based on Audience Response System [14]. Different measurements, such as speech quality or didactics quality should be specified to return useful feedback to the students. Finally, we propose to implement the designed course and analyze the behavior of the students. The obtained results combined with the assessment criteria will be used to refine the pedagogical aspects of the course.

6.REFERENCES

[1] Basart J.M, 2008. Hindrances to Engineering Ethics Appraisal. In Proceedings of the First International Conference on Ethics and Human Values in Engineering, Barcelona. pp. 35-38

[2] Biasutti, M. 2011. The student experience of a collaborative e-learning university module, Computers & Education.

[3] Bratsas, C., Kapsas, G., Konstantinidis, S., Koutsouridis, G., Bamidis, P.D.;, A semantic wiki within moodle for Greek medical education, Computer-Based Medical Systems, 2009. CBMS 2009. 22nd IEEE International Symposium on , vol., no., pp.1-6, 2-5 Aug. 2009

[4] Brooke, S. 2006. Using the Case Method to Teach Online Classes: Promoting Socratic Dialogue and Critical Thinking Skills. International Journal of Teaching and Learning in Higher Education, 18, 2, 142 – 149.

[5] Demiray, U. and Sharma R.C. 2009. Ethical Practices and Implications in Distance Learning. Information Science Reference. Hershey, New York.

[6] Dreyfus, H. L. 2001. On the Internet, Routledge.

[7] Dyrud, M. A., 2004. Cases for teaching engineering ethics, . Frontiers in Education, (Oct. 2004) FIE 2004. 34th Annual , Vol. 3, 20-23 DOI= http://dx.doi.org/10.1109/FIE.2004.1408693

[8] Gobbo, F. and Lanzarone G. A. 2006. A wiki-based active learning system; how to enhance learning material in epistemology of computer science and computer ethics, in Current Development in Technology-Assisted Education, Vol. II, Formatex, Badajoz (Spain): 757-761

[9] Goold A. and Coldwell J. 2005. Teaching ethics in a virtual classroom. In Proceedings of the 10th annual SIGCSE conference on Innovation and technology in computer science education (ITiCSE '05). ACM, New York, NY, USA, 232-236.

[10] Grodzinsky, F. S. 2000. The Development Of The 'Ethical' ICT Professional. Computers and Society, vol. 30, no. 1, pp. 3-7.

[11] Habermas, J. 1984. The Theory of Communicative Action, I, Beacon Press, Boston.

[12] Harris, C.E., Pritchard, M.S., and Rabins, M.J. 2009. Engineering Ethics: Concepts & Cases. Belmont, 4th ed . CA: Wadsworth Publishing.

[13] Kolhberg, L. 1976. Moral stages and moralization. In T. Lickona (Ed.). Moral development and behaviour. Holt, Rinehart and Winston, New York.

[14] Konstantinidis, S.T., Bamidis, P.D., Kaldoudi, E. Active blended learning in medical education - Combination of WEB 2.0 problem based learning and computer based audience response systems, Computer-Based Medical Systems, 2009. CBMS 2009. 22nd IEEE International Symposium on , vol., no., pp.1-6, 2-5 Aug. 2009

[15] Ram, P., Ram, A., Spregue, C., Hill, P. (2011). Open Social Learning Communities To Engage Digital Millenials in Learning. In Proceedings of Society for Information Technology & Teacher Education International Conference 2011 (pp. 677-683). Chesapeake, VA: AACE.

[16] Regueras, L. M.; Verdu, E.; Verdu, M. J.; de Castro, J. P.; 2011, Design of a Competitive and Collaborative Learning Strategy in a Communication Networks Course, Education, IEEE Transactions on , vol.54, no.2, pp.302-307.

[17] Rodríguez, M.E., Serra M., Cabot J., and Guitart, I. 2006. Evolution of the Teachers' Roles and Figures in E-learning Environments. IEEE Computer Society Press, 512 – 514.

[18] Salmon, G. 2011. E-moderating: the key to teaching and learning online. 3nd edition, Routledge Falmer.

[19] Serra M. and Basart J.M. 2010. A dialogical approach when learning engineering ethics in a virtual education frame. Ethicomp - The "backwards, forwards and sideways" changes of ICT, 483 - 490.

[20] Sieber, J.E. 2005. Misconceptions and Realities about Teaching Online. Science and Engineering Ethics, 11, pp.329 – 340.

[21] Toulmin, S. E. 1968. An examination of the place of reason in ethics, Cambridge University Press, 172-174.

Designing a System to Create a Community: The GEMviz Project

Peter Abrahamsen, Anna Delamerced, Doug Divine, Christopher Nguyen, Mark Zachry
Human Centered Design & Engineering
University of Washington
423 Sieg Hall
(206) 543-2567
{peidran, avmd, rddivine, chris480, zachry} @uw.edu

ABSTRACT

In this poster, we describe the development of GEMviz, a web-based visualization generator with supporting user interaction tools intended to create a sense of community among a loosely connected group of researchers and educators.

Categories and Subject Descriptors

H.5.2 [**User Interfaces**]: Prototyping, user-centered design.

General Terms

Design, Human Factors.

Keywords

Genre ecology models, visualization tools, social media.

1. INTRODUCTION

The GEMziv project addresses the design-use challenge of creating a shared tool and related resources in order to create a community where only individuals with loosely related shared interests existed before. Our poster describes the process of using community-focused design techniques to develop a system that represents the ideas of dispersed researchers and educators with uncoordinated interests in genre ecologies.

2. COMMUNITY-FOCUSED DESIGN

Recognizing the increasing frequency with which the concept of genre ecologies was being discussed by scholars working independently, our team took on the challenge of designing a system that would reflect the loosely connected ideas of those scholars. This design process involved recurring interactions with potential users to establish needs for a system as well as the features and functionality of the system.

A unique objective in our design process was to develop a community where only individuals with thematically connected ideas had existed before. Specifically, we wanted to explore whether a system could be developed to support patterns of activity that would be of interest to participants as exhibited in an ongoing conversation about those practices. Consequently, with periodic input from the potential community of users, we developed a working prototype system that includes a tool and a forum for sharing and discussing artifacts created with that tool.

3. VISUALIZATION GENERATOR

A primary motivation for the GEMviz project was to create a web-based tool for generating genre ecology models (GEMs). In the absence of this tool, GEMs have been created by researchers and students using ad hoc means of production (e.g., computer-based drawing tools, hand-drawn images. Our visualization generator (see Figure 1) is designed to provide an accessible utility that will help standardize model-creation choices, reflecting best practices expressed by the scholars engaged in this work.

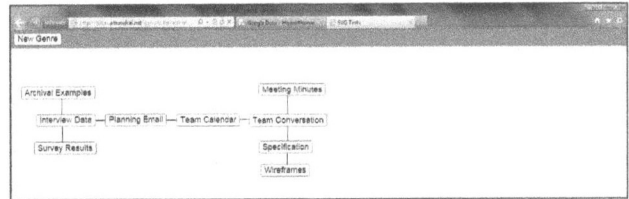

Figure 1. Tool for generating GEM visualizations.

4. GALLERY INTERACTION FORUM

To facilitate community-based conversations about GEMs, the system includes a gallery space (see Figure 2) in which people may display their work, comment on the work of others, and rate contributions.

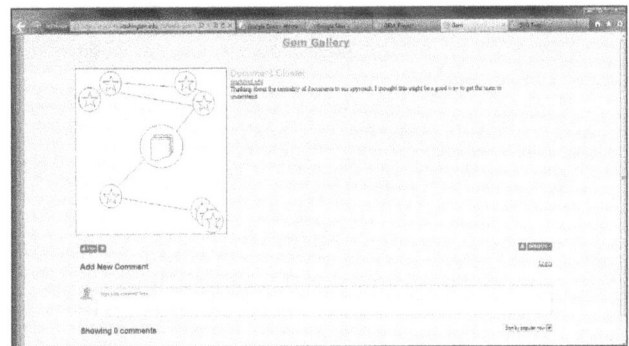

Figure 2. Gallery space for displaying GEMs and interacting with others about them.

SIGDOC'11, October 3–5, 2011, Pisa, Italy.
ACM 978-1-4503-0936-3/11/10.

ImREAL: Immersive Reflective Experience-based Adaptive Learning

Lucia Pannese
Imaginary srl
via Mauro Macchi 52 I- 20124 Milan
lucia.pannese@i-maginary.it

ABSTRACT

The poster describes the vision of the ImREAL FP7 project about the design of immersive, simulated environments for experience-based adaptive learning in the scenario of multicultural dialogues and pinpoints the differences to current practice in learning. Real world modeling linked to semantic content augmentation will guarantee a constant alignment of the virtual with the real world for an effective experience-based training.

Categories and Subject Descriptors: H.m

General Terms: Human Factors.

Keywords: Adaptive Learning, Experience-based Learning, Dialogue Simulation, Real World Modeling, Semantic Augmentation.

1. INTRODUCTION

Immersive simulated environments for experiential learning are growing in popularity and will play a key role in tomorrow's technologies for adult training. The major challenge is to effectively align the virtual learning experience with the 'real-world' context and 'day-to-day' job practice. This poster describes how the ImREAL FP7 project provides a new class of cost effective adaptive systems adjusted to adult learners' needs to seamlessly link the simulated learning experience and 'real-world' job-related experiences. The ImREAL framework exploits and significantly extends advances in distributed architectures, context modelling, dialogic systems, semantic web, ontological reasoning, and follows pedagogical models of adult self-regulated learning to deliver an evolving model of 'real-world' job activities, linked to storytelling and semantic content augmentation, an extended model of the learner and context and affective meta-cognitive scaffolding to motivate and engage learners and promote self-reflection, self-evaluation and self-awareness. The chosen validation context is Interpersonal Communication focusing on Multi-cultural Awareness.

2. CURRENT PRACTICE-ImREAL VISION

ImREAL is aimed at enhancing existing low-cost simulated environments for experiential learning available on the market by integrating psycho-pedagogically driven innovative intelligent functionalities to substantially improve learning efficacy without increasing the cost for implementation of the simulated environment. ImREAL is developing a knowledge-enhanced open source framework compliant with existing semantic web standards and based on relevant service-oriented architectures. In current practice the trainers provide content to create sequences of simulated situations while the learners practice job activities in the simulated situations. Simulated context represents some activity aspects but does not capture the range of aspects the same activity can have in real life. The ImREAL vision foresees services that will provide 'middleware' to connect reality and simulated environments. In addition to practice with simulated situations, learners can make connections to real job experience in an interactive open learner model which helps them become aware what they are good at, or need to improve. An affective 'coach/mentor' will offer positive encouragement and feedback, help learners identify alternative techniques, and encourage them to reflect on their experiences in the simulated environment and relate this experience to real world job experience.

3. SCENARIO: JOB INTERVIEWS

For the simulation scenario of job interviews research must combine two aspects: a) the focus is on the learners/users of the simulator needs to enhance self-regulated learning relying on andragogy principles and b) the technological aspect of augmenting the present simulator with semantic based intelligent services must be brought forward. In order to experiment this, free content dealing with the topic of job interviews taken from YouTube will be analyzed together with comments given by the users. The content will address topics and competences such as being able to recognize verbal and non-verbal cues; showing an adaptive behavior; emotional intelligence; being aware of cultural issues that determine communication and act as a filter in its meaning and interpretation.

4. OUTLOOK AND NEXT ACTIVITIES

The envisaged roadmap foresees a roadmap with three main steps: development of semantic based intelligent services to align contents to the real world and mainly support the development of the simulation; augmentation of the user's satisfaction in terms of enhancing the quality of learning; organization of services for meta-cognitive scaffolding and therefore self-regulated learning. All services will be built around and not within the simulator. In such a way ideally it will be possible to apply them to a different simulator in the future.

ACKNOWLEDGMENTS: The research leading to these results has received funding from the European Union Seventh Framework Programme (FP7/2007-2013) under grant agreement no ICT 257831 (ImREAL project).

Applying Cultural Knowledge to Multimedia Resources to Enrich Contextualized Applications

Rafael L. P. da Silva, Junia Coutinho Anacleto, Fernando Cesar Balbino
Advanced Interaction Laboratory (LIA)
Department of Computing - Federal University of São Carlos (DC/UFSCar)
Rod. Washigton Luis KM 235 – São Carlos-SP – Brazil
rafaelkuasy@gmail.com, {junia, fernando_balbino}dc.ufscar.br

ABSTRACT

This work aims to enlarge the OMCS-Br Project's potential. Contextualized applications have been developed to take advantage from the cultural knowledge base provided by it, but we had not considered multimedia resources yet. Thus, we have developed a new engine which allows people to store images and "add" cultural knowledge to them, enriching the possibilities to design contextualized applications where multimedia resources can be used according to users' cultural background.

Categories and Subject Descriptors

H.1.2 [**User/Machine Systems**]: Human Information Processing – *cultural knowledge processing*; H.1.m [**Miscellaneous**]: *contextualized multimedia resources*.

General Terms

Design, Human Factors.

Keywords

OMCS-Br, cultural knowledge, contextualized multimedia.

1. INTRODUCTION

The Open Mind Common Sense Brazil (OMCS-Br) Project focuses in doing computers "think" as human beings do [1] and it provides means of developing contextualized applications based on Brazilians' cultural background. Minsky's relations [2] are used to establish semantic relations between words, e.g. "a tire is PART OF a car"; here the relation *PartOf* is used. The set of relations forms the ConceptNet, a semantic net which can be represented as a large graph and which contains all the cultural knowledge collected from people with different profiles. Anyone can access the project's website, register and "donate" his/her cultural knowledge through templates related to different themes, like slangs, emotions and folklore knowledge. All the collected cultural knowledge can be used by contextualized applications, i.e. applications that take advantage of the cultural knowledge base and provide functionalities which "fit" users' culture. In this work our goal is to expand the potentialities of OMCS-Br to enable users to: a) store and name images and; b) apply Minsky's relations to the images through appropriate templates. As result, we want to make the computer understand things like "what are the possible usages for the objects in an image?", "what are they made of?", "are they part of something?" etc.

2. "CONTEXTUALIZED" IMAGES

The engine we are developing will allow users to store new images, name them and to enter semantic information to new and existing images through templates, which represent Minsky's relations in natural language. Stored images will be shown randomly and beside them will appear a template (Figure 1). The user will be asked to fill the blank field(s) in a template (Figure 1); after that, the processing of data entered by the user will aggregate cultural knowledge to the ConceptNet in such a way that meaningful semantic relations will be applied among the entered cultural concepts and the respective image. Thus, contextualized images will be obtained, i.e. images will not be only textually labeled, but they will associated to cultural knowledge and semantic meaning. For instance, an image of a white dress can be linked to the *UsedFor* relation if a person's cultural knowledge says that a white dress is used for wedding.

is a kind of

template

Teach! Doesn't make sense next random

Figure 1. A prototype of the OMCS-Br's new functionality

3. FINAL CONSIDERATIONS

To develop mechanisms of storing images in the cultural knowledge base and associating semantic values to them is a first step towards further works which can cover other types of media, such as sound and video files. An entire new set of functionalities can be developed, and new kind of applications may rise to explore the contextualized multimedia resources in the cultural knowledge base. One of the potential applications is the semantic retrieval of images in the Web.

4. REFERENCES

[1] Anacleto, J. C., Carvalho, A. F. P. Improving Human-Computer Interaction by Developing Culture-sensitive Applications based on Common Sense Knowledge. Advances in HCI. Vienna: In-Teh, 2008, p. 1-30.

[2] Liu, H., Singh, P. 2004. ConceptNet – a pratical commonsense reasoning tool-kit. IN *BT Technology Journal*, v. 22, n. 4, pp. 211-226. October 2004.

Kairos-OJS Plugin Project: Tools for Scholarly Multimedia

Kathie Gossett
Iowa State University
Department of English
203 Ross Hall, Ames, IA 50011

kgossett@iastate.edu

Cheryl Ball
Illinois State University
Department of English
Campus Box 4240, Normal, IL 61790

cball@ilstu.edu

Douglas Eyman
George Mason University
Department of English
4400 University Drive 3E4, Fairfax, VA 22030

deyman@gmu.edu

ABSTRACT

This poster presents the plugin developed for PKP's Open Journal System (OJS) to facilitate editing and publishing scholarly multimedia.

Categories and Subject Descriptors

D.2.2 [**Software Engineering**]: Design Tools and Techniques – *Modules and interfaces.* H.5.1 [**Information Interfaces and Presentation**]: Multimedia Information Systems – *Evaluation/methodology.* H.5.3 [**Information Storage and Retrieval**]: Group and Organization Interfaces – *Web-based interaction.*

General Terms

Management, Design, Standardization.

Keywords

Scholarly Multimedia, Multimedia Publishing, User Interface Development, Metadata

1. INTRODUCTION

Scholarly multimedia (also called webtexts) are article- or book-length digital pieces of peer-reviewed scholarship designed using media-rich elements to enact the author's argument. They incorporate interactivity, digital media, and different argumentation strategies such as visual juxtaposition and associational logic and are published in online, peer-reviewed journals and presses. Scholarly multimedia cannot be printed and retain the author's argument because such texts are composed of webpages with links, animations, images, audio, video, scripts, databases, and other multimedia elements, including but not limited to written text. These publications are unique in that each webtext is individually designed, which makes basic editorial processes such as reviewing, copy- and design-editing, publishing, and indexing significantly more complicated than print-based or linear (e.g. PDF-like) scholarship.

In order to support the publication of scholarly multimedia works, the editors of *Kairos* secured an NEH Digital Humanities grant to build a new editorial management system and reader tools for scholarly multimedia. We chose to build our system as a plug-in to the open-source, editorial management system Open Journal System (OJS), which has been widely adopted but currently only handles the editorial process for digitized print scholarship.

2. THE NEED FOR BETTER PUBLISHING TOOLS

Kairos: A Journal of Rhetoric, Technology, and Pedagogy is a free, independent, open access, digital journal that has been publishing scholarly multimedia on the Web since 1996. *Kairos* is a no-money-in, no-money-out operation. Editors of other scholarly multimedia journals keep asking us what our technological secrets are to editing and publishing this work. The dirty secret has been that for 15 years, the journal has cobbled together unrelated technologies (YahooGroups, instant messaging programs, S/FTP programs, gifted servers, etc.) to support our publishing stream. It became clear that the journal needed a more robust system to support its collaborative review and copy- and design-editing process.

3. DESIGN DECISIONS AND TECHNICAL REQUIREMENTS

In 2007 the editors of the journal *Kairos* decided it was time to redesign the journal and its support structure. This project was subsequently divided into two phases: the interface and the backend. The new interface (phase one) was launched in fall 2008 and received several awards from various academic publishing venues. Phase two included plans to build a system to handle webtexts from the earliest author queries, through the review and editing processes, up through the actual publication of webtexts in each issue of the journal. This section of the poster reviews those plans and discusses how the decision to build a plugin for the OJS system, rather than build and maintain a homegrown system, has impacted the design and development of the system from the metadata schema to the database design to the technologies used to accomplish the editorial and publication work of the journal.

4. READER TOOLS

This section of the poster presents a mockup of the tools we are developing for readers. The focus of these tools is to allow flexibility in the use of these scholarly works for both teaching and research purposes. While the editorial functions of the project are primarily not publicly available, the reader tools are designed to give users the opportunity to select, re-arrange, comment upon, and more easily cite the digital works published in *Kairos*

Browsing as a Learning Practice in the Information Management Work of Technical Communicators

Stewart Whittemore
9030 Haley Center
Auburn University
Auburn, AL 36801
1-334-844-9028

whittemore@auburn.edu

ABSTRACT

This poster reports data from a case study of the information management practices technical communicators at a software company in the U.S. Midwest. The study found that the technical communicators preferred location-based file folder browsing for their information finding and retrieval activities. Building on situated cognition theories of learning, the researcher speculates that file folder browsing may serve a learning purpose for the technical communicators by helping them internalize technical information about their products and social information about their work teams and processes.

Categories and Subject Descriptors

Documentation

General Terms

Management, Documentation, Performance, Design, Theory

Keywords

information management, technical communication, file browsing, searching

1. POSTER PROPOSAL

Jones and Teevan (2007) define information management activities as "activities people perform to acquire, organize, maintain, retrieve, use, and control the distribution of information items" [1, p. 3]. Examples of these activities include: a) Finding and re-finding activities like searching for a document in a file cabinet or a computer file or performing a keyword search using Google; b) Keeping activities like saving a downloaded PDF to a local computer; and c) Meta-level activities like setting up folder structures on a computer disk drive; cleaning out an email inbox.

During the first decade of the 21st century, new communication technologies and work arrangements greatly increased the need for effective information management in the workplace. These developments include flattened organizational hierarchies, which led to more team-based collaborative work environments in which information must be shared vertically and horizontally [2]; new communication technologies (e.g., wikis, blogs, Campfire) enabled distributed work arrangements like telecommuting, remote teams, and flexible work hours, which resulted in a much larger information stream to maintain team awareness and enable joint cognition [3]; and the introduction of new work methodologies (e.g., content management, Agile software development) greatly expanded the need for speedy, secure, and accurate information transfer among work teams [4].

Because of their expertise in communication, technical communicators are often perceived as the best members of their work teams to handle the new information management tasks enabled by new technologies and methodologies. To better prepare future graduates for these types of work, we need to better understand the information management preferences and needs of technical communicators.

This poster reports an intriguing finding from a case study of a group of technical communicators at a software firm. This finding was that the technical communicators displayed a definite preference for file folder browsing over searching when engaging in re-finding activities. While this is not an entirely unusual finding, it did appear out-of-place given the exigencies of the particular research site and participants. That is, given that browsing has been shown to be generally less efficient and more time-consuming than searching, why did a group of well-trained and tech-savvy technical communicators in a fast-paced and dynamic workplace rely so heavily on antiquated file folder browsing to keep and re-find their information? Turning to social theories of cognition and learning, including especially situated cognition theory [6], I speculate that navigating these structures served important social and technical learning functions.

2. REFERENCES

[1] Jones, W., and Teevan, J. 2007. Introduction. In *Personal Information Management*, W. Jones & J. Teevan, Eds. Seattle: University of Washington Press, Seattle, 3-20.

[2] Amidon, S., and Blythe, S. 2008. Wrestling with proteus: Tales of communication managers in a changing economy. *Journal of Business and Technical Comm.* 22, 1 (Jan. 2008), 5-37.

[3] Slattery, S. 2007. Un-distributing work through writing: How technical writers manage texts in complex information environments. *Technical Communication Qtrly.* 16, 3 (July-Sept. 2007), 311-325.

[4] Mott, R. K., and Ford, J. D. 2007. The convergence of technical communication and information architecture: Managing single source objects for contemporary media. *Technical Comm.* 54, 1 (Feb. 2007), 27-45.

[5] Brown, J. S., Collins, A., and Duguid, P. 1989. Situated cognition and the culture of learning. *Educational Researcher.* 18, 1 (Jan. 1989), 32-42.

Author Index

www.ingramcontent.com/pod-product-compliance
Lightning Source LLC
Chambersburg PA
CBHW082108220326
41598CB00066BA/5792